Giuseppe Picarella

Mitsubishi Babs vol. II

The world's first high-speed strategic reconnaissance aircraft

STRATUS

Published in Poland in 2023
by STRATUS s.j.
ul. Żeromskiego 6A,
27-600 Sandomierz, Poland
e-mail: office@mmpbooks.biz
as
MMPBooks,
e-mail: rogerw@mmpbooks.biz

http://www.mmpbooks.biz

ISBN
978-83-67227-16-2

Editor in chief
Roger Wallsgrove

Editorial Team
Bartłomiej Belcarz
Robert Pęczkowski
Artur Juszczak

Proofreading
Roger Wallsgrove

DTP
Stratus sp. j.

Printed by
Wydawnictwo
Diecezjalne i Drukarnia
w Sandomierzu
www.wds.pl

PRINTED IN POLAND

Table of contents

This book is dedicated to all of the reconnaissance pilots and ROs (see Notes, Aircrew and terminology) of WWII. Typically operating unarmed and unescorted aircraft, these brave individuals were truly the eyes of their respective nations, providing governments and military planners with the vital information needed to formulate long-term strategies, invasion plans and defences measures. Where once their missions held the highest priority, the very clandestine nature of such operations has served to obscure their services, and ultimately their sacrifices. I would also like to dedicate this second volume to my late mother Barbara, my very own "*Babs*".

Introduction and Acknowledgements

For more than eighty years the RAF has widely been credited with pioneering the concept of high-speed strategic reconnaissance aircraft, thanks to the unorthodox theories and avant-garde activities of visionaries such as Sidney Cotton and F/O. Maurice Longbottom. Their unwavering belief that specialised high-performance reconnaissance aircraft could fly to predetermined targets, deep inside occupied Europe, evading all defending fighters by virtue of their high-speed capabilities alone, was initially viewed with disbelief and a measure of contempt by the establishment. Despite official misgivings their concepts were put to the test during the autumn of 1939 and the resulting stream of reconnaissance photographs quickly dispelled the critics and, for the want of a better word, served to "refocus" the photographic reconnaissance and the intelligence gathering community. For the first time British military commanders had access to what was almost "real-time" intelligence of the day (collected within hours of official requests rather than days or weeks later) and the subsequent recognition and adoption of RAF reconnaissance practices by the USAAF in 1942 has only served to reinforce the accepted Western chronology of high-speed strategic reconnaissance operations.

Mitsubishi *Babs* vol.I and vol.II were written to redress this imbalance and tell the true story behind the development and operational deployment of the world's first high-speed strategic reconnaissance aircraft, which began 6,000 miles further east and four years prior to the momentous events in Europe, under the guidance of the Imperial Japanese Army and Mitsubishi Heavy Industries Co Ltd. Faced with similar preconceptions, technical arguments and a very rigid operational doctrine, the Mitsubishi *Babs* was developed during a brief golden aeronautical period (between the mid 1930s and early 1940s) when the Japanese aircraft industry flourished under constant military aircraft competitions and production orders. Free from prying eyes and shrouded within a self-imposed veil of secrecy, the Japanese developed numerous designs that were equal to and in some cases ahead of contemporary Western manufacturers. By 1940 the Imperial Japanese Navy arguably possessed the most advanced carrier-borne aircraft designs in the world, thanks to the A6M *Zeke* (*Zero*) Carrier-borne Fighter, B5N *Kate* Carrier-borne Torpedo Bomber and D3A *Val* Carrier-borne Dive Bomber. While the Imperial Japanese Army also developed many advanced combat types during this period, it would excel in the field of high-speed strategic reconnaissance or "Command Reconnaissance" aircraft, as the concept was known in Japanese service, in order to monitor its perceived long distance adversary of the period, the Soviet Union.

The origin of these two books date back to the summer of 2010, following the completion of my previous title: *Japanese Experimental Transport Aircraft of the Pacific War* (Stratus/MMP Books – ISBN 978-83-61421-41-2). With that major work finally published in 2011, my mind turned to summer days and generally avoiding the process of researching extinct Japanese aircraft. Unfortunately I'm a creature of habit and the seed of a book detailing the development and operational history of the Mitsubishi Ki-46 *Dinah* sat firmly at the back of my mind, as I had previously acted as the Japanese technical advisor for the RAF Museum's Ki-46-III *Dinah* restoration. Suffice to say that several months into writing the *Dinah* book, I naively decided to include a chapter on the Ki-15 *Babs*, in order to tell the full story of how Japan conceived the concept of Command (Strategic) Reconnaissance aircraft. That chapter soon outgrew the confines of the planned Dinah book and initiated what will ultimately become a series of books on Imperial Japanese Reconnaissance aircraft of WWII.

As is always the case, a book of this size cannot be written without the help of others and I gratefully acknowledge the assistance of many Japanese aviation friends and associates whom contributed data and photographs, including: Showzow Abe, Tetsuya Inoue, Kenji Miyazaki, Tomoaki Shimamoto, Takashi Doi – Yokohama WWII Japanese Military Radio Museum, Tomiharu Taima, Shawn DuBois, Taizou Nakamura, Ryusuke Ishiguro, Jim Lansdale, Shigeyoshi Kanda of the Japan Aeronautical Association (JAA), Robert Mikesh, René Francillon, Bernard Millot, Nick Millman – aviationofjapan.com, Shoichi Tanaka, K. Natsuya, Todd Pederson, Ron Cole, Henry Sakaida, Mitsubishi Heavy Industries, George Eleftheriou – Arawasi.jp, Darryl Ford, Aireview, Yuri Svoyski, the Nauchno-Issledovatel'skiy

Institut Voyenno-Vozdooshnykh Seel (NII VSS) – Soviet Air Force Scientific Research Institute, Kagamigahara Aerospace Museum, Richard Dunn, James Payne, Richard Lane, Andy Robinson – IWM, Justin Taylan – pacificwrecks.com, the Public Records Office, Brett Stolle and the Staff of the National Museum of the U.S. Air Force, Philip Jarrett, Flight International and Aeroplane Monthly, Katsuyuki Kodama – Peace Memorial Imperial Japanese Army and Navy Museum, Brian Harrison and Hubert Miller.

Giuseppe "Joe" Picarella MRAeS
Hatherleigh, Devon
January 2023

Ground instructional Ki-15-II airframes of the 10th Kyoiku Hikotai, at Tachikawa Airfield in late 1945 (Darryl Ford)

Notes

Aircraft nomenclature

Within the context of this second volume of Mitsubishi Babs, the breakdown of specific Japanese designations issued to the Babs family of aircraft fall into three main groups, although there are many more individual subtypes. These groups are:

Army:

- Army Type-97 Command Reconnaissance Plane Model-I, or Ki-15-I
- Army Type-97 Command Reconnaissance Plane Model-II, or Ki-15-II
- Plus the experimental third version of the aircraft, or Ki-15-III

Navy:

- Navy Type-98 Reconnaissance Plane Model-11, or C5M1
- Navy Type-98 Reconnaissance Plane Model-12, or C5M2

Civilian:

- Karigane-I Communications Aircraft (Ki-15-I airframes)
- Karigane-II Communications Aircraft (Ki-15-II airframes)

In addition to this the Allies issued the codename *Babs* to the Ki-15-I, and for a short period of time the newly identified examples of the C5M1 and Ki-15-II were identified as *Norma*, before the family name was standardised back to *Babs*. In order to better understand the complicated and specialised nature of the Japanese Army, Navy and civilian nomenclature systems, please refer to the Notes section (pages 5-8) in Volume I.

Aircrew and terminology

Unlike the Allied air forces, there was no official designation for the rear crewmember carried on Army or Navy reconnaissance aircraft and two seat fighters, and Mitsubishi's own documentation often describes the second crewman as the "passenger" and even the "co-pilot". For the sake of consistency throughout this book, the reconnaissance/radio operator/observer is referred to as the "RO".

The terms "port" and "starboard" are used to identify structure, systems and equipment locations plus exterior reference points on the aircraft, while "left" and "right" are used inside the cockpits.

Volume I Addendum

Following the publication of Mitsubishi Babs Vol. I, the accompanying photograph was discovered showing Army Ki-15-IIs operated by the 10th Kyoiku Hikotai (Operational Flying Training Unit).

10th Kyoiku Hikotai

The unit was established at Kagamigahara on February 25th 1944, for the purpose of training Ki-46 Dinah reconnaissance pilots. While it is known that this unit was issued with Ki-46-II Dinah, Ki-54a Hickory and Ki-36 Ida aircraft, the use of Ki-15-II Babs aircraft is undocumented and goes someway to confirm the belief that Babs airframes were allotted too, or absorbed into, many of the new Dinah units due to their specialized role and high-speed envelope.

The unit's aircraft carried a black circle with two horizontal red bars.

The photograph shows a group of six Ki-15-II airframes, which were discovered by personnel of the *17th Photographic Reconnaissance Squadron (B)*, when they occupied Tachikawa Airfield in Tokyo Prefecture during September 1945. Although it is likely that these aircraft were original used for strategic reconnaissance flight-training purposes, it would seem that they had been relegated to ground-training duties by the end of hostilities. Under the terms of the surrender negotiations, all offensive arms, including combat aircraft, were to be rendered inoperable or non-airworthy. This would allow overflying US observation aircraft to visually confirm that Japanese aircraft were not a threat and would also make it difficult for rebellious Japanese personnel to continue fighting or performing Kamikaze missions with these aircraft. Rendering the aircraft inoperable typically took the form of removing propellers, deflating tyres, removing wheels or damaging flight controls, etc., but this practice was not entirely complied with or needed, as the surrender became a reality. As can be seen, all of the aircraft retained their propellers, but are devoid of their outboard wings. This, combined with the canvas covers over the engine cowls, would indicate that they were possibly still in use as for ground-training – starting procedures, taxiing, etc.

The photograph is a perfect example of – what paint schemes did Japanese aircraft use in service? All six aircraft within this one unit carry different paint schemes ranging from Type "O" Army (Mitsubishi) grey-green, through to heavily mottled Type "B" camouflage.

The furthest aircraft seems to be in the standard Mitsubishi/Army grey-green, and carries the "accepted" markings of the *10th Kyoiku Hikotai* on the fin and rudder, although the markings on the fabric-covered rudder are worn.

The next aircraft has a very lightly applied mottled camouflage over the grey-green. It carries the faded remnants of the unit markings, but the rudder (and unit markings) are over painted with the individual katakana character "me".

The next aircraft carries a mottled camouflage over the airframe and the unit markings!

The next airframe carries a heavily mottled camouflage scheme (possibly even two-tone green and brown) over the grey-green, plus an all-over brown propeller.

The next aircraft carries a mottled paint scheme over grey-green, which covers the entire airframe including the spinner. It also includes two nonstandard access panels ahead of FS.2 and may even carry yellow/orange leading-edge identification markings on the wing leading edge?

The nearest aircraft is finished in standard grey-green.

A chronological error appears on page 73. The Coronations of King George VI took place on May 12th. This error does not affect the timeline, dates or events listed for *Kamikaze*. Mea culpa and apologies to the King.

Following the publication of Vol. I, questions were raised in relation to the validity of *Kamikaze's* official *Fédération Aéronautique Internationale* record application. For many years the FAI official website gave the impression that Capt. Yuuzou Fujita's (May 13th 1938) long-range flight (11,652.01km) aboard the Gasuden Koken, was the first FAI record awarded to Japan. Because the author has a copy of the official *FAI* "*Certificat de record*" for *Kamikaze*, he contacted the FAI directly to clarify the situation. They responded by confirming that Masaaki Iinuma and Kenji Tsukagoshi (aboard *Kamikaze*) were in fact issued with an official *FAI* record for the: "Journey [between] Tokyo – London. Duration: 94h. 17m. 56s. Speed [average]: 162.854 km/h". The *FAI* representative explained that for many reasons: "Unfortunately not all past records have been entered in the [online] *FAI* Record database". They assured me that the database would be updated to show *Kamikaze's* official *FAI* record in due course. My thanks go out to the staff at *FAI*.

Chapter 1

Brothers in arms

"The failure of the Hankow Assault Unit to locate the target, despite such favorable conditions as a full moon was due to a reliance on a map, and to an unexpected flood. It taught us the necessity of pre-assault photographic reconnaissance."

Hisazumi Tadao, former Commander IJN

When the second Sino-Japanese war began in July 1937, the Imperial Japanese Navy found itself embroiled in a war that was outside its natural scope of operations and despite the fact that they were operating outmoded and obsolescent aircraft at that time, the *Kaigun Koku Hombu* (Naval Air Headquarters) was adamant that they would share in the victory over mainland China. Within the first week of the conflict the Army and Navy had agreed upon their specific responsibilities; the Army would provide tactical and close air support for its ground troops in northern China, and the Navy would assume responsibility for combating and destroying the Chinese Air Force in central and southern China.

Taking the lead in a major land-based war left the Navy in the position of having to collect strategic reconnaissance, plus tactical pre – and post-strike photographs of fixed and often well defended targets. Unfortunately for the Navy, not only did they lack experience in such strategic reconnaissance duties, they were also devoid of both carrier and land-based aircraft capable of performing reliable long-range, unescorted reconnaissance missions over defended territory. For the Navy, the role of "reconnaissance" aircraft had always been divided into two basic categories – Patrol and Reconnaissance.

Patrol or scouting duties simply expanding the range of a carrier's vision and formed the initial basis for the introduction of aircraft into the Navy, as they searched for enemy ships in order to forewarn the fleet of potential threats and targets. The Japanese Navy's first carrier, the *Hōnshō*, had in fact been designed specifically for such reconnaissance duties around the fleet. The patrol process involved collecting notes on the number of vessels, including their range, heading and possible intentions. But as the aircraft carrier evolved into an offensive weapon, the importance of reconnaissance aircraft began to diminish and other combat aircraft, such as attack bombers, were tasked with patrol duties. Regardless of the aircraft type, carrier-borne reconnaissance aircraft, by the very nature of ship-based operations, were limited in size and weight, and as such they possessed a relatively short range.

Reconnaissance duties on the other hand performed the same basic role, but at much greater range. These missions were flown with specially designed flying boats that were capable of long-range flight, at the expense of slow cruising speeds.

Regardless of the definition (patrol or reconnaissance) the Navy was now handicapped in two primary areas; its aircraft were not designed for, or capable of, performing strategic reconnaissance duties over mainland China, and its crews had not been trained to perform such a role.

Initially this was not a major problem, as the Navy did not participate in bombing missions until mid August, when the new Navy Type-96 Attack Bomber, G3M *Nell* entered the war.

On August 14th, 18 G3M2s of the *Kanoya Kokutai (Kanoya Koku Sentai)* or *Kanoya Naval Air Group*, operating under the control of the *First Combined Air Group*, departed their base at Taipei, Formosa (Taiwan). It should be noted that the Navy did not specifically differentiate between land-based and carrier-based divisions at that time, referring to them all as *Kōkū-Sentai*, meaning Air Group or Air Divisions. For the sake of clarity, we have chosen to use *Air Flotilla* for land-based squadrons and *Carrier Division* for carrier-based squadrons.

During that mission the *Kanoya Kokutai* travelled 2,012km (1,086nm) through typhoons in order to attack Chinese air bases at Hangchow and Kwangteh. This was the longest bombing mission in the world up until that point in time and its audacity caught the attention of the international press. But this mission and numerous subsequent missions from Formosa and Kyushu (on the Japanese mainland) were not the panacea that the Navy had hoped for. While the Navy basked in the glory of its revolutionary new weapon and sang its praises to the Japanese people, the number of bombers being lost in combat was escalating rapidly, due to poor defensive armament, a lack of fuel tank protection and the increasing performance and experience of Chinese fighters that opposed each mission. On the first three raids alone, nine of the 38 bombers had been shot down and several others were badly damaged, leaving just 18 operational aircraft for subsequent missions. The nature of these missions, flying deep into China, was also handicapped by a lack of fighter support over the target, due to the long distances involved. The Navy's current fighter at the beginning of the conflict was the Navy Type-95 Carrier Fighter, A4N1, which was incapable of supporting the new bombers over such distant targets. This problem would be partially addressed by the arrival of the new Navy Type-96 Carrier Fighter, A5M *Claude* at the end of the year, but until those aircraft entered service the bombers had to fend for themselves.

In addition to these technical issues, the Navy's lack of suitable reconnaissance aircraft also meant that they were increasingly reliant on the Army for intelligence gathering, thanks to its newly introduced strategic reconnaissance aircraft, the Ki-15 *Babs*. As mentioned in Chapter 1, Volume I, the slow speed and lack of defensive armament rendered the C2N totally unsuited for combat operations. While at the other end of the spectrum, the Ka-9 program had produced a remarkable aircraft from a development and manufacturing perspective, and its ability to travel long distances would have been a useful attribute over China, but its mediocre speed rendered the aircraft a sitting duck even for China's obsolete fighters, as the Navy had quickly discovered with its direct descendant the G3M.

Nakajima Navy Carrier Reconnaissance Aircraft – C3N1

One aircraft that could have potentially fulfilled the Navy's reconnaissance needs during the initial conflict over China was the Navy Type-97 Carrier Reconnaissance Aircraft, C3N1, but this aircraft had been cancelled earlier in 1937, as it was deemed superfluous to operational needs!

In essence the Navy had cancelled its only dedicated reconnaissance aircraft, which was capable of 387km/h (208kt), in favour of a three-seat bomber (the Navy Type-97 Carrier Attack Bomber, B5N *Kate*), which was capable of 368km/h (199kt). And to add insult to injury, both C3N1 prototypes continued to perform excellent long-range reconnaissance duties over China for some time after the cancellation of the project.

The reasons for this decision were probably based on the widely held belief that the new aircraft entering service with the Navy were more advanced than anything that the Chinese could field. Such beliefs surrounded the newly accepted G3M2, B5N and the A5M, which stunned the world with their capabilities and performance, lead to an air of invincibility being attributed to them. These views were so prevalent in Japan that some high-ranking naval offices suggested that Navy fighter units could be wholly replaced with bomber units!

These opinions soon evaporated in the skies over China as the Navy's reconnaissance needs became glaringly obvious in the face of increasing long-range bomber missions and the improving performance of Chinese fighters. Slowly but surely, the Navy came to the conclusion that it too needed a high-speed, long-range reconnaissance aircraft that was capable of evading interception, similar to the qualities possessed by the Army's new Ki-15.

As the Navy took stock of the situation, their first reaction was to try and utilize existing aircraft to perform such a role, but a brief review of their operational equipment revealed that nothing was capable of fulfilling these needs. But there was one possible candidate in the form of the Seversky A8V1.

A Nakajima Carrier Reconnaissance Aircraft (C3N1) of the 12th Kokutai. *(Shorzoe Abe)*

Land and Carrier-based Navy reconnaissance aircraft 1935 to 1937

Operational period	Manufacture/model	Role	Max speed	Range/ endurance	Quantity built
1933-1940	Nakajima Navy Fokker Reconnaissance Aircraft C2N1/C2N2	Mapping	231km/h 144mph	Estimated 5.5hrs 550miles 885km	20
1934	Mitsubishi 8-Shi Special Reconnaissance Aircraft Ka-9 G1M1	Strategic	230km/h 143mph	3,830km 2,380miles	1
1936-1940	Nakajima Navy Carrier Reconnaissance Aircraft C3N1	Recon	387km/h 240mph	2,277km 1,415miles	2
1937	Seversky Navy Type-S Two-seat Fighter A8V1	Strategic	465km/h 289mph	3,138km 1,950miles	20
1938	Aichi Navy Experimental 13-Shi High-speed Recon-naissance Aircraft C4A1	Strategic	–	–	Paper project only
Total					43

Seversky Navy Type-S Two Seat Fighter – A8V1

By the end of 1937 it was obvious to all involved that the G3M was far from invincible, despite the introduction of the improved G3M2. What the bombers desperately required was an escort of fighter aircraft, which would accompany them over the target area and provide credible air cover. In defence of the Navy this requirement had already been identified and would eventually be fulfilled by the A5M, but as a stopgap measure the Navy agreed to purchase 20 Seversky 2PA-B3 long-range two-seat fighters.

Developed from Seversky's ever-changing SEV-3 Amphibian design, which would ultimately evolve into the P-47 Thunderbolt, the 2PA-B3 boasted a top speed of 508km/h (273knots) and a range of 3,138km (1,695nm), but all was not as it seemed with this design. Seversky was a master of marketing and sales, and because every customer could include whatever modifications they required, engine changes and long-range fuel tanks etc., the specific performance figures for these aircraft were constantly in a state of flux. Just what the Navy expected from the 2PA-B3 is unclear, as the standard 2PA airframe is listed in the 1939 issue of *Jane's All the Worlds Aircraft* as having a loaded weight of 2,732kg (6,022lb), with a range of 1,086km (675miles) and a top speed of 459km/h (285mph). Performance figures for the much heavier A8V1, which was reportedly 3,474kg (7,659lb), due to increased fuel capacity and reconnaissance equipment, was actually in the region of 465km/h (251knots or 289mph) at 5,000m.

When the 2PA-B3s (C/n 122 to C/n141) were finally assembled in Japan during the spring of 1938, they were found to be much heavier than anticipated, most likely due to the inclusion of long-range fuel tanks, so their performance and handling fell well below Japanese practices of the day. It should be highlighted that Japanese Naval fighter pilots at that time considered the wing loading of their latest monoplane fighter, the A5M2, to be "high" at 84.3kg/sq/m (20.5 lb/sq/ft). Just what they made of the Seversky's wing loading of 170kg/sq/m (34.8 lb/sq/ft) is not recorded.

A Seversky Type-S Two Seat Fighter (A8V1).

Initially and somewhat prematurely the aircraft was accepted into service as the Type-S (Sikorsky) Limited Area Fighter (period Japanese terminology for Interceptor) or A8V1, and were passed to the *3rd Kokutai* for evaluations in China. It rapidly proved to be unsuitable for the Japanese in its intended role due to slow climb speeds and high wing loading. In light of this failure and with the growing bomber losses, the aircraft was briefly evaluated as the Type-S Long-range Fighter, in an attempt to fulfil the desperately need fighter escort role, but by this point in time the requirement for escort fighters had been partially fulfilled by the A5M2, which had begun operating from bases on mainland China from in September 1937.

The failure of Limited Area Fighter and Long-range Fighter programs left the Navy with an aircraft it did not need or want, but in the light of the growing requirement for a high-speed reconnaissance aircraft, the A8V1 was given a short reprieve, as it was still faster in a straight line than almost all Japanese Navy aircraft at that time. Six A8V1s were subsequently issued to the *12th Kokutai*, where they performed reconnaissance duties alongside the unit's other aircraft in the air above Shanghai and Nanking.

Ultimately, when the Navy's own C5M1s entered service the A8V1s were quickly replaced and by October 1938 the Navy had already leased one A8V1 to Asahi Shimbun (Asahi Press) as J-BAAN *"Shiokaze" (Salty sea breeze)*, followed by J-BAAQ *"Umikaze" (Sea breeze)* in March 1941 and a third A8V1 to Nichi-Nichi Shinbum (Tokyo Daily News). Given the fact that Sikorsky 2PA-B3s had been sold to Japan, the Allied Technical Air Intelligence Centre (TAIC) wisely issued the codename *Dick* to this aircraft type, although it would become obsolete long before the Pacific war started.

In the meantime, with only a handful of A8V1s and C3N1s to fulfil the strategic reconnaissance needs of central and southern China, the Navy rapidly came to the conclusion that it also needed to develop all-new dedicated land-based reconnaissance aircraft to correct the shortfall in its operational capabilities.

AM-20 – Aichi Navy Experimental 13-*Shi* High-speed Land-based Reconnaissance Aircraft – C4A1

To save precious time, the contract for the Navy Experimental 13-*Shi* High-speed Land-based Reconnaissance Aircraft was issued directly to Aichi, who had produced more than 60 seaplane and flying boat reconnaissance aircraft, and one land based observation aircraft, for the Navy since 1924.

As with most of the Japanese aircraft and engine manufacturers, Aichi had aligned itself with Western companies during the 1920s and 1930s to acquire manufacturing rights and purchase research aircraft for study and evaluation purposes. In Aichi's case, Heinkel Flugzeugwerke of Warnemünde, Germany, had been their company of choice and Heinkel engineers and working practices had been welcomed into the Aichi factory. By 1937 Aichi was working hard to embraced modern aeronautical practices and several of its new monoplanes would prove to be as advanced as contemporary Western designs. The Navy Experimental 11-*Shi* Carrier-based Dive-bomber requirement would result in the company producing the Aichi Monoplane design number 17 (AM-17), or D3A *Val*, which was the most advanced carrier-based dive-bomber in the world when it was thrust onto the world stage at Pearl Harbor in December 1941. Likewise, Aichi's designs for the Navy Experimental 12-*Shi* Three-seat Reconnaissance Floatplane (AM-19), would lead to the Navy Type-0 Reconnaissance Seaplane, E13A *Jake*.

Despite these advance designs, Aichi's attempt at entering the world of high-speed aircraft was not without problems. When the contract was initially awarded, Aichi had not built an advanced aircraft with retractable undercarriage, nor for that matter had it produced an aircraft that was capable of surpassing 386kp/h (240mph). When the Navy issued the requirements for its high-speed land-based reconnaissance aircraft, Aichi's management appointed Mr. Noiro Ozaki to act as the chief engineer on the project, which was assigned the company designation AM-20. Few details survive of this project, but it is generally believed that Mr. Ozaki took the same design route as Mr. Kouno and the original Ki-15, by utilizing an existing advanced design and redeveloping it to fit the Navy's requirements. In this particular case, such an approach would have allowed Mr. Ozaki to utilize new data and manufacturing techniques from both the Aichi AM-17 and AM-18 designs, such as the highly streamlined canopy and fixed main landing gear, together with engine installations details.

The subsequent layout of the AM-20 was based around a low-wing monoplane design, with fixed "spatted" undercarriage. It was powered by a Mitsubishi MK2A *Zuisei* 12 (Ha-31-12), rated at 850hp, driving a two-blade constant-speed propeller. The layout of the aircraft include two-crewmen, an aerial camera, radio and one Type-92 7.7mm machine-gun.

Unfortunately, the Navy's high-speed reconnaissance needs were more urgent than they had first predicted, forcing them into the highly unusual position of purchasing examples of the Army's Ki-15-II design "off the shelf" in late 1938, while the AM-20 was still under development.

The exact details of the AM-20 program are somewhat confusing, as the Navy allowed Aichi to continue with the design and development of the C4A1, as it had become known under the Short Designation System, through to the spring 1939. At which point the preliminary design was frozen and a wooden mock-up was made available for inspection during March.

It is generally assumed that the AM-20 project was officially cancelled following the inspection of the mock-up, as the first C5M1 left Mitsubishi's production line within one month of the decision. The reason for the rapid change of direction is unknown: was the Navy simply "hedging their bets" by allowing the development phase of the program to continue up until March, or did the predicted performance figures for the C4A1 offer a potential improvement over Ki-15-II? We simply don't know the answer, but as matter of record, Aichi's 1,300hp Navy Experimental 16-*Shi* Reconnaissance Seaplane, E16A1 *Paul* (built in 1943), would only be 37km/h (20knots) faster than the 1939 vintage Ki-15-II/C5M.

C5M1

Off the shelf design?

In light of the A8V1 fiasco, it would seem that the Navy took the wise decision to test two Ki-15 airframes before committing to a production order. The first aircraft to be evaluated was **J-BAAL** *Asakaze* (Morning Breeze), which had been operated by Asahi Press since April 27th 1937. This was transferred from its civilian owner in August 1938, and it would seem that the aircraft piqued the interest of the Navy. But given the fact that *Asakaze* was the 3rd prototype of the Ki-15-I series, complete with its low canopy, the Navy decided that it would be prudent to also evaluate the newer Ki-15-II, which was then undergoing flight-testing. At that time the Army had already given permission to Asahi Press to receive an early production examples of the Ki-15-II, but the Navy managed to obtain permission from the Army and Asahi Press for the temporary transfer of two aircraft for testing and evaluation purposes.

Navy test pilots would describe the aircraft as having very limited visibility on the ground, instability at low speed and was susceptible to spinning on approach, a trait that was put down to the lack of wash-out on the wings. That said, its top speed and overall performance was better than any other reconnaissance aircraft in the world, or for that matter any fighter aircraft in the Chinese theatre, including the Navy's newest fighter, the A5M4!

On the face of it, the decision to utilize an aircraft designed specifically for the strategic reconnaissance role, albeit an Army aircraft, may have seemed like the perfect solution to the Navy's problem. But, in traditional naval fashion this acquisition would not simply be an "off the shelf" purchase, as the whole aircraft would need to be navalized, from "stem to stern" to use an appropriate phrase.

These changes included a "new" engine, redesigned cockpits, additional structural safety features and aerodynamic refinements. In addition to this, naval radios, cameras and armament, would need to be fitted. A full listing of all known Ki-15-II/C5M1 modifications is included within Chapter 4, **Technical Description.**

Surprisingly, the biggest modification to primary systems, the installation of the Mitsubishi *Zuisei* 12 engine, was the most straightforward, as it was practically identical to the Ha-26-I, except for navalized fittings and the inclusion of a 12Volt starter and generator system. The Navy also took this opportunity to remove the propeller spinner and *"Hucks"* type starter dog, which was a common practice on their aircraft at that time, despite the increase in drag that was incurred.

While the engine-mounted electrical-system modifications were easily accomplished, the reason for them was a little more convoluted, as the entire electrical installation would need to be converting from the Army's 24Volt system to the Navy's 12Volt system, in order to be compatible with naval equipment such as the radio and camera installation. In addition to theses changes, the aircraft also received navigation and formation lights on the tail and wing tips.

At some point during 1938, it seems that Navy flight-testing had highlighted a possible flight control issue, specifically the fact that the Ki-15 could suffer from elevator flutter in some regions of its flight envelope, which is a common occurrence with high-speed aircraft designs. To solve the control issues, mass-balance weights were designed and retrofitted above the upper elevator surfaces, in order to move the centre of gravity forwards, inline with the control surface hinge datum. It is interesting to note that while all C5M1 and C5M2s would receive elevator mass balance weights, no such modifications were fitted to the Ki-15-I or Ki-15-II. Engineering drawings in the Ki-15-II manual do not show modifications to the elevators, nor do they include elevator leading edge or horn-balance weights in the elevator structure whatsoever.

A beautiful study of J-BAAO Amakaze. During 1939, the aircraft was evaluated by the Navy and several modifications were made to the airframe, including the installation of elevator mass balance weights. Note the standard (Army) Ki-15-II oxygen bottle hoop mounts inside the centre canopy tunnel and the drop tank attachment fittings.

In addition to these aerodynamic modifications, the throttle system may also have been reversed to match Navy practices. At that time the Navy used the British system of throttle movements, whereby the low power setting (throttle closed) was fully back towards the tail of the aircraft and high power (throttle open) was fully forwards towards the nose of the aircraft. The throttle system employed by the Army had traditionally been based on the French system, which was opposite to that of the Navy, but during the very late 1930s the Army began to change over to the British system, so it is unlikely that this would have been an issue for the Navy.

A new instrument panel was installed with instruments calibrated to nautical measurements – Knots or Nautical miles per hour instead of the Army's kilometers Km/h (1 knot = 1.825 km). The Army master compass was also removed from the cockpit lip and its naval equivalent positioned in the centre of the panel, as per the standards of the day.

The RO was furnished with a Navy Handheld Aerial Camera 25cm F-8 Type and a Navy Type-96 *Ku* Mk.2 "Command" radio, the latter item having a profound affect on the RO's cockpit layout, as the this new radio did not fit inside the Ki-15-I radio cabinet. This required the whole radio installation to be move forwards by one fuselage frame, from FS.6 to FS.7. In addition to this, the installation of a roll-over pylon inside the centre canopy tunnel necessitated the relocation of the oxygen bottles back inside the fuselage. The combined effect of these changes reduced the RO's already cramped cockpit by 400mm in length.

A Navy Type-92 7.7mm flexible machine-gun was installed in the rear fuselage and additional dorsal spine transparencies and a modified gunner's window were incorporated to provide an improved the field of view for tracking attacking aircraft.

With these modifications in place, the Navy deemed the aircraft as acceptable for service and ordered it into production in April 1939. The aircraft was officially accepted into service on November 17th 1939, as the Navy Type-98 Reconnaissance Plane Model-11, C5M1.

Once the first production order of C5M1s had been fulfilled in August 1939, the Navy's need for Ki-15-II test aircraft ended, and they duly returned them to Asahi Shimbun, who registered C/n2012 as **J-BAAO**, *Amakaze* (Heavenly Wind) and the second airframe as **J-BACK**, *Kinshi* (Golden Eagle). It is interesting to note that both aircraft continued to operate for a period with C5M elevator mass balance weights, before they were subsequently removed and the aircraft reverted back to standard Ki-15-II/*Karigane*-II configuration.

For a short period of time J-BAAO retained the elevator mass balance weights after the aircraft was returned from Navy testing, but these were subsequently removed.

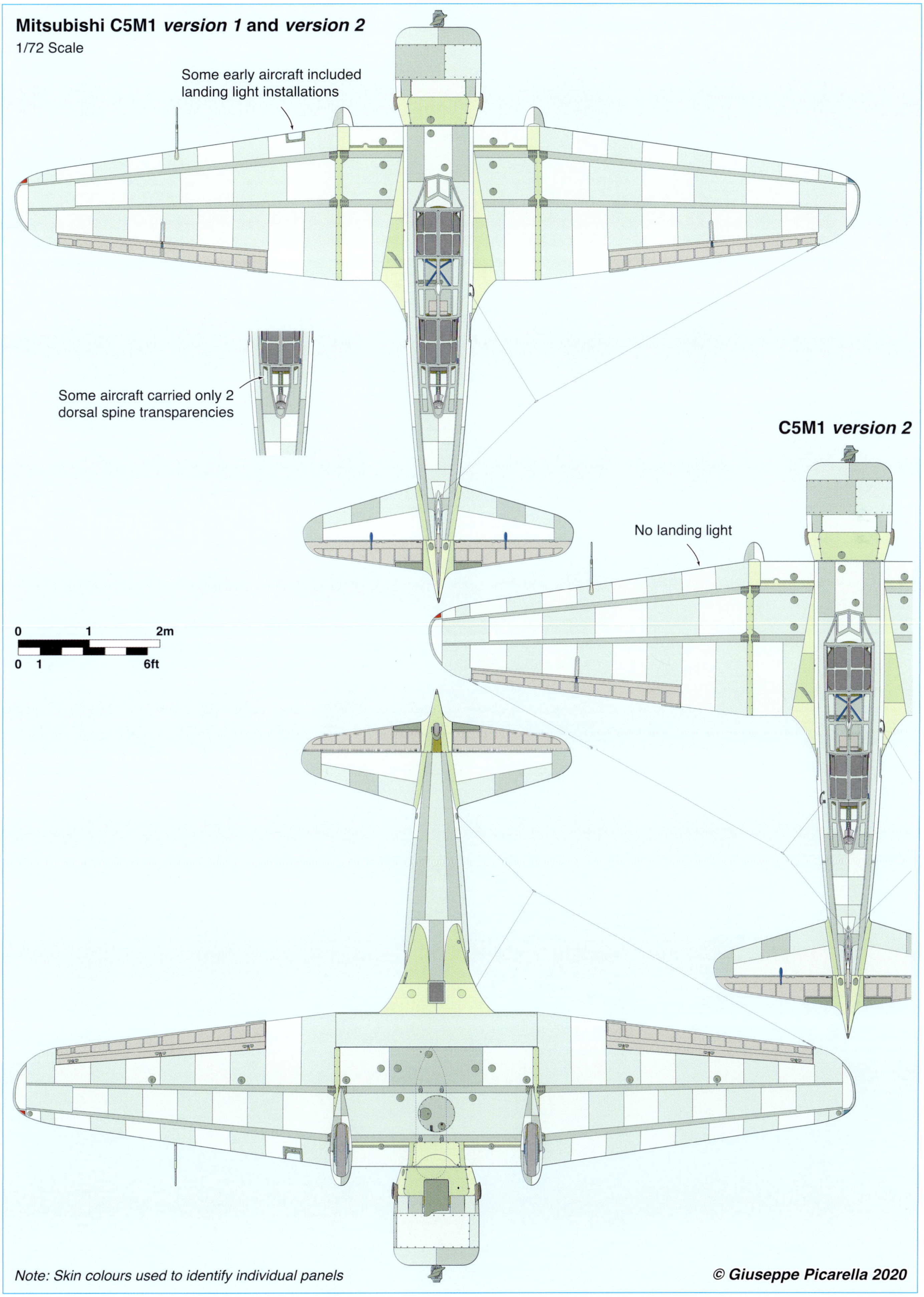
Mitsubishi C5M1 *version 1* and *version 2*
1/72 Scale
Some early aircraft included landing light installations
Some aircraft carried only 2 dorsal spine transparencies
C5M1 *version 2*
No landing light
0 1 2m
0 1 6ft
Note: Skin colours used to identify individual panels
© Giuseppe Picarella 2020

Mitsubishi C5M1 *version 1* and *version 2*

1/72 Scale

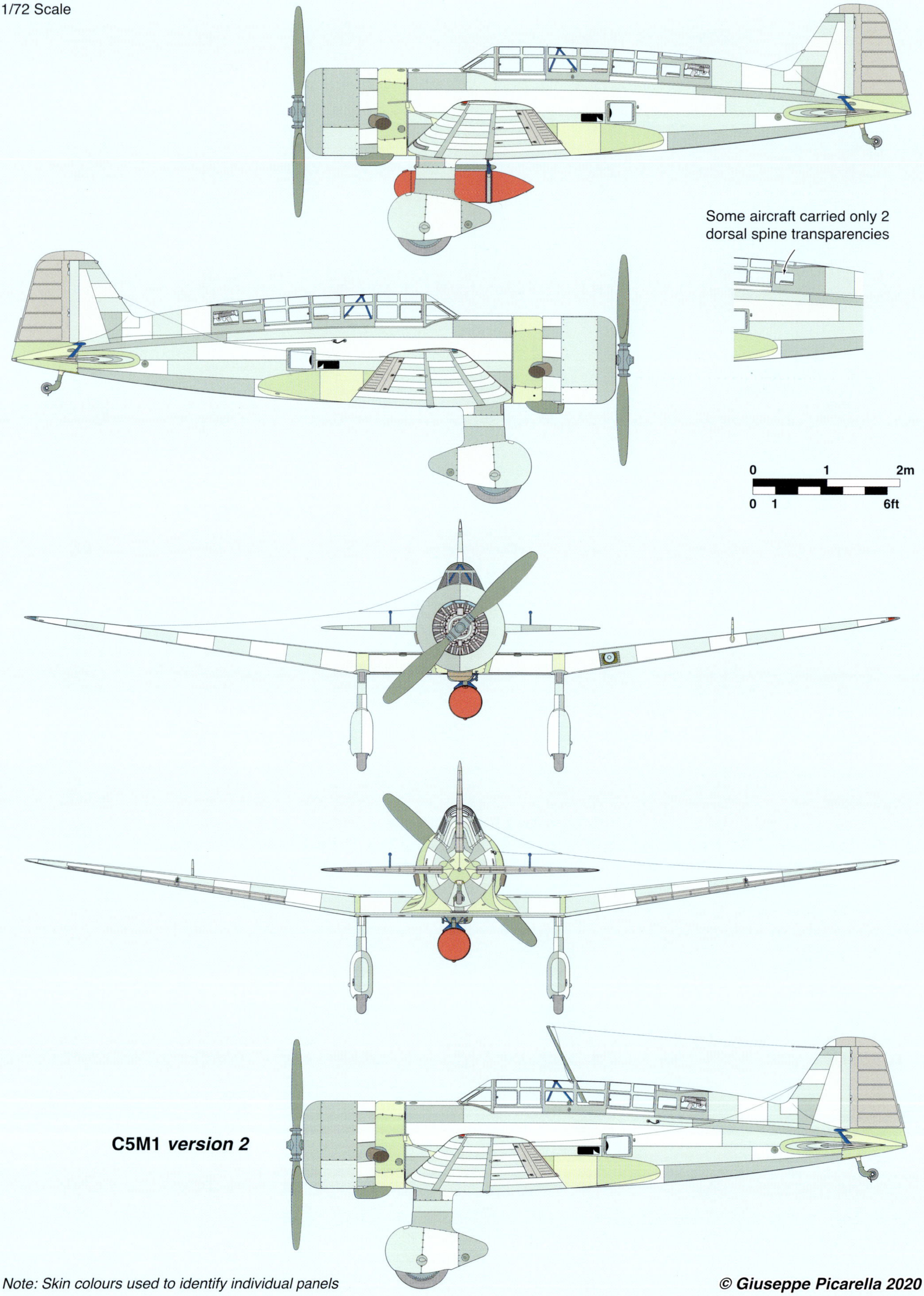

Note: Skin colours used to identify individual panels

Into service

With the arrival of the C5M, the Navy was finally able to bridge the shortfall in its land-based long-range reconnaissance requirements and the new aircraft quickly proved its strategic capabilities over China, which impressed the Navy. But, despite the looming Pacific war, the Navy slowly returned to a policy of tactical reconnaissance – action and reaction – with few thoughts of long-term strategies and US Navy analysts would later go on to describe the Japanese Navy's attitude towards photographic reconnaissance as possessing little value:

"*...beyond the immediate tactical phase and apparently made no effort to use photos in planning or anticipating new offensives.*"

This attitude was considered to be a failing of Japan's high command structure, which was unable to establish and therefore implement a standard set of operating procedures for photographic evaluation, interpretation and dissemination, unlike the massive emphasis placed upon such data by the Allies.

This was optimized by the piecemeal approach to reconnaissance aircraft procurement in its 5-year expansion plans, and hampered further still by the lack of interest in any aircraft that was not capable of offensive operations. The first relevant 5-year expansion plan, in the context of the *Babs* story, occurred in 1937, with the Navy's decision to increase the size and strength of its forces by 1940. This included an increase in the number of air squadrons from 39 to 53, equipped with 1,915 operational aircraft. These figures included two carrier-based reconnaissance "training" units with a total of 32 aircraft, as there were no land-based reconnaissance aircraft in service at that time.

An amendment to the 5-year expansion plan was initiated in 1939, which proposed an increase in the number of air squadrons up to a 160, with 5,499 operational aircraft, to included two operational carrier-based reconnaissance squadrons with a total of 48 aircraft. Yet, despite the operational value of the C5M1 in China and the loss of face regarding its reliance on Army reconnaissance material throughout 1937, the Navy neglected to include land-based reconnaissance aircraft in the expansion plans. After the defeat at Midway in 1942, the Navy proposed a greatly modified expansion program, calling for the establishment of 659 air squadrons, with a total compliment of 16,174 aircraft. At this point in time the Navy finally recognized the necessity of land-based reconnaissance aircraft. In all, nine land-based reconnaissance squadrons operating 162 aircraft, 11 carrier-based reconnaissance squadrons equipped with 198 aircraft and 21 floatplane reconnaissance squadrons with 252 aircraft were included within these figure. Scheduled for completion in 1947, this final expansion plan would ultimately remain unfulfilled.

Colour schemes and production markings

As far as we know, all C5Ms were delivered with an overall Type "O"* Navy (Mitsubishi) glossy grey finish – most likely a J3 *Haiiro* (grey) – as per the 1938 *Temporary regulation No117* requirement. Some of these paints were notoriously unstable and prone to discolouration and the glossy surface could oxidize to leave a dull and chalky surface.

National markings, in the form of the Hinomaru, were applied to the upper and lower surfaces of the wings and the fuselage sides, but this was not always the case, as the *3rd Kokutai* operated aircraft both with and without fuselage Hinomaru markings. Initially, the front face of the propeller was polished aluminium, with two 30mm wide red warning bands applied 30mm apart, 100mm from the tip, while the rear face was painted matt black or brown. By 1943 the Navy adopted a 50mm red stripe (yellow on dark propellers) similar to that of the Army, followed in 1944 by a 100mm deep, yellow tip on brown or black propellers.

The airframes received the various naval information stencils, including the obligatory "No step" on areas of the wing, a Navy aircraft data box on the port side of the rear fuselage and access panel closing lines. In line with Navy practices, most construction number markings were stencilled on the inside of removal panels, although the main landing gear spats retained their C/ns on the outboard surface.

* *In the 1960s, the author Donald Thorpe was the first person to introduced a system of categorising the exterior colours and paint applications on Japanese military aircraft and system is still in use today:*

Unit markings

Once delivered to training or operational units, aircraft received unit markings. In the case of the Imperial Japanese Naval Air Force, individual unit markings were typically confined to the fin and rudder of the aircraft. These markings were composed of an identifier in the form of a unit Kana or Kanji character, code numbers or letters, followed by the aircraft's individual position within the *Kokutai.* This system was constantly evolving due to the increasing number of aircraft and units, plus the deployment of individual *Chutai* to other fleets, armies or taskforces, etc. By the end of 1942 a new system was launched, which simplified the ever increasing list of unit markings. By allotting specific number ranges (shown below) to Fighter, Attack Bomber, Reconnaissance units, etc., it was possible to identify an in-

C5M Standard finish and markings

1/72 Scale

C5M1

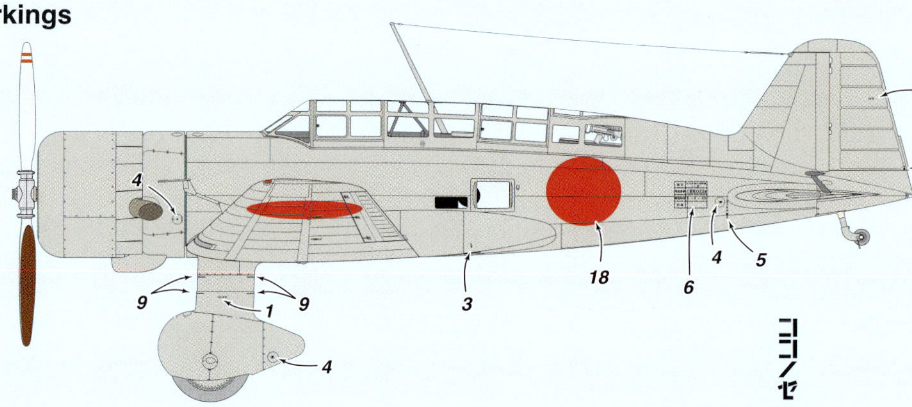

1 XXXX左 XXXX右

Serial number – left and right

2 XXXX

Serial number

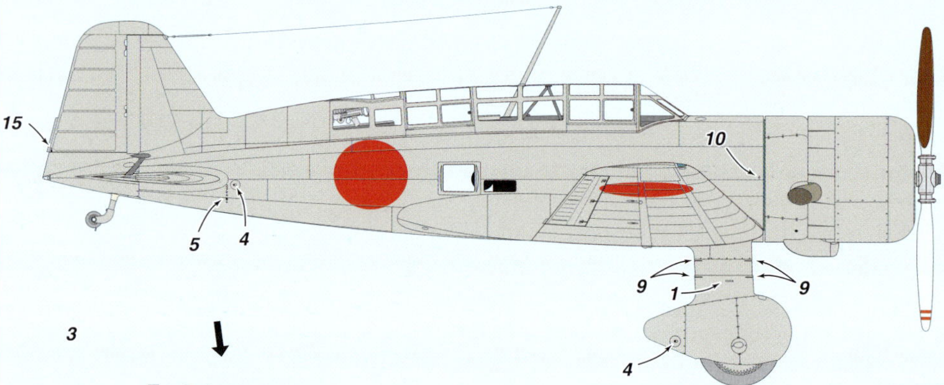

3

Foot step arrow

4

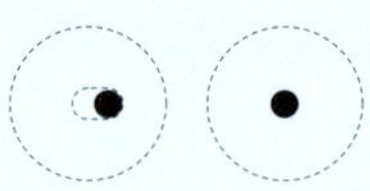

Access panel spot

5

Trestle markings

6

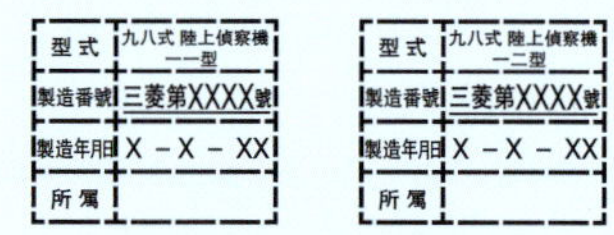

Aircraft data stencils
C5M1 (Model-11) and C5M2 (model-12)

7

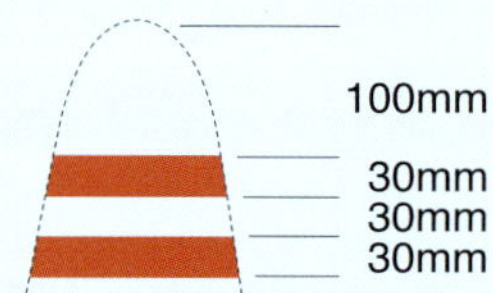

Propeller tip markings

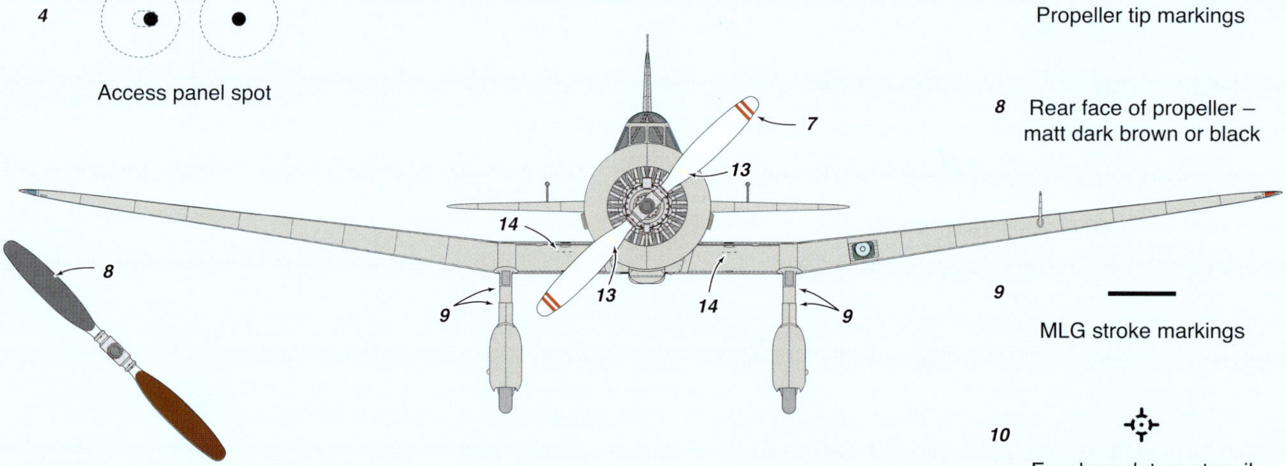

8 Rear face of propeller – matt dark brown or black

9

MLG stroke markings

10

Fuselage datum stencil

11

Centre of gravity stencil

12

Rearmost centre of gravity stencil

13

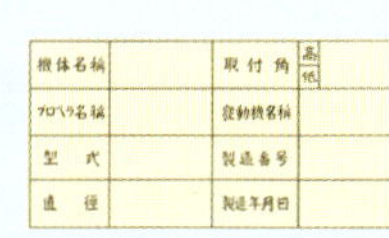

Propeller decal

C5M2

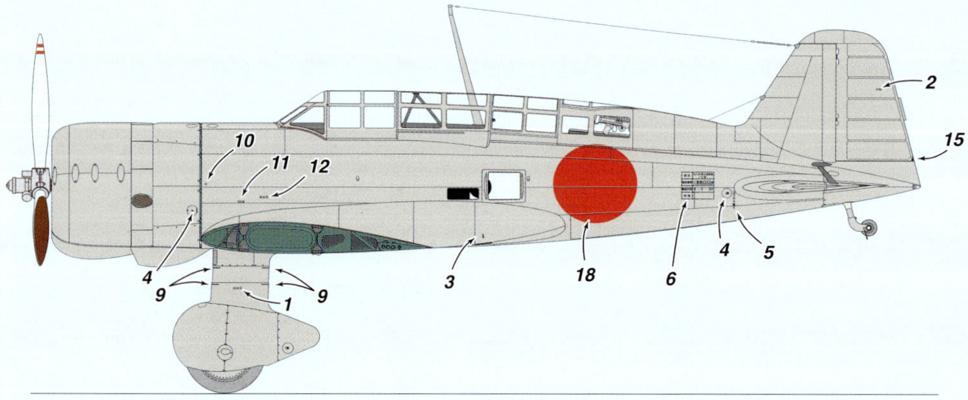

© Giuseppe Picarella 2020

C5M Standard finish and markings

1/72 Scale

Mitsubishi/Navy J3 Ash Grey (gloss)

Mitsubishi/Navy black (satin) – cockpit/centre canopy tunnel top surface

Hinomaru red (gloss)

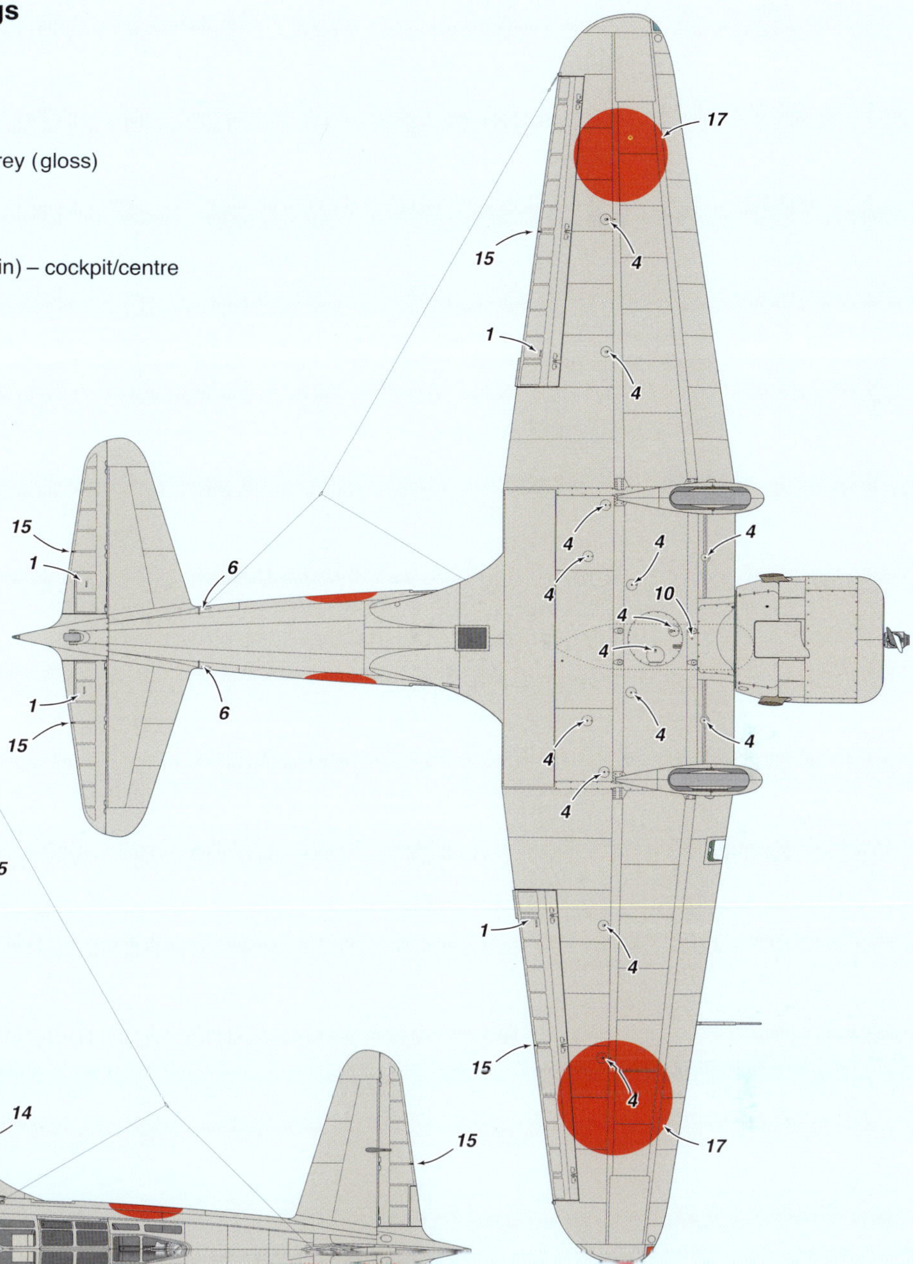

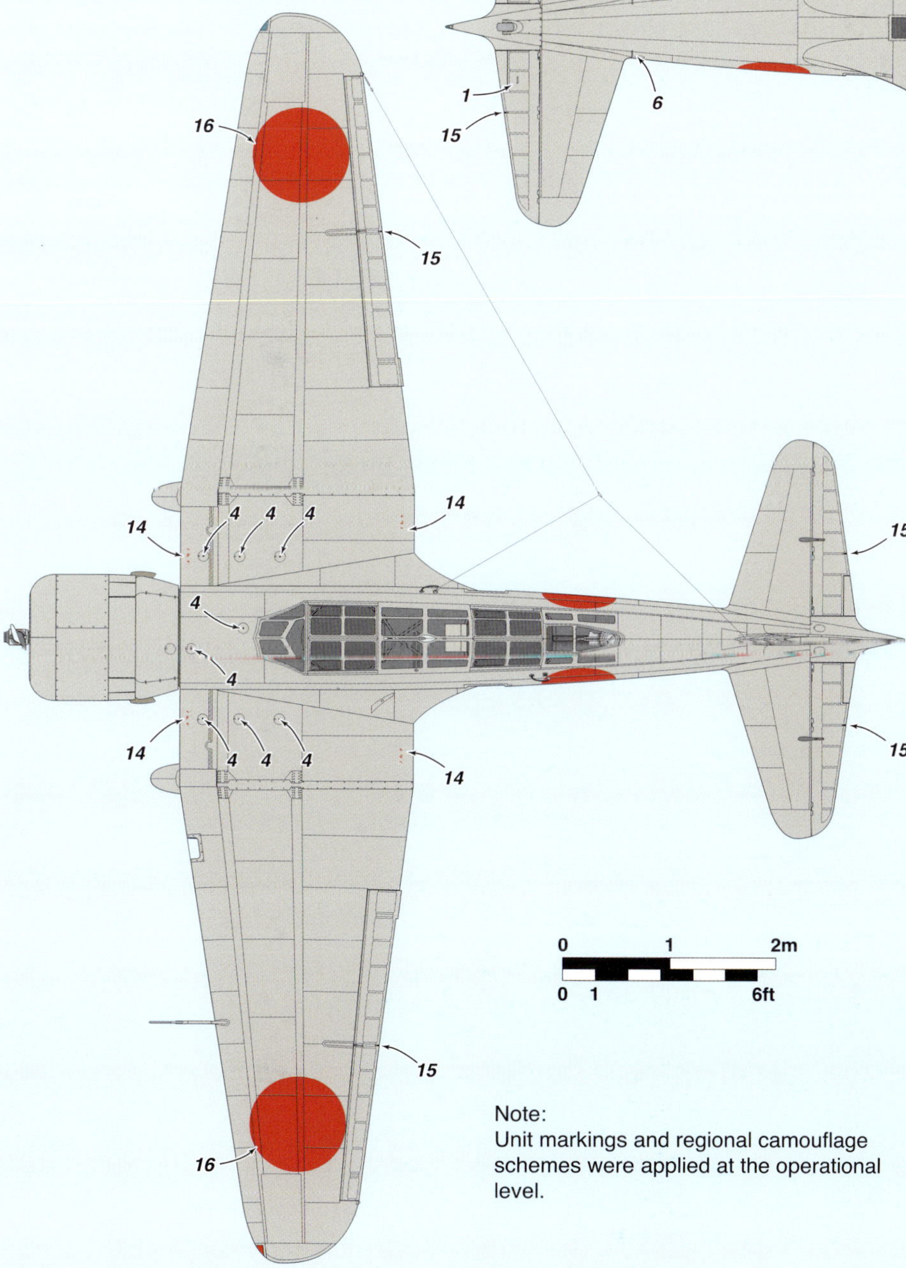

0 1 2m
0 1 6ft

Note:
Unit markings and regional camouflage schemes were applied at the operational level.

14 ノ ル ナ
No Step warning

15 測
Control surface measuring/ rigging point stencil

16
Hinomaru markings (upper wings) – approximately 90cm diameter

17
Hinomaru markings (lower wings) – approximately 90cm or 110cm diameter

18
Hinomaru markings (fuselage) – approximately 70cm and 80cm diameter

dividual unit and also its designated combat role. Unfortunately, because C5Ms were often embedded within fighter or bomber units, etc., they often adopted the markings of those units.

- 100–199 Reconnaissance unit.
- 200–299 Fighter unit.
- 300–399 Interceptor unit.
- 400–499 Seaplane unit.
- 500–599 Torpedo and Carrier Bomber unit.
- 600–699 Land-based unit aboard a carrier.
- 700–799 Attack Bomber unit.
- 800–899 Flying boat unit.
- 900–999 Patrol and anti-submarine unit.
- 1000+ Transport unit.

Fuselage bands

Unlike the Army's ubiquitous white identification band, the Navy used fuselage bands and chevrons (of various colours) to identify an aircraft's specific position within a unit, or as command markings for *Chutai* leaders, etc. The small numbers of fuselage bands depicted on C5Ms seem to be white in colour. They ranged from 100 to 150mm wide and were located between FS.11 and FS.13.

Given the limited number of C5Ms and their operational roles, fuselage bands were most likely used to denote either an attachment to a higher organization, such as a fleet identifier, or an individual *Chutai* within a *Kokutai*.

Camouflage

During operations in China, some C5M aircraft would have adopted the standard two-tone (green and brown) camouflage scheme, similar to the Navy's bomber aircraft. Following the beginning of the Pacific war, those C5Ms that remained embedded within island-based combat units would have quickly adopted regional camouflage. Unfortunately, no photographs of camouflaged C5Ms have thus far been traced. Those aircraft that were still in service during 1943, would have received yellow/orange wing leading-edge recognition markings.

C5M Operational markings
1/48 Scale

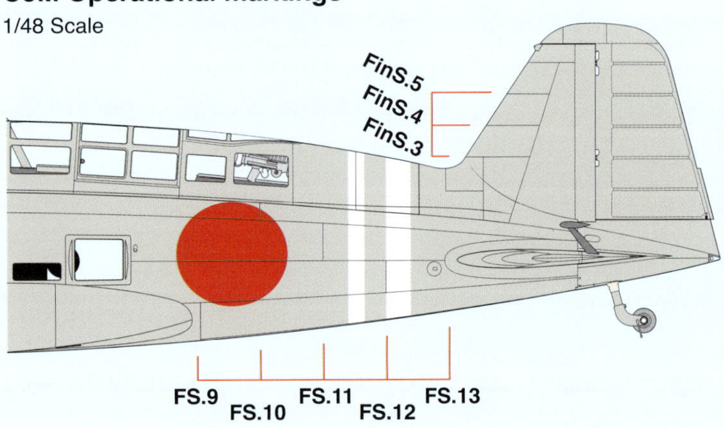

Typical width and placement of the Navy fuselage bands and hinomaru.

Unit markings were confided to the fin and rudder of the aircraft, between FinS.3 and FinS.5. These markings were typically composed of an identifier letter or numeral, followed by the aircraft's individual position within the Kokutai.

Given the limited number of C5Ms and their operation deployment, fuselage bands were most likely used to denote either an attachment to a higher organization or an individual Chutai within a Kokutai.

Fin Station (FinS) points
Frame Station (FS) points

© Giuseppe Picarella 2020

Reconnaissance duties over China

Between April and August 1939, Mitsubishi delivered 10 C5M1 airframes to the Navy, which was very slow in comparison to Ki-15 production, which amounted to 51 airframes for the same period. What is more, the figure of 51 airframes did not including the manufacture of C5M1 "rolling airframes", which actually raised the Ki-15 output up to 61 deliveries! With such low delivery numbers it is most likely that the first one or two C5M airframes would have been considered as prototypes, or at best, pre-production examples. As such, these aircraft would have been passed on to the *Yokosuka Kokutai* for official Navy evaluations, together with examples going to the various *Kokutai* for operational training. Historically the Navy had always undertaken advanced and specialized training within its operational units, for both operational and budgetary reasons, but as the air arm of the service expanded, it was deemed necessary to establish advanced and specialized aircrew training courses in 1938. In general, the Japanese naval aircrew-training program was considered to be of the highest standard before the outbreak of the Pacific war, with training typically being undertaken at several locations around Japan and its empire.

Once type conversion onto the aircraft had been completed the Navy was eager to deploy the C5M1 into service, as a matter of pride, in order to reduce its reliance on the Army for strategic and tactical reconnaissance material, damage assessments and weather reports in the Chinese theatre. At that time though, the Navy had not devised an overall working plan for it new land-based reconnaissance aircraft, but they eyed the Army's operational usage of the Ki-15 with great interest. If their C5M1 was going to operate in a similar pre-strike and weather observation role it would need to be able to communicate with other aircraft in the air, which is not as easy as it might seem. In 1939, Navy bombers tended to use the wireless-telegraph (Morse code) system, in order to communicate over long distances back to their home bases. Bulky wireless-telephone (voice) equipment had also made an appearance onboard bombers operating over China, allowing them to communicate with ground forces and airfield control towers, but such communications were generally frowned upon, because "radio silence" was the order of the day. Radio transmissions would not only alert the Chinese of their approach, but radio triangulation could also track the source of the transmissions and pinpoint the location of the bombers, allowing fighters to be vectored to intercept them. In addition to this, only coded wireless-telegraph communications could be considered safe for transmitting combat information. Radio equipment fitted to fighter aircraft was still a novelty, with the first operational examples being installed on a small number of A5M2bs, before appearing as standard on the A5M4 during the latter half of 1938. Weight limitations and single-pilot operations meant that fighter aircraft could only used the smaller, lighter, short-range Type-96 Ku Mk.1 wireless-telephone device, as it would have been impossible to tap out Morse code on a wireless-telegraph key while engaged in a dogfight!

Luckily, the RO's radio installed aboard the C5M1 was capable of communicating via both wireless-telegraph and wireless-telephone devices, but this assumed that they had somebody to talk to in the air. Therefore, the decision concerning which units would receive the C5M1 in China would in part be based on whether a unit's existing aircraft were radio-equipped. The Navy finally chose the *12th*, *13th*, *14th Kokutais* during the late summer and *15th Kokutai* in November, but with only six or seven C5M1s available for combat operations, between June and December 1939, it is unclear how many aircraft were allotted to each unit and what role they played in combat.

- *12th Kokutai* – 30 A5M4 and 12 Type-96 Carrier Attack Bombers, B4Y1.
- *13th Kokutai* – 40 G3M.
- *14th Kokutai* – 12 A5M4, 18 G3M and 18 B5N1.
- *15th Kokutai* – 27 G3M.

While the *Kaigun Koku Hombu* did not fully grasp the true value of the strategic reconnaissance aircraft at that time, many of its frontline officers did, as the Navy's long-range "reconnaissance" tasks in China were typically undertaken by G3M bombers, which were not immune to interception and required fighter escorts when operating deep into enemy territory. Also, and perhaps most crucially, in addition to the standard reconnaissance duties provided by Ki-15s of the *18th Dokuritsu Chutai*, Army

Two unidentified C5M1 Version 2 aircraft seen in China. Note the drop-tank installation on the closest aircraft, which was airbrushed out on some press photographs. (Authors collection)

pilots had been operating alongside Navy bombers on actual attack missions, providing real-time information to the bombers, both before and during the bomb runs. These Command & Control or "God's eye" type operations, as we would call them today, provided valuable support to the bomber crews, by identifying enemy fighters as they appeared around the bomber formations and directed escorting Japanese fighters to intercept them.

In this regard the Army's Ki-15s were providing a much broader service than standard reconnaissance duties and this concept interested the Navy, which slowly began to formulate its own ideas concerning the use of the C5M.

On January 15th 1940 a new type of *"Reconnaissance Unit"* was activated as part of the *13th Kokutai* and placed under the command of Navy Lt. Takehiko Chihaya, who quite wisely decided to ask the Army for assistance in training his men with regards the deployment and operation of strategic reconnaissance aircraft. This request was duly sanctioned by both services, and from the beginning of February 1940 the Navy received specialized tuition from Army Capt. Aramaki and the men of the *18th Dokuritsu Chutai.* Once this training was completed the *18th Dokuritsu Chutai* officially handed over its land-based reconnaissance duties to the Navy's *13th Kokutai* and their new C5M1 aircraft. In the meantime, Navy Commander Toihata had reviewed the Army's Ki-15 operations and developed a new set of Navy tactics, which would allow for the similar use of C5Ms in conjunction with G3Ms. Toihata's system proved successful and his diligent work caught the attention of Admiral Yamamoto, who transferred Toihata onto the joint staff of the combined fleet to assist in preparing for the war with the US.

C5M-led Command & Control operations soon became standard practice for Navy bomber missions over China, such as the May 22nd raid on Chungking, when three C5M1s controlled and monitored a formation G3M2s of the *2nd Combined Kokutai.* After advising the bombers to orbit 92km (50 nautical miles) from the target, the C5M1s counted the Chinese fighters and waited for them to land and begin refuelling, at which point the bombers were ordered to commence their attack runs, which resulted in five fighters destroyed on the ground plus numerous others damaged. As a matter of interest it would seem that some C5M1 aircraft carried an additional blue "command" stripe on the rear fuselage, in order for these aircraft to be easily identified in the heat of combat, as they possessed a similar silhouette to the A5M.

To their credit the Chinese were quick learners, as the Japanese tried the same tactics on the 26th, and the Chinese attempted to chase the three C5M1s away from Chungking, but the mission continued regardless and one bomber from the *1st Combined Kokutai* was shot down.

Babs biographies: Takehiko Chihaya 1913

Takehiko Chihaya was born on September 26th 1913, in Tansui (Dansui), Taibeizhou, Taiwan as the second son of Seijiro Chihaya, a Japanese government official attached to the Government General of Taiwan. After completing his elementary education in Taiwan, he entered Kagoshima Middle School in Kagoshima, Kyushu, where he passed the entrance examination of the Navy Academy and was enrolled in the 62nd Class. After graduating in November 1934, his first sea bound assignment was aboard the light cruiser Kiso, *then the torpedo boat* Hiyodori, *before being posted to the battleships* Fusõ *and* Mutsu.

While on the Mutsu *he was crucially selected to be a "Reconnaissance Officer" in the Naval Air Force, entering the Kasumigaura Kokutai as part of the 29th Class in September 1937 and completing the course on May 3rd 1938.*

Initially assigned to Yokosuka Kokutai, he was soon posted to the aircraft carrier Soryu *before becoming a squadron leader in charge of carrier dive-bombers in the Usa Kokutai.*

On January 15th 1940 he was given the responsibility to form and lead the new "Reconnaissance Unit" attached to the 13th Kokutai, which was then fighting in China.

After taking command of the "Reconnaissance Unit" his operational flying came to an end and he served with distinction throughout the remainder of his career.

"Reconnaissance Unit" – 13th Kokutai

The *13th Kokutai* was organized on July 11th 1937, by the Ōmura *Kokutai.* Operating two *Daitai* (squadrons) of A5M fighters, the group moved to Kunda Airfield, Shanghai, on September 5th and participated in the support missions over the city, followed by bomber escort duties to outlying targets such as Nanking, Nanchang and Hankow. In March 1938 the

"Reconnaissance Unit" – 13th Kokutai

1/48 Scale

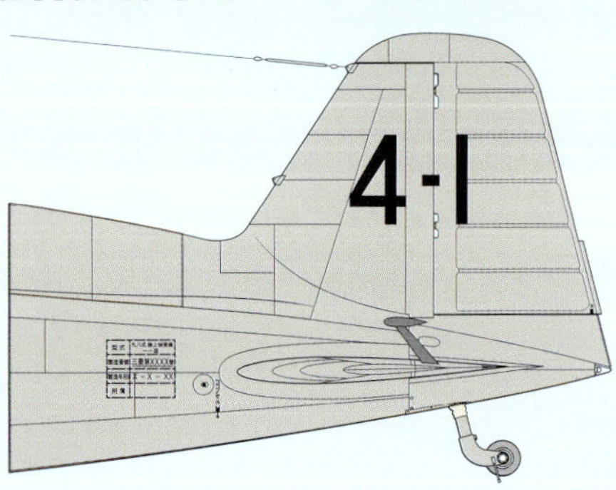

© Giuseppe Picarella 2020

group was reorganized as a land attack group with two individual squadrons. One continuing to operate the A5M for escort duties and the other was issued with 14 G3M2 bombers. In addition to operating bombers the *13th Kokutai* would be the first Navy unit to operate a small number of C5M1 aircraft in combat. As bomber operations increased over China the unit slowly dissolved its fighter unit, which was disbanded official in November 1940, while the bomber unit continuing operations until it too was disbanded in April 1941.

Between October 1937 and April 1941 the unit code of the *13th Kokutai* was **4**.

A match made in heaven

When the new *"Reconnaissance Unit"* was formed within the *13th Kokutai*, the Navy was still experiencing major problems concerning fighter escort missions over China. While combat performance of the A5M was judged to be outstanding, its operational range was not capable of supporting such long-range missions. This meant that the fighters could only escort the G3M when missions were within range of Japanese fighter bases. The answer to Japan's bomber escort problems lay in its new fighter, the A6M *Zeke*, which was capable of more than doubling the range capabilities of the A5M.

With initial service trials completed in early July 1940, the Navy decided to commit a batch of early production A6M2s to actual combat trials in China, reassigning 15 examples from the *Yokohama Kokutai*, to the *12th Combined Kokutai*. On July 15th, some 16 days before the aircraft was officially accepted into service as the Navy Type-0 Carrier Fighter, the first flight of six A6M2s, led by Lt. Tamotsu Yokoyama, departed Omura Air Base on route to Hankou, China. The flight was guided on its journey by a G3M, as was the second flight of nine A6M2s lead by Lt. Saburo Shindo, which departed soon after.

Such rapid and early deployments of new aircraft types were not without their issues however. Pilots of the *12th Kokutai* were not only receiving conversion training on to a new and untested aircraft, they were also operating early production airframes, which suffered from numerous issues, which differed from one airframe to the next. The most common problems were excessive temperature rises related to the engine installation, together with problematic drop tank jettison systems. Most of the initial "bugs" were eventually solved by the efforts of Lt. Shou-ichi Takayama, Lt. Osamu Kokutaiano and Engineer Sototsugu Uzai, but it still took almost a month to declare the *12th Combined Kokutai* operational on the A6M2.

The first combat mission occurred on August 19th, when 12 A6M2s led by Lt. Tamotsu Yokoyama, provided escort duties for a flight of 54 G3Ms on a bombing mission against Chongqing. For the first time the A6M2s were able to escort the bombers throughout the entire mission, although no Chinese fighters were intercepted on that day. This was an anticlimax for the *12th Kokutai*, but it was far from accidental, as the Chinese were already well aware of the existence of Japan's new fighter and wanted to assess the aircraft before committing to battle. Further missions were conducted on August 20th and September 12th, but once again the Chinese refused to intercept the raiding aircraft. For the bomber pilot's these few perfect missions displayed Japanese air superiority and joint operations at their best, but for the fighter pilots they were disappointing, as they desperately wanted to test their aircraft in combat. The only positive outcome

Aircraft "1" is a C5M1 Version 2 of the 15th Kokutai. Note the high gloss finish and elevator mass balance. (Jim Lansdale)

The RO keeps a lookout while this unidentified C5M1 Version 2 taxis through parked aircraft. Note the unit codes on the fin and rudder have been removed from this photograph. (Japan Aeronautical Association)

of these missions was the fuel management experience that had been gained during the long-range flight from Hankou to Chongqing and back, which was in the order of 1,850km (1,000 nautical miles).

While these missions will forever be remembered as the first combat operations of Japan's infamous *Zeke (*or *Zero* as it would become popularly known), what is often overlooked was the support and interaction provided by the C5M1. With its high speed and long-range the C5M1 was capable of operating in tandem with the A6M2 over much of the mission, which presented many possibilities to the Navy. After all, if the Army's real-time support of Navy bombers over China was possible with the Ki-15, then the symbiotic relations between the C5M1 and A6M2 would rapidly become a match made in heaven. This working relationship was soon paying dividends, as previous post-strike reconnaissance reports by Lt. Chihaya's C5M1 crews had observed that shortly after Japanese bombers and fighters had departed the target area, a force of approximately 32 Chinese fighters had appeared over the city and flew a "show-of-force" demonstration for approximately 20 minutes, before returning to a nearby airfield. Some 20 minutes later, after refuelling, the Chinese fighters took off once again and disappeared to the north-west in the direction of Chengdu, where they were no doubt based. This type of intelligence allowed Navy pilots to employ new tactics on the 13th, when 27 G3M2 bombers, supported by 13 A6M2s and one C5M1, mounted an attack mission to Chungking. As prearranged the C5M1 arrived high over the target area well ahead of the attack force, in order to relay weather, wind-speed and aircraft activity via its Navy Type-96 *Ku* Mk.2 "Command" radio. Once the attack was completed, the bombers and fighters departed back to Hankou, but the C5M1 loitered high above Chungking. As predicted, Chinese fighters once again appeared over the city, performing their morale-boosting flight for the benefit of Chungking's citizens, but this time they were in for a shock. While the Japanese fighters had appeared to "depart" back to base to provide an escort for the homeward bound bombers, they had in fact merely vacated the immediate area and were orbiting some 64km (40miles) to the east of the city. The RO onboard the C5M1 informed the A6M2s of the situation and Lt. Shindou's formation rapidly turned around and headed back to Chongqing, gaining altitude as they approached. Upon arrival they swarmed over the 27 Chinese fighters, which consisted of Russian-built Polikarpov I-15bis biplanes and I-16 monoplanes. Within 10 minutes the action was over, with the *12th Combined Kokutai* claiming the destruction of all 27 Chinese fighters, with no Japanese losses. In actual fact the Chinese reported losing 13 fighters outright, with 11 heavily damaged, which was a substantial number of defending aircraft, but the psychological affect of the battle proved to be much more dangerous. Later that same day a flight of Navy Type-99 Carrier Bomber, D3A1 *Val* dive-bombers attacked Chungking once again, followed by another raid on the 15th by B5N Carrier Attack Bombers. Despite both types of aircraft being susceptible to Chinese fighter interception, due to their speed, no attempt to intercept either of these raids was made and the legend of the A6M's invincibility was born – with the direct support of the C5M.

12th Kokutai

The 12th *Kokutai* had been activated on July 11th 1937 at Saeki Naval Air Base, Kyushu, and was rapidly deployed to Kunda in China on August 7th. Operating a mixed unit of A5M fighters, D1A and B5N bombers, the unit provided convoy support until the end of the month, before being posted back to mainland Japan and then on to Shanghai on September 5th. In March 1938, the unit was reorganized into a dedicated fighter unit, operating A5Ms until eventually being chosen to perform combat testing of the A6M in China.

At some point after arriving in China, the *12th Kokutai* was issued with its own C5M1s, in order to provide Command & Control services similar to those offered by the *"Reconnaissance Unit"* of the *13th Kokutai.*

The unit code applied to aircraft of the *12th Kokutai* was 3.

Known C5M aircraft include:

C5M1: **3-1, 3-3 and 3-6.**

12th Kokutai

1/48 Scale

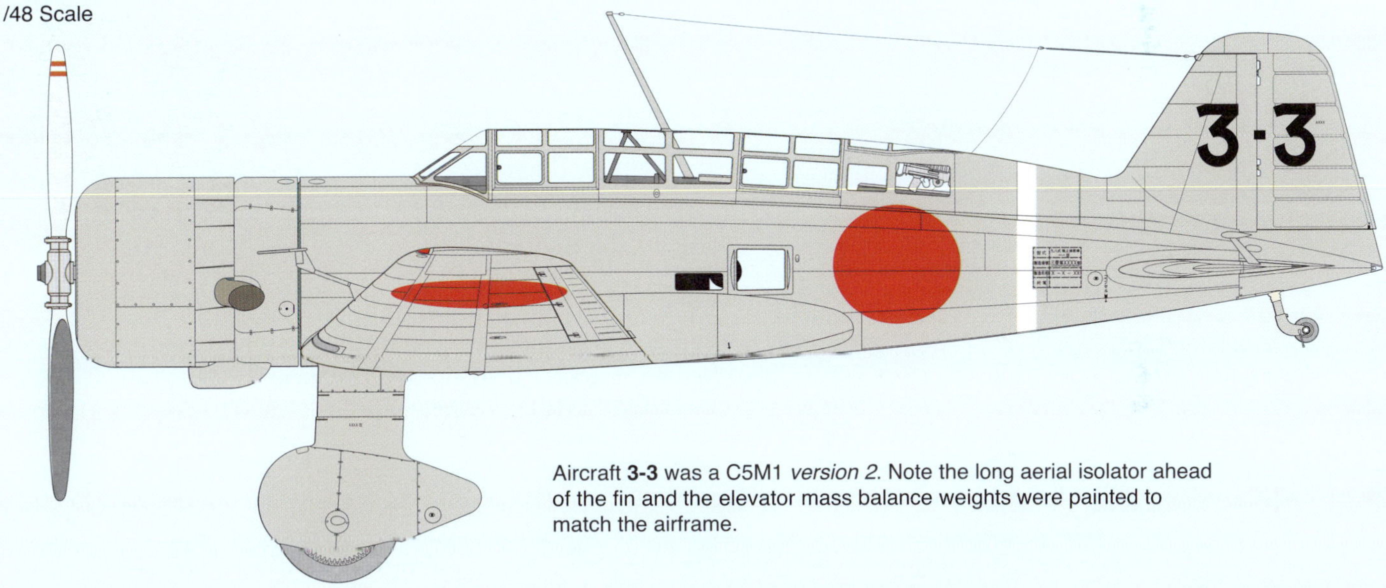

Aircraft **3-3** was a C5M1 *version 2.* Note the long aerial isolator ahead of the fin and the elevator mass balance weights were painted to match the airframe.

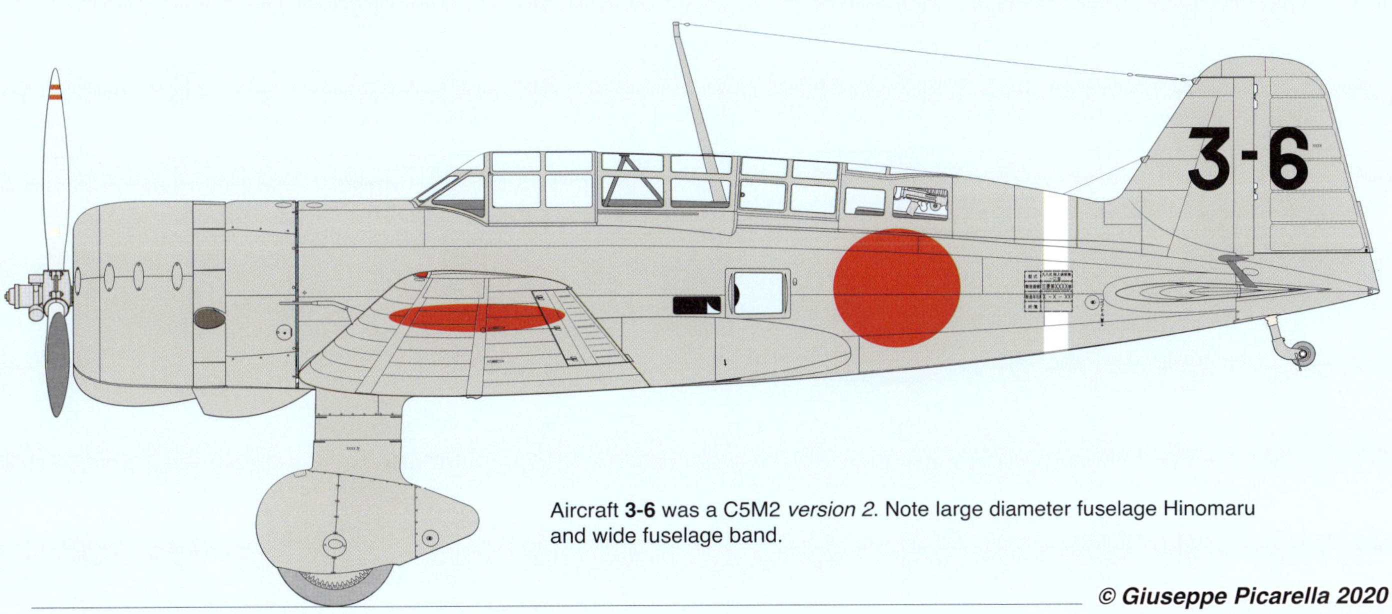

Aircraft **3-6** was a C5M2 *version 2.* Note large diameter fuselage Hinomaru and wide fuselage band.

14th Kokutai

The *14th Kokutai* was formed on April 6th 1938, as a mixed unit operating A4N, A5M2, B4Y and D1A aircraft within three individual *Daitai*. After training the unit was dispatched to Santsao Island on the peninsular of Macao, where it was tasked with both local surveillance missions and regional duties against targets such as Liuchow and Kwangtung, but the unit's A5M2s were involved in very few battles. In December the unit was enlarged and re-equipped with 18 G3Ms and 18 B5Ns. In November 1939 the unit was once again reorganized and reduced in size down to two *Hikotai* (Flying groups), one with 18 A5M4 fighters and the other with nine D1A2 carrier bombers. From that point onwards the unit was involved in heavy combat over Liuchow, then Hankow from May until September 1940, before the fighter group converted over to the A6M2. In June 1941 the *14th Kokutai* was relocated to Hanoi and began operations against Kunming, where it was involved in heavy fighting until the unit was deactivated on September 15th. The unit would rise once more on October 1st 1942 as a seaplane unit, operating the Navy Type-0 Observation Seaplane, F1M1 *Pete* and Navy Type-2 Floatplane Fighter, A6M2-N *Rufe*, in the Solomon Islands, before being reorganized once again to form the *802nd Kokutai* on Novemebr 1st 1942.

While operating the C5M1, the unit code of the *14th Kokutai* was **9**.

14th Kokutai
1/48 Scale

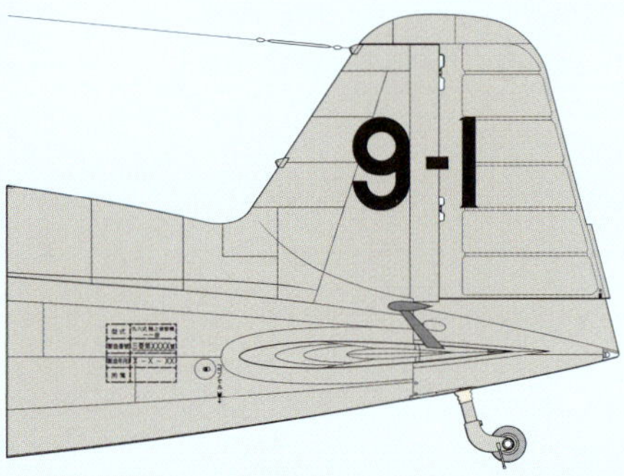

Speculative layout based on contemporary 14th Kokutai markings.

© Giuseppe Picarella 2020

15th Kokutai

The *15th Kokutai* existed in two forms during the Sino-Japanese war. The original unit was formed at Omura Naval Air Base on June 25th 1938, operating A4N, A5M2, B4Y and D1A aircraft within three individual *Daitai*, with the unit code **10**. As the year progressed the unit was slowly upgraded to include newer equipment, including the A5M4 fighter and B5N1 attack bombers, before being disbanded on December 1st 1938.

The second incarnation of the *15th Kokutai* was activated at Kanoya Naval Air Base on November 11th 1939, as a dedicated bomber unit, complete with 27 G3M bombers and two C5M1 land-based reconnaissance aircraft. Operating from Zialam in southern China and then Hanoi in French Indo China, the unit participated in attacks on the Kunming aircraft plant at Loiwing and the Shinetsu Railways, before being disbanded on November 15th 1940.

The unit code applied to aircraft of the second formation of the *15th Kokutai* was **8**.

Known C5M1 aircraft: **8-1** and **8-2**.

15th Kokutai
1/48 Scale

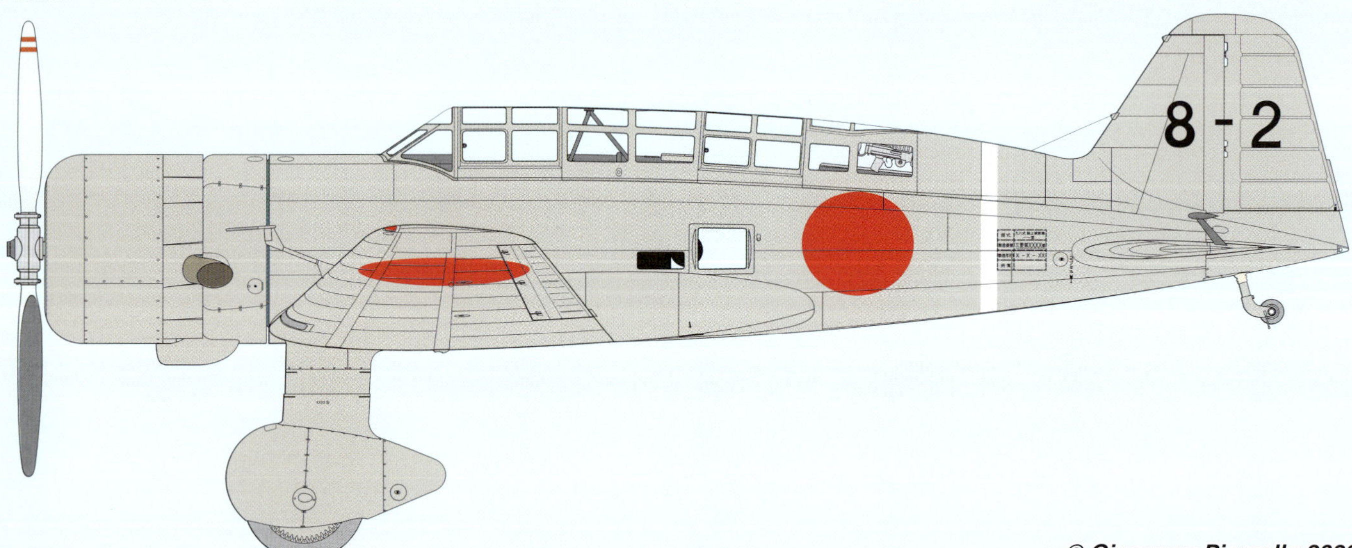

© Giuseppe Picarella 2020

While the concept of distributing C5Ms to every frontline fighter and bomber unit in mainland China would have been welcomed by the *Kokutais*, the reality of this idea was operationally impractical and numerically unworkable. The Navy only purchased 20 C5M1 land-based reconnaissance aircraft during 1939, so by discounting the two or three examples needed for flight and maintenance training in Japan, the Navy was left with left 17 or 18 frontline aircraft for operational use across all of central and southern China. On September 15th 1940, the A6M2 and C5M1 aircraft of the *12th* and *13th Kokutais* were re-allocated amongst the fighter unit attached to the Headquarter of the *22nd Air Flotilla*, and the *3rd* and *Tainan Kokutai* under the *23rd Air Flotilla*. The strength of each unit at that time stood at:

22nd Air Flotilla

Kanoya Kokutai (fighter unit) – 27 A6M2.

Kanoya Kokutai (Reconnaissance unit) – six C5M1.

23rd Air Flotilla

3rd Kokutai – 45 A6M2, three C5M1 and two G6M1-L2 *Betty* bomber-transport conversions.

Tainan Kokutai – 45 A6M2, three C5M1 and two G6M1-L2.

The attack on Chongqing had proven the value of the A6M and the Navy was so delighted with their new fighter that the Commander in Chief of the China Area Fleet issued a unit citation to the *12th Combined Kokutai* for its outstanding victory, within which special recognition was also made regarding the land-based reconnaissance aircraft.

The C5M1 Version 1 aircraft of the 15th Kokutai. While rollover pylons are visible on all three aircraft, note that the nearest aircraft does not have a landing light on the wing leading-edge. (Shoichi Tanaka)

To: No.12 Kokutai
Fighter Force Commanded by Navy Lt. Shindou.
On September 13, 1940, this force escorted attack bomber aircraft in the bombing of Chungking, penetrating, at long range, over the mountain ranges of Sczechuan Province, at one time making a seeming manoeuvre to withdraw in order to draw out enemy aircraft, then penetrating Chungking airspace a second time, ***and with the co-operation of a land-based reconnaissance aircraft****, succeeded in spotting and making contact with 27 enemy fighter aircraft, and through courageous and vigorous combat, definitely shot down all of them, such action being a tremendous feat of arms.*
In recognition of the foregoing this citation is hereby presented.
October 31, 1940
China Area Fleet
Commander in Chief Shigetaro Shimada

After two weeks of maintenance and mission planning, additional A6M2 flights were staged in support of long-range bomber missions, penetrating deeper and deeper into Chinese territory, most of which being supported or guided to their target by their own C5M1s.

By this point in time the Chinese were well aware of the abilities of the *Babs*. They understood that once such reconnaissance aircraft were observed in the vicinity of cities and military establishments, attack missions soon followed, but few aircraft were capable of matching the speed of these potent reconnaissance aircraft. On November 2nd an attempt to intercept a C5M was made by Gloster Gladiators of the 26th Pursuit Squadron over Wuming airfield, Kwangsi. Knowing the high-speed capabilities of the C5M, Capt. Arthur "Art" Sui-tin Chin positioned two Gladiators over opposing sides of airfield and was able to make a single head-on attack as the aircraft departed the area. His plan partially worked, as he badly damaged the *Babs*, injuring the RO, Sub-Lt. Yonetaro Ueda in the process, but it failed to down the aircraft, which returned safely to base.

C5M2

Despite the Navy's ambivalence to the concept of land-based strategic reconnaissance, its value in the tactical reconnaissance role was much appreciated by commanders in the field, who utilized the aircraft for a variety of additional roles, including that of a navigation lead-ship, Command & Control aircraft and long-range weather observation aircraft. But as the 1930s drew to a close, the technological lead that the Ki-15-II/C5M1 once held over the Chinese was slowly being eroded by more advanced Soviet and Western fighters. Recognizing this shortfall the Navy began to outline an improved C5M model, which could also better complement their new A6M fighter.

In order to increase the performance of the C5M, Mitsubishi redesigned the aircraft from the firewall (FS.0) forwards, with a completely new engine, propeller and cowling. The engine chosen for this upgrade was the Nakajima NAM, or *Sakae 12*/NK1C, the same 940hp two-row 14 cylinder radial engine as fitted to the A6M2. The decision to utilize this engine was twofold: it would increase the performance of the aircraft, while engine commonality with the A6M would also allow for easier maintenance and simplify supply-chains in theatre. Commonality of parts also extended to the constant-speed, three-blade propeller hub, a modified A6M cowling assembly, cowl flap installation, engine mount and oil cooler assembly. In effect the redesign amounted to the installation of an A6M-type "power-egg" onto the front of the C5M1 airframe.

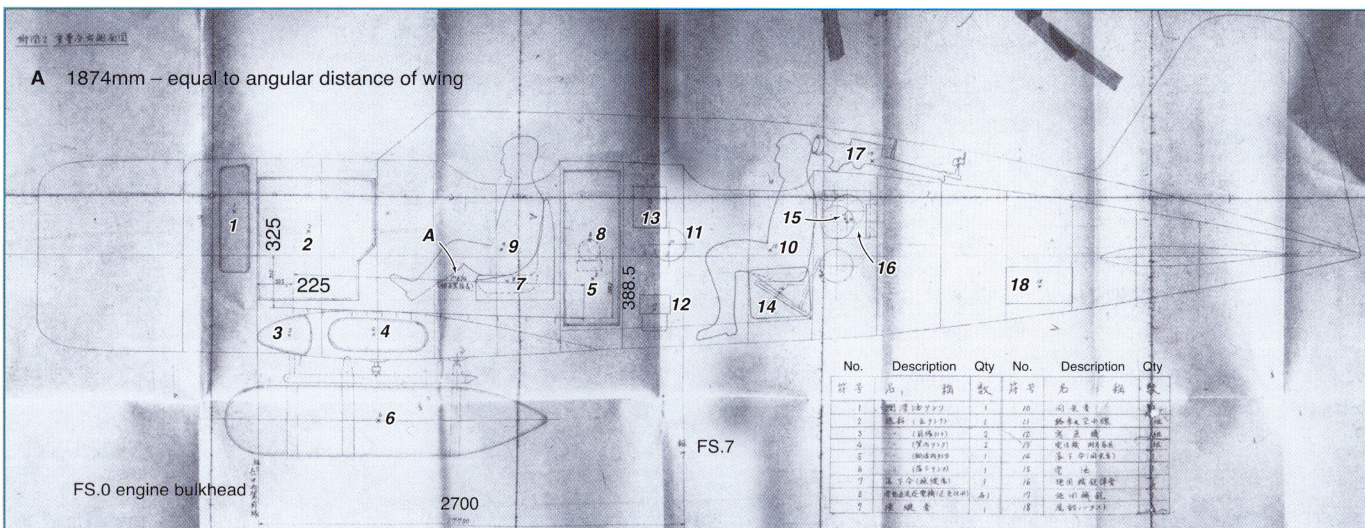

C5M2 Inboard profile

An original Mitsubishi engineering drawing.

1 Oil tank – 1
1 Fuel (main tank) – 1
3 Fuel (leading-edge tank) – 2
4 Fuel (wing tank) – 2
5 Fuel (fuselage tank) – 1
6 Fuel (drop tank) – 1
7 Parachute (pilot) – 1
8 Direct current generator – 1 right side
9 Pilot – 1
10 Copilot/passenger – 1
11 Reel and antenna – 1 full set
12 Camera – 1 full set
13 Radio installation – 1 full set
14 Copilot parachute – 1
15 Battery – 1
16 Machine gun magazine – 6
17 Flexible machine gun – 1
18 Tail ballast – 1

Sakae 12/NK1C engine – prosperity of range

Originally conceived with the Navy in mind, the NAM engine was first adopted into service by the Army during 1938, for installation in the Type-1 Fighter, Ki-43 *Oscar*, under the Ha-25 designation. In this configuration the engine was specifically tuned to produce its maximum power at take-off, which exceeded 980hp. This figure came tantalising close to fulfilling the Navy's requirement for an indigenous two-row radial capable of producing 1,000hp and the engine was soon ordered into production under the *Sakae 11*/NK1B designation, for installation in the Type-97 Carrier Attack Bomber Model-12, B5N2 *Kate*.

Jiro Horikoshi had originally selected the 870hp *Zuisei 13* engine (a *Zuisei 11* fitted with a machine-gun interrupter) for use on the new 12-*Shi* Carrier Fighter, as it offered the best chance of meeting the performance requirements of the program, a decision that was also swayed by the desire to utilize a Mitsubishi engine, rather than one of its competitors, as had been the case with the A5M. Unfortunately, history would repeat itself again, as despite meeting almost all of the performance requirements of the program, the *Zuisei 13* could not propel the first two prototypes of the A6M1 to their required top speed. At that point the Navy instructed Mitsubishi to install the *Sakae* engine in to the 3rd prototype for comparison purposes, redesignating the aircraft as the A6M2. While the Navy's decision may have upset Mitsubishi, there was method to their madness as this new variant of the engine, the *Sakae 12*/NK1C, had been specifically tuned for better altitude performance, and more crucially, it was producing very encouraging lean cruise performance, which could edge the A6M closer to its stringent range and power loading requirements. In addition to the obvious performance improvements, the Navy was also of the opinion that the *Sakae* engine offered better growth potential than the *Zuisei*, especially in regards to the incorporation of a two-speed supercharger. The resulting marriage of A6M airframe and the *Sakae 12*/NK1C engine would produce the finest naval fighter in the world at that time.

But how does all of this impact upon the design of the C5M2? Despite being almost identical in overall size and layout to the A6M, Mitsubishi's Engineering Dept. was well aware that the adoption of the *Sakae 12*/NK1C engine would not greatly increase the C5M2s top speed, in fact it would only prove to be 10kt (19km/h or 12mph) faster than the C5M1. The reason for this relatively modest increase in performance was simple aerodynamics. By the beginning of 1941, the *Babs* lagged behind the aerodynamic refinements of the A6M2, which possessed a smaller (fuselage) wetted area, an improved aerofoil section and a retractable landing gear. The cumulative effect of these design features meant that the A6M2b airframe, with the same *Sakae 12*/NK1C engine, was 25kt (47km/h or 29mph) faster than the C5M2.

So why did the Navy expend time, effort and money on what at first glance appears to be a mediocre upgrade to 30 airframes? The answer lies in the extremely low fuel consumption rate of the *Sakae 12*/NK1C. Following its entry into service the long-range capabilities of the A6M2 were explored and perfected, to the point where it could be coaxed to "sip" as little as 63 litres per hour, giving a range in excess of 3,100km, based on its 865lt fuel capacity!

Despite being less aerodynamically clean, such range figures were exactly what the Navy needed to extend its land-based reconnaissance capabilities during the opening phase of the of the Pacific war. Unfortunately, the exact range figures for the C5M2 are shrouded in confusion, with 600nautical miles (690miles or 1,110km) being listed in Mitsubishi documentation. See Chapter 6, **Dimensions and performance figures.**

In addition to the engine modifications, the flight control systems were once again amended to "Navy" standards, with changes made to the rudder horn-balance assembly and the pitot head. The pilot's canopy was also extensively redesigned to allow it to slide fore and aft, rather than the original bi-fold arrangement of the Ki-15. The full listing of all known C5M2 modifications are included within Chapter 4, **Technical Description.**

Little is known about the C5M development programs, but one interesting photograph shows what is thought to be a development airframe exhibiting several unusual features, including a three-blade constant-speed propeller fitted to a standard Ki-15-II/C5M1 straight cowling. While the C5M2 would

This unusual photograph potentially depicts the Mitsubishi/Navy C5M1/C5M2 development airframe, complete with a three blade propeller and elevator mass balance installation. Note the black or brown oil system access panels and the square (Ki-46 style) boarding step. (Jim Lansdale)

ultimately receive a three-blade propeller, production aircraft were fitted with subtly shaped cowlings, similar to the A6M2 installation. To be fair, the aircraft in the photograph could have been fitted with the new Nakajima *Sakae* 12 engine (of 1,115mm diameter), or the standard Ki-15-II/C5M1 Mitsubishi Ha-26-I *Zuisei* 12 engine (of 1,118mm diameter), plus a three-blade propeller. While the latter installation is not unique, as the Army Type-LO transport *Toby* (Lockheed Model 14-38) utilized such an installation in 1939, it is unusual to say the least, but it would have been a quick and easy way of testing the *Babs* airframe with a three-blade propeller. The inclusion of a Navy data stencil on the rear fuselage is also telling, because it would indicate that the aircraft is most likely a Navy development airframe for the C5M1 and C5M2 programs, rather than a Mitsubishi development airframe, used across all the development programs. It is also interesting to note that the ROs cockpit was a fitted with a larger boarding step, similar to the step that was subsequently adopted on the Ki-46 *Dinah*.

Development and testing of the C5M2 began in the latter half of 1940, but the whole process was afforded a low priority by the Navy and Mitsubishi, which was struggling at that time to develop the next generation of Army and Navy combat aircraft in the form of the Ki-46, A6M and G4M *Betty*. Testing was finally completed during the winter and the aircraft was ordered into production in January 1941 and officially accepted into service on July 3rd as the Navy Type-98 Reconnaissance Plane Model-12, C5M2. In total, 30 examples of the C5M2 would be built between January and August 1941. See Chapter 7, **Production figures and construction numbers**.

C5M development airframe

1/48 Scale

Believed to be the development aircraft for the C5M program, this C5M1 airframe exhibited several unusual features.

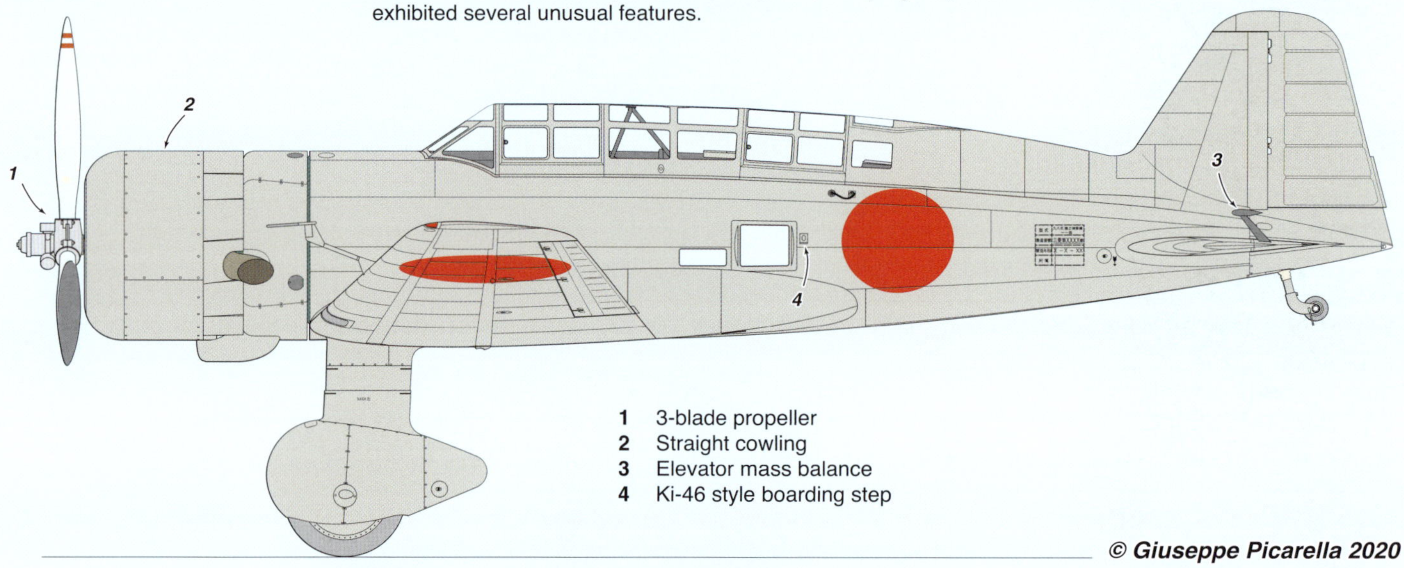

Vibration and resonance testing

During the winter of 1940 the Kaigun Koku Hombu, Department of Engineering were involved in a prolonged test program, investigating the vibration characteristics and resonant frequencies of operational and development airframes. This process was accomplished by hoisting each aircraft into a horizontal flying configuration and running the engine. Test results were monitored and recorded on specialized sensors located on the RO's cockpit floor, exactly 245cm aft of FS.0. Examples of the C5M1 and C5M2 were included in the test program between December 11th *and* 16th *December. The subsequent 27-page report entitled* ***"Type-98 Ground Reconnaissance Aircraft (Kamikaze model). Mitsubishi test No217 – Ground Vibration Test Section"*** *detailed the purpose of vibration test as: "To investigate the vibration condition of Type 98 Ground Reconnaissance Plane in respect to propeller installations – 2 blades fixed joint, 2 constant-speed blades and 3 constant-speed blades." Testing was performed at the Hangar of the Aero Experimental Division Ground Team and was managed by Navy engineers Matsudaira and Hata. Mitsubishi support was provided by Technicians Esashi, Degawa, Abe and Tajiri. It is interesting to note that Engineer Tadashi Matsudaira would later go on to assist in solving the flutter issues experienced by the A6M Zeke.*

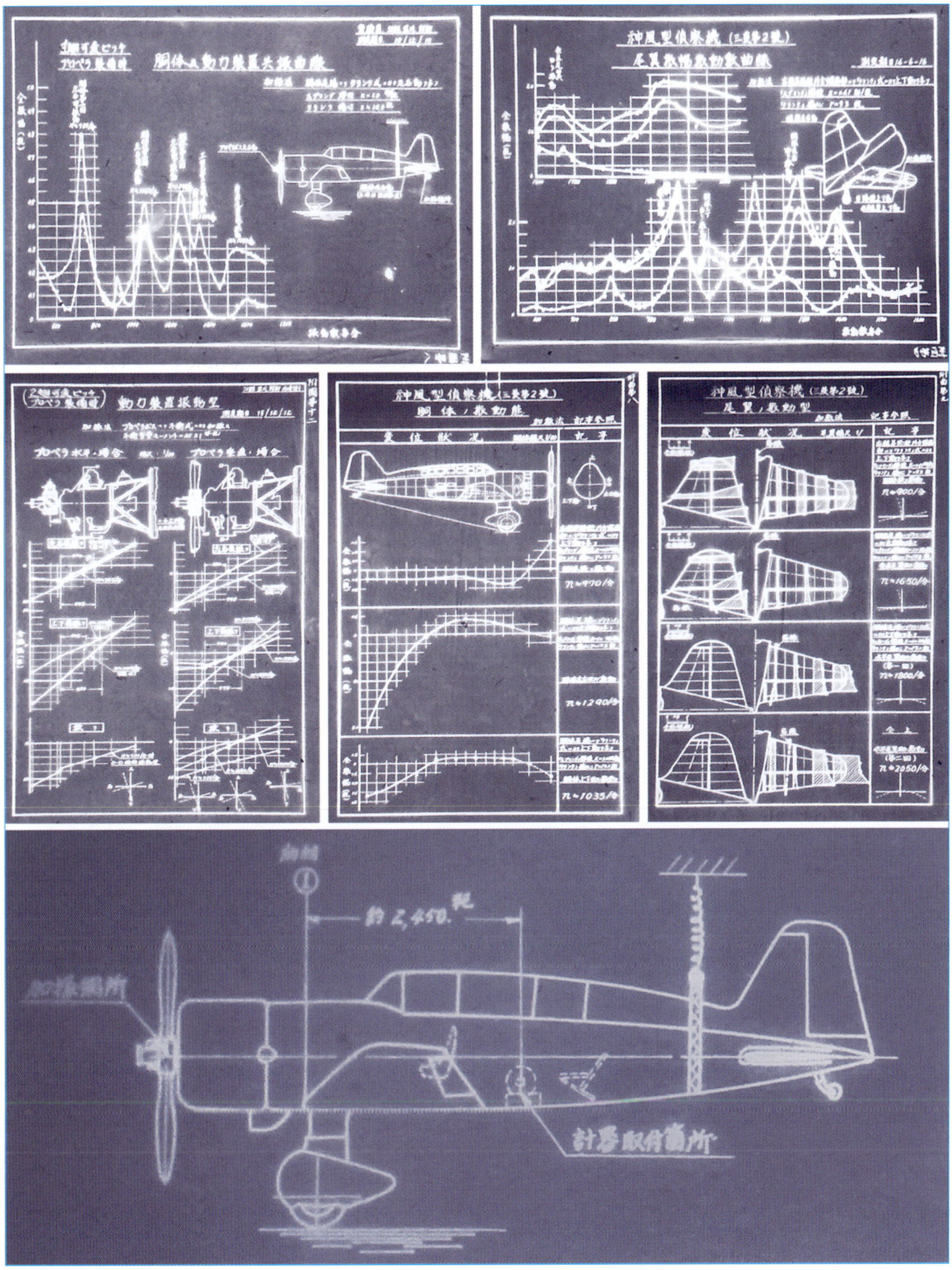

Vibration report.

Takao Kokutai and "Operation 101"

The *Takao (Kaohsiung) Kokutai* was activated at Takao Naval Air Base, Formosa, on April 1st 1938. It was the fourth land-based attack bomber unit to be formed by the Navy, after the *Tateyama Kokutai*, *Kisarazu Kokutai* and *Kanoya Kokutai*, and the first *Kokutai* to be established in Formosa. Equipped with 12 operational and six spare G3M bombers, it was organized (together with the *Kanoya Kokutai*) with the capability of fielding six operational and three spare Navy Type-95 Carrier Fighters, or A4Ns. The first combat mission of *Takao Kokutai* was against the airfield at Fuchou, China on April 27th 1938 with 12 G3Ms, after which time the unit was almost continually involved with attack missions until September, when it was brought back up to standard strength. On the 15th, the unit was deployed to San-a, on Hainan Island, in order to participate in bombing missions against military facilities in Wuzhou, Guilin, Liuzhou, Longzhou and Guiyang in southern China, including the first attack on the capital of Yunnan Province, Kunming, on September 28th. After participating in bombing operation against the Guangdong area in October, the unit returned to Takao in mid November and continued to fly extended attack missions against airfields in the two provinces of Guanxi and Hunan.

Mitsubishi C5M2 *version 1* and *version 2*

1/72 Scale

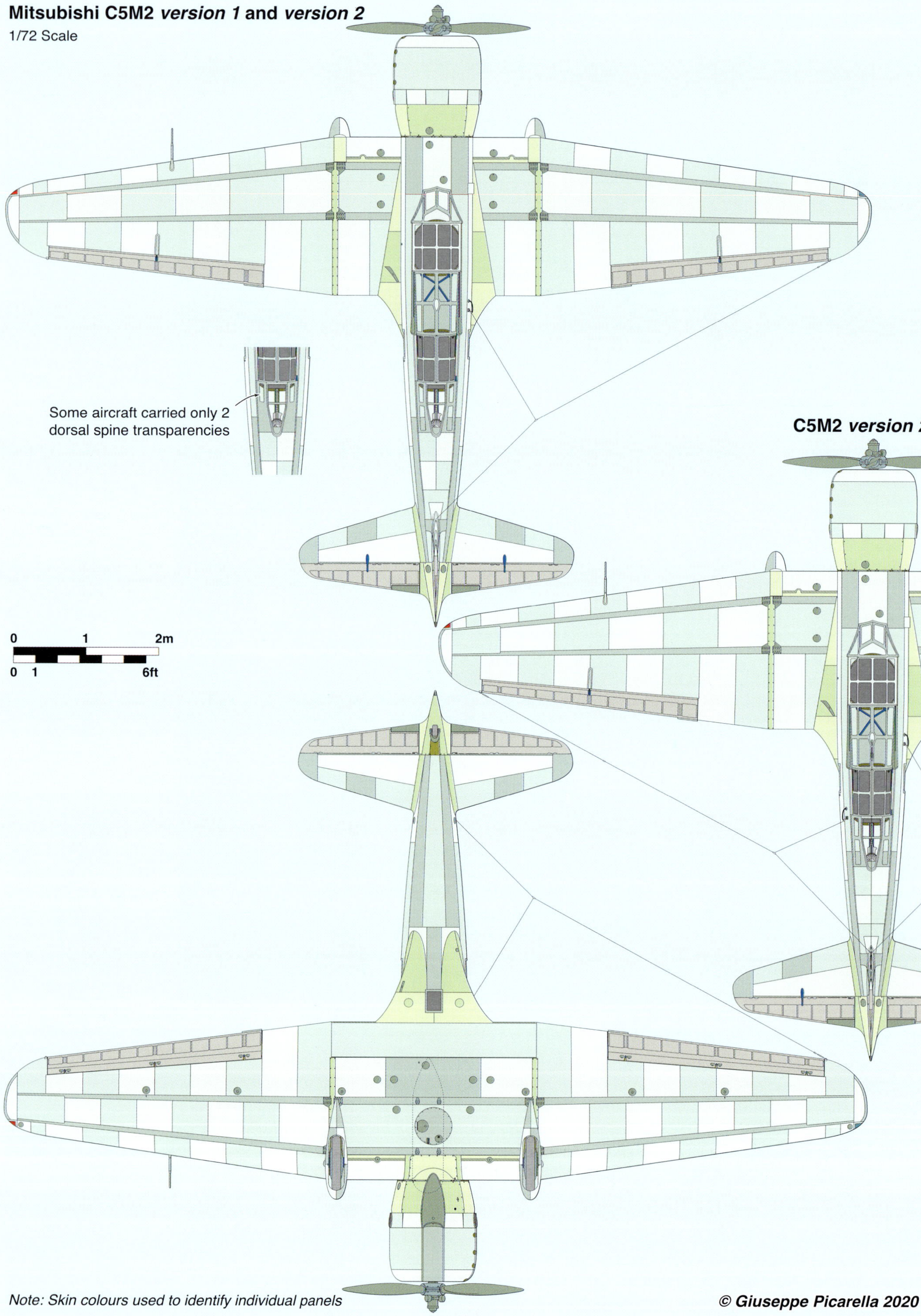

Note: Skin colours used to identify individual panels

Mitsubishi C5M2 *version 1* and *version 2*

1/72 Scale

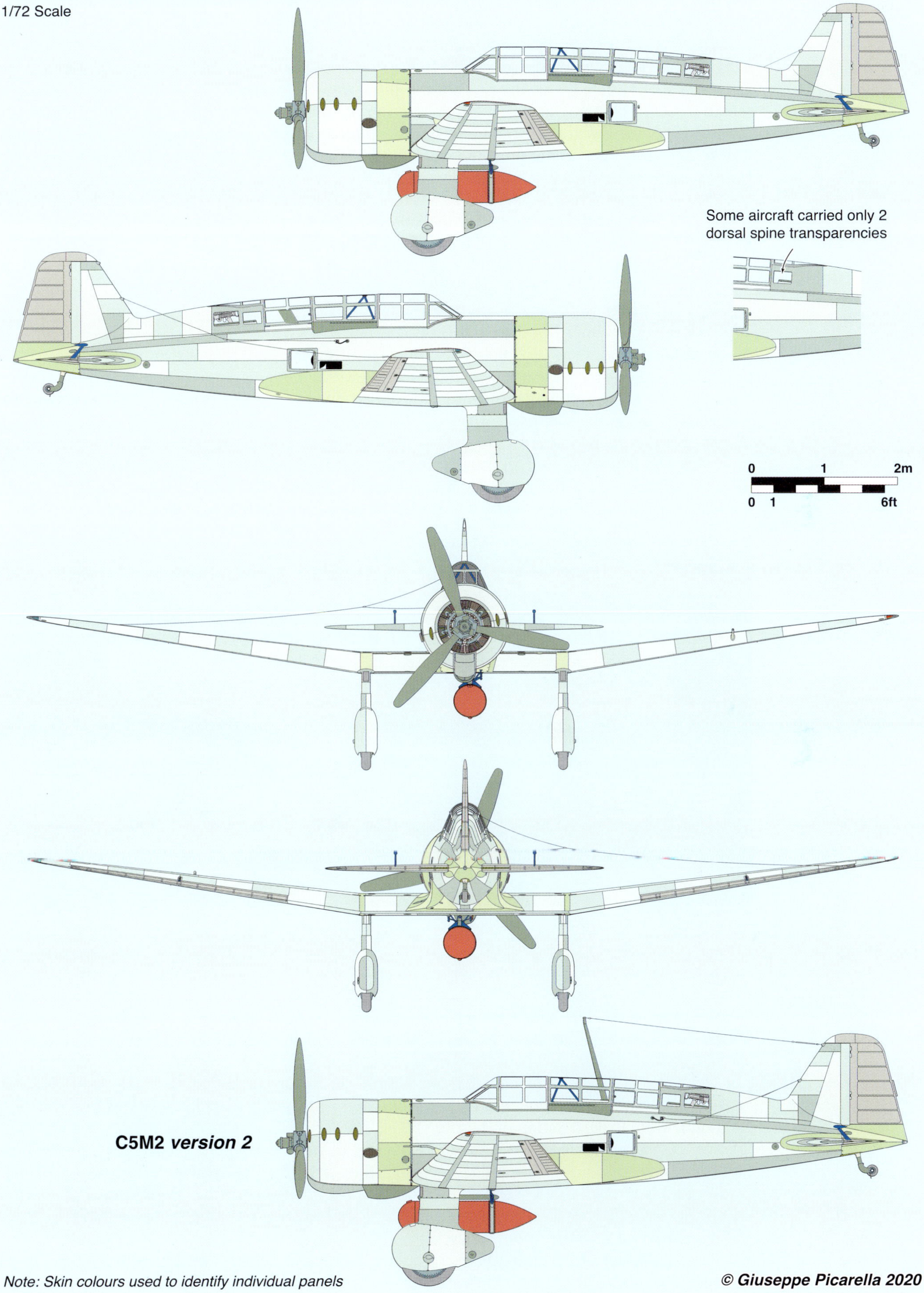

Note: Skin colours used to identify individual panels

By the end of 1938, the *Kaigun Koku Hombu* was becoming concerned that many of its new land-based attack units and aircrews had only experienced land-based aerial bombing missions in support of the Army forces on the China mainland, so it began a series of deployments intended to re-qualify their land-based attack bomber units in the art of open-sea or anti-shipping operations. In late November the *Takeo Kokutai* was once again deployed to San-a, to participate in such training, which it completed on December 12th. During the winter of 1939 the *Takao Kokutai* proceeded to southern China once again to participate in bombing missions, before returning home to continue anti-ship training. From January 15th 1940, the *Takao Kokutai* and *Kisarazu Kokutai* took turns being assigned to the *1st Combined Kokutai* for open-sea training until the end of April. On May 11th, the unit proceeded to base-W at Hankou, with orders to participate in "Operation 101", the strategic air operation against Chongqing and Chengdou, which was undertaken between May 17th and September 5th. The attack force included:

- The *1st Combined Kokutai* formed of the *Kanoya Kokutai* and *Takao Kokutai*.
- The *2nd Combined Kokutai* formed of the *12th Kokutai* and *13th Kokutai*.
- The *3rd Combined Kokutai* formed from a partial deployment of the *14th Kokutai* and the *15th Kokutai*.

During "Operation 101" great use was made of the *"Reconnaissance Unit"* of the *13th Kokutai*, with its C5Ms supporting long-range bombing missions to strategic points such as Chongqing and Kunming. Typically taking off ahead of the main G3M and newer G4M bomber force, their C5Ms approached the target area at altitudes of 7,000m (22,965ft) and higher, from where they reported on weather conditions and enemy movements. The bomber crews were highly appreciative of this information, but command and reporting paths continually undermined such support missions, because the C5Ms were directly under the command of the *13th Kokutai* and *15th Kokutai*, and as such the *Takao Kokutai* and *Kanoya Kokutai* had no operational control over their duties! Even for the Navy this situation was somewhat absurd, but rather than forming an independent reconnaissance service which could support the needs of the whole Naval Air Force, it was decided to form a 5th *Chutai* (division) within the *Kanoya Kokutai*, as a *"Reconnaissance Unit"*, specifically for use within the two bomber groups!

Aircraft "6" was a C5M2 Version 2 of the 12th Kokutai. *(Showzow Abe)*

Kanoya Kokutai

The *Kanoya Kokutai* had been organized on April 1st 1936, at Kanoya Naval Base and despite being established specifically as a land-based attack aircraft unit, the first aircraft to be operated were A4N1 fighters. In October the unit received the new A5M fighter and G3Ms, which were used operationally in China from July 1937 onwards. The unit would go on to deploy the G4M and A6M throughout the remainder of its illustrious career (including its reorganizations into the *751st Kokutai*), until its deactivation on July 10th 1944. The *Kanoya Kokutai's* operational use of the *Babs* within its *"Reconnaissance Unit"* was somewhat short lived, because once preparations for the invasion of northern French Indo-China were initiated in early 1941, the whole *"Reconnaissance Unit"* was transferred to the *Takao Kokutai*, becoming known thereafter as the *"Reconnaissance Unit"* of the *Takao Kokutai*, with its experienced commanding officer and reconnaissance expert Lt. Chihaya being transferred accordingly on January 25th, 1941.

Between January 1938 and October 31st 1940, the *Kanoya Kokutai* unit code was **Y**, changing to **K** from November 1st 1940 until the spring of 1943.

"Reconnaissance Unit" – Kanoya Kokutai
1/48 Scale

Speculative layout based on contemporary Kanoya Kokutai markings.

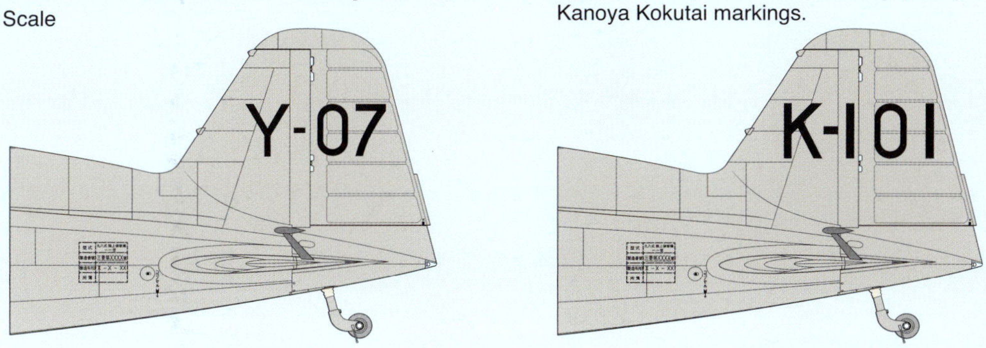

© Giuseppe Picarella 2020

"Reconnaissance Unit" – Kanoya Kokutai

On October 1st the *"Reconnaissance Unit"* of the *Kanoya Kokutai* was formed and placed under the command Lt. Chihaya, who had been responsible for forming and moulding the highly effective *"Reconnaissance Unit"* of the *13th Kokutai.*

Preparations for war

From October 1940 the Navy slowly began to withdraw many of its frontline bomber and fighter units from China, passing those duties over to the Army, as it reorganized and prepared for operations in South-east Asia. At that time the Navy decided to reorganize its air power into one "Air Fleet" rather than individual carrier fleet divisions, bringing both sea and land-based units under one command, allowing better oversight and combined training. On January 15th 1941, the *11th Air Fleet* was established as an expeditionary force, comprised of the *21st Air Flotilla*, the *22nd Air Flotilla* and the *24th Air Flotilla*, expanding to include the *23rd Air Flotilla*, *Destroyer Divisions 34*, *Auxiliary Aircraft Transport vessels* and the *Special Naval Landing Forces* (paratroop forces) as the Navy's strategic plans progressed.

In order to manage the vast tracts of land and sea within the sights of the expanding Japanese Empire, *Kaigun Koku Hombu* divided the Western Pacific and South-east Asia into six Fleet Areas, each of which had at its disposal a fleet of surface vessels, ground forces and an Air Flotilla.

- **Home Island Naval Districts** – Japanese home Islands including, Okinawa, Formosa and the Korean peninsular.
- **North Eastern Area** – Aleutians and Northern Pacific.
- **China Area**
- **Central Pacific Area** – Mariana Islands, Marshall Islands, Caroline Islands, Guam and Saipan etc.
- **South Eastern Area** – Papua New Guinea, the Bismarck Archipelago, Solomon Islands and the Coral Sea.
- **South Western Area** – Philippines, New Guinea (Papua Indonesia), Northern Australia, Dutch East Indies (South Sumatra and Java), Borneo (Indonesia), Malaya (Malaysia), French Indio China (Vietnam), Thailand and Burma (Myanmar).

Despite Japan's occupation of north-eastern China and Mongolia, it was unable to control the vast interior of the country with its limited military resources. As the Chinese resistance withdrew inland, Japan changed its strategy to one of isolation and began to capture China's coastal ports. From March 1941, the Japanese Navy and Army slowly leapfrogged down the south-eastern coast of China, capturing one port after another until it had reached the boarder of French Indo-China (Vietnam) in May. This effectively cut off China's access to the sea, leaving only the narrow-gauge railway from the port of Haiphong in French Indo-China and the Burma Road to deliver military supplies into the centre of the country. In June, France surrendered to Nazi Germany and Japan entered French Indo-China because the French were powerless to stop them. At the same time the Japanese demanded that the British should close the Burma Road, and fearing that they would have to start a second front against the Japanese, just as Germany threatened to invade, the British government reluctantly agreed to close the road on June 18th. China was effectively isolated and Japan could momentarily breathe, but this was only a short respite. In response to the partial occupation of French Indo-China and subsequent agreement with Vichy France, the US froze Japanese assets and established an embargo on steel, oil and gasoline exports in late July and early August. This move alarmed the Japanese and forced them back to the negotiation table because the US supplied 80% of their material needs at that time. While Japan was willing to relinquish its air bases in the south of French Indo-China and also agreed not to move further south into the South China Seas, they stipulated that the US, Britain and the Netherlands would also need to stop supporting China and lift all sanctions on imports. In late November the US countered this request with a demand that Japan should vacate China. In the eyes of Japan and its new military Prime Minister, Hideki Tōjō, this was unthinkable. Faced with real material shortages within an estimated two years, Japan looked towards the "Southern Area" – Malaya and the Dutch East Indies. War in the Pacific was now inevitable.

Reconnaissance shortfalls

Faced with long-range attack missions during the opening stages of the Pacific war, it was vitally important for the Navy to acquire accurate intelligence on possible targets. Unfortunately the Navy lacked sufficient numbers of dedicated land-based reconnaissance aircraft to perform such tasks, so an order for specially modified G3M2 Model-21 *Nell* Attack Bombers was placed on March 21st 1941. Outwardly identical to a standard G3M2, these "Long-Range Reconnaissance Attack" aircraft carried a mapping camera beneath the cockpit floor and were operated up to altitudes of 9,000 (29,527ft), over a maximum range of 3,460miles (5,569km). These aircraft were assigned to the newly formed *3rd Kokutai,* which was temporarily tasked with the role of performing clandestine flights over US territories in the South China Sea, specifically the Philippines, which represented the largest US threat to Japan's plans.

The crew of a 3rd Kokutai C5M2 Version 2 prepares to depart for the Philippines on the morning December 8th 1941, in order to provide en-route navigation and Command and Control services to the attacking force of G4M1 Betty bombers and A6M2 Zeke fighters. (Shoichi Tanaka)

In addition to the *Nell* reconnaissance flight, high altitude strategic reconnaissance flights with C5Ms of the *23rd Air Flotilla* were made over the Philippines during the last week of October, together with flights over Luzon on November 20th, in order to identify troop landing sites and airfield locations. As such missions were totally clandestine in nature, all national markings (Hinomaru) were removed from these aircraft, together with unit markings, and in some cases all exterior evidence of Japanese ownership was obliterated with a black-green paint scheme.

On November 10th 1941 the *Southern Expeditionary Fleet* was formed by combining the *15th* and *25th Armies*, together with the *22nd Air Flotilla,* comprised of 72 G3M and 27 G4M bombers, 12 A5M and 25 A6M fighters and 6 C5Ms. As the main *Southern Force* left the inland sea on November 24th, heading for the main staging point near Formosa (Taiwan), on its journey to the Philippines, the *Southern Expeditionary Force* was brought up to speed on Hainan Island and in French Indo-China, with aircraft

of the *22nd Air Flotilla* moving to air bases at Saigon and Thu Dau Mot, in order to support the Malaya Force, which would be ready by December 6th.

While Japan's main carrier striking force was tasked with attacking Pearl Harbor, the remaining forces of the Combined Fleet were distributed amongst the *Southern Combined Fleet*, including an air contingent comprising two Raiding Groups:

The *1st Raiding Group* was comprised of the *21st Air Flotilla* (minus the *Kanoya Kokutai*), which amounted to 36 G3M bombers, plus 24 H6K flying boats.

The *2nd Raiding group* was made up of *23rd Air Flotilla* (minus the *Tainan Kokutai*), which was comprised of 54 G4Ms, 12 A5Ms and 45 A6Ms and 6 C5M land-based reconnaissance aircraft.

Reconnaissance duties in the Pacific

On December 8th (December 7th on Hawaii) the Japanese began combat operations against the Allies in Malaya, the Hawaiian Islands and the Philippines, with the first air operations over enemy territory occurring over the latter location.

Following the outbreak of Pacific war, tracking C5M operations becomes more difficult. With only 40 C5M airframes spread-out over the rapidly expanding front lines of the new empire, these valuable aircraft were deployed when and where they were needed, before being relocated or redeployed to assist other units. By the mid of 1942, such deployments of multiple or single C5Ms were often identified in reports as a "*land reconnaissance plane* dispatched to…"

The Philippines, Celebes, Borneo, Timor, Java and Australia.

3rd Kokutai – 23rd Air Flotilla and 24th Air Flotilla

3rd Kokutai

The *3rd Kokutai* was formed as a land-based bomber unit on April 10th 1941, at Kanoya Naval Air Station and affiliated within the shore-based *11th Air Fleet*. In actuality the unit had been earmarked to operate a force of 36 G3M2 Long-range Reconnaissance Attack aircraft. With these reconnaissance duties completed in the autumn, the unit moved to Hainan Island, before returning to Kanoya, where it converted to a fighter unit on September 15th, absorbing combat veterans from the *12th Kokutai* and fighters from the *1st Kokutai*, which had been reorganized into a land-based attack bomber unit at the same time.

The *3rd Kokutai* and the subsequent *202nd Kokutai* applied the unit code X to its aircraft, up until July 1944.

Known C5M aircraft include

C5M2: **X-3, X-8, X-9, X-11, X-12 and X-14.**

By November the unit was equipped with a mixture of 12 A5M4s and 45 A6M2s fighters, together with nine C5M2s. Most of these aircraft were deployment to Hanoi, in preparations for the possible invasion of the Philippines. In addition to this, a small temporary unit was formed from elements of the *3rd Kokutai* and *Tainan Kokutai*. Known as the *Yamada Unit*, its 13 A6M2, nine A5M2 and three C5M2 aircraft were deployed to southern Indo-China to assist the *22nd Air Flotilla* with their planned operations in Malaya. By November 22nd they had been tasked with providing fighter cover over the Southern Area of operations, so the main group of the *3rd Kokutai* was deployed to Takeo on Formosa, where fuel management and extreme navigation training prepared the fighter and reconnaissance pilots for a long-range 1,930km (1,200mile) round trip flight to Manila and back. This flight occurred on December 8th, when three C5M2s and 43 A6M2s provided air cover for G4M1s of the *Takao Kokutai* and *Kanoya Kokutai* during the attack on Clark and Iba airfields. The C5M2s once again proved their worth to the Navy during the initial attack on the Philippines that day, providing navigation, Command & Control and reconnaissance roles to and from the targets.

On December 11th a lone C5M2 guided nine A6M2s to attack PBY Catalinas of *Patrol Wing 10* on Laguna Bay, to the south of Manila. This was followed by a similar long-distance flight on the 12th, in support of Lt. General Homma's invasion of the Philippines, when a C5M2 led 18 G3Ms together with their escort of 25 A6M2s back to Clark Field. Support was also provided by the *Tainan Kokutai* in the form of 29 A6M2s led by another C5M2. In addition to these actions, two groups of 27 G4M1s from the *Takao Kokutai*, escorted by 22 A6M2s of the *Tainan Kokutai* were led to the Nichols and Del Carmen airfields by a C5M2 of the *3rd Kokutai*. Another mission followed on the 13th, when bombers attacking Nichols Field were escorted by 33 A6M2s and one C5M2 of the *3rd Kokutai*, plus two C5Ms of the *Tainan Kokutai*.

By the beginning of January 1942, the *11th Air Fleet* listed a complement of 12 C5Ms on its books, seven of which were attached to the *3rd Kokutai* at Davao and three with the *Tainan Kokutai* at Jolo and two at Legaspi.

From their new bases on the Philippines, a three-pronged offensive towards Java was set in motion as Japan tried to close the gap and capture the Dutch East Indies. The western arm would soon sweep through to Sumatra and capture the oil fields at Palembang. The central arm, which was led by the *16th Army*, was tasked with capturing the oil fields of Borneo, while the eastern arm would take the Celebes and Timor.

On January 11th, men of the *Special Naval Landing Force (SNLF)* embarked on the first Japanese paratroop operation of the war at Manado in the Celebes. This operation was part of a combined air and sea offensive, planned to capture the airfield at Langoan and the seaplane base at Kakas. Leading the way was the *Yokosuka 1st SNLF*, which consisted of an HQ unit, a signals unit, plus the 1st and 2nd Companies of regular *SNLF* troops totalling 336 fighting men. Deployed with great accuracy by 28 Mitsubishi L3Y2 *Tina* transport aircraft, the force landed in near proximity to the target area. This precision drop accounted for high casualties, as many of the targets were well fortified. Along with the 12 paratroops deployed from each aircraft, the force dropped one para-drop container from inside the cabins and five containers from the external bomb racks of each aircraft. These supply containers carried additional weapons, ammunition and ration packs. The following day, with the support of 10 A6M2s and a C5M of the *3rd Kokutai*, a further 18 L3Y2s dropped 74 men of the 3rd Company onto the besieged airfield as reinforcements, together with additional cargo containers. With the airfield in Japanese hands, local missions could be supported more efficiently.

On the 12th, a flight of five RAAF Hudson bombers, which had been dispatched from Ambon, Ceram in the Dutch East Indies, in order to support the fighting in the Manado area, was intercepted by seven A6M2s and a C5M2 operating out of Davao, and four of the five bombers were destroyed. On the 15th, a flight of 18 A6M2s, guided by a C5M2 of the *3rd Kokutai*, attacked the airfield at Amboina, claiming two P-35s shot down and a transport destroyed on the ground. The aircraft they had destroyed were in fact Brewster 339 Buffalo fighters of the Dutch *1-VLG-IV*. On the following day a C5M2 guided four A6M2s to Ambon, where the fighters strafed two Catalina flying boats of the USN VP-22. A similar flight was made the next day with four A6M2s and a single C5M2, leading to the destruction of another Catalina.

On January 23rd, the *3rd Kokutai* relocated to Davao, Mindanao, and began missions southwards, with C5M2s leading the charge. On the 29th a C5M2 guided seven A6M2s to Tarakan Island in Northern Borneo, where seven Brewster Buffalo fighters were destroyed in combat, without loss to the Japanese. A similar flight was made over airfields on Timor during the 30th, resulting in the destruction of aircraft on the ground and the Empire flying boat "*Corio*" (VH-ABD) operated by Quantas.

On February 2nd, the unit leapfrogged down to Palikpapan, Borneo, and the following day deployed a C5M2 to lead a flight of 54 A6M2s of the *3rd Kokutai* and *Tainan Kokutai* over a distance of

An interesting photograph of C5M2 aircraft attached to the 3rd Kokutai. *Taken at Kendari Airfield Island, Celebes in February 1942, aircraft "14" in the foreground is a C5M2 Version 1, while the two aircraft behind are C5M2 Version 2 airframes. (Shoichi Tanaka)*

800km (498miles) to attack Surabaya, Java. On the 26th, two additional sorties involving C5Ms and A6Ms were flown over Timor and Ambon, resulting in more than a dozen enemy aircraft destroyed or damaged.

On the morning of February 27th a C5M2 spotted the aircraft carrier *USS Langley* to the south of Java, as it transited from Fremantle to Java. It was loaded with pilots of the *3rd* and *13th Pursuit Squadrons*, plus 32 Curtiss P-40s of the latter unit. The *USS Langley* and the *MS Sea Witch*, which was carrying an additional 27 fighters in crates, were part of Convoy MS-5, under the protection of the cruiser *USS Phoenix*. As the convoy approached the Cocos Islands the carrier broke away from the main group at a prearranged point and headed towards its destination of TJilatjap. It was supposed to be escorted for the remainder of its journey by the destroyers *USS Whipple* and *USS Edsall*, but confusion with regards a change of orders and support from a Dutch minesweeper caused the carrier to waste valuable time. Spotting an opportunity the C5M2 quickly called in air support from a routine patrol of G4Ms of the *Takeo Kokutai*, which appeared shortly before 11:40 and dropped 250 kg bombs, five of which struck their target. Set afire and listing 10° degrees to port, the carrier was finally sunk with gunfire and two torpedoes from the *USS Whipple*.

Australia

By the end of January, the Philippines were to all intents in Japanese hands, with the US and Philippine Armies both withdrawn on to the Bataan Peninsular and Corregidor Island. After gaining air superiority over Java and Timor the *3rd Kokutai* reached the extent of its southern deployment, when it was relocated to Koepang, Timor, where it began air operations over Australia's Northern Territory (NT), Western Australia (WA) and Queensland (QLD).

The first combat mission over Australia occurred on February 10th, when a C5M2 of the *3rd Kokutai* departed Ambon and flew directly to Darwin, NT, where it counted 27 ships in the harbour and 30 aircraft at both the civilian aerodrome and the RAAF Air Station. The intelligence gathered during this flight was processed and subsequently passed on to the *1st Carrier Fleet*, which had departed Palau on the 15th, heading to the Ceram Islands, from which point it would strike at Darwin on the 19th. The intent of their mission was to neutralize the large amount of Allied military shipping that had vacated the Dutch East Indies and Malaya during the previous weeks, specifically the aircraft carrier *USS Langley*, before the *1st Carrier Fleet* transited to the Indian Ocean. This initial attack would be followed later that same day by a land-based attack force of 27 G4Ms from the *Kanoya Kokutai* and 27 G3Ms of the *1st Kokutai*. The raid was aimed at neutralizing the RAAF Air Station, and a single C5M2 was tasked with providing both reconnaissance and Command & Control duties.

On March 2nd a reconnaissance flight was made over Broome and Cape Latouche Treville, WA, which reported at least eight aircraft on the ground. The next day two individual attack groups left Koepang airfield (Air Base 335), with C5M2s initially acting in the navigation role for each group. The first group of nine A6M2s was guided directly to Broome harbour by their C5M2, which was flown by 1st Sergeant Akira Hayashi, with Shinobu Nagasawa acting as his RO, while the second C5M2 led a group of eight A6M2s to Wyndham airfield, WA. During the actual attack on Broome, the A6Ms came under the Command & Control of the C5M2, which was operating at high altitude above the target. With the attack unfolding directly below them, the C5M2 could identify individual targets or threats and direct the fighters accordingly. This process worked incredibly well and the raid resulted in the destruction of all the aircraft in the vicinity of the town, including a DC-3 which unfortunately approached the airfield during the attack. In all, eight landed-based aircraft and 15 flying boats at anchor were claimed.

At Wyndham the second attack group operated in the same manner, but only found one de Havilland D.H.84 Dragon on the ground, which was quickly destroyed. The operation cost two A6M2s, one of which was shot down during the attack and the second was forced to ditch on the return flight.

On March 4th, attacks were launched against Broome and Darwin. Both incorporated flights of A6Ms, under the control of C5M2s, in what would become standard working practice over Australia. The first group, comprised of three A6Ms and a C5M2, had to aborted en route due to bad weather, while the latter group of nine A6Ms and a C5M2 resulted in the destruction of Lockheed Hudson at Darwin RAAF Air Station.

Reconnaissance flights were dispatched over Broome and Darwin on the 10th, but little activity was detected at either base. The next attack on Broome occurred on the 20th and was divided into three elements. The first element consisted of a lone C5M2 reconnaissance over-flight to assess weather conditions. As everything was conducive for a raid, the second element, consisted of seven G4Ms bombers of the *Takao Kokutai*, was dispatched to the target as the C5M2 made its way home. Soon after, a second C5M2 arrived over the Broome, complete with an escort of four A6Ms. Its job was to identify specific targets and reassess the situation, before passing the details to the inbound bombers. Despite this extravagant process, only two aircraft were destroyed on the ground.

On the 21st, Petty Officer Akira Hayashi with Shinobo Nakasawa acting as the RO, undertook a long-range reconnaissance mission into the Northern Territory. Departing Koepang, they flew to Pine Creek and then onto Katherine, where they orbited for 40 minutes before returning to base. The straight-line distance for this mission (to and from the target, plus 40 minute loiter) amounted to approximately 2,342km (1,455miles), with an endurance of 7 hours 20 minutes. This is far in excess of the officially quoted range figure for the C5M2 (1,112km (691miles), even without factoring in a fuel safety margin or detours for weather or evasion, etc. It is entirely possible that the C5M2 used that day was aircraft "X-3", which had been specifically modified to accept either an additional oxygen cylinder for longer duration, high-altitude operations, a different long-range radio installation, or both.

The following day a bombing mission was launched against Katherine, while C5M2 "X-3" flew a reconnaissance mission over Darwin, together with an escort of three A6Ms. Piloted by Petty Officer Shigiki Mari with Shinobo Nakasawa as the RO, "X-3" completed its reconnaissance task without any difficulty and began its return to base. Unbeknown to the Japanese, the flight had been detected by No.31 Radar Station, which had been installed a few weeks earlier at Dripstone Caves near Casuarina, to the north of Darwin. Finally calibrated and deemed operational, the radar station had detected the "bandits" as the flight departed Darwin and headed out over the Timor Sea. Ordinarily this one event would not have been a major issue for the *Babs*, as its speed and altitude typically provided a buffer against interception. But on the 22nd the odds were fatally stacked against "X-3" because Darwin's air defences had also been bolstered by 12 P-40E Kittyhawk fighters of the 9th Squadron/49th Pursuit Group, USAAF, which had arrived one week earlier! The combination of these two factors would lead to the only *Babs* loss over Australia. With fighters vectored along its projected route, aircraft "X-3" was finally intercepted at 6,010m (20,000ft) heading west, and eventually shot down over Bynoe Harbour 45km (28miles) south-west of Darwin by Lt. Poleschuk and Lt. Harvey, who shared their misidentified kill.

Lt. Poleschuk's after action report stated:

"We sighted one Nakajima Type 97..... I delivered a thirty [degree] beam attack at less than 200 feet in a slight climbing turn, fired 100 rounds..... The enemy plane was shot down in flames, the pilot bailed out."

While Lt. Harvey reported added:

"We sighted Nakajima Serial #3 at 19,000 feet.... The Nakajima started burning and pilot jumped in chute."

On the 23rd a bomber raid was made against Wyndham (WA) by G4Ms of the *Takao Kokutai*, supported by a C5M2 and three escorting A6Ms, but little damage was reported. Another escorted reconnaissance flight was made on the 28th, this time to Drysdal, WA, culminating in the A6Ms strafing the airfield before the flight returned to Koepang.

The RAAF Air Station at Darwin was once again attacked on the 31st, when eight G4Ms of the *Takao Kokutai*, together with their fighter escort of eight A6Ms came under the Command & Control of a C5M2. One bomber was lost.

April 3rd saw another uneventful escorted reconnaissance flight to Broome. Similar flights were made against Darwin on the 15th and the 22nd. The latter was in preparation for the last bombing raid to be launched from Koepang. This occurred on the 25th, when a force of 27 G4Ms of the *Takao Kokutai*, supported by nine A6Ms and a Command & Control C5M2 of the *3rd Kokutai* created havoc on the air station, but it was not without incident. Approximately 50 P-40Es attacked the Japanese as they departed the area that day, resulting in the loss of four bombers and one fighter, together with major damage inflicted on several of the returning aircraft.

During this period the majority of the *3rd Kokutai* would remain at Koepang airfield, Kendari and Ambon in the Dutch East Indies, but following the battle of the Coral Sea in early May 1942, 27 A6M2s

Four C5M2 aircraft including "8" and aircraft "9" of the 3rd Kokutai *at Kendari Airfield. (Shoichi Tanaka)*

and three C5M2s, were transferred to Rabaul, in the New Guinea, by the escort carrier *Kasuga Maru* (a converted ocean liner that was later renamed *Taiyō* on August 31st 1942), where they were absorbed into the *Tainan Kokutai*.

A solo reconnaissance fight was also made to Drysdale on the May 25th, together with escorted reconnaissance missions on the 26th and 27th, but the Japanese found no targets on the ground.

On the 27th, a weather reconnaissance mission was also flown high over Darwin, well above the service ceiling of resident P-40s. Fighters were scrambled to intercept the aircraft, but the C5M2 was relatively immune at 10,670m (35,000ft) where it even found time to slow down and release a weather balloon before returning to base. A short time later a force of 17 G4Ms of the *Takao Kokutai*, supported by 21 A6Ms, struck the air station. In the ensuing combat one bomber was shot down, but the escorting A6Ms managed to down four of the defending P-40s as retribution. In addition to the bomber, a C5M2 was also lost in the vicinity of Koepang later that day. It is unclear if the accident occurred during its departure or on its return to base, but the pilot Tadashi Kobayashi went down with the aircraft. The fate of the RO is unrecorded.

On June 15th, 27 G4Ms and 21 A6Ms attacked Darwin under the Command & Control of two C5M2s, each with an escort of three A6Ms. No Japanese aircraft were lost that day, but the defenders lost two P-40s during the encounter.

On the 17th a solo C5M2 of the *Tainan Kokutai* flew over Batchelor Airfield on Horn Island, before heading deep into Cape York (QLD), proceeding all the way down to Cairns, before returning to Lae, Papua New Guinea, without being intercepted. This flight was notable for the fact that it covered a straight-line distance of 2,606km (1,620miles), which is the longest documented operational sortie of a C5M2.

Two reconnaissance flights over Horn Island, Cooktown and Cairns, WA, were undertaken on the June 24th, followed by two additional flights flown out of Rabaul on July 6th, as the *Tainan Kokutai* attempted to chart the State of Queensland. While flights from Rabaul covered a greater distance than those staged out of Lae, they had the luxury of being able to land at Lae, to rest and refuel if required, before completing their journey back to Rabaul. A pre-strike solo reconnaissance flight was made over Batchelor Airfield on the 7th, clearing an inbound attack force of 18 G3M2s of the *4th Kokutai*, with a second *Tainan Kokutai* C5M2 performing in the Command & Control role during the attack.

Solo and escorted reconnaissance flights were undertaken over Darwin on July 10th, 15th and 18th, and while defending aircraft were scrambled to intercept them, contact with the Japanese aircraft was not made.

The 15th also saw two uneventful *Babs* reconnaissance flights made over Wyndham and Drysdale, while on the other side of the Australia, the last recorded C5M flight over the State of Queensland occurred on 20th.

Additional solo reconnaissance missions were made by the *3rd Kokutai* over the State of Western Australia's coastline on the 24th, 25th, 26th and 27th. The extent of these flights are unrecorded, but since bombing missions were made against Port Headland on the 30th, it would seem that they flew at least that far south.

A solo reconnaissance flight was tracked on radar on August 24th over Joseph Bonaparte Gulf, encompassing Wyndham and Port Keats, NT, but no interception was made. A similar flight was tracked on the 25th, in the vicinity of Bathhurst Island, NT, but once again no action was taken.

On November 1st the *3rd Kokutai* was officially reformed into the *202nd Kokutai*. While this name change did not initially affect the day-to-day operations of the *Kokutai*, changes were on the way. On the 13th the C5M officially bowed out of operations over the Western Australia, when a solo mission was flown to Cape Latouche Treville, Broome, Wyndham and back to Koepang. Despite its performance capabilities, the appearance of Spitfires in late 1942, working under the guidance of radar units, meant that *Babs* operations were becoming untenable. Lacking a suitable replacement aircraft for such high-speed reconnaissance missions, the Navy requested support under the pre-war joint air operations agreement with the Army. In response to this the *3rd Hikodan* deployed Ki-46-II aircraft of the *70th Dokuritsu Chutai* to Kendari, which were tasked to support of the *23rd Air Flotilla* and provide reconnaissance of the Darwin area and Timor Sea.

Such was the pace of reconnaissance missions over northern Australia that a further nine C5M2 missions would be flown to Darwin between November 21st and December 3rd. The initial solo and escorted flights were in support of night bomber raids that occurred on the 22nd and the 25th, while the last four assessed the damage that the previous raids had inflicted.

For a while the C5Ms were relegated to other duties and prepared for distribution to other units, but following the losses of two Ki-46 over Darwin in February and early March 1943, the *Babs* was called back into frontline operations for one last encore. Reconnaissance missions were staged against Darwin on March 11th, 12th and 13th, but all failed to get through of the target due to severe weather conditions in the area. Finally on the 14th, one aircraft did manage to reach Darwin, but the weather was once again deemed to be atrocious, but improving. This mission would prove to be the last *Babs* reconnaissance flight over Australia, and the attack planned for later that day was postponed until the next day. From that point forward the Ki-46 *Dinah* would be responsible for all subsequent high-speed reconnaissance missions over Australia.

In all, 207 air raids and dedicated reconnaissance missions would be staged against northern Australia between February 1942 and July 1944, with C5Ms of the 3rd, 202nd and *Tainan Kokutai* participating in at least 58 of them, for the loss of two C5Ms.*

C5M2 operations over Northern Australia February 1942 – April 1943

Target/Dates	State of Western Australia	Northern Territory	State of Queensland
February 10th **1942**		Darwin	
February 19th		Darwin	
March 2nd	Broome		
March 3rd	Broome/Wyndham x 2		
March 4th	Broome	Darwin	
March 10th	Broome	Darwin	
March 20th	Broom x 2		
March 21st		Darwin	
March 22nd		Darwin*	
March 23rd	Wyndham		
March 28th	Drysdale		
March 31st		Darwin	
April 3rd	Broome		
April 15th		Darwin	
April 22nd		Darwin	
April 25th	Drysdale	Darwin	
April 26th	Drysdale		
April 27th	Drysdale	Darwin*	
June 15th		Darwin x 2	
June 17th			Horn Is./Cairns
June 24th			Cooktown x 2
July 6th			Cairns
July 7th			Horn Island x 2
July 10th		Darwin x 2	
July 15th	Wyndham/Drysdale x 2	Darwin	
July 18th		Darwin	
July 20th			Horn Island
July 24th	Broom – Port Headland		
July 25th	Broom – Port Headland		
July 26th	Broom – Port Headland		
July 27th	Broom – Port Headland		
August 24th	Wyndham		
August 25th		Bathhurst Island	
November 13th	Cape Latouche Treville, Broome, Wyndham		
November 21st		Darwin x 2+	
November 22nd		Darwin	
November 24th		Darwin	
November 25th		Darwin	
November 26th		Darwin	
November 27th		Darwin	
November 29th		Darwin	
December 3rd		Darwin	
March 11th **1943**		Darwin	
March 12th		Darwin	
March 13th		Darwin	
March 14th		Darwin	
State/Territory totals	20	30	7
Mission total	58		

3rd / 202nd Kokutai

1/48 Scale

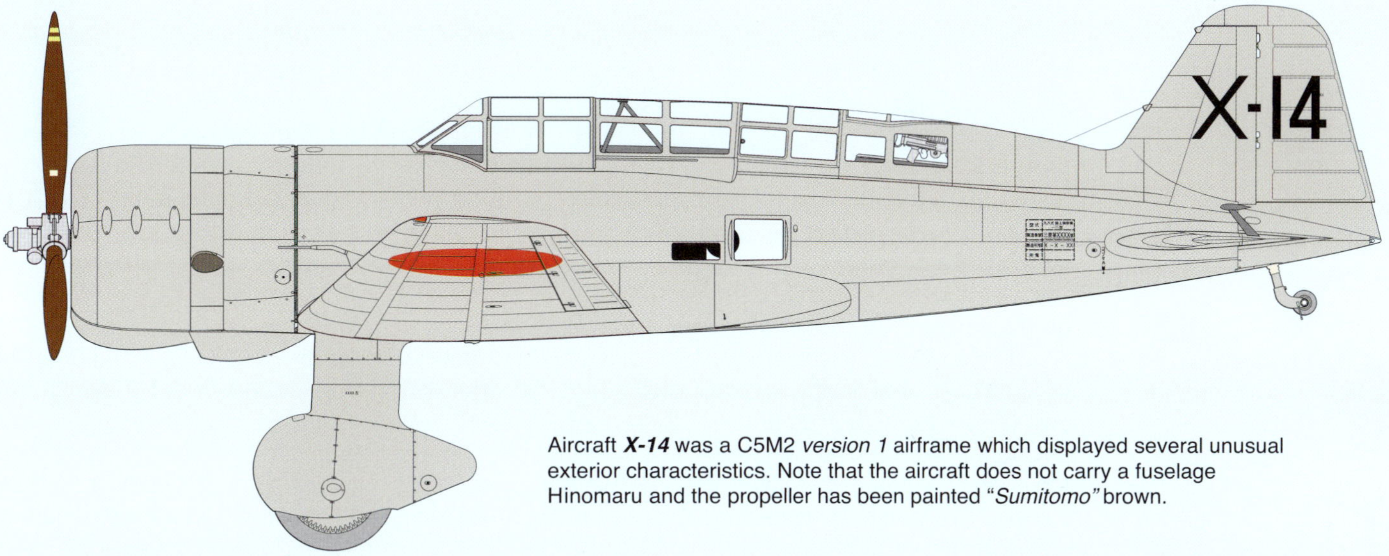

Aircraft ***X-14*** was a C5M2 *version 1* airframe which displayed several unusual exterior characteristics. Note that the aircraft does not carry a fuselage Hinomaru and the propeller has been painted *"Sumitomo"* brown.

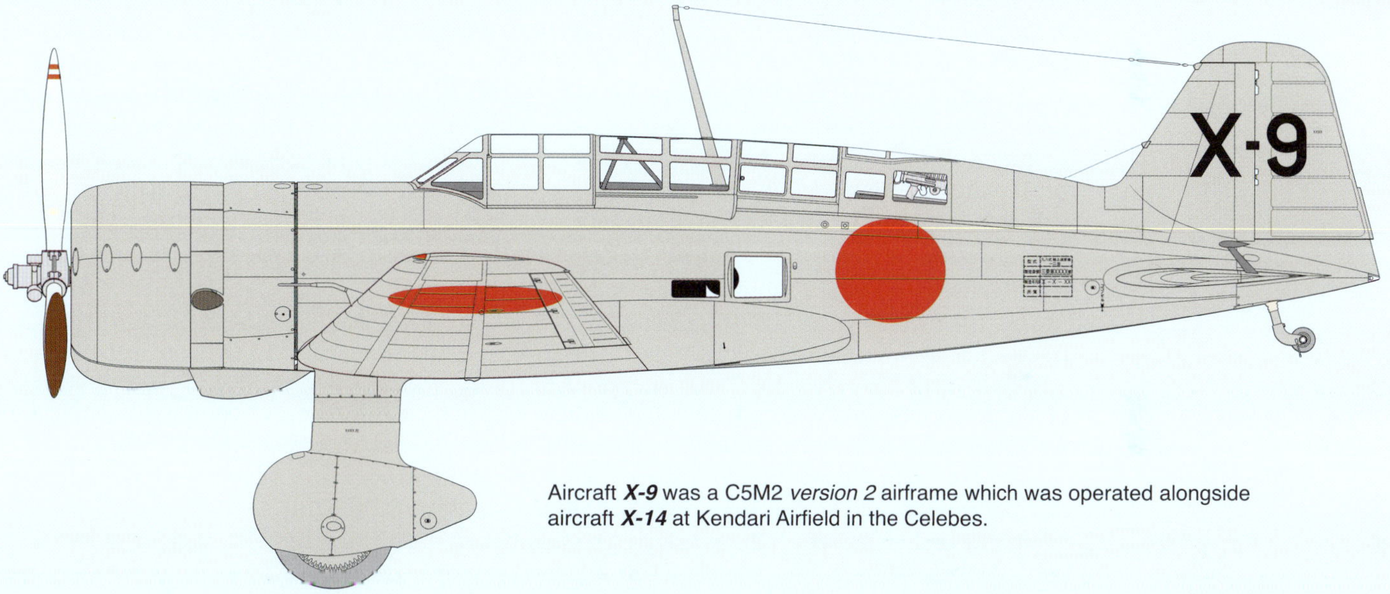

Aircraft ***X-9*** was a C5M2 *version 2* airframe which was operated alongside aircraft ***X-14*** at Kendari Airfield in the Celebes.

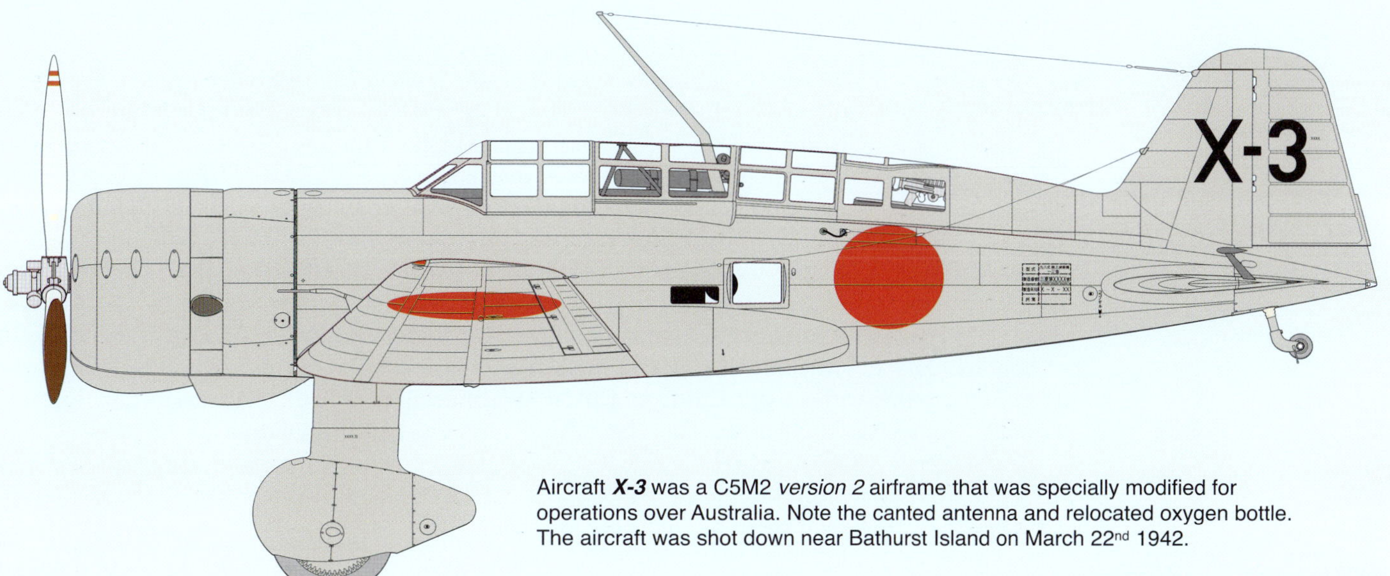

Aircraft ***X-3*** was a C5M2 *version 2* airframe that was specially modified for operations over Australia. Note the canted antenna and relocated oxygen bottle. The aircraft was shot down near Bathurst Island on March 22nd 1942.

Thailand, Malaya, Burma, Ceylon and Bismarck Archipelago

Kanoya Kokutai – 22nd Air Flotilla and 24th Air Flotilla

On December 8th 1941, a C5M2 of the *Kanoya Kokutai (22nd Air Flotilla)* conducted a reconnaissance sweep of the Singapore area, looking for the British Far East Fleet. The Japanese were specifically looking for the *HMS Prince of Wales* and *HMS Repulse*, which represented the most dangerous threat to Japan's naval operations in the area. Both battleships, plus two cruisers and four destroyers, were observed in port that day and a similar reconnaissance flight on the morning of the 9th recorded the same results, but by 17:10 that evening, the fleet was sighted by submarine *I-65* some 225 miles from Paulo Tioman Island. The Japanese fleet was quickly vectored to intercept the British vessels, with plans to attack them on the morning of the 10th. Unable to make contact, Admiral Kondo ordered his most southerly submarines, of the *18th Submarine Division*, to attack the vessels at the earliest opportunity, but they too had been left behind by the rapidly moving fleet.

At 06:25 that morning an assortment of 9 G3Ms bombers, under the overall command of Lt. Makino, took off from Saigon together with two C5M2s from Soc Trang and proceeded to search an the area of 160° through 216°, out to a distance of 600nm (1,111km/690miles). Shortly after 11:45, patrol aircraft No.3 (a C5M) spotted the battleships and called in the coordinates to the to the main bomber force, which amounted to sixty G3Ms of the *Genzan* and *Mihoro Kokutai*, plus 26 G4Ms of the *Kanoya Kokutai*. By 14:50 both battleships, the pride of the Royal Navy, had been sunk and the age of the battleship had given way to air power. Upon hearing the news Winston Churchill would later write:

"In all the war I never received a more direct shock..... There were no British or American capital ships in the Indian Ocean or the Pacific except the American survivors of Pearl Harbor, who were hastening back to California. Over all this vast expanse of waters Japan was supreme, and we were weak and naked."

At noon on the morning of January 16th two C5M2s of the *Yamada Unit* were dispatched to reconnoitre Singapore following an early morning raid on Seletar, which had been made by 24 G3Ms of the *Genzan Kokutai*, supported by 12 A6Ms of the *22nd Air Flotilla*. One C5M headed for Tengah, where 21 aircraft were observed on the ground, while the second C5M searched the sea-lanes for a battleship that had been spotted by one of the returning bombers. This C5M was intercepted by a flight of Brewster F2A Buffaloes of 243 Squadron. Believing the aircraft to be a Type-97 *Nate*, Sqn Ldr Howell positioned his himself behind the Japanese aircraft and:

"... I let him have a good burst. The enemy immediately went straight down, bursting into flames as it went, and before the crash one wing came off altogether."

On January 18th two C5M2 and 11 A6M2s of the *22nd Air Flotilla* provided air cover for 26 G4Ms of the *Kanoya Kokutai* over Singapore. A similar raid occurred on the 21st composed of one C5M2, 53 G3Ms and G4Ms of the *Mihoro* and *Kanoya Kokutais, together* with nine A6Ms.

This was followed on the 22nd with an almost identical formation of Japanese aircraft although on that occasion it was controlled by two C5Ms in the skies over Singapore.

By the end of January, Malaya was in Japanese hands, with Singapore surrendering on the 15th. Japan's desire to capture the resources of the Dutch East Indies had taken a back seat to the tactical invasion of the Philippines and Malaya. With both of these prizes in hand, the Dutch East Indies needed to be seized as quickly as possible to prevent retaliation from the Allied nations, especially their air forces. The western arm of the Dutch East Indies campaign was begun.

On February 5th, 21 A6M2s and three C5M2s of the *Yamada Unit* were deployed to Kuching, Sarawak, where they remained until the 18th. The Army's invasion plan of Sumatra began on February 14th under the designation "Operation L", spearheaded by the Paratroop *Hikotai*, which took off from Kahang Airfield, Malaya, and soon rendezvoused over Batopaha with 27 Ki-21-II *Sally* bombers of the *98th Sentai* from Kluang, Malaya. The formation manoeuvred into two groups: the first group was to assault and secure the airfield, while the second group was to take the oil refineries. Both drops were satisfactory and within 72 hours the Japanese had control of Palembang airfield and the oil refinery, with air losses during the operation amounting to three transports and one bomber. On the 18th, 15 A6M2s and three C5Ms moved on to Muntok, Sumatra, followed by nine A6Ms and two C5Ms of the *3rd Kokutai.*

On February 25th the *22nd Air Flotilla* mounted its first mission against Java, when it dispatched 27 G3Ms, together with a single C5M2 and 13 A6Ms against Batavia. One A6M was lost on the mission, together with a C5M2, which was shot down by a Hurricane of 242 Squadron.

On March 4th 18 G3Ms of the *Genzan Kokutai* were escorted from Thailand to Mingaladon in Burma by 18 A6Ms and a C5M of the *22nd Air Flotilla*. The capture of Burma represented the furthest point west that the *Babs* would be operated during the Pacific war.

Yamada Unit – 22nd Air Flotilla

The *Yamada Unit* was established November 22nd 1941, as a fighter squadron assigned to the *22nd Air Flotilla* during the invasion of Malaya and the Dutch East Indies. Made up of aircraft from the *3rd Kokutai* and *Tainan Kokutai*, the unit comprised 27 A6M2, nine A5M and six C6M aircraft, placed under the command of Commander Yutuka Yamada. The unit operated over French Indochina, the Dutch East Indies, Java and Thailand, before returning to the 22nd Air Flotilla on March 15th.

During the life of the *Yamada Unit* the code applied to its aircraft was **II**.

Yamada Unit

1/48 Scale

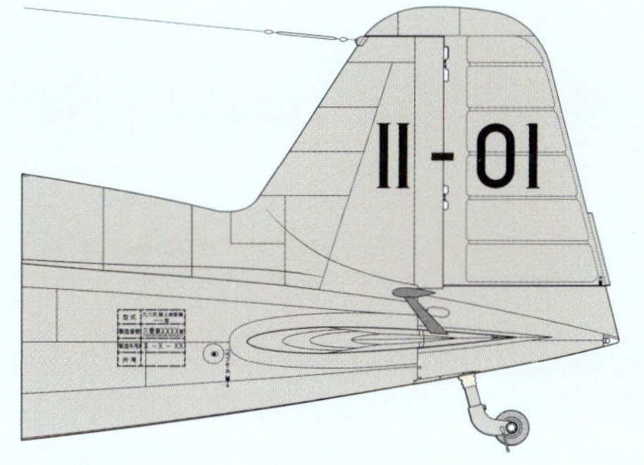

Speculative layout based on contemporary Yamada unit markings.

© Giuseppe Picarella 2020

Tainan Kokutai – 23rd Air Flotilla

Established on October 1st 1941, at Tainan, Formosa, the Tainan Kokutai is perhaps the most famous squadron of the Japanese Navy. Formed as a fighter unit on the eve of the Pacific war, the unit was assigned to the 23rd Air Flotilla and issued with 45 front line A5M fighters (plus 18 reserve) and six C5M1s. It was subsequently resupplied with more modern A6M2 fighters by the start of hostilities, when examples of the C5M2 were also issued to the unit.

During the operational career of the Tainan Kokutai the unit code applied to its aircraft was V.

Known C5M aircraft include:

C5M2: **V-10, V-11** and **V-16.**

On January 7th 1942, two C5M2s and seven A6M2s of the unit were moved to Jolo Island in the Philippines to await the arrival of A6M2s and 11 G4Ms of the *Takao Kokutai*. Nine of the fighters were later dispatched, together with two C5M2s, to Tarakan on the 16th, to begin operations from that airfield, but the conditions were marginal at that location and the aircraft returned to Jolo while the airstrip was made serviceable. By the 20th Tarakan was deemed acceptable for fighter operations, so four A6M2s and a C5M2 undertook flights over southern Borneo, attacking targets of opportunity, including a PBY on the Barito River during the 20th and one Martin bomber destroyed on the ground at Balikpapan during the 26th.

On the 27th a flight of six A6M2s, led by a C5M2, departed Tarakan on an attack mission to Bandjermasin airfield, where they destroyed and damaged 10 bombers on the ground. Their return flight though was marred with issues, as the C5M2 and two of the fighters made forced landings at Balikpapan. The reason for these landings remains unclear, as Allied fighters did not intercept the aircraft, so it is most likely that either flak damage or extreme weather was the cause of the problem.

Aircraft were subsequently deployed to Balikpapan on the 30th, including two C5Ms, 12 A6M2s and nine D3A *Val* dive-bombers.

On February 1st three C5M2s were sent out to reconnoitre the US airfields around Surabaya and one aircraft failed to return. The information provided by the remaining two aircraft resulted in an attack mission being mounted the following day, with a single C5M2 guiding 17 A6M2s from Balikpapan back to Maospati, where considerable damage was inflicted.

On the morning of the 3rd, two large flights of bombers were dispatched against US airfields. The first flight, which was comprised of 26 G3Ms of the *Takao Kokutai*, headed to Surabaya with an escort of 17 A6M2s and a C5M2 from the *Tainan Kokutai*. The second flight targeted Madioen with 27 G4Ms of the *Kanoya Kokutai*, escorted by 27 A6Ms and two C5Ms of the *3rd Kokutai*. The melee that followed above Perak airfield, the Naval base, Singosari airfield and Surabaya Bay saw more than 35 Dutch and US aircraft shot down, destroyed on the ground or heavily damaged, with three A6Ms and a C5M2 lost in the action. The C5M2 was crewed by NAP 1/C Minoru Morita and the RO was Lt. Tetsutaro Suzuki, both of whom were killed when their C5M2 passed too close to a landing PBY, while attempting to cause the aircraft to abort its landing, only to be shot down by the PBY waist gunner!

Several ships were spotted in the vicinity of the attack and a second raid was launched on the 4th, in an attempt to locate and destroy them with 56 G3M and G4M bombers guided by seven C5M2s. The Dutch Navy's HNLMS *De Ruyter*, USS *Houston* and USS *Marblehead* were attacked and hit, with the latter sustaining heavy damage. One G4M failed to return from the mission.

Yet another attack occurred on the 5th, when 27 A6Ms of the *Tainan Kokutai* were led to Surabaya by a C5M2, while a second C5M2 of the *3rd Kokutai* led 10 A6Ms to strafe Denpassar on Bali, in support

Tainan Kokutai

1/48 Scale

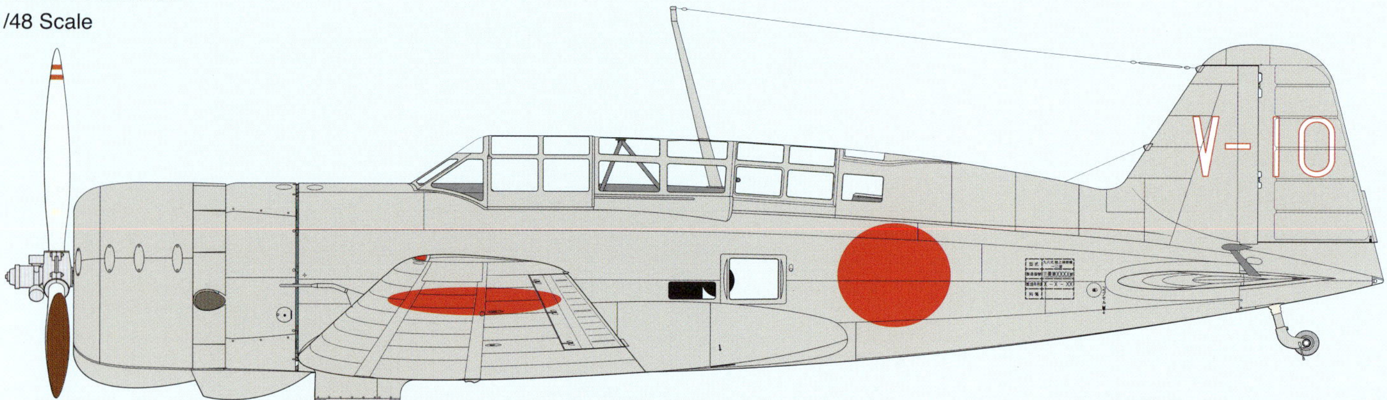

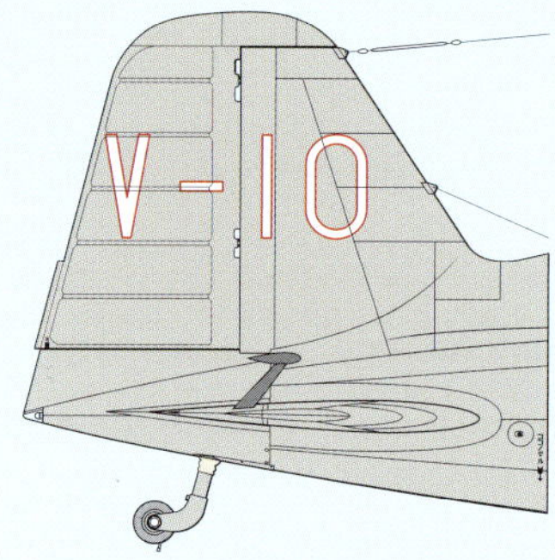

Aircraft ***V-10*** was a C5M2 *version 2* airframe, which included a single pane gunner's window and single pane dorsal spine transparencies.

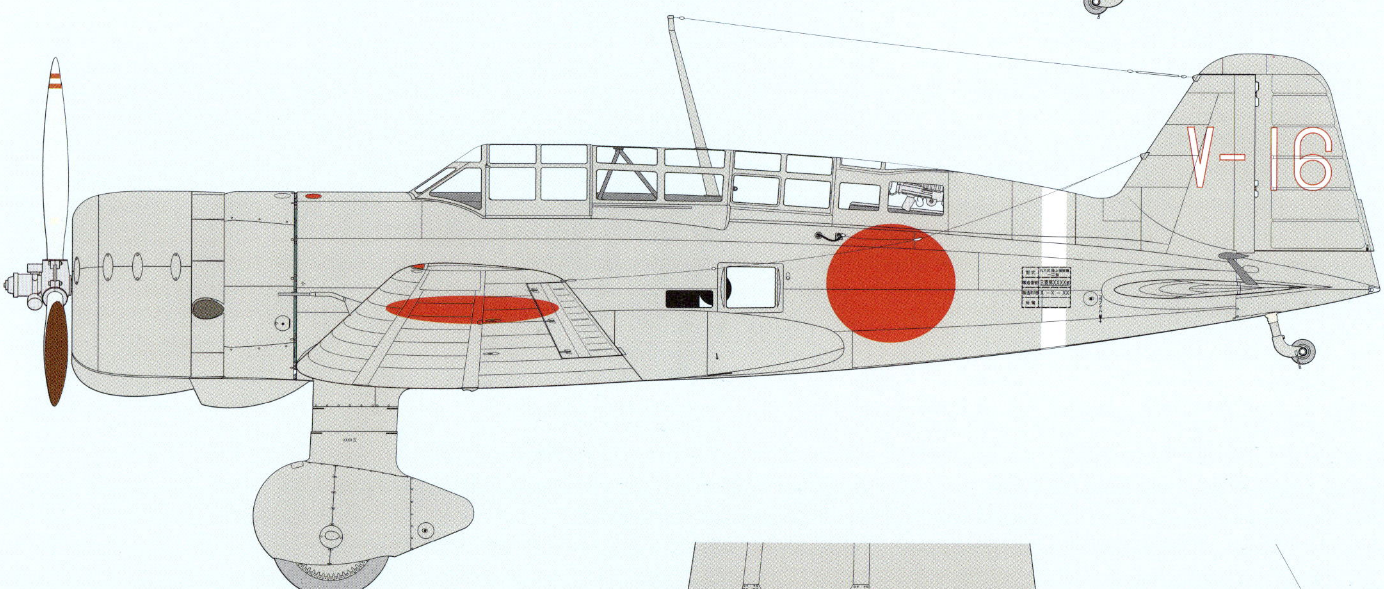

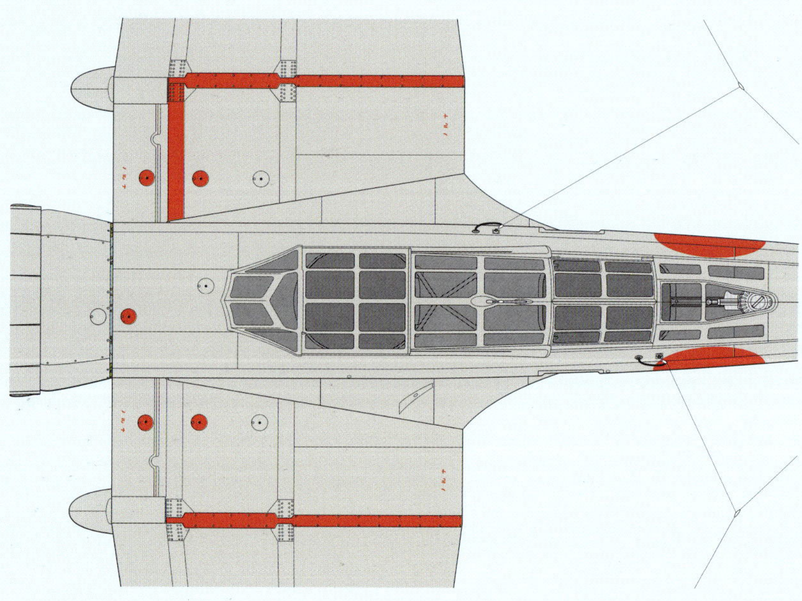

Some C5Ms exhibited unique markings, the best example of which was aircraft ***V-16*** of the Tainan Kokutai.
This C5M2 *version 2* airframe included a red boarder applied to the fairings between the centre wing section and outboard wing panels. These markings may have also extended inboard along the forward main spar chord-plate. Both possibilities are depicted (right).

It is assumed that these markings were cosmetic rather than functional, as they cannot act as "no walk" boundaries, because the area of wing behind the rear main spar was of lightweight construction and included its own dedicated "No Step" stencils.

In addition to these boarders, the fuel filler access panels were also painted red.

of a bombing mission of 31 aircraft. The Surabaya mission resulted in the destruction of seven aircraft for the loss of three A6Ms, but for the first time, Allied fighters activity in the area meant that the C5M2 needed to be escorted back to base by two A6Ms, which subsequently shot down a Dutch Catalina that strayed across their return path. The attack on Denpassar resulted in the loss of seven P-40Es from a group of 12 aircraft being ferried to Saurabaya.

On the 8th a second mission against Denpassar was attempted, but bad weather forced all nine A6Ms and the single C5M to return to base. On the return trip the flight came across nine B-17Es of the 7th BG and promptly shot two aircraft down and badly damaged two more. On the 18th, Maospati airfield became the next target, when a flight of 15 A6Ms guided by a C5M2, was dispatched from Banjermasin.

After taking Guam the *Fourth Fleet* turned towards the Bismarck Archipelago, but the campaign was devoid of land-based air support due to the isolated nature of the location. Once The Solomon Islands and New Guinea were targeted, the lack of land-based air support became evident and the Navy was forced to form a *Kokutai* of land-based aircraft within the *24th Air Flotilla*, the first of which was the *4th Kokutai* on February 10th.

On February 25th a C5M2, complete with an escort of two A6M2s of the *3rd Kokutai*, flew from Bali on a reconnaissance mission over Surabaya. During the mission they intercepted and shot down a Catalina of *Patrol Wing 10*.

With Rabaul as its base, the air element the *24th Air Flotilla*, known locally as *"the Base Air Force"*, could cover the whole of the archipelago including New Guinea, the Solomon Islands and the Coral Sea. As operations increased the *24th Air Flotilla* was allotted additional support, which arrived on April 1st in the form of the *Tainan Kokutai*, which had been reorganized as the *25th Kokutai*, with some pilots returning to Japan and the remainder posted to Rabaul and then Lae in support of Guadalcanal operations. Along with A6M2 fighters, the *Tainan Kokutai* also brought its C5Ms to Rabaul, as the unit was listed as having: *"45 0-type fighters"* based at Lae and *"6 land reconnaissance planes"* as part of the *"The Base Air Force in the Rabaul Area"*. After the plan to capture Port Moresby *"Operation Mo"* had been formulated, the *Fourth Fleet* established the *"5th Air Attack Force"* in addition to the *"The Base Air Force"* specifically for offensive support missions and the aircraft of the *Tainan Kokutai* were listed as part of this force on April 10th.

On May 1st the strength of the *"5th Air Attack Force"* included:

- 4 – A5M
- 24 – A6M
- 27 – G3M
- 28 – G4M
- 16 – Type-97 Flying boats (H6K *Mavis*)
- 3 – *"land reconnaissance plane"*

The latter "3" aircraft were marked as being dispatched to that zone, with 8 C5M flight personnel (four crews) available for operations. In the end, the Port Moresby landings were cancelled due to the Battle of the Coral Sea (May 4th to May 8th) although the air element did begin operations. By May 25th six land reconnaissance planes were reported as attached to the *Tainan Kokutai*.

Between June 19th and August 5th the *Tainan Kokutai* managed to retain six *"land reconnaissance planes"*, three of which were included in attacks on Port Moresby on the 19th June and four on the 21st July.

The following entries from unit records represent a snapshot of the missions undertaken by *Babs* aircraft, in supporting reconnaissance, interception and attack missions on Lae and Rabaul between June 19th and August 4th. Three of these missions are also identified in the **Australia** subsection listed above. It should be pointed out that this is only a fraction of the combat operations undertaken by the *24th Air Flotilla* during the dates show, but it does illustrate the value of the C5M. The missions were divided into three categories within the records: Attack (**A**), Interception (**I**) and Reconnaissance (**R**). It is assumed that these terms refer to missions where the C5M either led bomber attack missions, led fighter interception missions, or performed dedicated reconnaissance and patrol duties.

In addition to these notes, only two *"Land recon planes"* were based at Rabaul on June 19th, while four were recorded on July 21st.

June 19th R – Reconnaissance of ?ieta (illegible) airfield (possibly Weipa): 1 reconnaissance plane
June 24th R – Reconnaissance of ?arkham (illegible): 1 reconnaissance plane
June 24th R – Reconnaissance of ?eandes (illegible) and Cooktown: 2 reconnaissance planes
June 28th A – Reconnaissance or Port Moresby: 1 reconnaissance plane
R – Road reconnaissance over New Guinea: 2 reconnaissance planes
June 30th R – Road reconnaissance over New Guinea: 1 reconnaissance plane and 4 fighters
July 2nd I – 1 Reconnaissance plane and 8 fighters over Rabaul
July 3rd R – Reconnaissance of Suna and Kokoda: 1 reconnaissance plane and 3 fighters
July 6th A – Attack on Horn Island: 16 attack planes and 1 reconnaissance plane

July 17th I – 2 Reconnaissance planes and 25 fighters over Rabaul
July 19th I – 1 Reconnaissance plane and 10 fighters over Rabaul
July 20th I – 2 Reconnaissance planes and 6 fighters over Rabaul
July 22nd I – 1 Reconnaissance planes and 6 fighters over Rabaul
July 23rd I – 1 Reconnaissance planes and 4 fighters over Rabaul
July 24th I – 2 Reconnaissance planes and 6 fighters over Rabaul
July 25th R – Patrol area A: 1 reconnaissance plane and 1 land-attack plane
July 26th I – 3 Reconnaissance planes and 8 fighters over Rabaul
July 27th R – Weather reconnaissance: 2 Reconnaissance planes
July 29th R – Patrol area A: 1 reconnaissance plane and 2 land-attack planes
I – Convoy in Buna: 27 fighters, 10 fighters and 1 reconnaissance plane
July 30th R – Patrol area A: 1 reconnaissance plane and 2 land-attack planes
I – 1 Reconnaissance plane and 8 fighters over Rabaul
July 31st I – 1 Reconnaissance plane and 13 fighters over Rabaul
August 1st I – 2 reconnaissance planes and 10 fighters over Rabaul
August 2nd R – Patrol area A: 1 reconnaissance plane and 2 fighters

A reconnaissance flight over Milne Bay ended in disaster on August 4th, when a C5M2 and two escorting A6M2s were intercepted by P-40s of 76 Squadron RAAF. The C5M2, which was flown by pilot Keiryu Hanahiro, with Kameichi Hasegawa as RO, quickly headed inland at high speed, but was shot down and crashed in the mountains, while the fighters survived the combat and returned to base. The wreckage was found two weeks later and contained a detailed sketched of 7-Mile Drome and the Kila Kila airfield (3-Mile Drome).

On August 6th the *"5th Air Attack Force"* listed only one *"Type 98 land reconnaissance plane"* and 19 A6Ms as part of the *Tainan Kokutai*. The C5M had been used on August 8th in conjunction with two H8K flying boats, one H6K flying boat and two G4Ms, as part of a large patrol extending 160km (100miles) to the south-east of Rabaul, in search of the US invasion convoy. The Convoy was sighted at anchor near Tulagi and Guadalcanal and its location was transmitted to the main attack force, which was comprised of 23 G4Ms and 15 A6Ms.

On August 9th the C5M together with four G4Ms and two flying boats repeated the search pattern and discovered several cruisers and destroyers to the south-west of Tulagi. The search team promptly relayed the information to the waiting attack force of 16 G4Ms and 15 A6Ms

One *"land-based reconnaissance plane"* was listed as part of the *Tainan Kokutai* at Rabaul on August 27th, but the preceding months had taken a heavy toll on the C5Ms and it was reported that:

"… the damage to scout planes was very heavy and replacement was very difficult, thus causing considerable trouble to operations."

After that date, A6M fighters and even G4M bombers were routinely used for reconnaissance tasks. Despite the low number of operational C5Ms, some aircraft were even used for bomber interception

Japanese air-to-air bombing in action. (Henry Sakaida)

missions during this period, due to their high-speed capability. These *Babs* attack aircraft carried a version of the "San-go" aerial burst bomb, which showered burning phosphorous pellets down on bomber formations. After extensive testing one B-17 kill and one probable was credited to PO2C Kudo of the *Tainan Kokutai* on August 29th. See text box **Babs shows her claws.**

"San-go" Type-99 No.3, Mk.3, Kai-1 aerial burst bombs attached to an A6M Zeke. (Authors collection)

Above: A detailed view showing Type-99, No.3, Mk.3, Kai-1 air-to-air bombs mounted on the wing of a Mitsubishi A6M2b *Zeke* with the aid of the Small Bomb Dispenser for Fighters. Note that the nose fuse spring-loaded safety arms are in place, even though the fuses are not yet installed – wooden transportation plugs are fitted in the fuse cavities of each bomb. Below: A general view of the complete installation as fitted to an A6M2b *Zeke*.

Babs shows her claws

PO2C Shigetoshi Kudo "The king of the night". (Henry Sakaida)

At least one Babs is known to have been involved in offensive operations during the Solomon Islands campaign, where it is claimed that a successfully interception and downing of two B-17 bombers occurred!

As the Allied bomber offensive began to increase during the summer of 1942, several equipment modifications and ad hoc interception techniques were developed by Japanese aircrews in the Rabaul area. In June a series of air-to-air bomb interceptions were flown by C5M2s of the Tainan Kokutai, utilizing a "San-go" Type-99 No.3, Mk.3, Kai-1 aerial burst bomb. This weapon contained up to 198 phosphorous pellets, which were dispersed when the weapon "bursts" after a pre-determined period, scattering burning pellets over a wide area. See Chapter 4, **Technical Description.**

Tests on a section of fuel tank from a downed B-17 confirmed that the pellets ignited effectively and resulted in flames, which spread over the whole tank, but flight-testing with a G4M bomber revealed numerous problems, which were slowly overcome. On the morning of August 29th a C5M2 of the Tainan Kokutai was dispatched to patrol the Rabaul area, piloted by PO2C (Aviation Petty Officer 2nd Class) Shigetoshi Kudo, who was an experienced reconnaissance pilot at that time. Instead of its usual reconnaissance duties, this aircraft had been specifically modified to carry a pair of "San-go" bombs, as PO2C Kudo's specific mission was to intercept an incoming enemy bomber formation. Climbing to 7,500m (22,860ft), PO2C Kudo began an hour-long pursuit of the bombers and finally positioned himself ahead of and above the left hand side of formation of aircraft, which he identified as B-17 bombers. Without the aid of a sighting system, PO2C Kudo and his RO began their attack run and the "San-go" separated perfectly from the Babs and detonated at the planned altitude, with its payload of phosphorous pellets raining down on to the bomber stream. The Babs crew observed strikes on the tail of one B-17, which suddenly exploded and broke into pieces. A second B-17, flying directly behind the first bomber was also hit and began to trail white fuel vapour. By this time the formation had broken up and the second B-17 was seen entering a cloud, still streaming fuel, and PO2C Kudo later recalled that:

"... if a bombsight had been available to use at the time, it would not have resulted in a better attack."

For his actions that morning PO2C Kudo was credited with one kill and one probable, however the USAAF do not record any losses on that day. Had this been a "one-off" claim, then it would be easy to dismiss, but PO2C Kudo's escapades and experiences at that time guided him into the field of night-fighter operations, which was beginning to be utilized at the same time over Rabaul. After converting on to the J1N1-S Irving, fitted with obliquely mounted cannons, CPO (Aviation Chief Petty Officer) Kudo would become Japan's first night fighter ace in the Pacific, credited with a total of nine kills, and would become widely know as "The King of the Night".

Armed C5M2 of the Tainan Kokutai

1/48 Scale

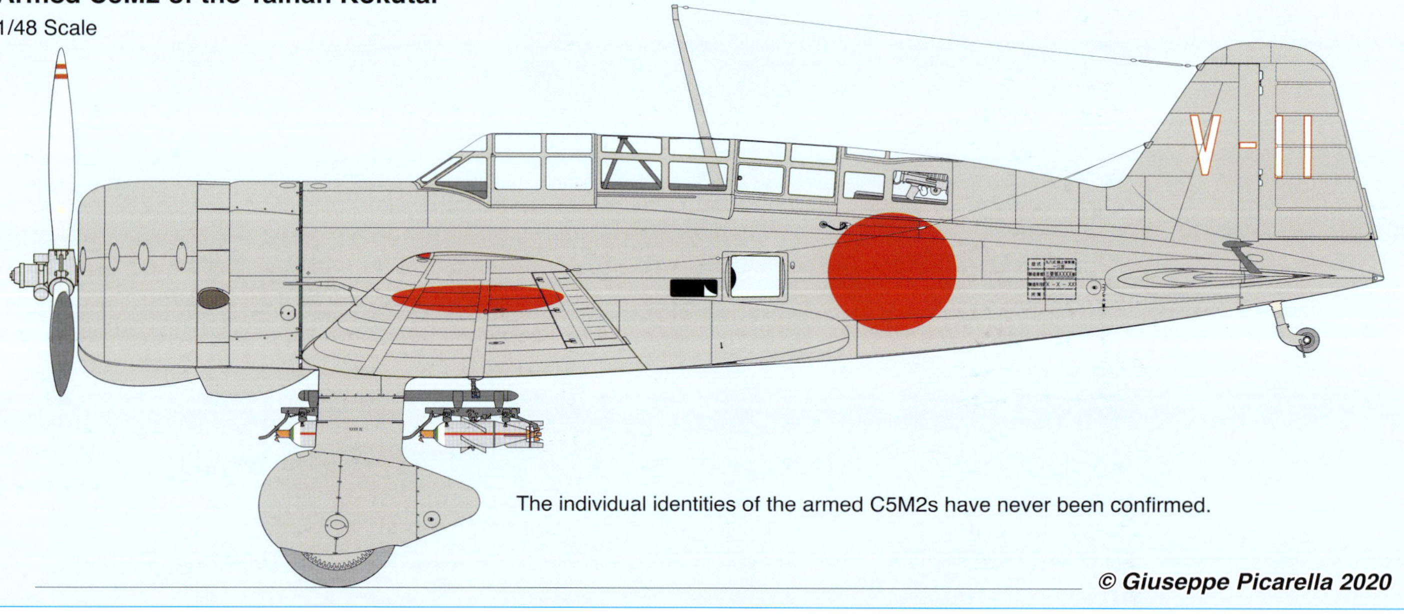

The individual identities of the armed C5M2s have never been confirmed.

One C5M performed a reconnaissance flight over San Cristobal Island on the September 11th and two C5Ms were dispatched on the 13th to support the Army's counter attack on Guadalcanal, which had begun the day before. The Navy's orders to the reconnaissance flight were:

"The land reconnaissance plane unit of 5 Air Attack Force shall dispatch two land reconnaissance planes and six Zero fighters at 04:30 hours; report on the situation of the ground combat on Guadalcanal Island as well as the possibility of landing there. If landing is possible one plane will land, contact the army and make preparations for the landing of fighters."

On September 14th one C5M and one of the Navy's new reconnaissance aircraft, the Yokosuka Navy Type-2 Carrier Reconnaissance Plane, D4Y1-C *Judy*, were sent out on a mission with 10 A6Ms, to reconnoitre the situation over Guadalcanal. The C5M and two of the A6Ms were lost.

A similar operation was performed on September 16th, with one C5M, 26 G4Ms and 24 A6Ms, but a developing storm front forced the mission to be abandoned. On September 19th a C5M was dispatched to report on weather conditions over Guadalcanal, ahead of 17 G4Ms and 39 A6Ms, but conditions deteriorated rapidly as the day progressed and the mission was recalled. The weather was no better on September 20th when C5Ms were once again dispatched to report on the situation over Guadalcanal and New Guinea. The weather was reported to have been *"favourable"* by the C5M crew over New Guinea on September 23rd, allowing a parachute resupply mission to be made in support of the *South Seas* and *Sasebo Detachment*.

A further weather reconnaissance flight was made by a C5M on September 24th, clearing the way for 27 G4Ms and 42 A6Ms to attack Guadalcanal. On September 25th a C5M was sent to report on weather conditions over Guadalcanal, but was forced to turn back in the face of the growing storm. Later that day a flight of nine A6Ms and one C5M were sent out to search for the crew of the Kamikaze-class destroyer *"Yayoi"*. The vessel, which was captained by Lt. Commander Shizuka Kajimoto, had been attacked by B-17s and B-25s after departing Rabaul on the September 11th, forcing it to make a dash for Normanby Island. Of the listed crew complement of 150 men, 83 survived and were later rescued by the destroyers *"Isokaze"* and *"Mochizuki"*. Unfortunately though, the reconnaissance/rescue flight was also compelled to turn back because of the bad weather. Another weather flight was conducted by a C5M on September 26th, but the weather had not improved and the aircraft returned to base.

On October 4th the weather conditions seemed to be improving, so a C5M and two B5N Carrier Bombers were sent on a weather observation flight over New Guinea. Conditions were reported to have been favourable and the following day a C5M and nine A6Ms made a photographic reconnaissance flight over Hood Point.

On the 12th, two unidentified cruisers were spotted by a C5M returning from a "secret" flight to Talugi and an attack mission was rapidly dispatched to intercept the vessels. 27 G4Ms from the *6th Air Attack Force* and 14 from the *1st Air Attack Force*, together with 21 A6Ms of the *5th Air Attack Force* headed for Savo Island, where the vessel had been reported, but the weather conditions had deteriorated once again and the aircraft were forced back to base.

One C5M and eight A6Ms attacked Guadalcanal and Talugi on the 25th, and on the 28th a C5M was dispatched to make weather observations over Kokoda, in preparations for parachute supply drop in support of the *South Seas Detachment*. Unfortunately foul weather caused the cancellation of the mission, but it was carried out the following day by nine G4Ms, supported by 15 A5Ms.

A C5M weather observation flight was also dispatched on the 29th to determine if an attack mission to Port Moresby was possible, but this was forced to turn back, although the weather had improved enough for the enemy to counter-attack Rabaul the next day.

At the end of October only three C5Ms remained operational on Rabaul and reports of their usage in combat reports become evermore sporadic, although four aircraft were later listed at Buin, Bougainville.

On November 31st the *Tainan Kokutai* was in the midst of being reorganized into the *251st Kokutai*, although this did not stop its C5Ms from continuing the fight. On April 3rd 1943, two C5Ms reported spotting five large, three medium, one small transport vessel and approximately 30 amphibious boats at Munda, in addition to approximately 45 enemy aircraft at Baniki. On the 14th, the *"full force"* of the *11th Air Fleet* was used to attack enemy ships anchored in Milne Bay, together with the aircraft located at Rabi airfield, all of which was overseen by two C5Ms performing Command & Control operations.

By the end of April the ferocity of the air war around Rabaul and the later influx of Navy Type-2 Reconnaissance Aircraft, J1N1-C *Irving* and Type-2 Carrier Reconnaissance Aircraft, D4Y1-C *Judy* reconnaissance aircraft marked the end of the Navy's reliance on the C5M on the South East Area.

As Japan's frontlines expanded and reacted to Allied actions, it was inevitable that units were modified in theatre, or reassigned and divided to form the nucleus of new *Kokutais*. This meant that C5Ms were often absorbed into those new units, albeit for a short period of time, until the commanding Air Flotilla reassigned aircraft more efficiently. These units included:

Kisarazu Kokutai

Formed at Kisarazu Air Field, Chiba, on April 1st 1936, the *Kisarazu Kokutai* was the first land-based bomber group to be formed in the Navy. Initially operating only six B4Y1, this figure rapidly increased on the eve of the second Sino-Japanese war, when aircraft of the *Tateyama Kokutai* and *Ōminato Kokutai* were absorbed into the unit. In 1937 the unit began operating A4N1 Carrier Fighters to protect its new G3M bombers, which were operating from bases in Shanghai and Nanking. In January 1940 the unit returned to Japan for re-equipment, training and homeland defence duties. By 1942 it had converted onto the G4M and it would seem that a single C5M2 was utilized for both Command & Control and reconnaissance duties within the unit. In August 1942 the *Kisarazu Kokutai* was deployed to Rabaul, where it became the *707th Kokutai* by November 1st, before being reorganized into the *705th Kokutai* in December.

The unit code was **Ki** between April 1936 and March 1942, changing to **R** in April 1942.

Mihoro Kokutai

Formed on Formosa on June 1st 1938, the *Mihoro Kokutai,* was initially equipped with G3M bombers, which were utilized almost immediately against targets in mainland China. Following an initial deployment to China in 1939, during which time it began to operate the C5M1, the unit soon returned to Formosa in the build up to war with the US. In November 1940 it was deployed to Northern French Indo-China, before being posted to Saigon, from where it formed part of the attack force that sank *HMS Prince of Wales* and *HMS Repulse*. Following operations through the Dutch East Indies the unit was dispersed amongst several small bases in Java during mid 1942, before being renamed the *701st Kokutai* on November 1st.

The unit code between June 1938 and November 1942 was **M**

6th Kokutai

The *6th Kokutai* was formed at Kisarazu Naval Air Base on April 1st 1942 as a dedicated fighter unit. Although the Navy assigned 60 A6M2 fighters and eight C5M2 land-based reconnaissance aircraft to the *6th Kokutai* on that date, it would only receive a mixture of six A6M2 and A5M4 fighters until the end of the month, when 29 A6M2s were finally delivered. Just prior to the Doolittle Raid on April 18th, the unit deployed 15 A6M2s to the Kanto Prefecture, where they would be utilized in the unsuccessful search for the US carriers. After carrier qualifications in late May, the unit was dived between the carriers *Kaga, Hiryu* and *Soryu*, to provide support in operations in the Aleutians and Midway, before being dispatching to Rabaul in August 1942. In October the remainder of the *6th Kokutai*, was dispatched from Kisarazu Naval Air Base, to Rabaul onboard the carrier *Zuiho*, where the unit was finally rejoined. On November 1st the *6th Kokutai* was renamed as the *204th Kokutai.*

The unit code applied to its aircraft was **U**.

204th Kokutai

The *204th Kokutai* and officially formed with a mixture of 60 A6M2 and A6M3 *"Hamp"* fighters, plus a compliment of eight C5M2s, but pressing combat and supply issues meant that these numbers were not initially fulfilled. Operating from Buin, Solomon Islands, the new unit continued to oppose US operations in Guadalcanal and provide air cover for Japanese convoys, aided by their C5M2s. With decreasing air superiority in the region and pilot fatigue, aircraft losses mounted and by the end of 1943, the unit listed no C5Ms on its books. Transferred to Truk in late January 1944, the unit was decimated in a matter of weeks and finally disbanded on March 4th 1944.

The unit code applied to its aircraft was **T2**.

251st Kokutai

On November 1st 1942, the *Tainan Kokutai* was reorganized into the *251st Kokutai* and ordered to return to Japan for retraining at Toyohashi Air Base, where it was issued with 60 A6M2 and A6M3 fighters, eight C5Ms and four transport aircraft. In May 1943 the unit returned to Rabaul by sea and air, with 58 of its remaining fighters and seven C5Ms, and was soon involved in fierce operations against Guadalcanal and the Russell Islands. By May the unit was operating examples of the J1N1-C, Type-2 Reconnaissance Plane *Irving* and losses of all aircraft began to increase. On September 1st the *Tainan Kokutai* converted to night-fighter operations with J1N1-S, Night Fighters.

The unit code was **U1** between November 1942 and May 1943, changing to **51** between May 1943 and July 1944, while some references also accredit **251** as the unit code.

253rd Kokutai

The necessity to provide fighter cover for bomber operations saw the *Kanoya Kokutai* receive approximately nine A6M2s in September 1942, increasing by an additional 24 fighters in October. On November 1st 1942, the *Kanoya Kokutai* was divided into the *253rd* and *751st Kokutais*, with the former operating A6M fighters and the latter operating G4M bombers. Issued with 48 A6M2 and eight C5M2 aircraft, the *253rd Kokutai* was placed under the command of the *21st Air Flotilla*, and remained at Kavieng, New Ireland, but individual flights were sent to operate from Buka, Rabaul and Surumi, where an increasing number of combat missions were launched against Guadalcanal. In May 1943, the unit was withdrawn to Saipan and by September it listed only fighter aircraft.

Between November 1942 and September 1943 (the most likely operational career of its C5M2 aircraft) the unit code employed on its aircraft was **U3**.

254th Kokutai

The *254th Kokutai* was activated on October 1st 1943, and posted to Hainan Island to provide air cover for the Hong Kong area, including convoy protection and general coverage of the southern China zone. Provisionally equipped with 24 A6Ms, four B5N2s and a single Navy Type-0 Transport, L2D *Tabby*, the unit grew to include 48 A6Ms and eight C5M2s* by November 1st 1943. Made up of newly qualified and inexperienced enlisted pilots, the unit's main activities involved bomber interception missions, but the appearance of increasing numbers of Allied P-40 and P-38 fighters took their toll on the unit. At one point fighter-bomber missions were initiated with poor results and in October 1944 a unit of aircraft was sent to support fighting on Formosa, before moving to Mabalacat, where operations over Leyte reduced the unit down to two aircraft. On January 1st 1945, what remained of the unit personnel were sent back to Hainan and absorbed into its parent unit, the *901 Kokutai*, which fell back to Shanghai in April 1945.

Between November 1942 and September 1943 (the most likely operational career of its C5M2 aircraft) the unit code employed on its aircraft was **54**.

The long goodbye

By the beginning of 1942 the Ki-15 design was almost seven years old and the Navy's C5Ms were all but obsolete. When they entered service in 1939 they still possessed a small speed advantage over most enemy fighters in China and South-east Asia, but with the arrival of modern fighters during 1941 their days of relative immunity were numbered. The subsequent arrival of Allied radar equipment in late 1941 and early 1942 effectively pre-warned the Allies of approaching Japanese formations and lone reconnaissance aircraft, which enabled defending fighters to be vectored to the right location and altitude, in order to wait and pounce on their targets at high speed.

In June 1942 the Navy was becoming desperate for land-based, long-range reconnaissance aircraft and the "action-reaction" mentality of the *Kaigun Koku Hombu* once again became prevalent in its planning. This lead to the conversion of two types of existing combat aircraft into "dedicated" reconnaissance aircraft, in the form of the J1N1-C *Irving*, which was unloved by the reconnaissance crews, and the carrier based D4Y1-C *Judy*, which was seen as a short term solution until the Navy Carrier Reconnaissance Aircraft, C6N1 *Myrt* was predicted to entered service in 1944. But with no real successor for the C5M available to the Navy, planners were once again forced to turn to an Army aircraft type in order to fulfilling their land-based reconnaissance aircraft needs. With appropriate approval granted by the Army, the Navy began operating a small number of the superlative Type-100 Headquarters Recon-

Kisarazu Kokutai

1/48 Scale

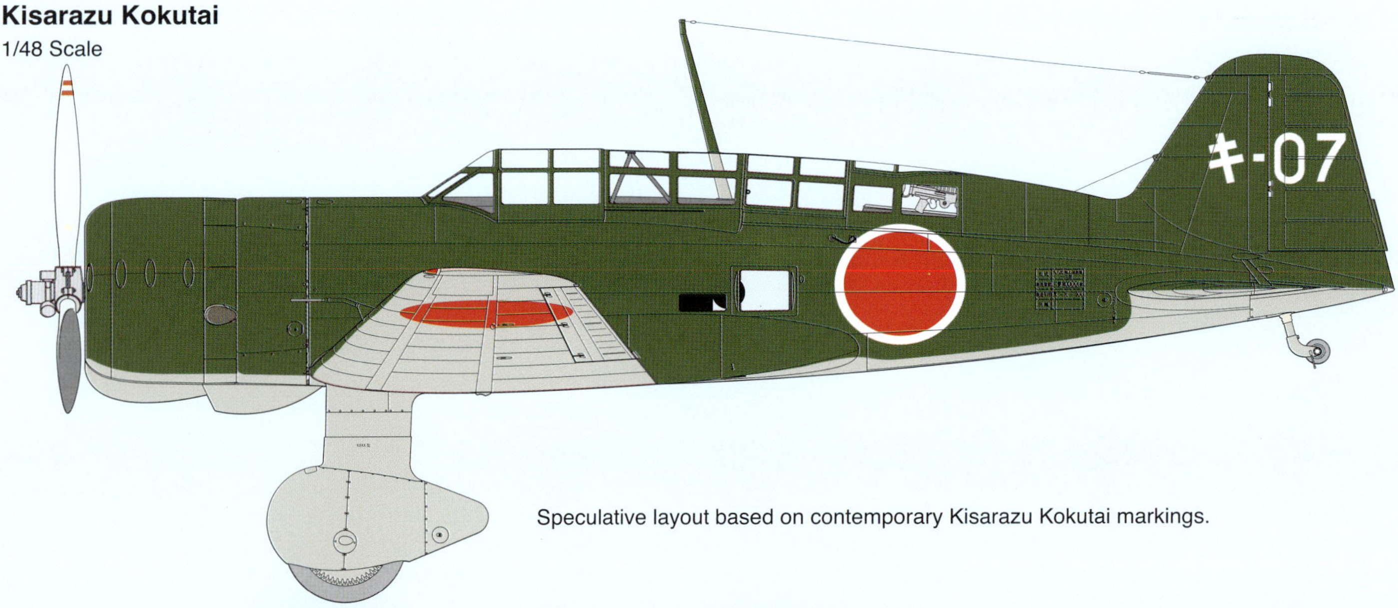

Speculative layout based on contemporary Kisarazu Kokutai markings.

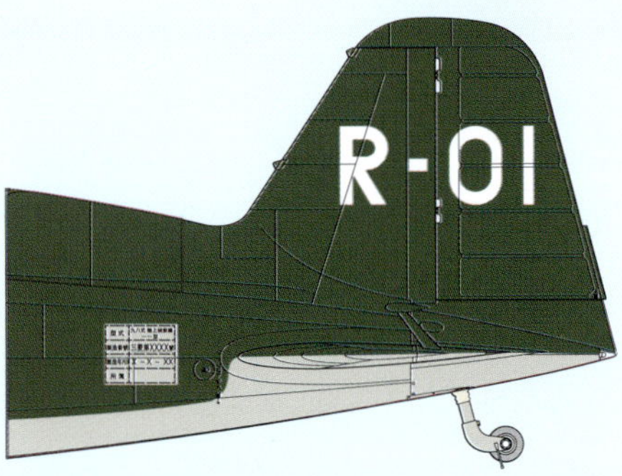

Speculative layout based on contemporary Kisarazu Kokutai markings.

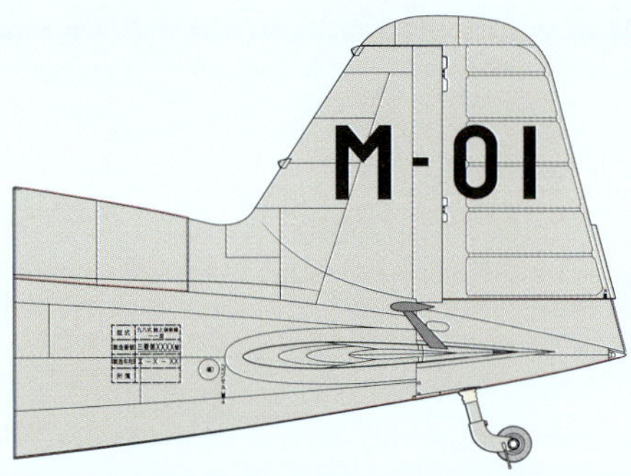

Speculative layout based on contemporary Mihoro Kokutai markings.

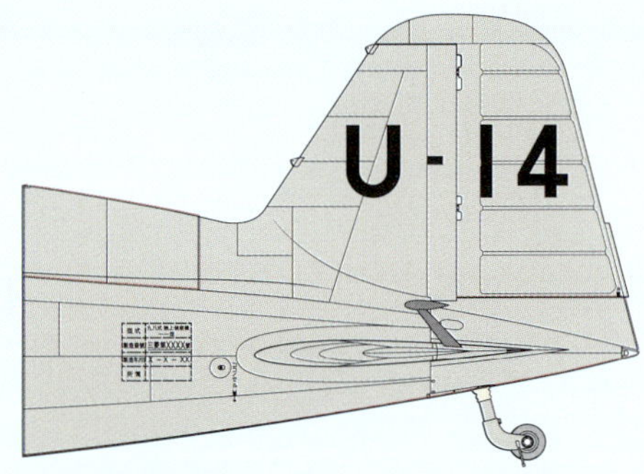

Speculative layout based on contemporary 6th Kokutai markings.

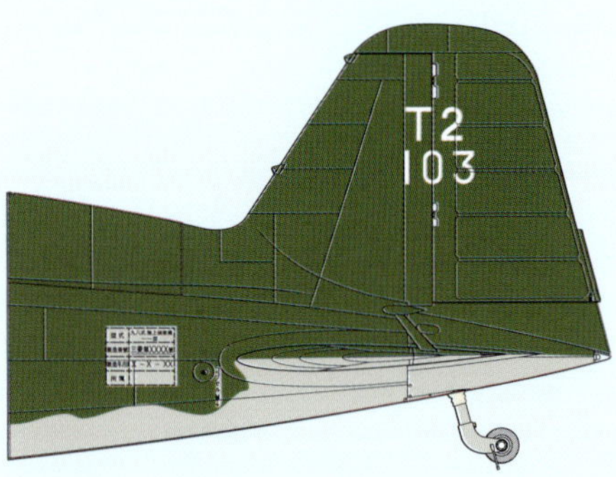

Speculative layout based on contemporary 204th Kokutai markings.

Speculative layout based on contemporary 253rd Kokutai markings.

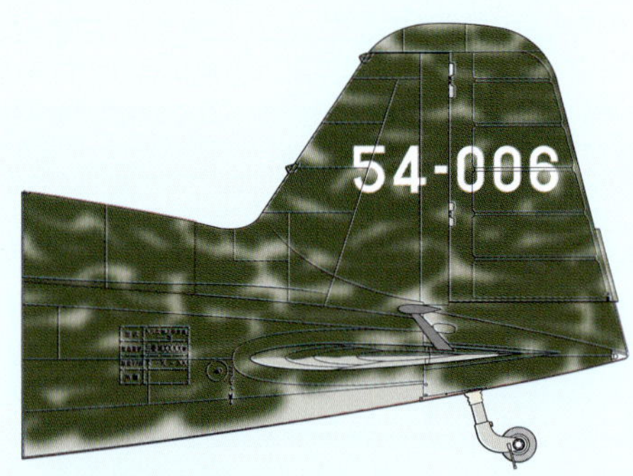

Speculative layout based on contemporary 254th Kokutai markings.

251st Kokutai

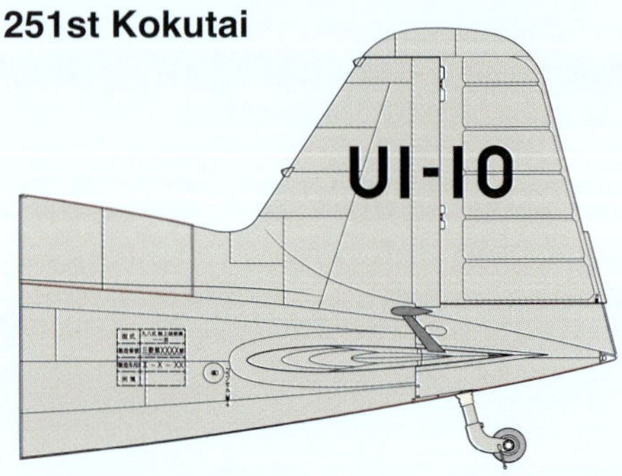

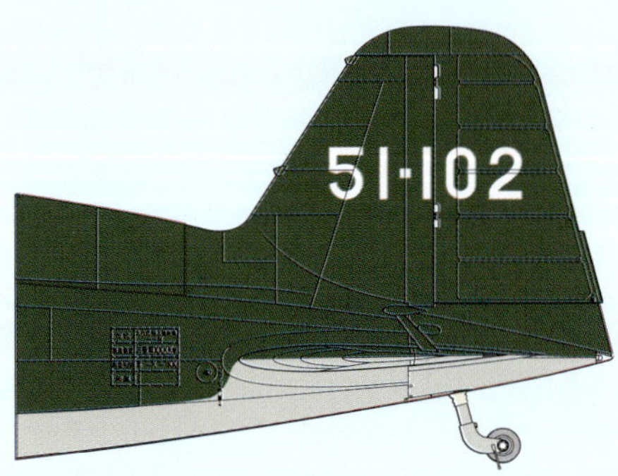

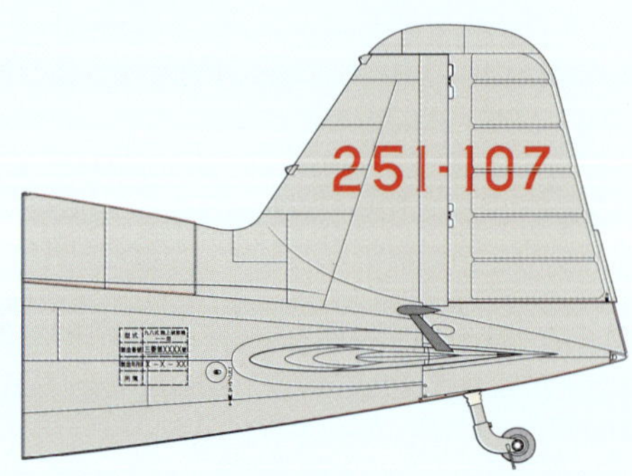

Speculative layouts based on contemporary 251st Kokutai markings.

Flight-test units and higher organizations

1/48 Scale

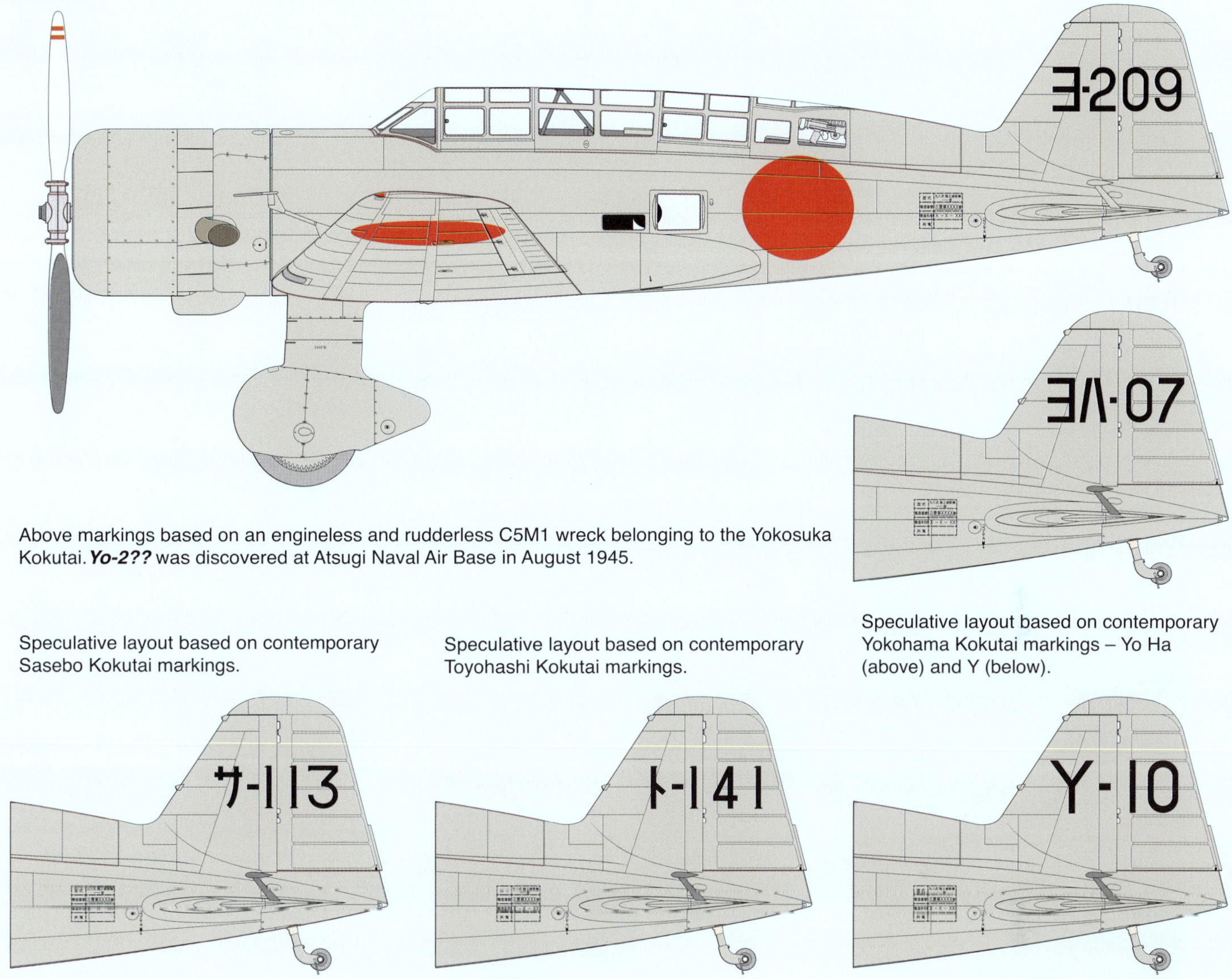

Above markings based on an engineless and rudderless C5M1 wreck belonging to the Yokosuka Kokutai. ***Yo-2??*** was discovered at Atsugi Naval Air Base in August 1945.

Speculative layout based on contemporary Sasebo Kokutai markings.

Speculative layout based on contemporary Toyohashi Kokutai markings.

Speculative layout based on contemporary Yokohama Kokutai markings – Yo Ha (above) and Y (below).

naissance Aircraft, Ki-46-II *Dinah*, until a solution to their reconnaissance aircraft requirements was found. This subject will be expanded upon in the next volume of this series.

By August 1944 only four (out of six) C5M airframes were listed as operational among the 408 aircraft attached to the *1st Air Flotilla* in the Philippines, which was comprised of the *22nd*, *25th*, *26th*, and *61st Air Flotilla's* and the *153rd*, *201st 761st* and *1021st Air Groups.* And because combat operations were becoming so frantic, it was duly noted that:

"Both the air reconnaissance plane group and the carrier bomber units were engaged in actual battle with hardly any time for training because of the shortage of materials."

In addition to the training establishments and operational *Kokutais*, some of the Navy's flight-test and higher organizations have also been identified as operating the C5M aircraft at one time or another. It is unclear if these aircraft were attached to these specific units for used as reconnaissance aircraft, or simply retained as fast communications and VIP aircraft. These units included the:

Yokosuka Kokutai – unit code katakana **Yo**. One C5M1 was photographed amongst numerous wrecked aircraft at Atsugi Naval Air Base in August 1945. The aircraft did not have a main landing gear, outer wing panels, an engine or rudder, so the unit code was incomplete **Yo-2??**

Yokohama Kokutai – unit code katakana **Yo Ha** then **Y**.

Sasebo Kokutai – unit code katakana **Sa.**

Toyohashi Kokutai – unit code katakana **To Yo.**

Operational deployment of C5M aircraft

Kokutai/Year	1939	1940	1941	1942	1943	1944	1945
12th Kokutai	– --	--------					
13th Kokutai	– --	--------					
14th Kokutai	– --	--------					
15th Kokutai	– --	--------					
3rd Kokutai		– -	---------	---------	---		
Yamada Unit			–	----			
Tainan Kokutai		– -	---------	---------	---		
Kanoya Kokutai		– -	--				
Takao Kokutai			---------				
251st Kokutai				– -	-----		
6th Kokutai				– -------			
204th Kokutai					---------		
Mihoro Kokutai	– -						
Kisarazu Kokutai			--				
253rd Kokutai				– -	--		
254th Kokutai					– -	--	

One of the few C5M airframes (right) to be recorded on the Japanese mainland was discovered at Atsugi Naval Air Base. Other photographs of this aircraft reveal the tail markings to be Yo-2?? of the Yokosuka Kokutai. *(Authors collection)*

Postwar extinction?

There is no documented evidence of any C5M aircraft being utilized by other nations after the war, unlike the Army Ki-15. Of the 50 examples built, it is unlikely that more than four or five C5M airframes survived to see the surrender of Japan, and those were probably being used as airfield decoys at the end. But one partial example managed to survive a little longer and may still be extant.

During the summer of 1943 a C5M2 of the *11th Air Fleet, 22nd Air Flotilla* was damaged on the ground at the Japanese Navy airfield at Gasmata, New Britain (Papua New Guinea). The Japanese Navy subsequently vacated the site at the beginning of 1944 and the airfield was soon bypassed by the Allies, as they island-hopped their way towards Japan. Located some 4,800km (2,982 miles) from its birth place at Mitsubishi's No.3 Airframe Works in Nagoya, this unidentified C5M2 was photographed by Charles Darby in 1974, together with half a dozen other Japanese aircraft wrecks, which had been dragged back onto the airfield as tourist attractions by the locals. It is currently unknown if this airframe still exists, but if it does it represents the only known *Babs* airframe in existence.

Possibly the last surviving Babs airframe was this C5M2 at Gasmata Airfield, New Britain (Papua New Guinea), which was photographed in the 1970s. (Charles Darby)

Chapter 2

Western intelligence reports

"BABS – Type 97 LIGHT BOMBER. KARIGANE MARK I – This light reconnaissance bomber is a single-engine, low-wing monoplane. Max. speed 210 mph, Armament – [Forward] fuselage: 2 x 7.7mm (fixed machine-gun), Max. bomb load: (est.) 1,100 lb."

Informational Intelligence – Summary. No.43-26. Japanese Aircraft and Armament, April 1943.

After a seven-year development and production program, the final *Babs* airframe rolled off the assembly line during August 1941. The concept of the high performance Command Reconnaissance aircraft had been vindicated in combat over China and a successor, in the form of the superlative Ki-46-II *Dinah*, had just entered production. But what did the Western Allies know about the *Babs*, or the new branch of aviation it ushered in?

In the years leading up to America's entry into World War II, it is known that Capt. Claire Chennault, acting as an advisor to the Chinese Air Force between 1937 and 1941, regularly reported back to the US Government on the activities of the Japanese Air Force, including specifics on their capabilities, procedures and equipment. During that period at least one *Babs* is known to have been damaged and force-landed, while participating in the Chongqing (Chungking) bombing offensive of August 1940. The Chinese subsequently recovered the airframe for inspection, but it is unclear if Chennault inspected or reported on its substantial remains when he arrived in the city two weeks later?

Following the attack on Pearl Harbor, US intelligence agencies frantically began to collect data on Japan's grossly underestimated military capabilities, only to be confronted by complex nomenclature systems and a veil of secrecy that the Japanese military had deliberately drawn around its aviation industry during the 1930s. In such a situation, one would assume that collecting information on a high-performance military reconnaissance aircraft, acting as the eyes of both the Army and the Navy, would have been a difficult task, but this was far from the case. Technical data for the *Babs* had in fact already been published in two British weekly aviation magazines, ***The Aeroplane*** and ***Flight***, following the arrival of *Kamikaze* at Croydon airport in April 1937.

This was followed by detailed and technically accurate inclusions for the Mitsubishi *Karigane* within the 1937 and 1938 volumes of ***Jane's All The World's Aircraft***. This information was further updated with entries for the more advanced *Karigane*-II within the 1939, 1940 and 1941 volumes, although the 1941 volume did include the spurious fact that the aircraft was known in the: "*... Japanese Army Air Corps as the Army Type 98 Light Bomber.*"

Given that such data was available in the public domain, it remains unclear why US Intelligence teams took so long to publish credible information on the aircraft, or even identify its actual role. As will be seen in the following reports and summaries, which represent the majority of the known Technical Air Intelligence Center (TAIC) references for *Babs*, the TAIC was responsible for disseminating a very meagre and somewhat confusing picture of the aircraft during the Pacific War. While it is entirely possible that the high performance capabilities and true nature of the aircraft may have contributed to it being overlooked, misidentified or misunderstood by the western Allies at the start of the conflict, these capabilities were well known to Allied pilots in the field. And the absence of *Babs* data, within the tens of thousands of pages of wartime TAIC documentation, no doubt eased the *Babs* into post-war obscurity.

It is worth pointing out that some in the West still believe that the Ki-15 design was based on the Northrop Gamma airframe, and the editor of ***The Aeroplane*** (C. G. Grey) possibly added to this misconception, as several assertions to that effect were made in the magazine's April 14th news story. The fact that *Kamikaze* was similar in appearance to contemporary US and British designs had come as a shock to many in the industry, which took the view that the Japanese were "copyists" at best. With hindsight it is somewhat laughable to assume that the Ki-15 was simply a copy of an existing design,

APRIL 14, 1937 439 THE AEROPLANE

The Heavenly Breeze

JAPANESE AEROPLANES rarely visit us, so the arrival of the Mitsubishi all-metal low-wing monoplane *Kamikaze*, in which Mr. Iimuma and Mr. Tsukagoshi have just flown from Tokyo to London, as reported elsewhere, is of particular technical interest. It is rather smaller than the Northrop monoplanes it is popularly supposed to represent, its undercarriage is cleaner. The long narrow ailerons and short broad flaps which end far short of the ailerons are entirely original.

The 550 h.p. Nakajima Kotobuki motor seems to be a Japanese-built Wright Cyclone.

The external finish of the machine appears to be very good indeed. The flush-riveting of both the wing and the fuselage is some of the finest we have ever seen. The whole surface has been covered with many layers of clear dope so that not the slightest inequality can be felt.

On the wings, the riveting has been done in panels of about 6 ins. by 4 ins. with about 1½ in. spacing between rivets. We were not able to get any information about the internal wing structure but it is probably of the multi-spar type.

Split trailing-edge flaps extend underneath the fuselage to within about 3 ft. of each aileron. There seems no obvious reason why the flaps are not carried right up to the ailerons.

Landing lights, covered with transparent sections shaped to the wing-contour, are housed in the leading edge of the wings on either side of the fuselage.

Elevators and ailerons appear to have cotton fabric covering in the American manner. Trimming tabs on the trailing edges of the elevators can be adjusted while flying.

There are generous fillets between the wing roots and the fuselage in typically Northrop fashion. Rather cunning footsteps disappear into the fillets when not in use. The cockpit cover fairs prettily into the circular section fuselage.

The cockpits are about four feet apart and the fuel tanks are between them. Both cockpits are roomy and neatly arranged. The rear cockpit has two small windows let into each side at seat level. Dual control is not fitted. The normal rudder-bar and control column are in the front cockpit.

Dome-type navigation lights on top of the cockpit hooding and below the fuselage are perfect copies of a British make. We could not see that any British instruments were used.

The motor is enclosed in a conventional N.A.C.A. long-chord cowling without baffles between the cylinders. The exhaust collector ring is placed inside the cowling immediately behind the cylinders where it must impede the air flow considerably, and discharges above the wing on the port side. The hot gases had considerably seared the wing between Tokyo and London.

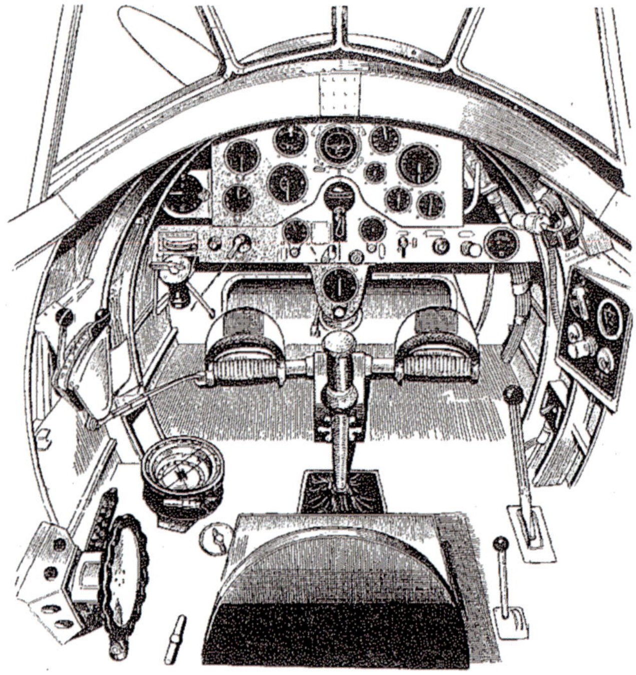

INSIDE THE PILOT'S COCKPIT.—The rudder-bar has loops over, and flat plates beneath, the toes.

The airscrew appears to be a Japanese-built version of the Hamilton. The hub is concealed by a very fine spinner, an excellent example of Oriental attention to detail.

The undercarriage is neatly done and appears to be a distinct improvement on the Northrop model. It has a very long travel which was especially noticeable when the machine was landed at a high sinking speed and yet squashed down with not the slightest tendency to bounce. There is a small solid-tyred tail-wheel which is fully castoring.

Altogether the machine seems a robust job. The Heavenly Breeze after which it is called must be a pretty hearty built-in tail-wind because on only 550 h.p. the machine does not appear to have the performance which it has just achieved.

LEADING PARTICULARS.—Span, 12 m. (39 ft. 4¾ in.). Length, 8.22 m. (27 ft.). Height, 2.8 m. (9 ft. 2½ in.). Wing area, 24 sq. m. (258 sq. ft.). Weight loaded, 2,000 kg. (4,410 lb.). Max. speed, 500 km.p.h. (310 m.p.h.). Range, 2,400 km. (1,490 miles).

PUT AWAY.—The Mitsubishi monoplane in the shed of Rollason Aircraft Services Ltd., which concern specialises in service to long-distance aviators. The relative positions and sizes of ailerons and flaps are interesting.

News story in The Aeroplane, April 14th 1937. Courtesy of Aeroplane Magazine, Key Publishing Ltd.

Saying it with flowers at Croydon (left to right): Mr. Iinuma, Mr. Tsukagoshi, Capt. W. A. Rollason (behind the petals) and, representing the R.Ae.C., Comdr. Perrin. Lower picture shows *Divine Wind*.

JAPAN MAKES HER MARK

Mr. Iinuma, Mr. Tsukagoshi and their Honourable Mitsubishi Monoplane

(*Flight* photograph.)

AT 3.30 p.m. on Friday a large welcoming crowd, largely consisting of the Japanese residents in London, who had been waiting since mid-day, saw a characteristically "over-nosed" monoplane coming in from the direction of Paris. Mr. Iinuma, the pilot, made two complete circuits of the aerodrome while two Leopards, bulging with Press photographers, made an abortive attempt to keep up with the machine, both by diving and by cutting off corners. Then he brought it in slowly and carefully to land neatly, with a burst of engine and straight off the glide, in the centre of the available landing area—which was restricted by flagged-off areas populated by various working parties.

Thus was the "goodwill" flight of Mr. Iinuma and Mr. Tsukagoshi from Tokio to London completed in 94 hours. The effort is of rather unusual interest in that the aircraft and engine were of Japanese manufacture.

The first section of the flight which was sponsored by the Tokyo *Asahi* Press, commenced from Tokio at 5.12 p.m. on Monday, April 5, and covered the 1,400 odd miles to Taihoku, Formosa. In spite of the weather conditions, which were the worst experienced on the whole trip, an average speed of almost 200 m.p.h. was maintained. After leaving Hanoi (French Indo-China), the next stop, bad visibility to Vientiane lowered the average a little and it was not until the Baghdad to Athens stage was covered that the average speed for a section exceeded 200 m.p.h.; in this case 1,280 miles was covered in 6 hours 17 mins., a speed of 202 m.p.h. Strong head-winds were encountered while crossing India.

Last Friday the final European stages were commenced; leaving Athens at 5.40 a.m., Rome was reached at 8.46 a.m. —710 miles at 219 m.p.h. After only 50 minutes the *Divine Wind* took the air again for Paris, arriving there at 1.33 after having put up an average of 230 m.p.h. for the 730 miles. Finally, at 2.15 on Friday, April 9, Mr. Iinuma took off for Croydon and had terminated his flight within 75 minutes.

Without fuss or bother the two members of the crew smiled gravely at their compatriots and disappeared into the seething crowd. They managed to obtain a good rest at Rome and did not appear to be particularly exhausted. In due

(*Concluded on page 376.*)

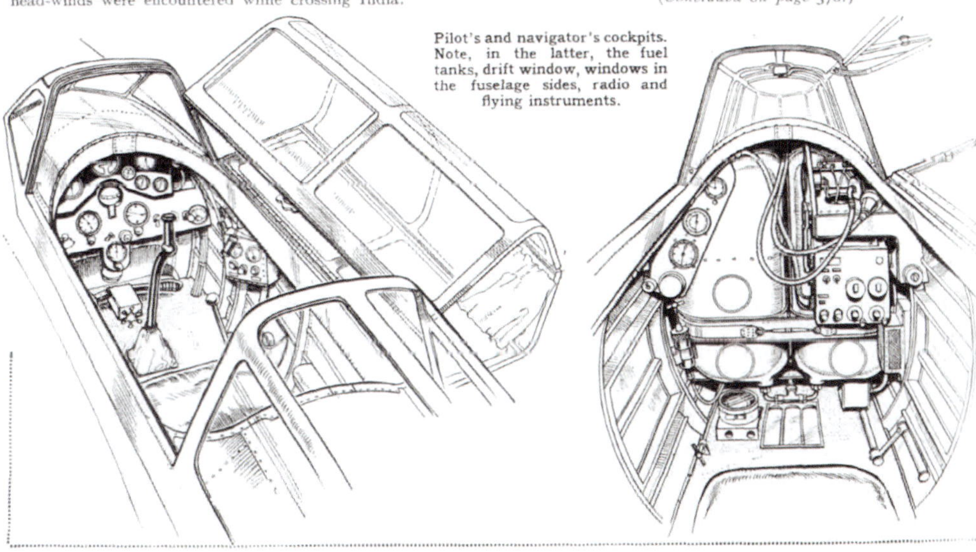

Pilot's and navigator's cockpits. Note, in the latter, the fuel tanks, drift window, windows in the fuselage sides, radio and flying instruments.

(*Continued from page 374.*)

course, mechanics wheeled the *Divine Wind* into the Rollason hangar and the inner doors slid in front of the eyes of the curious.

Contrary to expectations, this Mitsubishi monoplane (which, incidentally was completed toward the end of March) and its engine do not appear to have been built under direct licence from any particular American firms. Its type-name is *Karigane*, or Wild Goose. It is reminiscent of the well-known Northrop series of single-engined mailplanes, but the resemblance is largely superficial and might apply to any machine built on the same lines and for the same purpose. The radial engine—a Nakajima Kotobuki III giving 550 h.p. (normal) at sea level and designed for a fixed-pitch airscrew, has points of similarity with the P. and W. Wasp and the earlier Wright Cyclones, but it obviously of Japanese design. Superior people would not find it difficult to discover similarities—and to talk of "copying"—in the case of such a machine built anywhere. Two additional aircraft of similar type, but with various improvements are being built for *Asahi*.

Except for the control surfaces, the machine is entirely of metal skin covering and the thin-section wing appears to be of cellular construction—and a very nice piece of work, too, with flush rivets and little sign of irregularities.

The wing area is given as 215 sq. ft. and the span is 39 ft. A range of just under 1,500 miles is claimed by the manufacturers.

The only noticeable British item of equipment was a "Demec" navigation light.

The centre part of the long, roofed cabin is devoted to the accommodation of the extra tanks, which give the machine a range of 1,500 miles, with the pilot's seat ahead and the radio operator's cabin at the rear. There does not appear to be any fairlead for a trailing aerial, but the fixed aerial is mounted well away from the fuselage. Presumably the "radio operator" was more of a navigator; certainly, a new and interesting type of combined slide-rule and calculator could be seen in one of the pockets, and he had both a compass and a selection of essential instruments for his own use. The pilot's instruments were of standard type, with an artificial horizon, a turn indicator, a rate-of-climb and so on. He used two compasses, one of the direct-reading bowl type and the other of the verge-ring type—the latter being on the floor of the cockpit. The maximum speed of this Mitsubishi monoplane is given officially as 310 m.p.h. This seems to be on the high side, but the machine had certainly been cruising at somewhere over 200 m.p.h.

At Croydon, Mr. J. C. Galpin, of the Air Ministry, gave the two airmen a message of welcome from Sir Philip Sassoon.

News story in Flight, April 15th, 1937. Courtesy of Flight International, DVV Media International Ltd.

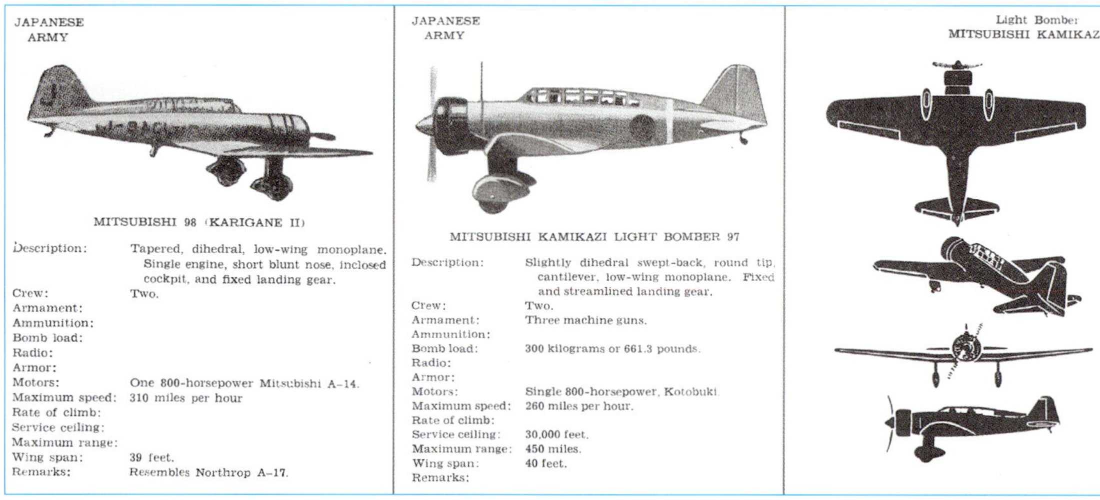

JAPANESE ARMY

MITSUBISHI 98 (KARIGANE II)

Description:	Tapered, dihedral, low-wing monoplane. Single engine, short blunt nose, inclosed cockpit, and fixed landing gear.
Crew:	Two.
Armament:	
Ammunition:	
Bomb load:	
Radio:	
Armor:	
Motors:	One 800-horsepower Mitsubishi A-14.
Maximum speed:	310 miles per hour
Rate of climb:	
Service ceiling:	
Maximum range:	
Wing span:	39 feet.
Remarks:	Resembles Northrop A-17.

JAPANESE ARMY

MITSUBISHI KAMIKAZI LIGHT BOMBER 97

Description:	Slightly dihedral swept-back, round tip, cantilever, low-wing monoplane. Fixed and streamlined landing gear.
Crew:	Two.
Armament:	Three machine guns.
Ammunition:	
Bomb load:	300 kilograms or 661.3 pounds.
Radio:	
Armor:	
Motors:	Single 800-horsepower, Kotobuki.
Maximum speed:	260 miles per hour.
Rate of climb:	
Service ceiling:	30,000 feet.
Maximum range:	450 miles.
Wing span:	40 feet.
Remarks:	

Light Bomber
MITSUBISHI KAMIKAZI

War Department. Basic Field Manual. FM 30-38, March 16th, 1942.

at a time when almost the whole industry was developing similar looking aluminium-alloy monocoque monoplanes with low-wings, radial-engines and spatted undercarriage! Regardless of this belief, the development phase of the Ki-15 is well documented and the chronology of events simply do not fit the facts. See Chapter 3, Volume I, **Strategic Reconnaissance – uncharted territory.** One export version of the Northrop Gamma 2E (C/n187), specifically identified as a Gamma 5A, was imported into Japan for technical evaluations by the Navy in late October 1935, but this aircraft (officially designated the BNX-1) arrived after the Mitsubishi design team had completed its critical design review of the Ki-15, and after the Army had inspected the wooden mock-up. If the Ki-15 *had* been a copy of the Northrop Gamma 2E/5A, modified to conform to out-dated Japanese capabilities, then it surely deserves to go down as possibly the best copy in history, because it was capable of travel at 481km/h (299mph) with an engine of 550hp, compared to the Gamma's 326km/h (202mph) with its 710hp engine! Following Navy tests the BNX-1 was sold to a civilian operator in September 1936 and registered J-BAGK, before being written off later that same year. A second export Northrop airframe, identified as a Gamma 5D (C/n291) was subsequently imported into Japan by the Navy in October 1936 and re-designated as the BNX-2. After testing the aircraft was loaned to the Nakajima Aircraft Company for further study, before being sold to the Manchurian Air Transport Co Ltd., in 1937. Registered as M-506, the aircraft was regularly utilized by the Army for aerial mapping and reconnaissance in the region, including large swathes of China and the Soviet Union. The aircraft was subsequently used for research and development activities by the airline until at least 1939.

Cruver cellulose acetate plastic identification model of the "JAP MITS T97 ALB", issued June 1942.

Confusion reigns

The first official identification book describing Japanese aircraft types was published on March 16th 1942. ***War Department. Basic Field Manual. FM 30-38. "Identification of Japanese Aircraft"*** was an attempt to rapidly provide desperately needed information to serving US personnel, but due to the almost total lack of available data, ***FM 30-38*** represented at best a scrapbook of figures that had been published in various pre-war US aviation periodicals. The first entry of any relevance occurs on pages 18/19 of the *"Single Engine Fighters:"* section of the manual, which contained a photo of *Karigane*-II (complete with civilian registration – J-BACL) entitled *"Fighter Mitsubishi 98 (KARIGANE II)"*. This may seem somewhat confusing to us now, but in early 1942 the *Karigane*'s airspeed was comparable to many front-line fighters of the period, so it is not difficult to understand why such high performance was confused with fighter-like capabilities. In addition to this, pages 42/43 contained a second entry for the *"Mitsubishi Kamikaze Light Bomber 97"*, with reference to its *"Three machine guns"* and bomb load of *"300 kilograms or 661.3 pounds"* – fictitious statistics that would follow the aircraft through its entire career.

While *FM 30-38* had provided some information to front-line soldiers, its amateurish format was of little practical value. What was needed was a more robust military system of cataloguing, amending and disseminating up-to-date information. This came in the form of ***Informational Intelligence Summary. No.41. "Japanese Aircraft and Armament***", which was issued by the Headquarters, Army Air Forces, Director of Intelligence, in July 1942. Within that publication, details of each new aircraft were set out on standard format forms, which could be amended, updated or superseded when needed. Identified in the summary as a *"Light bomber and reconnaissance – T-97 Army and Navy (Kamikaze)"* the *Babs* was once again quoted as being capable of carrying a 660lb/1,000lb (300kg/450kg) bomb load and fitted with two machine guns, although they were listed as *"positions uncertain"*. Given the listed performance figures it is most likely that the aircraft had been confused with the Mitsubishi Army Type-97 Light Bomber (Ki-30) *Ann*, which carried one machine gun in the wing and one in the rear cockpit.

As the intelligence community released data concerning enemy aircraft developments, Western aviation periodicals of the day were quick to disseminate such details to its readers, who were eager for any information, regardless of it accuracy. The September 24th 1942 issue of the ***The Aeroplane Spotter*** perfectly illustrates the general lack of knowledge surrounding Japanese aircraft types, as it identifies three different types of aircraft (the Mitsubishi *Kamikaze*, Mitsubishi Ki-30 *Ann*, and Tachikawa Ki-36 *Ida*) as Mitsubishi KARIGANE I, KARIGANE II and KARIGANE III Light Bombers. And, with the exception of the *Kamikaze* wingspan, all of the supporting dimensions, performance figures and editorial are wholly inaccurate.

Enemy aircraft table in "The Aeroplane Spotter", September 24th, 1942.

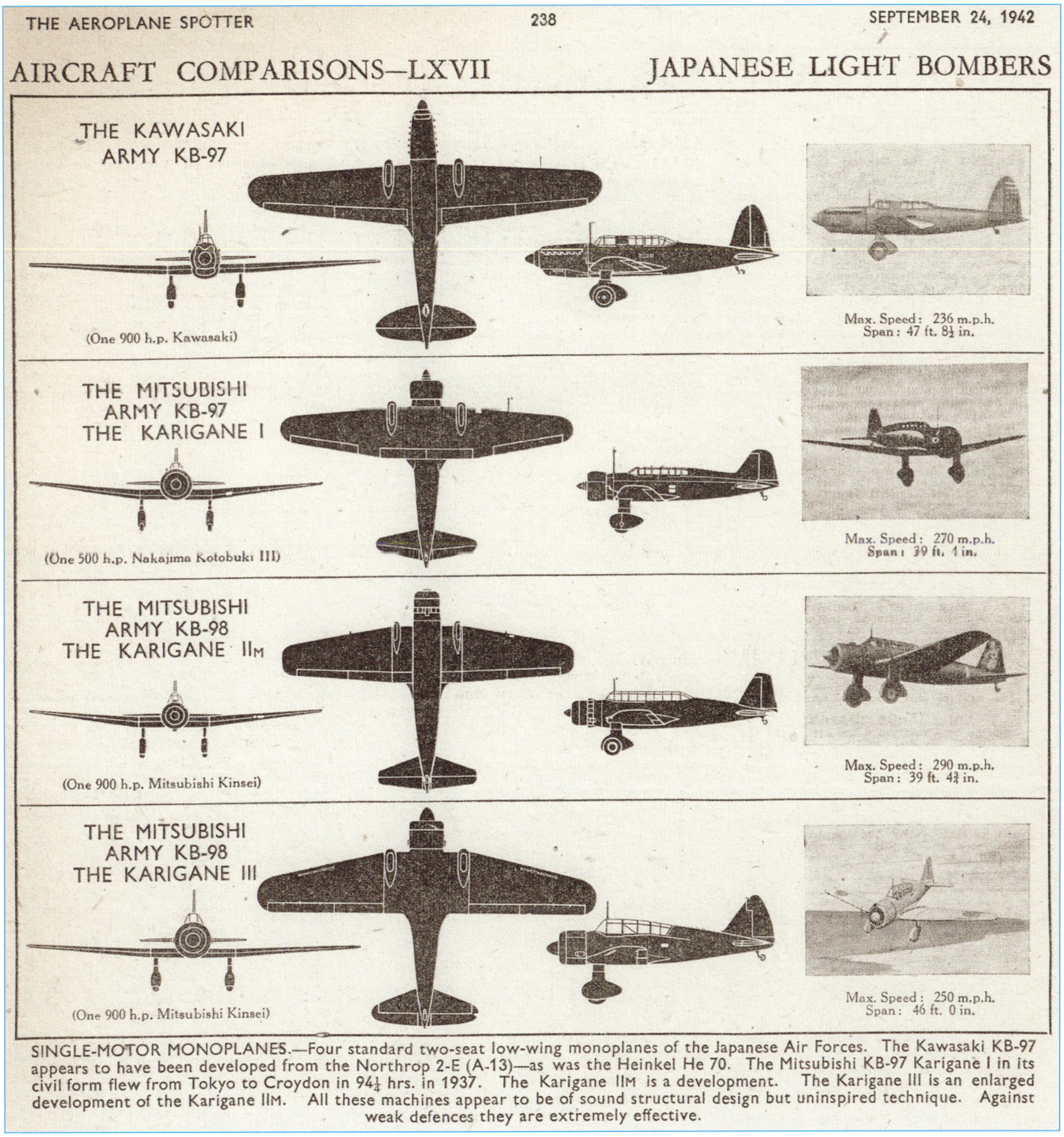
THE AEROPLANE SPOTTER 238 SEPTEMBER 24, 1942

AIRCRAFT COMPARISONS—LXVII JAPANESE LIGHT BOMBERS

THE KAWASAKI ARMY KB-97

(One 900 h.p. Kawasaki)

Max. Speed: 236 m.p.h.
Span: 47 ft. 8½ in.

THE MITSUBISHI ARMY KB-97 THE KARIGANE I

(One 500 h.p. Nakajima Kotobuki III)

Max. Speed: 270 m.p.h.
Span: 39 ft. 4 in.

THE MITSUBISHI ARMY KB-98 THE KARIGANE IIM

(One 900 h.p. Mitsubishi Kinsei)

Max. Speed: 290 m.p.h.
Span: 39 ft. 4¾ in.

THE MITSUBISHI ARMY KB-98 THE KARIGANE III

(One 900 h.p. Mitsubishi Kinsei)

Max. Speed: 250 m.p.h.
Span: 46 ft. 0 in.

SINGLE-MOTOR MONOPLANES.—Four standard two-seat low-wing monoplanes of the Japanese Air Forces. The Kawasaki KB-97 appears to have been developed from the Northrop 2-E (A-13)—as was the Heinkel He 70. The Mitsubishi KB-97 Karigane I in its civil form flew from Tokyo to Croydon in 94¼ hrs. in 1937. The Karigane IIM is a development. The Karigane III is an enlarged development of the Karigane IIM. All these machines appear to be of sound structural design but uninspired technique. Against weak defences they are extremely effective.

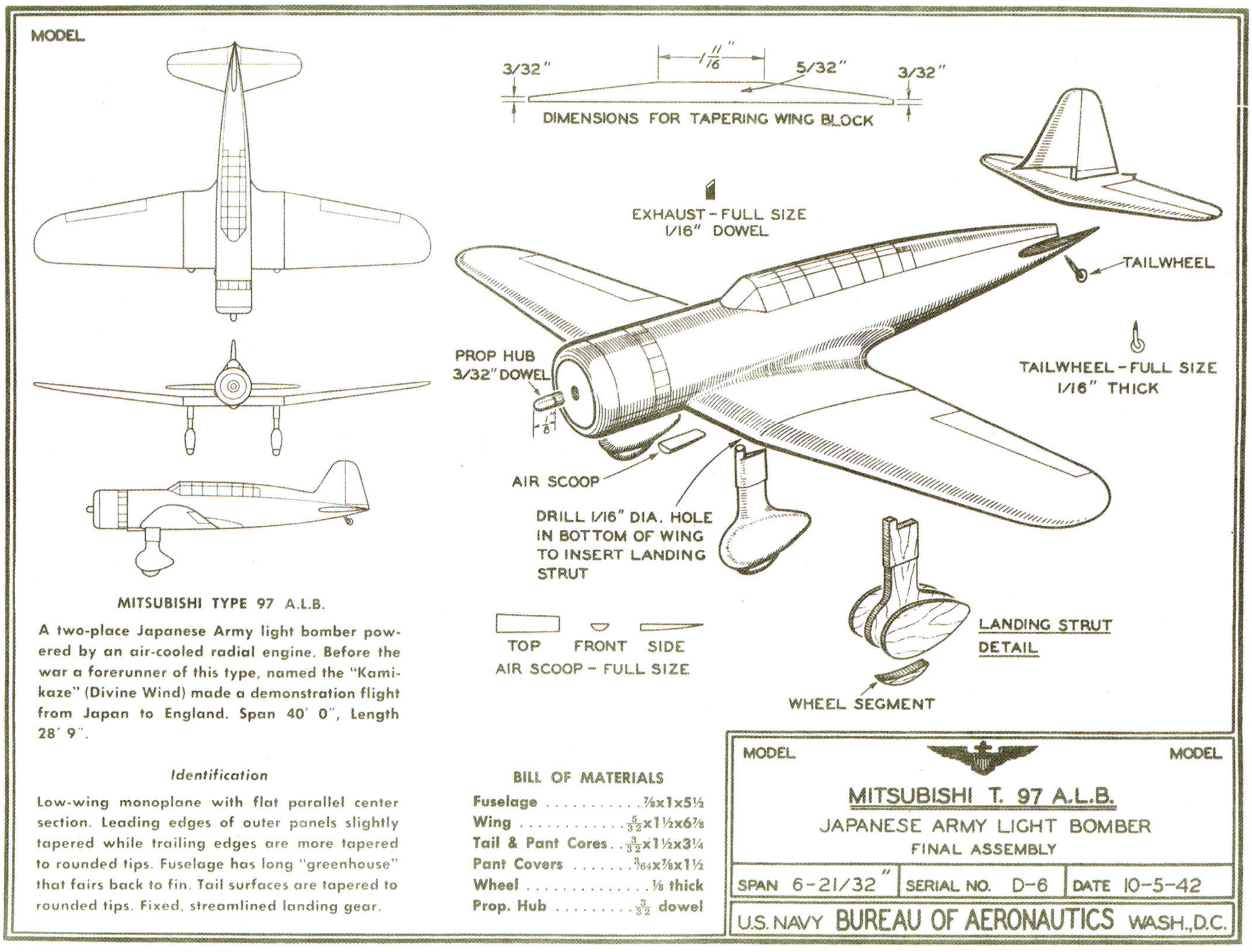

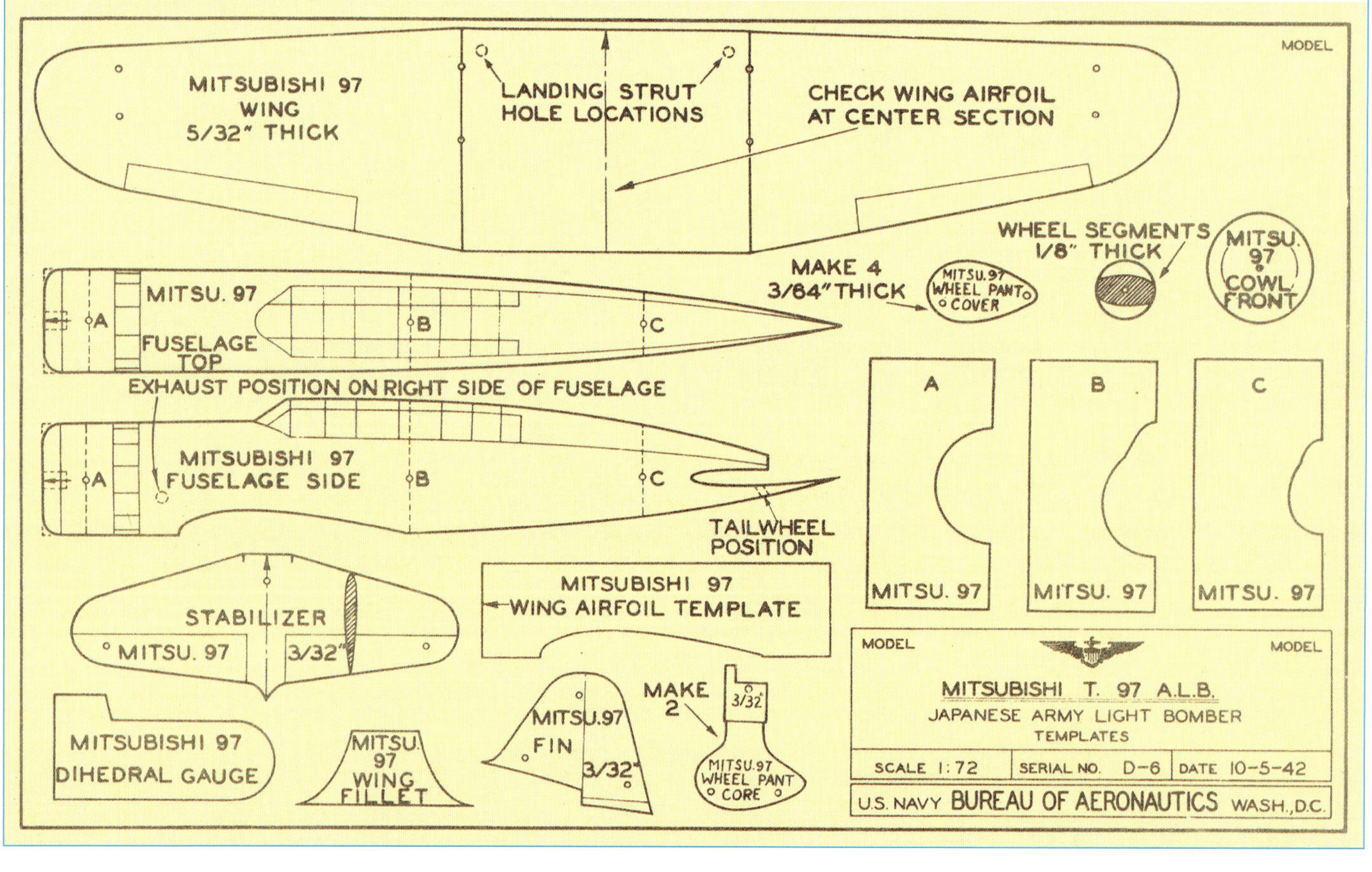

The Comet Model Airplane and Supply Co. supplied a wooden model kit to the US Navy, issued October 1942.

The general state of confusion concerning Japanese aircraft nomenclature was eased in September 1942, following the distribution of ***Informational Intelligence – Memorandum No.12. "Japanese Air Service and Japanese Aircraft***". The memorandum set out a new Code Name system for identifying Japanese aircraft, which had been developed during the summer of 1942, by Captain Frank T. McCoy Jr. and Technical Sergeant Francis M. Williams, of the *Material Section, Directorate of Intelligence, Allied Air Forces, Southwest Pacific Area.* By simply allocating boys' names to fighters and floatplanes, and girls' name to bombers, land based reconnaissance, flying boats and transports, the need to know any actual details concerning the original manufacturer or Japanese designation system was removed. This meant that pilots simply needed to be able to visually identify an aircraft and remember its allotted

An example of the assembled Comet Model Airplane and Supply Co. "MITSUBISHI T.97 A.L.B. (Jim Lansdale)

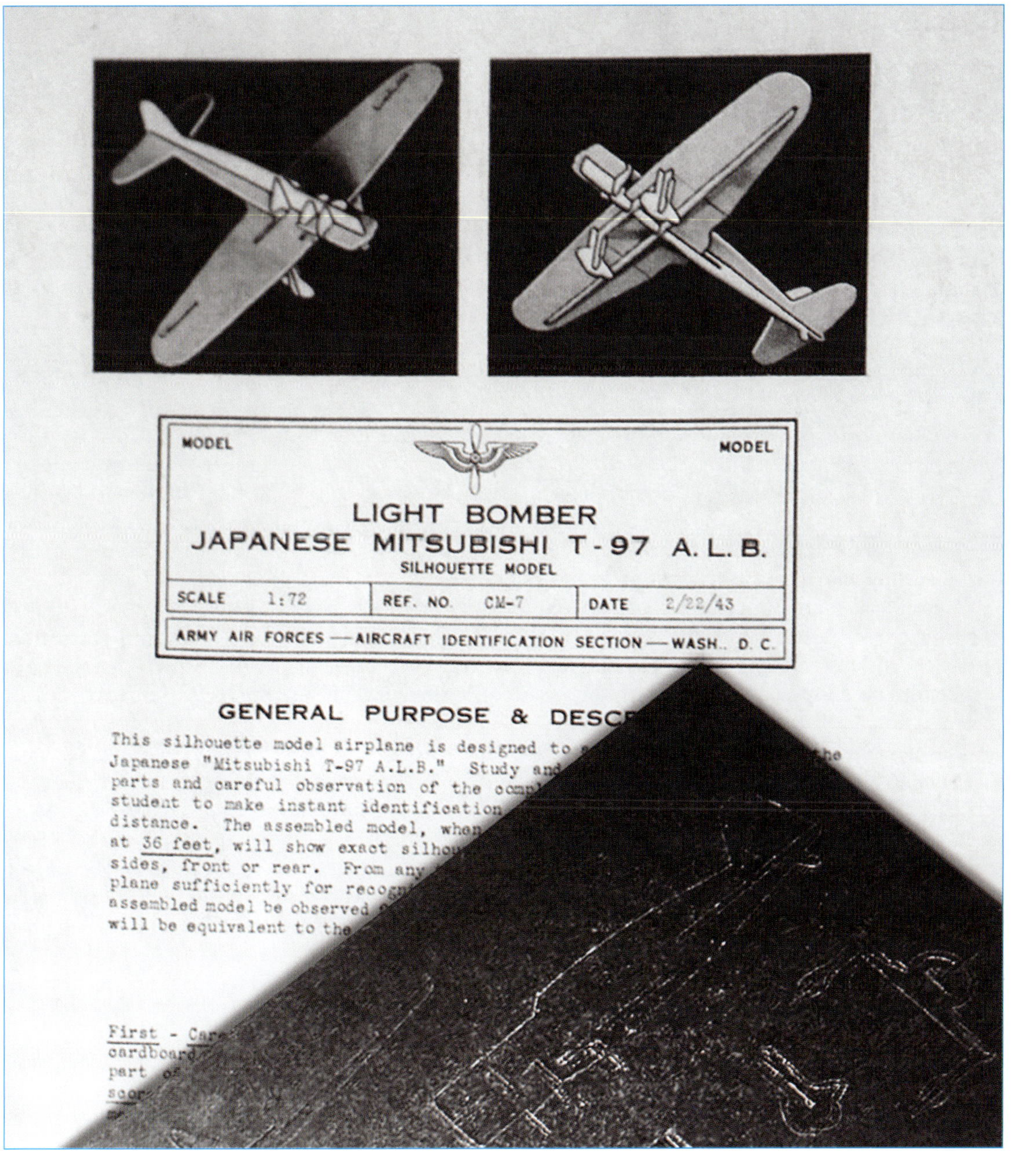

MODEL MODEL

LIGHT BOMBER
JAPANESE MITSUBISHI T-97 A. L. B.
SILHOUETTE MODEL

SCALE 1:72	REF. NO. CM-7	DATE 2/22/43

ARMY AIR FORCES — AIRCRAFT IDENTIFICATION SECTION — WASH., D. C.

GENERAL PURPOSE & DESC

This silhouette model airplane is designed to
Japanese "Mitsubishi T-97 A.L.B." Study and
parts and careful observation of the comp
student to make instant identification
distance. The assembled model, when
at 36 feet, will show exact silhou
sides, front or rear. From any
plane sufficiently for recog
assembled model be observed
will be equivalent to the

First - Car
cardboard
part of
scor

A USAAF press-out cardboard silhouette training aid of the "Japanese Mitsubishi T – 97 A.L.B", issued February 1943.

code name. As the memorandum was initially issued to higher-level organizations, its value to operational units was limited and as such it actually took several mouths to be fully embraced by all branches of the service.

On January 7th 1943, ***Informational Intelligence – Summary. No.43-3. "Code Names of Japanese Aircraft***" was issued to all squadrons for immediate use. It reaffirmed the launch of the new system and updating the list of code names. Within the listings was the "Type 97 LB (Light Bomber) Mitsubishi", which had been allotted the code name *Babs* for the first time.

Following a further review and consolidation of Japanese aircraft types, ***Informational Intelligence – Summary. No.43-26. "Japanese Aircraft and Armament***" was published in April 1943. In this publication, *Babs* was identified as the *"Type 97 LIGHT BOMBER. KARIGANE MARK I"*, and listed as *"Japan 201"* within section II (Light Bombers). With the exception of the dimensions, the performance and technical description was pure fiction and a retrograde step from ***Informational Intelligence Summary. No.41***. With a quoted maximum speed of 210mph, range of 700 miles (1,089 miles actual) and a pair of 7.7mm wing-mounted machine guns, it seems most likely that the aircraft had this time been confused with the Mitsubishi Army Type-99 Assault Plane (Ki-51) *Sonia*! At that point in the war the TAIC was still struggling to accurately identify Japanese aircraft types and it is fairly safe to say that any Japanese two or three seat, low-wing, radial-engined aircraft fitted with fixed-undercarriage was likely to be confused with the *Babs*. To illustrate the point, the next entry within ***Summary No.43-26*** was listed as the *"Sonia Type 97 Light Bomber, KARIGANE Mark II."* And to further confuse matters, the photographs accompanying this entry included one Ki-51 *Sonia* and two Mitsubishi Ki-30 *Ann* aircraft! It is, though, interesting to note that within the "Additional Technical Data" section for the *Babs*, reference is made to a second version of the aircraft fitted with a *"...twin-row engine similar to the Nakajima "Sakae" of about 910 h.p."*

The *Babs* entry within the updated August 1943 issue of ***Informational Intelligence – Summary. No.43-26. "Japanese Aircraft and Armament***" was modified to read *"BABS Mk.III. Type 98 Light Bomber, Mk.III"* and included more credible performance figures. Interestingly the data table identifies the aircraft as being fitted with a *"Mitsubishi "Kinsei" 44, 14 cyl., twin-row, air-cooled radial."* and *"3-blade, constant speed, variable pitch, Hamilton type"* propeller. This would indicate that technical data for the C5M2 was available to the TAIC at that time.

A further updated version of ***Informational Intelligence – Summary. No.43-26. "Japanese Aircraft and Armament***" was issued in September 1943, and while the *Babs* entry remained unmodified, the *Sonia* was at least correctly identified as the *"Type 99 Single-engine Light Bomber"* instead of the *"KARIGANE Mk.II"*.

Norma

During mid 1943, the confusion over the various *Karigane* Lighter Bomber types reached its peak. The long cowling installation of the Ki-15-II had visually set it aside from the Townend ring equipped Ki-15-I, so in late 1943 the TAIC issued the codename *Norma* to this "new" aircraft, describing it as a "Type-97 Reconnaissance and Light Bomber". This designation was short lived though as the TAIC soon recognised their mistake, and in an attempt to simplify the codename system for combat pilots, they made the wise decision to identify all Ki-15s as *Babs*.

It should be pointed out that codename *Norma* was originally issued to the *"Mitsubishi Type-97 Light Bomber – Darai 108"* in late 1942, before being dropped from the TAIC listings in June 1943. In fact the *"Mitsubishi Type-97 Light Bomber – Darai 108"* was a totally fictitious twin-engined light bomber design, supposedly copied from the unsuccessful Bennett BTC-1, which was an all wood light transport aircraft of 1937 vintage.

The updated ***Informational Intelligence – Summary. No.44-11.*** of March 1944 containing the same inaccuracies as previous editions, but for the first time the *Babs* was correctly identified as a Reconnaissance Landplane and moved to section V (Reconnaissance) of the summary as entry *"Japan 501"*. More than any other, this publication illustrated how confusing the Japanese designation system and Allied Code Name system could be when merged, as the *Babs* was attributed to the Army and described as the *"Type 98 Mk.3, Babs Mk.3"*. It would seem that the TAIC had also decided that the Ki-15-I was a *Babs* Mk.1, the Ki-15-II/C5M1 was a *Babs* Mk.2 and the C5M2 was the *Babs* Mk.3. The accompanying recognition page contained a mixed collection of captured photos depicting *Kamikaze*, a Ki-15-I, Ki-15-II and the C5M development aircraft! It also included a wholly inaccurate field of fire diagram, showing the predicted coverage of the rear 7.7mm machine gun, plus the fictitious pair of forward firing 7.7mm machine guns! Given that the description still included the forward-firing machine guns, an exhaust stack location similar to the Ki-15-I and the annotation *"Fuel tanks probably in each wing root"*, it would indicate that the TAIC had still not physically examined a *Babs* airframe by this date, but this would soon change.

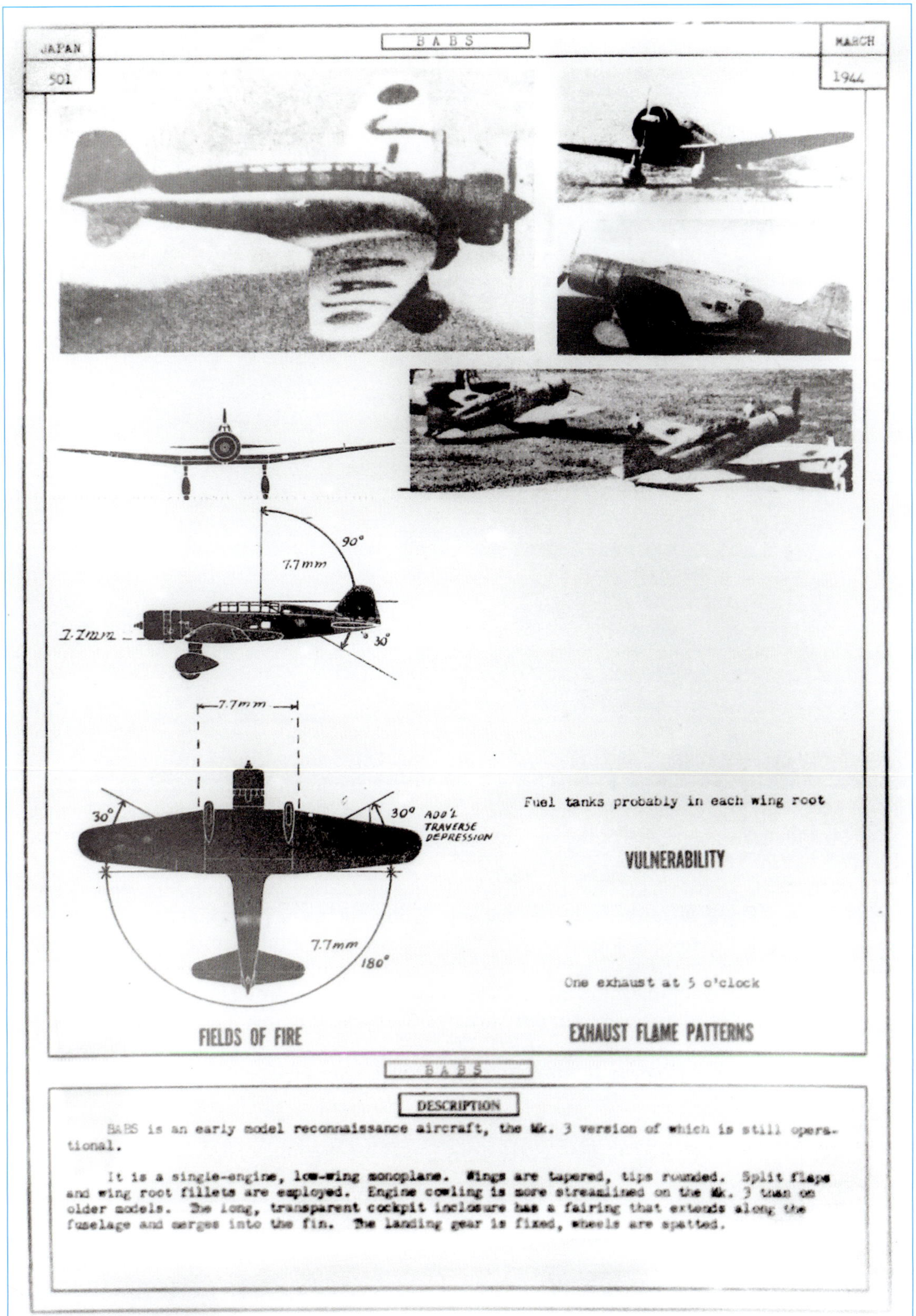

JAPAN 501 — BABS — MARCH 1944

BABS

DESCRIPTION

BABS is an early model reconnaissance aircraft, the Mk. 3 version of which is still operational.

It is a single-engine, low-wing monoplane. Wings are tapered, tips rounded. Split flaps and wing root fillets are employed. Engine cowling is more streamlined on the Mk. 3 than on older models. The long, transparent cockpit inclosure has a fairing that extends along the fuselage and merges into the fin. The landing gear is fixed, wheels are spatted.

Informational Intelligence – Summary No.44-16 was issued on May 20th, and within its "*Notes on Enemy Aircraft*" section, a report was published on a "crashed aircraft." Of the hundreds of Japanese airframes that were surveyed throughout the Pacific war, this is the only documented *Babs* airframe to have been examined by personnel of the TAIC. From the report and accompanying low quality photograph it is unclear if this C5M2 had in fact crashed or been damaged by Allied bombing (probably the latter), but it is likely that the rear fuselage was badly damaged or missing because only the span of the aircraft was provided. Given the obsolescence of the aircraft at that time, it would seem that the report was a brisk one at best, which resulted in some unusual and possibly misleading details pertaining to the fuel tanks.

Photograph of the a C5M2 wreck featured in "Notes on Enemy Aircraft", Informational Intelligence – Summary No.44-16, May 20th.

As the Allies captured more and more Japanese documentation and technical information, the TAIC began to include Japanese model designations within the code name system. ***Technical Air Intelligence Center, Summary #2. "Revision of Allied Code Names for Japanese Aircraft"*** was issued on August 15th 1944, and included portions of the Japanese Navy Type Number system, which modified *Babs* entries to read "*Babs 11*" and "*Babs 12*".

The retrieval of operational data from prisoner interrogations, captured documents, reports, equipment and the surveys of aircraft wrecks, together with all important data plates and Construction numbers (C/n), allowed the TAIC to produce "estimates" of Japanese monthly and yearly aircraft productions capabilities. Despite the fact that only one *Babs* is known to have been surveyed by the TAIC, a rudimentary estimate of production figures appeared as part of a larger report in a September 1944 intelligence report entitled: ***Japanese Aircraft Maker's Plates and Markings – Report No.49.***

"Cumulative Total of Japanese Combat Airplane Production – 1940 – 1944"

Year / Quarter *Model*	*1940*				*1941*				*1942*				*1943*
	1st	*2nd*	*3rd*	*4th*	*1st*	*2nd*	*3rd*	*4th*	*1st*	*2nd*	*3rd*	*4th*	*1st*
BABS 11	9	28	36	16	-	-	-	-	-	-	-	-	-
BABS 12	-	-	-	-	15	45	75	105	135	165	195	225	240
Estimated totals	89				240				720				240

Seemingly unaware of the prefix codes allocated to the *Babs* program (See Chapter 7, **Production figures and construction numbers**), the report wildly overestimated the total production figure for the *Babs* family of aircraft by more than 250%, predicting that 1,289 aircraft had been built instead of the actual figure of 498. In addition to this the TAIC were also under the impression that *Babs* production had continued into the summer of 1943, some two years after the final C5M2 airframe had left the Mitsubishi production line.

The final official entry for the *Babs* within Allied intelligence reports of World War II appeared in ***Technical Air Intelligence Center, Summary #29. "Japanese Aircraft Nomenclature"*** of April 1945. This entry was most likely included to reacquaint combat troops with all of the possible aircraft types that could be used for kamikaze attacks. Bizarrely though, the Navy "*Babs 11*" was omitted from the list, despite the inclusion of the Army "*Babs 1*".

Know your Enemy!

Despite the numerous inaccuracies and glaring mistakes included within the above mentioned reports and publications, the ultimate purpose of gathering intelligence on enemy equipment and aircraft is twofold: to estimate the strength and disposition of the opposing side, then to form a strategy with which to combat such equipment. The first requirement was accomplished by inspecting captured documentation, aircraft, maker's plates and Construction number (C/n) data, etc. The second requirement was to identify an aircraft's strengths and weaknesses, in order to work out how best to fight it in the air.

In order to achieve success in air combat, a fighter pilot first needs to correctly identify his opponent and this skill is typically accomplished with visual training aids, such as posters and silhouettes, all the way through to training films and recognition models. Several identification models and silhouettes were produced for the *Babs*.

In June 1942, a pre-assembled cellulose acetate plastic model was produced by the Cruver Company of Chicago, which identified the aircraft as the "JAP MITSU T-97 ALB". While most Cruver recognition models included the Allied codename on its lower surface, the *Babs*, *Claude*, *Ida*, *Kate*, *Mary*, *Nell*, *Sonia* and *Val* only carried Type numbers, because these models were produced one month prior to the official adoption of Allies Code Name system. In early October 1942, the Comet Model Airplane and Supply Co., also issued a simple wooden model kit of the "MITSUBISHI T.97 A.L.B – Japanese Army Light Bomber" to the US Navy, under the designation "D-6". In essence this crude DIY kit included several wooden blocks and assembly instructions, which allowed the builder to whittle the aircraft into shape!

US Navy View-Master 3D training images of the "Mitsubishi Babs Type 97 ALB Jap Light Bomber", issued 1943.

The final recognition aid for the *Babs* was a press-out cardboard silhouette, dated February 22nd 1943. These simplified and vastly cheaper identification aids were produced in their thousands, for all of the fighting services and US Civil Defense organizations. It is a little surprisingly to note that even by 1943, the *Babs* was still being referred to as the "Japanese Mitsubishi T – 97 A.L.B".

The *Babs* was also represented in cellulose training aids. Sawyers of Portland, Oregon was responsible for producing the various "View-Master" 3D aircraft identification training images, including the 1943 reel: ***U.S. Naval Aviation Training Division, Study Reel S39 – Mitsubishi Babs Type 97 ALB Jap Light Bomber.*** In addition to this, a short-duration aircraft identification training film was produced for the *Babs* by the USAAF.

Stills of the "Babs" taken from a USAAC training film, produced in 1943.

Chapter 3

Soviet intelligence reports

"…. in production since 1935, with its 316kmh [196 mph] maximum speed, by the end of the second half of the Thirties it was an easy target, as proved in the Spanish Civil War when (Natashas) [Polikarpov R-5 reconnaissance aircraft] could only hope to fulfil their task with solid fighter escort, suffering significant losses in all cases. Similar aircraft equipped the Soviet reconnaissance forces, explaining their low effectiveness…."

Japan against Russia – In the sky of Nomonhan. Dimitar Nedialkov, Propeller Publishing, 2005.

While the Western Allies had struggled to accurately describe or even categorise the *Babs* over a four-year period, the Soviets thoroughly understood the capabilities of the aircraft. With their own reconnaissance pilots flying out-dated aircraft, the Soviet Air Force was well aware of Japan's high-speed reconnaissance machine, as it was still reeling from the "*Nononhan Incident*". This all changed on the night of February 11th 1940, when an *early model* Ki-15 strayed too close to Soviet airspace and was caught in searchlights near to Spassk, in the Spassky District of Primorsky, 150miles NE of Vladivostok. Unfortunately the details of the incident become a little confusing thereafter, as it is reported that the dazzled and confused pilot became disoriented attempting to outmanoeuvre the searchlights, before flying into the snow-covered terrain on the Soviet side of the of the Amur River. The only problem with this story is that the Amur River is 500 miles NW of Spassk! These conflicting details offers two possible solutions: firstly, the aircraft came down on a river bank in the Spassk area, possibly the Song'acha River, which divided Manchuria from the Soviet Union, or the pilot became lost as a result of the incident over Spassk and eventually force-landed on the banks of the Amur River, near Blagoveshchensk, after running out of fuel. We shall probably never know the truth, but regardless of the location, the force-landing was under the control of the pilot, as the flaps were lowered before touchdown. Despite this attempt to slow down, the impact tore both main landing gear and the port main-plane from the aircraft, buckled the main fuselage in the area of the pilot's cockpit (between FS.4 and FS.5), and damaged the windscreen, pilot's canopy and rudder horn-balance. Miraculously the pilot survived the impact with only minor injuries and subsequently posed for photographs, with a suitably bandaged head, when Soviet forces arrived.

It is claimed that the pilot was alone during the flight, which might indicate that he was either on an orientation flight, a delivery flight, or undertaking a test flight when the crash occurred. But that story does not seem quite right for several reasons. Firstly, single-pilot operations in close proximity to the Soviet border were incredibly hazardous and radio or air-to-ground communications were vitally important in a region where anti-aircraft gunners were typically "neutral" when it came to unidentified aircraft. Prearranged radio frequencies and specific day code responses would need to be issued in order to identify your aircraft as friendly, but such communications would have been impossible for the pilot of the Ki-15, because he could not typically operate the radio from the front cockpit. Secondly, it is also implausible to assume that the pilot was on a "lone" photographic reconnaissance mission, as it was also impossible for the pilot to operate the camera from the front cockpit, not to mention the fact that the Soviet forces found no camera equipment in the aircraft.

Likewise, if the flight had been intended as a clandestine visual reconnaissance mission, similar to flights that would be made over French Indochina, Thailand and Burma (See Chapter 5, Volume I, **Changing the rules of the game**), then all Japanese markings would probably have been removed from the aircraft and the pilot would have worn civilian clothing, but this was not the case. In addition to this, the aircraft was operating at night, so visual reconnaissance would not have been possible.

Given the description of the incident, two possibilities exist: The aircraft was either on a delivery or test flight, when it became lost and strayed into Soviet territory or, it was in fact on a late afternoon reconnaissance mission along the border? While the first possibility could have occurred with just a pilot

The captured Japanese pilot, complete with improvised field dressing to his head! Note the flush riveting, recessed windscreen panes and streamlined fairing over the upper navigation light. Ahead of the windscreen is the fuselage main fuel tank filler and it is interesting to note that that the cockpit sill (inside the windscreen area) is the same colour as the fuselage exterior. (NII VVS via Y. Svoyski)

on board, this would have been highly unusual, given the proximity to the Soviet border. If an RO was in fact on board, it is not unreasonable to believe that, when faced with approaching Soviet troops and an unconscious pilot, he decided to cross the river back into Manchuria, carrying the camera and the machine-gun, which was also missing from the aircraft?

Whatever the background to this intriguing set of events, it is presently assumed that the aircraft was assigned to the 2nd *Hikodan*, operating out of Jiamusi, which is coincidently located halfway between both possible crash locations. Sadly there are no records of these specific markings being assigned to any Japanese units.

The damaged Ki-15 was subsequently examined and described in detail by a Soviet Engineer from the 25th Air Brigade. His report and accompanying photographs were filed with the appropriate departments and quickly forgotten during the turmoil or WWII. After languishing in the Soviet Air Force Research and Development Institute Archive for almost 80 years, the report was discovered by historian Yuri Svoyski.

SECRET

BRIEF DESCRIPTION OF CONSTRUCTION OF A JAPANESE RECONNAISANCE AIRCRAFT R-97 WITH 550 HP NAKAJIMA 94 ENGINE, NR.181

Section 1:

The aircraft is a riveted all-metal low-wing monoplane. Equipped with two cockpits – the pilot's cockpit and the navigator's cockpit, the fuselage is built as a single unit, integrally with the centre wing section. The fuselage is a stressed-skin [semi-] monocoque design with four longerons. Longerons, formers, and stringers are box-section members with solid rivets. All the exterior surfaces are flush-riveted.

Wing centre section's principal fore and aft members are two longerons, each designed as a built-up I-beam comprising L-shapes, strips, and channel-shape struts and braces. Centre section's ribs are box-sections and I-shapes. Rivets are solid, external surfaces are flush-riveted. Fuselage, wing centre section, and longerons are fabricated of aluminium alloy.

The [outboard] wings are of two-spar design. Reinforced ribs are I-shapes, non-reinforced ribs are rolled open shapes. All ribs are of truss design. The spars, similar to the centre section's longerons, are built-up. Solid riveting is used, with exterior surfaces flush-riveted.

Empennage design is similar to that of the wings, with the exception of the rudder, which is a fabric-covered metal structure.

The aircraft is equipped with a single hydraulically operated flap, mounted under the centre section.

The fuselage is oval in section. The wings and horizontal tail plane members are tapered in plan, with rounded wingtips.

Devoid of a fuselage Hinomaru, C/n181, displays the unconfirmed markings of the 2nd Hikodan on its tail. Note the standard "Army Secret" stencil applied to the rear fuselage centreline, just aft of FS.9 (NII VVS via Y. Svoyski)

Dimensions:
Fuselage length with engine 7.81 meters
Height in three-point position 2.9 meters
Wing span 11.92 meters
Chord at centre section and wing joint 2.2 meters
Half-wing length 4.6 meters
Centre section length 2.72 meters
Weighing could not be performed.

Section 2:

The aircraft carries no bomb armament. The only armament is a machine gun installed in the navigator's cockpit, covering rear and top aspects. The field of fire in the horizontal plane is 12 deg. left and right of the fin, and 45 deg in the vertical plane (these numbers should be treated with reserve, as the machine gun was not installed and no precise measuring was possible).

No armour protection is provided for the crew.

Section 3:
Cockpit equipment:
Pilot's cockpit:

a. Elevator, rudder, and aileron controls (see photo 12 and diagrams).
b. Brake control.
c. Flap control indicating the angle of deflection (see photo 13).
d. Throttle and high-altitude mixture control quadrant.
e. 3 fuel shut-off valves.
f. Instrument panel (see photo 11).
g. Oxygen station (see photo 15).
h. Control device and wiring for electrically heated flight suit.
i. Elevator trim control wheel indicating the angle of deflection.

Navigator's cockpit:

a. Photo equipment mount.

The underside of the Starboard wing carries the aircraft C/n stencil on the aileron and outboard wing panel. Note the high gloss finish of the Hinomaru. *(NII VVS via Y. Svoyski)*

b. *Radio equipment (see photos 39, 40, 41, 42, 43).*
c. *Oxygen station (see photo 15).*
d. *Control device and wiring for electrically heated flight suit.*
e. *Navigation instruments (altimeter, air speed indicator, magnetic compass and clock).*

Section 4.
Engine and airscrew assembly:

Engine NAKAJIMA 94, 550 hp, manufactured in September 1939, serial number 3073 (apparently a license-built Wright Cyclone type, as no differences were identified by visual inspection).

The airscrew is a 2.9m 2-blade fixed-pitch type 97 "top secret" Nr.293 airscrew with the blade pitch at 0.75 of the radius measured at 29 deg. 39 min.

See photo 16 and 17.

See photo 12.

An interesting feature of the engine mount to fuselage connection is that coupling bolts pass through a rubber damping sleeve enclosed in a steel shell and affixed to the 1st former by the firewall.

<u>Pilot's control panel</u>

The instrument panel is grouped in two parts, the top panel housing flying and engine instruments, and the bottom one with auxiliary equipment controls. The top panel is mounted on damper springs, designed to protect flight instruments from vibration damage. The bottom panel is rigidly affixed.

The panel is equipped with navigation equipment (see photo 11):
1. *Air speed indicator.*
2. *Turn indicator.*
3. *Artificial horizon (can be turned off).*
6. *Altimeter.*
7. *Clock.*
   Electric-heated vertical compass (see photo 24) is fitted above the control panel, aft of the pilot's windscreen.
5. *Electrical air thermometer.*

See photo 11.

Engine instruments
4. *R.P.M meter.*
8. *Fuel oil pressure gauge.*
9. *Oil pressure gauge.*
10. *Oil pressure gauge.*
11. *Magneto switch.*
12/14/18. *Fuel gauge.*

The engine cowling on C/n181 was finished in the standard semi-gloss black, while the nose fairing and spinner were the same colour as the fuselage. The front face of the propeller was polished aluminium with a 50mm wide red warning band positioned 50mm from the tip. The rear face was most likely matt black in colour. With the spinner cap removed it is possible to see the front-plate assembly, which was finished in dark Aotake and also carried the C/n stencil for the aircraft in white. (NII VVS via Y. Svoyski)

13. Throttle [control] switch for heating pilot's legs with warm air from the engine.
15. Inertial electric magneto.
16. Primer.
17. Altimeter.
See Photo 24.

HAMILTON-type airscrew hub

See photo 17.

Starting aids

Engine starting equipment includes manual eclipse-type inertia self-starter, fuel primer (see photo 11) and a manual inertial magneto, actuated by a pull wire from the pilot's cockpit.

When tested, the magneto provided a 14-mm spark of high intensity. Magneto operation for starting the engine is very simple and reliable.

See photo 38.

Flying controls

Flying controls are quite similar to those of a typical aircraft and follow a conventional design and construction.

Aileron control is rigid – via duralumin push-pull rods. Rod end connections are ball bearings.

Elevator control is mixed, with rods up to the navigator's cockpit and then cables up to elevator bell-crank. Each half of the elevator has its own bellcrank unit (see photo 30), even though both halves are rigidly interconnected with a tube. Two 3mm cables run to each bellcrank.

Rudder control is done by cable. Cable diameter is 6 mm.

The control system, especially the rudder and elevator controls, is very easy to inspect. For inspection, the quick-detachable rear fuselage fairing needs to be removed, and all bell cranks and brackets become easily accessible. Photo 30 was taken with the rear fairing removed, and all linkages are clearly visible.

For easier steering, ailerons have a slight hinge offset. No trim tabs are provided.

Rudder is horn balanced; no trim tabs are fitted.

See photo 30.

Horizontal stabilizer is fixed and constructed as a single unit (see photo 31).

Elevator is fitted with trim tabs, apparently to simplify take-off and landing.

Elevator trim tab control wheel, equipped with a deflection indicator, is located to the left of the pilot's seat. The tabs are operated via cables and worm drive. The cables run to a length of chain, which turns via a gear connection the spool with a worm nut, which moves the worm. The worm, in turn, deflects the trim tab via cables and a link.

See photo 31.

Flap.

See photo 22.

Flap control.

Flaps are hydraulically operated with the system represented on the diagram.

See photo 13.

The hydraulic system comprises (see photo 12): [annotated on photo] hydraulic fluid reservoir **1**, *flap valve* **2**, *hand pump* **3**, *servo pump* **4** *to actuate bracket* **5**, *with a pushrod* **6** *actuating flaps via bracket and link (see photo 22). As the pump moves, cable 7 pulls an indicator slide graduated for flap deflection degree angle.*

Maximum deflection is 60°. The hydraulic fluid used is a mixture of some kind of mineral oil and gasoline. The mixture is highly fluid. The system performs well (even after the accident) and is reliable in operation, but may distract the pilot's attention when landing and requires a lot of additional action when operating the hand pump to pressurize the system.

See photo 12.

Oxygen equipment

Oxygen equipment consists of oxygen cylinder **1**, *with a pressure reducing valve* **2**, *and a fitting for attaching a low-pressure rubber tube* **3**, *and oxygen flow regulator* **4**, *graduated up to 12 (apparently for flow regulation at altitude).*

No automatic altitude-dependent flow regulation is provided.

There is no gauge to enable monitoring the oxygen supply remaining.

Each cockpit is equipped with its own oxygen supply system.

Oxygen cylinder with approximately a 4-5 litre capacity is designed for operating pressure of 140 atm.

See photo 15.

Fuel system

Total fuel tank capacity is 550 litres. There are 6 fuel tanks: two 103-litre tanks between the longerons of the central section, two 45.5-litre tanks in the central section's leading edge, a 135-litre tank in the fuselage behind the pilot, between the pilot's and the navigator's cockpit, and one tank of approximately 120 litres (precise capacity could not be measured) in the fore part of the fuselage, just aft of the firewall.

The stored fuel capacity provides 6-6.5 hours of flight time at the speed of approximately 280-300 kph.

See photos 23 and 24.

The tanks were manufactured by a Mitsubishi, Ltd. aircraft factory in Nagoya in February-April 1939. The tanks were rated for overpressure of 0.2 kg/cm^2.

Fuel system diagram

See photo 18.

The fuel system is controlled with three 3-way valves:

Valve 1 *– with the valve in the position shown in the diagram, fuel is supplied to the engine from two central section tanks of 103 litres each. When turned 90 degrees clockwise, the valve shuts off the central section tank line and switches to fuel supply from the tank located in the fore cockpit just aft of the firewall. Accordingly, top and bottom tanks cannot be used simultaneously.*

Valve 2 *– with the valve in the position shown in the diagram, fuel is supplied from the wing central section leading edge tanks. When turned 90 degrees, this valve shuts off these tanks and connects the fuel feed system to the tank located between the two cockpits (valve 3 must be set to the position shown in the diagram).*

Valve 3 *– connects the fuel tank located between the cockpits as described above and, if turned 90 degrees, connects the tank to drainage pipeline.*

Based on the above, it may be concluded that, while being considerably complex in operation, the fuel system automatically eliminates the possibility of drawing fuel simultaneously from top and bottom tanks and precludes fuel down-flow from fuselage tanks to the wing tanks.

It may be assumed that the pilot is supposed to first use up the 4 tanks located in the centre section first, then the tank between the pilot and the navigator, and finally the tank aft of the firewall.

See photo 22.

Photos 21 and 22 provide a clear view of the fuel manifold connecting all fuel piping from tanks and feeding into the main line to engine fuel pump and carburettor.

See photo 21.

Oil system

Simplified oil system diagram

The oil tank has a capacity of 30-35 litres (no exact measurements were performed). The system comprises an oil tank, shut-off valve, oil-filter, drain valve, and oil supply and return mains. The oil tank is affixed directly aft of the engine, forward of the firewall (see photo 8). The tank is insulated with a special cotton-lined cover case. Oil lines are also insulated with cotton wool and covered with fabric.

See photo 33.

Electric system

Power is supplied by engine-driven dynamo generator and a battery. The generator's operating range is 3000 to 6000 rpm. The system's voltage is up to 28 V, operating voltage is 24 V. To enable combined use of generator and battery, the aircraft is equipped with a regulator switch box. The regulator switch box is a system comprising over and under relays.

The aircraft's electric equipment is of excellent quality.

The battery and regulator switch box are installed just aft the engine, forward of the firewall (see photo 8).

On-board generator, type 97. Capacity 400. 25 V, 16 A. RPM settings: 3000 and 6000. Weight 1.5 kg. Manufactured by Oomori factory of central limited company in July 1939.

See photo 25.

Side view of the regulator switchbox.

See photo 26.

Electric diagram.

See photo 37.

Regulator switch box, top view.

See photo 28.

Dynamo generator installed on Nakajima 94 engine.

See photo 29.

The 30V 16A battery installed in the aircraft consists of 2 serially connected cells. While small in size, the battery is large in capacity. One of the cells was not heavily damaged in the crash and can be tested to obtain more data.

The aircraft is not equipped with navigation lights in our conventional sense of the term. The top part of the canopy has a teardrop-shaped fairing (behind the pilot's cockpit, see the first photograph), which is fitted with three lamps (red, green, and white). These are not visible from the ground.

On the left wing the aircraft has 2 large landing lights and a smaller light, all mounted flush with the leading edge. The smaller light is most likely a signal lamp used for communicating with the ground.

Tail wheel assembly

The construction of the tail wheel assembly is clearly shown on in photo 36. The assembly consists of a round rod with the fork **1** *for the wheel* **3***, cast strut* **2***, air-oil shock unit* **4** *and shock cords* **5***.*

The wheel is mounted on ball bearings. The tire is airless solid rubber. The rotation of the wheel is restricted by two shock cords **5***. All shock absorption is provided by an oleo-pneumatic shock unit.*

The design of the tail wheel assembly is very good and the construction is very rugged, but the weight of the assembly is also quite considerable. The tail cone fairing is very well designed. Once the fairing is removed, all of the tail wheel assembly components become easily accessible for inspection.

(photograph taken with the fairing removed.)

See photos 36 and 37.

Photo 37 is a photo of instruction plate located at the lower fairing of the assembly.

Caution: Maintenance of the Tail Skid Shock Absorber

1. *Only use hydraulic oil*
2. *Check oil level and pressure periodically, as it requires precision*
3. *Oil level and pressure checking procedure:*
    - i. *After lifting the plane to reduce the weight on the shock strut, remove the oil-pour cap, insert the oil-check tool carefully. Avoid directly facing the oil pit hole and turn the screw cock once.*
    - ii. *If the oil flows first and air second, the oil is fine. If the air comes first and oil second, add more oil since it means that oil level is too low. After adding oil to the proper level, tighten the screw cock.*

This photograph clearly shows the glossy exterior finish that was typically applied to Ki-15s in order to reduce airframe drag to a minimum. The wing leading-edge fuel tank is shown to good effect together with the filler cap and "No Step" stencil. (NII VVS via Y. Svoyski)

iii. *Connect the oil-check tool to the high-pressure machine in order to pressurize the oil tank. Set the pressure to 215. Then, gently loosen the screw cock. Make sure the oil pressure is at 215 in the shock resistance strut, and if so loosen the screw cock to close the oil cap.*

Main landing gear

Main landing gear is non-retractable, covered with aerodynamic fairing. The landing gear is of fully cantilever design, and, as a result, the strut was designed very rugged (see photo 33 and 34). The struts are oleo-pneumatic.

See photo 36.

Pneumatic shock absorber, serial nr. 401, manufactured on 16.9.39. Okamoto Ltd.

The legs do not have any support struts or bracing. The wheels are equipped with mechanically actuated brakes. Brake controls are foot-operated and located on the rudder pedal bar.

The fork is welded and very sturdy. Neither fork was damaged in the crash, even though the impact was very strong (as evidenced by the overall damage).

Radio unit

Could not be tested, so no data available. Two of the receiver lamps were broken on impact.

See photos 39,40, 41, 42, 43, 44 and 45.

GENERAL NOTES

Aircraft nr.181 type R-97 with 550 hp Nakajima 94 engine 3073 was manufactured in December 1939 and is an upgraded version of R-97 type aircraft.

To improve airspeed and ceiling performance, bombing equipment has been removed. It should be specifically noted that the upgrade has not been completed, as all oxygen equipment, wiring, and electric heating equipment are not permanently affixed, but simply held in place by wires and tie strings.

Radio equipment has been recently upgraded, as the new radio equipment does not fit into the allocated mounting area.

Photo album and brief explanations developed by:
Deputy commander for maintenance, 25 Air Brigade.
Commissioned engineer 2nd rank Romashkin.

Chapter 4

Technical description

Mitsubishi Ki-15-I, *Kamikaze*, Karigane-I, Ki-15-II, *Karigane-II*, C5M1, C5M2 and Ki-15-III

"The external finish of the machines appears to be very good indeed. The flush riveting of both the wings and the fuselage is some the finest we have ever seen."

"The Heavenly Breeze" editorial in The Aeroplane, April 14th 1937.

The following technical descriptions are based on official Army specifications, Mitsubishi Ki-15-II maintenance manuals (March 1941), engineering documents, C5M2 Provisional maintenance manual (March 1941), Western and Soviet intelligence documents and period photographs.

Note: While the official designation "Ki-15-I" was applied retrospectively, following the introduction of the improved "Ki-15-II", it is used here from the outset, to avoid confusion.

Ki-15-I early and late model

When new aircraft types enter service, their specific idiosyncrasies and faults are quickly identified and shared between other units and maintenance teams, and any field modifications or technical observations are passed back to the manufacturer for attention and review. While small changes in equipment or layout are commonplace, larger modifications are typically included in official airframe upgrades and receive an amendment to the Model number of the aircraft, such as –Ia or –II, etc. Sometimes though, several major modifications can be included in the middle of production run, without a subsequent Model number upgrade. This occurred on the Ki-15-I production line during late 1939, when the standardized oxygen system was relocated to the centre canopy tunnel, together with the incorporation of the new lateral camera window and surround.

While no official Model number or amendment was ever issued for these important and very visible modifications, they clearly indicate the maturity and standardization of the Ki-15-I airframe. In order to differentiate between the two airframe types – built before and after these changes – the two models are identified (in italics) as ***early model*** or ***late model*** aircraft within this text.

Mitsubishi Ki-15-I

Army Type-97 Command Reconnaissance Plane Model-I – *Early model* and *late models*

Fuselage

The fuselage of the Ki-15 was divided into two specific zones:

The nacelle assembly, which extended forward of the firewall (Frame Station 0 – FS.0), including the engine mount, forward fuselage fairings and cowlings.

The single-piece semi-monocoque main fuselage, which extended aft from FS.0.

It should be pointed out that when the aircraft was assembled at the factory, the wing centre-section was permanently attached to the main fuselage, but for the purposes of clarity, the fuselage and wing centre-section are described separately in this technical description.

Mitsubishi Ki-15-I *early model* inboard profile – with initial fuel system

1/48 Scale

© Giuseppe Picarella 2020

Airframe component colour

Ki-15 airframe components were typically manufactured (cut, pressed and formed) then built up into sub-assemblies, such as individual wing ribs or spars, etc., before being painted with a dark *Aotake* (bamboo-blue/green) coloured phenolic varnish. In general, items and areas that were exposed to wear and tear received a coating of *Aotake*, such as the wing panel attachment points and firewall, etc. In addition to this, many of the sub-assemblies would have been manufactured well in advance of individual numbered airframes, which means that the thickness and application of the *Aotake* varnish could vary, as could sub-assemblies supplied by other companies. Items made of steel received a coating of satin black paint to prevent rust, including the undercarriage legs, engine mount, hinge fittings and support brackets inside the canopy structure, handles and steps, etc. Internal equipment and systems, such as electrical boxes, etc., may have been painted in slightly different shades of *Aotake* or even a Mitsubishi olive green. That being said, the Army had applied a grey-blue interior finish to some of its aircraft during the early and mid 1930s, so it is entirely possible that first few Ki-15s may have received this alternative internal colour.

The pilot's instrument panel was finished in a matt black "crackle" finish.

Externally, the airframe would have received a pale primer over all exposed surfaces, before the glossy topcoat of Mitsubishi/Army grey-green was applied, together with a satin black engine cowling – on the Ki-15-I only.

Ki-15 interior colour

1/48 Scale

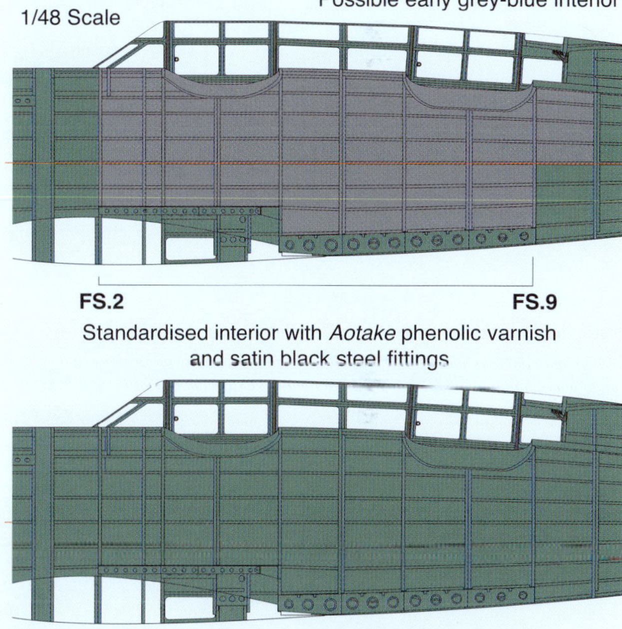

© Giuseppe Picarella 2020

Nacelle assembly

The cowling installation for the Ki-15-I was as aerodynamically refined as the state-of-the-art would allow in 1935. It consisted of a nose fairing, Townend ring, engine rear fairings, primary firewall and forward fuselage fairings.

Nose fairings

The three-section nose fairing bridged the gap between the back-plate of the propeller-spinner and the front of the engine cylinders. The assembly was attached to the forward face of the engine's reduction-gearbox casting via support arms and a ring frame. The rear portion of the nose fairing was scalloped to fit tightly around the engine cylinders, with additional fairings extend aft between cylinders No.2/No.3 and No.8/No.9 in order to provide mounting surfaces for the engine accessory-bay ram-air cooling intakes. The fairings were attached to their neighbouring section with two round-headed fasteners and a flange strip on the left-hand side of each panel.

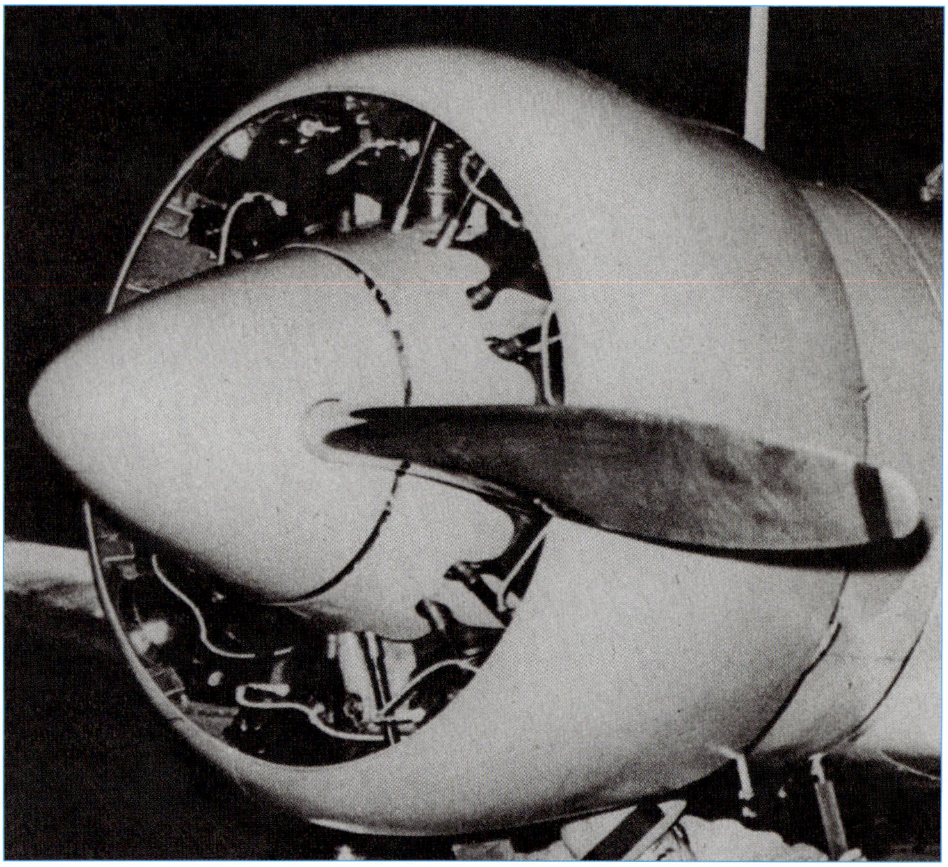

Townend ring

A long-chord Townend ring was fitted to the Ha-8-I engine in order to reduce the drag generated by the top of the engine cylinders and rocker covers. Each half of the two-part assembly was comprised of an aluminium-alloy aerofoil-section outer skin, with a beaded leading edge and doubled trailing edge. The ring was located in position by way of 18 individual felt-lined "top-hat" section brackets, which were riveted to the inner face of the ring. Once the brackets were located on the engine rocker covers, two latches on each segment of the ring were fastened tightly together. These latches were adjustable, allowing for a very tight fit, with no tendency to vibrate.

Engine rear fairings

In order to continue the same lofting lines (exterior envelope of the airframe) as the spinner and nose fairing assembly, five aluminium-alloy rear fairings, similarly scalloped to fit around the rear of each engine cylinder, were located behind the exposed engine cylinders. These fairing bridged the gap between the rear of the engine and the forward firewall, and were attached with round-headed fasteners.

The tightly fitted nose fairing and Townend ring of the Ha-8 engine installation. (Shorzoe Abe)

Forward firewall

The forward firewall assembly was sandwiched between the engine crankcase and the engine-mounting frame, providing a support frame for the engine rear fairings and forward fuselage fairings. Located approximately 660mm ahead of FS.0, this oval-section aluminium-alloy panel was stiffened at its out-

The forward firewall and engine mount are visible on Ki-15-I "Ro". (Kagamigahara Aerospace Science Museum)

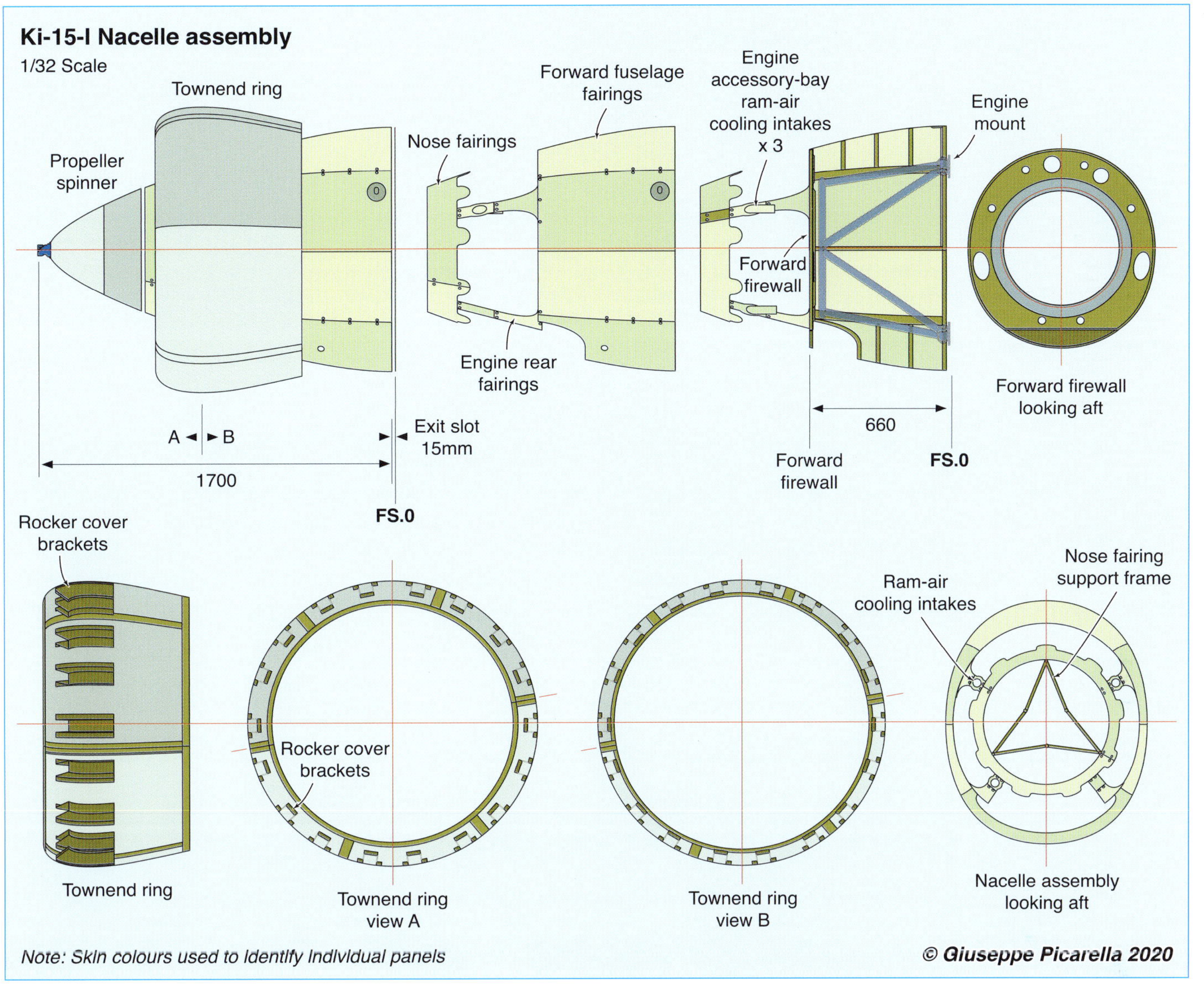

board edge with the aid of a forward flanging L-section former and four rear flanging lightening hole cut-outs, which also provided access for the carburettor and accessory bay ram-air cooling ducts.

Forward fuselage fairings

The four-part forward fuselage fairings were delicately shaped to follow the same curved lines as the nose fairing, while morphing from a circular cross-section behind the engine into the oval fuselage cross-section at FS.0.

The upper fairing contained a cut-out along its rear edge, to accommodate the antenna mast at top dead centre (TDC), while the lower panel contained a small hole on the lower port side, to accommodate the engine inertia starter handle. An access hatch was fitted to the top of the port side panel, to allow access to the oil tank filler. The lower fairing contained a cut-out section at its forward edge to allow the carburettor to project out into the airstream, just behind cylinders No.5/No.6. Shielded by the lower engine cylinders, this lower intake would most likely have been closed during ground running and taxiing in order to reduce the ingestion of dust and debris, with air being supplied to the carburettor via the ram-air intakes located between the engine's upper cylinders No.2/No.3 and No.8/No.9. Each of the aluminium-alloy fairing panels were edged and stiffened with formers and stringers, and attached to the aircraft with domed Dzus-type fasteners. The fasteners engaged four C-section support strips, attached along the outboard horizontal sections of the engine-mounting frame.

A tightly controlled exit slot (of approximately 15mm width) was incorporated into the rear edges of the fuselage fairings just ahead of FS.0, in order to ensuring adequately cooling of the engine accessory bay and oil tank.

The nacelle assembly was approximately 1,700mm long, from the tip of the "Hucks" type starter on the spinner to the rear edge of the forward fuselage fairings, 15mm forward of FS.0.

Main fuselage

The semi-monocoque main fuselage assembly was constructed of aluminium-alloy frames, longerons, formers, stringers and skins.

Fuselage frames

The main fuselage was comprised of 16 full fuselage frames (and one sub-frame) between FS.0 to FS.15. This gives a dimensioned length of 5,900mm between FS faces. The actual length of the forward fuselage, from the front of the engine attachment fitting to the rearmost skin flange aft of FS.15, was approximately 5,950mm. The fuselage had a constant cross-section from FS.0 to FS.4, thereafter the flat-bottomed frames morph into the oval cross-section rear fuselage, before becoming fully circular from FS.14 aft. All of the frames were pressed and formed assemblies with multi-directional flanged webs. Constructed of 1mm thick aluminium-alloy, with the exception of FS.0 (which was 1.4mm thick), the frames were divided into three distinct groupings – the forward group, centre group and aft group.

The forward grouping (between FS.0 and FS.3) was the most densely constructed section of the fuselage, as it incorporated the main longeron assemblies required to support the engine and also provides the mounting interface for the centre-wing section. Frame station spacing throughout the main fuselage was predominantly 400mm, with the exception of FS.1 to FS.2 (350mm) and FS.2 to FS.3 (350mm). Sub-frames are detailed individually.

Secondary firewall

The secondary firewall assembly was mounted on the front face of FS.0. This two-section panel was press formed, with scalloped cut-outs around the four engine mounts. The main Z-section alu-

The secondary firewall was attached to FS. 0 and provided support for the antenna mount, oil tank, battery and voltage regulator. (NII VVS via Y. Svoyski)

The fuselage structure was flush riveted with all lap joints facing aft or downwards. A high gloss finish was applied to the exterior of the airframe on factory fresh aircraft, although later applications of "field camouflage" were often matt or satin in finish. (NII VVS via Y. Svoyski)

minium-alloy frame was attached to FS.0 with approximately 34 screws. The steel centre panel was riveted to the forward face of the frame, sitting approximately 30mm ahead of FS.0. The front face of the secondary firewall also accommodates the oil tank mounting frame, battery mount and antenna support frame.

FS.0 was oval in section with a flat bottom – a lower panel section was attached to the base of the frame to complete the oval cross-section ahead of the wing leading edge and to act as an access route for various systems. FS.0 was manufactured with a frame width of 80mm and rearward flanging 30mm C-section flange (80 x 30mm).

The lack of fuselage longerons or stiffening structure in the vicinity of the lower engine mounts was initially troubling during the preparation of this technical description. But it is believed that there was a tubular steel tie-rod attached to the rear of FS.0, transferring the load path to the front spar, at the intersection of FS.1 and Wing Station 2 (WS.2), which is in keeping with Japanese structural practices of the period.

FS.1 was an oval section frame with an open flat bottom. Constructed of two C-section (15 x 60mm) frames placed back-to-back (spaced 100mm apart in order to accommodate the wing spar), this "twin-frame" acted as the fuselage forward mainframe, providing the primary load-path for the forward wing spar. Cut-outs were included in each frame between FS.1 and FS.14 to accommodate longitudinal stringers.

From approximately 350mm below the aircraft centreline (CL), FS.1 through FS.5 had their lower sections canted inwards at 15° to act as a mounting surface for WS.2.

FS.2 was similar in form to FS.1, but incorporated an intercostal frame to provide a forward mounting structure for the pilot's cockpit floor. The frame was comprised of a single rearward flanging C-section (15 x 80mm) outer and inner upper flange, with a forward facing lower inboard flange. The increased (80mm) frame width found on FS.0 and FS.2 provided mounting surfaces for the modular fuel tank design.

FS.3 was generally similar to FS.1 as it acted as the rear mainframe, providing the primary load-path for the rear wing spar. A dedicated C-section intercostal spanned the aft frame to provide support for the pilot's cockpit floor.

The centre group of frames (FS.4, FS.4A and FS.5) housed the flight control conversion quadrants and also provided the transition zone between the flat-bottomed forward group and oval-section rear group.

Fuselage structure

1/48 Scale

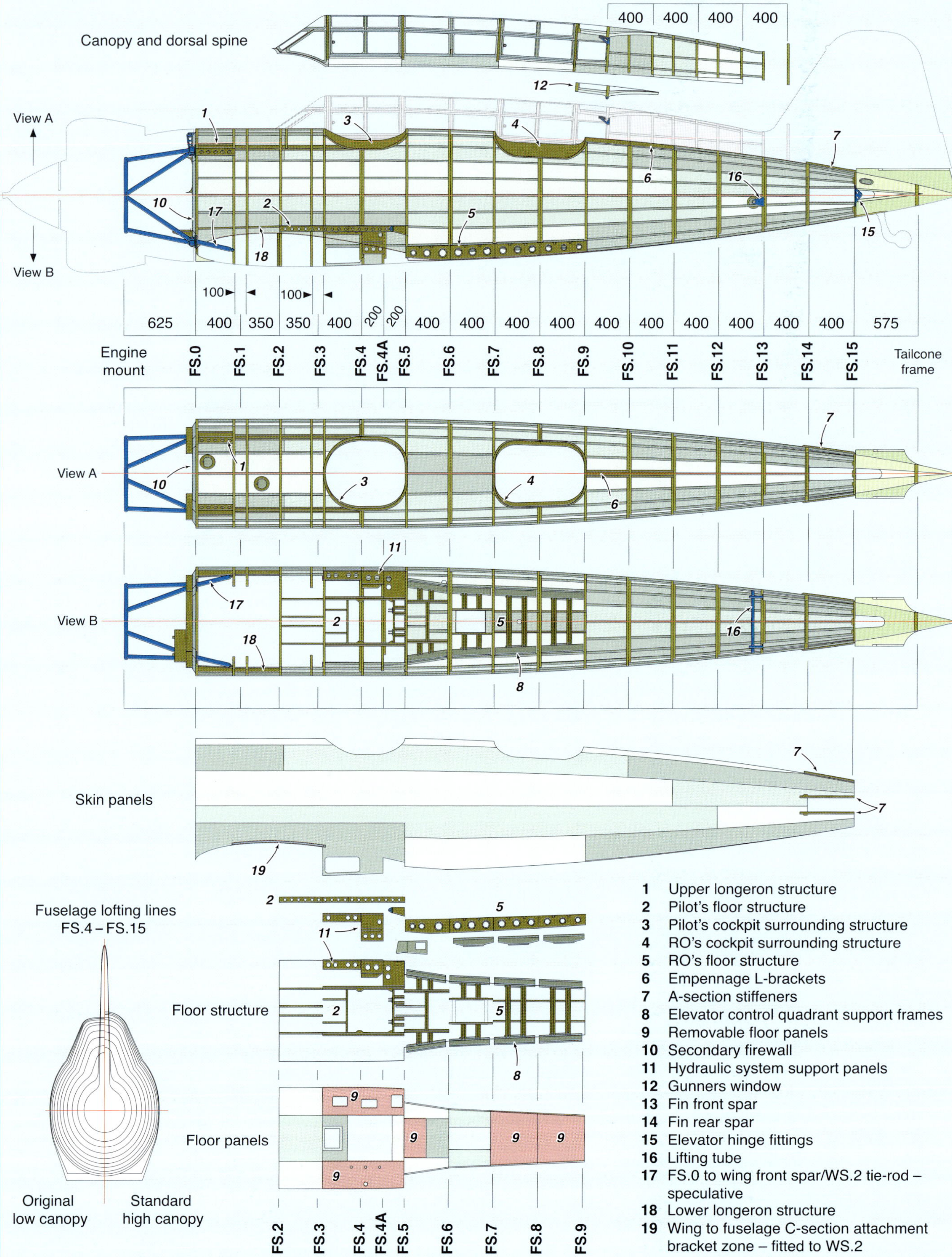

1 Upper longeron structure
2 Pilot's floor structure
3 Pilot's cockpit surrounding structure
4 RO's cockpit surrounding structure
5 RO's floor structure
6 Empennage L-brackets
7 A-section stiffeners
8 Elevator control quadrant support frames
9 Removable floor panels
10 Secondary firewall
11 Hydraulic system support panels
12 Gunners window
13 Fin front spar
14 Fin rear spar
15 Elevator hinge fittings
16 Lifting tube
17 FS.0 to wing front spar/WS.2 tie-rod – speculative
18 Lower longeron structure
19 Wing to fuselage C-section attachment bracket zone – fitted to WS.2

Note: Skin colours used to identify individual panels

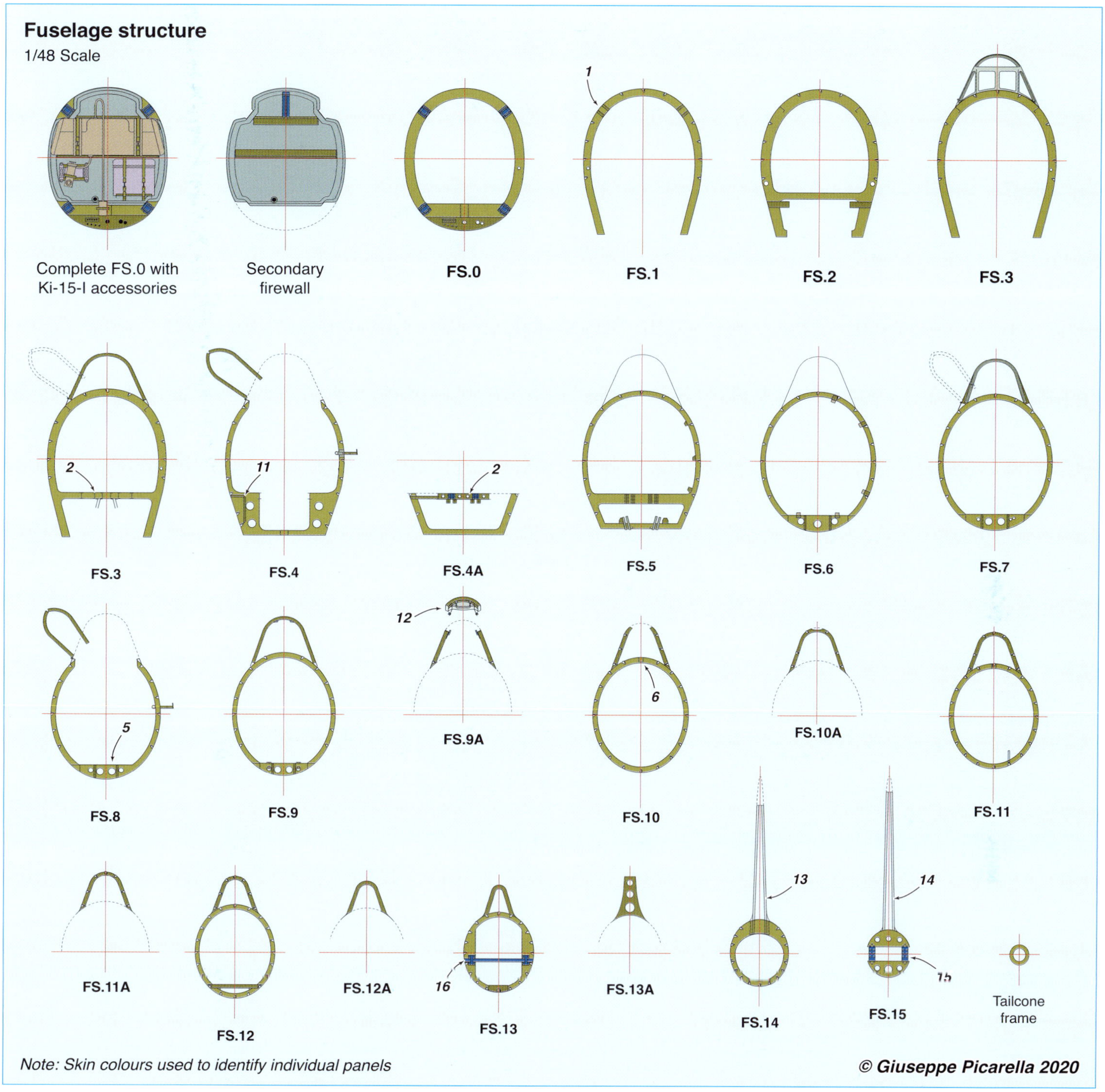

FS.4 carried the same cross-section and flat-bottomed profile as preceding frames. The Z-section frame (15 x 40mm) was open at the top, to provide access to the pilot's cockpit, but included additional area approximately 275mm below the aircraft CL. This additional structure formed the elevator conversion quadrant and crank torsion-box, and also provided support for the longitudinal frames of the cockpit floor.

FS.4A was located 200mm aft of FS.4. This sub-frame was broadly similar to the lower section of FS.4 and formed the rear portion of the elevator control torsion-box. It also provided support structure for the centre wing-section auxiliary (flap) spar.

FS.5 was the last flat-bottomed fuselage frame. The C-section (15 x 40mm) frame included a floor-level intercostal, which provided the rearmost support frame for the pilot's cockpit floor and the hinge points for the elevator conversion quadrant. FS.5 also acted as the forward attachment frame for the "additional fuel tank", with two attachment brackets located at the base of the frame and three located up the port side. The base of FS.5 was above the lofting line prescribed between FS.4A and FS.6, as this area formed the recess for the land flap well.

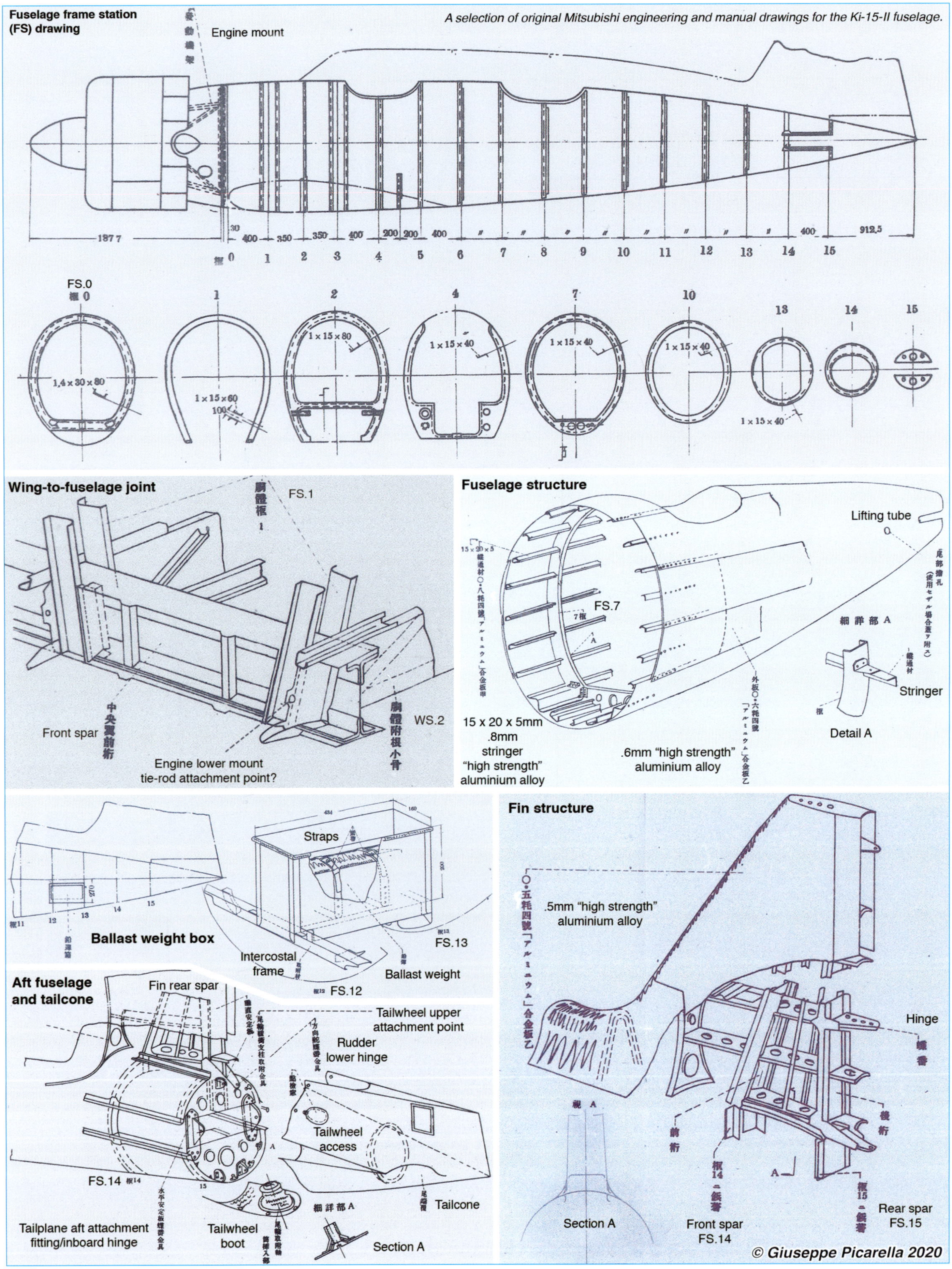

Fuselage frame station (FS) drawing
A selection of original Mitsubishi engineering and manual drawings for the Ki-15-II fuselage.
Engine mount
FS.0
Wing-to-fuselage joint
FS.1
Front spar
WS.2
Engine lower mount tie-rod attachment point?
Fuselage structure
Lifting tube
FS.7
Detail A
Stringer
15 x 20 x 5mm .8mm stringer "high strength" aluminium alloy
.6mm "high strength" aluminium alloy
Straps
Ballast weight box
Intercostal frame
FS.12
FS.13
Ballast weight
Fin structure
.5mm "high strength" aluminium alloy
Hinge
Section A
Front spar FS.14
Rear spar FS.15
Aft fuselage and tailcone
Fin rear spar
Tailwheel upper attachment point
Rudder lower hinge
Tailwheel access
FS.14
Tailcone
Tailplane aft attachment fitting/inboard hinge
Tailwheel boot
Section A
© Giuseppe Picarella 2020

The rear group of fuselage frames (FS.6 through FS.15) were oval in section, with FS.14 and FS.15 forming true circular cross-sections. All of these frames, except FS.14, had a frame width of 15 x 40mm, with localized support-structure.

FS.6 was a Z-section frame, which acted as the rear attachment frame for the "additional fuel tank", with two attachment brackets located at the base of the frame and three located up the port side. FS.6 through FS.9 included a flat internal section, which acted as the support structure for the rear cockpit floor.

FS.7 was a rearward flanging C-section frame.

FS.8 was a Z-section frame with an opening at the top, to provide access to the RO's cockpit.

FS.9 was a rearward flanging C-section frame, which acted as the rear bulkhead for the RO's cockpit and provided the mounting structure for the storage cabinet.

FS.10 was a forward flanging Z-section frame, which provided the aft mounting structure for the storage cabinet.

FS.11 was a forward flanging Z-section frame.

FS.12 was a forward flanging Z-section frame carrying a riveted horizontal intercostal frame that provided the forward support for the ballast weight container.

FS.13 was a forward flanging Z-section frame with additional vertical surface area, which provided the primary mounting surfaces for the rear fuselage lifting tube fittings. An additional horizontal and vertical intercostal acted as the rear support frame for the ballast weight container.

FS.14 was a forward flanging C-section frame with an increased outer flange width of approximately 30mm, which was required to carry the load of the tailplane horizontal attachment fittings. Additional area on its upper section was provided to act as the forward attachment interface for the fin front spar.

FS.15 took the form of two individual semi-circular rearward flanging Z-section frames, a design that enabled the installation of the completed single-piece tailplane. The frame provided the aft attachment interface for the tailplane horizontal attachment fittings, with the upper segment providing the rear attachment interface for the fin rear spar. FS.15 also acted as the mounting bulkhead for the tailwheel attachment fittings. Once the tailplane was fitted, both frames were stiffened by the installation of the elevator central hinge fittings, which bridged the gap between the upper and lower frame segment.

Tailcone

The tailcone was fabricated from upper and lower aluminium-alloy segments, extending aft 912.5mm from the face of FS.15, and was stiffened by a single support frame located approximately 575mm aft of FS.15. In order to streamline into the elevator and rudder root profiles, portions of the tail-cone were cut away and flared fairings were riveted into position. The unit was attached to the rear fuselage skin panels by 14 countersunk screws, engaging into anchor-nuts installed on the aft facing flange of FS.15. To allow for the compression of the tailwheel shock-strut, a removable panel was installed on the lower segment, at the forward end of the tailcone. This was attached with an additional six countersunk screws and a canvas boot was provided to fit around the tailwheel leg, to prevent debris and mud from entering the structure. Access to the tailwheel upper shock-strut fitting was facilitated by the inclusion of two inspection hatches located on either side of the upper tailcone.

Support structure – longerons, formers, stringers and skins

In order to transmit the loads from the upper engine mounts into the fuselage, two box-section longerons were installed in the upper forward fuselage between FS.0 and FS.2. These aluminium-alloy longerons were constructed of two 60mm deep C-section channels with a closing panel on the inboard face. Aft of FS.1, the box-section reduced in depth as it transited to FS.2. From that point aft, the upper fuselage was devoid of longerons, but the pilot and RO's cockpits were both surrounded by ring shaped C-section formers, which stiffened the upper fuselage between FS.3 and FS.5, and FS.7 and FS.9. A "Top hat" section stiffener was attached at the top dead centre of the rear fuselage between FS.9 and FS.11, to act as a support for the machine gun runner. In the extreme rear fuselage, four machined aluminium-alloy L-section brackets provide localised support structure for the installation of the tailplane. These were located on the exterior of the fuselage, bridging FS.14 back to FS.15.

The lower engine mounts transferred their load back to FS.1, where the wing and fuselage were mated at the canted wing ribs – WS.2, which transferred loads back to FS.4A (See **FS.0**). Between FS.4 and FS.5, the cockpit floor/elevator conversion quadrant torsion-box stiffened the centre fuselage. Aft of this point, stiffening was provided by the main floor structure of the RO's cockpit between FS.5 to FS.9.

Almost all of the stringers on the Ki-15 were 0.8mm L-section, roll-extruded high strength aluminium-alloy of 15 x 20 x 5mm. From FS.0 to FS.5 the pattern varies from 13 to 17 stringers per frame, with 15 stringers present in the oval fuselage section between FS.6 to FS.9. Between FS.10 and FS.13 there were 20 stringers, but the diminishing diameter of the fuselage and tailplane cut-out reduced the stringer count down to 17 aft of FS.14. Stringers were attached to the fuselage frames by right angle brackets, with a single rivet passing through the stringer and a two rivets passing through the fuselage frame. Two C-section stringers (40 x 20 x 5mm) were installed adjacent to the camera window (FS.6 and FS.7) in the RO's floor.

The fuselage skin panels were 0.6mm pressed and rolled high strength aluminium-alloy, fitted with low-drag, lapped and flush panel joints. All skin panels were attached longitudinally to the fuselage, with countersunk/flush riveting throughout the whole wetted area of the airframe.

Floor structure

The floor of the pilot's cockpit was located 275mm below the aircraft CL, extending between FS.2 and FS.5. In addition to the lateral support offered by FS.2, FS.4, FS.4A and FS.5, dedicated C, L and H-section frames provided longitudinal support for the floor panels and rudder pedal pivot. The pilot's seat was designed to be removable in order to allow access to the elevator conversion quadrant, as were the floor panels located outboard of the pilot's seat between FS.3 and FS.5, which allowed access to fuel and hydraulic systems. An aperture was also provided for the control column to pass through. Localized support structure was included below the right-hand side of the cockpit floor, between FS.3 and FS.5, to provide ridged mounting points for the hydraulic hand pump and selector assembly.

The RO's cockpit floor was on a separate level to that of the pilot and was also canted upwards by 2°. The forward and rear edges were 460mm and 410mm below the aircraft CL respectively, as the floor panels rested on the flat internal section of each fuselage frame, extending between FS.5 and FS.9. In addition to the A-section stiffeners between FS.6 and FS.9, which supported the outboard edges of the RO's floor panel, two longitudinal C-section support frames were located inboard, to support the centre of the floor panels. Lateral floor support was provided by two sets of Top hat section stringers located between each frame station. The floor panels were fixed between FS.5 and FS.7, although the forward central panel, between FS.5 and FS.6, could be removed for maintenance of the elevator control quadrant. The floor panels between FS.7 and FS.9 were removable, allowing access to the control cable pulleys located beneath them. The vertical camera window was installed between FS.6 and FS.7.

Canopy

It is unclear if Fumihiko Kouno's initial sketches for the "Two-seat high-speed aircraft" incorporated partially open cockpit layouts, as the aircraft's inception occurred during a period of aeronautical

The first three or four prototype airframes incorporated low profile canopies. (Japan Aeronautical Association)

Low profile bi-fold canopies shown in the open position. (Japan Aeronautical Association)

transition. The development of all-metal airframes, coupled with more powerful engines, was the state-of-the-art in the mid 1930s, as the field of "aerodynamics" became the dominant design criteria in aeronautical engineering. Despite attempts to streamline and clean up airframe designs, internationally most operational biplane fighters did not have fully enclosed cockpits, including Mitsubishi's own experimental 9-*Shi* Single-seat Fighter. The accepted norm for high-speed aircraft, including fighters and racers of the period, still embraced exposed cockpit layouts, which allowed unlimited visibility, especially during combat and it could be argued that the same requirements were desirable during ground or target alignment in the case of a reconnaissance aircraft.

Following the acceptance of the 9-*Shi* Carrier-borne Fighter into service as the A5M1 *Claude* in 1937, Mitsubishi was eager to develop an improved version of the aircraft. When the new A5M2b entered production in 1938, it incorporated a fully enclosed cockpit and rearward-sliding canopy, which was a first for a Japanese production fighter. Mitsubishi though was surprised to discover that the majority of battle-hardened pilots returning from combat over China universally shunned this feature. Many of the first 100 A5M2b aircraft to enter service would subsequently be operated with their canopies removed and Mitsubishi's production lines reverted back to the earlier open cockpit configuration for the remainder of the production run.

Original Mitsubishi manual drawing for the Ki-15 canopy.

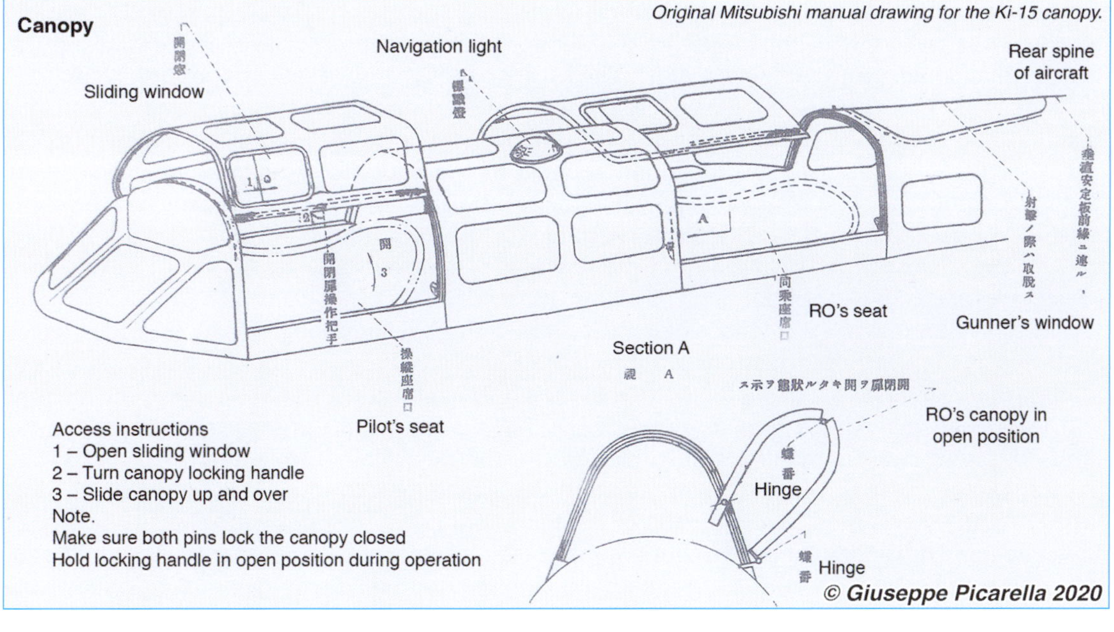

As can bee seen in this photo of J-BAAL Asakaze, the top of Toshio Omata's head is in line with the canopy rear runner frame. (Japan Aeronautical Association)

Operational requirements and pilot preferences aside, once the preliminary Ki-15 aerodynamic calculations had been studied in detail, they showed the need for an incredibly smooth and, more importantly, a very low canopy profile, in order to meet the required performance figures. The extent to which Kouno studied parasitic drag is quite amazing for the period and his solutions were equally impressive. For example, all of the canopy transparencies were manufactured with 2mm bevelled edges on their outer surfaces, which allowed them to fit flush with the windscreen or canopy framework, thus removing all steps on the external surface of the canopy installation!

The ergonomic restrictions of the Ki-15 cockpit were all too evident in the configuration adopted for the initial prototypes, which included an upper canopy profile that extended only 250mm above the fuselage profile – which was barely the height of a pilot's head from chin to crown! Ultimately this meant that the pilot's seated position would have to be located very low in the fuselage, impacting on visibility, especially during take-off and landing. It is not known if the headroom issues was mentioned during the inspection of the wooden mock-up in October 1935, but it is most likely that Mitsubishi would have held their ground on this issue due to the required performance figures.

Ki-15-I – prototypes

The canopy was comprised of four assemblies – the windscreen, pilot's canopy, centre canopy tunnel and RO's canopy. All skins and stiffeners were of aluminium-alloy, with steel brackets and hinges, with glass and Plexiglas used for the transparencies.

The windscreen was designed with a central frame at its leading edge, to cut through the air. The five-pane windscreen installation positioned four direct-vision flat panes of glass on its forward and side faces, with a moulded Plexiglas upper panel. The flat panes were sandwiched into position by internal stiffeners, with a rearward-facing machined aluminium C-section (forward) canopy runner provided rigidity to the installation. The three front vertical frames were parallel in layout and angled back at approximately 55° to meet at a horizontal mid frame, which was located approximately 175mm above the fuselage profile, to align with the canopy mid frame installation. From the mid frame line the upper panel curved back to meet the forward canopy runner, which prescribed a flat-topped arch. The outer frame of the windscreen was flanged to fit the profile of the forward fuselage between FS.1 and FS.3, where it was riveted into position.

The pilot's canopy was a sideways hinging, bi-fold design (660mm long by 650mm wide), which eliminated any lips or ridges that threatened to project into the airstream. The two-piece canopy was attached to the fuselage by a piano hinge fitted to the sill structure on the starboard side of the fuselage, with a secondary piano hinge running along its TDC position. When the pilot opened the canopy, the left-hand canopy panel moved upwards, guided by two rollers which following the C-section forward and rear canopy runners. The TDC hinge allowed the canopy to fold in half as the left-hand panel passed over the pilot's head, across the top of the frame and down the right-hand side of the canopy runner frames. The canopy contained eight transparencies, two of which (side-windows) could slide aft, to provide ventilation and access. A metal knob fitted to the forward edge of each sliding windowpane was mounted on an internal plate, with its outside section flush with the glass. The attention to aerodynamic cleanness extended to every component of the canopy, even the sliding-window access knob, which was hollow in section and required a finger to slide the window open when entering from the outside. The pilot's canopy frame was divided by a single vertical bar, a TDC hinge/bar and a horizontal mid-frame bar, the latter of which carried internal J-sections, which acted as the upper runner for the sliding ventilation windows. The canopy was locked and unlocked by turning a circular handle on the left-hand side lower frame, which controlled two horizontal locking pins on the forward and rear edges of the canopy. A second handle, located ahead of the circular handle, was used to manoeuvre the canopy into the required position.

The glass and Plexiglas panes of the windscreen and canopy were beveled by 2mm in order to remove the step between the glass and the framework. Note that the fuselage skin panels, inside the windscreen and centre canopy tunnel, match the high gloss exterior paint scheme. (NII VVS via Y. Svoyski)

The centre canopy tunnel was approximately 890mm long and mirrored the pilot's canopy layout. The forward edge of the installation was positioned vertically, as it included the forward facing C-section frame for the pilot's canopy (rear) runner. Both runners needed to be parallel in order for the bi-fold system to operate. The canopy line was canted aft from FS.5 along the length of the aircraft to match the fuselage lines. In order for the runner frames of the RO's canopy to be installed in a parallel position, the centre canopy tunnel (aft) frame had to be canted rearwards in order to remain perpendicular with the TDC profile. The centre canopy tunnel included a Plexiglas blister at FS.6 for the navigation light, and the upper retractable handhold cut-out was located in the port canopy lower fairing ahead of FS.6.

The RO's canopy dimensions were 660mm long by 640 wide and the whole assembly was canted aft by approximately 3.7° in order to remain perpendicular with the fuselage profile. While it was similar in design and operation to the pilot's bi-fold canopy, there was one very important difference. Whereas the pilot's canopy was parallel in design and guided by two sturdy C-section runners, the RO's canopy reduced in width to match the rear fuselage lines. This required a different hinge system and two articulated guide arms to facilitate canopy movement. The tapered profile of the RO's cockpit meant that the rear hinge fitting protrude slightly into the airstream, in order for the canopy hinges to remain parallel. In its closed position the RO's canopy frame sat on Z-section flanged frames at the rear of the centre canopy tunnel and the front of the dorsal spine structure at **FS.8A**, which was located approximately 130mm ahead of FS.9. See **Dorsal spine.**

The canopies could not be opened at speeds in excess of 200km/h.

Ki-15-I – production model

The stunning performance figures displayed by the 1st prototype were only marred by the test pilot's dislike of the low canopy and its lack of visibility during take-off and landing.

Content in the knowledge that the performance of the aircraft was well within its requirements, the development of a slightly taller canopy structure for production aircraft was approved. It is unclear how many low canopy Ki-15 prototypes were built. We know that the 1st prototype (C/n1501), the 2nd prototype *Kamikaze* (C/n1502) and 3rd prototype *Asakaze* (C/n1503) all included these design features, but no additional photographs of low canopy Ki-15s exist between these three prototypes and the 7th airframe (C/n107), which incorporated the high canopy.

The new canopy arrangement was almost identical to the original design, differing only above the mid frame line, where the flat upper profile was replaced with a hemispherical arch. These modifications not only raised the height of the pilot's canopy by approximately 50mm to 300mm, it had the additional benefit of increasing the dorsal spine profile height, which also improved field of fire for the machine gun. Mitsubishi also took this opportunity to modify the RO's canopy design to match that of the pilot's, with C-section runner frames fore and aft, but in order to for the bi-fold canopy to open smoothly, a new two-piece hinge design was incorporated. The front hinge remained inside the fuselage lines, but the rear hinge fitting required an "offset" design, which moved to canopy outboard as it opened, thus keeping the two hinges parallel. Unfortunately, when closed, the offset hinge bracket protruded slightly into the slipstream on the starboard side of the fuselage.

The bi-fold canopy allowed the installation to close without any edges protruding into the airstream, while the centre canopy tunnel was delicately faired into the fuselage sides. Note the black or dark Aotake speaking tube. (NII VVS via Y. Svoyski)

In all fairness it should be pointed out that the bi-fold canopy was not the most user friendly of designs, as it required the crewmembers to "hunch" down in their seats as they opened and closed the canopies. This was not so much of an issue for the RO, as the rear cockpit was longer and lower, but it was awkward for the pilot, who could not lean too far forward because of the cockpit sill structure. While this issue was never fully resolved, the improved visibility offered by the introduction of the higher canopy did appease the Army.

Dorsal spine and gunner's window

In order to fair the cockpit canopies into the rear fuselage, a dorsal spine structure was fitted to the existing oval cross-section fuselage frames. The leading edge of the dorsal spine (FS.8A) included the Z-section flange (low canopy prototypes) or canopy runner (high canopy production aircraft) for the RO's canopy, followed by eight C-section formers, which morphed from the flat-sided profile of the rear canopy, into a slightly concave cross-section at FS.13A, at which point fairings blended the spine structure into the fin root fairing. Located between FS.8A and FS.9A were two gunner's windows, which were used for rearward observation while operating the machine gun.

A removable "gunner's" window panel was located in the upper section of the dorsal spine between FS.9 and FS.10A. Designed to match the upper contours of the dorsal spine, the gunner's window was constructed of aluminium-alloy C-section frames, with a mid support frame, skin and a Plexiglas panel. The mid frame extended downwards and contained guide rollers fitted to each extension. These guide rollers engaged into track fittings located in the dorsal spine structure at FS.10A, for securing the window into place. A handle and locking catch were fitted to the leading edge of the window frame to assist in removing and fitting the assembly.

Dorsal spine frames at FS.9A and FS.10 were partial frames due to the gunner's removable upper window panel. Both frames canted forward at an increasing angle in order to align with the vertical frames at FS.10A, which was shaped to support the end of the window frame at TDC.

Dorsal spine frames FS.11, FS.11A, FS.12, FS.12A and FS.13 were all (vertical) full frames. The dorsal spine was fitted with aluminium-alloy skins, supported by four L-section stringers between FS.9 and FS.10, after which point seven stringers travelled aft to FS.12A, where they reduced to six at FS.13. Between FS.13 and FS.13A the dorsal spine skin panels blended into the fin support frame and extended down each side of the fin to form a fixed fairing over the fin-to-fuselage support strips.

The flat upper dorsal spine profile of the prototype aircraft was also redesigned to match the hemispherical profile of the production aircraft, with all changes occurring ahead of FS.12A.

Empennage

Fin (vertical stabilizer)

The cantilever fin was comprised of two built-up I-section spars, ribs, stringers, hinge fittings and skins. Manufactured independently from the fuselage, the whole unit was permanently installed onto the fuselage during final assembly with 0° offset or deflection. The leading edge of the fin was swept back at 32° and the trailing edge of the rudder was swept forward at 14.5°.

The front spar was comprised of four L-section stiffeners attached to the web, with spar caps on both sides of the assembly, providing localized support for the ribs. The spar was riveted to the face of

FS.14 and supported with additional L-section stiffeners on its outboard edges. It extending vertically until it exited the fuselage profile, from which point it was canted 18° aft and extend upwards to Fin Station 6 (FinS.6). The rear spar was similar in design with the spar caps extending between FinS.1 and FinS.6, providing localized support for the ribs and rudder hinges. The rear spar was attached to the face of FS.15 with the aid of outboard stiffeners, before extended vertically to FinS.7. Seven ribs were incorporated into the fin structure, evenly spaced approximately 200mm apart. Each rib was of aluminium construction with a 15mm flange. The ribs displayed a variety of construction techniques, from solid format with lightening holes, through to shaped formers with and without intercostal stiffeners.

FinS.1 spanned between the front and rear spars and was inclined upwards at approximately 8°, in order to clear the top skin panel between FS.14 and FS.15. Aft of the rear spar, the rib was horizontal, extending aft to match the lowest rudder rib adjacent to FinS.1. All successive fin ribs were positioned horizontally.

FinS.2 was a three-piece rib with lightening holes, spanning from the fin rear edge to the fin support frame located between FS.13 and FS.14.

FinS.3 through **FinS.7** each spanned from the trailing edge of the fin to the leading edge of the fin.

Rudder hinges were located adjacent to FinS.1, FinS.3 and FinS.6, which were 165mm, 643.5mm and 1243.5mm above the aircraft CL respectively.

Each side of the fin contained two stringers for rigidity, one located ahead of the front spar between FinS.3 and FinS.6, and one between the front and rear spars, bridging FinS.1 and FinS.4.

The arrangement of skin panels on the fin was novel to say the least. In all, 10 individual skin panels of 0.5mm sheet aluminium-alloy were used. The upper panel was attached to FinS.7 and FinS.6, spanned from the rear spar skin joint, forwards around the leading edge and back to the opposite rear spar joint. The next three leading edge skin panels spanned from the front spar skin joint only, passing around the leading edge to the opposite front spar joint. Two skin panels (one per side) were attached to the skin panel in an arc, between FinS.2 and FinS.3. Two skin panels (one per side) filled the A-space between the front and rear spar skin joints from FinS.1 to FinS.6. Two trailing edge skin panels (one per side) completed the fin trailing edge, aft of the rear spar. Two L-section support strips (one per side) secured the lower edge of each fin centre section skin panel to the fuselage skin, adjacent to support stringers located inside the fuselage. These strips were faired over by the trailing edge of the dorsal spine skin.

Rudder

The 1,250mm high horn-balanced rudder was constructed of an aluminium-alloy structure with an Irish linen skin. The spine of the rudder was built-up around two, back-to-back, C-section frames, formers and outboard capping panels. Ahead of this "box-spar" construction, eight nose ribs and two hinges were contained within the leading edge skin panels, with cut-outs adjacent to the centre and up-

The single piece tailplane and rear-fuselage interface. Note the Aotake finish on the front face of the spar. (NII VVS via Y. Svoyski)

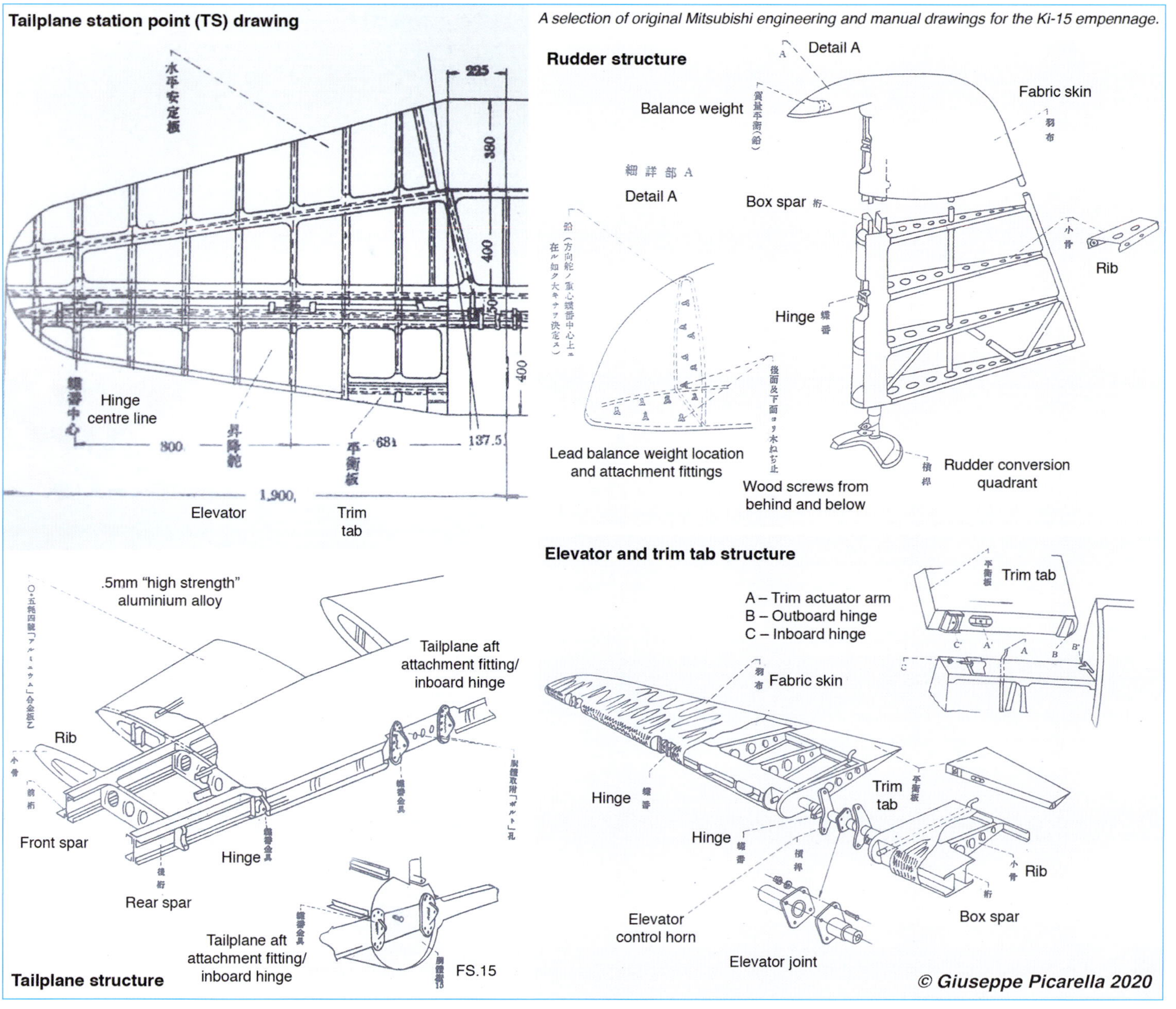

A selection of original Mitsubishi engineering and manual drawings for the Ki-15 empennage.

per hinge points. Aft of the spar, seven downward-flanged C-section main ribs (with integral lightening holes and rib-stitching eyelets) were aligned to the corresponding fin stations. A vertical support tube was installed between FinS.1 and FinS.7, with supplementary diagonal tubes located between FinS.1 and FinS.2, in order to stiffen the structure, and a full-height V-section frame completed the trailing edge. Rudder FinS.7 extended from the trailing edge, to the leading edge of the fin, just above fin FinS.7. The tip of the rudder was comprised of three aluminium-alloy fairings, supported by an aft flanging C-section former and the box spar. A lead balance weight was screwed to the forward face of the former.

The rudder was actuated via a torque tube and conversion quadrant, attached to the lower rib.

Rubber tab

There is no evidence of ground adjustable trim tabs being installed on the Ki-15 prototypes, due to the high quality finish on these early aircraft. But as airframes began to accumulate operational hours in the harsh combat environment of China, the need for fixed trim tabs became apparent, in order to allow the ground-crew to rig individual aircraft to fly true, despite wear and tear. The tab was fitted to the trailing edge of the rudder, spanning upwards from FinS.7 to FinS.5, and was easily adjusted by hand or with a pair of pliers.

Tailplane (horizontal stabilizer)

The 3,800mm wide, single-piece cantilever tailplane was comprised of two built-up I-section spars, ribs, stringers, hinge fittings and skins. Manufactured independently from the fuselage, the whole unit

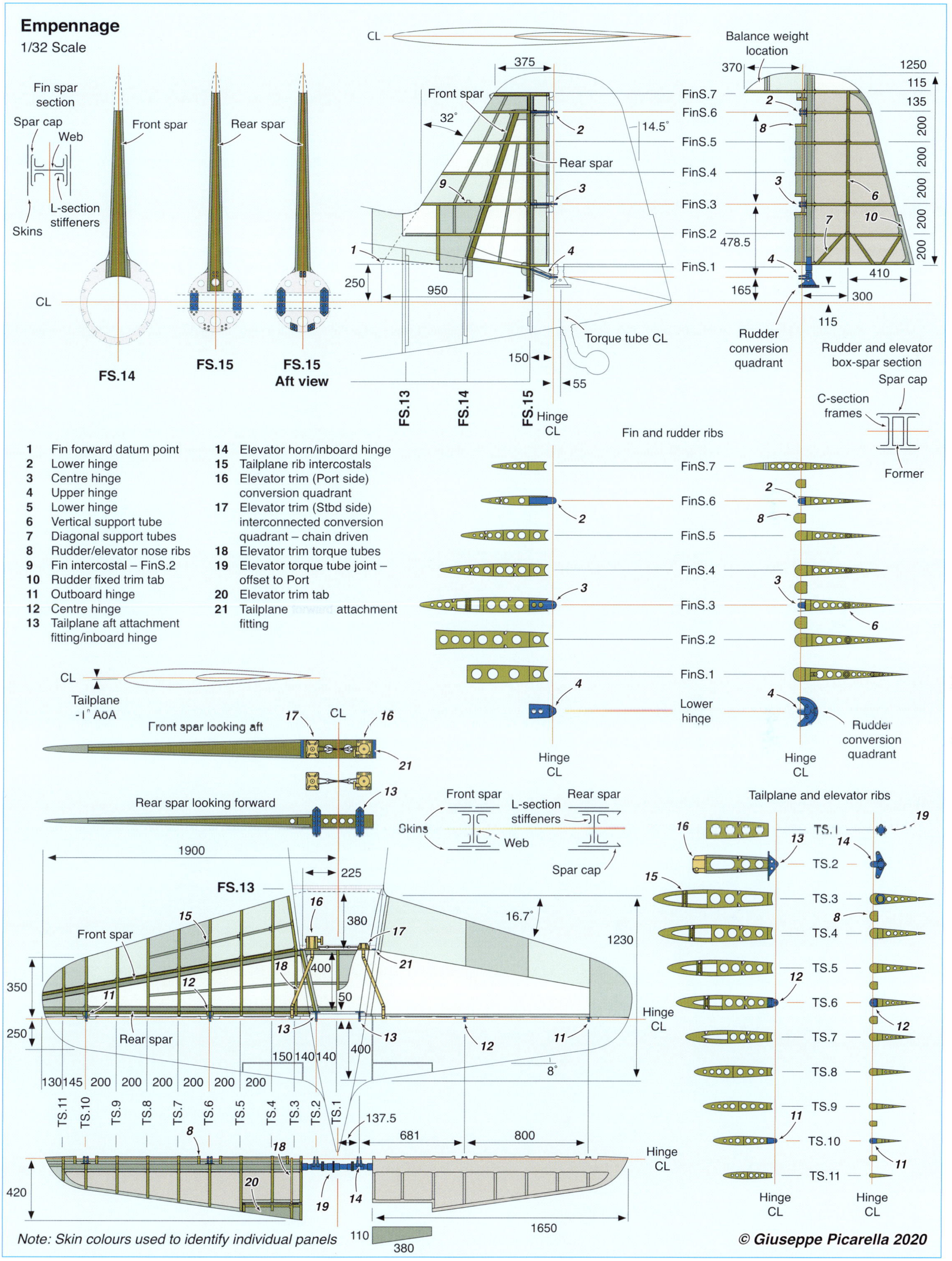
Empennage
1/32 Scale
Fin spar section
Spar cap
Web
L-section stiffeners
Skins
Front spar
Rear spar
CL
FS.14
FS.15
FS.15 Aft view
Balance weight location
Torque tube CL
Hinge CL
Rudder conversion quadrant
Rudder and elevator box-spar section
Spar cap
C-section frames
Former
Fin and rudder ribs
Lower hinge
Tailplane -1° AoA
Front spar looking aft
Rear spar looking forward
Tailplane and elevator ribs
1 Fin forward datum point
2 Lower hinge
3 Centre hinge
4 Upper hinge
5 Lower hinge
6 Vertical support tube
7 Diagonal support tubes
8 Rudder/elevator nose ribs
9 Fin intercostal – FinS.2
10 Rudder fixed trim tab
11 Outboard hinge
12 Centre hinge
13 Tailplane aft attachment fitting/inboard hinge
14 Elevator horn/inboard hinge
15 Tailplane rib intercostals
16 Elevator trim (Port side) conversion quadrant
17 Elevator trim (Stbd side) interconnected conversion quadrant – chain driven
18 Elevator trim torque tubes
19 Elevator torque tube joint – offset to Port
20 Elevator trim tab
21 Tailplane attachment fitting
Note: Skin colours used to identify individual panels
© Giuseppe Picarella 2020

was detachable for transportation and maintenance. For rigging purposes the tailplane was installed on the fuselage with a – 1° angle of attack. The leading edge of the tailplane was swept back at 16.7° and the trailing edge of the elevator was swept forward at 8°.

The I-section front spar was built-up of an aluminium-alloy web, four L-section stiffeners and spar caps at the top and bottom, the later providing localized support for the ribs and hinges. The 450mm wide centre-section sat within the lines of the fuselage and was attached to FS.14 by one bolt on each side of the assembly. These attachment brackets were located on the face of the front spar, protruding below the lower spar cap to facilitate installation. Outboard of these attachment points the front spars were canted 9° aft.

The straight rear spar took broadly the same form as the front spar, attaching to FS.15 via the upper and lower segments of the central hinge fittings.

The tailplane centre torsion-box contained 21 ribs, typically spaced 200mm apart – 10 each side and one central rib – Tailplane Station 1 (**TS.1**) – while the leading edge panels each contained nine aluminium-alloy ribs with a 15mm flanges.

TS.2 of the centre torsion box carried the load for the elevator central hinge fittings and represented the deepest section of the tailplane, at 120mm. TS.2 was also canted 15° outboard to provide support for the tailplane support brackets between FS.14 and FS.15.

TS.3 through **TS.9** were similar in construction, each with or without an intercostal stiffener, depending on the rib depth.

Due to their small depth, **TP.10** and **TS.11** were most likely single-piece ribs with lightening holes.

The leading edge structure contained 9 ribs on each side, which aligned with the central torsion box ribs **TS.3** through **TS.11**. These nose ribs typically took the form of shaped formers (between TS.3 and TS.9) both with or without intercostal stiffeners. TS.10 and TS.11 were most likely sold ribs with lightening holes due to their depth.

Aft of the rear spar, auxiliary ribs supported the trailing edge skins ahead of the elevator.

Each side of the tailplane contained two sets of stringers for rigidity, two located within the leading edge structure between TS.3 and TS.8, and two between the front and rear spars, spanning from TS.1 to TS.8.

Elevator hinges were located adjacent to TS.1, TS.6 and TS.10, which were 137.5mm, 818.5mm and 1,618.5mm outboard of the aircraft CL respectively.

In marked contrast to the fin skin layout, the tailplane contained only six individual skin panels (per side) of 0.5mm sheet aluminium-alloy. Each centre torsion box (port and starboard) received an upper and lower skin panel, spanning from TS.1 outboard to TS.10. Each of these main panels extended over the auxiliary ribs, ending with stiffening flanges on their trailing edges. Two-part (top and bottom) tailplane tips spanned TS.10 and TS.11, while the leading edges consisted of three skin panels per side, spanning TS.3 to TS.5, TS.5 to TS.8 and TS.8 to TS.10 respectively.

Elevator

Each elevator panel was approximately 1,665mm wide and constructed of aluminium-alloy with an Irish linen skin. As per the rudder, the elevators were built-up around two back-to-back C-section frames, formers and capping panels. Ahead of this "box-spar" construction, 11 nose ribs and two hinges were contained within the leading edge skin panels, with cut-outs adjacent to the centre and outboard hinge points. Aft of the spar, nine inward-flanged C-section main ribs (with integral lightening holes and rib-stitching eyelets) were aligned to the corresponding tailplane stations TS.4 through TS.11.

The two inboard ribs (TS.2 and TS.3) were truncated with a transverse C-section spar extending out to TS.4. This carried two hinges and formed the mounting surface for the all-metal trim tab. The elevators were bolted together on the tailplane CL, via their individual torque tubes, which also contained the elevator inboard hinge points and control-horns.

Elevator tab

An elevator trim tab was fitted to each of the elevator panels. Controlled via a pilot actuated cable and pushrod mechanism, these 400mm wide aluminium-alloy tabs were construction with a C-section spar, two hinges, an articulation fitting, upper and lower skins and four internal ribs.

Tailplane fairings

A fixed, two-piece aluminium-alloy fairing streamlined each side of the tailplane into the fuselage. To ensure a close fit and reduced drag, countersunk screws were used on all fairings, which engaged into anchor-nuts that were pre-installed inside the fuselage and tailplane skins. The trailing edge of the fairing fitted tightly against the leading edge of the tailcone.

Wing

The cantilever wing was comprised of three sections – the centre wing section and two outboard wing panels. Each section was built up of spars, stringers, formers, attachment brackets and skins.

Centre wing section

Kouno designed the Ki-15 wing around a modified Blackburn B-9 aerofoil section set at 2° incidence, with the thickest section of the aerofoil located at approximately 35% chord. Mitsubishi had already achieved excellent performance with that aerofoil on the Ka-14/A5M *Claude*. With further development the aerofoil would ultimately result in the MAC-118 profile, as used on the company's A6M *Zeke* and early G4M *Betty*.

The three-spar centre wing section had a span of 2,800mm between outboard wing panel attachment bracket centre points, and a constant chord of 2,200mm. It is no accident that the centre wing section span was identical to that of the A5M, as these dimensions allowed for the aircraft to be dismantled and transported in a flat orientation aboard standard width railway carriages.

The front (or forward) and rear main spars (as they formed widely spaced box-spar) were located 400mm and 1,100mm aft of the leading edge respectively, with the auxiliary (or flap) spar located at the 1,700mm point. The positioning of the spars (400mm, 1,100mm and 1,700mm aft of FS.0) coincided with the main fuselage frames at FS.2, FS.3 and FS.4A. This enabled the centre wing section, which was constructed independently from the fuselage structure, to be permanently joined to the fuselage during final assembly.

The forward and rear (main) spars were built-up, high strength aluminium-alloy I-section assemblies. The forward spar incorporated (at the top and bottom faces) a 0.8mm chord plate, a 2-3mm cap plate, two 2-3mm L-section stiffeners and a 0.5-1mm web. The rear spar was similar in construction, with the exception of the main web, which was 0.5-0.8mm thick.

The Rohrbach-type forward and rear spar layout attached to the fuselage at FS.1 and FS.3 respectively, with each I-section spar passed between the back-to-back fuselage frames. The inboard faces of the fuselage frames were attached to the spars by four L-section box-brackets, while the outboard faces were connected to outboard webbing plate of Wing Station 2 (WS.2). In addition to these attachment fittings, a C-section bracket, attached along the top surface of FS.2 (above the wing upper skin panel, between the front and rear spars) was also riveted to the fuselage skin panels when the wing and fuselage were permanently joined.

The centre wing section contained six Wing Stations on each side of the centre line, typically spaced 250mm apart. The positioning of the spars effectively divided the wing into four rib zones, the leading edge, box-spar, aft section and flap well.

The centre wing-section to outboard wing-section, forward spar attachment fittings. The large round-headed rivets, on the wing attachment doubler-plates, were the only raised rivets found on the exterior of the Ki-15 airframe. (NII VVS via Y. Svoyski)

There were no WS.1 or WS.2 nose ribs ahead of the forward spar, as this region was within the envelope of the fuselage, but the front webbing plate at WS.2 did extend forward of the FS.1 in the form of a localized extension with an attachment eye. This is believed to be the fuselage lower load distribution path from the lower engine mounts located on FS.0, a practice entirely consistent with contemporary Japanese designs. The remainder of the wing leading edge contained three Z-section nose rib frames at **WS.3**, **WS.4**, and **WS.5**, each connected to the forward spar via Z-section stiffeners, supported by localized extensions of the chord plate at the top and bottom of the spar.

The outermost rib was **WS.6**, this C-section rib acted as both the end rib of the leading edge and the attachment frame for the forward aerodynamic wing joint fairing. Two 15 x 20 x 5mm L-section stringers supported the leading edge skin, which is thought to be 0.5mm aluminium-alloy, as per the outboard wing panels. Outboard of WS.6 the front face of the forward spar was built-up to incorporate a mounting structure for the main landing gear fittings, which was further stiffened by the outboard wing panel attachment fittings.

The upper and lower skin panels of the box-spar zone each contained a 500mm wide circular access hole, for fuel/flight control installation and maintenance. This cut-out effectively truncated **WS.1** into a forward and aft rib-let, with loads distributed through the C-section stiffener that bordered the access hole.

WS.2 was canted 15° inboard from its upper edge, to provide a primary attachment interface between the wing-to-fuselage joint. Spanning between FS.1 and FS.3, the rib was built-up from C-section formers at the (outboard) top and (inboard) lower, connected by a Z-section web and stiffened with diagonal L-section Warren-truss frames. A hole in the webbing adjacent to FS.2 accommodated the wing fuel tank inboard locator bolt.

The area between **WS.2** and **WS.6** contained the modular wing tank and was therefore devoid of truss structure. **WS.3**, **WS.4** and **WS.5** were comprised of Top hat section formers, attached to the spars with similar section stiffeners.

WS.6 was formed from box section upper and lower formers with a flanged webbing plate extending from the forward to the rear spar. The webbing plate contained an aperture into which the fuel tank could be fitted. The vertical flange on the fuel tank sat against WS.6 and was secured in place by 26 screws. Two L-section stringers were attached to the upper and lower skins, with circular inspection hatches provided (on the upper surfaces) for fuel tank system access.

The aft wing area, between the rear spar and auxiliary spar, contained no ribs at WS.1 and WS.2 as this was within the fuselage envelope, but WS.3, WS.4 and WS.5 contained L-section ribs braced with a vertical and diagonal C-section Warren truss structure. WS.6 continued the box-section end rib structure all the way back to the trailing edge of the wing, with a web and lightening hole used to stiffen the forward section, adjacent to the flap actuator arm. Two L-section stringers supported the skin panels on the upper and lower surfaces, together with inspection hatches (on the lower surfaces) for access to the flap and aileron control systems.

The centre wing section and outboard wing panels were connected via machined steel brackets located at the end of each spar. These L-section brackets, with a centralized flange, were riveted to the spar caps and localized support structure, with the flange spliced onto the spar web. An additional capping panel was also included on each spar cap for localized support. The forward attachment fittings were slightly larger than the rear fittings and also contained locator holes for the installation of the main landing gear attachment bolts. It is interesting to note that the only domed or non-flush rivets found

Just like the forward spar fittings, the centre wing-section rear spar attachment fittings were designed to be flush with the wing surface, in order for the wing joint fairing to remain flat. The outboard wing panel rear spar fitting is seen resting on top of the wing. (NII VVS via Y. Svoyski)

Wing (centre section) structure

1/48 Scale

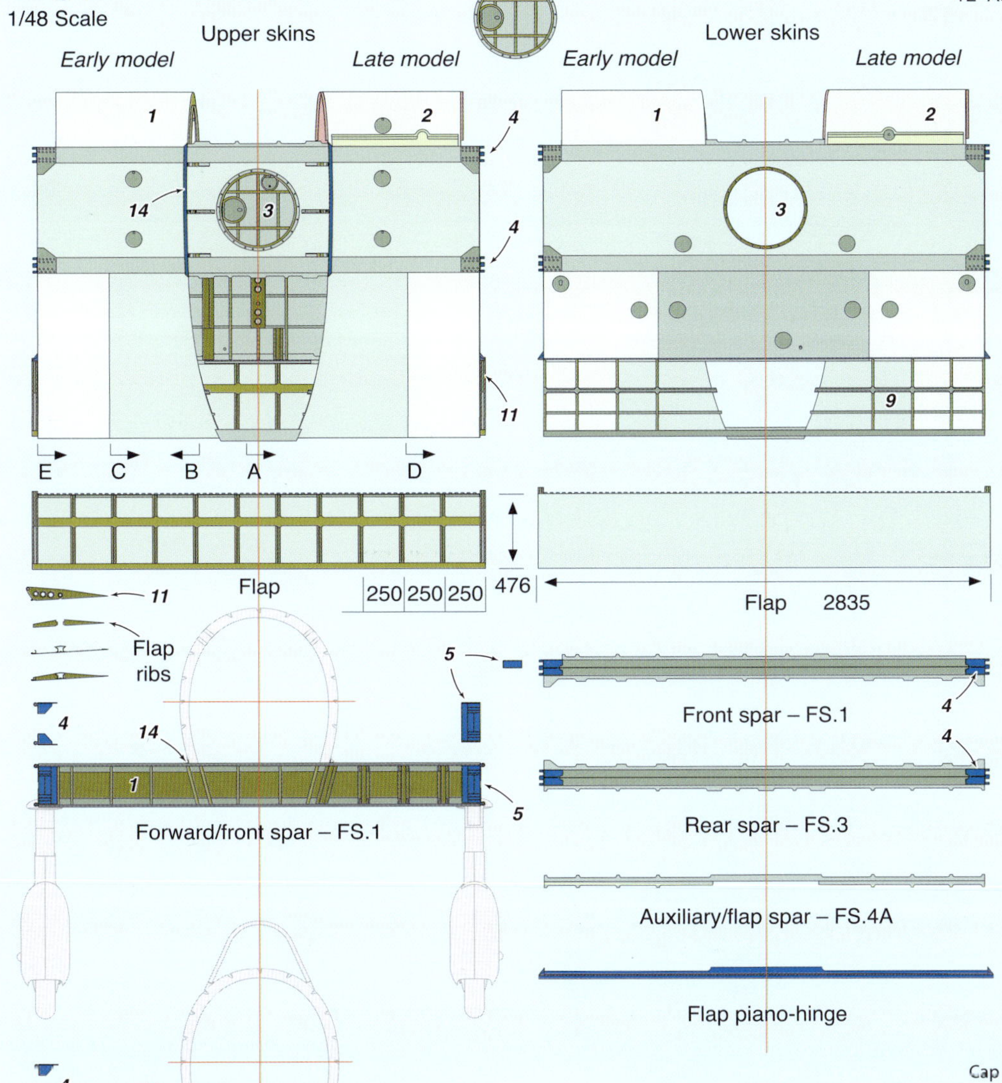

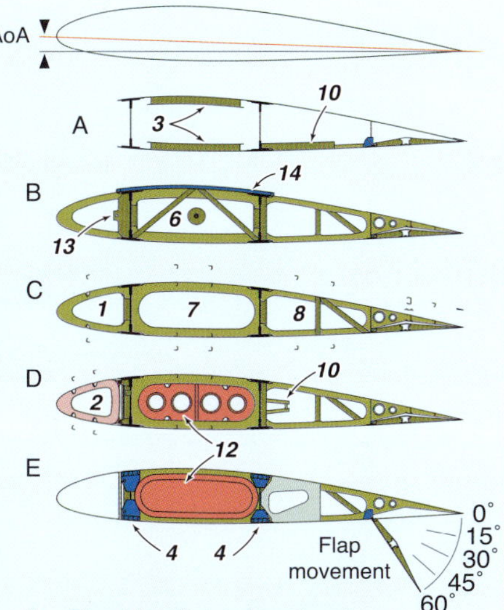

1 Fixed leading-edge structure – **initial and intermediate** fuel system
2 Leading-edge fuel tank – **standard** fuel system
3 Fuel system access hatch
4 Outboard wing attachment brackets
5 MLG attachment structure
6 **WS.2** canted frame – 15°
7 Forward and rear spar bay – Top hat section support ribs
8 Aft wing area – Warren truss structure
9 Flap well
10 Flap/aileron and systems support structure
11 Flap actuator arm end-fitting
12 Modular wing tank
13 FS.0 tie-rod attachment point
14 Wing to fuselage C-section attachment bracket zone – fitted to WS.2

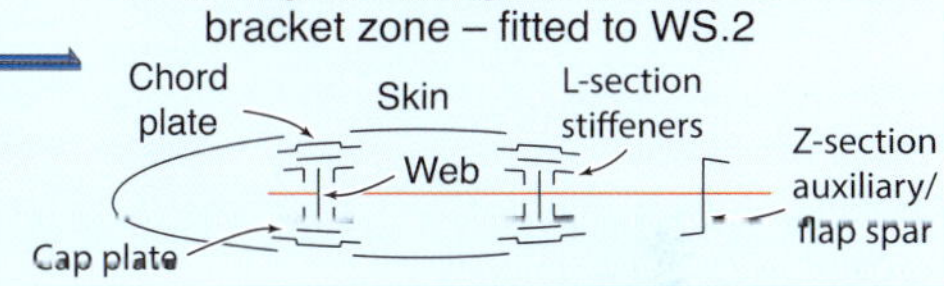

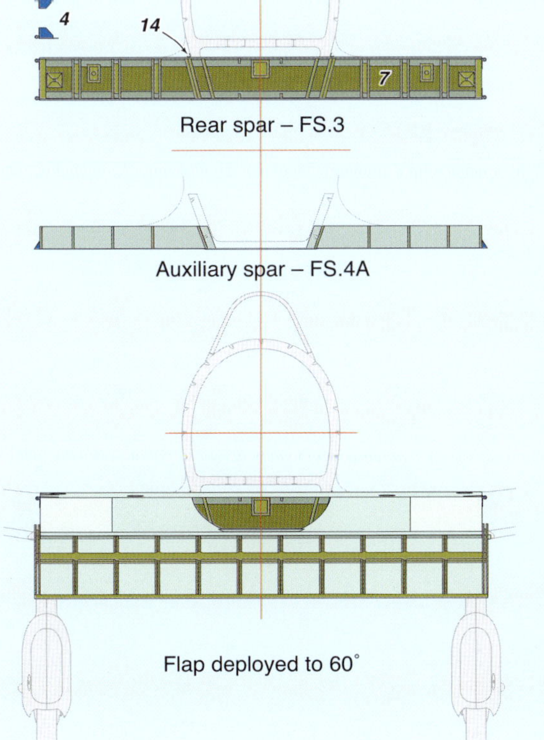

Wing stations (WS)

1/32 Scale

See fuel system for tank structure

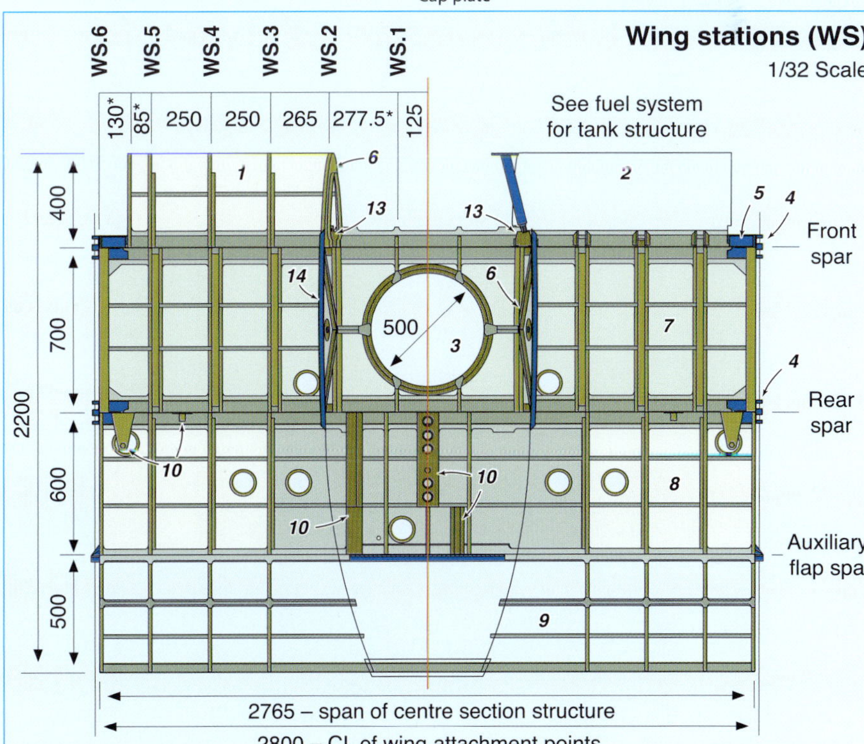

Note: Skin colours used to identify individual panels

* Estimated dimension based on CAD model

A selection of original Mitsubishi engineering and manual drawings for the Ki-15 wing.

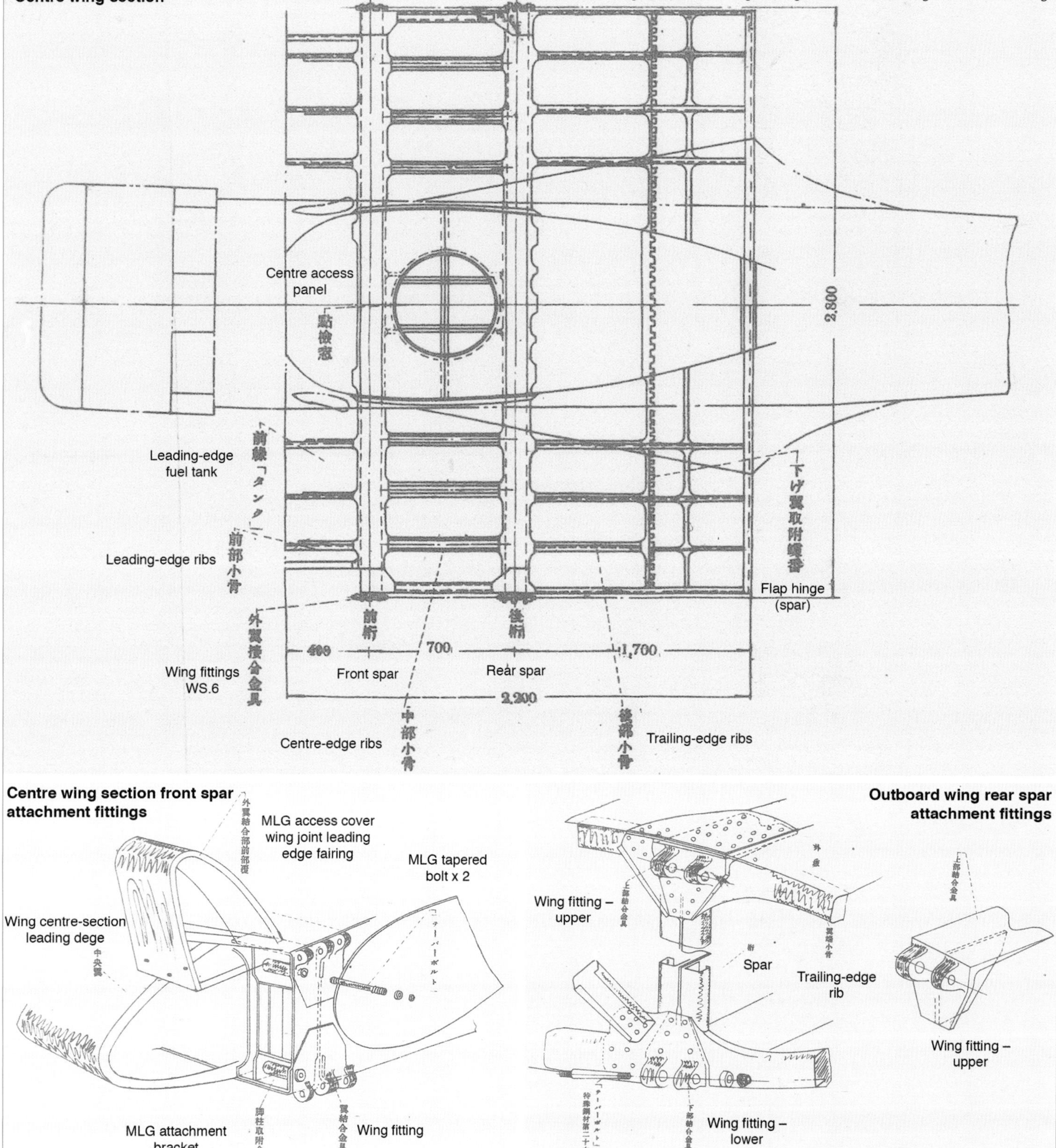

© Giuseppe Picarella 2020

on the exterior of the Ki-15 airframe were those of the wing attachment brackets and no attempt was made to fair these fittings.

The centre wing section attachment fittings each contained three attachment lugs, while the corresponding outboard wing panel contained two lugs per attachment fitting. Tapered 26mm diameter "Special steel" bolts were used to join the wing panels. Unlike similar installations on contemporary Japanese aircraft, the Ki-15s attachment fittings were designed to lie below the surface of the wing, allowing them to be totally covered by the closing fairing.

The landing flap actuator arm occupied the gap between the centre wing-section and outboard wing section. The aluminium wing structure, steel attachment fittings and flap control linkage appear to have been liberally coated with Aotake *varnish. (NII VVS via Y. Svoyski)*

The auxiliary spar was a forward-facing Z-section frame designed to provide a ridged mounting surface for the landing flap. As the spar passed through the fuselage envelope at FS.4A, its lower forward flange was enlarged and elongated to better distribute loads to that frame. The lower edge of the spar carried a full span (2,800mm) piano hinge for mounting the split-type landing flap.

The flap well contained C-section formers on its upper section, at WS.3, WS.4 and WS.5, with a single L-section stringer supporting the upper skin panels. A full width, V-section stiffener completed the trailing edge of the centre wing section and also provided a mounting interface for the lower wing-to-fuselage fairing. A welded bracket was located outboard of WS.6, in the space between the centre wing section and outboard wing section, which acted as the outboard hinge fittings for the flap.

Landing flap

The span of the landing flap was slightly wider than the centre wing section at 2, 835mm, as it partially bridged the gap between the centre wing section and outer wing panels. It was 476mm deep and the leading edge contained a piano hinge, sandwiched between an L-section stringer and the 0.6mm aluminium-alloy skin panel, while the trailing edge was fitted with a V-section stiffener. A box-section spar with an intricately pressed "mushroom-section" profile, with flanged edges, and a lower capping plate spanned the flap at its midpoint. The flap included 12 station points, positioned broadly inline with those of the centre wing section. Ten of the Z-section ribs were produced in two halves, each forward section located in front of the spar, with the rear section located aft of it. The ribs were further supported by localized extensions on the upper capping plates. The two outboard ribs were of a box-section construction, with two C-section frames sitting back-to-back. The leading edge of each arm extended forward and above the hinge line of the flap to act as an actuator arm fitting.

Outboard wing panels

The 4,600mm span outboard wing panel (measured through the CL of the wing mounting bracket eyes, adjacent to the "mean camber line", inboard of WS.7) continued the same basic construction methods of the centre wing section, with a chord of 2,200mm at the wing joint and 1,100mm at WS.23. The spars were located 400mm and 1,100mm from the leading edge at WS.7, diminishing to 200mm and 560mm at WS.23. Set with a dihedral of 8°, measured through the centreline of the spar, the wing thickness reduced from 300mm at WS.7, down to 100mm at WS.23. The leading edge of the wing was swept back at 8.5°, while the trailing edge of the wing was swept forward at 7.15°.

It is interesting to note that, due to the high-speed nature of the Ki-15's role, the aircraft did not receive Mitsubishi's new leading edge wash-out design.

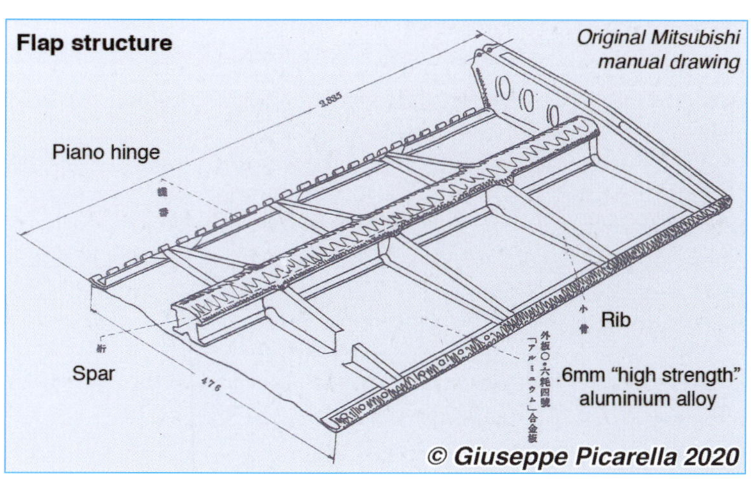

A rare photograph of Ki-15 with the landing flap in the down position.

While this cutting-edge technology would have vastly improved landing performance, it would also have impacted upon the maximum speed. Such a drop in high-speed performance would have been unacceptable for the design team, so the wing retained its 2° angle of attack across its entire span, at the expense of poor stall characteristics throughout the operational career of the *Babs*.

From the machined steel mounting brackets at **WS.7**, the forward and rear I-section spars were swept back at 5.75° and .65° respectively, with the auxiliary (aileron) C-section spar swept forward at 4.65°. There were 19 ribs in each outboard wing panel, spanning **WS.7** through **WS.25**. In general the leading-edge (nose) ribs (ahead of the forward spar) were of Z-section aluminium-alloy construction, attached to the spar webs by Z-section stiffeners, which typically took the form of shaped formers, both with or without intercostal stiffeners. Two L-section stringers were included to stiffen the skin panels between WS.7 and WS.23.

The area between the forward and rear spar contained a Warren-truss type structure, constructed from Z-section formers on the top and bottom skins, with tubes used as trusses. The 12mm diameter high strength aluminium-alloy tubes, with a wall thickness of .4mm, were squeezed together at each end to provide a mounting surface on the formers. The truss and formers were attached to the spars with Z-section stiffeners and bracket plates supported by localized chord-plate extensions. Four L-section stringers were included to provide support for the skin panels. The ribs between the rear spar and auxiliary spar utilised C-section trusses. In point of fact, WS.7 was slightly different to the other ribs in the outboard wing panel as it contained box-section upper and lower formers between the spars, similar to WS.6, plus a pressed C-section aft assembly, complete with lightening holes. These modifications allowed sufficient area to attach the centre wing section-to-outboard wing panel fairing.

Measured from the intersection line between the centre wing section and outboard wing panel, WS.8 was located approximately 232.5mm outboard of WS.7, from which point the ribs were spaced 250mm apart through to WS.23. Ribs WS.7 through WS.11 were all of full-chord design, with trailing edge ribs and V-section stiffener, but the ribs located between WS.11 and WS.23 all terminated at the auxiliary spar. Aft of the auxiliary spar were three aileron hinge brackets (spaced 1,250mm apart) plus eight rib-lets to support the extended upper skin panel.

WS.23 was a full-chord rib and outboard of this point WS.24 and WS.25 were spaced 215mm and 200mm apart respectively. It is likely that the shallow nature of the wingtip structure would have rendered these three ribs of solid design, with lightening holes. Also, the modified skin panels and chord-plates, located between WS.22 and WS.25, indicate that the I-section spars transformed into C-section spars at WS.24 and terminated at WS.25, from which point a pressed aluminium rib carried the load of the wingtip skins.

There were few apertures or external fittings in the outboard wing panels. A conformal landing light installation was included in the leading edge of the Port wing, between WS.9 and WS.10, and a pitot tube was installed outboard of WS.15. On the lower surface of the wing, a narrow tie-down eye was fitted to the forward face of the rear spar between WS.17 and WS.18, and two aileron control system

Wing (outboard panel) stucture

1/48 Scale

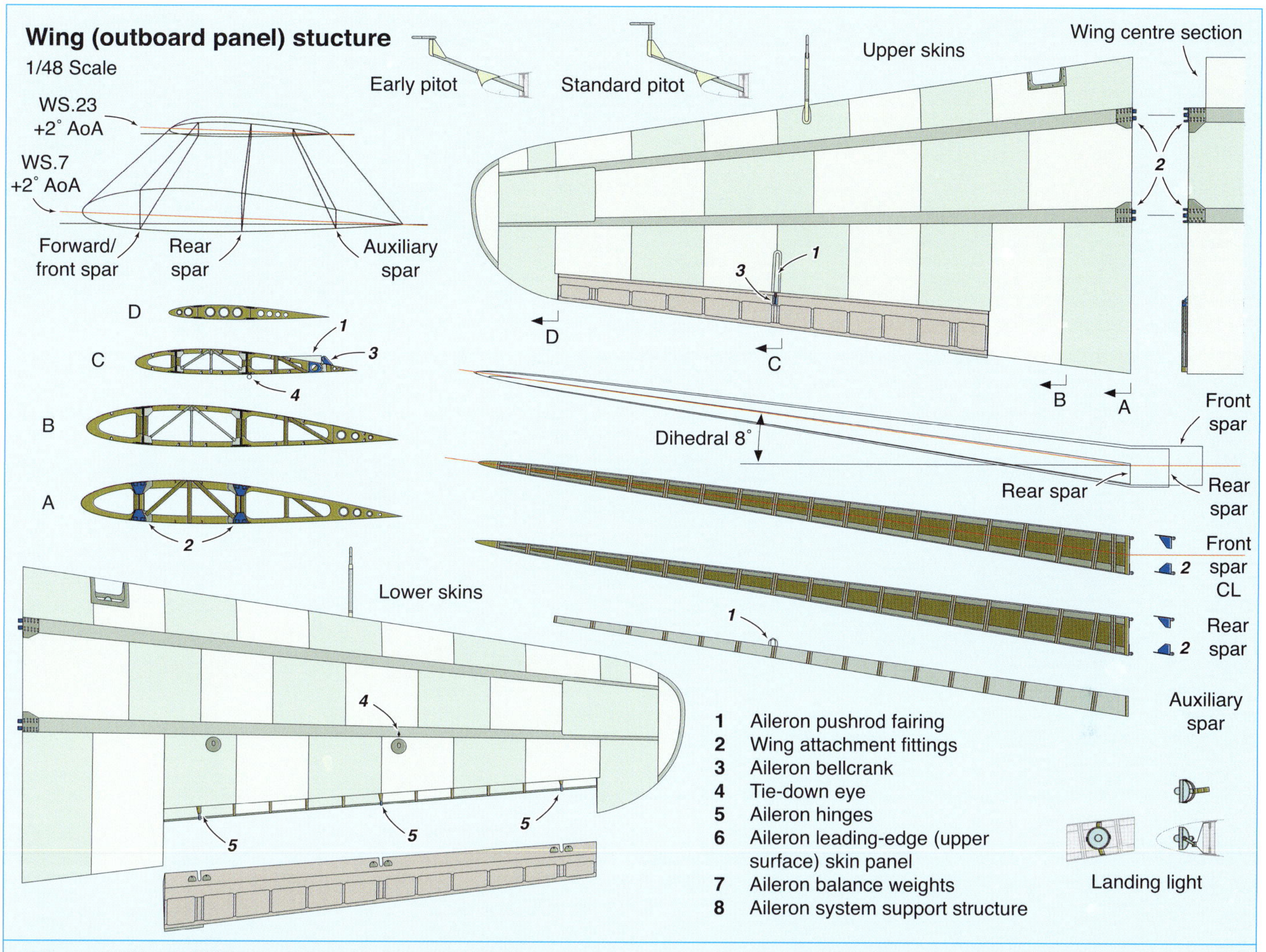

Wing stations (WS) – shown in true plan form

1/32 Scale

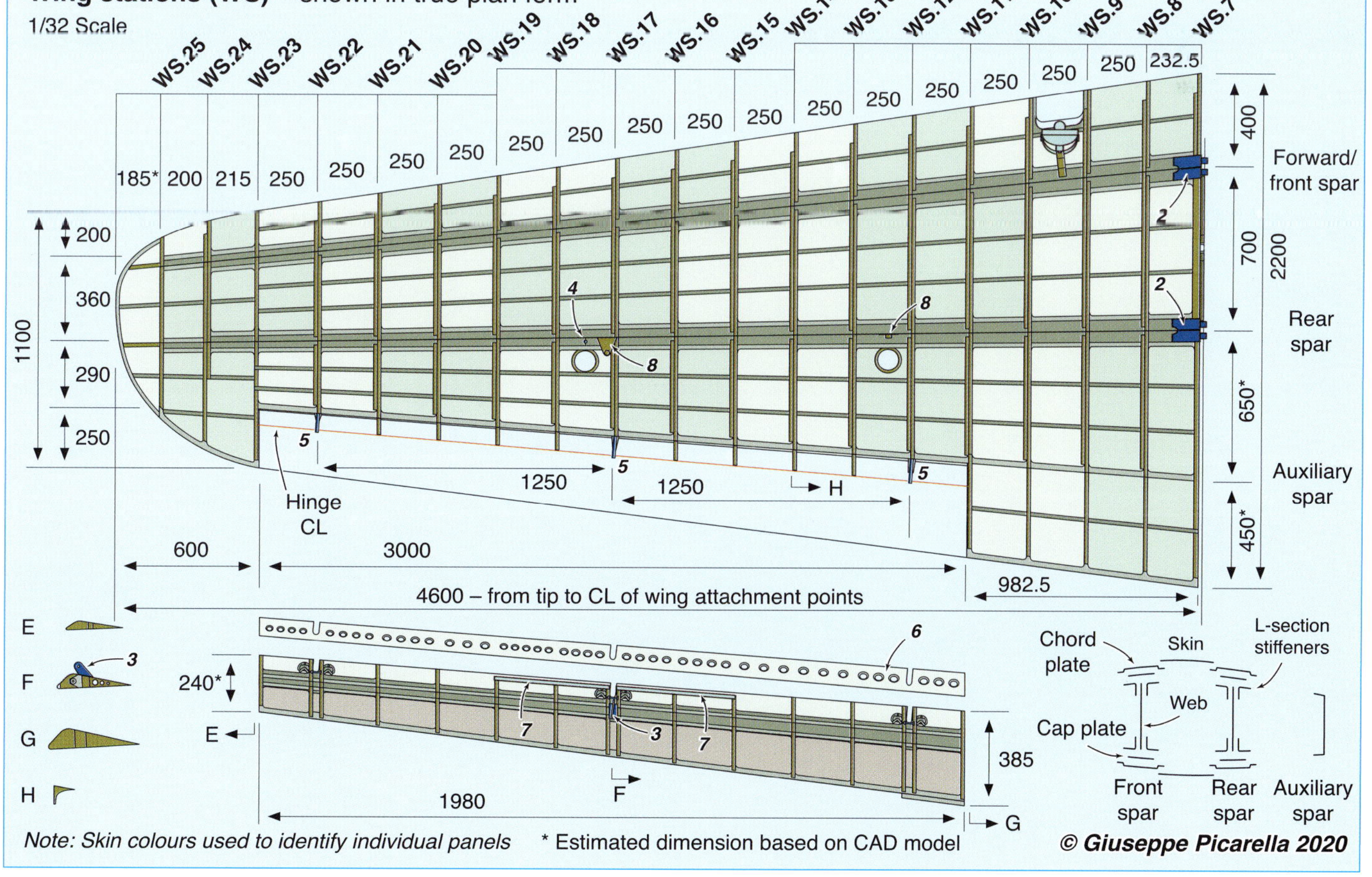

Note: Skin colours used to identify individual panels * Estimated dimension based on CAD model

Outboard wing station (WS) drawing

A selection of original Mitsubishi engineering and manual drawings for the Ki-15 wing.

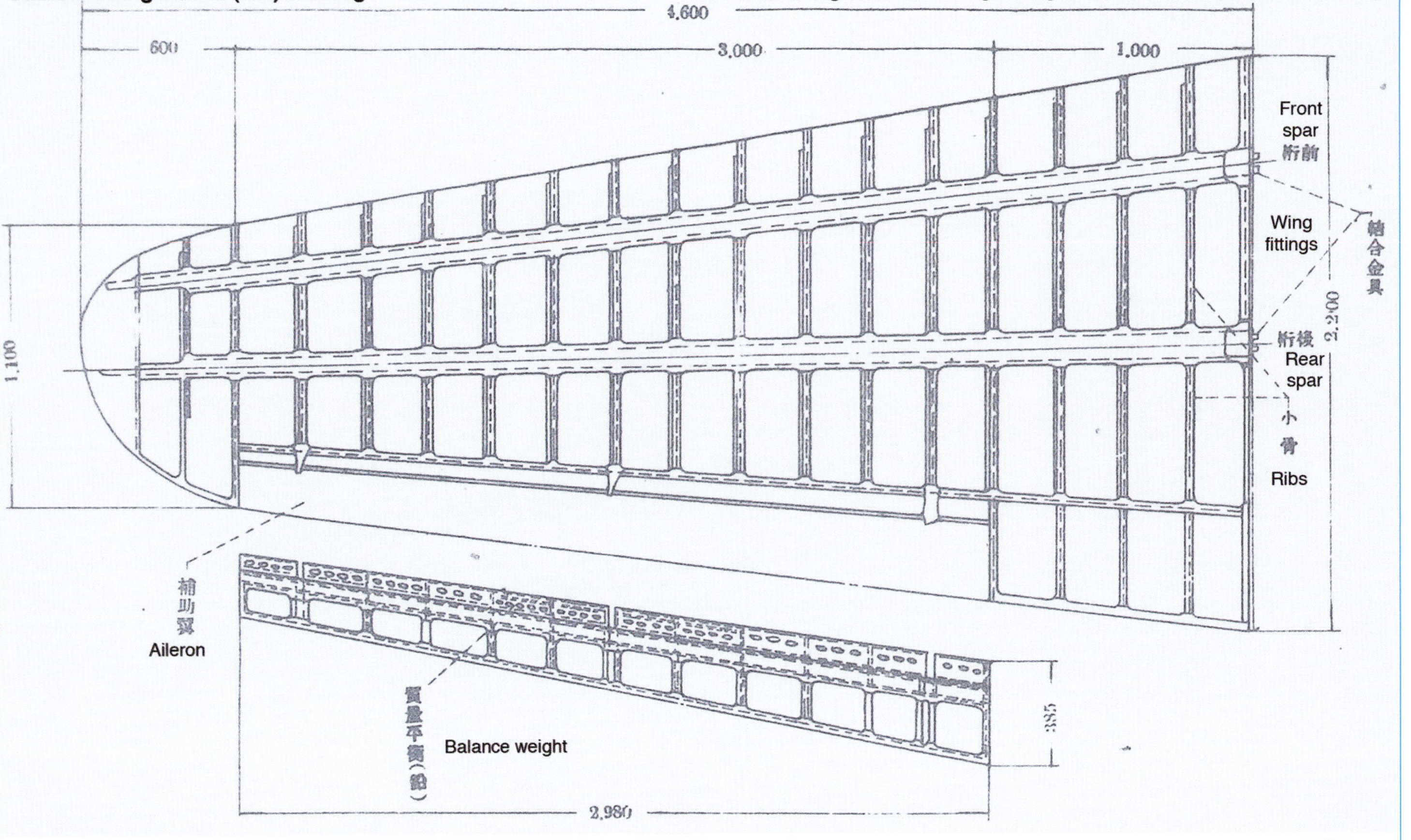

Outboard wing structure

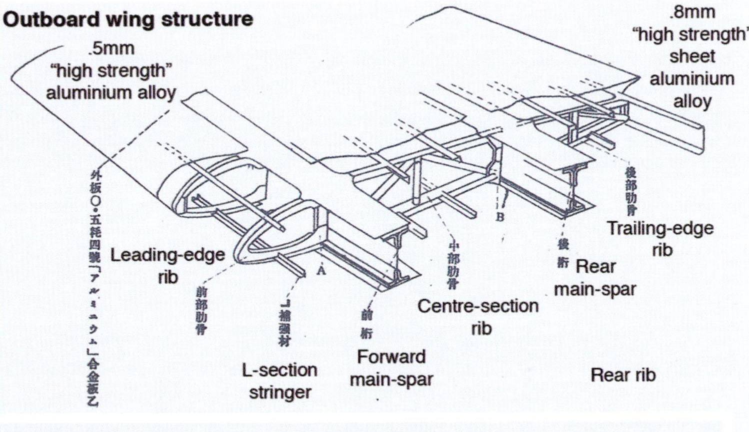

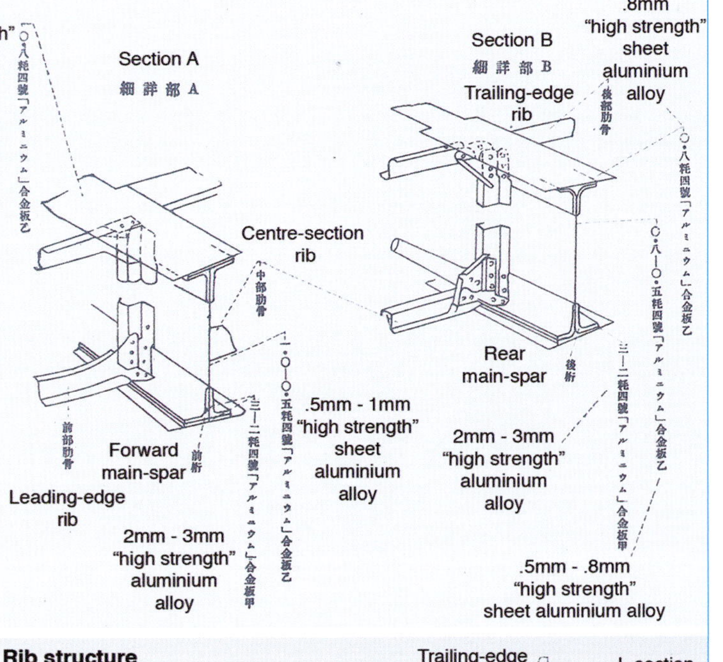

Aileron structure

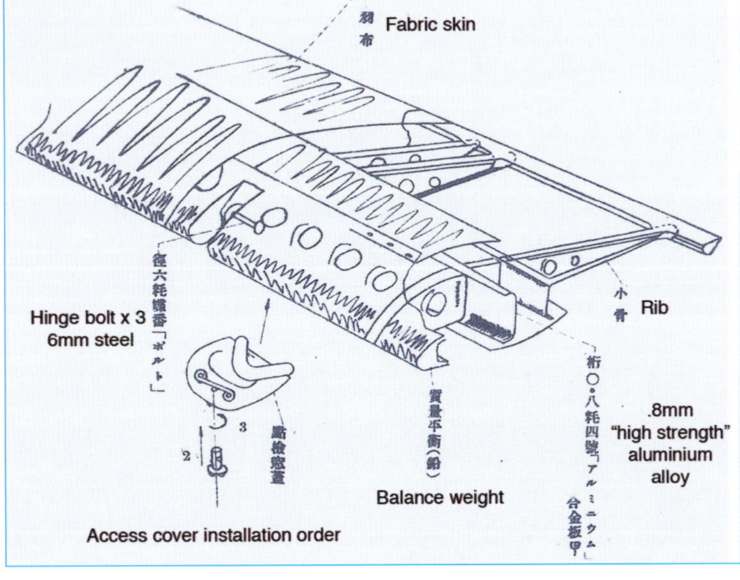

Rib structure

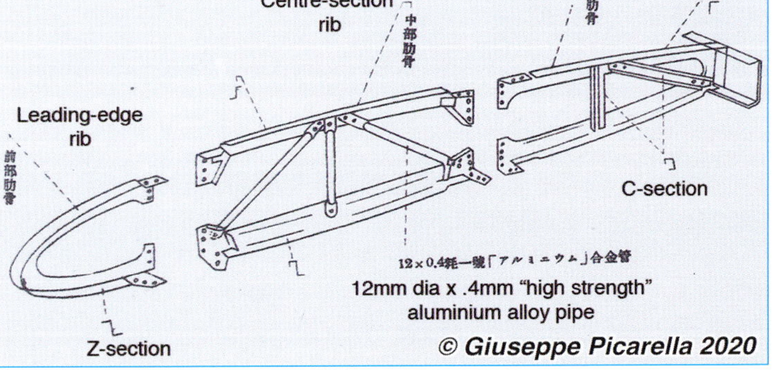

access panels located aft of the rear spar. The upper surface contained an aileron pushrod opening and fairing inboard of WS.17.

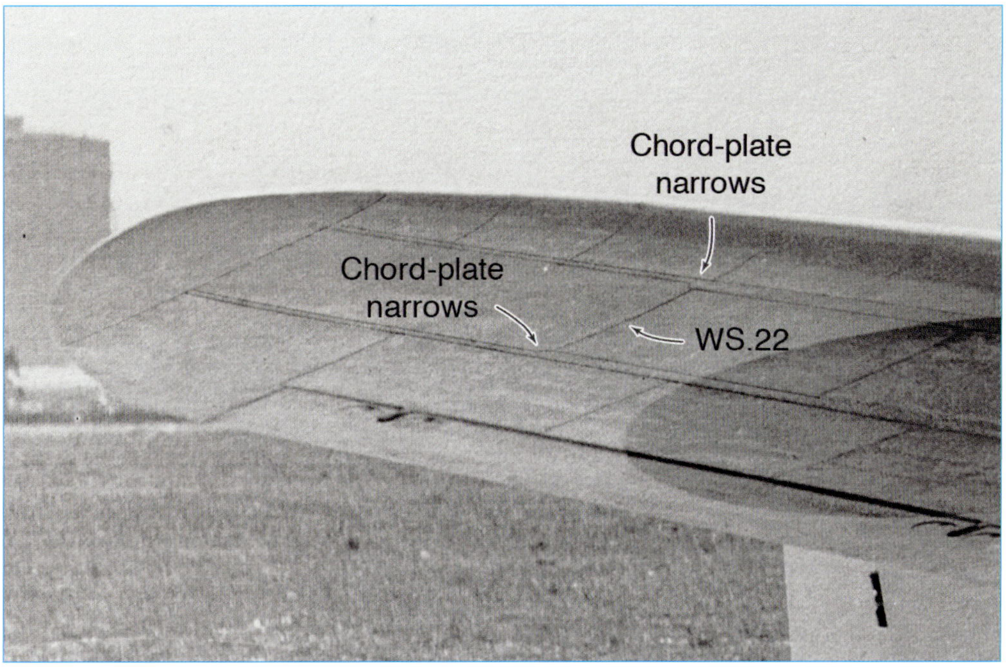

The construction of the wing spars was lightened towards the wingtip, resulting in narrower chord-plates between WS.22 and WS.25. This resulted in wider centre skin panels between the spars.

Ailerons

The aileron was approximately 2,980 wide with a 385mm chord at the inboard edge. Constructed of aluminium-alloy with an Irish linen covering, the ailerons were of similar design to the other flying surfaces, with a box-spar comprised of two, back-to-back, C-section frames of 0.8mm high strength aluminium-alloy and closing skin panels. Ahead of the box-spar construction were 13 nose ribs (arranged to align with WS.11 through WS.23) and three hinges contained within the leading edge skin panels, with cut-outs adjacent to the hinge points. The leading edge skin panel contained additional lightening holes on their upper surfaces, which were hidden by the linen covering. Two C-section stiffeners were installed in the leading edge skin panel between WS.15 and WS.19, which acted as the attachment surfaces for the aileron balance weights. Aft of the spar, 13 C-section main ribs (with integral lightening holes and rib-stitching eyelets) were aligned to the match the leading edge ribs.

Aileron ribs **WS.12**, **WS.17** and **WS.22** were double ribs, positioned back to back to act as localized support for the hinges. To allow for access to the aileron installation, two access panels were installed adjacent to each 6mm hinge bolt. Located on the lower surface of the aileron, these aluminium-alloy panels were pulled flush to the surface with the aid of locator lugs and a Dzus-type fastener.

Aileron rib **WS.17** also contained the aileron horn fitting on its upper surface.

A closing strip, most likely made of wood, was installed at the lower trailing edge of the auxiliary spar, between **WS.11** and **WS.23**. This would have been closely fitted to sit just ahead of the leading edge of the ailerons.

The gaps between the aileron end-ribs and the opposing trailing-edge wing ribs were kept within a 10mm tolerance.

An interesting photograph of the underside of the Kallang Ki-15-II. This image shows many of the under-wing and fairing access panels, some of which are still unopened (items 1), plus the trailing antenna down-tube (item 2). (Darryl Ford)

Aileron tab

As with the ground adjustable trim tab fitted to the rudder, early Ki-15s were devoid of these fitting, but received them as production progressed. The tabs were fitted to the trailing edge of the aileron, spanning from WS.11 to the outboard rib of WS.12. The tab was made of aluminium-alloy and was easily adjusted with a pair of pliers.

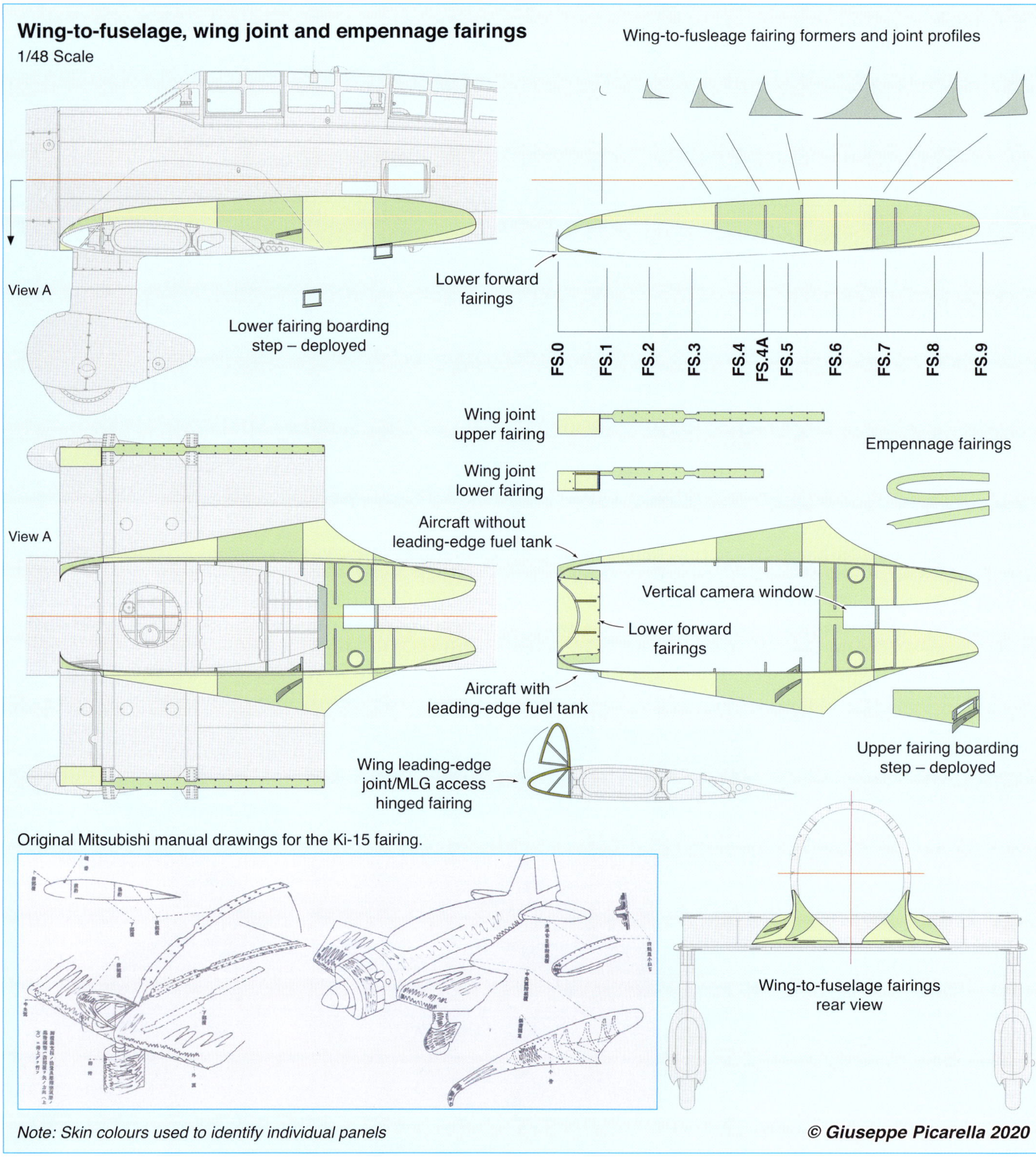

Fuselage and wing fairings

Two types of fairing were fitted to the Ki-15 wing, a wing-to-fuselage fairing and a centre wing section to outboard wing panel closing fairing.

The wing-to-fuselage fairing delicately blended the wing into the oval-section fuselage frames, extending from the extreme leading edge of the wing, adjacent to FS.0, back to a point midway between FS.8 and FS.9. The fairings were divided into 4 sections on each side of the fuselage, with a fixed aft assembly passing under the rear fuselage. The detachable front section was screwed into location between FS.0 and the front frame of FS.1. The remain three side panels were also screwed into position, with the forward panel extending from FS.1 to aft of FS.3, the middle panel from aft of FS.3 to aft of FS.5 and the rear panel from aft of FS.5 to just ahead of FS.7. The fixed (riveted) aft assembly not only faired the wing's upper surface into the fuselage sides, it also provided a flat surface, aft of the landing flap zone, for the installation of the ventral camera window. Six aluminium-alloy formers supported the fairings on both sides of the fuselage, with the port side formers providing localized support structure for the pull-out and pull-down boarding steps. No detail survives for the layout of these formers with regards to lightening holes, etc. The single-piece leading edge fairings extend forward, from above the front spar, to the same position below the wing. Bridging the two leading-edge fairings was the two-piece lower forward fairing. This fairing blended the profile of the forward fuselage fairings at FS.0, into the flat underside of the wing, just in front of the centre wing section front spar, with the aid of 12 Dzus-type fasteners.

The centre wing section-to-outboard wing panel closing fairing bridged the gap between WS.6 and WS.7. Unlike contemporary wing joint fairings, the Ki-15 fairing was designed to fit totally flush with the wing surface, due to the design of the wing attachment fittings. The fairing was divided into three sections, an articulated leading edge section and upper and lower fixed sections. The leading edge section was shaped to match nose ribs of the wing leading edge, but could be hinged upwards to allow access to the main landing gear (MLG) and brake fittings. The fairing was attached to a piano hinge located on the leading edge of the forward spar upper chord-plate. Its profile was stiffened with diagonal braces and the whole unit was locked into position by three screws on the MLG fairing. The upper fairing spanned the wing gap from the forward spar back to the trailing edge and was screwed into place along WS.6 and WS.7. Small cut-outs were included in the fairings to allow them to sit absolutely flush with the spar end capping panels. The lower panel mirrored the upper panel, but only extended back to the landing flap hinge.

Landing gear

The Ki-15 was designed at a time of great change within the aeronautical industry and the development of landing gear highlighted the technological problems that were beginning to be encountered by designers all around the world. While fully retractable landing gear was the aerodynamicist's ultimate goal, the fact was that contemporary retractable assemblies were heavy, bulky and unreliable. These installations typically required thicker, heavier wings, together with the inclusion of complex hydraulic, electrical or manual retraction mechanisms, all of which impacted upon the aircraft's performance. While the fixed 3-point undercarriage arrangement may have looked outdated by 1935, Masakichi Mizuno had in fact developed the most efficient design solution for the Ki-15's very rigid performance specifications. Balancing available engine output, weight, drag, range and (perhaps most importantly) fuel capacity, Mizuno's calculations demonstrated that a fixed and closely "spatted" oleo-pneumatic main landing gear (MLG) would best suit the Ki-15 design.

Below, left: This main landing gear installation is still attached to a section of the front wing spar aircraft C/n181 (81st). (NII VVS via Y. Svoyski)

Below: Main landing gear upper attachment fittings. (NII VVS via Y. Svoyski)

Another interesting insight into this period of aeronautical design is highlighted by the fact that the initial drawings of the Ki-15 displayed a tailskid arrangement instead of a tailwheel. Times were rapidly changing and one "new" modification could have far reaching effect on other aspects of the design. As aircraft engines became more powerful, maximum take-off weights increased, runways became longer and began to be paved. The age of the tailskid was drawing to a close.

Main landing gear

Each of the MLG legs included an oleo-pneumatic main leg, fork fitting and Bendix-type wheel assembly. The main leg incorporated a machined steel casing (painted black) and oleo shock strut. The upper end of the oleo cas-

ing incorporated four machined attachment lugs that were attached to the MLG attachment structure incorporated into the forward spar, outboard of WS.6. Fully extended, the whole unit was 804mm long, from the top of the leg to the fork fitting, with a maximum piston stroke (compression) of 150mm. The wheelbase was 2690mm wide. In order to pressurize the oleo, an air valve was located on the upper section of the oleo casing, inboard of the attachment lugs. When installed on the forward spar, the MLG leg was canted aft at 3.33° with the lower end of the shock strut fitted into a receptacle in the top of the fork fitting, and retained by a tapered bolt. The hollow fork fittings were fabricated out of pressed and welded sheet steel. Landing gear fairing attachment fittings were located up both sides of the flat-sided fork, which measured 475mm in length from the top of the fitting to the CL of the wheel axle holes. The axle holes were strengthened with steel doubler-plates, with the inboard plate containing four bolts for the attachment of the fixed drum brake assembly. Fairing attachment fittings also extended below the axles, with small lightening holes machined into these fittings. A tie-down fitting was incorporated on the inboard section of the axle, while the outboard end contained a grease fitting for axle lubrication.

The wheels were kept as narrow as was practical, in order to fit within the streamlined spats, with the "high pressure" tyres measuring 750mm x 125mm. The tyres contained inner tubes.

Brakes

As with all tailwheel aircraft, the braking system on the Ki-15 performed both braking and steering functions. The Bendix-type, Bowden-cable operated differential brakes were controlled by pedals located on the rudder bar. The actuation cables ran through shrouds below the cockpit floor to the front face of the forward spar, where brass cable guides directed them to each undercarriage leg. A 90° bellcrank at the top of each leg redirected the cable down to another shroud and end fitting on the inboard side of the undercarriage fork, to the drum-brake lever. No parking brake system was installed on the aircraft.

The highly streamlined main landing gear fairing reduced drag and removed the need for a heavy retractable landing gear installation. (Japan Aeronautical Association)

The tailwheel was comprised of a lower yoke fitting and upper shock strut installation. (NII VVS via Y. Svoyski)

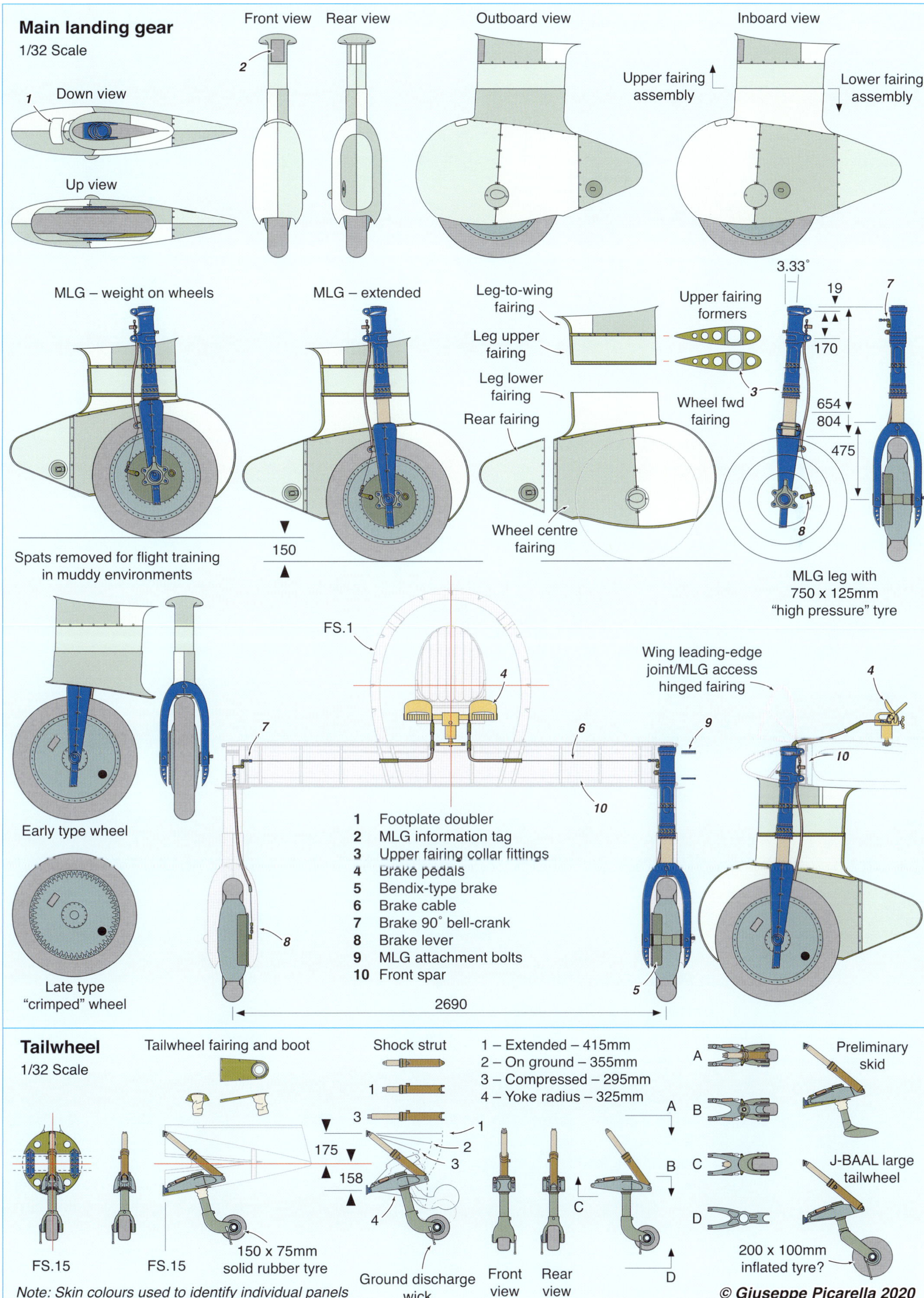
Main landing gear
1/32 Scale
Front view
Rear view
Outboard view
Inboard view
Down view
Up view
Upper fairing assembly
Lower fairing assembly
MLG – weight on wheels
MLG – extended
Leg-to-wing fairing
Leg upper fairing
Leg lower fairing
Rear fairing
Upper fairing formers
Wheel fwd fairing
Wheel centre fairing
3.33°
19
170
654
804
475
150
Spats removed for flight training in muddy environments
MLG leg with 750 x 125mm "high pressure" tyre
FS.1
Wing leading-edge joint/MLG access hinged fairing
Early type wheel
Late type "crimped" wheel
1 Footplate doubler
2 MLG information tag
3 Upper fairing collar fittings
4 Brake pedals
5 Bendix-type brake
6 Brake cable
7 Brake 90° bell-crank
8 Brake lever
9 MLG attachment bolts
10 Front spar
2690
Tailwheel
1/32 Scale
Tailwheel fairing and boot
Shock strut
1 – Extended – 415mm
2 – On ground – 355mm
3 – Compressed – 295mm
4 – Yoke radius – 325mm
Preliminary skid
J-BAAL large tailwheel
175
158
FS.15
FS.15
150 x 75mm solid rubber tyre
Ground discharge wick
Front view
Rear view
200 x 100mm inflated tyre?
Note: Skin colours used to identify individual panels
© Giuseppe Picarella 2020

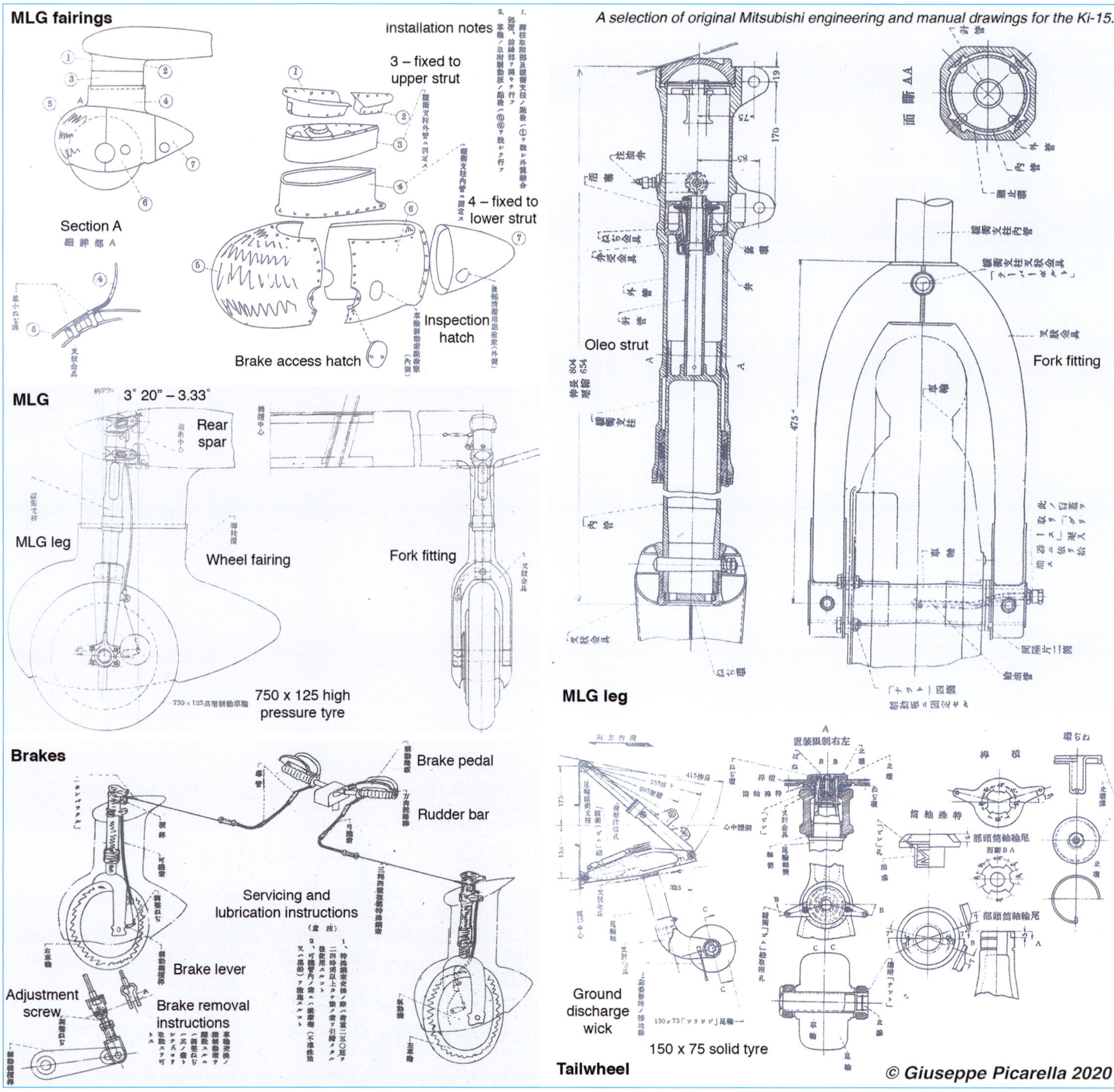

A selection of original Mitsubishi engineering and manual drawings for the Ki-15.

Main landing gear fairings

To reduce drag, Mizuno fitted a highly streamlined fairing or "spat" to each of the legs. The aluminium-alloy structure was divided into two main assemblies, a fixed upper section, and an articulated lower section.

The upper section was dived into two groupings, the leg upper fairing and the leg-to-wing fairing. The streamlined leg upper fairing was attached to the top of the MLG cylinder by an internal rib and collar fitting. This fixed fairing was blended into the lower wing with the aid of the two-piece leg-to-wing fairing.

The articulated lower fairings were comprised of a wheel fairing assembly and a leg lower fairing. The wheel fairing was a three-piece assembly with a forward, centre and rear section. The flat-sided forward and centre fairings contained beaded edges along their bottom apertures, while the rear fairing streamlined and terminated the whole assembly. The wheel fairing contained four access panels, one on each side of the axle CL. The outboard access panels featuring a teardrop fairing over the axle grease fitting and an inspection panel in the rear fairing, while the inboard access panels covered the MLG tie-down fitting and brake lever. The forward, centre and leg lower fairing were attached to a mounting frame, which was fixed to the shoulders and side forks of the MLG, all of which could telescope

(150mm) up and down over the leg upper fairing, as the MLG oleo strut was compressed and extended during taxiing. All fairing surfaces were flush fitted and secured with countersunk screws. Early in production it was found that ground-crew had a tendency to use the front of the wheel fairing as a step up to the wing, so a square footplate panel was added to the top of the fairing to reduce damage.

Tailwheel

The tailwheel assembly was comprised of a main yoke, oleo shock strut, fully castoring leg and tyre. The Y-shaped main yoke assembly was fabricated from cast and machined aluminium-alloy and painted grey-green. It was attached to mounting brackets located on the lower section of FS.15. The lower end of the shock strut attached to the tail of the main yoke, with its upper end fitted into a mounting bracket on the upper section of FS.15. This installation acted as a damped A-frame, with the oleo stroke ranging from 295mm at it maximum compression through to 415mm with no load, and 355mm under normal load.

The tailwheel leg passed through the main yoke and was fitted with a cast aluminium-alloy fork fitting, which contained a ground discharge wick on the port side. A wheel and solid rubber tyre (150mm x 75mm) completed the assembly.

The fully castoring tailwheel was fitted with a spring-loaded upper friction plate, fitted with a preset detent, with two bungee cords holding the tailwheel inline with the fuselage during take-off and landing. The use of brakes or rudder during taxiing produced sideways pressure on the tailwheel, allowing it to slip the detent and castor freely.

A canvas boot was fitted between the tailwheel leg and fuselage to keep dirt and debris out of the tailcone assembly.

Powerplant

Kouno's decision to select an engine of lower horsepower than that specified by the Army was bold to say the least, but wind tunnel testing had shown that the lighter 550hp Army Type-94 (Ha-8) nine-cylinder single-row radial engine would be better suited to the planned airframe. Built by Nakajima and identified under its designation system as the NAP (Nakajima – N, air-cooled – A, model P), the *Hikari* or "Splendour" engine would become a reliable and much respected powerplant, but the true development story of the Ha-8 is a little more convoluted. Initially conceived as an scaled-up development of the NAH *Kotobuki* or "Congratulations" engine, elements of the larger NAP design drew inspiration from the front section of the Wright R-1820 Cyclone, so when the engine was chosen for mass production (in the Nakajima Army Type-94 Reconnaissance Aircraft or Ki-4), the Army instructed Nakajima to acquire the regional production rights for the R-1820, which it did in late 1934. Following this acquisition, the engine was reworked during 1935 to include additional R-1820 details, but was never copied directly.

The Nakajima Ha-8 engine was ideally suited to the Ki-15 airframe, with the installation delicately faired into the profile of the airframe. Aircraft C/n131 (31st airframe) is seen being maintained at Kagamigahara airfield, of note are the engine mount, the rarely seen lower carburettor (at the bottom) and the bifurcated carburettor intake extending forwards between cylinders No3 and No.4. Note that the oil tank of this early machine appears to have been painted Aotake. (Kakamigahara Aerospace Science Museum)

Initially known as the 550hp Army Type-94 (Ha-8), this designation was retrospectively amended to the 550hp Army Type-94 Model-I (Ha-8-I) after Nakajima developed the Army Type-94 Model-II (Ha-8-II) engine. To add further confusion, several versions (and subtypes) of the Army Type-94 engine were developed and produced. Some utilised a downdraught carburettor intake, located at the top of the engine rear casing, while others had an updraught carburettor located at the

The bifurcated carburettor intakes are clearly shown in the head-on view of Kamikaze*. The component located between the lower cylinders is the oil system scavenge pump. (Japan Aeronautical Association)*

Damaged airframe C/n181 shows the engine accessory bay to perfection. The engine mount was attached directly to FS.0, with the secondary firewall joggled around the anti-vibration fittings. Below the oil tank is the electrical system voltage regulator (left) and the battery mount (right). The Secondary firewall is dark Aotake, the engine mount is satin black and oil tank is fabric covered and sealed with aluminium dope. (NII VVS via Y. Svoyski)

bottom of the casing. The engine installed in production Ki-15-I airframes was the 550hp Type-94-I (Mk.2) (Ha-8-I Mk.2), which should not be confused with the Hikari-I-*Kai* or Type-94-II (Ha-8-II)!

It incorporated an updraught carburettor at BDC (unlike the Cyclone), an inertia starter on the aft thrust-line of the accessory casing, magnetos on either side of the starter, a generator at the top of the casing and a vacuum pump.

The engine could be started by the either the inertia-starter, via a removable starter handle, or a "Hucks" type starter vehicle. The starter handle was inserted in the port side lower forward fuselage fairing. The engine casing was painted medium grey-blue and the cylinders were gloss black.

The starter ignition system included twin magnetos, an inertia generator, an isolator switch/cock, an ignition switch and a "Starter generator-operating device" or manual inertial magneto. The "Starter generator-operating device" was located in the centre wing section, aft of the front spar on WS.1, and was accessible via the fuel system access hatch on the lower surface of the wing. The device consisted of an electric coil, driven by a spring-loaded mechanism, which was wound-up by pulling the "starter handle" on the right-hand side of the lower instrument panel. When operated (released), the unwinding action of the unit caused the electrical coil to generated a spark for the magnetos, while simultaneously retracting the starter cable and handle back into the instrument panel.See Chapter 5, **Pilots operating manual.**

Nakajima 550hp Army Type-94-I/Ha-8-I/*Hikari*-I (Mk.2) specifications

Rated power	550hp
Compression ratio	5.6
Capacity	32.6 litres
RPM	1,900
Bore/stroke	160/180mm
Length	1,245mm
Height	1,354mm
Width	1,354mm
Weight	420kg

The Nr.293 propeller installation of the Ki-15-I carried the engraving "Type-97 "Top Secret" airscrew". (NII VVS via Y. Svoyski)

Carburettor intakes and dust screens

The carburettor fitted to the Ha-8-I engine could be fed via two intake systems – a single lower unit or a bifurcated upper installation. The purpose of these individual intake systems is unknown, but it likely to be heating or power/speed related. Possibly the lower main intake was used when carb-heating was required, as the ram-air had to pass between the warm cylinders of the engine in order to enter the intake, while the upper bifurcated intakes were used when the aircraft was travelling at high speed or at high power settings? The carburettor was fitted with a pilot-operated manifold boost control, which allowed the aneroid controlled intake to override the rated altitude limiter, so it is conceivable that this control opened both carburettor intake systems at the same time?

The main (lower) carburettor air-intake was located out of sight – BDC behind the engine's lowest two cylinders (No.5/No.6). In this location the intake was exposed to the airstream, but also shielded by the engine cylinders and Townend ring assembly. The only surviving photograph of the lower intake seems to include a particle filter, as would be expected.

The (upper) bifurcated ram-air intakes protruded forward of the engine face, between cylinders No.3/No.4 on the left-hand side and No.7/No.8 on the right-hand side. Each intake was protected by a wire mesh and natural sponge particle filter, and was routed aft through the forward firewall before merging into a combined intake chamber located just ahead of and slightly below the carburettor.

A drain line was fitted to the base of the combined intake chamber to remove any fuel or water that collected at this point.

Engine mount

The engine-mounting frames used by the *Babs* family of aircraft were of contemporary design, constructed of welded molybdenum-steel tubing, webbing plates, mounting ring and machined attachment fittings. This structure distributed the load of the engine from the mounting ring (640mm forward of FS.0), aft along eight convergent tubes to four transverse attachment bolts and brackets located at FS.0, which distributed the load of the engine along lateral longerons and fuselage frames.

Nakajima 550hp Army Type-94-I/Ha-8-I/Hikari-I engine

1/32 Scale

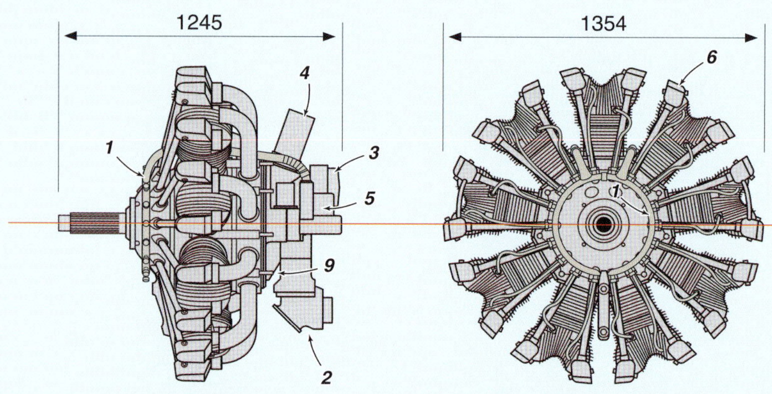

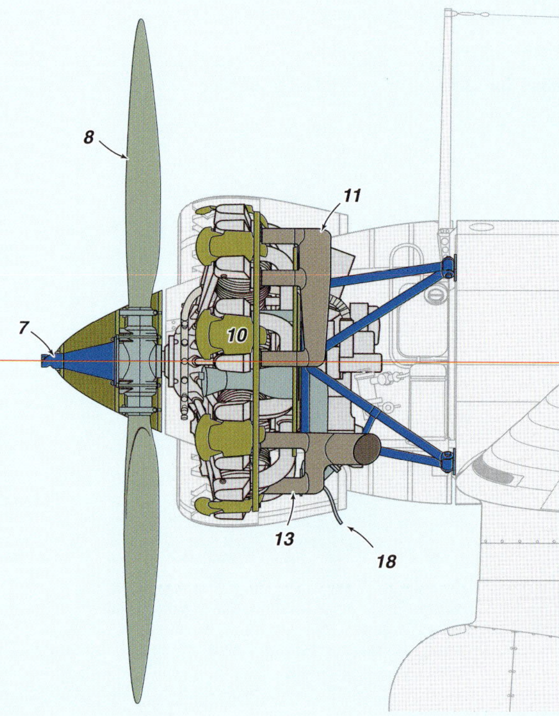

1 Ignition harness
2 Carburettor
3 Inertia starter
4 Generator
5 Magnetos
6 Rocker covers

7 "Hucks" starter
8 Type-97 "Top Secret" airscrew
9 Engine attachment bolt x 9
10 Rocker cooling baffles and ring
11 Exhaust – upper section
12 Exhaust – Port section

Dressed engine, mount and propellers

1/48 Scale

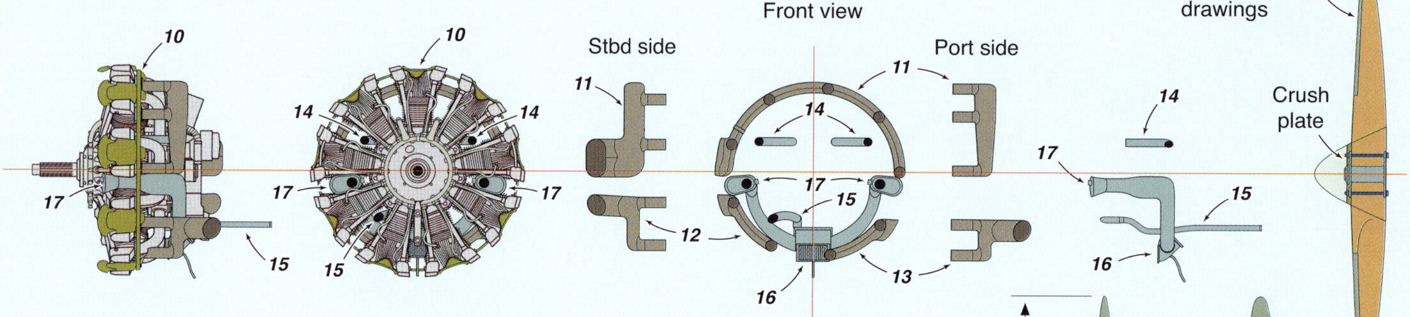

Engine mount

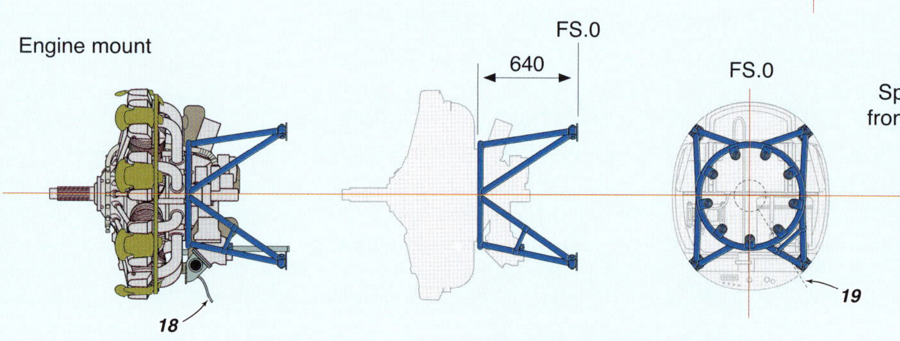

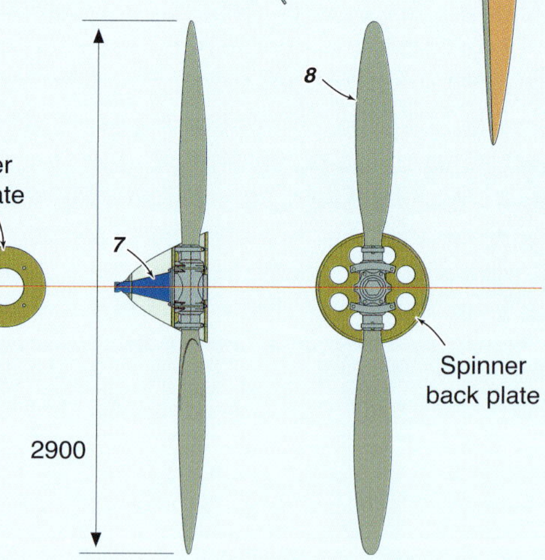

13 Exhaust – Stbd section
14 Accessory bay ram-air cooling
15 Cockpit ram-air intake

16 Carburettor (high-speed) intake
17 Carburettor (low-speed) intake
18 Carburettor drain
19 Inertia starter handle position

© Giuseppe Picarella 2020

The mounting ring connected directly to the engine crankcase via nine attachment eyes, which were welded onto its inner circumference. Each eye was fabricated out of steel plate and contained a steel bushing, which was dampened by a rubber vibration mount.

The engine-mounting frame also served as an anchor for the forward firewall and various brackets and control systems that were routed through the engine accessory bay. It also provided a substantial support frame for the hand starter and attachment points for the forward fuselage fairing support frames.

All *Babs* engine mounts were painted black.

Propeller and spinner

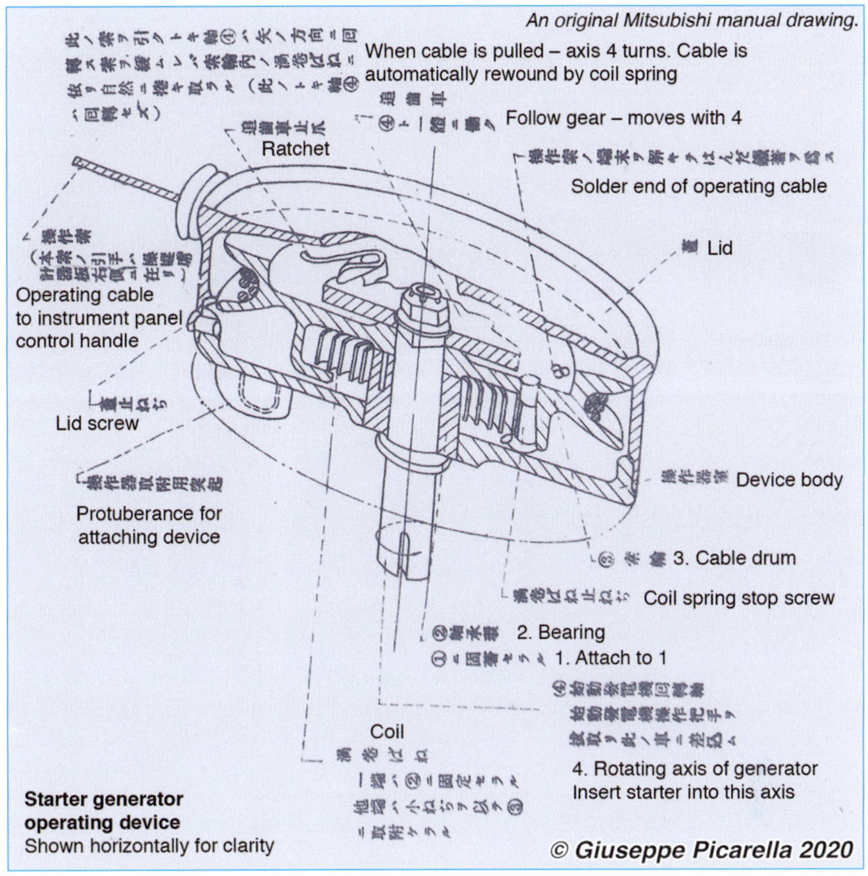

Initially the Ki-15 was designed to utilize a wooden propeller, as early engineering drawings included a propeller hub complete with front and rear crush-plates. But, just as the tailskid installation had been rendered obsolete during the design phase of the aircraft, the pace of aeronautical development during the mid 1930s soon favoured the inclusion of a metal propeller installation. To fulfil this requirement, Sumitomo Metal Industries provided a license-built (Hamilton Standard type) 2,900mm (114.2 inch) diameter, two-blade fixed pitch metal propeller, typically set between 30° to 33°pitch, with a weight of approximately 65kg (143.2 lb). The **Nr.293** propeller was in fact specifically designed for use on the Ki-15 and even came with the inscription *"Type-97 "Top Secret" airscrew"* stamped on the central boss and its highly polished narrow chord blades were configured for maximum cruise speed at the expense of climb performance. A red warning band of approximately 50mm was painted on the front face of the propeller blades, approximately 50mm from each tip, while the rear faces of the blades were painted matt black to reduce reflective glare on the pilot.

The propeller was enclosed within with a two-piece streamlined spinner that faired into the engine hub fairing, guiding the airflow in an unbroken profile through the engine cylinders and over the fuselage. Composed of a spinner cap, front plate, back plate, skin and "Hucks" adapter, the assembly was approximately 450mm long and 600mm in diameter. Including the length of the "Hucks" adapter, the length of the spinner was approximately 500mm. The spinner cap was single-piece spun dome approximately 280mm long and 440mm in diameter. The tip of the spinner was reinforced with a circular cap, attached to which was the forward "Hucks" mount and a machined and threaded fitting, with the dome screwed onto the spinner front plate. The aluminium-alloy front plate was made up of a rear flanging frame, with two L-section stiffeners on the front face. A centre cut-out was provided for the propeller shaft, plus two rectangular cut-outs for the balance weights and two circular aft-flanging lightening holes. Details of the back plate are unknown, but this was most likely similar to the front plate. The skin panel is believed to have been a single-piece pressing, riveted to the front and back plates. Close-fitting cut-outs were included for the propeller blades, with closing plates aft of the blades. Unlike most spinners of the period, no part of the propeller cuff fittings was allowed into the airstream to produce drag.

Details of the Ki-15-I "Hucks" adapter are unknown, but examples fitted to other aircraft and civil *Karigane* models typically took the form of a steel cone, attached with six bolts to the front face of the propeller boss. This assembly extended forwards through the threaded end-frame fitting and terminated with the starter-dog cut-outs.

Primary systems

The primary systems on board the Ki-15 included: the flight control system, fuel system, oil system, hydraulic system and electrical system. Secondary systems are covered within **Cockpits and secondary systems.**

Flight control system

The flight control system (FCS) of the *Babs* family of aircraft included an elevator, elevator-trim tab, ailerons and rudder. While independent in operation, it should be pointed out that the elevator and aileron control systems were interconnected at the pilot's control column via a bellcrank fitting attached to the aft face of the centre wing section rear spar, located directly below the pilot's cockpit.

Elevator and elevator trim system

The lower end of the control column was designed with a fork fitting that sat on the top of the aileron centre bellcrank. A bolt allowed the control column to pivot forwards 14.5° and aft 20°. A 30mm diameter pushrod was attached to the control column 122mm above the pivot point and transferred fore and aft movements to the lower front pivot of the elevator control lever. The elevator control lever was a cast and machined aluminium alloy (inverted) A-frame, attached to brackets below the pilot's seat, ahead of FS.5. Fore and aft movement was transferred via two 20mm diameter push rods on the rear face of the lever, to twin conversion quadrants located aft of FS.5, from which point cables were routed back to the elevator control horns via guide pulleys at the base of FS.9 and FS.14. The elevator surface movements were 33° up and 22.5° down.

The elevator conversion quadrant located below the pilot's seat (forward is left). (NII VVS via Y. Svoyski)

The elevator-trim system was controlled by a trim-wheel and indicator attached to the port side cockpit wall aft of FS.4. A bevel gear at the rear of the trim-wheel rotated a three-piece drive shaft with a worm-barrel fitting at its base. The trim cable forward end was wound around the worm-barrel, routing aft to the trim system rear sprocket via fairleads located at FS.6, FS.8 and FS.9. The aft end of the trim cable was fitted with a chain assembly, which engaged a sprocket mounted on the front face of the tailplane front spar. The sprocket actuated the port elevator trim tab via a bevel gear driving torque tubes fitted with universal joints. The trim tabs on the starboard side were slaved off the longitudinal driveshaft via two pulleys connected by an endless cable. As the trim tab torque tubes rotated, they moved forwards or aft, activating an armature inside the tab, which moved the tab up or down ±15°. No part of the trim mechanism or linkage was exposed to the airflow.

The cable operated rudder control quadrant can be seen above the tailwheel shock strut, while the elevator torque tube passes between the shock strut and tailwheel fork assembly. Note that the tailwheel fork is painted grey and the structure and controls are finished with Aotake. (NII VVS via Y. Svoyski)

The elevator trim tab gearbox (left) was located on the front spar of the tailplane. This unit drove the Port side tab, while the Stbd side trim tab was slaved off the gearbox via cables and a chain (right). (NII VVS via Y. Svoyski)

Ailerons

Sideways movement of the control column rotated the aileron bellcrank around its pivot mount, pushing/pulling the aileron pushrods laterally. The pushrods were connected to vertical bellcranks that were attached to the aft face of the rear spar, outboard of WS.5 and WS.12, with a final right-angle bellcrank located outboard of WS.17. The final bellcrank attached to the aileron push rod, which exited the upper wing skin and attached to the aileron through a highly streamlined fairing. The ailerons could be deflected 21.5° up and 18° down

Rudder

A rudder bar was mounted on the cockpit floor between FS.2 and FS.3, which controlled the rudder via control cables. The rudder bar could be deflected port and starboard by 28.5° and was connected via a torque tube to a set of control horns below the cockpit floor. Control cables were routed from the rudder control horns via pulleys located at FS.4, FS.9 and FS.14, to the rudder control quadrant located at the base of the rudder. Rudder deflection was 30° port and starboard.

For pilot comfort on long missions, the position of the bar could be adjusted fore and aft by 80mm (total), with the aid of a worm gear controlled by winding "spider" fitted to the front of the assembly. This rugged design allowed the pilot to adjust the pedals with the heel of his heavy flying boots and it seemed to work well, as the same system was adopted on the Ki-46 *Dinah*.

Ballast weight

For weight and balance requirements, trimming ballast was installed in the rear fuselage. The installation consisted of an aluminium alloy box (spanning between FS.12 and FS.13) which contained two

Flight control systems

1/48 Scale

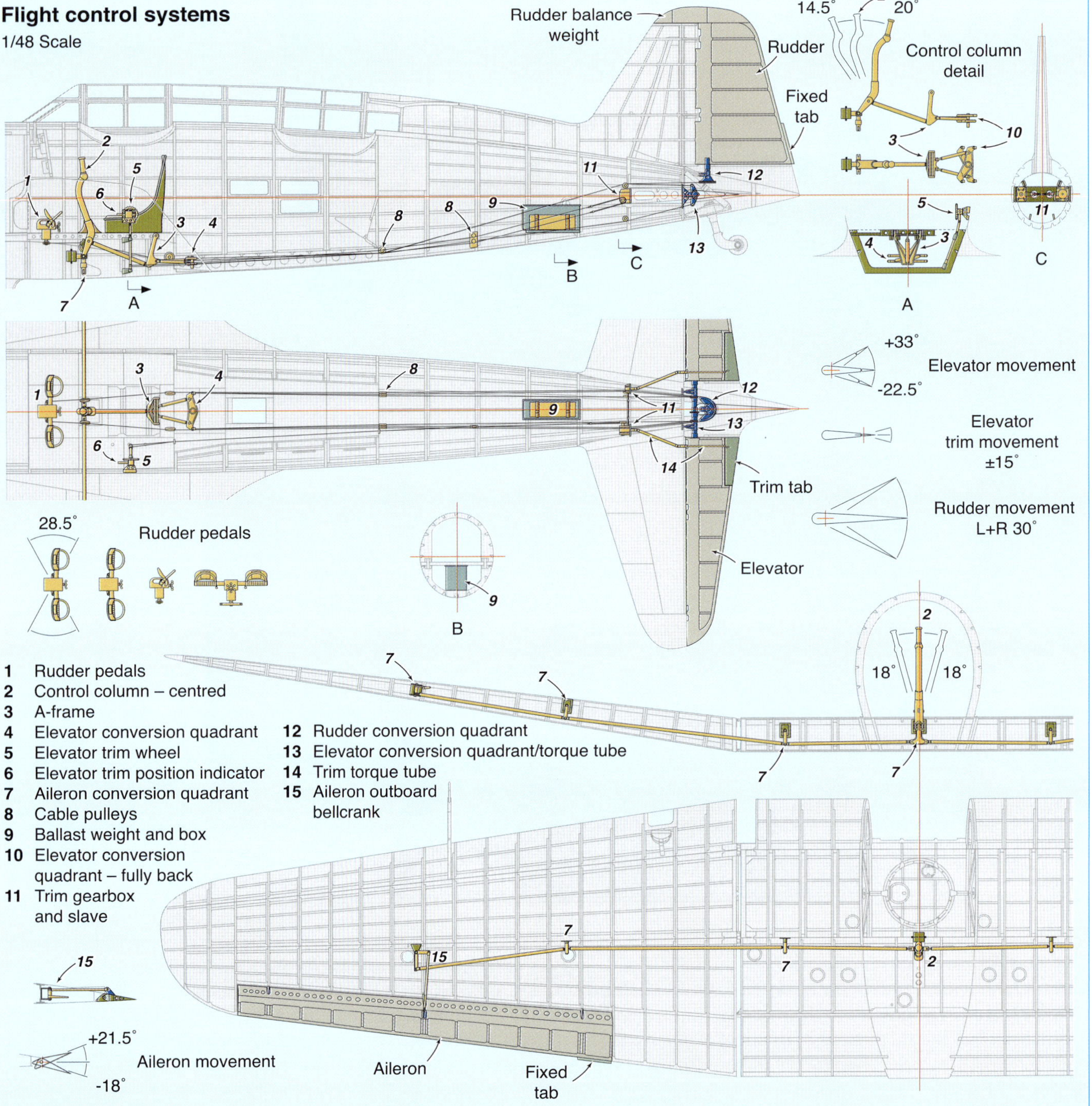

1. Rudder pedals
2. Control column – centred
3. A-frame
4. Elevator conversion quadrant
5. Elevator trim wheel
6. Elevator trim position indicator
7. Aileron conversion quadrant
8. Cable pulleys
9. Ballast weight and box
10. Elevator conversion quadrant – fully back
11. Trim gearbox and slave
12. Rudder conversion quadrant
13. Elevator conversion quadrant/torque tube
14. Trim torque tube
15. Aileron outboard bellcrank

Flap and hydraulic system

1/32 Scale

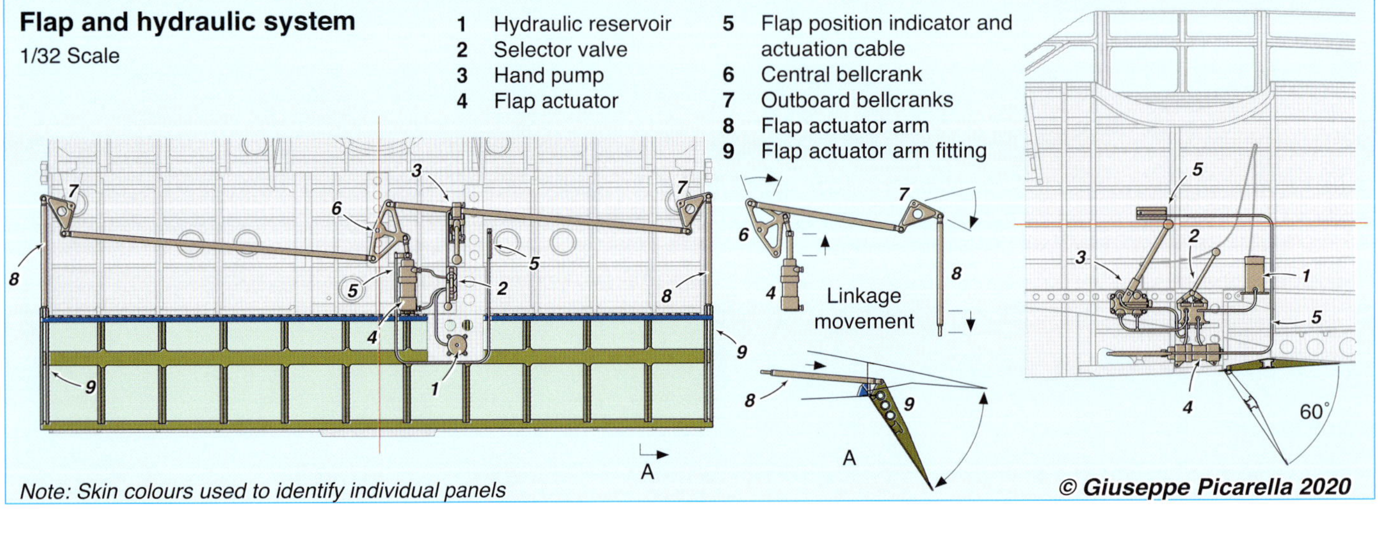

1. Hydraulic reservoir
2. Selector valve
3. Hand pump
4. Flap actuator
5. Flap position indicator and actuation cable
6. Central bellcrank
7. Outboard bellcranks
8. Flap actuator arm
9. Flap actuator arm fitting

Note: Skin colours used to identify individual panels

Flight control system

A selection of original Mitsubishi manual drawings for the Ki-15 flight controls.

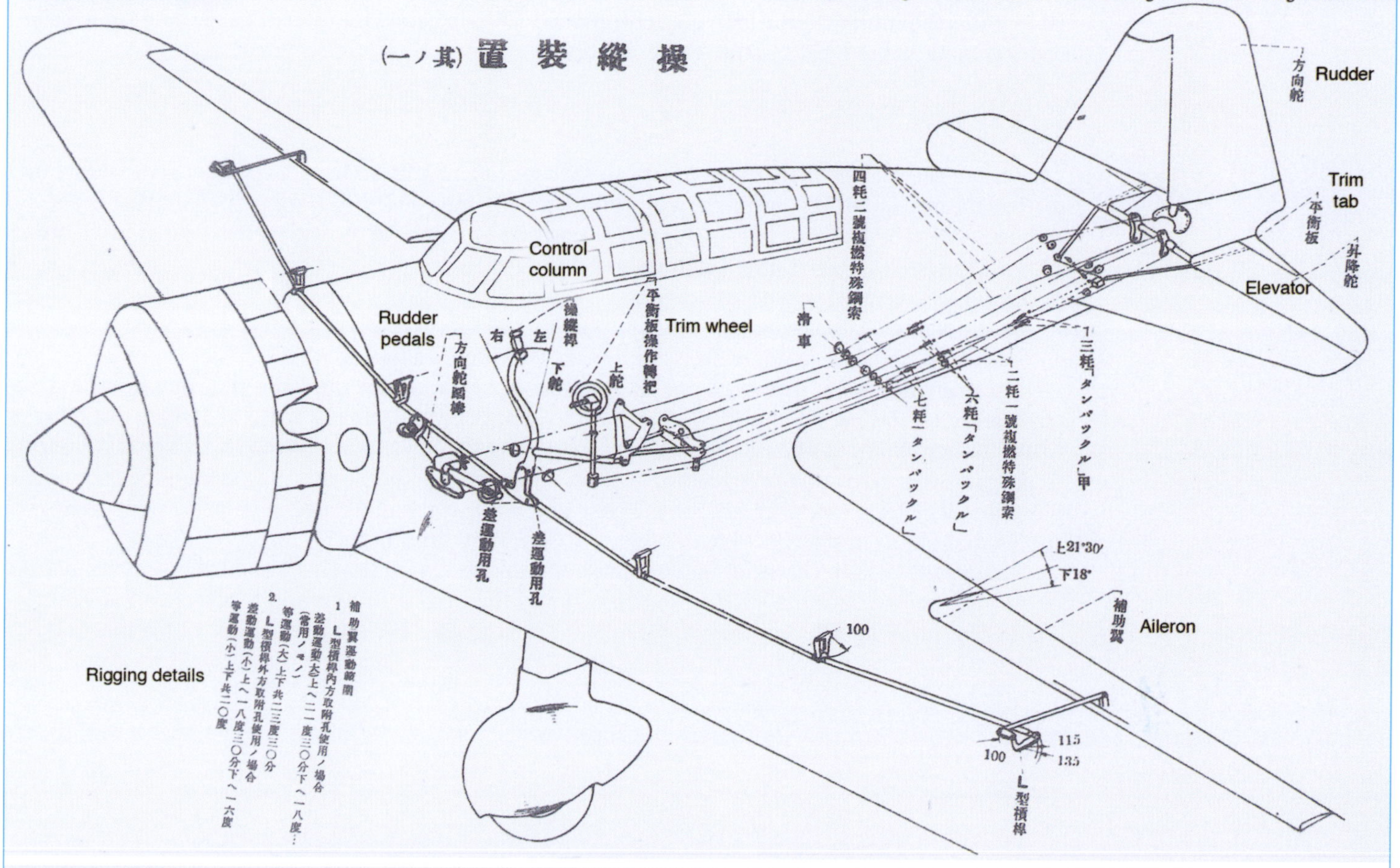

Elevator controls

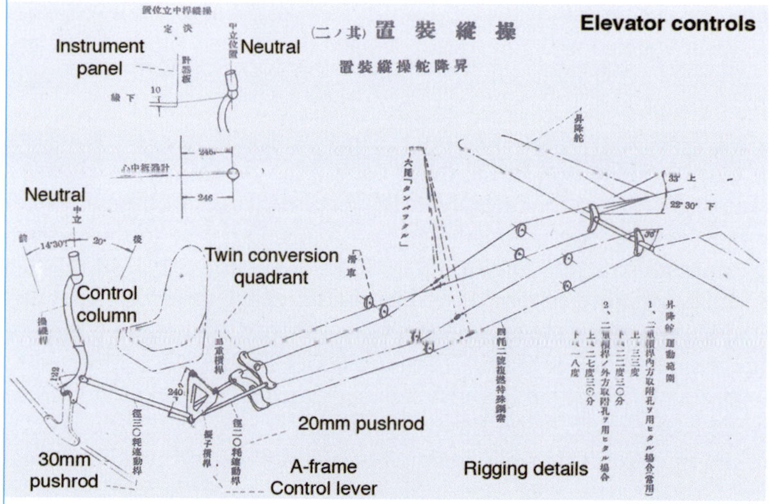

Rudder controls

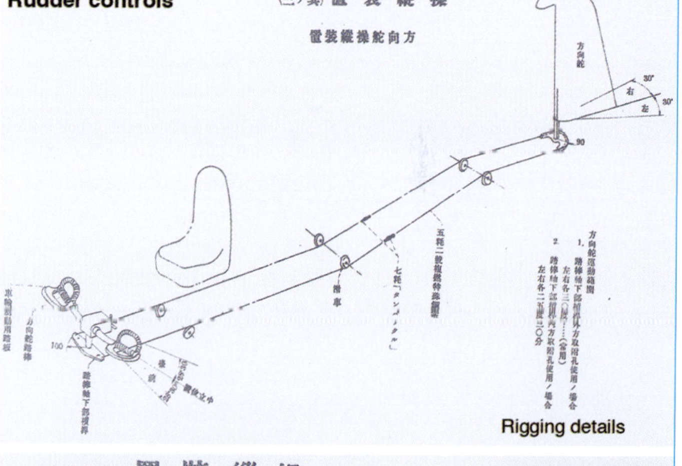

Elevator trim system

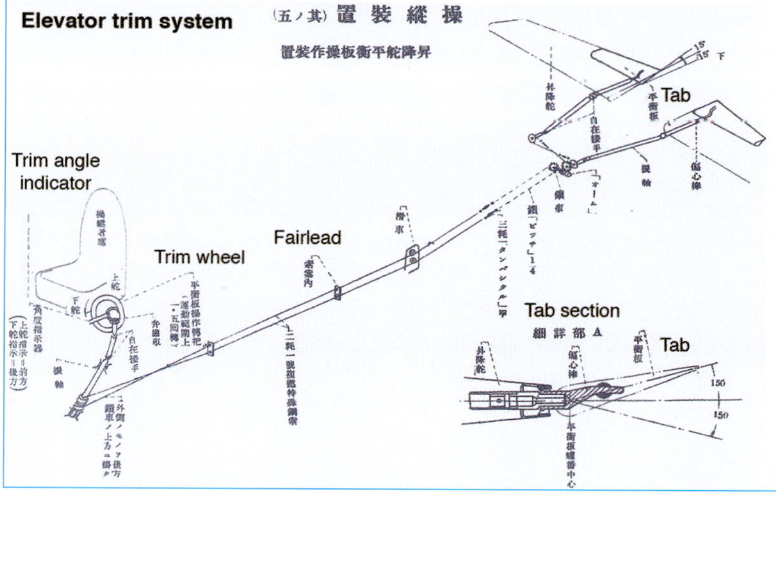

Rudder pedals

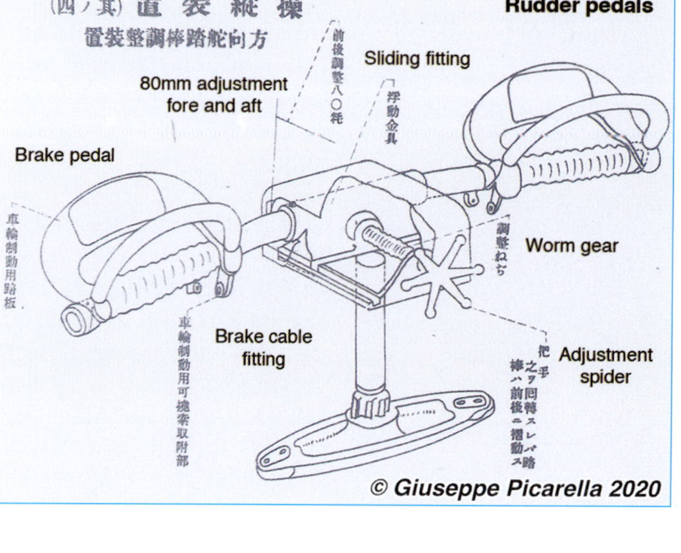

leather straps in order to secure the required lead ballast into position. The dimensions of the box were 434 x 160 x 200mm, with the base panel positioned 270mm below the aircraft CL. Access to the ballast box was made via the rear cockpit of the aircraft.

Fuel system

It is not unusual for fuel systems, fitted to such period aircraft, to be in a constant state of flux over the operational life of the airframe, with improvements introduced following development trials and combat usage. The Ki-15 *early model* was no exception to this pattern, with three distinct installations adopted in service – **initial, intermediate** and **standard**.

- **Initial** – Fuselage main and wing tanks
- **Intermediate** – Fuselage main, wing and "additional fuel" tanks
- **Standard** – Fuselage main, wing, "additional fuel" and leading edge tanks

The Army originally stipulated a 400km radius of operation for the *Babs*, plus one hour over the target area. It is unclear if "time over target" was to be at the stipulated full speed of 450km/h (279mph), to avoid interception by the enemy's fighter forces, or at the lower cruise speed of 320km/h (199mph), to perform what we would now refer to as "loiter" operations? While this may seem to be an ambiguous point, its effects were very real for the crew of a *Babs*, as the difference in range between these two speeds could be as much as 130km (80miles), or almost 50 litres of fuel.

Tomio Kubo was in charge of fuel systems and tank design on the Ki-15 and his ingenious method of utilizing flanged faces on the fuel tanks, removed the need for mounting brackets and attachment straps. This not only reduced structural weigh, it also increased the useable volume of the fuel tank.

Fuselage main fuel tank

Ki-15-I *early model*

The 389 litre fuselage main fuel tank was located ahead of the pilot's cockpit, between FS.0 and FS.2. Constructed of sheet steel, the tank was comprised of two end-walls, an upper skin and a lower skin. The forward end-wall of the tank was fabricated with a vertically flanged face, which allowed the tank to be attached directly on to the forward face of FS.0. For safety purposes the secondary firewall panel was then secured over the forward end-wall.

The rear end-wall of the tank was fabricated with a horizontal flange, which allowed the fuel tank to be slid (aft) inside the fuselage cavity and connect to the inner flanged face of FS.2, with felt strips lining the inner flange face of FS.1 in order to hold the fuel tank firmly in place. This attachment system not only secured the fuel tank to the airframe with minimal fuss, it also adding rigidly to the forward fuselage structure, by introducing a tubular structure to FS.0, FS.1 and FS.2. The lower half of the fuel tank rear end-wall was recessed to allow for movement of the rudder pedals, which were located immediately aft of the fuel tank. To avoid damaging the skin of the fuel tank a shaped aluminium bulkhead (attached to FS.2) separated the fuel tank and rudder pedals. The tank upper skin panels conformed to the internal shape of the fuselage frames, while the flat lower skin panel matched the cockpit floor line, allowing systems and pipes to travel uninterrupted below the cockpit floor.

The internally construction of the fuselage main tank consisted of one vertical and two horizontal baffle frames running the full length of the tank, plus supporting stringers. The baffle frames, which included lightening holes for weight reduction and rigidity, also served to reduce fuel movement or "sloshing". The tank was fitted with a fuel quantity probe, gravity filler port (to the starboard of TDC), fuel-screen, fuel expansion vent, fuel feed and fuel drain line.

Wing fuel tanks

The interconnected wing fuel tanks were located between the front and rear spars of the centre-wing section, extending outwards from WS.2 to WS.6. The modular wing tanks were designed in a similar fashion to the fuselage main fuel tank, with a flanged outboard fitting and a locator bolt on the inboard face. Built of sheet steel, the tank structure was comprised of two end-walls and a two skin sections. The outboard end-wall was designed around a vertical flange, allowing the entire fuel tank to be slid into the wing cavity and secured with 26 screws, which engaged nut-plates attached to the outboard face of WS.6. Felt strips lined the inner flange faces of WS3 through WS.5, in order to hold the fuel tank firmly in place. The inboard end-wall was canted 15° to sit against the canted face of WS.2, where its integral locator bolt passed through this wing frame and was secured by a wing-nut and washer. Access to this single inboard attachment point was provided through the centre-wing section lower access hatch.

Mitsubishi Ki-15-I *late model* inboard profile – with standard fuel system
1/48 Scale

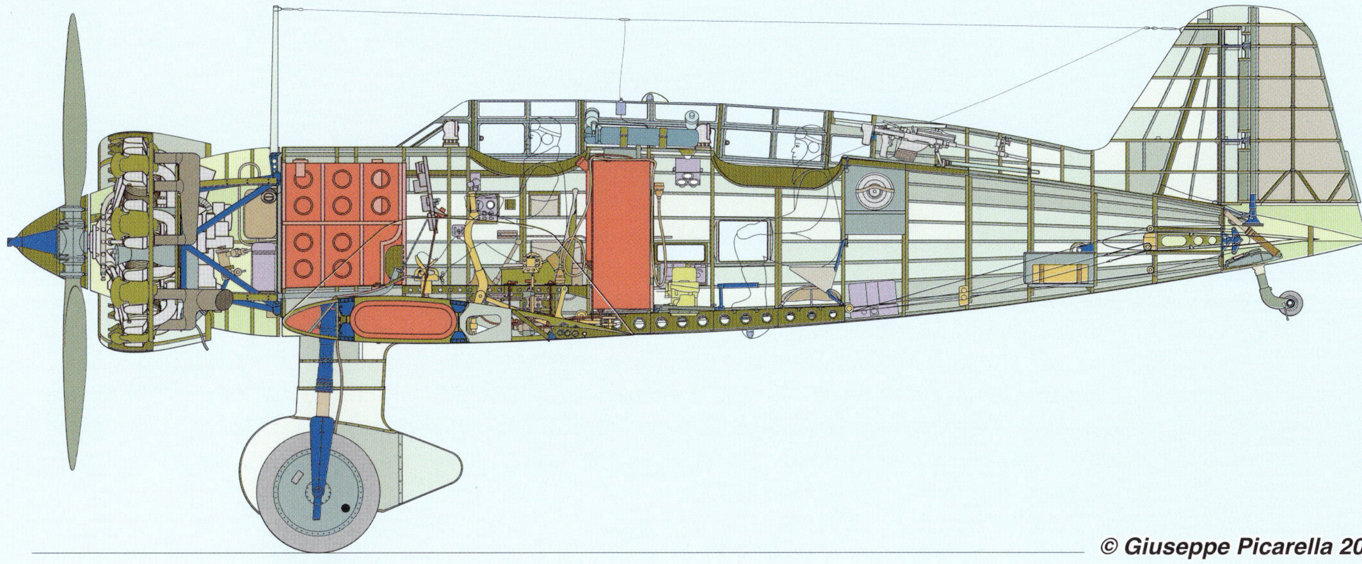

© Giuseppe Picarella 2020

The sheet steel internal construction of the wing fuel tanks consisted of three transverse baffle ribs, one longitudinal baffle frame and supporting stringers. All baffle-frames incorporated lightening holes and the forward and rear skin panels joined at TDC and BDC along the longitudinal baffle frame. Each of the two 105 litre wing tanks contained its own fuel quantity probe, gravity filler port, fuel-screen, fuel expansion-vent, fuel feed and fuel drain line.

Fuel expansion system

A fuel-expansion system was fitted to each fuel tank via a series of 20mm, 10mm and 6mm aluminium pipes, connected by flexible rubber joints. These pipes allowed the fuel to expand and vacate the system during warm conditions, without over pressurizing and rupturing the tanks, or overflowing the individual filler ports. The wing fuel tanks were interconnected up-and-over the fuselage main tank, fore and aft of FS.1, before joining the main fuel tank expansion system. The combined system then descended down on the right-hand side of the fuselage main tank forward of FS.1, exiting the lower wing-to-fuselage fairing, just ahead of FS.0. In order to allow a free flow of expanded fuel, without the fear of air pressure forcing fuel back up the pipe during forward flight, an internal back-pressure syphon was included just above the main exit pipe. The fuel expansion pipe system also ensured that a vacuum-free environment existed within the fuel tanks, thus preventing restricted fuel flow and erroneous quantity readings.

Initial fuel system capacity – Ki-15-I

Tank location	Capacity in litres
Fuselage main tank	389
Wing tanks – starboard	105
Wing tank – port	105
Total:	**599**

"Additional fuel tank"

Following the outbreak of the Sino-Japanese war, the true value of the Ki-15 became readily apparent to the Army and their initial indifference to the aircraft was soon replaced with calls for improved performance and range.

Mitsubishi was not blind to this requirement and plans were already underway to improve the overall fuel capacity of the aircraft, but the need for increased range was an urgent one. Luckily the Engineering Dept. had a quick solution to the problem, which came in the form of a fuel tank that could be fitted into the centre fuselage – in a similar fashion to the long-range installation on *Kamikaze*. On the face of it this was a simple task, but unlike *Kamikaze*, the Ki-15-I was a working reconnaissance aircraft fitted with a large aerial camera and the rear cockpit had been designed specifically for this purpose. The location of the vertical camera window was integral to the airframe structure and fixed in relationship to the RO's crew-station. Fitting a new mid-fuselage tank installation would not only impact upon the

Looking up through the circular access hole on the lower surface of the centre wing-section (forward is up) of aircraft C/n181. At the right of the photograph is the fuel tank controller. The rudder bar bell-crank is at the bottom (attached to the centre fuselage/cockpit floor structure), while the large pipe at the top centre is the pilot's ram-air ventilation system. The smaller pipe and stop cock is the fuselage main fuel tank drain pipe. The small diameter tube with a cable exiting (between the fuel tank controller and ram-air pipe) is the left (Port) main landing gear brake cable. Note the inner upper wing surface and upper circular access hole structure is visible behind the various fittings, and the liberal application of Aotake over all of the internal structure. Of additional interest is the painted coloured bar, located aft of the access panel (at bottom of photo). This mid colour (possibly blue) bar could be a Sentai Hombu marking? (See Vol I, Chapter 5). (NII VVS via Y. Svoyski)

operation of the camera, it would also require the relocation of radio equipment. While the layout and relocation of associated equipment had not been an issue with *Kamikaze*, it was impractical for the Ki-15, as the RO needed to also operate the rear-facing machine gun.

After studying several options, all of which required drastic changes to the RO's cockpit, the only viable solution was to design a shaped "additional fuel tank" (as it became know in Mitsubishi literature), which was located directly behind the pilot's seat, between FS.5 and FS.6.

The 137 litre "additional fuel tank" was constructed of sheet steel and comprised of two end-walls and several skin panels. The tank was fabricated in a similar manner to the main fuel tank, with a vertical flange on the forward end-wall and a longitudinal flange on the rear end wall. But unlike the main fuel tank, the "additional fuel tank" was designed to slide forwards, from the RO's cockpit, into the fuselage cavity directly behind the pilot's seat. The forward flange of the tank was attached by way of five brackets located on FS.5, while the rear flange was supported by five bolts, engaged through rubber suspension dampers on FS.6. Initially designed to match the oval section of the centre fuselage frames, as per *Kamikaze*, the right-hand upper quadrant was cut away to fit around the radio equipment cabinet installation. Similarly, the base of the tank was truncated to match the level of the front cockpit floor, giving the tank an L-shaped profile when viewed from the rear cockpit.

The internal construction of the additional fuel tank would have matched that of the fuselage main tank, with a series of vertical and horizontal baffle frames. The tank was fitted with a gravity filler port and fuel-screen (which protruded up behind the pilot's left-hand shoulder), a fuel quantity sight-glass on the left-hand side of the front end-wall, a fuel expansion vent and feed line.

It is unclear what colour these fuel tanks would have been painted, but given their steel construction they were probably painted satin black.

Intermediate fuel system capacity – Ki-15-I

Tank location	Capacity in litres
Fuselage main tank:	389
Wing tanks – starboard	105
Wing tank – port	105
Additional fuel tank	**137**
Total	736

While the "additional fuel tank" installation had gone a long way to extend the aircraft's endurance and range, Mitsubishi began to investigate the possibility of installing more fuel tanks in the existing centre-wing section, which was suitably near to the aircraft's CG to offer realistic results. The only location that was capable of accepting addition fuel tanks was the leading edge of the wing, but Kubo's modular fuel tank system was impractical in this area, as the double-skinned layout would have severely reduced the capacity of these tanks, so another option was needed.

At that time Mitsubishi's production lines were starting to deliver production examples of the Mitsubishi Navy Type-96 Attack Bomber (G3M1) *Nell*, and the Navy was rightly proud to be accepting one of the world's most advanced bombers into operational service. One of the many interesting design features used on the *Nell* was that of low-drag integral fuel tanks, fitted to the leading edge of the wings. Initially designed by Kubo as part of the Experimental 8-*Shi* Special Reconnaissance Aircraft (G1M1) project, these "wet" fuel tanks also acted as leading edge torsion boxes for the wing, so they needed to be specially sealed in order to stop any fuel leakage. This type of leading edge tank had several advantages over an internally mounted fuel tank:

1. It was lighter than an internally mounted tank, as it did not require to be fitted inside existing leading edge structure.
2. It produced a larger volume tank, as it did not require a double skin.
3. It was easy to fit, remove and maintain.

Kubo quickly adapted the low drag design to fit the existing B-9 aerofoil section, and the new leading-edge tanks were rapidly assembled and tested on the production line jigs, where it was confirmed that they had little impacted on the overall wing assembly. In essence the modifications consisted of deleting the leading edge skin panels and replacing all three of the leading-edge nose

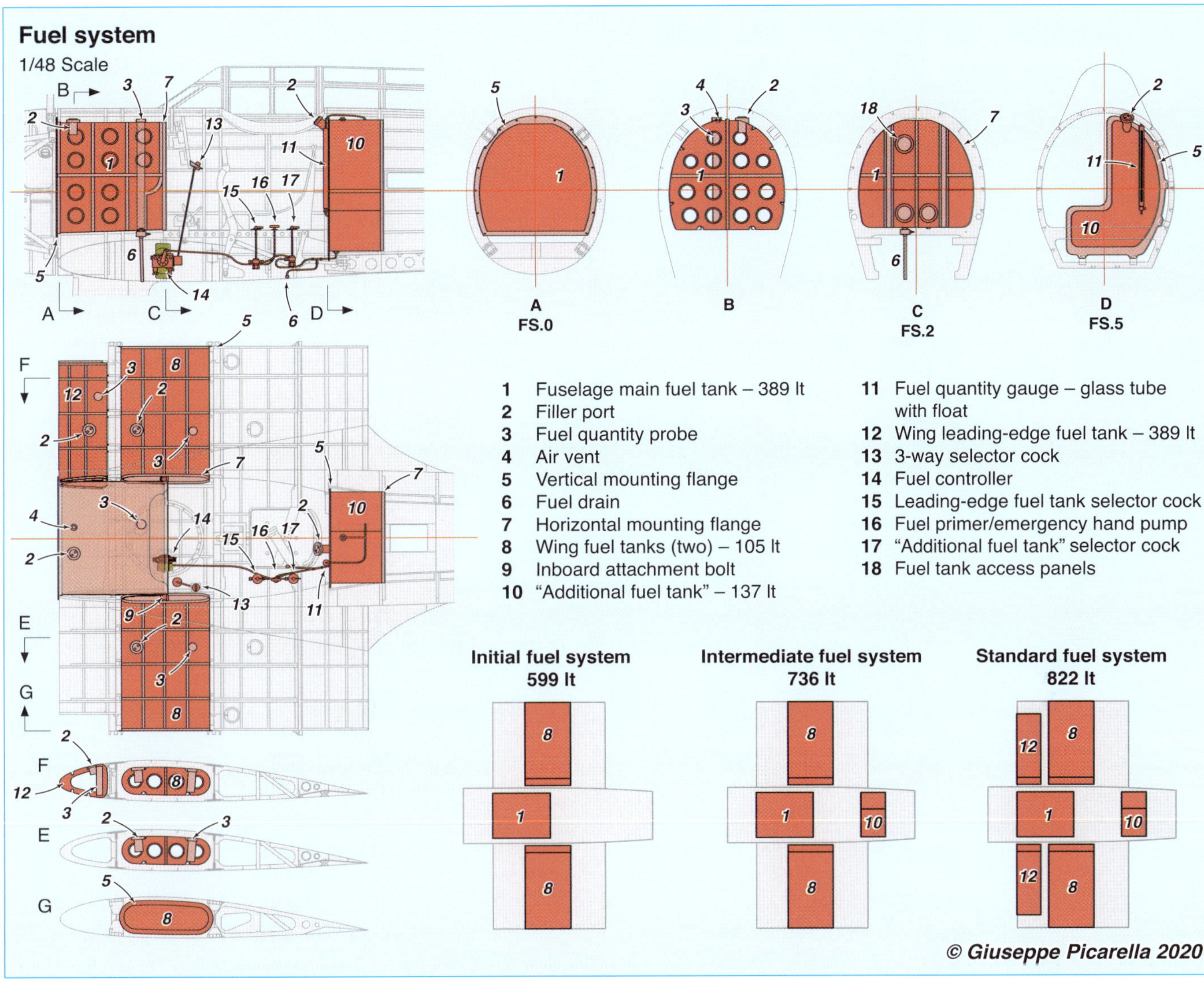

ribs with new fuel tank attachment fittings. The fuel tanks were then attached to the wing and aerodynamic cover-plates sealed the gap between the tank and wing skin. This concept worked so well in fact that Mitsubishi went on to adopt this type of leading-edge fuel tank design on many of its later designs, including the *Nate, Sally, Ann, Dinah, Sonia, Betty* and *Peggy*.

Leading-edge fuel tanks

The interconnected semi-monocoque leading-edge "wet" fuel tanks were located ahead of the centre-wing section front spar, extending outwards from a point adjacent to WS.2 through to WS.5, Each of the 43 litre capacity tanks was built of sheet steel, with each assembly comprised of two end-walls and two skin sections. The outboard end-wall formed the closing bulkhead for the forward aerodynamic wing joint fairing. The inboard end-wall was inclined approximately 15° to align with WS.2.

The internal construction of each tank each consisted of four transverse baffle ribs and supporting stringers. All baffle-frames incorporated lightening holes and the forward and rear skin panels joined along the rear TDC and rear BDC edges. Four sets of attachment brackets were located on the rear face of the tank, which engaged into the appropriate spar mounted attachment fittings. In order to attach the aerodynamic cover plates to the fuel tank and streamline the assembly into the wing, a low profile fairing strip was attached to the upper and lower edges of the tank. The cover plate assemblies were simply pushed under the tank fairing strips and held in position with locator screws on the opposing wing skin flanges. The outboard fairing strip contained an added doubler-strip to engage with the wing joint fairing.

Each of the leading-edge tanks contained its own fuel quantity probe, gravity filler port, fuel-screen, fuel expansion vent, fuel feed and fuel drain fittings.

It is unclear what colour these fuel tanks would have been painted, but given their steel construction they were probably painted satin black.

Standard fuel system capacity – Ki-15-I

Tank location	Capacity in litres
Fuselage main tank	389
Wing tanks – starboard	105
Wing tank – port	105
Wing leading edge tank – starboard	43
Wing leading edge tank – port	43
"Additional fuel tank"	137
Total	822

The fuel expansion system was of course modified to incorporate the new fuel tanks installation. The main modifications concerned the (four) wing fuel tanks, which were interconnected up-and-over the fuselage main tank, fore and aft of FS.1, before joining the main fuel tank expansion system. The combined system then descended down the starboard side of the fuselage main tank forward of FS.1, exiting the lower wing-to-fuselage fairing, just ahead of FS.0. The rear "additional fuel tank" expansion system, which incorporated the breather pipe for the visual quantity probe, travelled forwards, below the cockpit floor, on the starboard side of the fuselage, before connecting to the main fuel expansion system vent pipe.

Fuel management system

Several pieces of equipment were required to operate and connect the Standard fuel system on the aircraft, including:

1. The **fuel tank controller** was the heart of the fuel system, interconnecting the fuel pump, carburettor, fuel primer, emergency hand pump and the fuel system loop via the "wing/body" fuel selector cock. With an integral fuel filter and water drain, the fuel tank selector was located on the left-hand side of the centre wing section at WS.2 adjacent to FS.2. It was accessible via a dedicated 170mm inspection panel located in the lower centre-wing section access hatch.
2. A **fuel primer** hand pump was fitted to the lower instrument panel. This primed the engine impeller with fuel prior to start-up.
3. The **Wing tank selector cock** was located outboard and aft of the fuel tank controller unit and controlled the selection of the wing fuel tanks. The control handle was located on the left-hand side of the lower instrument panel and connected to the selector body by a torque tube routed through the cockpit floor.
4. The **Wing leading edge fuel cock** was located on the cockpit floor, to the left of the pilots seat and allowed the selection of the wing leading edge tanks.
5. A **manual fuel pump** handle was located on the cockpit floor aft of the wing leading edge fuel cock. This was a vertical plunger type handle that actuated a lever on the rear of the fuel controller via a flexible shaft. This pump was used to prime the carburettor before starting the engine, which then took over the pressurization of the fuel system. The manual fuel pump also acted as an emergence fuel pump if the engine-driven pump failed in flight.
6. Two/three individual **fuel quantity gauges** were installed in the instrument panel, depending on whether the aircraft incorporated the Initial, Intermediate or Standard fuel system. These provided readings for the fuselage main fuel tank, wing fuel tanks and wing leading edge fuel tanks.
7. A **fuel quantity sight-glass** was provided for the "addition fuel tank".

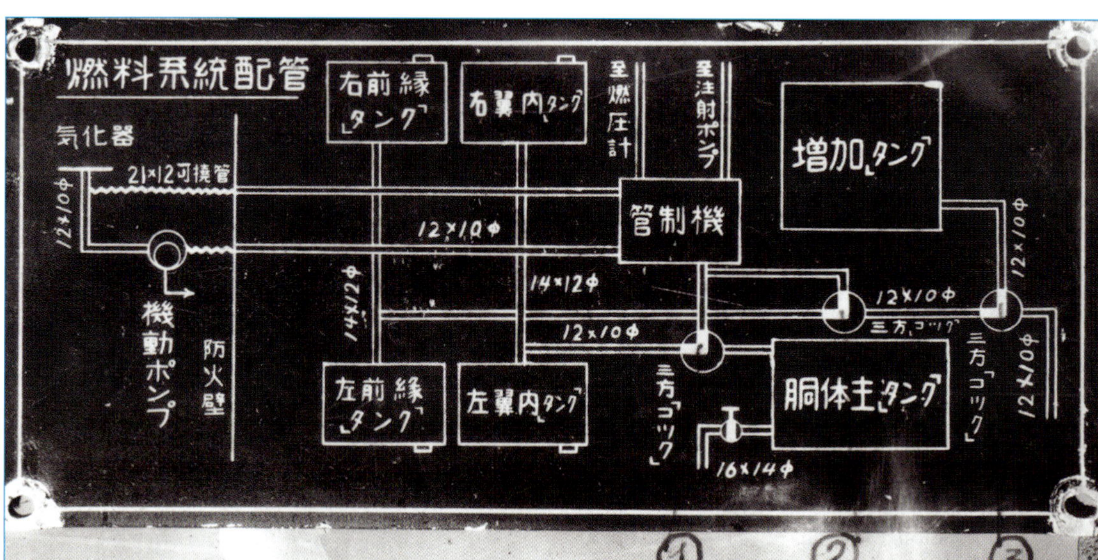

Airframe mounted fuel-system placard – Standard fuel system shown. (NII VVS via Y. Svoyski)

A selection of original Mitsubishi engineering and manual drawings for the Ki-15 fuel system.

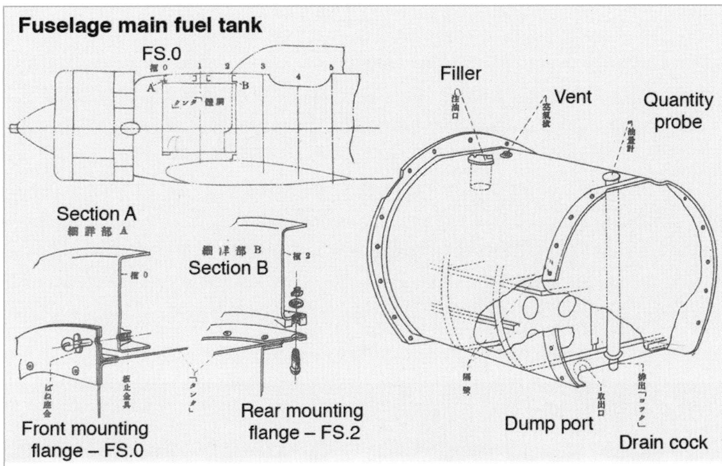

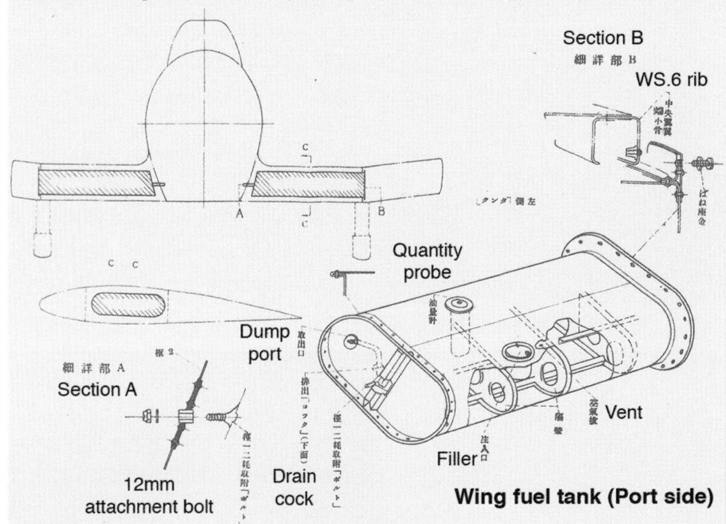

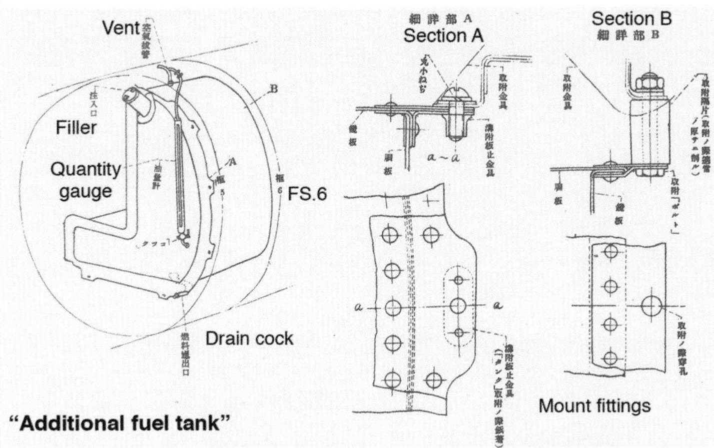

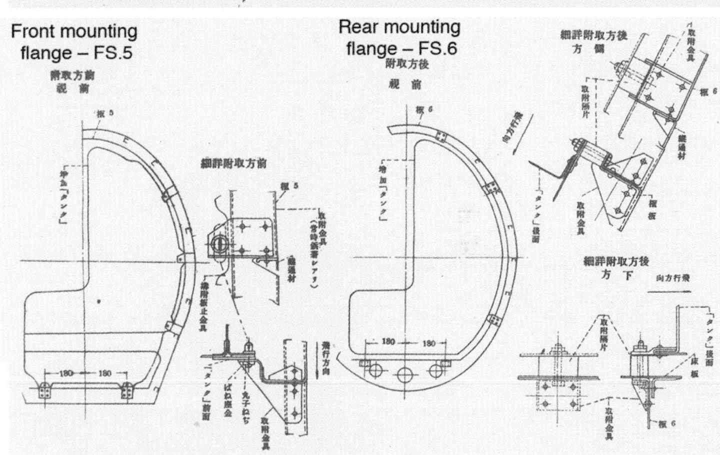

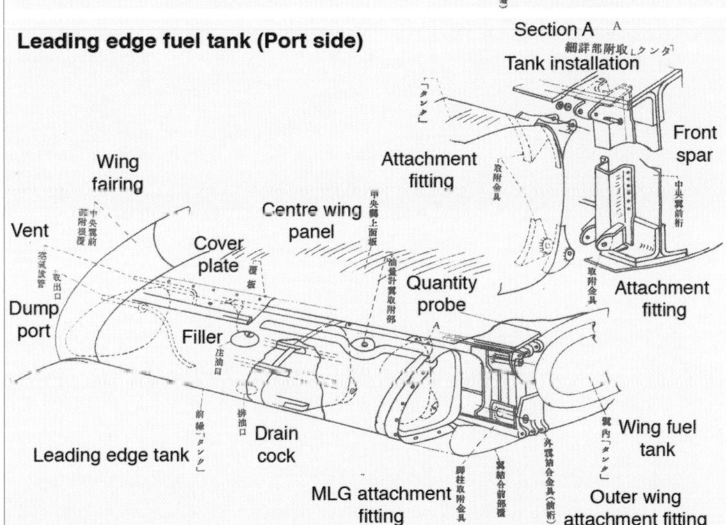

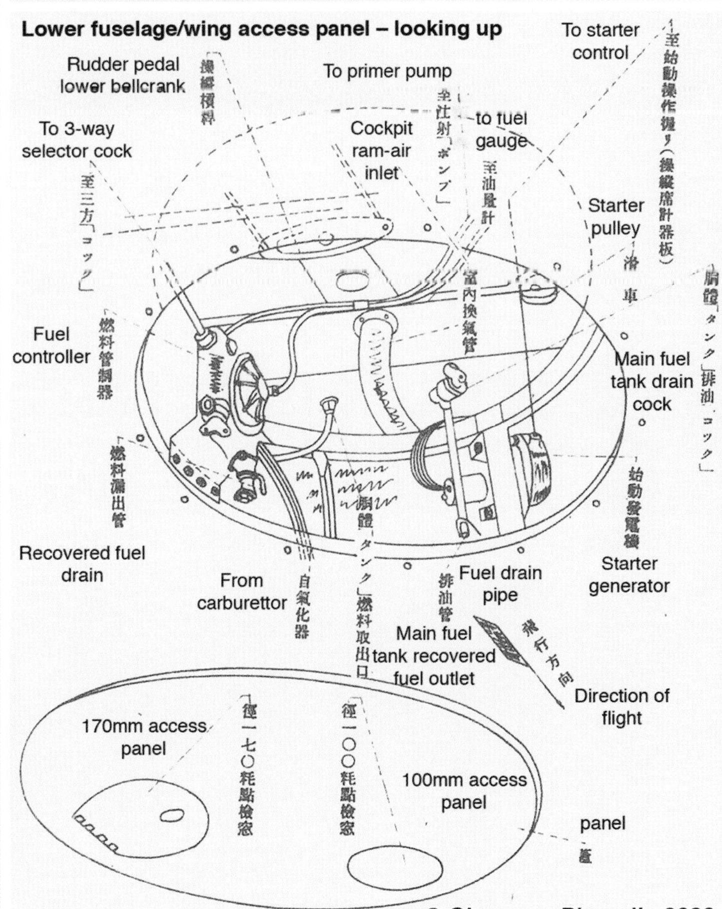

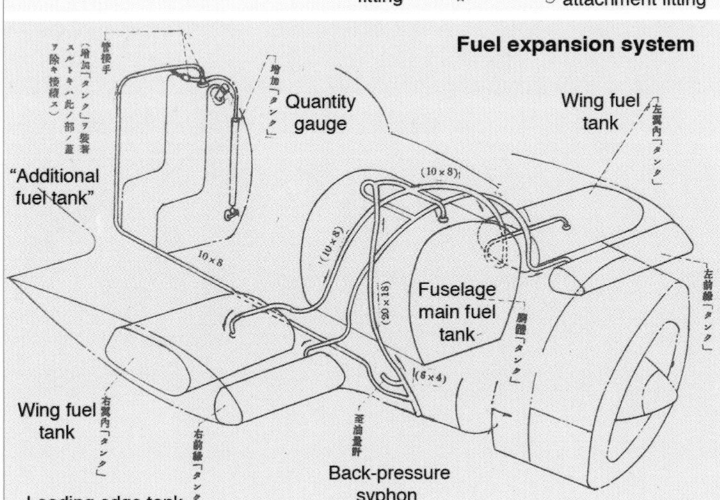

Oil system

By choosing to use the relatively low horsepower (550hp) air-cooled Nakajima Ha-8 radial engine, coupled with a highly efficient Townend ring design, Kouno was able to dispense with the need for a dedicated oil cooler, as this engine was capable of being cooled solely by the airstream throughout its operating range.

The oil lubrication and cooling system consisted of a 45 litre oil tank attached to the front face of FS.0. It was fitted with an integral air space and breather pipe, a system stop-cock, filter and drain located on the starboard side of the engine accessory bay. Oil pressure was controlled solely by the engine driven oil pump, which was located on the accessory gearbox of the engine. On early examples of the aircraft the oil tank was painted *Aotake*, but on later models (Prior to aircraft C/n181) the tank and associated piping was insulated with a rubber-impregnated cotton covering, which was finished with aluminium dope.

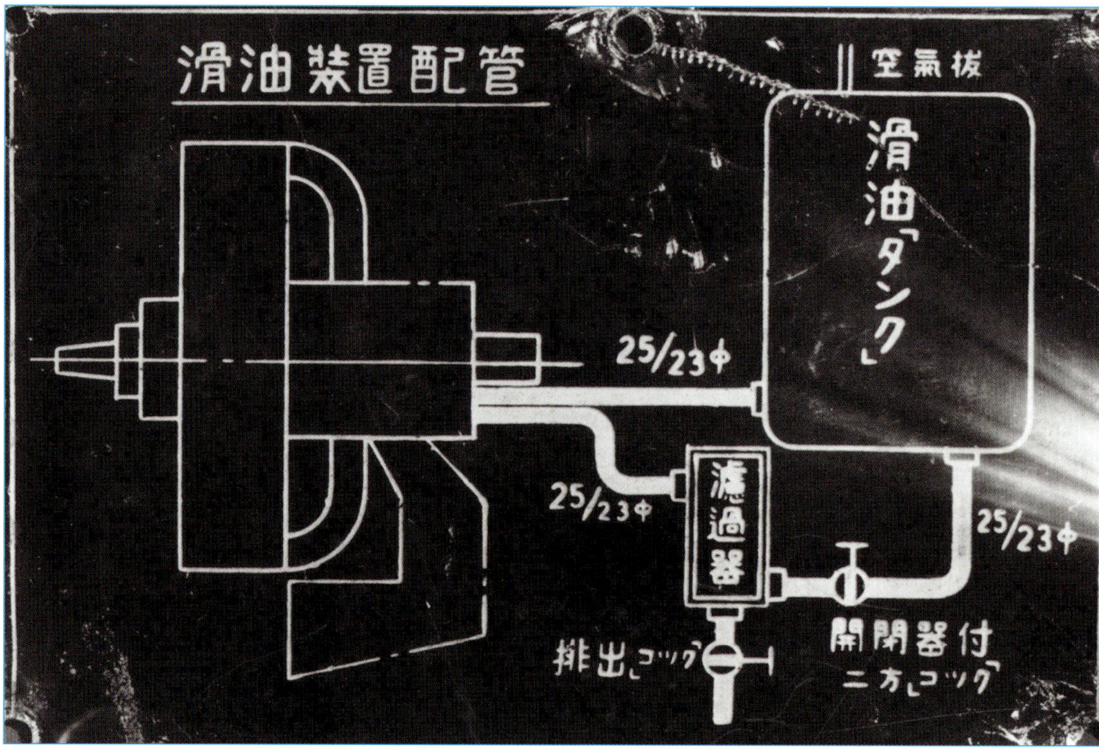

Airframe mounted oil system placard. (NII VVS via Y. Svoyski)

Hydraulic system

The hydraulic system installation remained constant throughout the life of the aircraft, due to its simplicity. Manually pressurized by the pilot, the hydraulic system controlled the landing flap actuation and retraction only. The whole system was comprised of a hand pump, selector valve, reservoir and actuator. The system was interconnected via 10mm tubing and used Type-2 No.1 hydraulic oil. No pressure gauge was fitted. The primary components of the hydraulic system were:

Ki-15-I Lubrication system

1/48 Scale

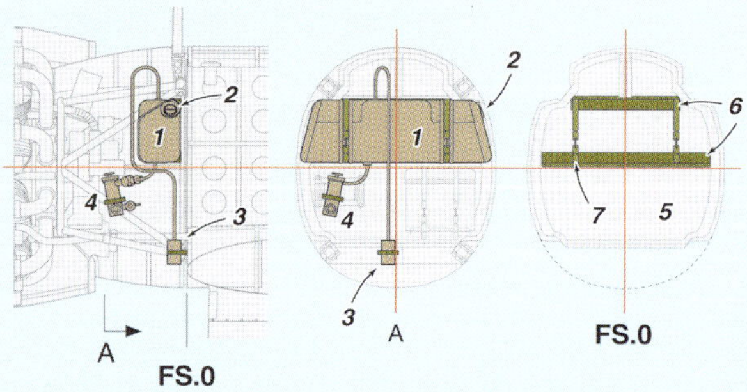

1 Oil tank – 45 lt
2 Filler port
3 Oil sump/drain
4 Oil filter and drain
5 Secondary firewall
6 Oil tank mount
7 Tank retaining straps

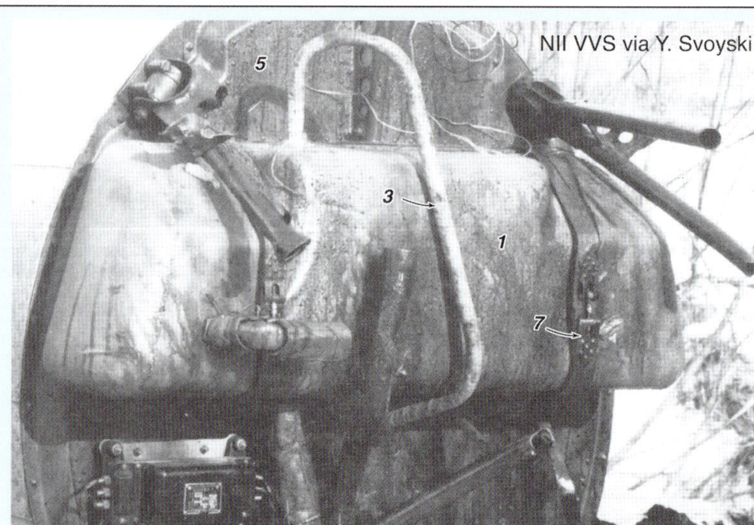

NII VVS via Y. Svoyski

1. The **hand pump** (**"oil pump"** as specified by the Japanese) was located below the cockpit floor on the right-hand side of the pilot's seat between FS.3 and FS.4.
2. The **selector "transfer" valve** was located below the cockpit floor on the right-hand side of the pilot's seat between FS.4 and FS.4A.
3. The **reservoir "oil tank"** was located to the right-hand side of the pilot's seat between FS.4A and FS.5. The reservoir was topped-up via a filler port on top of the reservoir.
4. The flap **actuator** was located below the cockpit floor on the right-hand side of the pilot's seat and attached to FS.4 and FS.4A.
5. The **flap position indicator** was located on the right-hand cockpit wall between FS.3 and FS.4. The indicator was connected to the flap actuator piston via a steel cable running along a brass tube. As the flap actuator piston extended, the cable was drawn along the brass tube, thereby moving the flap position flag fitted to the position indicator. Settings of 0°, 15°, 30°, 45° and 60° were denoted on the indicator, but actual flap positioning was governed by the pilot's use of the hand pump.

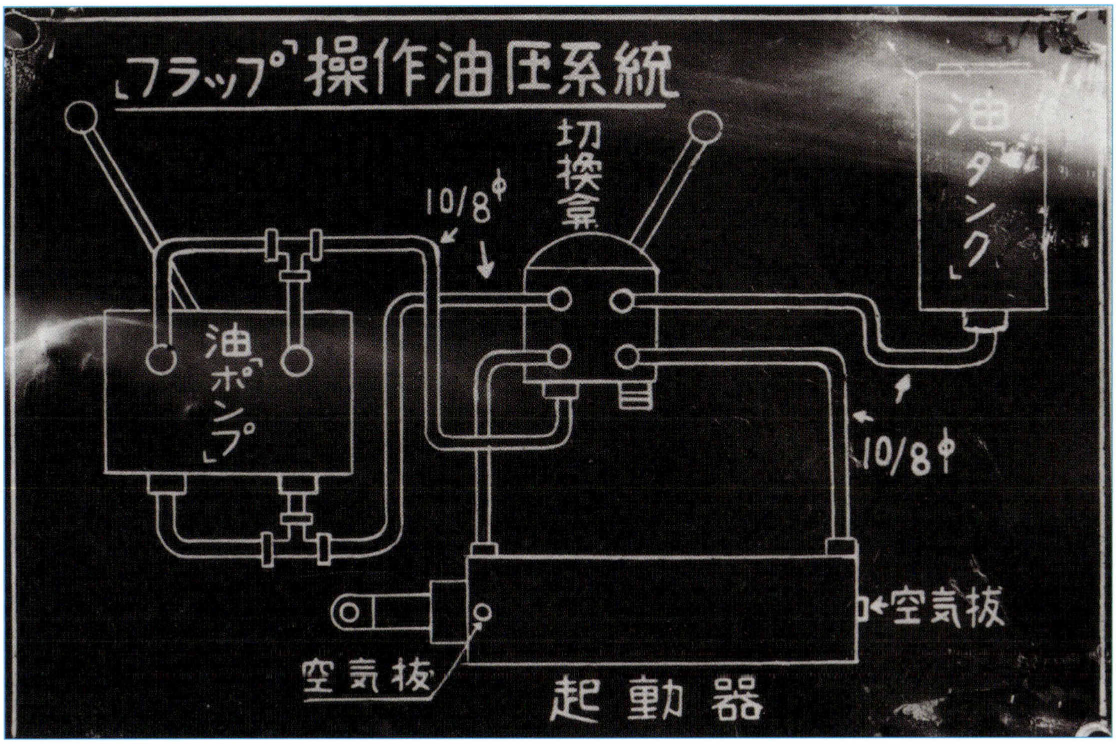

Airframe mounted hydraulic system placard. (NII VVS via Y. Svoyski)

Electrical system

No electrical system information survives for the Ki-15-I, although a sketch of the *Kamikaze* cockpit produced by "*The Aeroplane*" magazine on April 14th, 1937, includes the main electrical panel, master

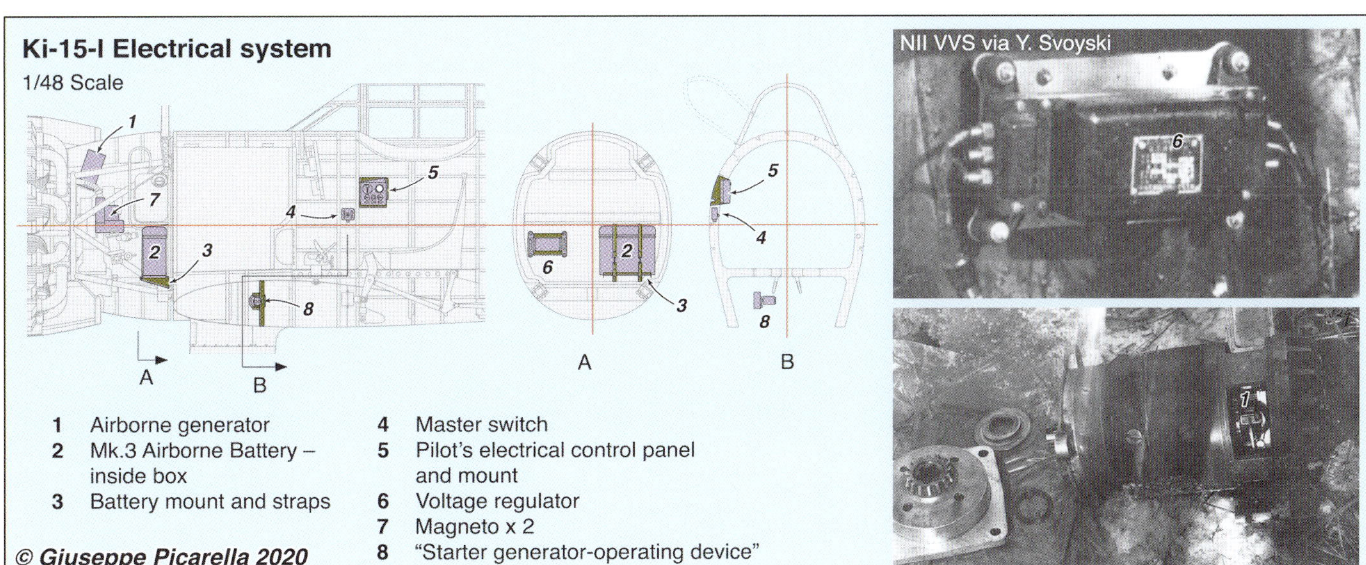

This photo shows the simple and compact hydraulic system fitted to the Ki-15 (forwards is left). The hydraulic reservoir "1" (with the circular information tag) is located at the top right of the photo. Item "3" is the hand pump for the system and "2" is the selector valve, fitted to the right of the pilot's seat. The flap actuator ram "4", flap bell-crank "5" and "7" flap position indicator cable are located inside the centre wing section, below the cockpit floor. Both are accessed through the base of the pilot's seat. (NII VVS)

switch and cockpit light, all of which matches the wiring diagram and layout found in the Ki-15-II maintenance manual. See **Ki-15-II technical description.**

Regardless of specific details, the 24Volt system fitted to the Ki-15-I would have included an engine-driven airborne generator, a battery, a voltage regulator, a main (master) switch and an electrical control panel.

We know that the 25Volt/350Watt airborne generator was located at the TDC of the Ha-8 engine accessory gearbox and Soviet photos of C/n181 confirm that the voltage regulator was mounted on the front face of secondary firewall FS.0, together with a two-cell Mk.3 Airborne Battery. The master switch and electrical control panels were located at FS.3 and between FS.3 and FS.4 on the right-hand side of the pilot's cockpit respectively.

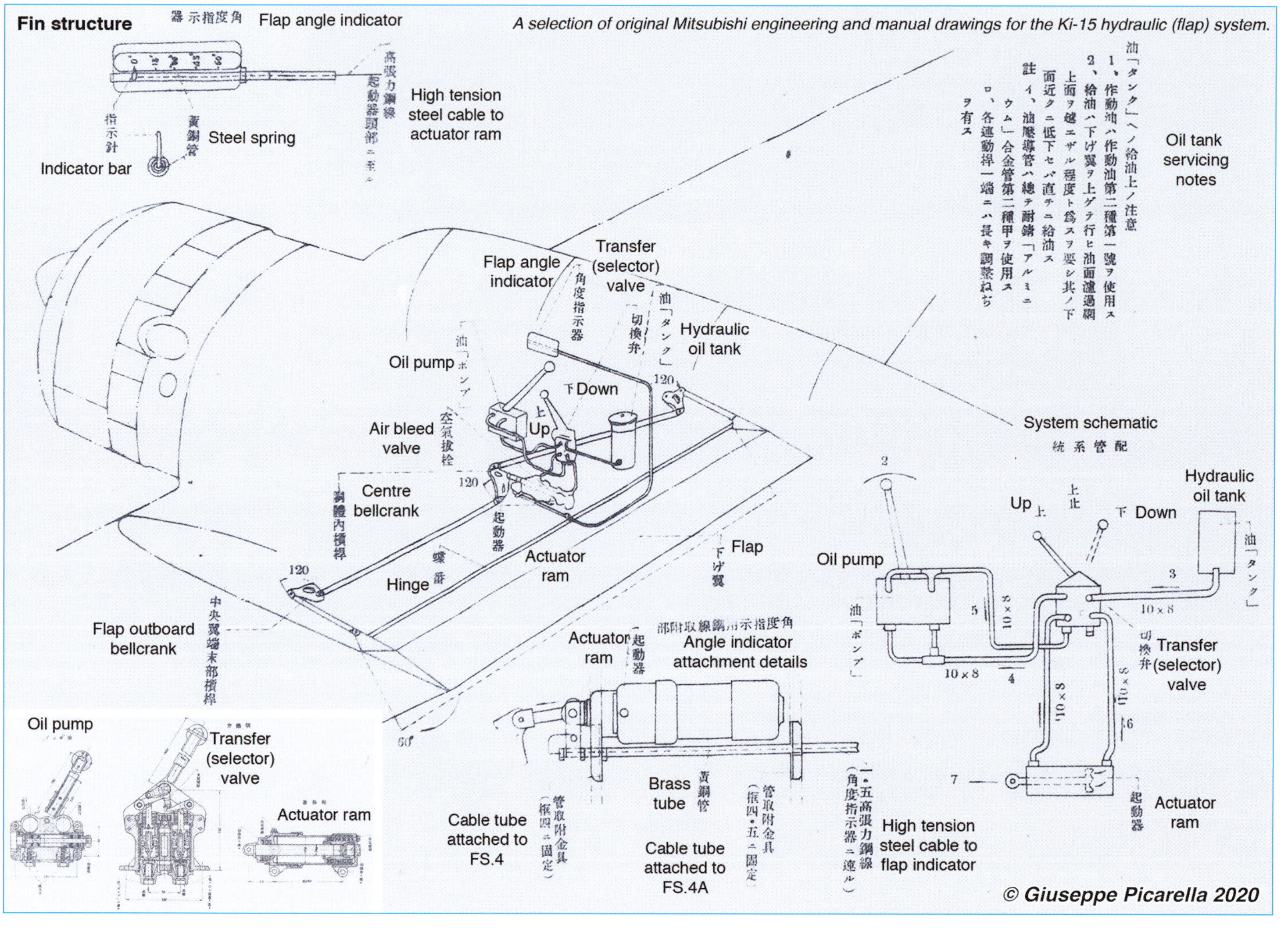

A selection of original Mitsubishi engineering and manual drawings for the Ki-15 hydraulic (flap) system.

In addition to other electrical functions, such as cockpit lighting, an electrically heated pitot system was installed on the aircraft. The master switch also supplied power to the RO's radio equipment.

External lighting

Typically the Ki-15-I was fitted with a single high power landing light and two smaller signal bulbs on the leading edge of the port wing between WS.8 and WS.9. This landing light included a bulb and concave reflector, mounted in a vertical support frame attached to the front spar. The connection between the support frame and the light unit was adjustable in two axes, allowing for alignment on the ground. Two smaller signal bulbs shared the same Plexiglas-covered bay as the landing light, but it us unknown if they were integral with the concave reflector or adjacent to it. The specific colours of these smaller lights is unknown, but red and green are most likely. An upper navigation light complete with three coloured bulbs (white, red and green) was located on the canopy frame TDC at FS.6 and a white lower navigation light was located BDC between FS.7 and FS.8. Both navigation lights were fitted within streamlined clear Plexiglas fairings and shielded with Grimes-type mounts on their forward hemisphere. This made them visible only (respectively) from above, below and behind the aircraft as per the international standards of the day.

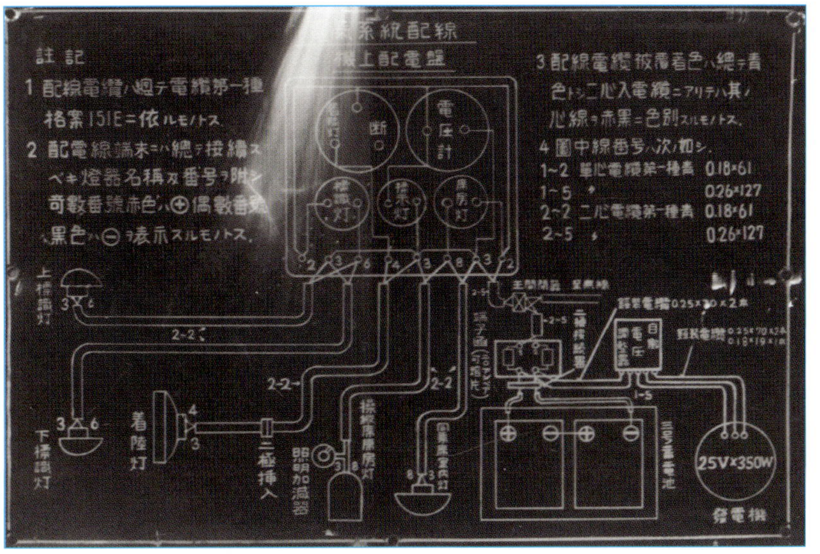

Airframe mounted electrical system placard. (NII VVS via Y. Svoyski)

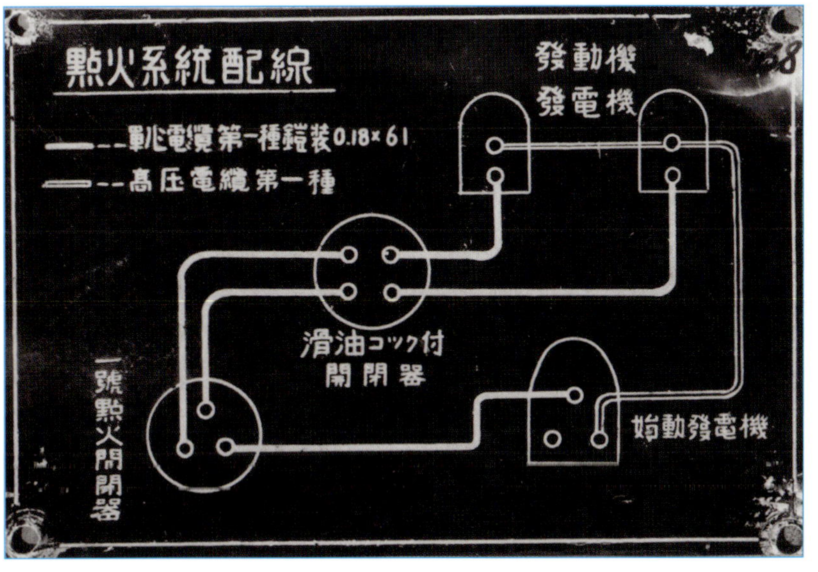

Airframe mounted magneto placard. (NII VVS via Y. Svoyski)

Cockpits and secondary systems

In the interest of clarity, the technical descriptions of the Pilot's cockpit and included systems have been separated from those of the RO's cockpit and systems.

Cockpit access

Access to the crew cockpits was accomplished with the aid of various steps and handholds located on the port side of the fuselage. Each of the spring-loaded steps contained release buttons to extend or lock each step into place when retracted. As with all aspects of the Ki-15, access handles and steps were designed to generate the least amount of drag possible when retracted. They consisted of:

1. A (vertical) boarding step located in the lower section of the wing-to-fuselage fairing adjacent to FS.7.
2. A (horizontal) mid fairing step between FS.5 and FS.6.
3. A (horizontal) rear cockpit step attached to FS.8.
4. A (flexible) upper handhold located within the canopy framework ahead of FS.6.
5. A (horizontal) forward cockpit step attached to FS.4.
6. A rear-cabin internal step located on FS.9.

In order to access the cockpits, the usual amount of balancing and leaning was required as for all such period aircraft. The pilot had to balance on the mid-fairing step while opening the sliding canopy window in order to swing open his canopy, whereas the RO had to face aft as he entered the rear cockpit in order to place his foot in the narrow slot in the centre of the storage cabinet – definitely a young man's game!

It is interesting to note that both spring-loaded cockpit steps (and presumably the vertical boarding step) could be retracted from inside the aircraft, but more importantly they could also be extended to assist crew egress when ground-crew were unavailable. It was typically the RO's responsibility to make sure that all the steps and handholds were retracted before taxiing.

Also of note is a "grip" section of the upper handhold, which is similar to the access straps or "whips" fitted to ease access onto the wing of various Japanese fighters of the period. This flexible handhold was constructed of plaited leather with a metal end-cap containing the release button. The whole handle retracted with the aid of a spring into a "U" section channel located on the upper deck of the centre canopy tunnel.

Pilot's cockpit and systems

General layout

The pilot's cockpit was position between FS.2 and FS.5 and conformed to typical layout practices of the day. It contained the instrument panel, pilot's seat, flight controls, electrical, hydraulic and fuel system controls. The pilot was responsible for flying the aircraft and navigating. He had no direct control over the operation of the radio or cameras.

Master compass

The location of the master compass migrated during the early development and operational career of the Ki-15-I. The prototype (C/n1501) was fitted with a Type-96 Magnetic Compass, attached to a large bracket, mounted centrally on the cockpit lip above the instrument panel. This was replaced with the Model-1 magnetic compass on production aircraft.

Aircraft access

An original Mitsubishi manual drawing.

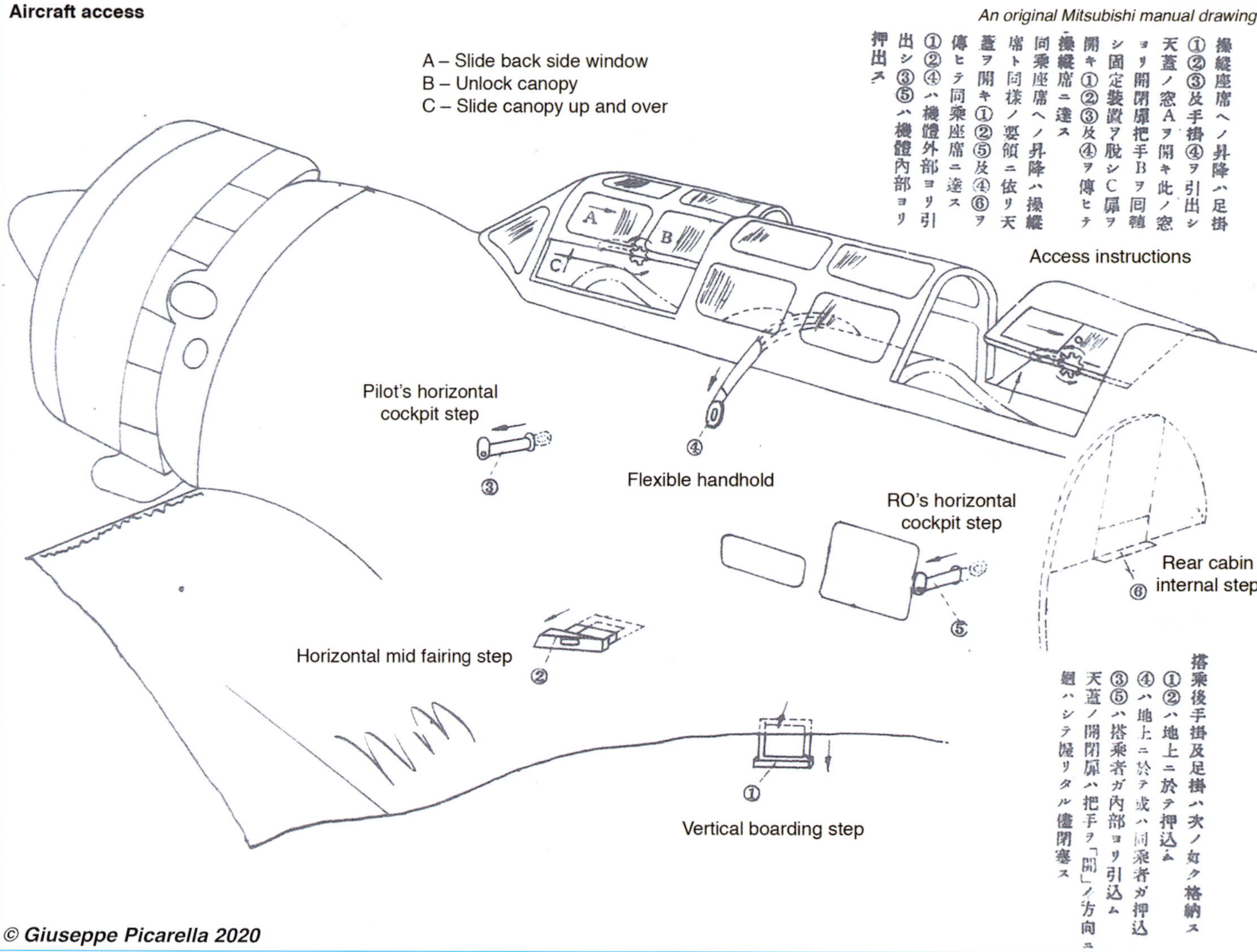

Instrument panel

All of the instrument panels fitted to the *Babs* family of aircraft were of a similar configuration, comprised of a fixed lower panel and suspended upper panel. The lower panel, containing engine and fuel systems, spanned the cockpit at a midpoint between FS.2 and FS.3 and was attached by brackets directly to the fuselage skin. The upper panel, containing the primary flight instruments, was fitted with rubber anti-vibration mounts. This panel was suspended between the fixed lower panel structure and an upper mount attached to fuselage skin. Because of the pilot's seated position, the low/narrow canopy installation and cockpit structure, the pilot could not see the upper third of the instrument panel, when sitting upright. An auxiliary panel was introduced to the right-hand side of the cockpit following the introduction of the wing leading edge fuel tanks. All panels were of pressed or built-up aluminium-alloy and photographs show that they were finished in a matt black "crackle" finish.

It should pointed out that due to drag restrictions, no venturi system was fitted to the *Babs* family of aircraft, so an engine driven vacuum was required for certain flight instruments.

Pitot system

An electrically heated pitot tube was installed on the leading edge of the port wing, outboard of WS.15. Mounted above and ahead of the wing leading edge, outside of the modified airflow, the T-shaped pitot head contained a pressure tube at the front and a static tube at the rear.

While the general pitot tube installation remained relatively unaltered over the life of the aircraft, several small modifications were evident between subtypes. The T-shaped pitot head on the Ki-15-I *late model* was raised approximately 150mm higher than that of the *early model* aircraft.

Flying controls

Flying controls were of the conventional type, with a centrally mounted control column, connected to the elevator and ailerons. The base of the control column was protected by a leather cover and zip, which stopped debris falling below the cockpit floor. The upper segment of the control column curved aft, terminating in a vertical handgrip that was wound with cord for extra grip. The rudder bar contained cable-operated toe brake pedals and fixed locator hoops to hold the pilot's feet in position. The elevator trim-wheel and trim position indicator was attached to a dedicated mounting structure located on the left side of the cockpit, aft of FS.4.

The cockpit layout of Ki-15-I – C/n181 (forward is left). The pilot's oxygen bottle is shown at the top right (photo number "N12" is written over the top), while at the bottom right is the "Additional fuel tank" filler cap. The structural item behind the seat is the floor panel, which would have covered the hydraulic systems located on the right hand floor of the cockpit. Fuel tank controls are located on the floor to the left of the seat and the control column is shown with a zip-up leather boot at its base. The seat pan has been removed, but the snap fittings for the seat-back padding are visible at the back. The dark shiny finish on the front lip of the pilot's seat would seem to indicate that the seat was painted with dark Aotake, similar to the floor frames and wing centre section structure below the seat. (NII VVS via Y. Svoyski)

Pilot and RO's cockpit and systems – Ki-15-I *early model*

1/32 Scale

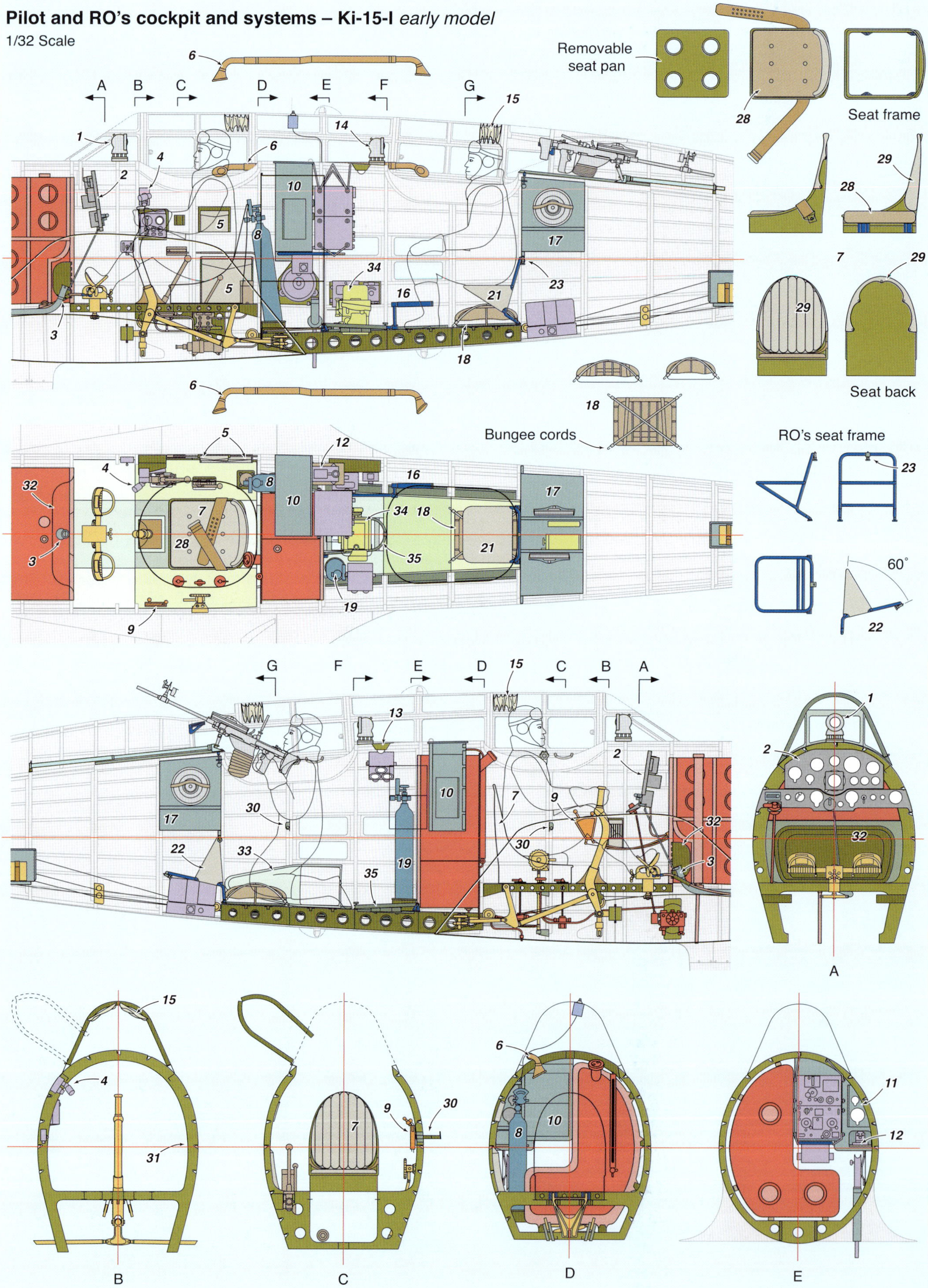

Note: Aircraft depicted with modified Type-94 Hi Mk.2 "Command" Radio installation

Representative of the production **Ki-15-I** when fitted with the *Initial* or *Intermediate* fuel systems

Upper panel

1 Altimeter Type-95
2 Airspeed indicator Type-96
3 Turn and bank indicator
4 Tachometer Type-14
5 Manifold pressure gauge Type-94
6 Chronometer Type-93
7 Artificial horizon Type-96
8 Fuel pressure gauge Type-95
9 Oil pressure gauge Type-94
10 Oil temperature gauge

Lower panel

11 Emergency boost control
12 Fuel tank selector cock
13 Starter control lever
14 Magneto switch Model-1
15 Fuel quantity gauge – fuselage tank
16 Cockpit ventilation control
17 Unidentified control – possibly the carburettor intake low/high-speed selector?
18 Fuel quantity gauge – wing tank
19 Fuel tank indicator selector – left/right
20 Starter generator
21 Fuel primer pump
22 Cylinder head temperature gauge
23 Master compass Model-1

Ki-15 prototype (C/n1501) – pilot's master compass installation

24 Compass correction card
25 Master compass Type-96
26 Compass mount

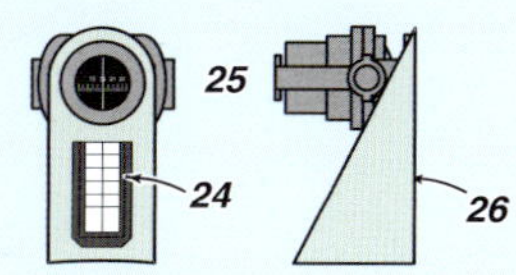

1 Pilot's master compass
2 Instrument panel
3 Fresh air vent
4 Cockpit light
5 Document case
6 Speaking tube
7 Pilot's seat
8 Pilot's oxygen cylinder
9 Throttle quadrant
10 Radio cabinet
11 RO's instrument panel
12 Writing table
13 Dome light
14 RO's master compass
15 Sunscreen
16 Engine inertia starter handle
17 Storage cabinet
18 RO's parachute
19 RO's oxygen cylinder
20 Camera plate and film holder – stowed
21 RO's seat
22 RO's seat – stowed positon
23 Seat catch
24 Storage bay retaining straps
25 RO's internal boarding step
26 RO's seatbelts
27 Rear fuselage canvas divider
28 Pilot's seat cushion
29 Pilots seat-back padding
30 Horizontal cockpit step
31 Pencil holder
32 Rudder pedal recess
33 Gunners window – stowed
34 Type-96 Aerial Camera – SK-96
35 Camera support frame

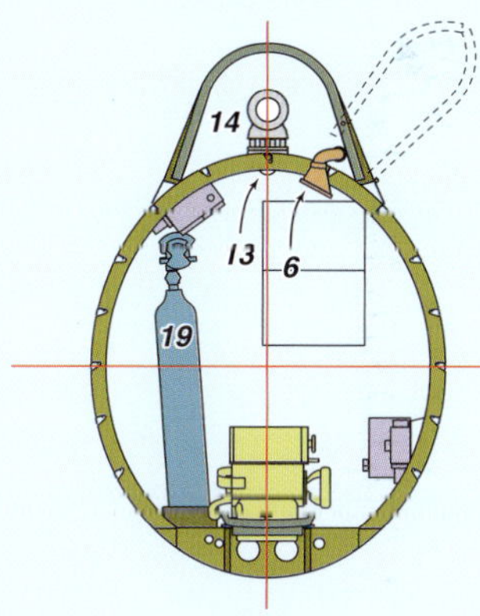

F

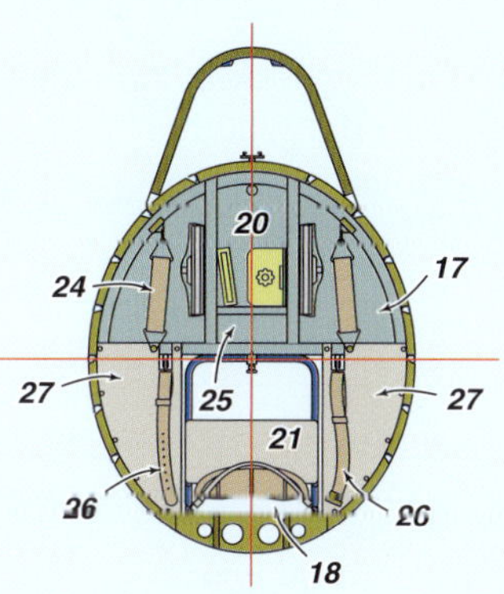

G

A selection of original Mitsubishi manual drawings for the Ki-15 fuselage.

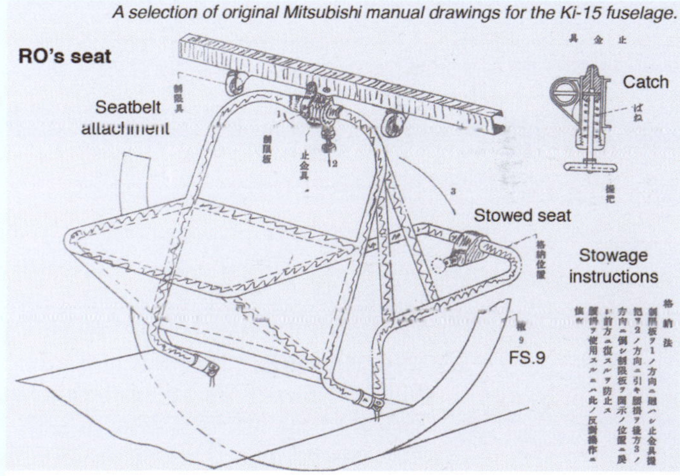

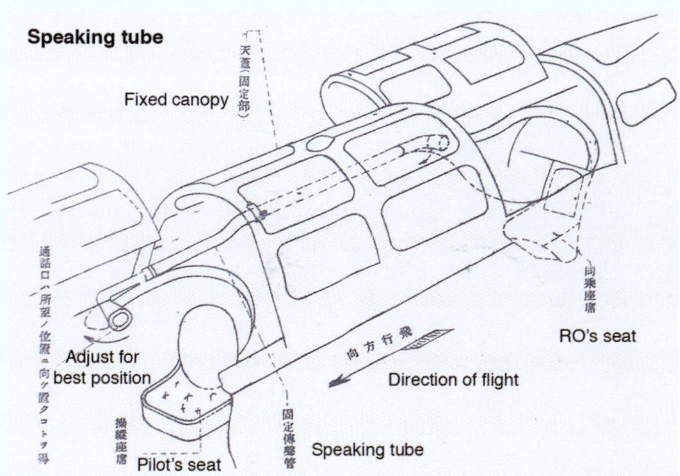

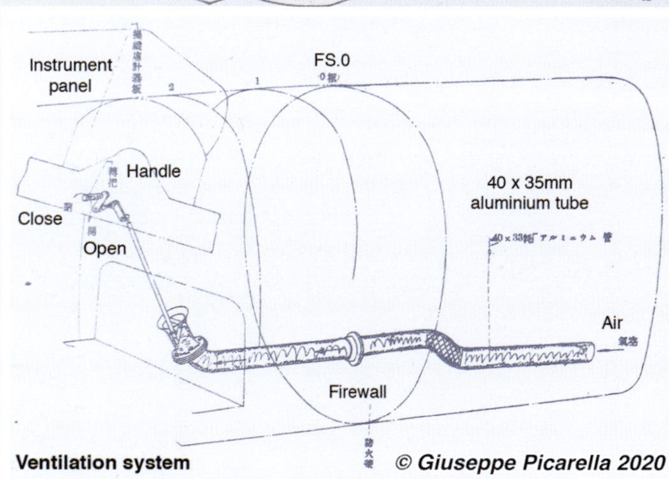

The two-part Ki-15 instrument panel is well illustrated, including the matt black crackle finish paint. The cockpit light and controller are to the upper right, and the electrical control panel is below. The control column is on the left. (NII VVS via Y. Svoyski)

Fuel system controls

Management of the fuel system was a major task for the pilot. While the fuel quantity gauges and fuel primer were located in and around the instrument panel, the system controls were all located down the port side of the cockpit for ease of operation.

1. The **Wing tank selector cock** was located on the left-hand side of the lower instrument panel.
2. The **Wing leading edge fuel cock** was located on the cockpit floor to the left of the pilot's seat, adjacent to FS.3 and FS.4,
3. A **manual fuel pump** handle was located on the cockpit floor aft of the wing leading edge fuel cock.
4. A **fuel quantity sight-glass** was provided for the "addition fuel tank". The pilot could look over his left shoulder to read the fuel quantity, as there was no fuel gauge provided for this system.

Engine controls

Engine controls were of the conventional arrangement, with a throttle quadrant located on the left-hand sidewall of the cockpit between FS.3 and FS.4. The quadrant contained a throttle and mixture control (high altitude lever), but it should be pointed out that the Japanese Army had historically used the French throttle system throughout the 1920s and 1930s, whereby the low power setting (closed throttle) was fully forwards, towards the nose of the aircraft, and high power setting (fully open) was fully aft, towards the tail of the aircraft. During the late 1930s the Army transitioned from the French system to the British system, as used by the Navy, with the full power setting (open throttle) in the forwards position. This change occurred during 1939 and 1941, so it is entirely possible that early examples of the Ki-15-I operated with the earlier "reversed" throttle linkage. It is assumed that early production examples were converted once the official changeover took place, as accidents were known to have occurred, for example when pilots operating the Ki-43-I *Oscar* transitioned over to the Ki-43-II!

Both controls levers were connected to braided steel cables, running through brass guide tubes. The tubes were attached with clamp fittings to FS.2 and FS.0, terminating with the appropriate connectors and fork fittings in the engine accessory bay.

During combat emergencies or for take-off at maximum all-up weight, the pilot could override the manifold boost pressure by operating the "Emergency boost" control, which was located on the left-hand side of the lower instrument panel.

Electrical system

The electrical system controls were located on the right side of the cockpit, with the master switch and cockpit light located on FS.3 and the electrical control panel located between FS.3 and FS.4. These control boxes would have had a matt black "crackle" finish.

Hydraulic system – flap actuation

The hand pump, selector valve and reservoir were located on the cockpit floor to the right-hand side of the pilot's seat, between to FS.3 and FS.5.

To lower the landing flap fully, the pilot selected "down" on the selector valve and pumped the hand pump approximately 10 times. To raise the flap, the pilot selected "up" on the selector valve and repeated the process. The pilot could select intermediate settings visually with reference only to the flap position indicator. See **Hydraulic system.**

Cockpit communications

Despite being the most advanced strategic reconnaissance aircraft in the world during the late 1930s, the *Babs* used an archaic internal communication system, relying on a fixed speaking tube or flexible Gosport Tubes for its entire service life. That said, the speaking tube was a proven piece of equipment that worked under all conditions and even continued to be used throughout the career of the high performance Ki-46 *Dinah*.

Initially, both the Ki-15-I and Ki-15-II used a fixed metallic speaking tube installed on the right-hand side of each the cockpit, travelling along the upper fuselage deck inside the centre canopy tunnel, from FS.5 to FS.7. Each end of the tube acted as both mouthpiece and earpiece, and could be rotated up and out of the way when not in use. On later models Gosport Tubes were employed with their rubber pipes following the same path along the upper deck, before being plugged into each crewmember's flying helmet.

Oxygen system

Ki-15-I *early model*

It is interesting to note that when the Army issued specifications for the Ki-15, they did not specify any oxygen equipment, choosing instead to stipulated a meagre operational altitude of between 2,000m – 4, 000m (6,561ft -13,123ft). Pilots operating without oxygen at altitudes between 3,657m – 3962m (12,000ft -13,000ft) are within the standard military limits of the period, but prolonged flight above 13,000ft would require a constant supply of oxygen for the aircrew. This would indicate that a fixed oxygen system was not originally planned for the aircraft, and as such the aircraft's altitude requirement revolved around human endurance limitations, rather than the 11,400m (37,401ft) service ceiling of the Ha-8 engine.

While this seems strange to us now, the role of Strategic Reconnaissance did not exist until the development of the Ki-15 and many within the Army could not come to terms with the concept, as slower aircraft operating at medium altitudes had accomplished all aerial reconnaissance tasks up to that date.

Given the aircraft's new reconnaissance role and the fact that oxygen cylinders were becoming standard issue amongst contemporary frontline fighters worldwide, one can only assume that oxygen equipment was issued as a field modification after the aircraft entered into service in China, as *Kamikaze* certainly did not carry any oxygen cylinders in early 1937.

Because the very first examples of the *early model* airframe did not utilize the "additional fuel tank", it is most likely that two oxygen cylinders (one for each crew member) would have been located close to the aircraft's (CG). The most obvious location for these large, heavy cylinders was on the opposite side of the fuselage to the original radio cabinet, between FS.5 and FS.6.

Following the adoption of the "additional fuel tank" (between FS.5 and FS.6) these bottles were presumably relocated fore and aft of the "additional fuel tank", in order to maintain the weight and balance of the aircraft. This assumption is confirmed in the Soviet report of aircraft C/n181 in February 1940, which found two (black) oxygen cylinders in the wreck. The pilot's cylinder was located over his right shoulder (behind FS.5), but canted forward, in to his cockpit, to avoid the radio cabinet structure. While it is likely that this was the standard installation of the day, it was obviously a field modification, as the Soviets reported that:

"*... all oxygen equipment, wiring, and electric heating equipment are not permanently affixed, but simply held in place by wires and tie strings.*"

Each oxygen installations consisted of a steel oxygen cylinder, a facemask and a flow-rate meter.

Ki-15-I *late model*

On *late model* aircraft a fixed oxygen system does finally make an appearance in the centre canopy tunnel. It was comprised of two identical and independent constant demand systems, located side by side,

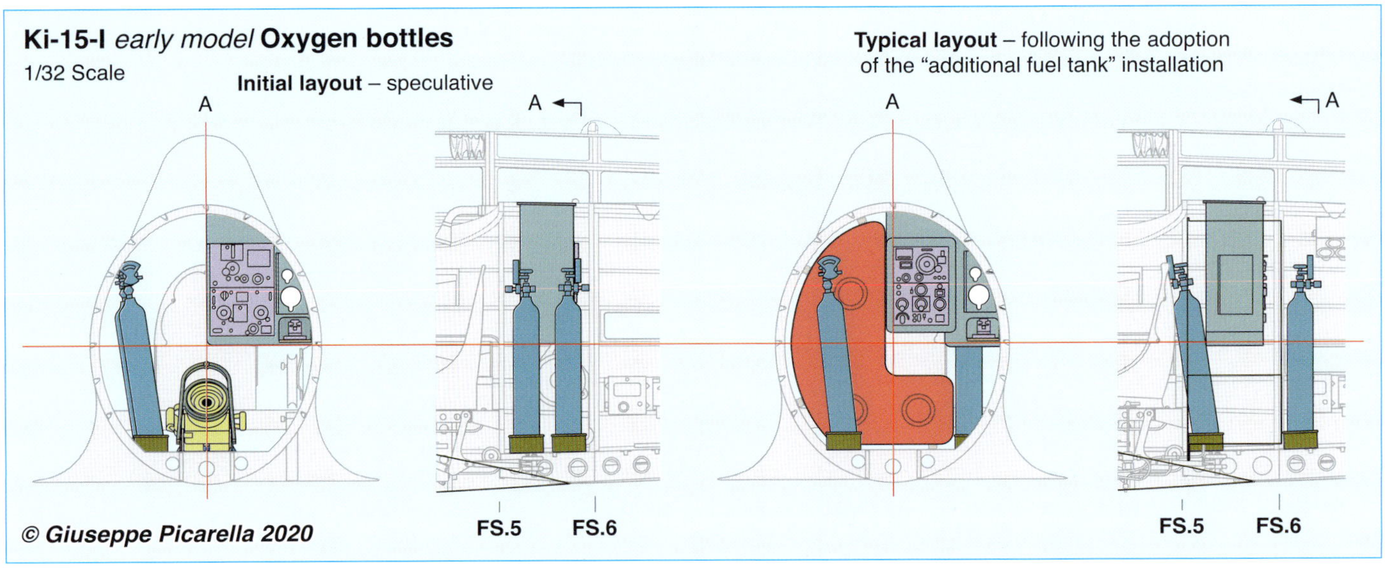

each incorporating a single oxygen cylinder, pressure/flow regulator, face mask, and supply line. Use of the oxygen system was achieved by simply turning on the flow of oxygen to the desired rate and donning the oxygen mask. The pilot's oxygen cylinder and system was mounted facing forwards, allowing the pilot to look over his should in order to set or read the pressure gauge. The RO's oxygen cylinder and system was rotated 180° to face aft. Each cylinder was attached to the fuselage by two felt-lined metal hoop mounts. The hoop mounts were hinged on one side and secured into position on the other side by a locking pin. This arrangement allowed oxygen cylinders to be rapidly removed for recharging or replacement on the ground.

The relocation of the oxygen system to the centre canopy tunnel is one of the differentiators between the *early model* and the *late model* Ki-15-I, but not in isolation. We know that the oxygen cylinders must have been repositioned after March 1939, because C/n181 does not carry such fittings, but before C/n188, as that airframe carried oxygen cylinders in the centre canopy tunnel, but these could have been retrofitted after C/n188 was originally delivered?

It should also be noted that it is highly likely that these ridged hoop mounts, when devoid of oxygen cylinders, are the cause of continued confusion regarding the installation of RDF antennas within the centre canopy tunnel of Ki-15 aircraft. See **Radio equipment and Antenna.**

Cockpit ventilation

Cockpit air was fed through an oval section (40x35mm) aluminium ram-air inlet tube, positioned between cylinders No.6 and No.7 on the right-hand side of the engine face. Protruding a little ahead of the cylinders to avoid engine fumes, the ram-air tube was routed back through the primary firewall and engine accessory bay to FS.0, where it passed through this secondary firewall, below the main fuel tank, before entering up through the cockpit floor ahead of the rudder pedals. The ventilation outlet pipe was fitted with a butterfly valve that was controlled by a pushrod connected to a bellcrank located on the lower instrument panel.

No direct ventilation was proved for the RO, but sliding side windows were provided on both sides of each cockpit canopy.

Cockpit heating

Cockpit heating at low and medium altitudes would not normally have been an issue on this class of aircraft, as the warm air from the engine bay would have percolated naturally through the airframe. In addition to this, the large greenhouse type canopy would have raised the cockpit temperature quite quickly on flights above cloud level.

For high altitude flights, the typical environment of the *Babs*, the lower external air temperatures would have been a real issue, especially in the skies over China, where winter temperatures above 9,144m (30,000ft) could easily plummet below – 58°F (–50°C). Flight crew would have dressed accordingly for such missions, wearing the heavy and restrictive fur-lined flying suits of the period, as warm-air cockpit-heating systems were not practical on such flights. Experience gained during early high altitude flights of the 1930s had proven that cockpit heating systems, combined with the respiration of the crewmembers, would cause condensation to freeze onto the inside surfaces of enclosed cockpits, obscuring canopies and the outside view. Electrically heated windows would be available on later aircraft, such as the Ki-46 *Dinah*, but even these were far from effective.

It is not known if early Ki-15-Is were capable of accepting electrically heated flight suits, as these were still a rarity in Japan at that time, found only on experimental aircraft, but the Army's initial medium altitude requirements may indicated that electrically heated flight suits were not compatible with early aircraft. This viewpoint would soon change over China and the Soviet report on C/n181 does confirm that that electrically heated flight suit controllers were included in both cockpits of that aircraft.

Sunscreens

Both the pilot and RO's bi-fold canopies could be fitted with concertina-type sunscreens. These fabric sunscreens ran along longitudinal wires spanning from the front frame to the rear frame of each canopy, which allowed them to stay extended even when the canopy was swung into the open position.

Pockets and cases

A pencil holder was located on the left side of the cockpit, between the back-to-back frames of FS.3, and a map case was positioned on the right side of the cockpit between FS.3 and FS.4.

Pilot's seat

The non-adjustable pilot's seat was constructed of sheet aluminium and fixed to the floor just ahead of FS.4 and back to FS.5. The seat consisted of a formed and pressed frame, back panel and seat-pan. The black or dark brown removable leather seat cushion and padded back support were attached to the seat structure with the aid of press-studs, and a leather lap-type seatbelt and buckle was fitted to the outside of the seat frame. The removable seat-pan allowed access to the four bolts that held the seat in position, and the systems routed beneath the cockpit. The depth of his parachute pack and the inclusion or removal of the seat cushion governed the pilot's seated position within the cockpit. Adjustable rudder pedals made this seating position quite comfortable, but it would have been difficult for the pilot to reposition himself on long flights.

Parachute

Army pilots wore contemporary seat-type parachutes, as the bucket seat was designed specifically for this purpose. Typically their parachute pack remained in the bucket seat and the pilot simply attached or detached his harness from the seat pack as he entered or vacated the cockpit.

Armour and crew protection

No armour plating, self-sealing fuel tanks, CO_2 or fire suppression equipment is known to have been fitted to the Ki-15 family of aircraft. Combat or field modifications to attach armour plating may have taken place at the local level, but no documentation exists to support this theory.

A hand-held fire extinguisher would have been carried in the aircraft, but no mention is made in the maintenance manual.

RO's cockpit and systems

General layout

Ki-15-I *early model*

The RO's cockpit was positioned between FS.6 and FS.9. It contained a reconnaissance camera, radio installation, RO's limited instrument panel, seat, storage cabinet and machine gun.

The RO was responsible for all photographic operations, radio communications and aircraft defence. He had no control over the aircraft, but would often assist the pilot with navigation duties. During taxiing, with his canopy in the open position, the RO would stand up and providing an additional pair of eyes during such ground operations. The RO would also hand-crank the engine when a Huck's starter or ground-crew were unavailable. To facilitate this role, a starter-handle was stowed in his cockpit.

Master compass

Ki-15-I

The location of the RO's master compass was relocated several times during the lifetime of the Ki-15-I. The prototype and early examples of the Ki-15-I were devoid of a compass above the cockpit lip and we know from an engineering drawing that a master compass was located BDC on the cockpit floor, between FS.5 and FS.6.

Later examples of the Ki-15-I saw the installation of a Model-1 compass standardized on the lip of the centre canopy tunnel

Radio cabinet

Due to the inclusion of the "additional fuel tank" and two different radio installations (the Type-94 *Hi* and Type-96 *Hi* "Command" radio) the layout of the RO's cockpit and the design of the radio cabinet offered three specific configurations. See **Radio equipment.**

In general, the radio installation was located to the right-hand sides of the RO's cockpit, between FS.5, FS.6 and FS.7. Depending on the fuel and radio layout, the self-contained aluminium-alloy cabinet housed the radio transmitter and receiver units, a stowable telegraph key, retractable writing table and the RO's flight instrument grouping, which included:

1. Chronometer.
2. Altimeter.

A trailing antenna reel was installed below the radio cabinet.

Internal lighting

A dome light was located TDC on the inner surface of the fuselage structure, between FS.6 and FS.7.

Oxygen system

Ki-15-I *early model*

The RO's oxygen bottle, flow regulator and face mask. The bottle and mask are black and mask surround is chamois leather. (NII VVS via Y. Svoyski)

No oxygen system was specified for the original Ki-15 design and Mitsubishi drawings provide no clues. Because of the "additional fuel tank", radio cabinet and trailing antenna reel installation (all located between FS.5 and FS.6), the most obvious location for freestanding oxygen cylinders would have been aft of FS.6 on the left-hand side of the cockpit, which would have placed the heavy cylinder close to the aircraft's CG.

Ki-15-I *late model*

See pilot's ***late model*** oxygen system notes above.

RO's seat

The RO's seat was of welded tubular steel construction with a canvas seat pan. The seat assembly was attached to the rear cockpit floor panel at FS.9, with hinge brackets. It was held in the seated position by a simple spring-loaded catch, which engaged into a C-section channel incorporated into FS.9. When the RO was required to use the machine gun, he stood up (in a stooped position), turned to face aft, released the seat catch, and then hinged the seat aft (60°) into its stowed horizontal position. A bracket was installed at the upper C-section channels, to limit the forward travel of the seat.

With the seat stowed in the horizontal position, the RO could turn to face the rear of the aircraft to operate the machine gun. Interestingly, no rear cushion or back support was provided for the RO's seat, as his standard working posture was biased towards a forward leaning position, in order to operate the floor mounted camera or radio. In practice the RO would obviously lean against FS.9 when seated upright for take-off or landing and a lap-type seatbelt was also fitted to the front face of the storage cabinet at FS.9.

Parachute

The RO's parachute pack was of the same type as the pilot, but his pack was stowed on the rear cockpit floor below his seat, with the aid of bungee cords. In this location the parachute pack acted as a kneepad when the RO was using the machine gun.

Storage cabinet

The rear cockpit contained an integral storage cabinet, which was located between FS.9 and FS.10. The cabinet spanned the full width of the fuselage, rising from stringer No.6 to the top of both frames and provided rigidity to the rear fuselage. Between stringer No.6 and floor level, two canvas covers were attached (with press-studs) to the front face of FS.9 on either side of the folding seat, in order to fully close the RO's cockpit. The storage cabinet was divided into four compartments. A central compartment and two outboard compartments were primarily designed for storage of machine gun ammunition drums (magazines), film containers and possibly the gunner's window when removed for combat. The outboard compartments were fitted with retaining straps. And the aperture below this compartment was in fact designed as a step, to facilitate the RO's entry or exit of the rear cockpit.

The area below the storage cabinet (between FS.9 and FS.10) contained the airborne transformer for the radio.

Aerial camera equipment

Aerial cameras of the late 1920s and early 1930s were typically large and bulky items, which were difficult to manoeuvre and operate. In specifying the requirements of its future airborne reconnaissance needs, the Army was wise enough to recognize the need to acquire an advanced aerial camera to be carried by such aircraft.

Army Type-96 Small Aerial Camera/SK-96

In 1933 Nippon Kogaku (Japan Optical Industries), better known as Nikon, began the development of a highly sophisticated small, lightweight camera. The aim was to deliver a modern, film-roll compatible and electrically heated aerial camera that was easy to use in handheld oblique operations, but would also offer excellent results in the fixed mapping position. For the mapping role the camera even included integral twin light projectors, capable of recording the tilt and declination of the camera onto each photographic exposure! The broad operating requirements, coupled with the complexity of the camera's systems, caused many development issues. Despite this the camera was specified within the Ki-15 requirements of July 1935 and officially accepted by the Army in 1936 as the Type-96 Small Aerial Camera (SK-96). The standard camera kit incorporated an aluminium alloy body (heated), 179mm lens (heated), folding view finder, wooden handles, roll film holder (canister), plate film holders x 4, optical view finder, viewing screen, bubble levels x 2, lens filters x 4, remote shutter release cable, power cord, lanyard and carry case.

Unfortunately it would seem that the complexity of the camera caused reliability issues and faced with these problems, the Army called for the camera to be replaced, but the small production run of SK-96 cameras soldiered on until 1940.

Army Type-96 Small Aerial Camera/SK-96

Manufacturer	Nippon Kogaku.
Shutter speeds	1/100, 1/150 sec
Finder	Frame type
Lense	179mm F4.5.
Stock type	Plate/film roll – 6 meter
Image size	12 x 16.5cm
Dimensions – width/height/depth	Approximately 38 x 25 x 36cm
Weight	9.5kg
Operation	Manual
Notes	Heated lens and body – 24 Volts

Type-96 Small Aerial Camera (SK-96) installation

1/32 Scale

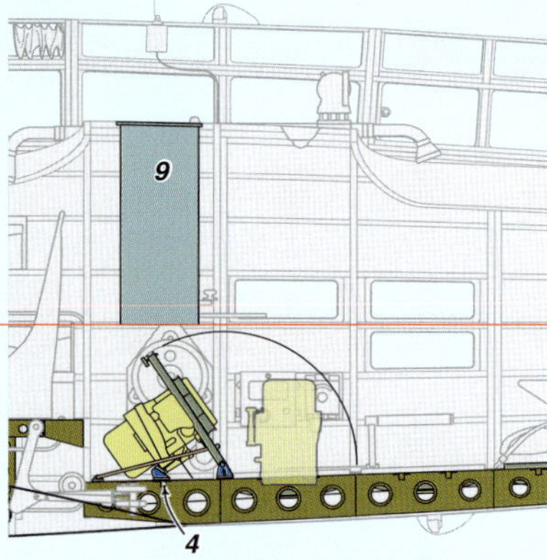

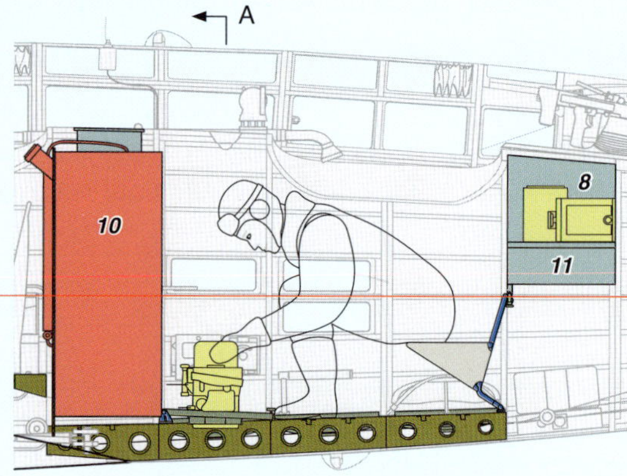

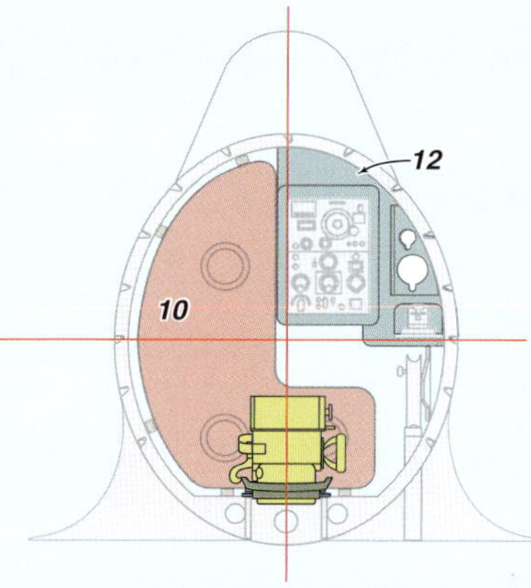

Ki-15-I *early model* with Initial fuel system – above and below

Ki-15-I *early model* with Intermediate/Standard fuel system

A

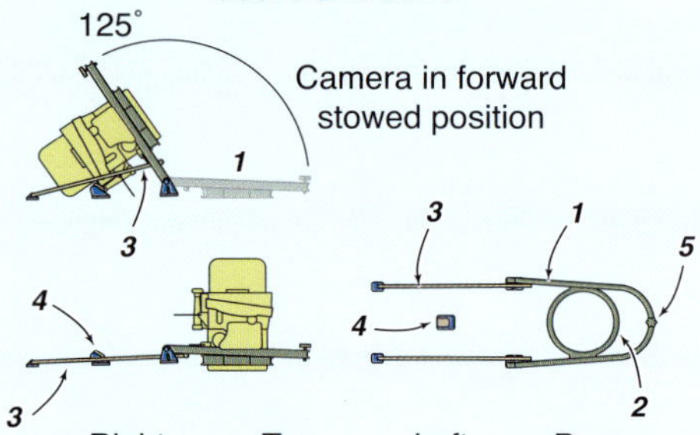

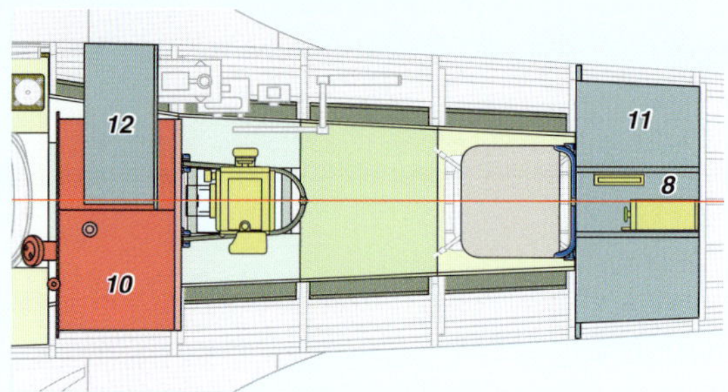

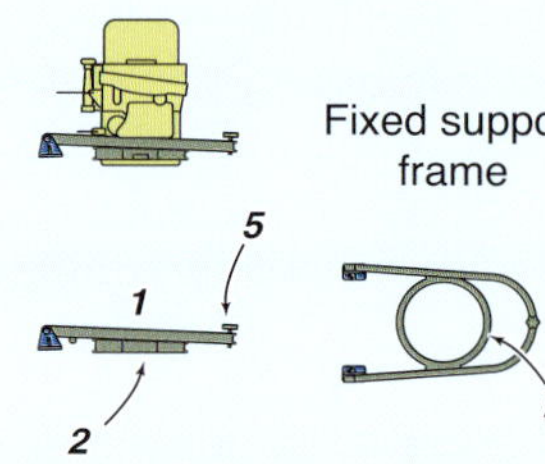

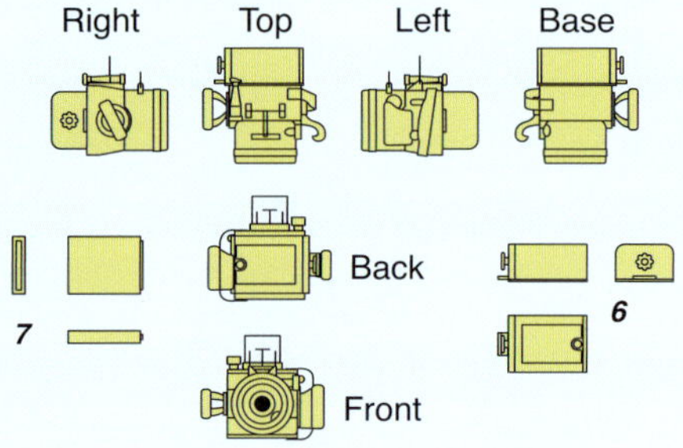

Army Type-96 Small Aerial Camera (SK-96)

1. Camera hinged support frame
2. Camera attachment ring
3. Bungee cord
4. Camera shock absorber – when stowed
5. Frame grip/locking screw
6. Film roll canister
7. Film plate
8. Film plate and roll canister stowage
9. Radio cabinet – Type-94 Hi Mk.2 Radio
10. "Additional fuel tank"
11. Storage cabinet
12. Radio cabinet – Type-96 Hi Mk.2 Radio

An RO inspecting his SK-96 camera

Camera equipment

An original Mitsubishi manual drawing for the Ki-15-I camera installation.

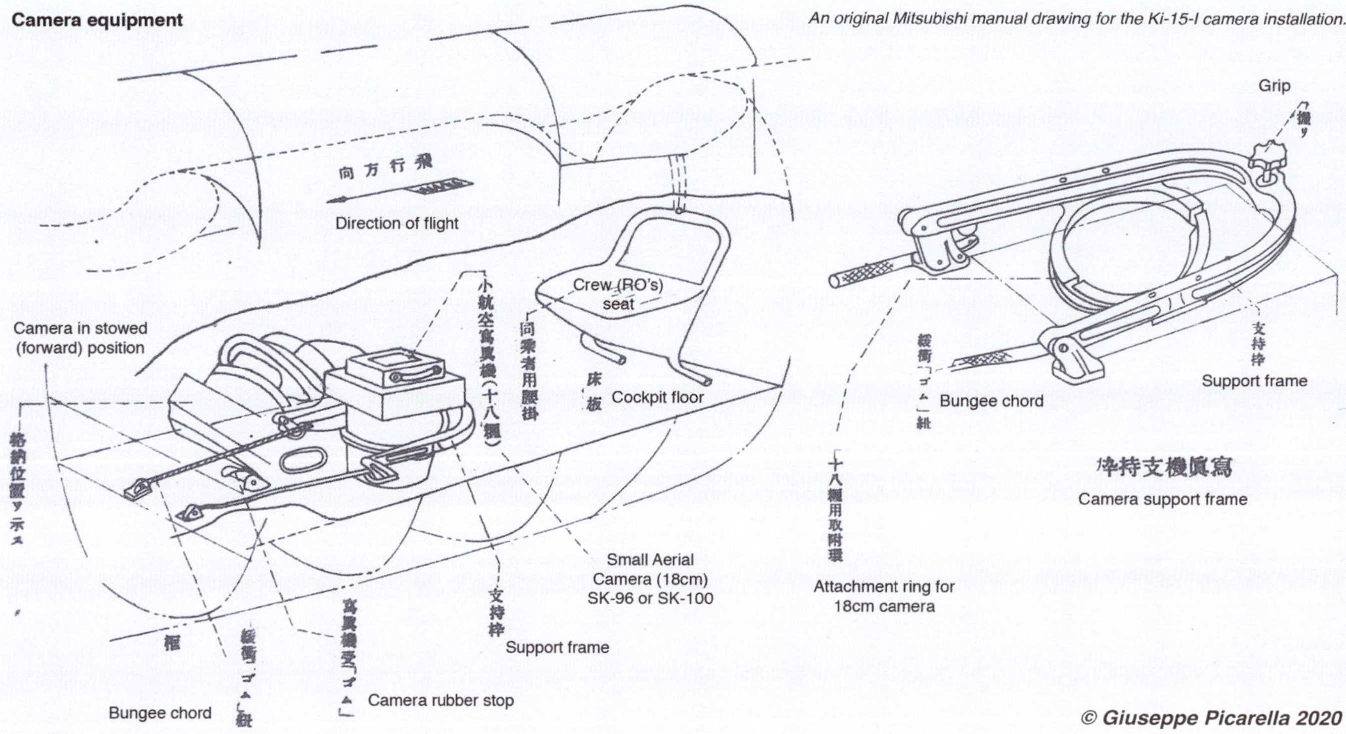

Camera support frame

The support frame for the Army Type-96 (and the subsequent Type-100 Small Aerial Camera) was manufactured from cast aluminium alloy and comprised two parts; the support frame and attachment ring.

The support frame was attached to the RO's cockpit floor by two brackets, located just aft of FS.6. These brackets allowed the frame (and attached camera) to be hinged forwards for storage, so that the RO could observe the approaching target area through the open vertical camera window. To assist the RO in manoeuvring the camera, the attachment frame was fitted with an elastic bungee or shock cord, which held the camera in either the deployed (vertical) position or the (horizontal) stowed position. The shock cord was attached in its forward extremity by two brackets mounted on the RO's floor just ahead of FS.5. When in the deployed position, the support frame was securely located with a retaining bolt at its aft end, which also acted as the handgrip for raising or lowering the frame.

The camera was secured to the support frame by way of a circular attachment ring, which bridged the frame and added rigidity to the installation. The ring was fitted with a simple bayonet fitting, which engaged with two locator pins on the forward bezel of the camera body.

The support frame (and attached camera) was designed to be manoeuvred through 125° from the deployed position to the stowed position, with the back of the camera resting on a shock absorber mounted on the RO's floor. In the stowed position, the camera and support frame was wholly located between FS.5 and FS.6, directly below the radio installation.

Theoretically, while the support frame was designed to be hinged forwards for stowage, the adoption of the "additional fuel tank" (between FS.5 and FS.6) effectively rendered camera stowage physically impossible. When the RO was required to use the vertical camera window (for target alignment, etc.,) the camera was typically placed on the cockpit floor (to the right of the camera window), or stowed in the rear storage cabinet.

Cameras by their very nature are precise instruments, susceptible to impact damage, dust and moisture, etc. For this reason aerial reconnaissance cameras (both hand-held and fixed) were typically removed from their aircraft when not in use.

Vertical (camera) window and lateral windows

The vertical camera window was located between FS.6 and FS.7, and contained an optically flat pane of glass, approximately 200mm x 350mm. Due to its location (in line with and downwind of the engine) is most likely that this window was hinged upwards into the RO's cockpit to facilitate cleaning or camera operations.

Mitsubishi engineering drawings show a slatted hatch cover located above the vertical camera window, in order to provide a single-level floor for the RO, while also protecting the vertical camera window. It is assumed that this cover, which allowed the RO to look vertically down below the aircraft, was utilised when the camera and frame was in the stowed position. But, given the redundancy of the frame stowage facility it is likely that the camera support frame remaining in place most of the time. Mitsubishi drawings also give the impression that this hatch was hinged on its forward edge, but this is unlikely. These hinge points are in fact the attachment fittings for the camera support frame, as it would be impossible to hinge the hatch forwards, because it would have conflicted with the camera support frame and the "additional fuel tank" installation.

Ki-15-I – prototypes

The RO's cockpit was a naturally dark environment due to the size and location of the upper fuselage structure. When leaning forwards on his seat, to operate the radio or camera, the working environment

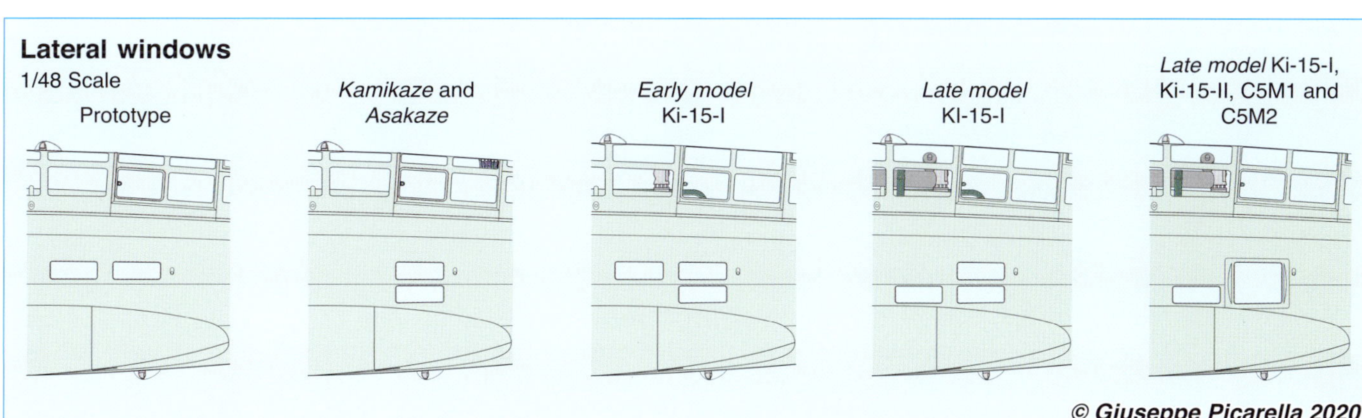

The Type-96 Small Aerial Camera. (Richard A Lane)

became darker still. A dome light provided some light, but in order to provide additional light the prototype Ki-15 (C/n1501) was fitted with two Plexiglas lateral window panels, located on both sides of the cockpit between FS.6, FS.7 and FS.8, sitting between stringers No.5 and No.6.

The 2nd prototype (C/n1502) *Kamikaze* carried a revised layout, with these lateral windows relocated to sit one above the other between FS.7 and FS.8, sitting between stringers No.5, No.6 and No.7. This modification was necessary due to the installation of the centre fuselage fuel tanks, which rendered the forward lateral window panels redundant between FS.6 and FS.7. While this modification did not increase the overall area of window, their relocation would have made the cockpit feel a little more open. The lateral window installation on the 3rd prototype *Asakaze* was identical to the 2nd prototype.

Ki-15-I *early model*

By the 7th production aircraft (C/n107) *Sochikaze*, the layout of the lateral windows had once again changed, with an additional panel included between FS.6 and FS.7, sitting between stringers No.5 and No.6. These windows not only increased the amount of light entering the RO's cockpit, they also served to provide a "slant" or sideways view of the ground below. While this was useful for confirming the position of the aircraft, and for keeping a lookout for intercepting aircraft, the idea of taking photographs through the lateral windows, given their small size and the profile of the Plexiglas panels was impractical. In addition to this, the height of the RO's canopy, coupled with the high cockpit sill, made it difficult for the RO to take lateral photographs through the main canopy. This would not have been an issue for the RO's of slower reconnaissance aircraft of the period, as they typically opened the cockpit canopy and leaned out of the aircraft with the camera, but for the Ki-15 this was awkward due to the narrow width of the canopy and its "up and over" movement. This flawed window installation remained constant up until at least aircraft C/n181, after which some aircraft had the additional window panel (between FS.6 and FS.7) relocated lower down to sit between stringers No.6 and No.7. Once again, this modification would have been more useful for downward observations, but still impractical for meaningful photography.

Ki-15-I *late model*

The double lateral panels occupying the area between FS.7 and FS.8 on the *early model* Ki-15-I were combined into a single, optically-flat photography window on the C5M1 and *late model* Ki-15-I in early and late April 1939 respectively. These panels were set into a special mounting frame that blended the curved fuselage at FS.7 into the flat glass windowpane and then back out to the curved profile at FS.8. In addition to this the curved single panels, ahead of the double panels, were also replaced with optically flat panes, but these were simply blended into the fuselage profile at their leading and trailing edges with putty.

No blinds or curtains were fitted to the lateral windows.

Radio equipment

Ki-15-I *early model*

As part of the initial Ki-15 specifications a Type-94 *Hi* Mk.2 wireless telegraph was included within the Army requirements. The defining Japanese character "*Hi*" or "flying" within the description identifies it specifically as airborne equipment. Little is known about the Type-94 *Hi* Mk.2 "Command" Radio as it was known, other than a few technical details listed in wartime intelligence documents. The radio operated in the frequency range of 1.4-7.9 megacycles, with an output of 15-20Watts. The transmitter/receiver weighed 16.3kg (36 lbs), while the weight of the airborne transformer (dynamotor), starter, ammeter and Mk.3 Airborne Battery would no doubt have doubled the overall weight of the installation. The transmitter and receiver were fabricated as individual units, which could be slotted into the original radio cabinet.

The Type-94 Hi Mk.4 wireless telegraph removed from Ki-15-I – C/n181. (NII VVS via Y. Svoyski)

The Type-94 *Hi* Mk.2 "Command" Radio installation found on Ki-15-I C/n181 — NII VVS via Y. Svoyski

1. Type-94 *Hi* Mk.2 receiver
2. Type-94 *Hi* Mk.2 transmitter
3. Telegraph (Morse) key
4. Ammeter
5. Starter unit
6. Input regulator
7. Transformer – cover removed
8. Radio suspension fittings
9. Antenna controller?
10. Microphone mouthpiece
11. Earphone
12. Battery cell

Type-94 Hi Mk.4 wireless transmitter and telegraph key. (NII VVS via Y. Svoyski)

Type-94 Hi Mk.4 wireless receiver. (NII VVS via Y. Svoyski)

Before the adoption of the "additional fuel tank", the radio installation in the Ki-15 would have been a straightforward exercise. But following this modification, space in the RO's cockpit was definitely at a premium. It is interesting to note that the Soviet report on C/n181 indicates that the Type-94 *Hi* Mk.2:

"Radio equipment has been recently upgraded, as the new radio equipment does not fit into the allocated mounting area."

This evidence would indicate that the combined Type-94 *Hi* Mk.2 "vertical" radio configuration could not be mounted within the new radio cabinet installation, as fitted to aircraft with the "additional fuel tank", a fact later confirmed on the CAD models produced for this book. Photographs of the radio installation removed from C/n181 show that bungee cord suspension fittings or "mushrooms" were still in place, which means that the radio was suspended from the fuselage structure, most likely between FS.6 and FS.7, in front of the new radio cabinet. Whether this stop-gap installation was a common occurrence, when the "additional fuel tank" first began to appear, is unclear, but the fact that the radio could not fit into the radio cabinet would indicate that either the Type-96 *Hi* Mk.2 radio was in

Radio dynamotor. (NII VVS via Y. Svoyski)

The Type-96 Hi Mk.2 "Command" radio. (Hubert Miller)

The Army Type-96 *Hi* Mk.2 "Command" radio was smaller and more compact than the earlier Type-94 *Hi* Mk.2. When installed inside a radio mount or cabinet, the external bungee cord suspension fittings "mushrooms" could be removed. © Hubert Miller 2021

Type-94 *Hi* Mk.2 "Command" Radio installations

1/32 Scale

Ki-15-I with Initial fuel system

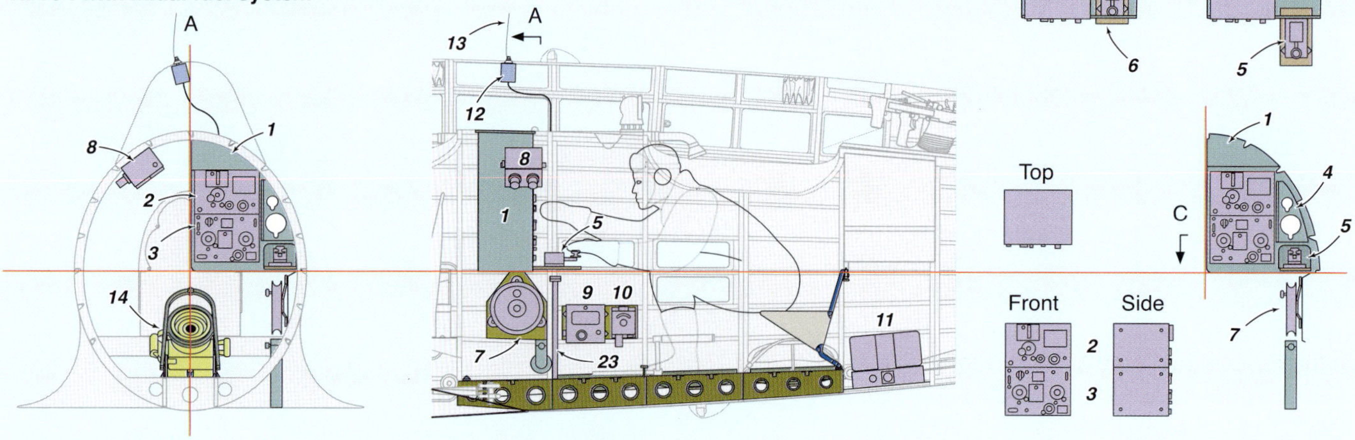

Ki-15-I with Intermediate/Standard fuel system – based on radio dimensions and Soviet report on aircraft C/n181

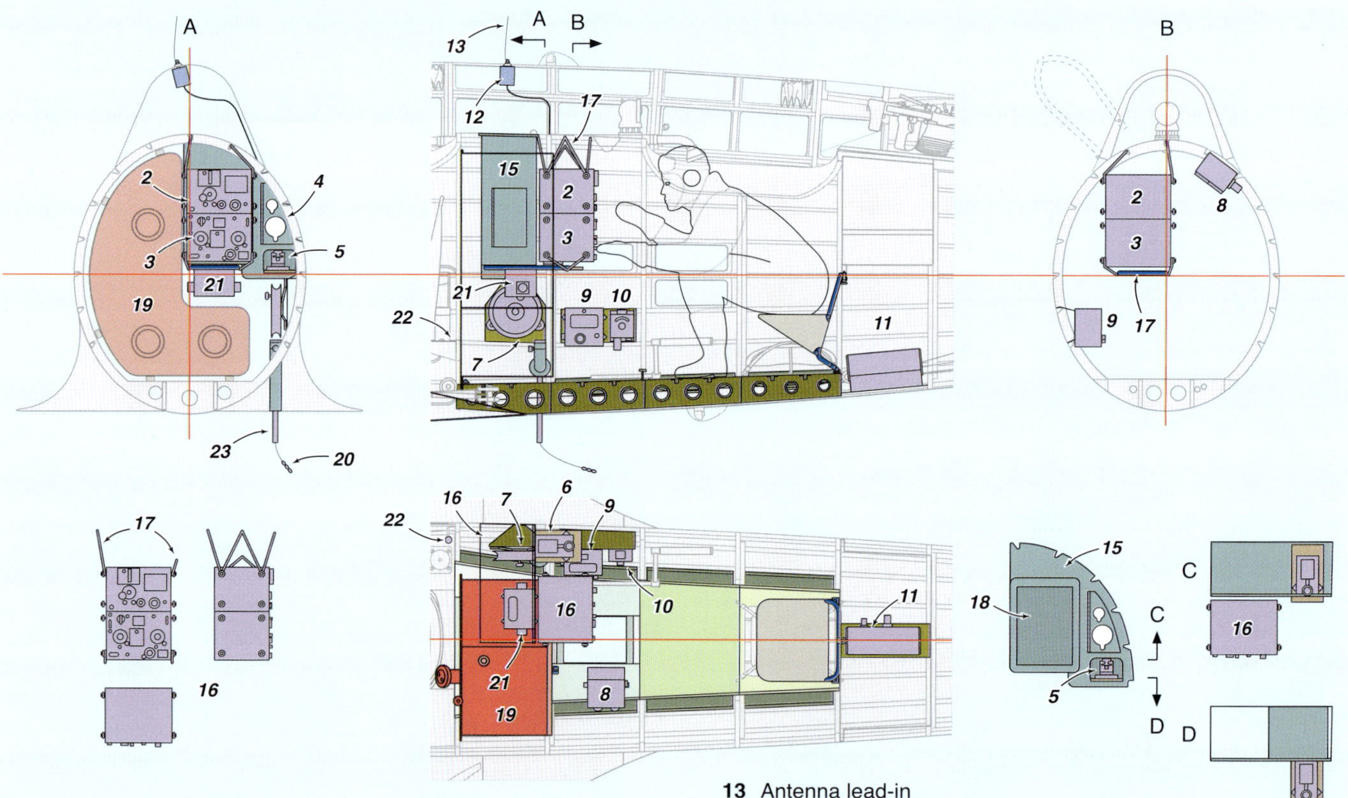

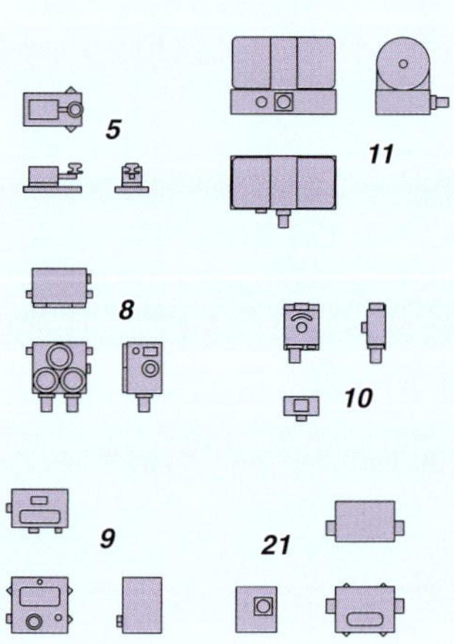

Typical installation

1 Radio cabinet designed specifically for the Type-94 *Hi* Mk.2 "Command" Radio
2 Type-94 *Hi* Mk.2 receiver
3 Type-94 *Hi* Mk.2 transmitter
4 RO's instrument panel
5 Telegraph (Morse) key
6 Retractable writing/Morse key table
7 Trailing antenna reel and guide tube
8 Ammeter
9 Starter unit
10 Input regulator
11 Transformer
12 Antenna connector
13 Antenna lead-in
14 Camera in forward stowed position

Aircraft C/n181 installation

15 Radio cabinet designed specifically for the Type-96 *Hi* Mk.2 "Command" Radio
16 Suspended Type-94 *Hi* Mk.2 radio
17 Radio suspension fittings
18 Empty radio aperture
19 "Additional fuel tank"
20 Trailing antenna
21 Antenna controller?
22 Radio power source connector
23 Trailing antenna insulator tube

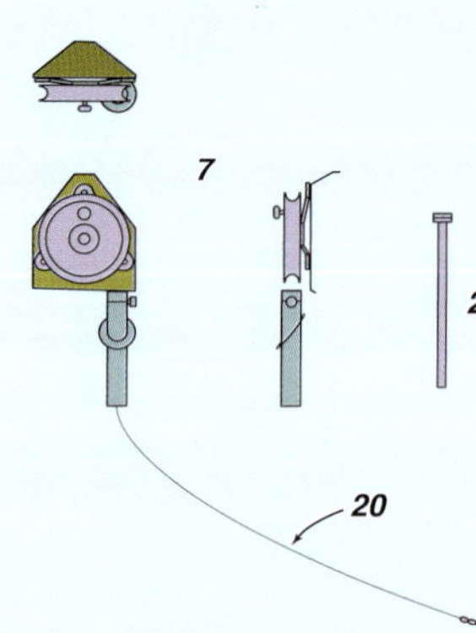

short supply, or that the "additional fuel tank" was retrofitted in the field and the newer radios had not yet arrived?

It should also be noted that while it may have been technically possible for the pilot to listen and talk on the radio (on lone delivery flights) by re-routing the RO's headphones and microphone through to the front cockpit, the pilot could not remotely control or tune the radio equipment in any way.

Ki-15-I *late model* and Ki-15-II

The standard radio installation of the Ki-15-I *late model* (and Ki-15-II) was the Army Type-96 *Hi* Mk.2 "Command" radio. This radio operated in the 0.2-0.5/1.5-7.5 megacycles range with 8-10Watts of power, weighing in at 37kg (82 lb) as a complete unit. The equipment was arranged in the following order: power was supplied via the Mk.3 Airborne Battery, or the aircraft main power switch to the single dynamotor, which was controlled by a starter switch. Power from the transformer was fed to the transmitter/receiver and then out to the aerial via a dedicated aerial ammeter unit. In its "slide-in" cabinet-mounted configuration the combined radio transmitter/receiver body was 330 x 230 x 178mm (13 x 9 x 7 inches) in size, and was suspended on the right-hand side of the cockpit between FS.5 and FS.6. When installed as a suspended configuration, with external "mushroom" fittings, etc., this radio could measure as much as 431 x 330 x 279mm (17 x 13 x 11 inches) in size.

The radio starter and input regulator were located on a shelf in front of the right-hand side lateral window between FS.6 and FS.7. The aerial ammeter was located in front and above the radio cabinet between FS.6 and FS.7. The transformer location remained unchanged.

The faces of the Type-94 *Hi* and Type-96 *Hi* "Command" radio transmitters/receivers and ammeters were all aluminium in colour.

Antenna

In order to retain aerodynamically clean lines the 1st prototype Ki-15 (C/n1501) did not carry an externally mounted antenna mast, but a standard antenna fitting was located at the top of the fin leading edge (FinS.7). The 2nd prototype (C/n1502) was fitted with a welded steel aerofoil-section mast, which was attached to the secondary firewall ahead of FS.0, by way of a fixed mounting bracket and three attachment bolts. It projected approximately 95cm above the fuselage and terminated in the form of a streamlined eye. The aerial typically exited the aircraft via a lead-in insulator located on the TDC frame of the centre canopy tunnel, midway between FS.5 and FS.6. On several aircraft this exit location migrating rearwards towards FS.6 and some insulators were located to the port side of the canopy frame, adjacent to the upper position light at FS.6. From the canopy insulator, the aerial travelled up to meet the forward insulator where it was routed aft to the standard rear insulator fitting on the fin. The forward section of rigging line between the aerial mast and lead-in insulator was inert.

Drawings of the prototype indicate that a trailing antenna reel and guide tube was fitted to the right-hand sidewall of the fuselage between FS.5 and FS.6, adjacent to stringer No.7. With the adoption of the "additional fuel tank", the location of the trailing antenna assembly and guide tube remained unaltered, because the right-hand side of the fuel tank was specifically truncated to provide space for the trailing antenna reel assembly. That being said, the location of the trailing antenna reel was not ideal and the installation was relocated on the Ki-15-II and Navy C5M airframes.

Radio Direction Finders

Various post-war sources have attributed Radio Direction Finder (RDF) equipment and specifically RDF Hoop antennas as being fitted to the Ki-15. These claims most likely stem from the misidentification of the oxygen cylinder hoop mounts located in the centre canopy tunnel of the *late model* Ki-15-I. Certainly these mounts, devoid of their oxygen cylinders, do look like RDF Hoop antennas. Despite these claims, no Radio Direction Finder (RDF) equipment or antenna loops have been observed or documented on Ki-15 aircraft. In addition to this, no such equipment is including within the Ki-15-II maintenance manual.

The installation of RDF equipment in Navy C5M aircraft is much more credible and the fact that the Ki-15 and C5M were both identified by the same Allied code name (*Babs*) within intelligence reports, has most likely added to this source of confusion.

Armament

When Capt. Fujita and Nario Ando wrote the original specification for the Ki-15, no mention of defensive armament was made because both men believed that the aircraft's high speed would render it immune to interception. This concept did not sit well with the Army, who firmly believed that combat aircraft should be armed, regardless of their role, and the Ki-15's specifications were duly modified to include a 7.7mm flexible machine gun.

Exactly which armament was initially intended for the production aircraft is open to debate, as the earliest Mitsubishi inboard profile shows an unusual weapon silhouette, similar to a Type-89 7.7mm fixed machine gun, but fitted with a pan type magazine located at the forward end of the receiver assembly, together with a large diameter barrel jacket and traditional Vickers style twin handgrips/trigger assembly. This weapon is believed to be the Te-1, which saw only very limited production between 1936 and 1938, before being replaced by more robust machine guns. While the Te-4 flexible machine gun would become the standard Ki-15-II defensive weapon (See **Te-4 7.7mm flexible machine gun**) the Ki-

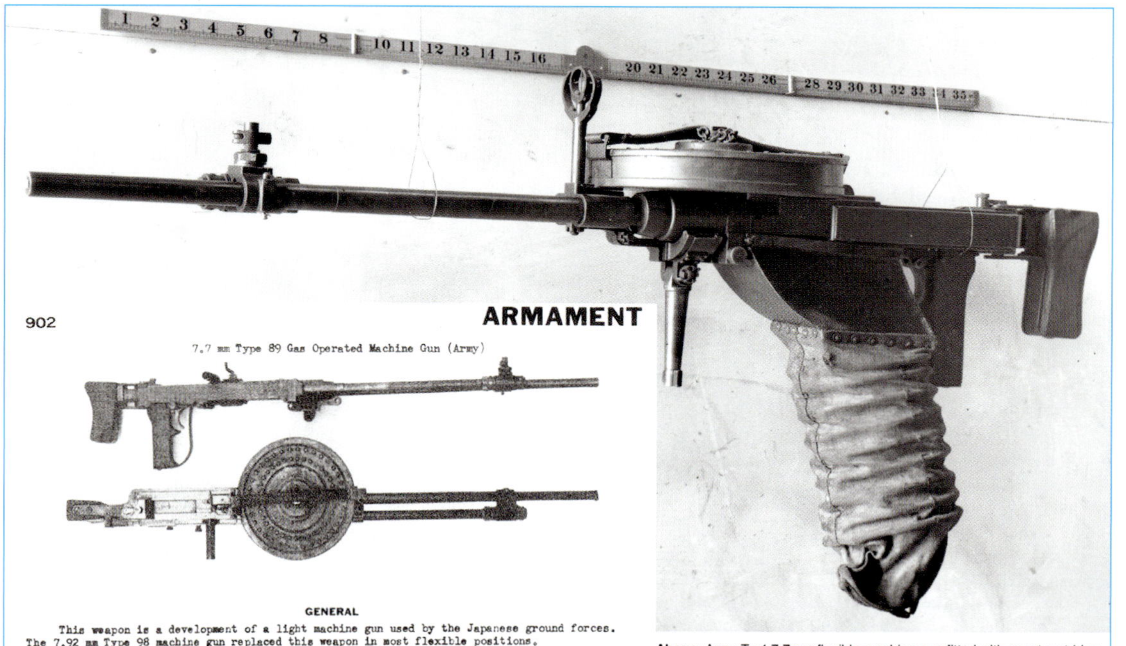

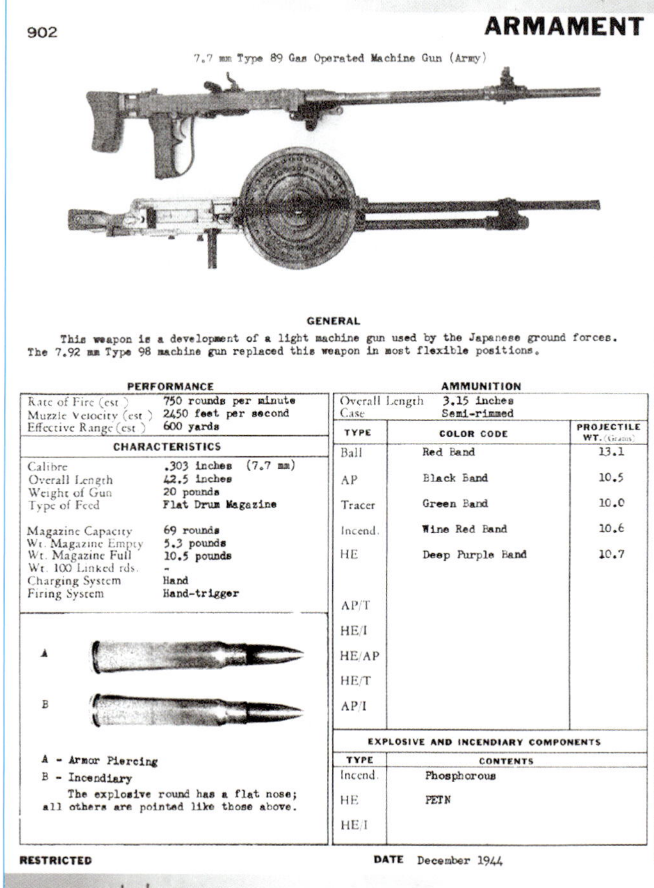

902

ARMAMENT

7.7 mm Type 89 Gas Operated Machine Gun (Army)

GENERAL

This weapon is a development of a light machine gun used by the Japanese ground forces. The 7.92 mm Type 98 machine gun replaced this weapon in most flexible positions.

PERFORMANCE

Rate of Fire (est.)	750 rounds per minute
Muzzle Velocity (est.)	2450 feet per second
Effective Range (est.)	600 yards

CHARACTERISTICS

Calibre	.303 inches (7.7 mm)
Overall Length	42.5 inches
Weight of Gun	20 pounds
Type of Feed	Flat Drum Magazine
Magazine Capacity	69 rounds
Wt. Magazine Empty	5.3 pounds
Wt. Magazine Full	10.5 pounds
Wt. 100 Linked rds.	-
Charging System	Hand
Firing System	Hand-trigger

A

B

A - Armor Piercing
B - Incendiary
The explosive round has a flat nose; all others are pointed like those above.

AMMUNITION

Overall Length 3.15 inches
Case Semi-rimmed

TYPE	COLOR CODE	PROJECTILE WT. (Grams)
Ball	Red Band	13.1
AP	Black Band	10.5
Tracer	Green Band	10.0
Incend.	Wine Red Band	10.6
HE	Deep Purple Band	10.7
AP/T		
HE/I		
HE/AP		
HE/T		
AP/I		

EXPLOSIVE AND INCENDIARY COMPONENTS

TYPE	CONTENTS
Incend.	Phosphorous
HE	PETN
HE/I	

RESTRICTED

DATE December 1944

Above: Army Te-4 7.7mm flexible machine gun fitted with spent cartridge concertina type bag. The forward and rear sights are not installed.
Left: TAIC listing for the Te-4 machine gun, although it is identified as the "Type-89 flexible machine gun".
Below: Contemporary film still showing the Ki-15 gunners window handle.
Bottom: This Te-4 is fitted with a "vane" drift sight at the front and fixed sight in the centre. Each individual aircraft type and weapon location (window or turret, etc.,) used the most affective sights for that installation.

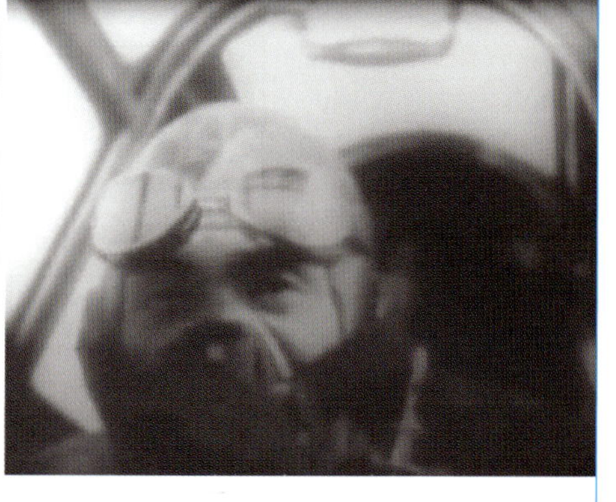

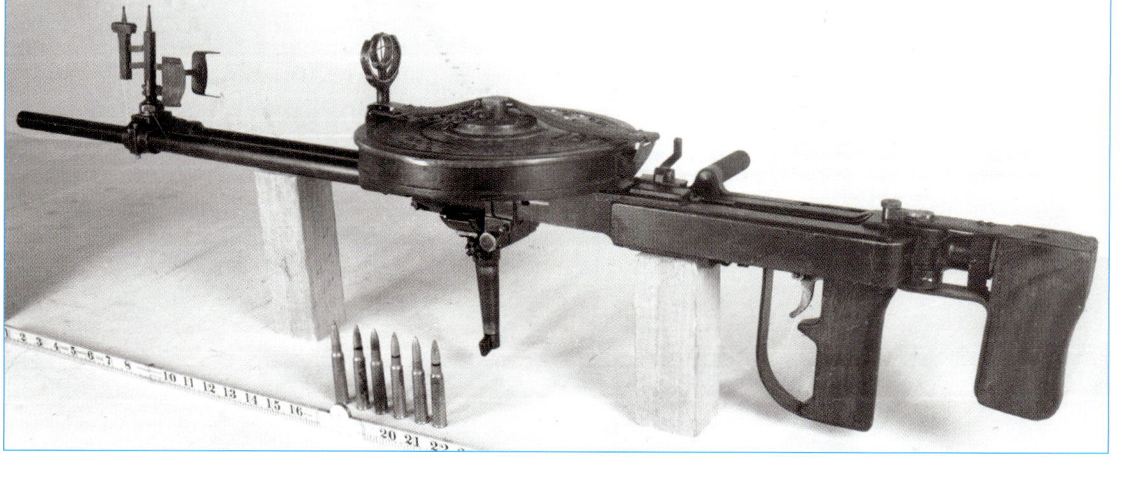

Ki-15 Machine gun installation

1/32 Scale

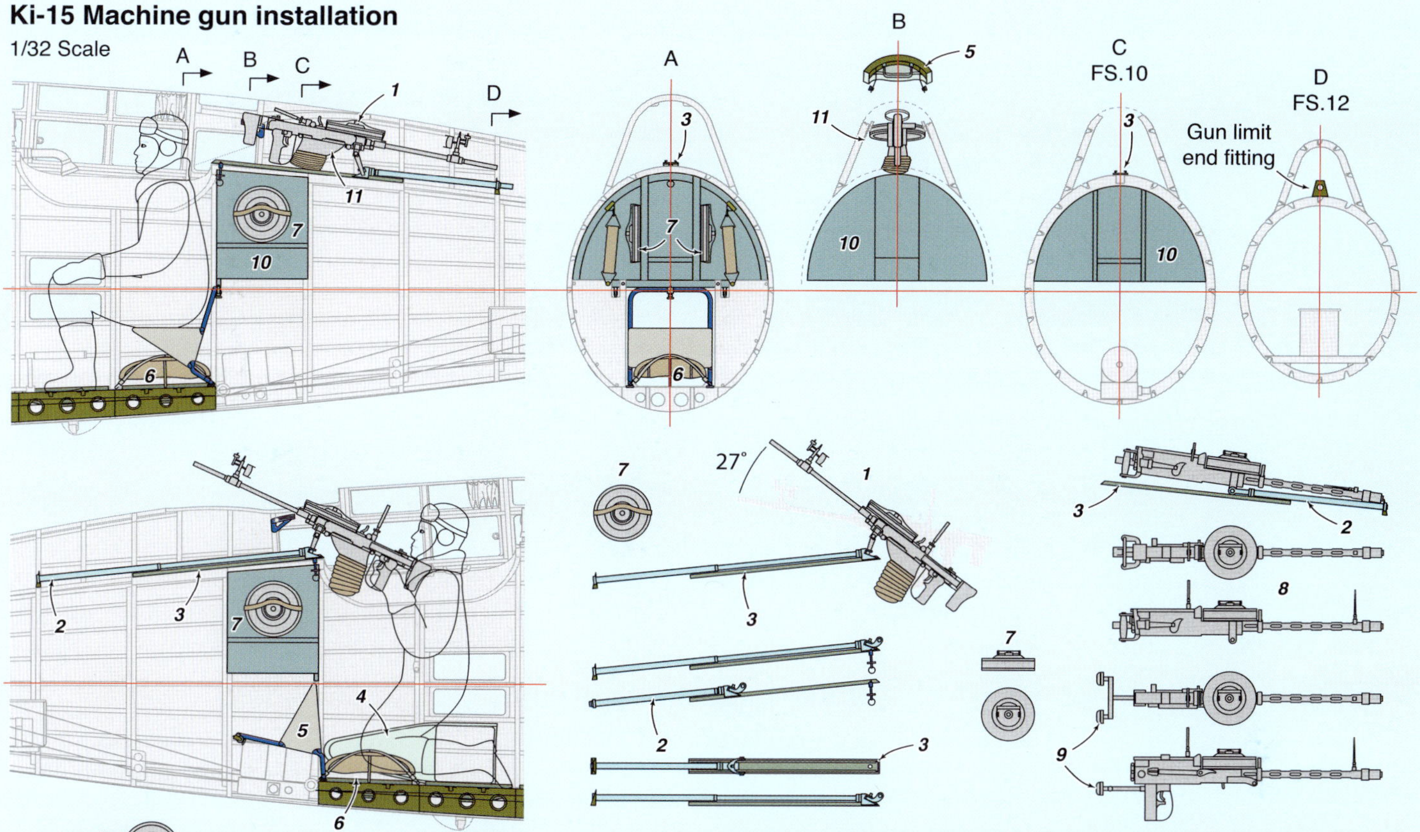

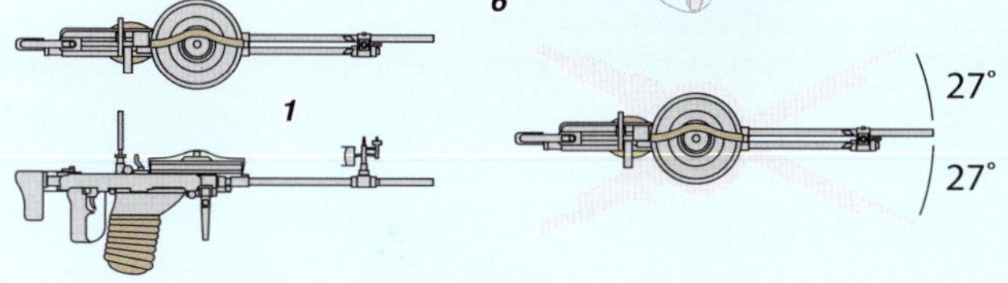

1 Te-4 7.7mm flexible machine gun
2 Gun limit fitting – telescopic strut
3 Gun track
4 Gunner's window – stowed
5 RO's seat – stowed
6 RO's parachute knee pad
7 Machine gun magazine
8 Te-1 single barrel rotary feed machine gun
9 Y-shaped shoulder stock
10 Storage cabinet
11 Machine gun – stowed

An original Mitsubishi manual drawing for the Ki-15 machine gun.

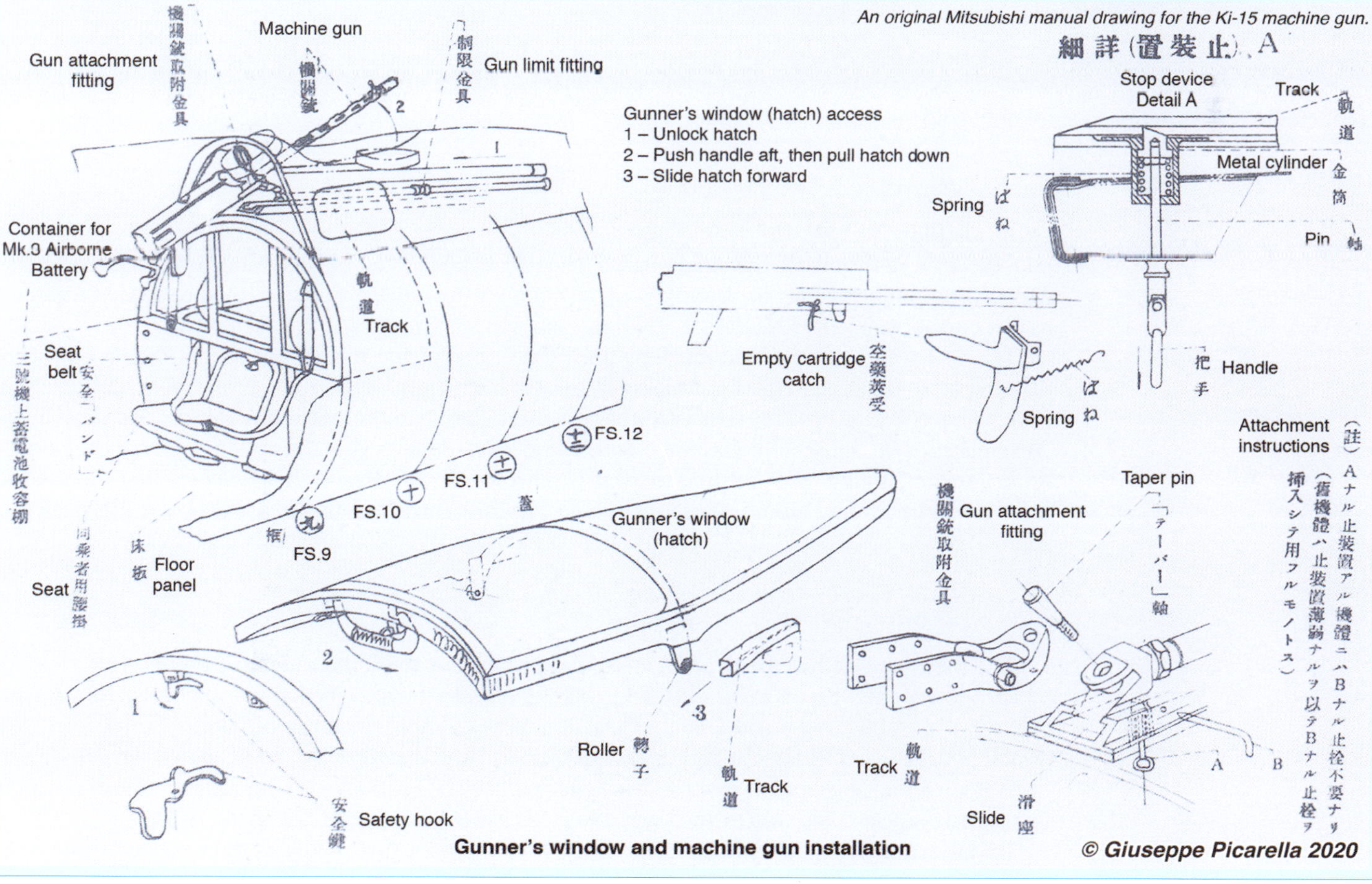

Gunner's window and machine gun installation

15-II maintenance manual incorporated many earlier illustration from the Ki-15-I manual, including a similar weapon to the Te-1 shown on the inboard profile, but fitted with Y-shaped shoulder stocks and an under-slung pistol grip trigger assembly.

Tracking down the actual weapon type depicted is complicated by the fact that several 7.7mm aircraft weapons were under development at that time! There were two totally different Type-89 7.7mm machine guns in service, together with another 7.7mm aircraft weapon that was often referred to a the Type-89 flexible machine gun, plus an experimental 7.7mm flexible machine gun, which would become known as the Te-1.

These weapons were:

- The Type-89 flexible machine gun (special). This was a twin barrel weapon derived from yet an earlier single barrelled weapon, also known as the Type-89 flexible machine gun, which was itself derived from the earlier Model-11 light machine gun. This obviously does not fit the technical specification or the actual aircraft, due to the twin barrels and restrictive size of the twin quadrant type magazines.
- The Type-89 fixed machine gun. This was a license-built Vickers E, which matches the profile of the Mitsubishi drawing, but utilized a horizontal feed assembly instead of an upper magazine feed. This weapon was typically mounted in upper cowlings or the wings of contemporary fighters, but was later adapted to fit into the tail section of the Mitsubishi Ki-21 *Sally* bomber and became know as the Te-1.
- Te-1 single barrel rotary feed machine gun.
- The Te-4, which was derived, during the mid 1930s, from the original single barrel Type-89 flexible machine gun.

Te-1 single barrel rotary feed machine gun

During the mid 1930s, several experimental aircraft weapons were under development by the Army, including a 700rpm weapon similar in layout to the Vickers Type-F flexible machine gun. This weapon incorporated a pan type magazine, located at the forward end of the receiver, and a Y-shaped shoulder stock for better comfort (as depicted in the Mitsubishi drawings), with rear mounted pistol grip trigger. Field modifications to increase the firepower of 60th *Sentai* Ki-21-Ia *Sally* bombers were undertaken in 1938, with a modified version (incorporating the under-slung pistol grip trigger assembly), but for some reason it was not accepted into service.

While this weapon would not prove to be successful, it would seem from its inclusion within the Ki-15-I manual that the Army had intended to place this weapon into widespread production with either twin grips or a pistol grip, depending on the specific aircraft type.

Due to the stowed location of this weapon on board the Ki-15 and the Army's tight censorship of the press, we shall never know if a limited number of Te-1 single barrel rotary feed machine guns were fitted to experimental or pre-production Ki-15-Is.

Te-4 7.7mm flexible machine gun

As mentioned above, the Te-4 7.7mm flexible machine gun was in limited production during the mid 1930s. A derivative of the single barrel Type-89 flexible machine gun, the Te-4 was never issued with a Type number during its development, although it subsequently drifted into production regardless of this bureaucratic omission during 1941 and saw service throughout the Pacific war.

The Te-4 was a gas-operated machine gun with a rate of fire of 730rpm and a muzzle velocity of 810m/s. A 70-round pan type magazine was located at the front of the receiver assembly and spent cartridges were collected in a concertina type bag. Several sighting options were available for this weapon, but when installed on the Ki-15 it was fitted with a "Norman Vane" type sight, which deflected the position of the forward aiming "pip" as the vane was exposed to the slipstream, thereby correcting the sight for drift. Three magazines (210 rounds in total) were typically carried by the Ki-15, although it is likely that addition magazines would have been carried in areas where interception was definitely expected.

Machine gun mount

The machine gun had an attachment fitting installed at the forward end of the receiver assembly, which allowed the weapon to be adjusted in elevation and azimuth. The base of the fitting was attached to a slide assembly, which slid along a C-section stowage rail, which ran aft along the top of FS.9 to a midpoint between FS.10 and FS.11. The rail allowed the machine gun to be stowed inside the rear fuselage upper fairing when not in use. Movement of the slide fitting was retarded with the aid of a gun limit fitting (a telescopic strut) which was attached to an end fitting in the region of FS.12.

With the machine gun withdrawn for use, a horizontal locking pin was used to secure the slide assembly into place for operation of the weapon. A spring-loaded retaining pin was located at the extreme

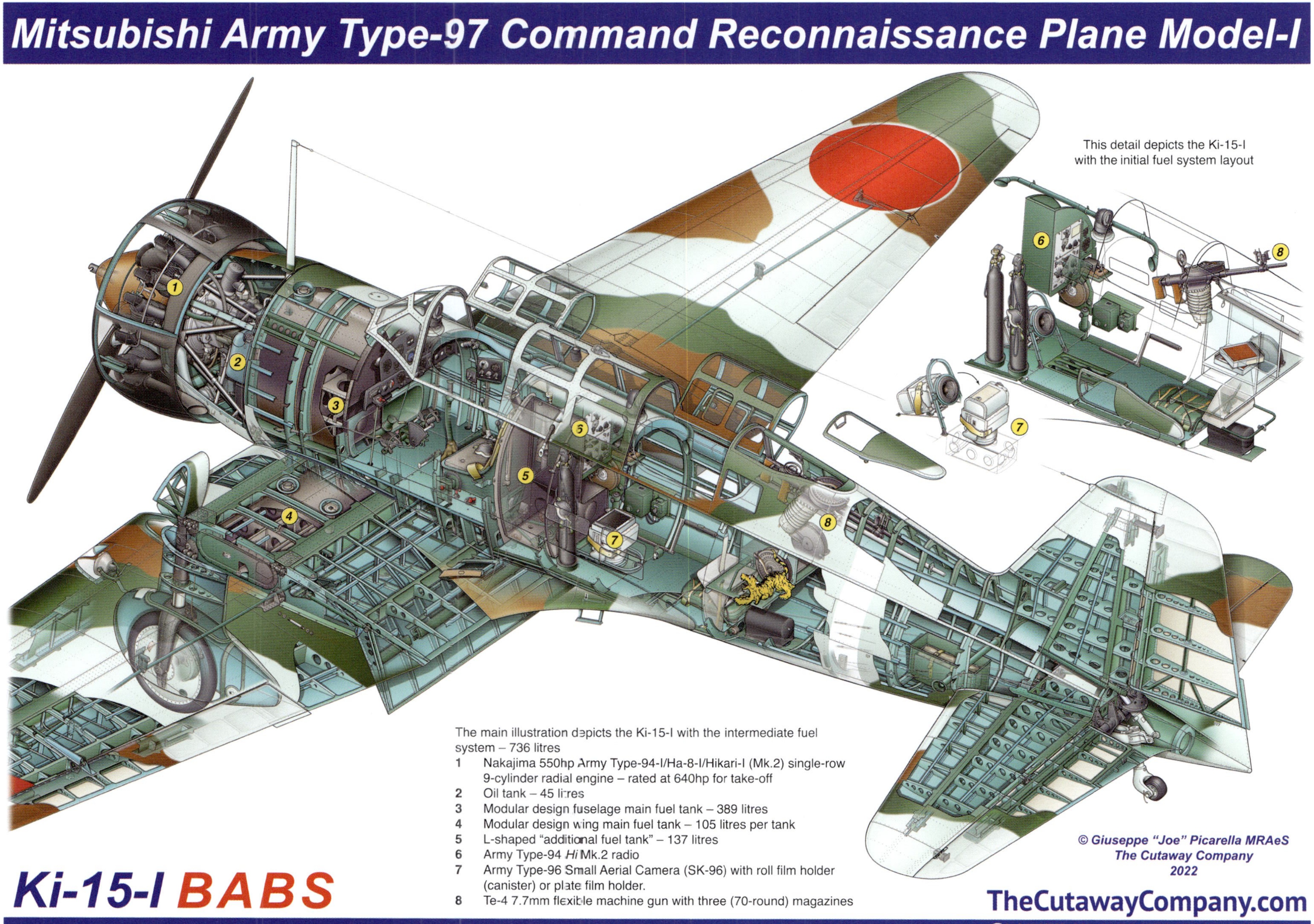
Mitsubishi Army Type-97 Command Reconnaissance Plane Model-I
This detail depicts the Ki-15-I with the initial fuel system layout
The main illustration depicts the Ki-15-I with the intermediate fuel system – 736 litres
1 Nakajima 550hp Army Type-94-I/Ha-8-I/Hikari-I (Mk.2) single-row 9-cylinder radial engine – rated at 640hp for take-off
2 Oil tank – 45 litres
3 Modular design fuselage main fuel tank – 389 litres
4 Modular design wing main fuel tank – 105 litres per tank
5 L-shaped "additional fuel tank" – 137 litres
6 Army Type-94 Hi Mk.2 radio
7 Army Type-96 Small Aerial Camera (SK-96) with roll film holder (canister) or plate film holder.
8 Te-4 7.7mm flexible machine gun with three (70-round) magazines
Ki-15-I BABS
© Giuseppe "Joe" Picarella MRAeS
The Cutaway Company
2022
TheCutawayCompany.com
CLARITY IN A COMPLICATED WORLD

rear of the stowage rail, which acted to limit rearward movement of the slide assembly, or to facilitate the removal of the machine gun.

The machine gun had an elevation of approximately 27°, with an azimuth of ±27°. While the weapon could be positioned at these angles, the RO would not have been able to aim the weapon accurately due to the confines of the canopy structure.

Flare pistol

A flare pistol would have been carried on the aircraft, although the type and stowed location are unknown. It would have been used for signalling and emergency purposes, rather than night-time photographic purposes.

It is unknown if the Ki-15 was used for night-time photographic reconnaissance purposes. If they were used in this manner, then parachute flares would have been utilized due to the intensity and duration of their burn, but with limited numbers of night qualified pilots capable of performing these tasks and even fewer night capable airfields in Manchuria and China before the Pacific War, such missions would have been rare. As night-time reconnaissance photographs are more tactical in nature than strategic, it is likely that aircraft such as the Ki-36 *Ida* and Ki-51 *Sonia* would have performed such roles if needed.

Kamikaze

The following technical description details the known differences between the Ki-15-I and the 1937 record breaking *Kamikaze* aircraft – J-BAAI, C/n1502. Unless specified, please refer to the Ki-15-I technical description for general details. While *Kamikaze* was in fact the first *Karigane* aircraft, it is included within its own section due to the specialized nature of its modifications.

Main fuselage

The construction and layout of the *Kamikaze* airframe was identical to the Ki-15 1st prototype. For the record flight to England, the whole aircraft received a low drag paint finish. The April 14th, 1937 issue of *The Aeroplane* magazine noted that:

"The external finish of the machine appears to be very good indeed. The flush-riveting of both wings and the fuselage is some of the finest we have seen. The whole surface has been covered with many layers of clear dope so that not the slightest inequality can be felt."

In fact there were so many layers of paint and lacquer that it is almost impossible to distinguish panel lines on the aircraft, other than removable fairings and access hatches.

***Kamikaze* inboard profile**

1/48 Scale

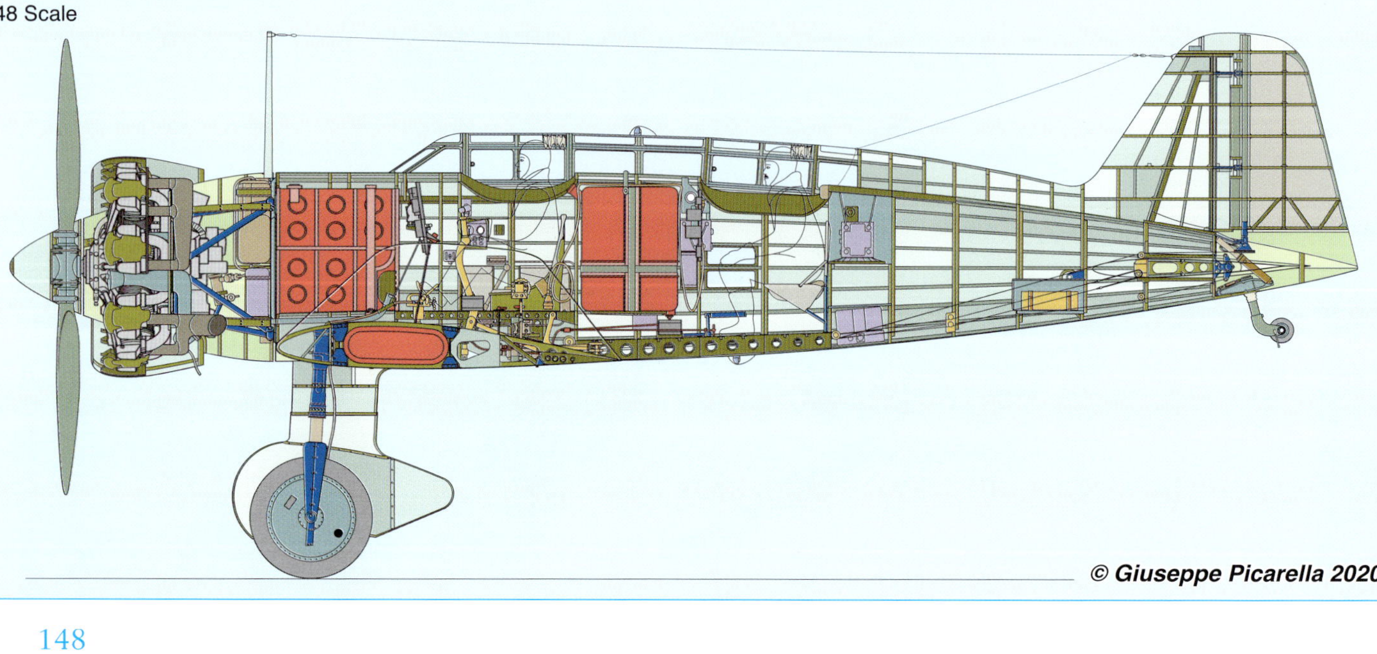

© Giuseppe Picarella 2020

The highly lacquered finish of Kamikaze *is evident in this photo, especially along the horizontal skin joint line. Note the location of the (retracted) cockpit steps and flexible handhold.*

Canopy

Because *Kamikaze* was the 2nd Ki-15 prototype, it was fitted with the original low profile canopy design. For the record breaking 1937 flight, both of the bi-fold canopies were fitted with concertina-type sunscreens along their upper sections.

Dorsal spine and gunner's window

The removal of the machine gun and associated fittings rendered the gunner's window obsolete, so the installation was deleted, although the upper window, located between FS.8A and FS.9A, was incorporated into the new upper skin panel.

Main landing gear

A servicing tag was attached to the front face of each MLG upper fairing, giving instructions on how to recharge the oleo strut.

Primary systems

Fuel system

The requirement to fly extremely long-distance legs during the flight to England (which in some cases were in excess of 2,230km) necessitated a reassessment of the fuel system fitted to *Kamikaze*. Following meetings with the Asahi Press team during the spring of 1937, Mitsubishi reviewed the aircraft's performance requirements and subsequently designed a 250 litre long-range fuel tank for installation in the centre fuselage of *Kamikaze*.

The two-part, interconnected oval-section fuel tanks were designed to conform to the internal shape of the fuselage frames, from FS.5 to a mid point between FS.6 and FS.7. The tanks were strapped together horizontally and supported on beams spanning the centre fuselage. Although they were quickly incorporated into the airframe, the large size of these tanks rendered the existing radio installation impractical, so the civilian type transceiver and receiver had to be located in various positions around the rear cockpit, wherever space was available.

The lacquer was applied liberally to all of the skin joints, which made their identification almost impossible in photographs. Note the deleted gunner's window. (Japan Aeronautical Association)

Fuel system capacity – *Kamikaze*

Tank location	Capacity in litres
Fuselage main tank	389
Long-range fuel tanks	250 approximately
Wing tanks – starboard	105
Wing tank – port	105
Total	850 approximately

Oil system

Oil consumption and lubrication was a major consideration for the *Kamikaze* flight, with some of the flight legs exceeding more than 7 hours in the air. While the *Hikari* engine was capable of such operational conditions, it was felt that the existing 45 litre oil tank was too small, so it was duly modified to increase the capacity by as much as 30%. This tank was located in the same position on the airframe, but was extended vertically, terminating just below the forward fuselage upper fairing. The upper section of the tank was fitted with an additional horizontal attachment strap and a new filler port.

Cockpits and secondary systems

Pilot's cockpit and systems

Instrument panel

The historic nature of *Kamikaze* has ensured that several cockpit photographs and contemporary illustrations were produced at the time of the record flight. Although the instrument panel was similar to that of the Ki-15, it should be remembered that some modifications were included for the long-distance flight. These including the installation of an additional fuel quantity gauge, a vertical speed indicator (VSI) and the removal of the Model-96 magnetic compass from the cockpit lip, in order to improve pilot visibility during the long flight. The latter item was replaced with an early model Type-1 magnetic compass, installed on pedestal behind the centre of the lower panel assembly, which was a common installation for the period. In addition to this a primary Master compass (similar in shape to a Army Master compass Model-2) was located onto the left-hand side of the cockpit floor, between FS.3 and FS.4.

Cockpit communications

Flexible rubber Gosport speaking tubes were fitted to *Kamikaze*. The twin tube installation was threaded beneath the centre decking between the cockpits, with each crewmember simply placing the

fur-covered earpiece under his flying helmet for the duration of the flight and speaking into the conical mouthpiece. Photographs indicate that other *Karigane* aircraft used a mixture of fixed metallic or rubber speaking tubes.

As Tsukagoshi guides himself into the rear cockpit, a member of the ground crew waits to pass him the engine starter handle, for stowage on the cockpit floor. Note the Gosport tube mouthpiece in the centre-canopy tunnel and the "NO STEP" marking on the centre wing section just below the mid fairing step. (Japan Aeronautical Association)

Oxygen system

No oxygen cylinders were carried by *Kamikaze* during its record-breaking flight, as the highest altitude that was recorded on the flight was 4,000 m (13,123ft). And since aircraft weight was a major concern, the deletion of any oxygen equipment would have been a simple decision to make.

A press release photograph of the *Kamikaze* crew holding a 20 litre liquid oxygen generator does exist, showing Tsukagoshi passing the generator to Iinuma while standing on the wing of J-BAAL *Asakaze* (C/n1503) This photograph was taken during high altitude/oxygen system tests in July 1941, which were connected to the Tachikawa A-26 (later Ki-77) project. The photograph would indicate that the oxygen unit was located in the front cockpit of the aircraft, which is the most likely location for several reasons. Firstly, weight and balance issues would require such a heavy item be located near to the CG of the aircraft and secondly, space for this unit was available to the left-hand side of the pilot's seat.

Cockpit ventilation and heating

It's not known if the *Kamikaze* was capable of accepting electrically heated flight suits, as these were still a rarity in Japan at that time, relegated to experimental aircraft only. Given the date of the flight and its intended middle eastern route, it is unsurprising that photographic evidence of the 1937 flight shows both crewmembers entering/exiting the aircraft at several of their destinations, wearing a mixture of flying suits or civilian clothes – jumpers, scarves and sports jackets, etc.

Pockets, cases and lockers

It is unclear what pocket or case modifications were made to the *Kamikaze* cockpits, but what is clear is that there was little space for the crew's personal belongings and clothes. Suitcases and bags were clearly stuffed into the centre canopy tunnel and dorsal spine during the record flight!

Every inch of Kamikaze *was utilized for storage space during the 1937 Coronation flight, including the centre-canopy tunnel, as can been seen following its arrival at Croydon.*

Navigator's cockpit and systems

General layout

The rear cockpit of the *Kamikaze* was cramped to say the least, as it had been extensively refitted to accommodate the long-range fuel tank and radio installation need for the record flight. A master compass was located on the left-hand side of the cockpit floor, adjacent to the vertical camera window, in place of the Model-1 magnetic compass typically fitted to the lip of the Ki-15 centre canopy tunnel, and the navigator's instrument panel had to be moved forwards and attached aft of FS.7, on the left-hand side of the rear cockpit. The panel included:

1. Chronometer.
2. Altimeter.
3. Airspeed indicator.
4. Master compass Model-2.

Several controls, handles and pumps were located below the long-range tanks, all of which were most likely fuel system related. The engine starter handle was also located on the floor, to the right of the vertical camera window aperture.

Vertical camera window and lateral windows

The absence of any camera equipment rendered the vertical camera window redundant, so the slatted hatch cover was used to provide a level cockpit floor.

Kamikaze also carried a revised lateral window layout, with the two lateral panels relocated between FS.7 and FS.8, sitting between ribs No.5, No.6 and No.7. This modification was due to the installation of the long-range fuel tanks in the centre fuselage.

Navigator's seat

The surviving photographs of *Kamikaze's* rear cockpit show the radio receiver located directly behind the navigator's seat, which looks to have been elevated in height and offset to the right-hand side of the cockpit. Because a parachute would be worn by Tsukagoshi at all times, the seat canvas was probably much looser than the standard Ki-15 seat, so that his head would not touch the canopy. The photographs also seem to indicate that the tubular backrest is folded flat against the seat pan. This makes perfect sense, because Tsukagoshi would need to turn 90° to the left in order to operate the receiver unit, and if the backrest were still in the vertical position, he would not have been able to operate the radio controls. An arched leather shoulder rest was located on FS.9.

Kamikaze cockpit layout and systems

1/32 Scale

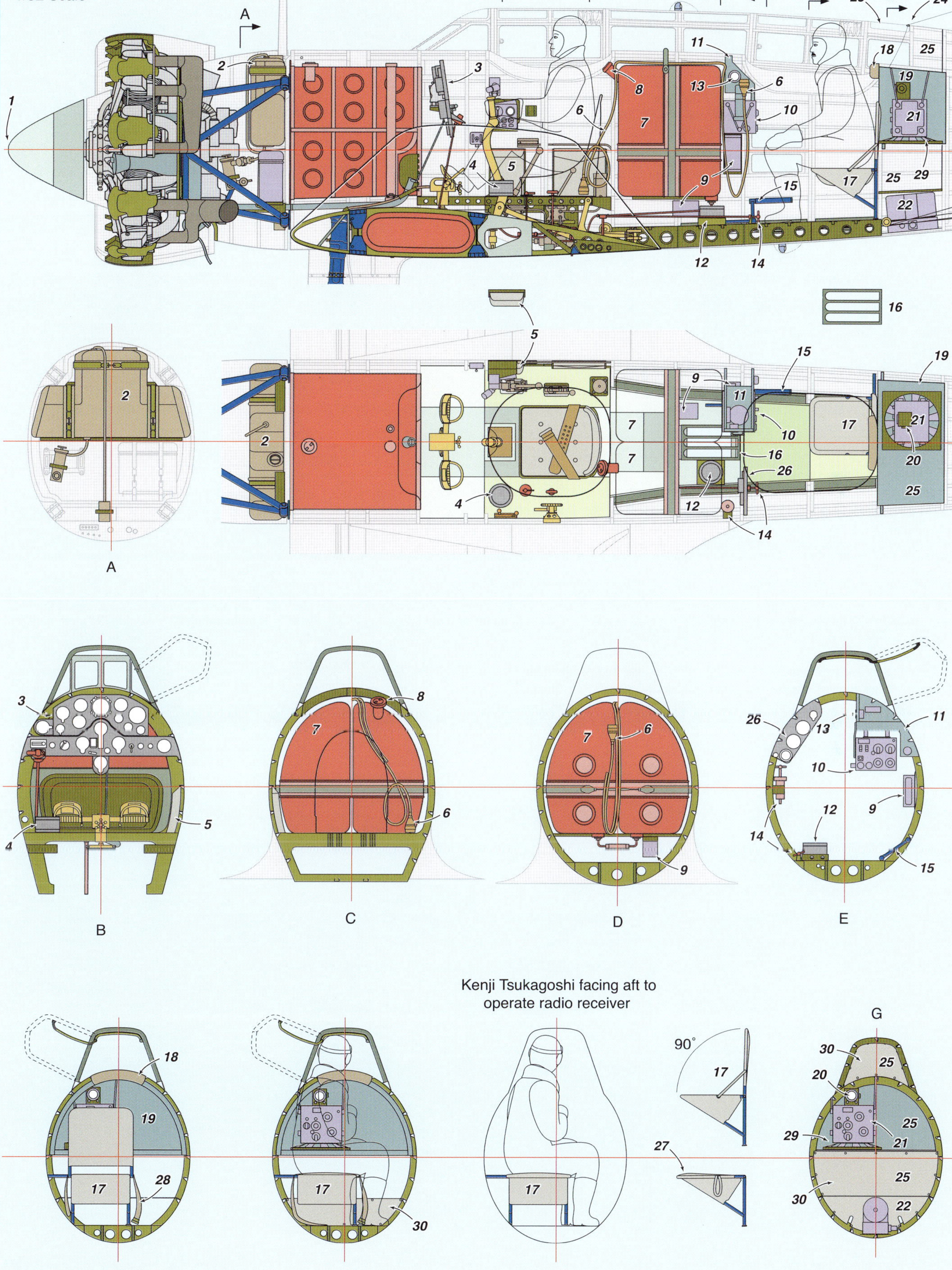

Navigator's panel

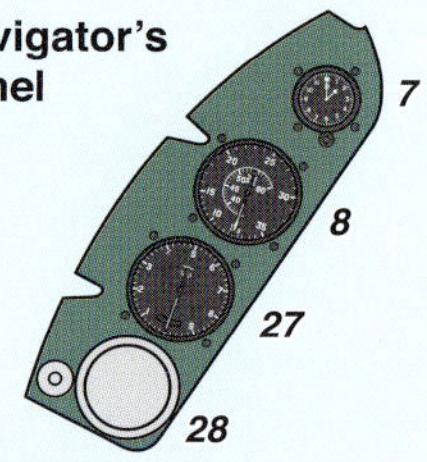

Kamikaze
Upper panel

1 Vertical speed indicator Type-95, Model-2
2 Altimeter Type-95
3 Turn and bank indicator Type-97
4 Artificial horizon Type-96
5 Manifold pressure gauge Type-94
6 Tachometer Type-14
7 Chronometer
8 Airspeed indicator Type-96
9 Fuel pressure gauge Type-95
10 Oil pressure gauge Type-94
11 Oil temperature gauge

Lower panel

12 Emergency boost control
13 Fuel tank selector cock
14 Starter control lever
15 Magneto switch Model-1
16 Fuel quantity gauge – fuselage tank
17 Compass correction card
18 Type-1 magnetic compass – early type
19 Cockpit ventilation control.
20 Fuel quantity gauge – long-range tank
21 Unidentified control – possibly the carburettor intake low/high-speed selector?
22 Fuel quantity gauge – wing tanks
23 Fuel quantity gauge – selector
24 Starter generator handle
25 Fuel primer pump
26 Cylinder head temperature gauge
27 Altimeter – unidentified type
28 Crew communications bell?

1 "Hucks" starter removed
2 Modified oil tank
3 Modified instrument panel
4 Pilot's Master compass
5 Additional document case
6 "Gosport" tube
7 Long-range fuel tank 251 litre
8 Long-range fuel tank filler
9 Radio support equipment
10 Radio transmitter
11 Transmitter mounting structure
12 Navigator's Master compass and mount
13 Transmitter ammeter
14 Long-range fuel system controls
15 Engine inertia starter handle
16 Camera window slatted hatch cover
17 Navigator's modified seat
18 Navigator's shoulder support
19 Modified storage cabinet
20 Receiver ammeter
21 Radio receiver
22 Transformer
23 Modified fuselage structure – former gunner's window
24 Aerial lead-in
25 Storage area
26 Navigator's instrument panel
27 Seat back – folded flat
28 Navigator's seatbelt
29 Receiver vibration mount
30 Rear fuselage canvas divider

Right: Pilot's cockpit with low canopy frame. Below: Navigator's cockpit looking forward. Below right: Navigator's cockpit looking aft, note that the seat frame is very close to the right-hand side of the cockpit – via Ron Cole

Mitsubishi Karigane-I Communications Aircraft *KAMIKAZE*

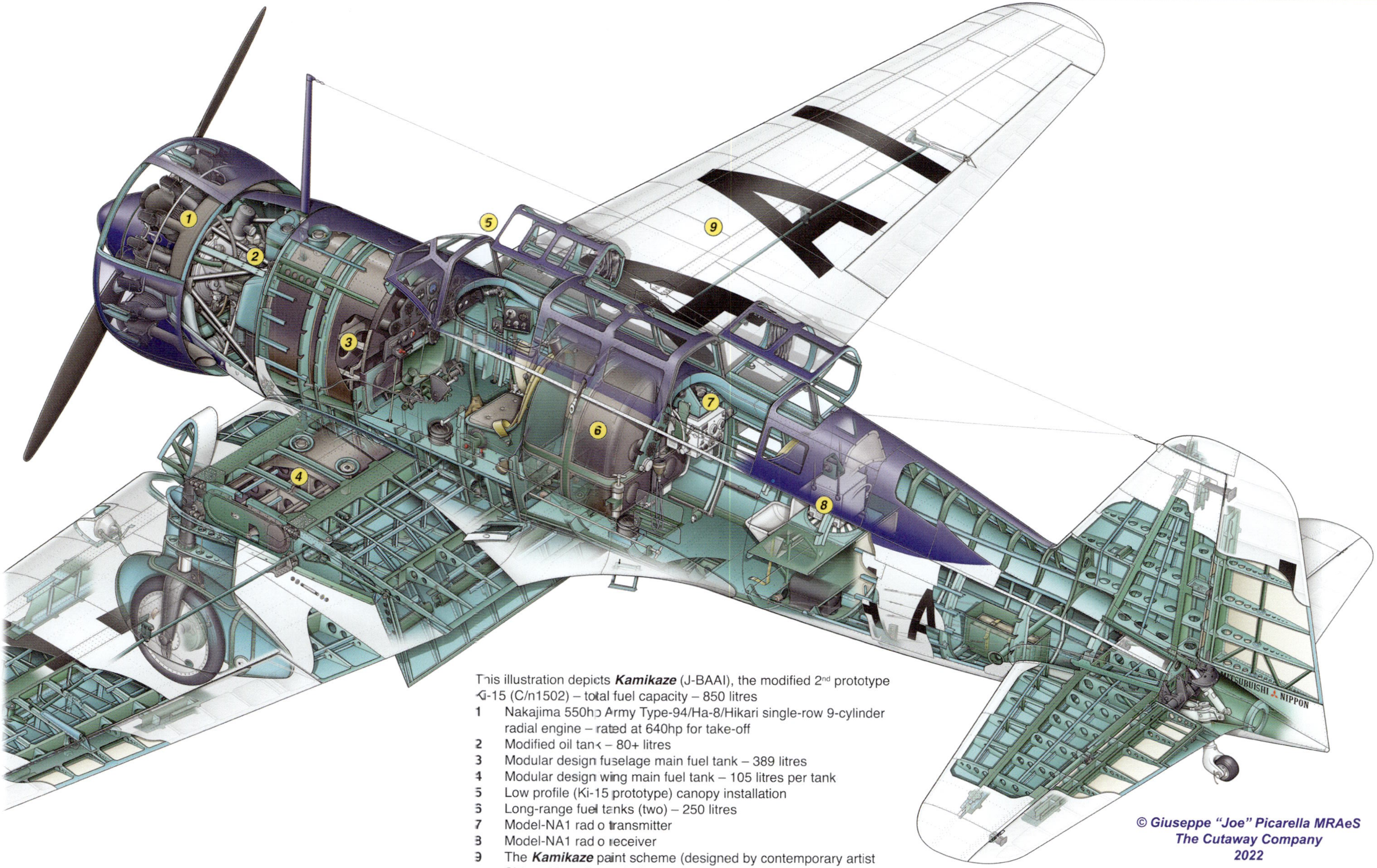

This illustration depicts ***Kamikaze*** (J-BAAI), the modified 2nd prototype Ki-15 (C/n1502) – total fuel capacity – 850 litres

1. Nakajima 550hp Army Type-94/Ha-8/Hikari single-row 9-cylinder radial engine – rated at 640hp for take-off
2. Modified oil tank – 80+ litres
3. Modular design fuselage main fuel tank – 389 litres
4. Modular design wing main fuel tank – 105 litres per tank
5. Low profile (Ki-15 prototype) canopy installation
6. Long-range fuel tanks (two) – 250 litres
7. Model-NA1 radio transmitter
8. Model-NA1 radio receiver
9. The ***Kamikaze*** paint scheme (designed by contemporary artist Shingo Yamaji) was built-up of several coats of lacquer, producing an exceptionally smooth exterior surface

Radio equipment

The radio installation fitted to *Kamikaze* consisted of a customized version of the Model-NA1, which was supplied to Asahi Shimbun by the Japan Radio Company in April 1937. It is unclear if the radio was of Japanese or Western origin, but it is known to have been modified to be more heat resistant and cold tolerant, due to the extreme climatic conditions that *Kamikaze* was expected to encounter on its planned flight. As the Army would discover in due time, the inclusion of long-range fuel tanks in the centre fuselage of the Ki-15 required a drastic redesign of the equipment layout within the rear cockpit. In the case of *Kamikaze* there was more freedom to relocate equipment, as the aircraft did not have to carry aerial camera equipment or a machine gun, etc.

Transmitter

A purpose built aluminium alloy radio mount was manufactured and fitted to the right-hand side of the cabin structure around FS.7, to accommodate the transmitter unit and aerial ammeter. The voltage regulator would have been mounted below the radio on the right-hand side of the fuselage between FS.6 and FS.7.

The transmitter specifications were: Frequency: 5660KHz, 6590KHz (crystal controlled.) Wave Form: A1 (telegraph), A2 (modulated telegraph), A3 (telephone). Output: A1-20W, A2/A3-10W Constitution: oscillation UY-47, power amp UX-202A, speech amp UX-12, modulation UX-202A.

Receiver

The aft storage cabinet structure was also heavily modified, with its vertical partitions removed in order to provide additional space for the installation of the radio receiver. The whole receiver unit was offset to the right-hand side of the aircraft, similar to the transmitter unit and presumably an airborne transformer was located on the floor below it, similar to the Ki-15 installation.

Receiver specifications were: Type: regenerative receiver. Constitution: RF amp RCA-78, Detector UY-37, AF amp UY-37/UY-38.

Both the transmitter and receiver units were painted light grey.

Antenna

The antenna installation on the *Kamikaze* was broadly the same as the Ki-15-I, but the route of the aerial differed. It exited between FS.9 and FS.10, by way of an insulator fitting located at the TDC position of the deactivated gunner's window, before terminated at the antenna mast via a standard fin fitting.

Karigane-I

Mitsubishi Karigane Model-I Communications Aircraft

With the exception of *Kamikaze*, three additional Ki-15-I airframes were supplied to civilian operators under the *Karigane* (Wild Goose) designation. It should be remembered that the designation *Karigane* Model-I would have been retrospectively adopted after the development of the *Karigane* Model-II airframes. As with the *Kamikaze* description, only modified items and equipment specific to individual *Karigane*-I aircraft are detailed within this technical description. For general layout details please refer to the Ki-15-I technical description.

Individual *Karigane*-I aircraft would have been fitted with radio equipment specified by their operators.

J-BAAL

It is assumed that *Asakaze* (C/n1503) was identical in construction to her sister ship *Kamikaze*, but several modifications were included on *Asakaze*, including a large inflated tailwheel assembly of approximately 200 x 100mm.

J-BAAL Asakaze *fitted with a large tailwheel assembly. (Japan Aeronautical Association)*

J-BAAM

Sochikaze (C/n107) appears to have been a standard Ki-15-I *early model*. The lateral window installation would indicate that this aircraft was devoid of an "additional fuel tank".

J-????

An unidentified third *Karigane*-I, possibly *Daimai* No.102, was operated by Osaka Mainichi Shimbun. It carried no antenna mast or visible aerials.

Mitsubishi Ki-15-II

Army Type-97 Command Reconnaissance Plane Model-2

The following technical description details the specific known differences between the Ki-15-I and Ki-15-II. Unless changes are specifically identified please refer to the Ki-15-I technical description.

Airframe component colour

With regards the Ki-15-II, it is entirely possible that the pilot and RO's cockpit areas were finished off with a Mitsubishi light olive green, similar in style to that of the C5M (See **C5M1**). This application would have lightened the confined workspaces considerably and was evident in later Army aircraft built by Mitsubishi, including the Ki-46 *Dinah*.

Nacelle assembly

The installation of the Mitsubishi Ha-26-I engine required a completely redesigned cowling and fuselage fairing for the Ki-15-II. The aerodynamically clean and close fitting assembly consisting of a nose cowling, access cowlings, cowl gills, forward firewall and forward fuselage fairings.

Nose fairing

The single-piece aluminium-alloy fairing smoothed the airflow between the 480mm diameter rear propeller plate and the base of the engine cylinders. Cut-outs were included in the fairing to accommodate the propeller speed governor mount (TDC) and the gearbox oil scavenge sump (BDC).

Nose cowling

Constructed with internal formers and shaped skins, the nose cowling was attached directly to engine cylinders via seven brackets, which engaged with integral castings on the front row of the Ha-26-I inlet manifold rocker covers. The aft flange of the nose fairing acted as the attachment interface for the access cowlings.

Access cowlings

Three tightly fitted long-chord access cowlings covered the main engine installation and were held in place with Dzus-type fasteners. The longitudinal edges were flanged with doubler-strips, which extended to act as tightly fitting attachment interfaces for adjacent cowlings. The inner surface of each fairing was fitted with an asbestos-webbing strip, which closed the gap between the fairing and each adjacent cylinder head, forcing the cooling air to pass through the engine via the engine cylinder baffles.

Cowl flaps

The multi-segment cowl flap assembly was of contemporary construction, comprising a tubular-steel support frame, attached to which was a cowl flap torque-tube assembly. The support frame connected directly to the engine via six A-frame brackets that engaged integral castings at the rear of the inlet manifold rocker covers, on the rear row of engine cylinders.

The individual torque-tube segments (together with their overlapping aluminium-alloy cowl gills) were attached to the support frame via steel brackets. These brackets not only held the cowl-gill universal joint assemblies in place, they also provided Dzus attachment fittings for the access cowlings. Five cowl gills were installed on each side of the nacelle assembly, each capable of being opened approximately 22°.

The upper quadrant of the cowl flap assembly was a fixed panel, to improve the pilot's view during approach, while the lower quadrant was cut-away to allow for the installation of the oil cooler intake. See **Oil system.**

Mitsubishi Ki-15-II inboard profile

1/48 Scale

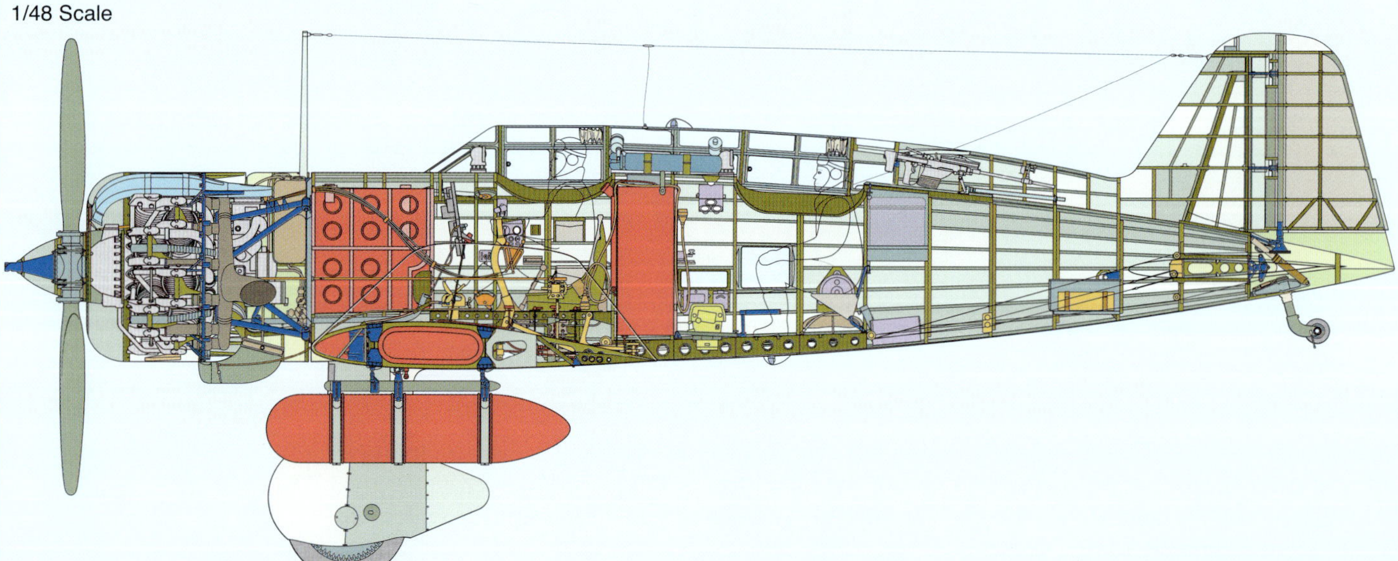

Ki-15-II Nacelle assembly

1/32 Scale

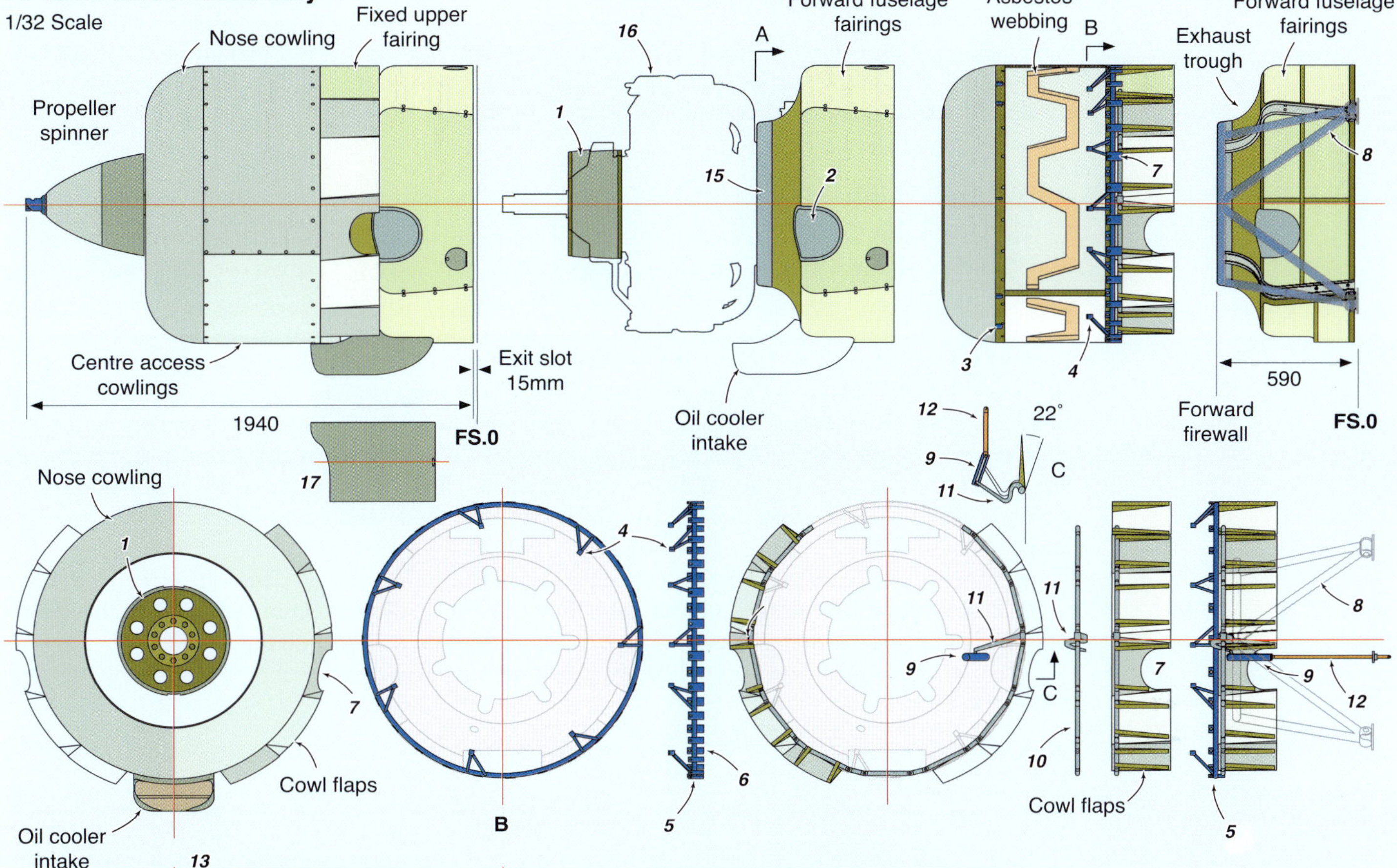

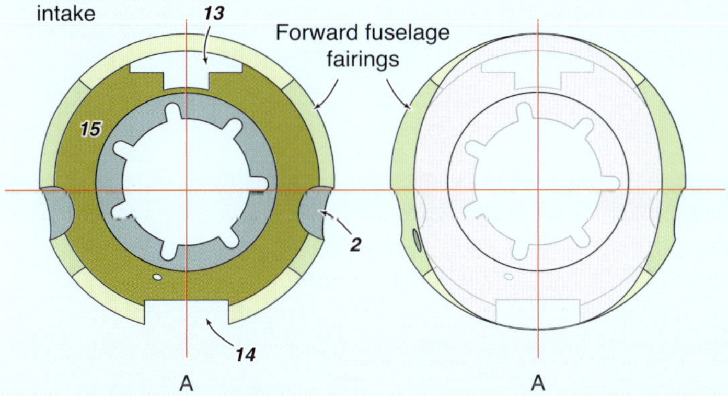

1 Nose fairing
2 Exhaust heat shield panels
3 Nose cowling-to-engine (fwd) attachment fittings x 7
4 Cowling-to-engine (aft) attachment fittings x 7
5 Cowling (aft) attachment frame
6 Cowl flap torque tube attachment fittings
7 Cowl flap exhaust aperture
8 Engine mounting frame
9 Cowl flap actuator collar fitting
10 Cowl flap torque tube
11 Cowl flap actuator arm
12 Cowl flap control torque tube
13 Carburettor aperture
14 Oil cooler aperture
15 Forward firewall
16 Mitsubishi Ha-26-II engine outline
17 Oil cooler intake – looking up

Note: Skin colours used to identify individual panels

A selection of original Mitsubishi manual drawings for the Ki-15-II cowling.

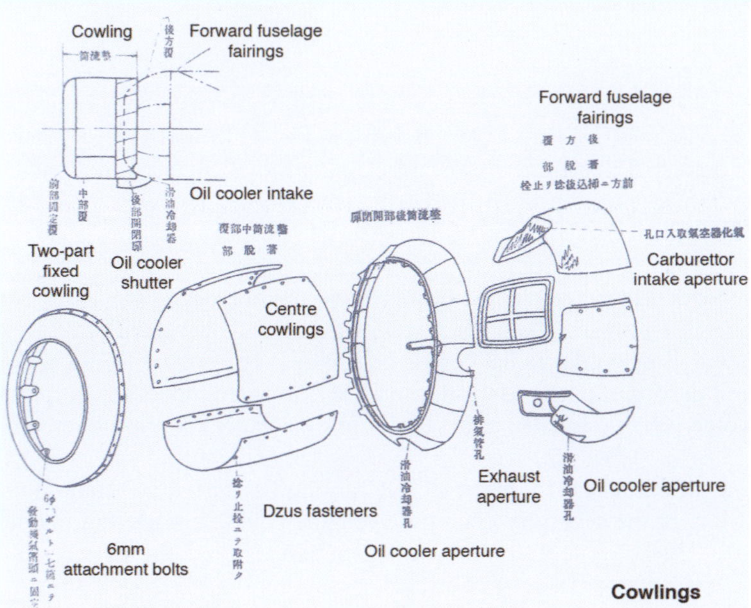

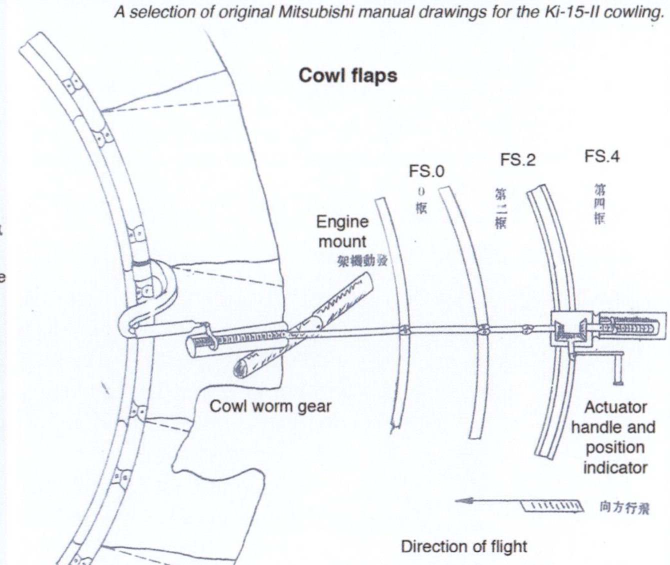

Forward firewall

A forward firewall assembly was sandwiched between the engine crankcase and the engine-mounting ring, providing a support frame for the engine rear fairings and forward fuselage fairings. Aft of the engine-mounting frame the firewall was troughed to accommodate the exhaust piper collector ring, which was located beneath the cowl flaps.

Forward fuselage fairings

The forward fuselage fairings were comprised of four individual panels. The upper fairing was shaped to fit around the downdraught carburettor intake on its forward edge, with a cut-out to accommodate the antenna mast at TDC on the rear edge. An access hatch for the oil tank filler was to the left of TDC.

The side fairings allowed general access to the engine accessory bay, with an access hatch fitted to the port side panel to allow access to the oil system stopcock. The lower panel was shaped to fit around the new oil cooler intake, with a small hole on the lower starboard side, to accommodate the engine inertia starter handle. A steel heat shield was included in the area adjacent to each exhaust outlet.

Each of the aluminium-alloy fairing panels were edged and stiffened with formers and stringers, and attached to the aircraft with domed Dzus-type fasteners. The fasteners engaged four C-section support strips, attached along the outboard horizontal sections of the engine-mounting frame. These support strips were visibly deeper than those of the Ki-15-I.

A tightly controlled exit vent (approximately 15mm width) was designed into the rear edge of the fuselage fairings at FS.0, ensuring a smooth transition into the fuselage structure, while allowing adequate pressure cooling of the engine accessory bay, oil cooler and oil tank installation.

The nacelle assembly was approximately 1,940mm long, from the tip of the "Hucks" starter on the spinner to FS.0.

Main fuselage

Visually there were very few difference between the Ki-15-I and Ki-15-II fuselage structures, but there would have been material and gauge changes to the airframe, plus construction, assembly and minor engineering modifications to accept the heavier engine and airframe loads.

Tailcone

The Ki-15-II manual shows an additional access panel was fitted to the port side of the tailcone, just aft of the circular support frame. It is believed that this was a manufacturing close-out panel.

Main landing gear

At some point during the production run of the Ki-15-II, modified side panels were incorporated into the MLG wheels. These new panels included a crimped design between the screw heads, most probably for increased rigidity.

Powerplant

When Mitsubishi began the development of its A4 (Air-cooled – model-4) *Kinsei* (Venus) series of engines in 1932, few would have predicted that this two-row 14-cylinder radial engine would become the backbone of the Japanese aircraft industry through the Pacific war. During 1937 the A14 *Zuisei* (Auspicious Star) was developed from the *Kinsei*, incorporating a reduced stroke length. This layout not only reduced the overall dimensions of the new engine, it also increased the torque. Army interest in this powerplant was rapid and coincidently in the context of this book, the first orders gained by Mitsubishi were for its proposed Ki-15-II. Following trials, the engine was officially accepted into service as the 900hp Army Type-99 Model-I, 14-cylinder radial engine or Ha-26-I. The engine would also be known as *Zuisei 12* when the naval derivative of the Ki-15-II, the C5M1, was developed. To complicate matters still further, the engine would be re-designated as the Ha-31 following the adoption of the joint designation system.

The engine was fitted with a downdraught carburettor at TDC, an inertia starter, a vacuum pump and a generator on the aft thrust-line of the accessory casing. The engine could be started in the field by the either the inertia starter or a "Hucks" type starter vehicle. When hand started, the starter handle was inserted in the starboard side lower forward fuselage fairing.

Mitsubishi 900hp Army Type-99-I/Ha-26-I/*Zuisei 12*/Ha-31 specifications

Rated power	875hp
Compression ratio	6.5
Capacity	28 litres
RPM	2,300
Bore/stroke	140/130mm
Length	1,564mm
Height	1,118mm
Width	1,118mm
Weight	542kg

Carburettor intakes and dust screens

The carburettor installation of the Ha-26-I engine was fed by a ram-air intake located inside the upper lip of cowling. The intake ducting was divided into three flat-oblong sections, passing between the

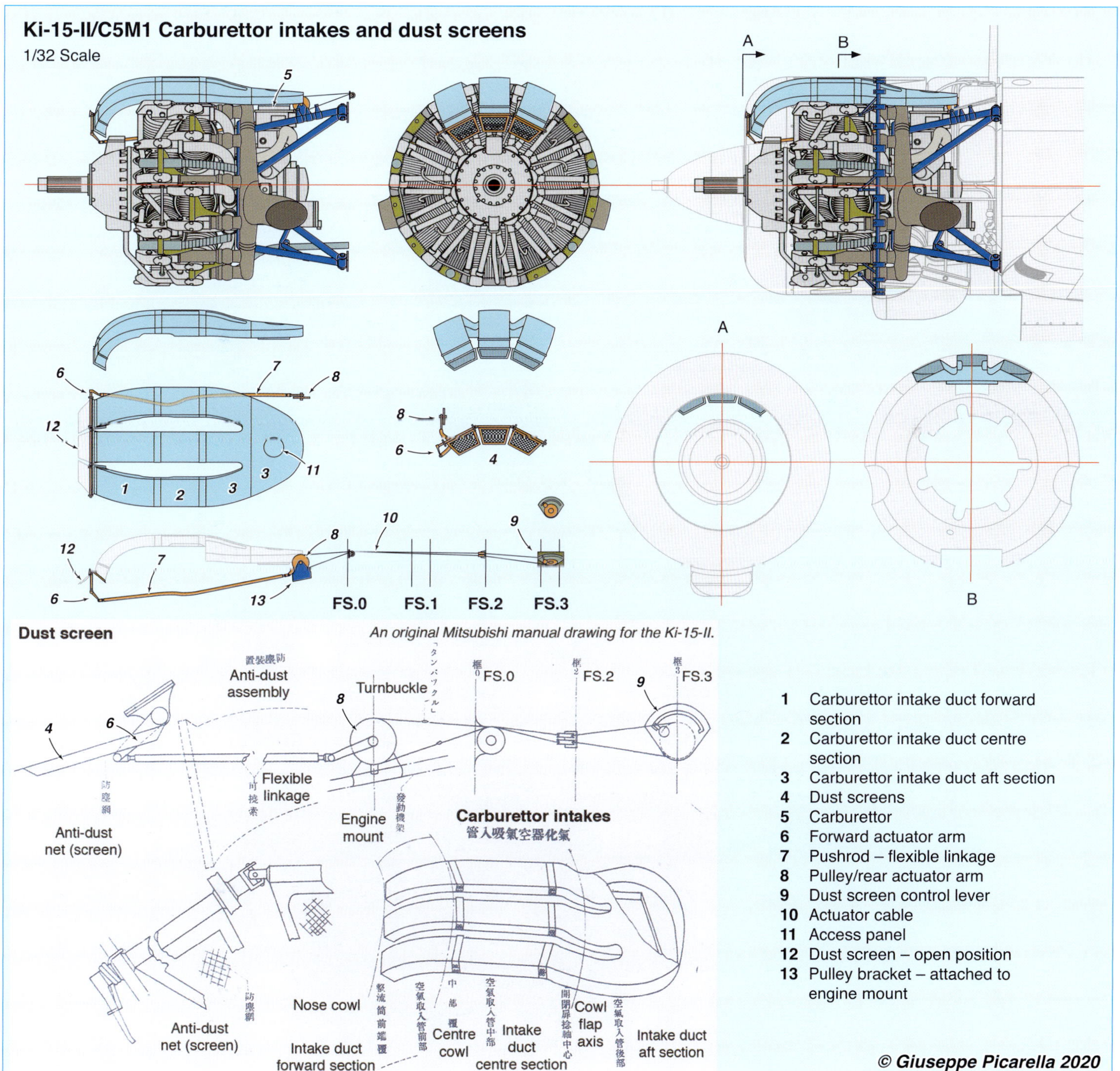

top cylinders of the engine and the inner surface of the cowling, before angling down to enter a master chamber above the carburettor. The limited space between the engine and cowling required intricate shaping and joggling of the intake ducting, a practice that was further refined on the Ki-46 *Dinah*.

The dust and sand rich environment of China had a detrimental affect on many Japanese aero-engines, restricting moving components and damaging carburettors in particular. Increased maintenance schedules rapidly became the order of the day and carburettor intakes were soon retrofitted with fixed sponge filters and wire screens. When the K-15-II was under development, specific attention was paid to the filter design and each ram-air intake was provided with an individual articulated cover containing a wire mesh particle screen. The covers were attached to the upper arch of the nose cowling and interconnected via two universal joints, controlled by an actuator arm on the port side of the assembly.

Engine mount

The engine-mounting frame on the Ki-15-II was similar to that of the Ki-15-I, albeit reduced to a length of approximately 590mm. The lateral tubes were increased in diameter to 32mm, with a wall thickness of 1.4mm, which attached to the (36mm diameter and 2mm wall thickness) engine-mounting ring, with the aid of webbing plates. The mounting ring connected directly to the engine via seven attachment eyes, which were welded onto its inner circumference. Each eye was fabricated from steel plate and contained a steel bushing and a rubber vibration mount.

Propeller and spinner

The Ki-15-II was fitted with a Sumitomo Metal Industries (license-built Hamilton Standard type) two-blade fixed pitch metal propeller. While it retained the same 2,900mm diameter of the Ki-15-I propeller, the chord of the blades was increased to absorb the high power output of the engine.

The two-part spinner had a length of 430mm (minus the starter dog) and a diameter of 480mm. Because the engine was encased in a full cowling assembly, the nose fairing was only required to align with the engine crankcase, rather than shroud the lower portions of the cylinders, as on the Ki-15-I. This smaller diameter nose fairing resulted in an equally reduced spinner diameter, which left the propeller cuff fittings partially exposed to the airstream. A red warning band of approximately 50mm was

Mitsubishi Ha-26-II engine.

Mitsubishi 900hp Army Type-99-I/Ha-26-I/Ha-31 engine
Navy Zuisei 12 engine

1/32 Scale

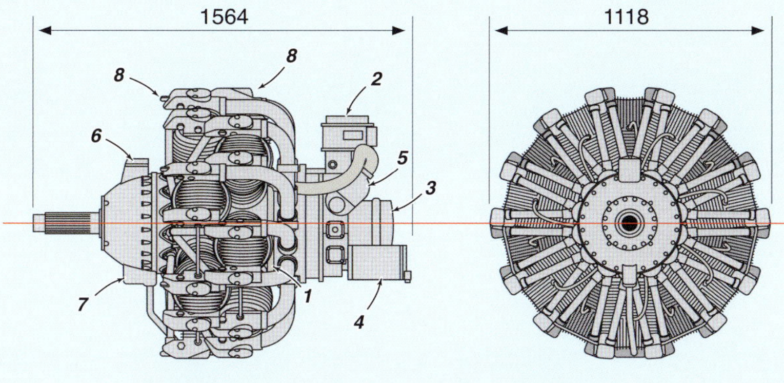

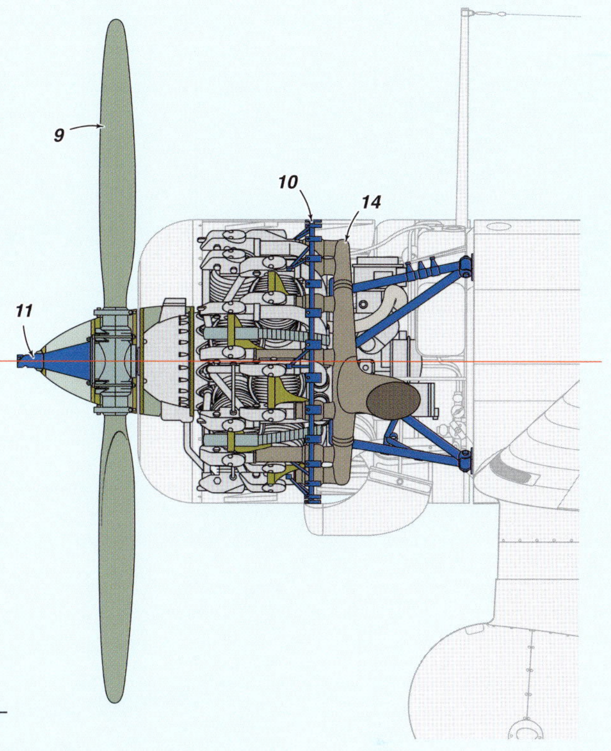

1 Ignition harness – rear mounted
2 Carburettor
3 Inertia starter
4 Generator
5 Magnetos
6 Propeller governor pad – redundant on Ki-15-II/C5M1
7 Gearbox oil scavenge line
8 Nose cowling-to-rocker covers attachment points – seven
9 Two-blade fixed pitch propeller – 2900mm
10 Cowling aft attachment frame
11 "Hucks" starter
12 Cockpit ram-air intake
13 Accessory bay ram-air cooling
14 Exhaust collector ring assembly – three sections per side
15 Cylinder cooling baffles
16 Inertia starter handle position

Dressed engine, mount and propeller

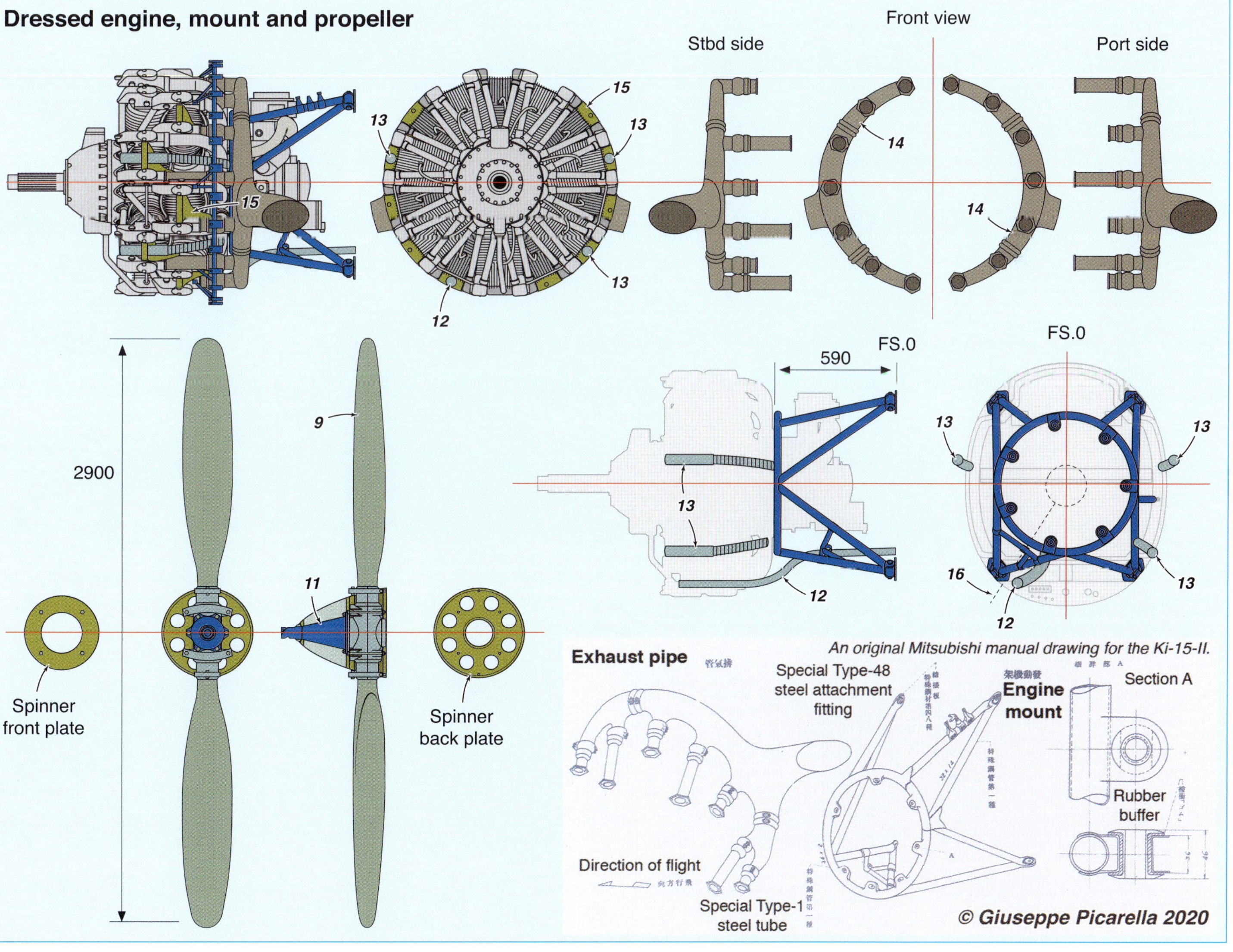

The Ki-15-II included a carburettor dust screen installation above the engine. This photograph shows the same triple-intake installation as fitted to a Navy C5M1. (Shoichi Tanaka)

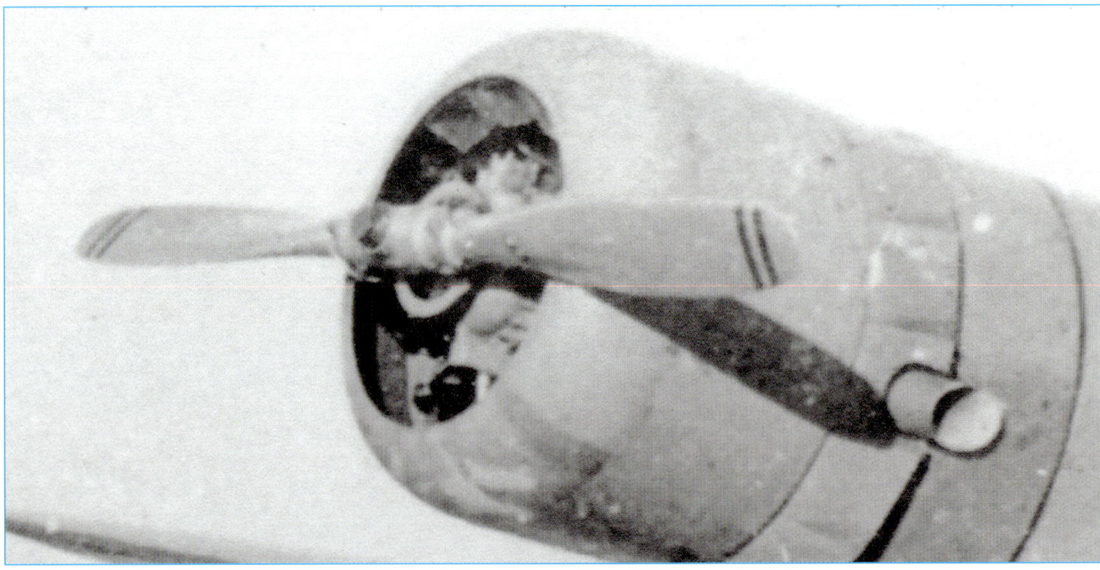

With the front of the spinner removed it is possible to see the Hucks starter fitting attached to the front of the propeller hub. (Ron Cole)

painted on the front face of the propeller blades approximately 50mm from each tip. The rear face of the blades were painted matt black to reduce glare for the pilot.

Primary systems

Fuel system

While the installation of the Ha-26-I engine would improve the overall performance of the Ki-15-II, the higher fuel consumption would undoubtedly take its toll on the endurance of the aircraft if the existing fuel capacity remained unaltered.

To compensate for the expected 973km (605 miles) shortfall in range (based on average fuel consumption figures), Mitsubishi once again turned its attention to increasing the aircraft's internal fuel capacity. Because the centre wing section had already been filled to capacity with the inclusion of the

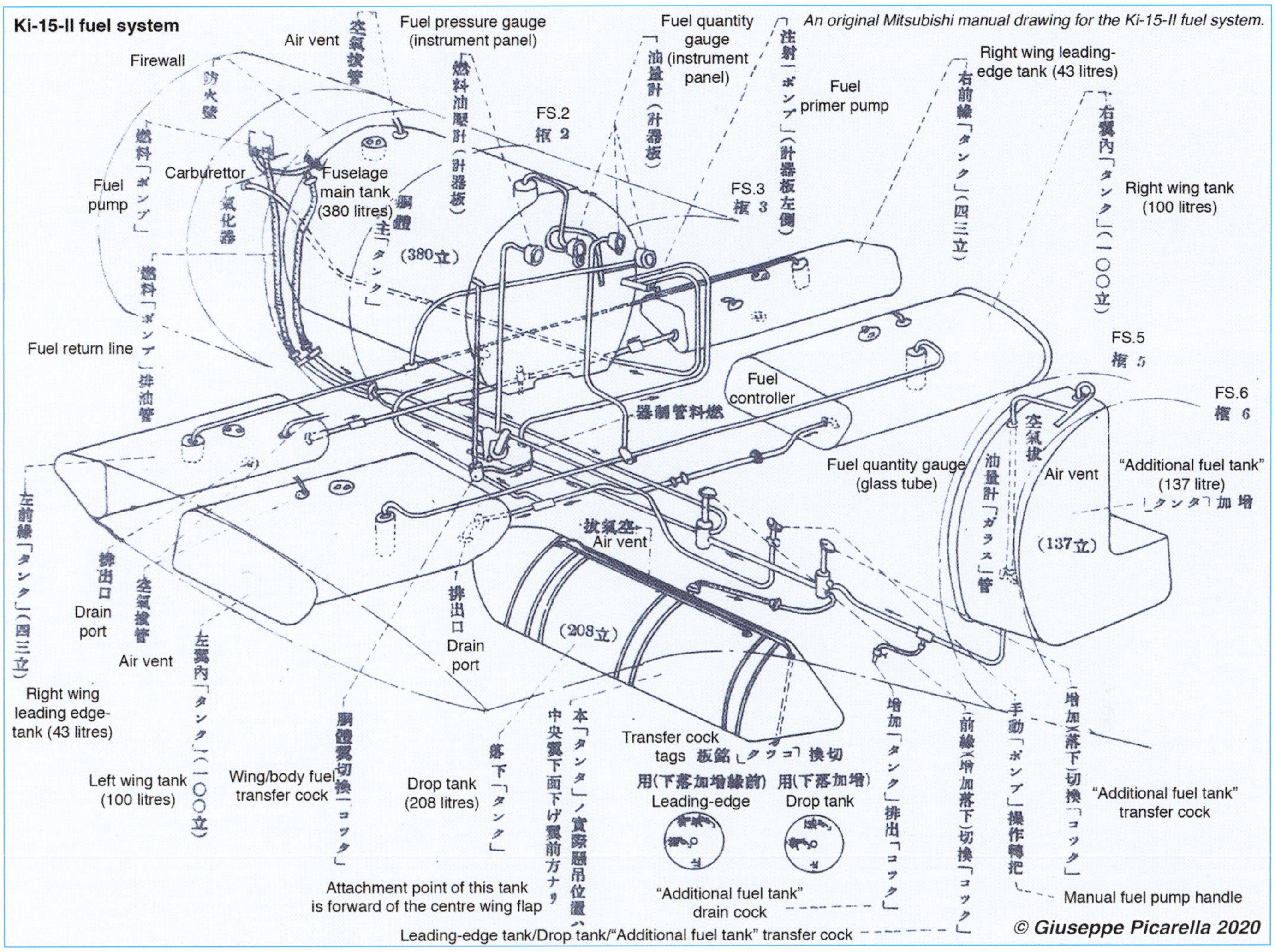

wing leading-edge tanks, and the fuselage had received the "additional fuel tank", this left only two viable options available to the design team; new tanks located in the outboard wing panels, or the inclusion of a drop-tank and its associated pylon fittings.

The concept of fitting additional tanks into the outboard wing panels of the Ki-15 was not impossible, but it was problematic. Mitsubishi's A5M2 *Nate* had this type of tank fitted to its outer wing panels, but these installations had been an integral part of the aircraft's development and the airframe had been specifically stressed to take the additional loading. The inclusion of such a system on the Ki-15–

The drop-tank fuel outlet pipe, attachment fitting (inside the circular access panel) and four sway-brace fittings (on the forward and rear main spars) are clearly visible on this Ki-15-II. Note the open vertical camera window aperture and boarding step. (Shoichi Tanaka)

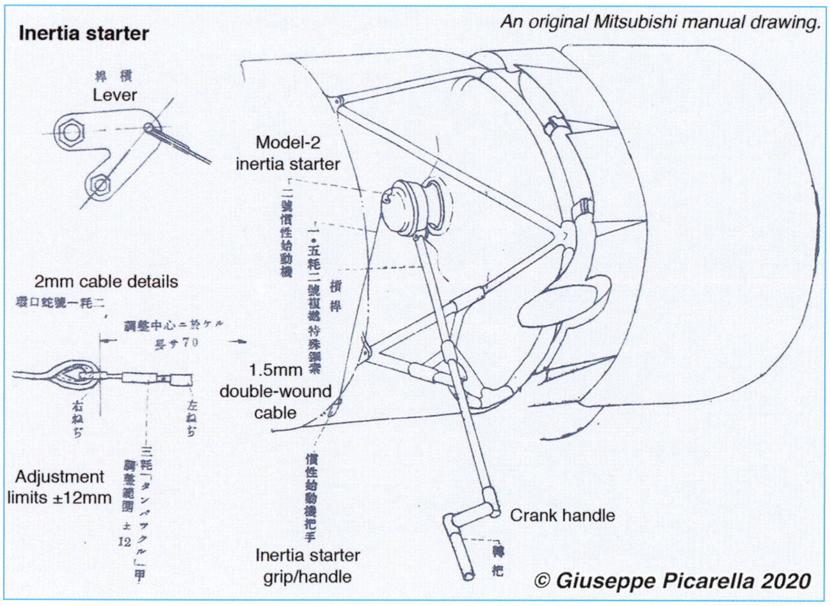

Inertia starter

An original Mitsubishi manual drawing.

II would have required re-stressing the outboard wings, wing attachment interfaces, centre wing section and localized fuselage attachment points, etc. With the design team working at full capacity on a completely new engine installation, the prospect of redesigning and re-stressing the wing would have been a major undertaking for Mitsubishi's engineers at that time and additional delays to the Ki-15-II program would have been inevitable.

That left the concept of fitting a drop-tank to Mitsubishi's highly streamlined airframe. While it is likely that the inclusion of a drop-tank and associated fittings had been discussed during the development of the production Ki-15-I, it is likely that the additional drag penalty incurred by such an installation was deemed undesirable to say the least. It would have been a conflict of aerodynamic interests for the design team to even consider "adding" such a large amount of parasitic drag to the sleek Ki-15 airframe. Times though had changed, extra range was desperately needed and a drop-tank could ultimately add another 150 or 200 litres of precious fuel to the aircraft. The use of drop-tanks to extend the range of military fighters had blossomed in the mid 1930s, as aircraft grew in size and power. But such installations, however clean, came at an aerodynamic price. Drop-tanks and their attachment fittings generate a lot of drag and on an aircraft like the Ki-15-II this could amount to loss of speed in the region of 64km/h (40mph)! While this reduction in speed would have had a devastating effect on the aircraft's ability to evade interception, the ability to "drop" the drop-tank and regain normal operating speeds was now considered acceptable, if a suitably "clean" attachment system could be developed.

A small change to the indicated fuel capacities was included in the Ki-15-II manual following the redesign. Specifically, the fuselage main fuel tank was listed as containing 380 litres, while the wing fuel tanks were amended to contain 100 litres (per tank). This is down from 389 litres and 105 litres (respectively) from quantities quoted for the Ki-15-I. It is unclear why these reductions occurred, but it is possible that these tanks were modified to fix operational or manufacturing issues. Alternatively these figures could imply that the fuel system was recalibrated to exclude any fuel that filters down into the associated fuel cocks, filters, pumps and interconnecting pipework.

It should also be pointed out that we do not know whether it was the Army or the Navy that first requested the inclusion of a drop-tank installation on the *Babs*, as the Navy was showing interest in the new Ki-15-II just as the 1st prototype was undergoing test flights in mid 1938. It is entirely possible that the Navy suggested the installation be included in future developments, as the first Ki-15-II capable of receiving a drop-tank was C/n2003 – a technical note in the maintenance manual specifies that aircraft C/n2001 and C/n2002 were not drop-tank compatible.

Drop-tank

Little is officially known about the drop-tank design used by the Ki-15-II, other than its capacity of 208 litres, but the patchwork of surviving engineering drawings detailing the layout of its attachment fittings, contain enough basic references to allow us to scale them against the fuselage station drawing. The results indicate that the installation was probably a modified version of the A5M2 *Claude* long-range (210 litre) drop-tank. This is unsurprising given that Mitsubishi's A5M2 was the most advanced fighter in Japan at the time and its drop-tank had been designed to complement its high performance characteristics. Incidentally, two different size drop-tanks were developed for the A5M2, the standard 160 litre tank with a pointed conical rear section and the 210 litre tank with a rounded rear section.

The *Babs* drop-tank was comprised of a nosecone, barrel section and tailcone. Its structure, based on other Japanese drop-tanks of the period, would have been aluminium alloy, with internal baffle frames and stringers. A horizontal pylon with three transverse hoop-frames supported the tank with aerodynamic end caps attached to each end of the support pylon. The upper (machined) segments of the hoop-frames were slid onto the pylon and bolted in place, while the lower section hoop-bands were tightened around the tank with a turnbuckle at the BDC. A forward sway-brace was located between the forward and centre hoop-frames, while the rear sway-brace was integral with the upper segment of

Ki-15-II Drop-tank and pylon

1/48 Scale

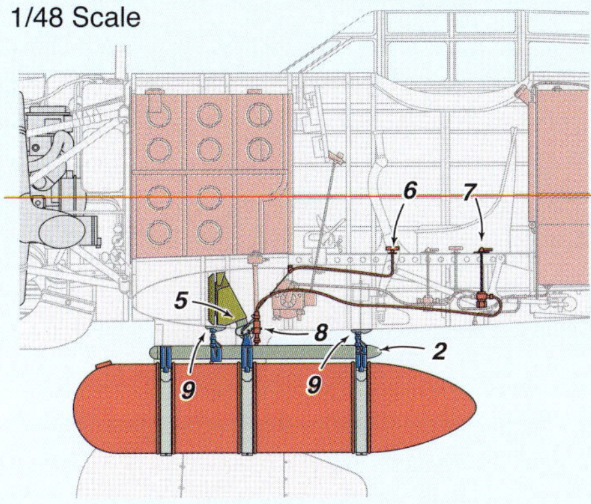

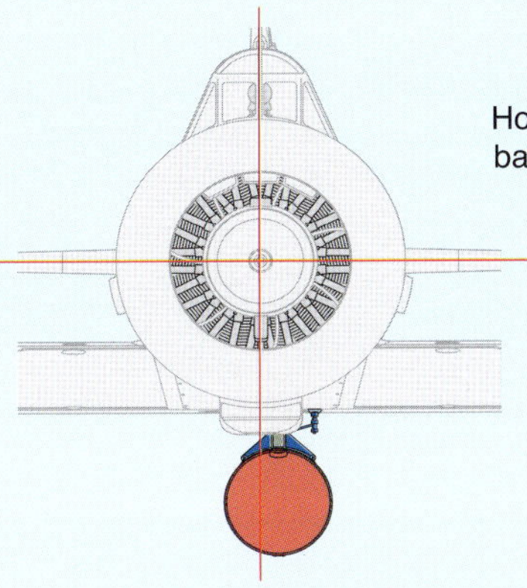

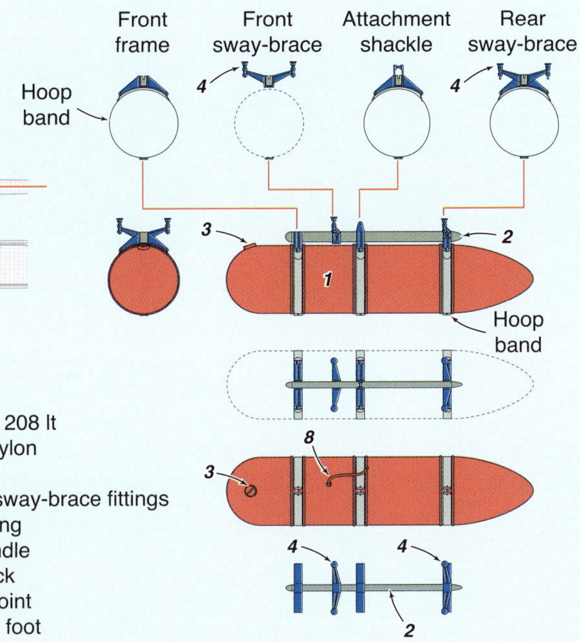

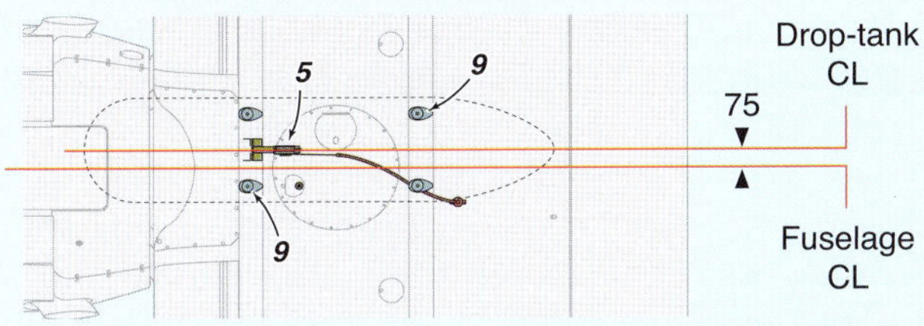

1. Drop-tank – 208 lt
2. Drop-tank pylon
3. Filler port
4. Adjustable sway-brace fittings
5. Release fitting
6. Jettison handle
7. Selector cock
8. Fuel outlet joint
9. Sway-brace foot

Drop-tank

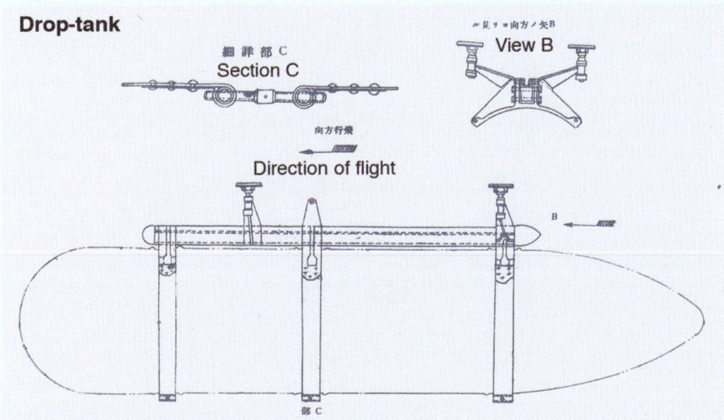

A selection of original Mitsubishi engineering and manual drawings for the Ki-15 drop-tank.

Drop-tank release fittings

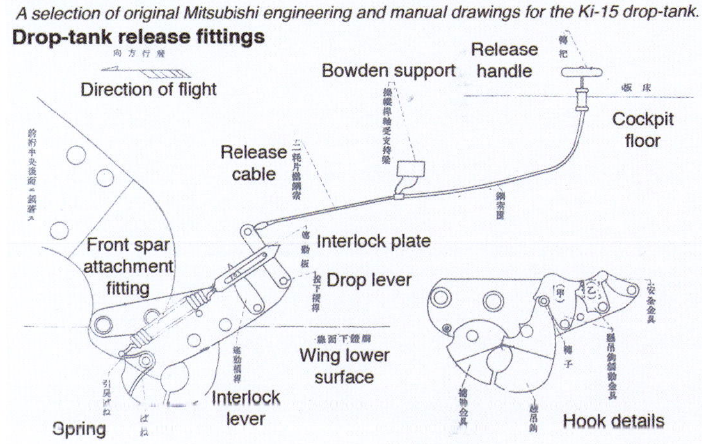

Drop-tank control system

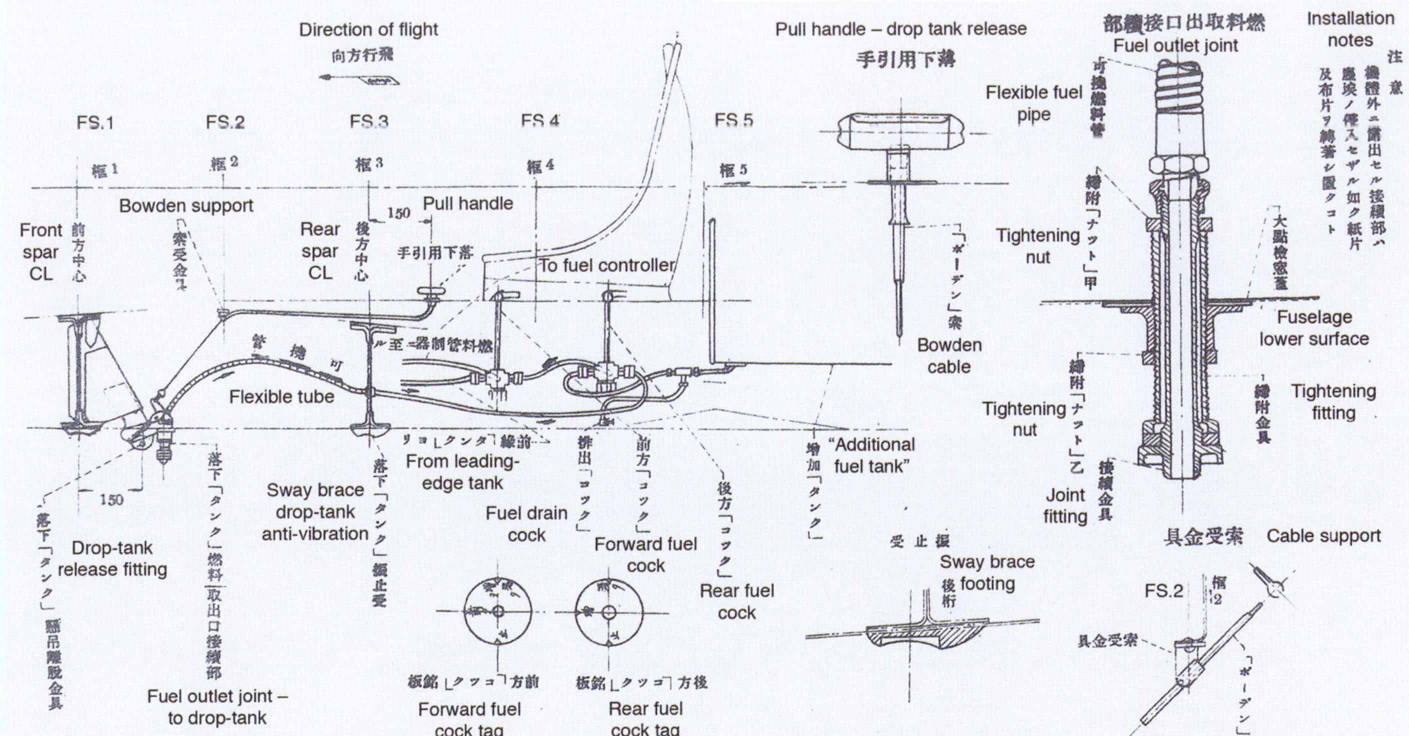

the rear hoop-frame. Each sway-brace contained adjustable vertical bolt fittings to steady the drop-tank installation when attached to the aircraft. The machined drop-tank support shackle was integral with the centre hoop-frame assembly.

The fuel system drawings are somewhat vague concerning the internal fittings of the tank, but these would have included a gravity filler cap and fuel screen, feed pipe and screen, vent pipe and drain fitting.

Interestingly, not one single photograph of an Army Ki-15-II carrying a drop-tank has ever been published, although they were probably used for long-range delivery flights. The Navy's C5M on the other hand routinely carried drop-tanks during both the Sino-Japanese and the Pacific war.

Drop-tank attachment fittings

The external drop-tank fittings were kept to an absolute minimum in order to reduce drag. The machined aluminium alloy and steel shackle-release fitting was attached to the rear face of the forward spar, with its jaws exiting the lower surface of the centre-wing section access hatch, approximately 75mm to the port side of the aircraft CL and 150mm aft of the FS.1. The jaws protruded approximately 50mm into the airstream. Two "teardrop" shaped sway-brace locators were fitted to each lower spar-cap, 150mm to the left and right of the drop-tank CL.

The fuel feed pipe exited the drop-tank to the starboard side of the support pylon and entered the lower surface of the aircraft via the fuel outlet joint. From there it was routed via a flexible pipe to the rear spar and then by copper pipe to the "aft fuel cock" located on the left-hand side of the cockpit floor between FS.4 and FS.5. Flow from the "additional fuel tank" and drop-tank was managed at the "aft fuel cock" before joining the main fuel system at the "forward fuel cock".

The spring-loaded support shackle was actuated by the drop-tank jettison handle located on the left-hand side of the cockpit floor between FS.3 and FS.4. The flexible release cable routed via support fittings to the jaws of the shackle, where an interlock lever ensured that the drop-tank could not be inadvertently released.

Fuel system capacity – Ki-15-II

Tank location	Capacity in litres
Fuselage main tank	380
Wing tanks – starboard	100
Wing tank – port	100
Wing leading edge tank – starboard	43
Wing leading edge tank – port	43
Additional fuel tank	137
Drop-tank	208
Total	**1,011**

Fuel management system

The Ki-15-I fuel system was modified to incorporate the "additional fuel tanks" and management system. It is shown in full for the purposes of clarity.

1. The **fuel tank controller** is the heart of the fuel system, interconnecting the fuel pump, carburettor, fuel primer, emergency hand pump and the fuel tanks loops via the "wing/body" fuel selector cock. With an integral fuel filter and water drain, the fuel tank selector was located on the port side of the centre wing section at WS.2 adjacent to FS.2. It was accessible via a dedicated 170mm inspection panel located in the lower centre-wing section access hatch.
2. A **fuel primer** hand pump fitted to the lower instrument panel. This primed the engine impeller with fuel prior to start-up.
3. The **Wing/body fuel tank selector cock** was located outboard and aft of the fuel tank controller unit. It controlled the selection of the wing fuel tanks or fuselage main fuel tank only. The control handle was located on the left-hand side of the lower instrument panel and connected to the selector body by a torque tube connected through the cockpit floor.
4. The **forward fuel cock** and **aft fuel cock** selectors were located on the cockpit floor, to the left of the pilot's seat. The forward fuel cock allowed the selection of either the wing leading edge tanks or the "additional fuel tank" and drop-tank into the main fuel system. The aft fuel cock controlled the connection of either the "additional fuel tank" or drop-tank into the forward selector cock.
5. A **manual fuel pump** handle was located on the cockpit floor between the "forward fuel cock" and "aft fuel cock". This was a vertical plunger type handle that actuated a lever on the rear of the fuel controller via a flexible shaft. This pump was used to prime the carburettor before starting the

engine, which then took over pressurization of the fuel system. The manual fuel pump also acted as an emergence fuel pump if the engine driven pump failed in flight.

6. The **Drop-tank jettison handle** was located ahead of the forward fuel cock.
7. Three individual **fuel quantity gauges** were installed in the lower instrument panels. These provided readings for the fuselage main fuel tank, wing fuel tanks and wing leading edge fuel tanks. A **fuel pressure gauge** was installed in the upper instrument panel, which was connected to the fuel tank controller unit.
8. A **fuel quantity sight-glass** was provided for the "addition fuel tank".

Above, left: *The rearward swept (starboard side) leading-edge of the oil cooler is clearly visible in this photograph, as too are the nose cowl leading-edge beading and the nose fairing. (Arawasi)*

Above: *The Ha-26 engine installation is clearly visible in this photograph of Toshio Omata and* Karigane-II *(Ki-15-II) J-BAAO* Amakaze. *The cowl gills are fully open and the oil tank, 2-way cock and oil filter can be seen behind the exhaust. (Japan Aeronautical Association)*

Oil cooling system

The installation of the (900hp) Ha-26-I engine and tightly fitted cowling necessitated a redesign of the oil system to incorporate an oil cooler to improve engine management. It is interesting to note that the Ki-15-II maintenance manual contains a general arrangement (3-view) drawing (See Chapter 6) of what is assumed to be an early Ki-15-II layout, which includes some unusual details. The front view depicts what seems to be a flat-sided annular oil cooler (radiator) assembly inside the cowling, a design similar to the type found on the Army Nakajima Army Type-97 Fighter (Ki-27) *Nate* or later Type-1 fighter (Ki-43-I) *Oscar*. In addition to this, the front view is also totally devoid of the fixed oil cooler intake beneath the cowling, while the side view drawing seems to hint at a retractable oil cooler scoop, similar to the design that would be installed on the Ki-46 *Dinah*. Could this be an example of a poor technical publication illustration, or does it show an oval-shaped annular oil cooler, from an earlier phase of the Ki-15-II development program? As all of the other circular items on the illustration, such as the propeller disc and wheels are drawn accurately, it seems unlikely that the engineer/illustrator found it impossible to draw a circular engine cowling or circular propeller spinner?

From a design point of view the inclusion of a low-drag annular oil cooler, for high-speed flight, supported by an auxiliary oil cooler (with a retractable intake) for take-off and climbing, would seem like the ideal solution. The fact that this installation was not included on the Ki-15-II may indicate that it was either unable to provide adequate cooling for the new engine, or the weight and complexity of a two-part (primary and auxiliary) oil cooler system rendered the installation problematic. While the Ki-43-I would use an engine of similar horsepower, a 950hp Nakajima Type-99 (Ha-25), it was not encased in such a highly streamlined cowling, with a small intake area.

Ki-15-II Speculative annular oil cooler

1/48 Scale

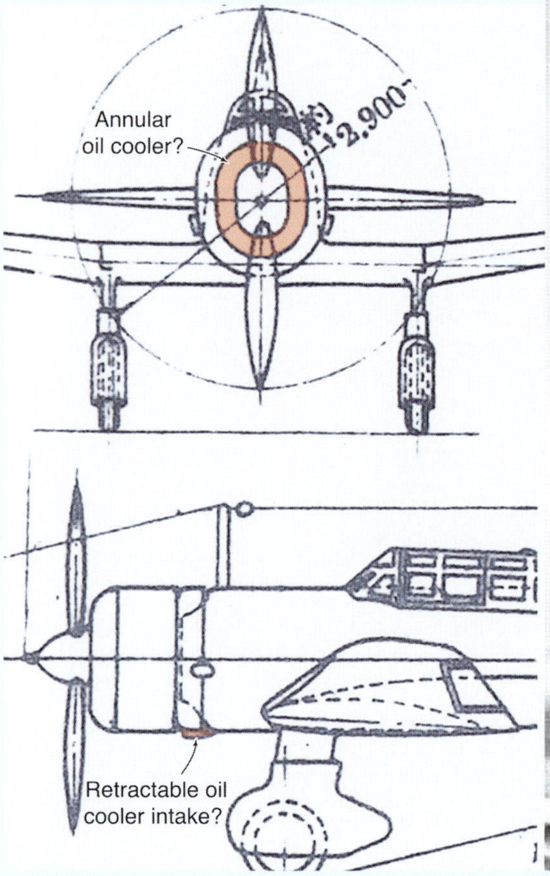

Illustration from March 1941 Ki-15-II manual

Nakajima Ki-27b *Nate* with annular oil cooler installation. Note the large intake area of the cowling.

Annular oil cooler speculative layout

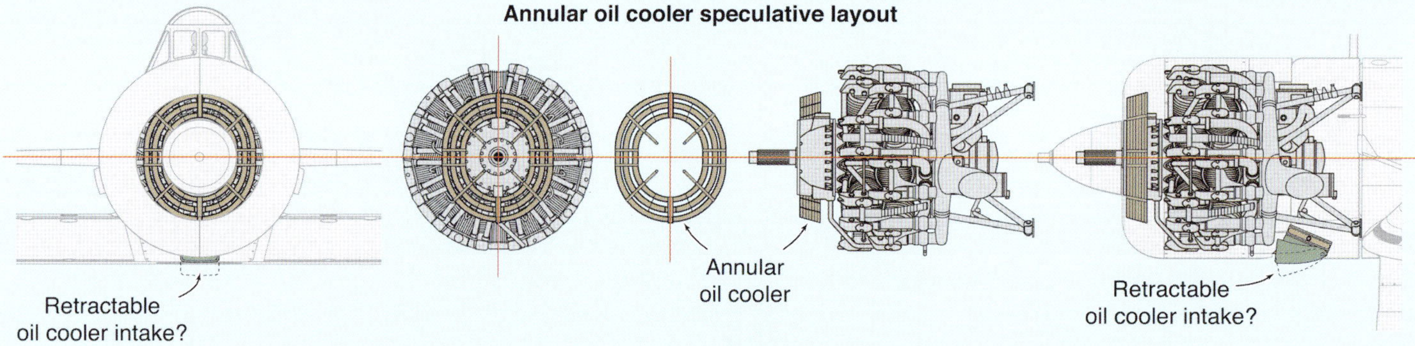

Ki-15-II Oil cooler

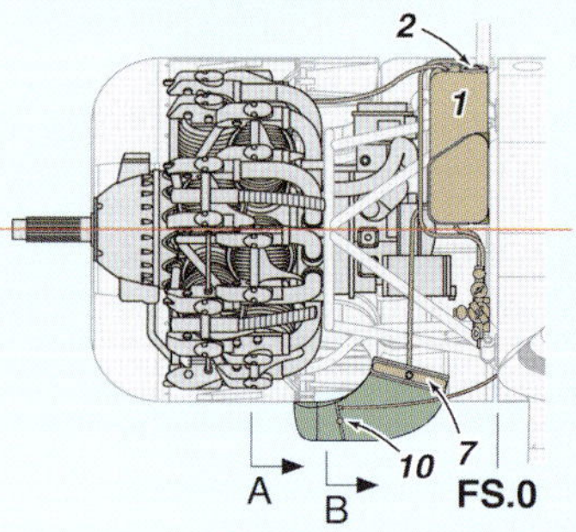

1 Oil tank – 73 lt
2 Filler port
3 Oil sump
4 2-way cock
5 Oil filter
6 Drain cock
7 Oil cooler
8 Oil tank mount
9 Oil tank retaining straps
10 Air-intake shutter and linkage
11 Inertia starter/oil tank recess
12 Air-intake and oil cooler – looking down

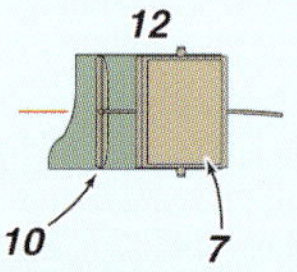

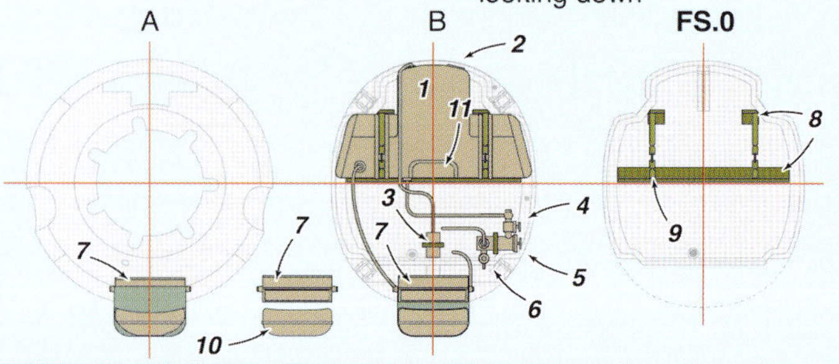

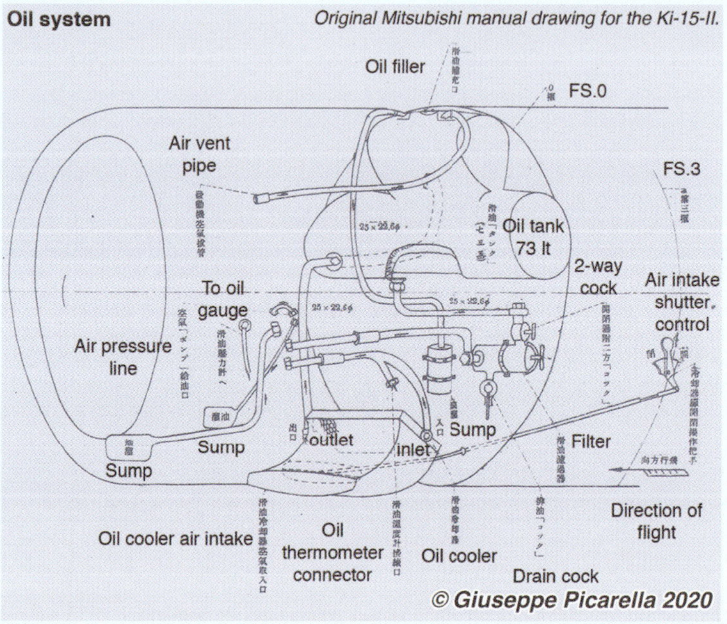

If the annular radiator installation was initially studied for the Ki-15-II, then it is also very likely that the design team considered installing a low-drag conformal oil tank on the leading edge of the wing. Without doubt this type of installation would have provided additional cooling and a very clean aerodynamic solution, as it was already proving its value on Mitsubishi's A5M *Claude*, which was in production at that time. Despite the possible benefits of this installation, it would seem that the necessity for additional fuel capacity took precedent; as such a leading edge oil tank would have robbed the fuel system of a least 105 litres.

After studying all options, the engineering team developed a low profile oil cooler installation with little or no impact on the existing airframe structure or fuel capacity. The system included an enlarged oil tank (73 litres) with an integral airspace and scalloped lower section (to allow clearance for the engine's accessory gearbox and equipment), an expansion sump, breather pipe, system stopcock, oil filter and oil cooler assembly. The oil filter and stop-cock were relocated to the port side of FS.0, while the new oil cooler was mounted on the lower portion of the engine mount, where it was supplied with ram-air through a dedicated air-intake located on the BDC of the accessory bay.

Because the intake was exposed to the airflow and was thus a potential source of drag, its design was closely controlled. The exposed dimensions were approximately 250mm wide by 100mm deep and the exterior surfaces were subtly curved to reduce parasitic drag. Perhaps the most interesting feature of the new air-intake, and an indication of the attention to detail lavished on the Ki-15, was the leading edge lip design. When running on the ground, there was a tendency for the closely cowled engine to overheat, and in an ideal world the air-intake would have worked more effectively if it had been enlarged and extended further into the airstream. While this solution would have assisted cooling on the ground, such a layout would have increased parasitic drag in the air. In order to avoid such additional drag, the starboard side of the intake lip was swept rearwards to allow the intake to receive more cooling air from the rearward "swirl" of the descending propeller blade, without affecting longitudinal airflow or drag during high-speed forward flight.

Oil pressure and flow were controlled by the engine driven pump and scavenge pipes reclaimed oil from the crankcase and gearbox sumps. Oil temperature was controlled by a butterfly valve located in the throat of the air-intake.

Electrical system

Electrical power for the Ki-15-II was supplied by an engine driven Model-2 Airborne Generator and a Mk.3 Airborne Battery. No ground power receptacle was fitted.

The engine generator was located on the centreline of the Ha-26-I accessory gearbox and provided 27V/400-650Watts of DC power to the electrical system while also recharging the single 24Volt Mk.3 Airborne Battery, which was located directly behind the RO's seat, in the aft storage cabinet between FS.9 and FS.10. See **Radio equipment**.

Power from either source was fed through the voltage regulator, which provided a constant 24Volt power supply to the main power (master) switch, which was located at FS.3 on the right-hand side of the pilot's cockpit.

The main power switch supplied power to the electrical control panel, which was located on the right-hand side of the pilot's cockpit between FS.3 and FS.4. It also supplied power to the RO's radio equipment via an airborne transformer.

Cockpits and secondary systems

Pilot's cockpit and systems

Instrument panel

The pilot's instrument panel layout of the Ki-15-II was identical to that of the Ki-15-I fitted with the *standard* fuel system.

Oil cooler lever

The oil cooler shutter control lever was located on the left-hand side of the cockpit, below the throttle quadrant on FS.3. The lever attached to a braided-steel cable, running through a brass tube, which passed below the fuselage fuel tank and exited the secondary firewall at FS.0. The cable operated a butterfly valve in the throat of the oil cooler air intake – forward was closed and aft was open.

Pilot and RO's cockpit and systems – Ki-15-II

1/32 Scale

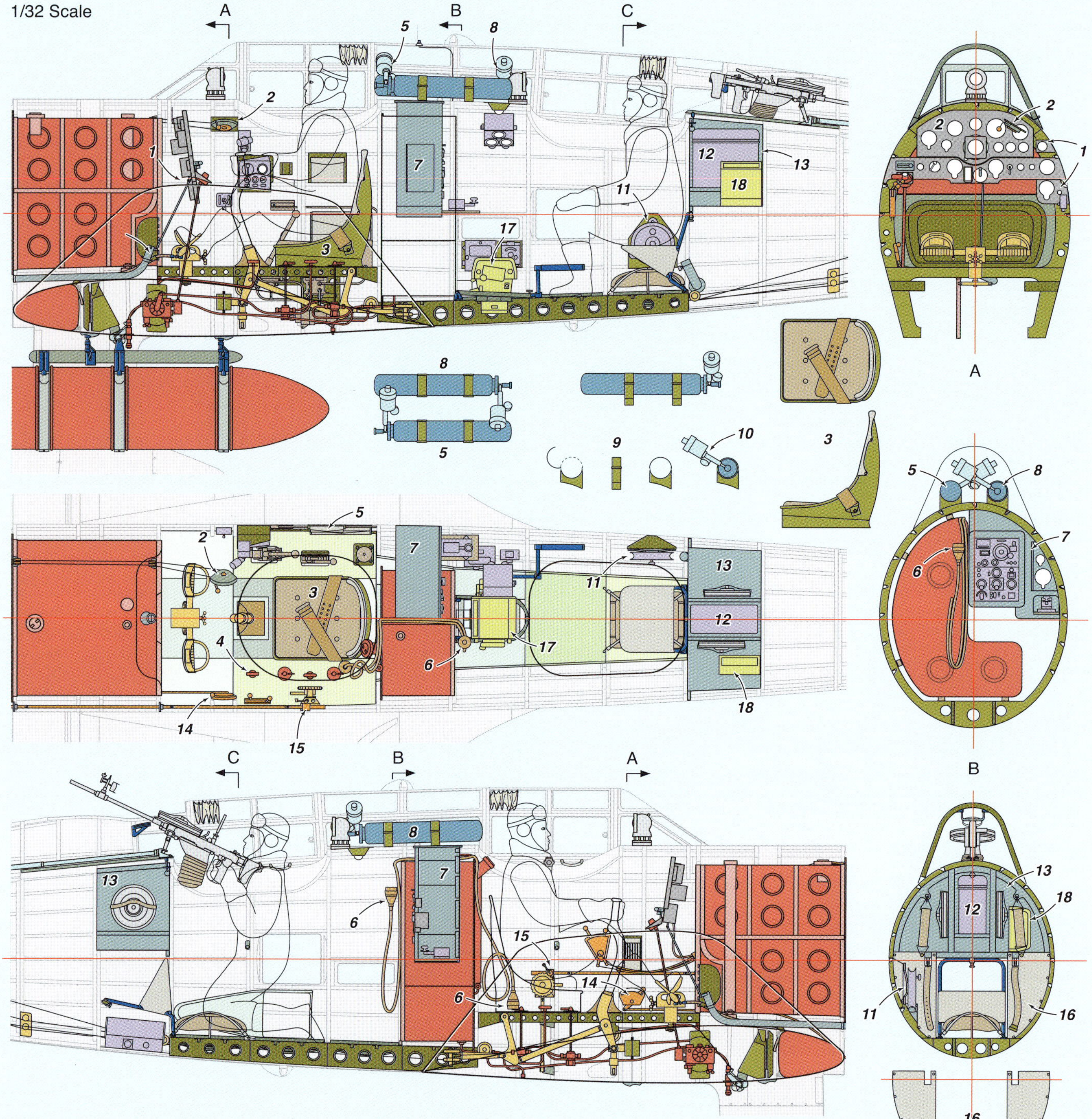

Engine controls

An original Mitsubishi manual drawing for the Ki-15-II engine controls.

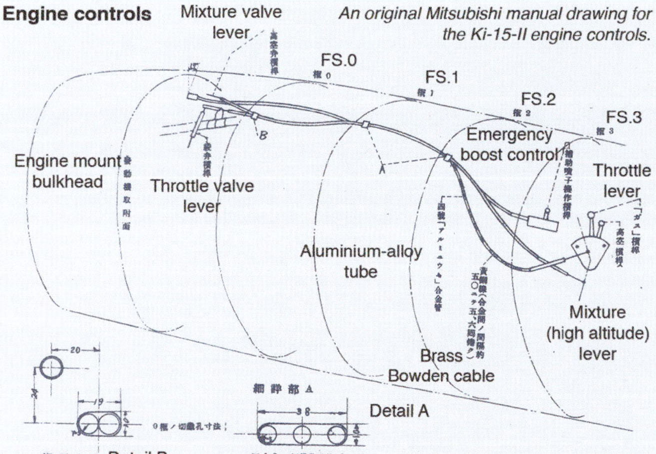

1 Auxiliary instrument panels
2 Carburettor dust screen control lever
3 Modified pilot's seat
4 Drop-tank jettison handle
5 Pilot's oxygen cylinder – left-hand side
6 "Gosport" tube
7 Enlarged radio cabinet
8 RO's oxygen cylinder – right-hand side
9 Oxygen cylinder hoop mounts – side hingeing
10 Oxygen valve and flow-rate meter
11 Possible relocation of the trailing antenna real and guide tube
12 Relocated Mk.3 Airborne Battery
13 Storage cabinet
14 Oil cooler shutter control
15 Cowl flap control and position indicator
16 Modified rear fuselage canvas divider – for trailing antenna guide tube
17 Type-100 Small Aerial Camera (SK-100) and support frame
18 Film roll canister

Representative of the production **Ki-15-II** and the *late model* **Ki-15-I** when fitted with the *Standard* fuel system

Upper panel
1 Altimeter Type-95
2 Airspeed indicator Type-96
3 Turn and bank indicator
4 Tachometer Type-1 Model-2
5 Manifold pressure gauge Type-94
6 Chronometer Type-93
7 Artificial horizon Type-96
8 Fuel pressure gauge Type-95
9 Oil pressure gauge Type-94
10 Oil temperature gauge

Lower panel
11 Emergency boost control
12 Fuel tank selector cock
13 Starter control lever
14 Magneto switch Model-1
15 Fuel quantity gauge – fuselage tank
16 Compass correction card
17 Cockpit ventilation control
18 Fuel quantity gauge – wing tank
19 Fuel tank indicator selector – left/right
20 Starter generator
21 Fuel primer pump
22 Cylinder head temperature gauge

Auxiliary panels
23 Fuel tank indicator selector – wing leading edge tank
24 Fuel tank indicator selector – left/right
25 Exhaust gas temperature gauge
26 Master compass Model-1

Electrical system

The electrical control panel was located on the right-hand side of the pilot's cockpit between FS.3 and FS.4. It also supplied power to the RO's radio equipment via an airborne transformer. See **Radio equipment** and **Antennas**.

The electrical control panel contained:

1. A landing light switch.
2. A voltage regulator.
3. A radio power source control.
4. A cockpit light – this is depicted as a dimmer unit and probably controlled the instrument panel light levels rather than the cockpit lighting.
5. Seat light.
6. Airspeed indicator heater – pitot heater.

In addition to the items controlled directly via this panel, a dedicated seat light with on/off control was provided for the pilot on the right-hand side of the cockpit at FS.3. The RO's seat light, on the other hand, was effectively controlled via the pilot's electrical control panel, although both seat lights could be manually dimmed if required.

Two-pin plug-type connectors for electrically heated flight-suits were also located on the right-hand side of both cockpits. See **Cockpit ventilation** and **crew heating.**

Cowl flaps

The cowl flaps were operated manually via a torque-tube, with a winding handle and position indicator attached to a bevel gearbox located at FS.4 on the left-hand side of the cockpit. The three-section torque-tube assembly, articulated with universal joints at FS.2 and FS.0, drove a threaded shaft located on the port side of the engine mount. As the torque-tube rotated, an actuator collar fitting, held in place by guide tube, moved along the threaded shaft. The fore and aft movement of the actuator collar fitting opened and closed the cowl flaps with the aid of a bellcrank.

Carburettor intakes controls

The carburettor intake covers were opened and closed via a selector lever located on FS.3, beneath the right-hand section of the instrument panel shroud. This two-position lever controlled an endless cable passing over two double pulleys located at FS.2 and FS.0, with a larger conversion pulley located on the upper port side segment of the engine mount. A pushrod directly connected the conversion pulley actuator arm to the intake cover actuator arm.

Pilot's seat

Circumstantial evidence would indicate that the pilot's seat fitted to the Ki-15-II was slightly modified when compared to the Ki-15-I seat. A fuel system engineering drawing in the Ki-15-II manual included a detailed side elevation of the seat, which incorporated a canted seat-pan plus a curved and enlarged seat back. It is assumed that these two small modifications were implemented to improve pilot comfort during long duration flights and a similar canted seat-pan design was also adopted on the Ki-46 *Dinah*. Neither modification impacted upon the shape and installation of the seat cushion and back support.

RO's cockpit and systems

Aerial camera equipment

Army Type-100 Small Aerial Camera/SK-100

While the Army respected the concept of the Type-96 Small Aerial Camera its reliability was a major issue. In light of these issues Konishi-Roku (Konica) took up the challenge of developed a camera of similar dimensions to the SK-96, but without the high tech additions. Konishi-Roku developed a removable mounting ring for their camera and decided to incorporate bayonet-type lens fittings, all of which proved to be rugged and easy to operate in the confines of a cold cramped cockpit. They also included a slide-out "bull's-eye" type spirit level on the right-hand side of the casing to allow the camera to be levelled when installed in the support frame. The Army accepted the camera into service in 1940, as the Type-100 Small Aerial Camera (SK-100) and 4,269 were produced over the next 5 years, making it the most widely produced Japanese aerial camera of the war. The camera kit incorporated an aluminium alloy body (heated), lens x 3 (heated), folding view finder, wooden handles, roll film holder (canister), lens filters x 3, remote shutter release cable, power cord and carry case.

Army Type-100 Small Aerial Camera/SK-100

Manufacturer	Konishi-Roku
Shutter speeds	1/100, 1/150, 1/200, 1/300, 1,400 sec
Finder	Frame type
Lenses	200mm F3.5, 400mm f6.3, 500mm f5.6
Stock type	Film roll – 6 meter
Image size	11.7 x 17.8cm
Dimensions – width/height/depth	Approximately 38 x 25 x 29/34cm
Weight	6.9kg
Operation	Manual or remotely operated
Notes	Heated lens and body – 24 Volts

Opposit page: The Type-100 Small Aerial Camera.

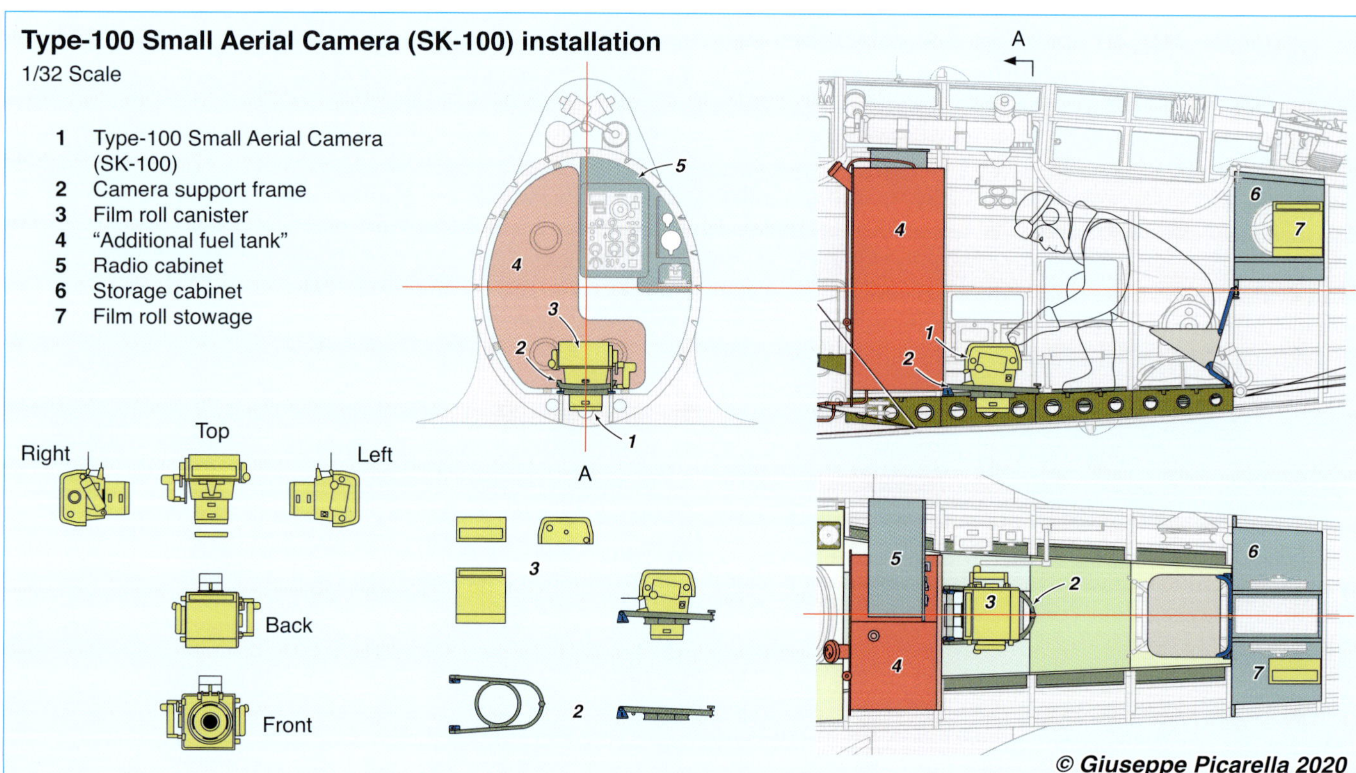

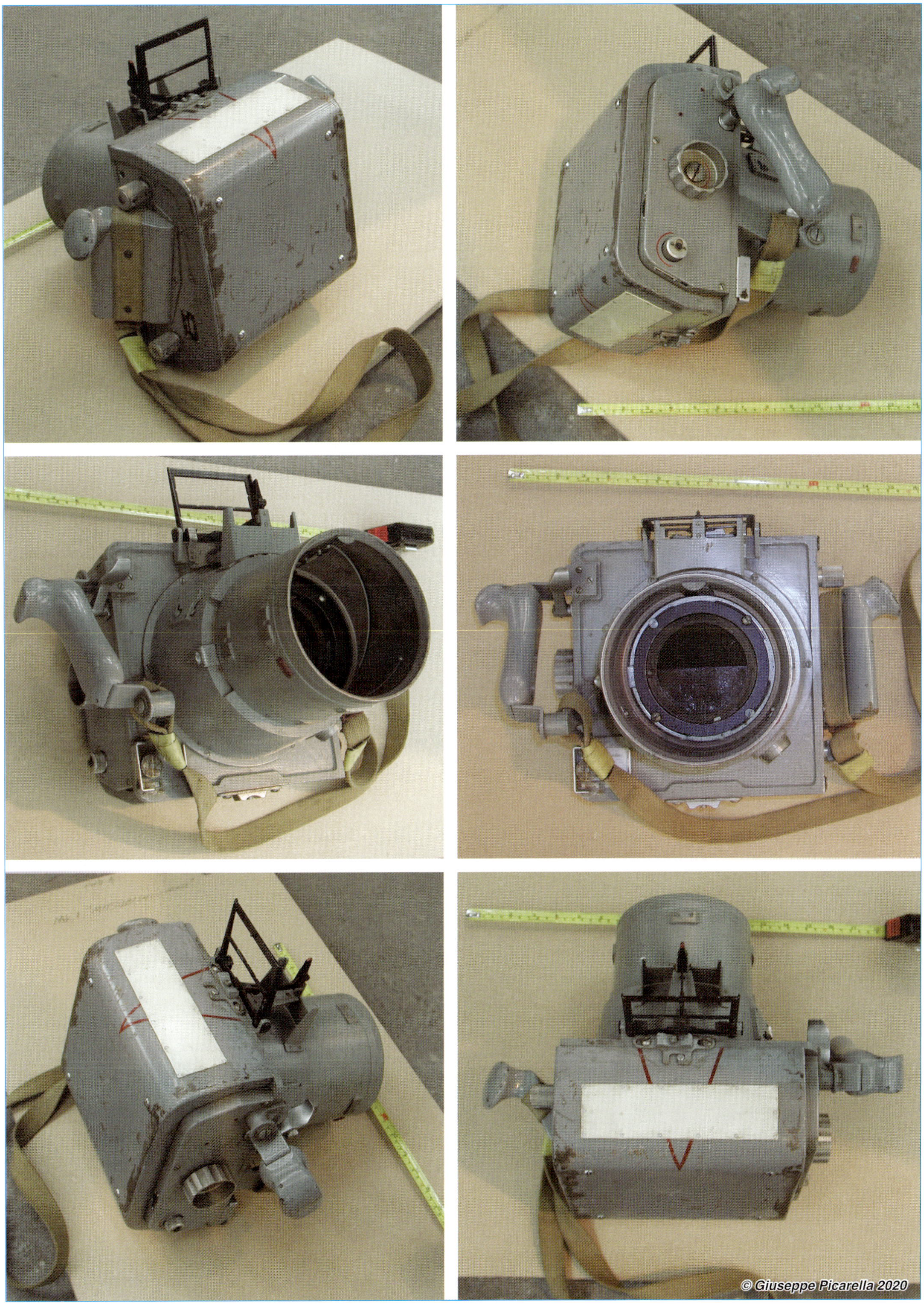
© Giuseppe Picarella 2020

Army Type-96 *Hi* Mk.2 "Command" Radio installation

1/32 Scale

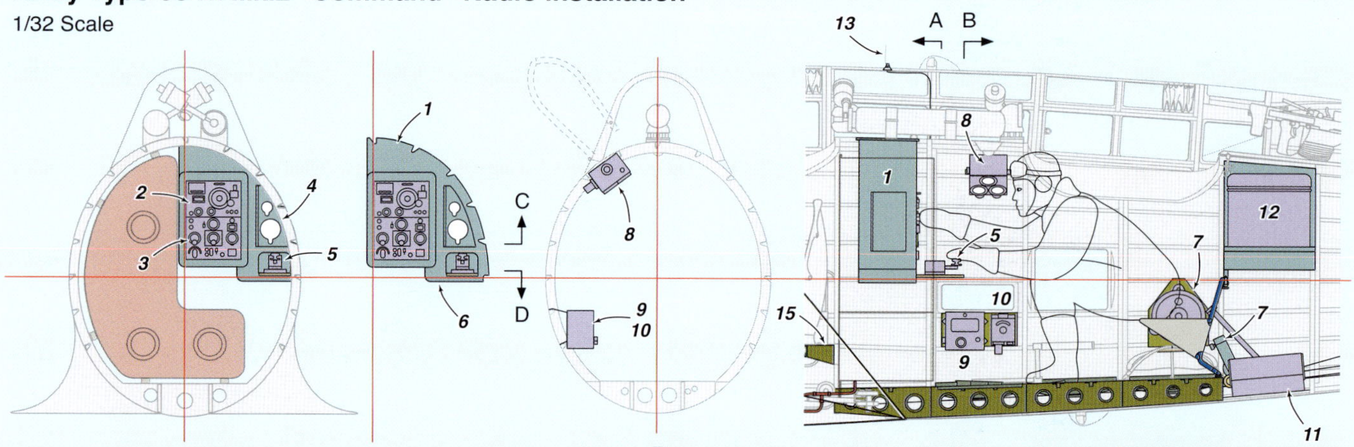

1 Radio cabinet
2 Type-96 *Hi* Mk.2 receiver
3 Type-96 *Hi* Mk.2 transmitter
4 RO's instrument panel
5 Telegraph (Morse) key
6 Retractable writing/Morse key table
7 Trailing antenna reel and guide tube
8 Ammeter
9 Starter unit
10 Input regulator
11 Transformer
12 Mk.3 Airborne Battery
13 Antenna lead-in
14 Trailing antenna – deployed
15 Radio power source connector
16 Trailing antenna insulator tube

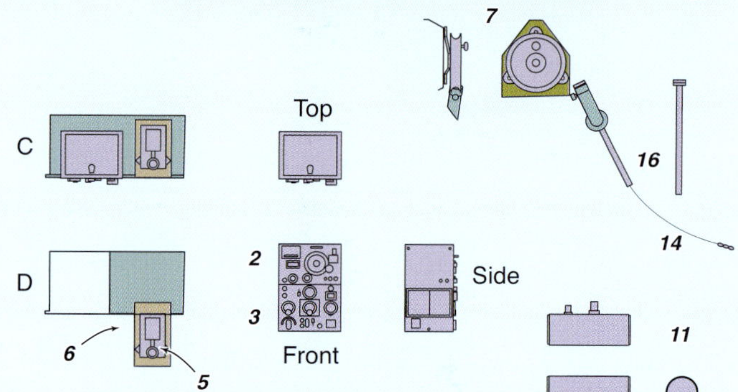

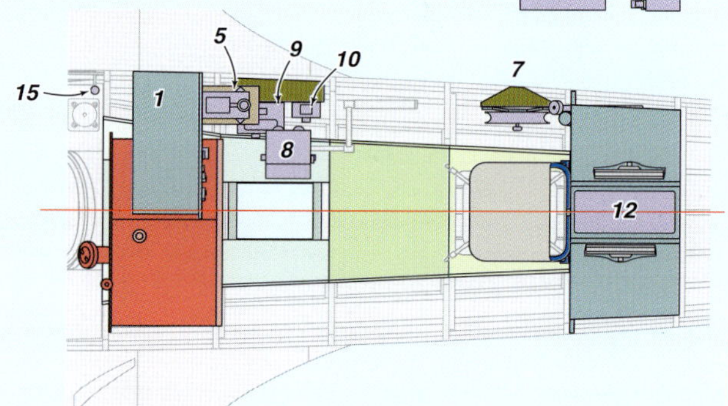

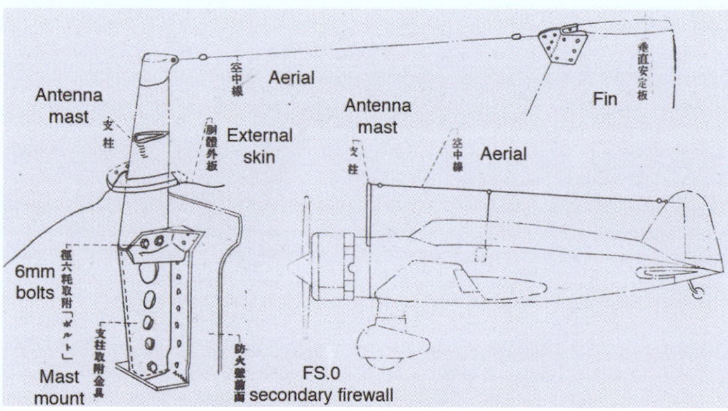

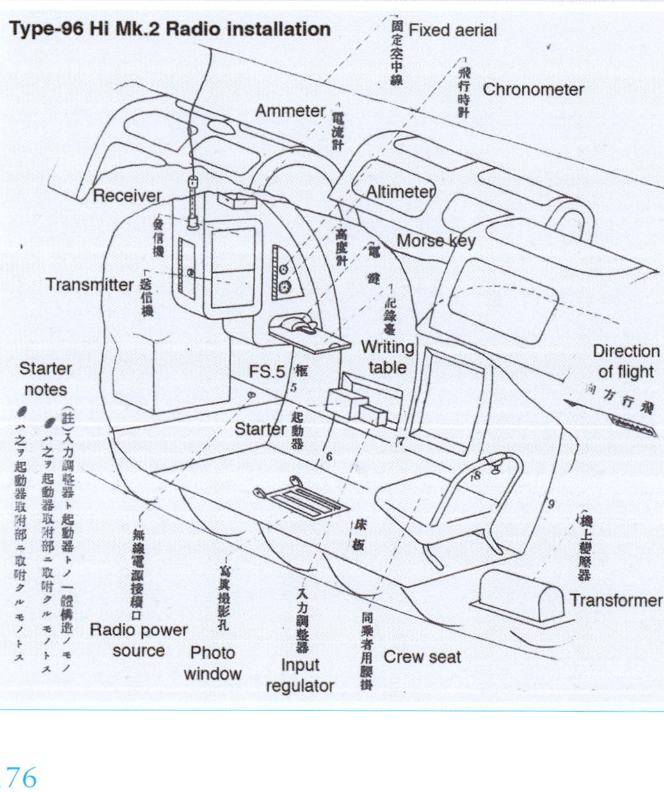

A selection of original Mitsubishi manual drawings for the Ki-15 radio system.

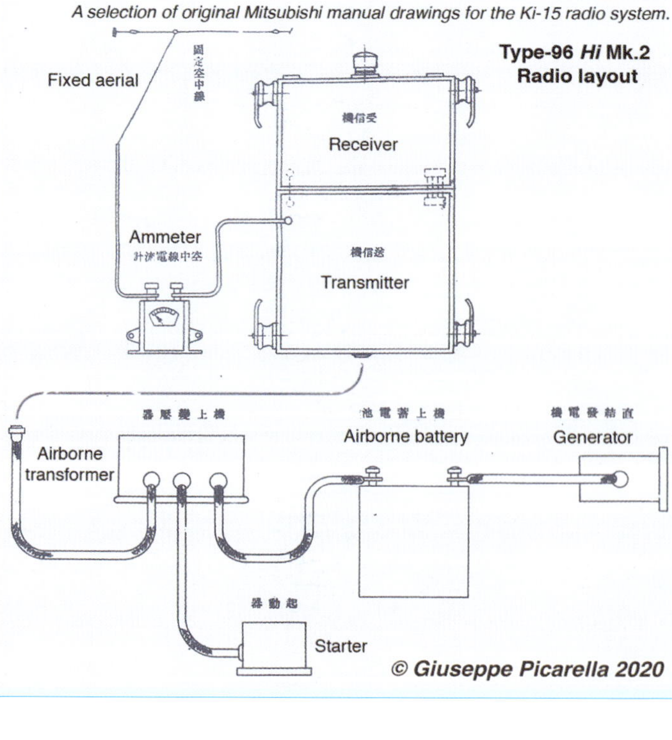

A selection of original Mitsubishi manual drawings for the Ki-15-II.

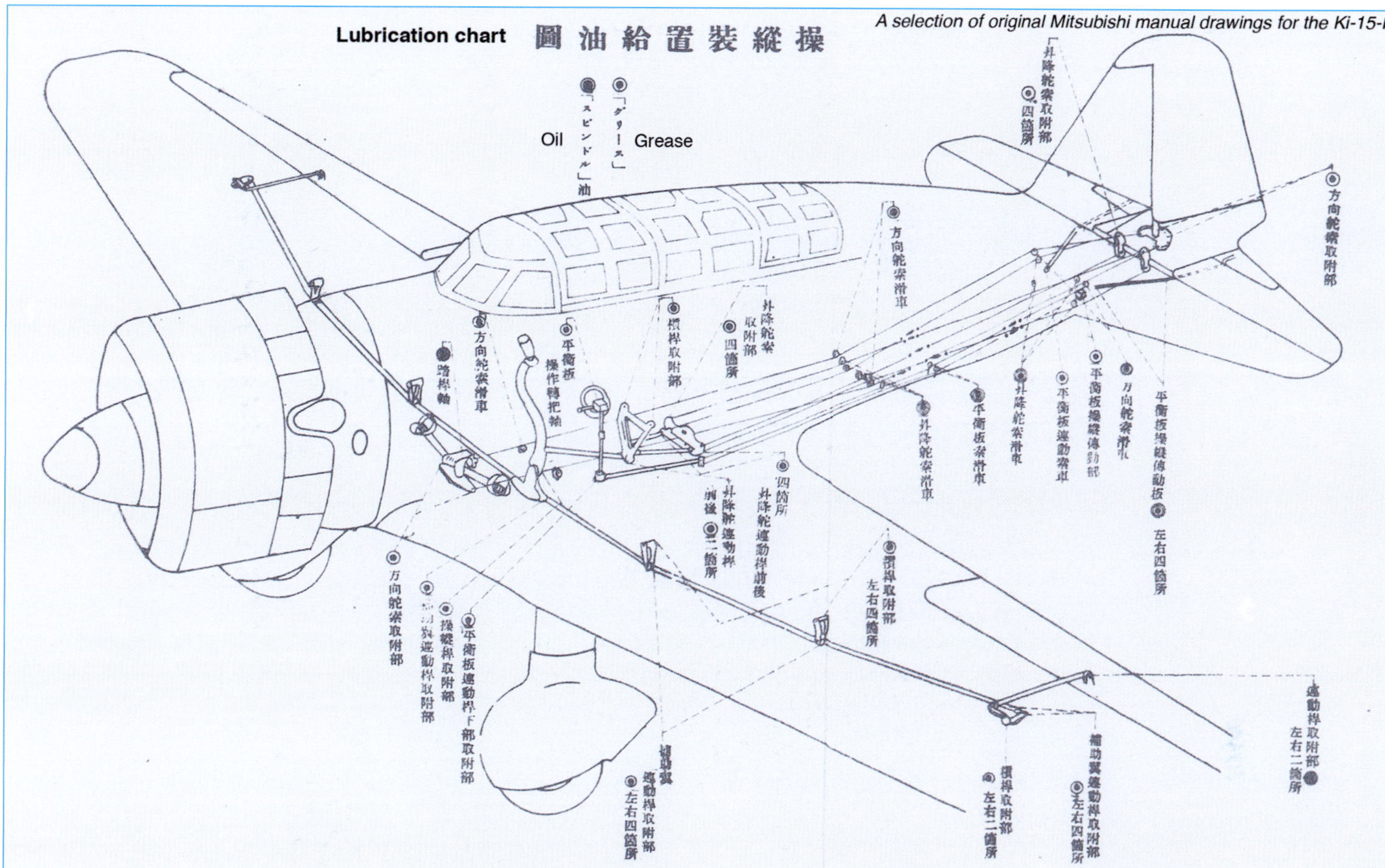

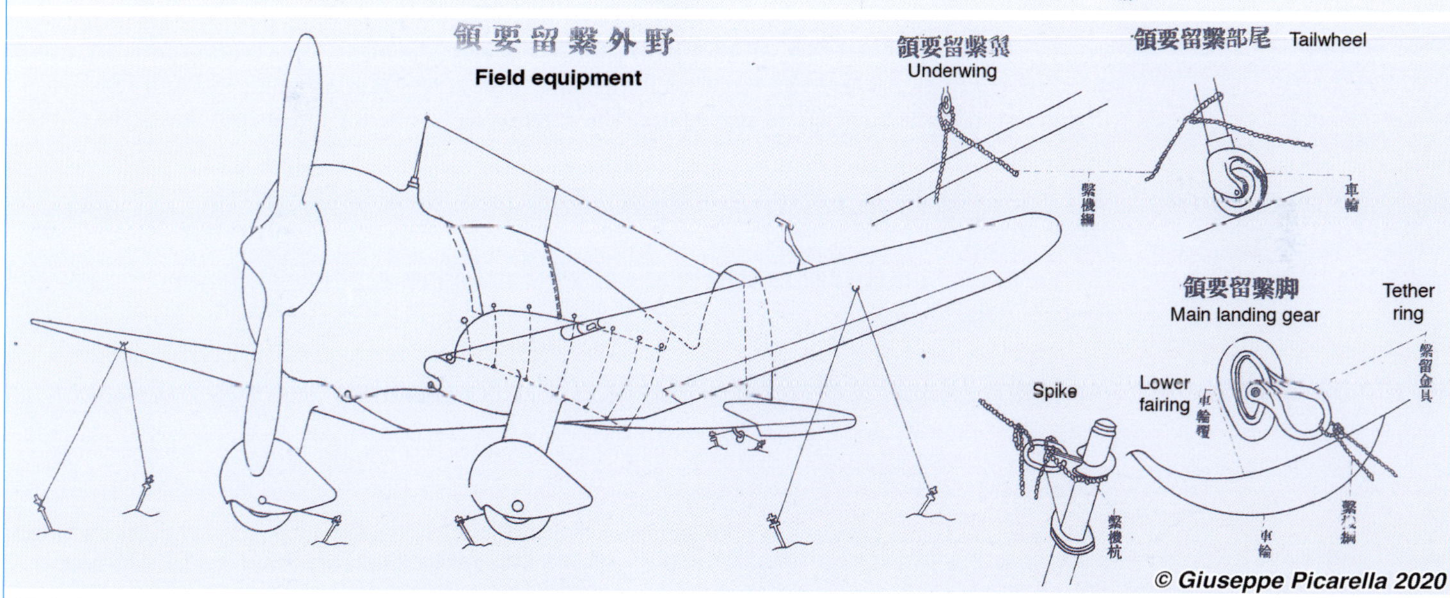

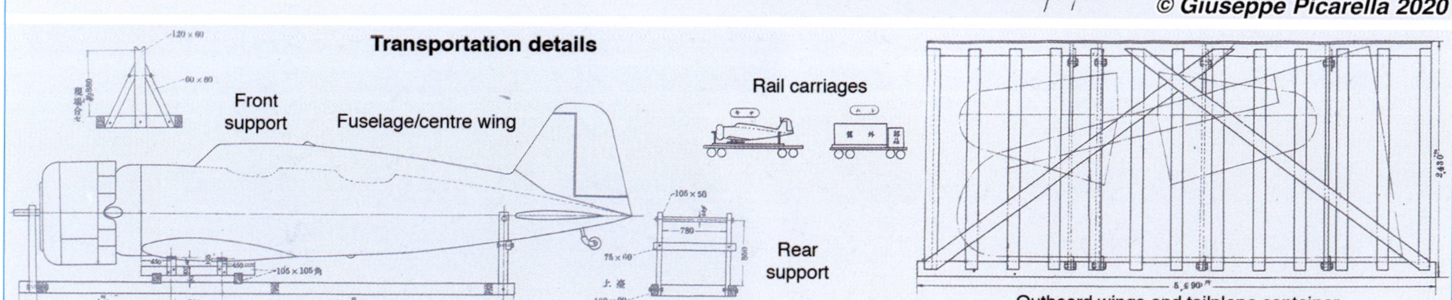

It is interesting to note that a captured SK-100 camera was evaluated by the US Naval Photographic Science Laboratory during November 1944. In comparison trials with a US Navy F-8 camera, it was concluded that the SK-100 held an advantage over the US camera with its:

1. Convenient detachable mounting ring.
2. Mounting for interchanging lenses.
3. Heating device.
4. Easy locking device on film spool holder.
5. More convenient shutter winding and film advance knob.

The report went on to recommend that:

1. Careful consideration should be given to the possible adaption on US Navy cameras of a more convenient shutter winding and film advancing knob similar to that found on the Japanese camera.
2. Serious consideration should be given to the possibility of including heater units in the US Navy F-8 camera. The speed of operation of the focal plane shutters has been observed to be seriously decreased at low temperatures.

Radio equipment

The standard radio installation of the Ki-15-II (and the Ki-15-I *late model*) was the Army Type-96 *Hi* Mk.2 "Command" radio. While these two installations were almost identical in format, there were definite modifications and upgrades to the Ki-15-II system. Firstly, the radio was installed inside the dedicated radio cabinet, located between FS.5 and FS.6. Secondly, whereas the airborne transformer on the Ki-15-I *late model* was controlled directly by a starter switch, the Ki-15-II installation included an integrated starter/input regulator, which was fitted in order to better control the power supply to the airborne transformer.

Antenna

Photographic evidence would indicate that Ki-15-II and civilian *Karigane*-II aircraft (such as **J-BAAO**) had the trailing antenna guide tube (and therefore the antenna reel) relocated further aft in the RO's cockpit, between FS.8 and FS.9. This location allowed easier deployment of the trailing antenna, free of the restricted space between the "additional fuel tank" and radio cabinet around FS.5 and FS.6.

Interestingly, the Navy would also relocate the antenna reel on their C5M aircraft due to the restricted space.

Armament

The Te-4 7.7mm flexible machine gun with three magazines (210 rounds) became the standard weapon of the Ki-15-II

Maintenance and transportation

Lubrication points

Periodic and daily lubrication charts were included within the Ki-15-II manual, for flight control hinges, flight control system linkage, runners, cranks, pulleys and gears, hydraulic actuators and landing gear.

Tie-downs and control surface locks

The Ki-15 would have been supplied with a tie-down kit, specifically designed for its airframe. This would have included ropes, pegs and shackles to secure the tailwheel, main landing gear and outboard wing panels. Removable wedge-type control surface locks were provided for the rudder, elevator and ailerons.

Protective covers

A two-piece canvas covering system was provided to protect the aircraft when stored outside. The forward section covered the nacelle assembly back to the windscreen, while the rear section extended back from the windscreen to the rear fuselage upper fairing. The edges of the covers were fitted with brass eye-fittings, which were used to secure the covers into place with the aid of cords. A pitot cover was also provided.

Mitsubishi Army Type-97 Command Reconnaissance Plane Model-II

The illustration depicts the Ki-15-II with the standard fuel system – 803 litres, increasing to 1011 litres when a drop-tank was utilised

1 Mitsubishi 900hp Army Type-99-I (Ha-26-I/Ha-31) two-row 14-cylinder radial engine – rated at 875hp for take-off
2 Oil tank – 73 litres
3 Modular design fuselage main fuel tank – 380 litres
4 Wing leading-edge fuel tank – 43 litres per tank

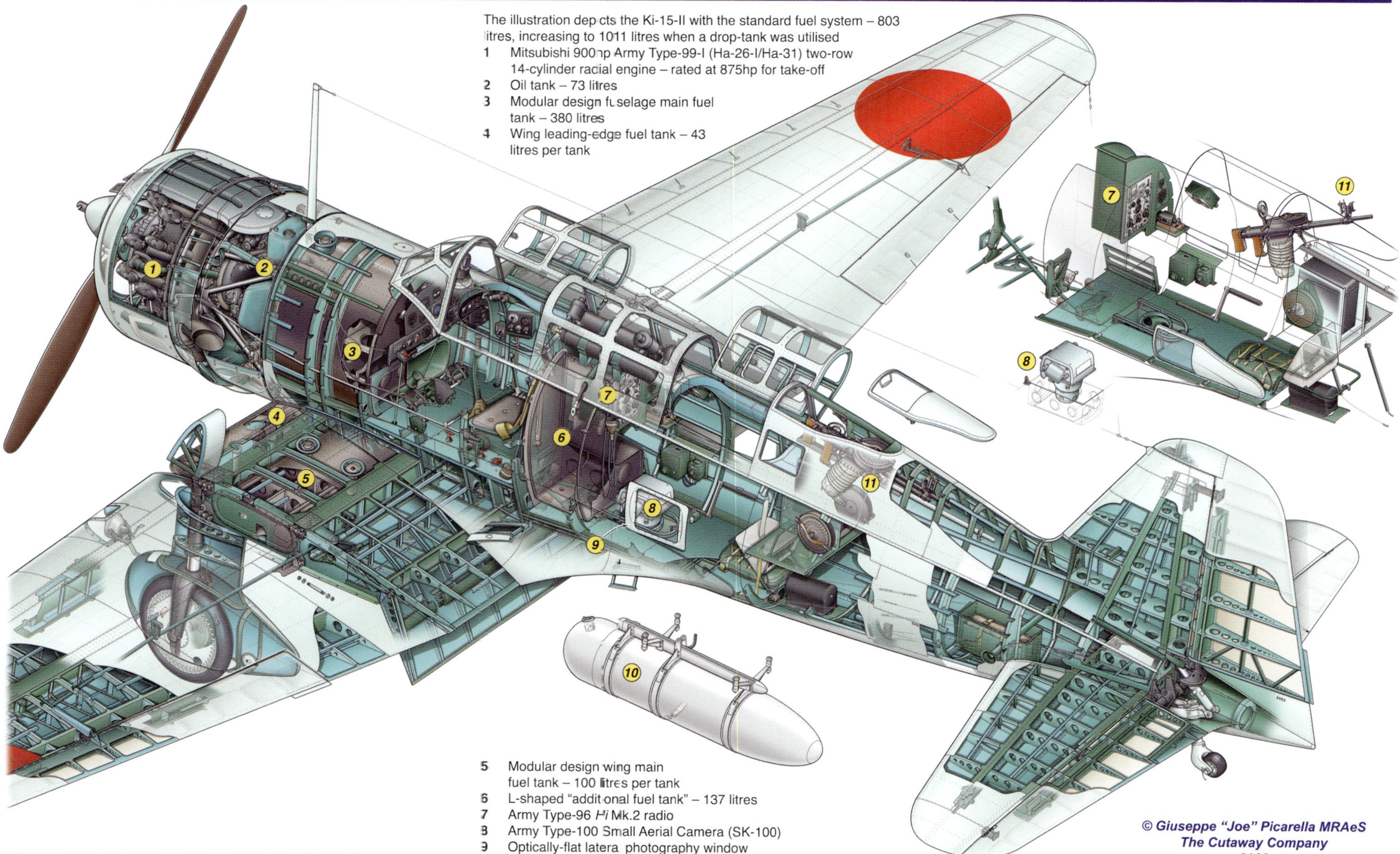

5 Modular design wing main fuel tank – 100 litres per tank
6 L-shaped "additional fuel tank" – 137 litres
7 Army Type-96 *Hi* Mk.2 radio
8 Army Type-100 Small Aerial Camera (SK-100)
9 Optically-flat lateral photography window
10 Aluminium alloy drop-tank – 208 litres
11 Te-4 7.7mm flexible machine gun with three (70-round) magazines

Ki-15-II BABS

TheCutawayCompany.com
CLARITY IN A COMPLICATED WORLD

Transportation

For delivery, overseas deployment or recovery, the Ki-15 could be dismantled for transportation. With the propeller, undercarriage, outboard wing panels and tailplane removed, the whole aircraft could be transported on two trailers, with the aid of purpose-built transportation stands and frames. The dimensions of the dismantled airframe, specifically the centre wing section, were designed to fit within a standard width railway carriage.

Karigane-II

The *Karigane*-II fleet represented a mixed assortment of Ki-15-II and C5M1 development and test airframes, with individual modifications differing between each aircraft. After receiving them, the various civilian operators slowly brought them back up to *Karigane*-II standard. With regards to civilian registrations numbers, most of these airframes fall out of production order. See Chapter 7, **Production figures and Construction numbers.**

Main fuselage

J-BAAO *Amakaze* (C/n2012) was leased to Asahi Shimbum by the Navy and initially operated in standard Ki-15-II configuration. It was later retrofitted with C5M type mass balance weights on the elevators and ground adjustable trim tabs.

J-BACK included a spinner, C5M type mass balance weights on the elevators and ground adjustable trim tabs, plus a large tailwheel.

J-BACL (C/n133) included the three-piece lateral windows of the Ki-15-I *early model.*

Powerplant

Most *Karigane*-II aircraft were fitted with Ki-15-II spinner assemblies, though **J-BACL** and **J-BECL** operated with exposed propeller hubs, similar to Navy C5M1 aircraft. In either case a starter dog exten-

J-BAAO Amakaze complete with gunners hatch, Model-1 compasses, and C5M mass balances on the elevators (Japan Aeronautical Association)

J-BACL (C/n2138) displays the pilot's concertina sunscreen inside the bi-fold canopy and the red identification stripe along the underside of the fuselage. Interestingly, J-BACL carried no spinner, no antenna mast, and was also fitted with early model Ki-15-I three-piece lateral windows. (Phil Jarrett)

Believed to be J-BACK Kinshi, *this is an interesting photo because it shows the machine-gun slide assembly inside the gunner's window, which would indicate that the photo was taken while the Navy was evaluation the aircraft. (Japan Aeronautical Association)*

sion fitting for "Hucks" type starts was installed. **J-BACL** was also fitted with a non-standard cowling with fewer Dzus fasteners.

Primary systems

Fuel system

Most *Karigane*-II aircraft seem to have had drop-tank attachment fittings, as they were completed as standard Ki-15-II airframes.

Cockpits and secondary systems

Oxygen system

Photographic evidence shows that despite some *Karigane*-II aircraft retaining their oxygen cylinder hoop mounts within the centre canopy tunnel, no oxygen cylinders have been observed fitted to these civilian aircraft. This is unsurprising due to the level of military control that was exercised over civilian organizations and Japanese airspace usage during the war.

Radio equipment

It is unclear what type of radios were fitted to the *Karigane*-II aircraft, as civilian customers could in theory specify equipment to best fit their existing fleet and requirements, but first they had to receive permission from the military to carry such equipment. From the limited CAB documentation that survives, we can see that **J-BAAO** was not issued with its permit for a radio installation until June 6th 1940, while **J-BACK** received its permit on July 25th.

It would seem that those aircraft without radios installed probably removed their antenna mast, to reduce drag, such as **J-BACL** and **J-BECL**. Both of these aircraft carried a standard Ki-15 insulator on the centre canopy tunnel and a rear fitting on the fin, but no aerial lead was installed.

J-BAAO was photographed with a 200mm+ extension exiting the lower fuselage between FS.9 and FS.10. This is assumed to be the extended tip of the trailing antenna lead.

C5M1

Navy Type-98 Reconnaissance Plane Model-1

While the following technical description details known C5M1 modifications, in direct comparison to the Ki-15-II technical description, these differences may not be complete by any means. As has already been highlighted, the production of the Navy C5M aircraft was not simply a continuation of the Ki-15 production line, as the Navy established its own completion line at Mitsubishi's No.3 Works. See Chapter 7, **Production figures and Construction numbers.**

Airframe component colour

While the majority of the airframe components were probably painted in a similar fashion to the Ki-15, Navy finishes and specifications were different to that of the Army. The aircraft may have received a coat of red/brown anti-corrosion primer. While this was typically only applied to carrier-based aircraft, there are land-based exceptions to the rule. Externally, the airframe received a glossy topcoat of Mitsubishi/Navy J3 Ash Grey.

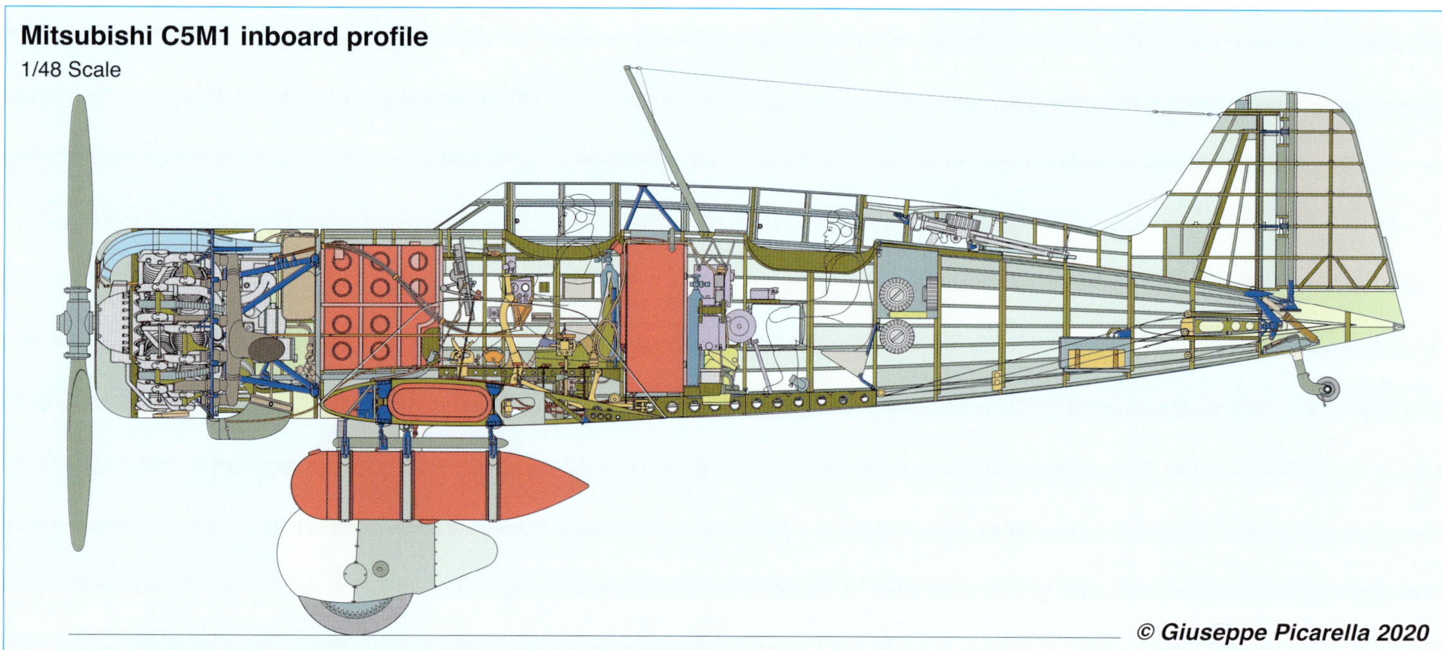

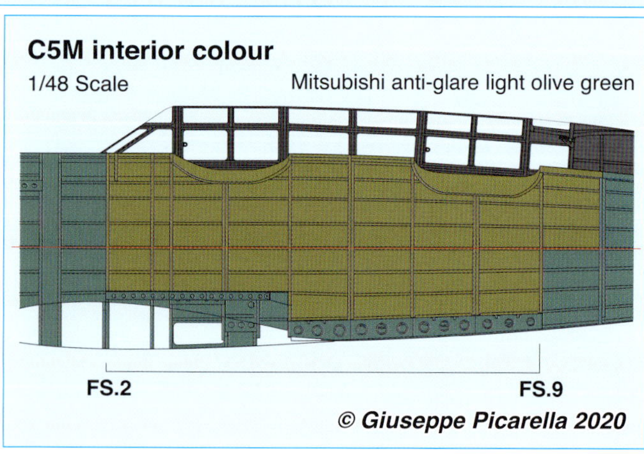

Internally, the pilot and RO's cockpit areas (between FS.2 and FS.10) would have been finished in the official 1929 paint standards formula of Chi-49 Type 4 (Mitsubishi anti-glare light olive green) which included the pilot's instrument panel. The upper surface of the fuselage skin (inside the windscreen/canopy tunnel) and interior of the canopy structure was painted flat black.

Main fuselage

Rollover pylon

The Navy was concerned about the C5M turning over during landing and take-off, so a rollover pylon was included in the redesign. The square pyramidal structure was fabricated from tubular steel, with a flat plate at the apex. The assembly was attached over stringer No.1 (left and right) at the interface of FS.5 and FS.6 inside the centre canopy tunnel. See **C5M2 Main fuselage**

This new structure rendered the centre canopy tunnel unusable for two oxygen cylinders.

Devoid of an antenna mast, this C5M1 version 1 shows the pyramidal roll-over pylon and wingtip navigation light. It also includes a leading-edge landing light. (Shoichi Tanaka)

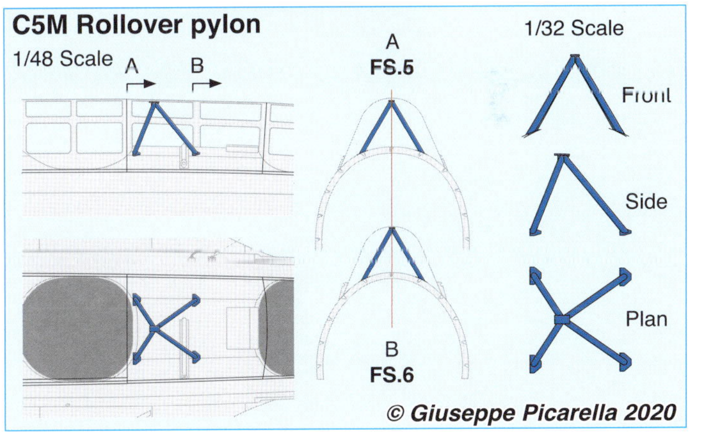

Canopy

C5M1 *version 1*

The general canopy was identical to the Ki-15-II installation with the exception of the central canopy tunnel, which had the upper navigation light Plexiglas dome removed from its FS.6 location and replaced with an aluminium-alloy closing panel.

C5M1 *version 2*

The upper navigation light aperture at FS.6 was utilized for the installation of a new antenna mast. A collar fitting would have stopped air or water entering the centre canopy tunnel during flight.

Dorsal spine transparencies and gunner's window

The dorsal spine transparencies and gunner's window installation both received modifications in order to improve rear visibility.

The original (forward) windows remained unchanged between FS.8A and FS.9A, but the new aft lateral windows, located between FS.9A and FS.10A, were taller and larger in area.

The assumption that early examples of the C5M1 simply copied the layout of the Ki-15-II, while later models included the double window installations, is tempting, but this is not the case, as two and four window examples are also found in the production run of C5M2 aircraft.

The gunner's removable window panel remained unchanged in shape, but was modified to be transparent along almost its entire length. This was accomplished by replacing the aft aluminium rear skin panel with Plexiglas.

Empennages

Elevator – mass balance weights

The C5M airframe received elevator mass balance weights, comprised of a C-section steel mounting plate, arm and balance weight. The mounting plate was fitted vertically over the elevator box-spar between TS.6 and TS.7, with wood packed into the voids beneath the C-section. Four bolts secured the mounting plate in place. The balance arm was welded to the top of the mounting plate, projecting forward and above the leading edge of the elevator assembly, with a 1.95kg aerodynamic balance weigh at its tip.

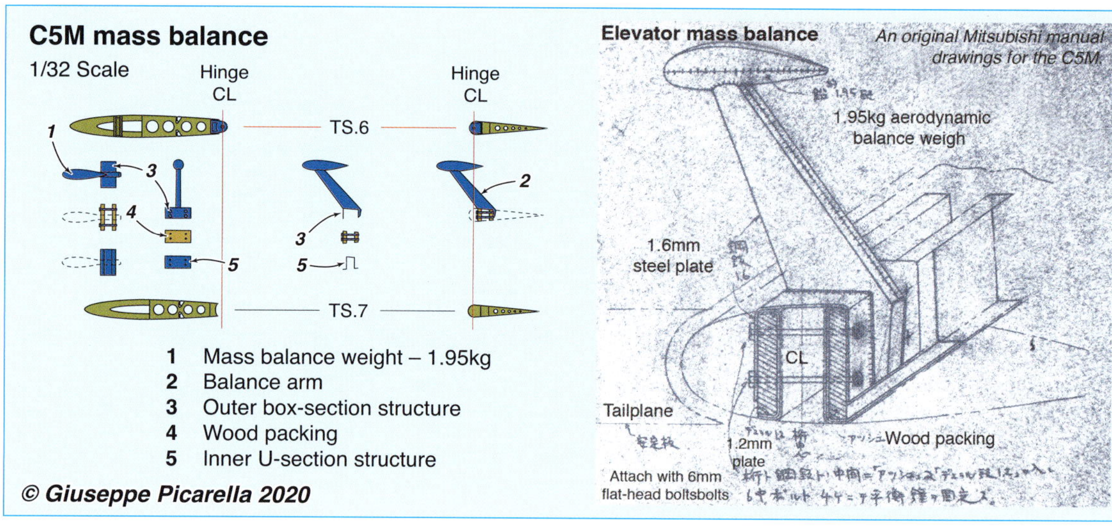

Wing

Outboard wing panels

The only known alteration to the outboard wing panels were the inclusion of conformal navigation lights outboard of WS.25, with associated access panels inboard of these modifications.

Powerplant

The Navy's version of the A14 *Zuisei* was the *Zuisei 12*. This was almost identical to the Ha-26-I, except for Navy-specific accessories.

Mitsubishi 875hp *Zuisei 12* specifications

Rated power	875hp
Compression ratio	6.5
Capacity	28 litres
RPM	2,300
Bore/stroke	140/130mm
Length	1,564mm
Height	1,118mm
Width	1,118mm
Weight	542kg

This C5M1 version 2 carries the new 1.2m antenna mast and is devoid of a leading-edge landing light. It is interesting to note that Navy censors airbrushed out the external drop-tank from this photograph for from security reasons. The original version of this photograph is depicted in Chapter 1, Brothers in arms.

Propeller and spinner

For some reason the Navy decided against the installation of a spinner on the C5M. While this practice was not uncommon for the period, it was an unusual stance to take with such a high-speed aircraft, as such modifications would have had a detrimental effect on the top speed of the aircraft. A circular back-plate sat between the propeller and the engine reduction gearbox.

Since no problems were encountered with Ki-15-II propeller and spinner, this configuration may indicate that the issue was one of weight and balance, as the Navy also deleted the "Hucks" type starter dog from the tip of the propeller hub assembly.

Primary systems

Fuel system

The fuel system of the C5M1 was almost identical to that of the Ki-15-II. See **Fuel system C5M2.**

Fuel system capacity – C5M1

Tank location	Capacity in litres
Fuselage main tank	380
Wing tanks – starboard	100
Wing tank – port	100
Wing leading edge tank – starboard	43
Wing leading edge tank – port	43
Additional fuel tank	137
Drop-tank	160
Total	**963**

Drop-tank

Photographic evidence confirms that the C5M probably used the 160 litre drop-tank developed for the A5M2 *Claude*, which included a small bulge below and behind the centre hoop-frame fitting for the drain/vent fitting.

It is interesting to note that Japanese wartime censors routinely airbrushed over drop-tank installations, along with many other pieces of equipment, effectively removing evidence of Japan's operational capabilities.

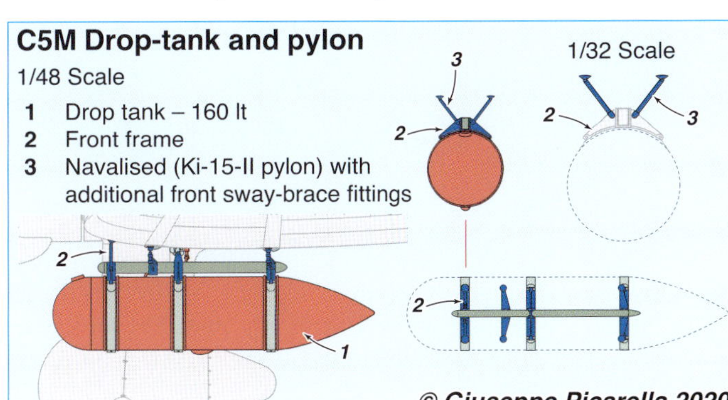

Drop-tank attachment fittings

The structure and sway-brace fittings were the same as Ki-15-II, but included an additional set of sway-brace fittings on the forward hoop-fitting.

Electrical system

The Army and the Navy used a different electrical voltage on their respective aircraft for most of WWII. While the Army had instituted a standardisation programme based on the 24Volt system during 1938, it would not be until April 1945 that the Navy followed suit. Until that time, a 12Volt electrical system powered all of its electrical airborne equipment.

Landing light and external lighting

The Navy installed a totally new external lighting system on the C5M1, which took the form of conformal navigation lights on the leading edge of the extreme wingtips and the rearmost tip of the rudder. The Ki-15 style centre canopy tunnel and ventral navigation lights and their Plexiglas domes were deleted.

While a landing light was installed on the wing leading-edge of some C5M1s, most airframes and all of the C5M2s were devoid of such equipment. The inclusion of a landing light on some C5M1s was probably confined to the initial production batch of 10 C5M1 airframes, as landing lights were not typically fitted to Japanese naval aircraft during that period.

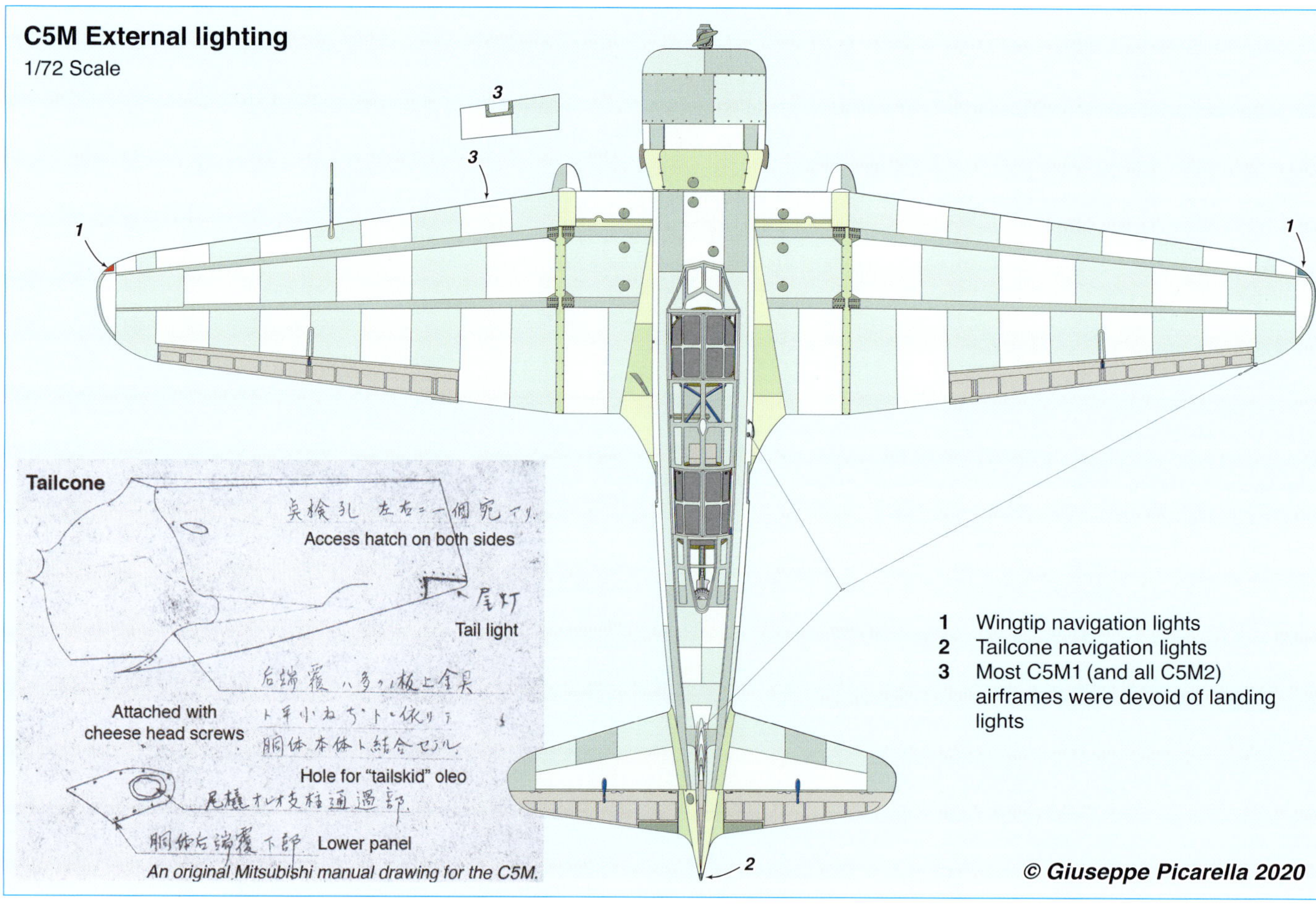

Cockpits and secondary systems

Pilot's cockpit and systems

General layout

No drawings or photographs depicting the C5M1 cockpits survive, but given the numerous changes applied to the airframe, it is most likely that the navalised instrument panel found on the C5M2 was also included in the C5M1. See **C5M2 General layout.**

Master compass

The Navy decided against locating a master compass above the cockpit lip, so it is most likely that one was installed in the centre of the instrument panel, as was the practice of the day. This lends some support to the assumption that a new instrument panel was installed in the C5M1.

Pitot system

The Ki-15 style pitot tube was modified by relocating the pressure head lower down and forward of the support arm, whilst also canting it downwards by approximately 3.5°.

Cockpit communications

The Navy favoured the flexible Gosport Tube in their aircraft, rather than fixed metallic tubes.

Oxygen system

No photographic evidence or engineering material survives regarding the oxygen systems fitted to the C5M1 or C5M2.

"Information Intelligence Summary No. 44-16" dated May 20th 1944," states:

"The following details of Type 98 Reconnaissance BABS are available as a result of examining a crashed aircraft. [item number 4] One or more oxygen cylinders were carried in the fuselage."

With the installation of the rollover pylon in the centre canopy tunnel, both cylinders were relocated inside the fuselage, but the new radio and ancillary equipment package was larger than any previous equipment fit in the cramped RO's cockpit. Fitting both cylinders aft of the "additional fuel tank" was difficult to achieve, based on the authors CAD drawings, but an installation similar to that found on the Ki-15-I *early model* produced a solution that kept the equipment close to the aircraft's CG.

Cockpit heating

It is likely that the Navy included electrically heated flight suit connectors in the C5M.

RO's cockpit and systems

Master compass

With the removal of the master compass from the cockpit lip, it is most likely that a Navy Navigator's Compass Model-1 was installed on the floor or in a similar location to that of the C5M2.

Pockets and cases

Some photographs hint at the possibility that a map or document case was installed on the cockpit lip, inside the centre canopy tunnel.

Aerial camera equipment

The Navy Handheld Aerial Camera – 25cm F-8 Type was the standard installation on the C5M1 and C5M2.

Navy Handheld Aerial Camera – 25cm F-8 Type

The Navy purchased and operated Fairchild F-8 cameras from the USA long before the outbreak of the Pacific war, after which Konica and Rokuoh-sha (Minolta) both manufactured examples of the camera in Japan. To date it is unclear if these were license-built copies or simply copies of the USAAC F-8 camera, but the fact that the F-8 designation was maintained throughout the war years may indicate that a license had been granted. While the F-8 was primarily designed as a handheld "oblique" aerial camera, a small number (possibly fewer than 30 examples) were specifically modified to include vertical mount fittings on the front of the body and two vertical spirit levels (see kit list below) for vertical use. By all accounts the vertically mounted F-8 camera installation was not considered to be wholly satisfactory, but it was considered to be excellent in the hand-held "oblique" role, leading some naval officers to state that the F-8 was as valuable to C5M as the 20mm cannons were to the A6M *Zeke*!

2,316 examples of this F-8 camera would be built in Japan.

The camera kit incorporated a built-up and pressed alloy body, lens (heated), folding view finder, brilliant view finder, handles, two "bulls-eye" spirit levels for aligning the camera in a vertical position, alternative film plate film holder, lens filters x 3, shoulder strap, vertical mounting brackets and carry case.

Navy Handheld Aerial Camera – 25cm F-8 Type

Manufacturer(s)	Konishi-roku/Rokuoh-sha
Shutter speeds	1/60, 1/100, 1/160, 1/250, 1/300, 1/400 sec
Finder	Frame type
Lenses	25mm f4.5 and 50mm f4.5
Stock type	Film roll – 3.7 meter/ Plate – 6 plates
Image size	13 x 18cm
Dimensions – width/height/depth	Approximately 36 x 28 x 36cm.
Weight	8kg camera,
Operation	Manual
Notes	Heated lens and body – 12 Volts

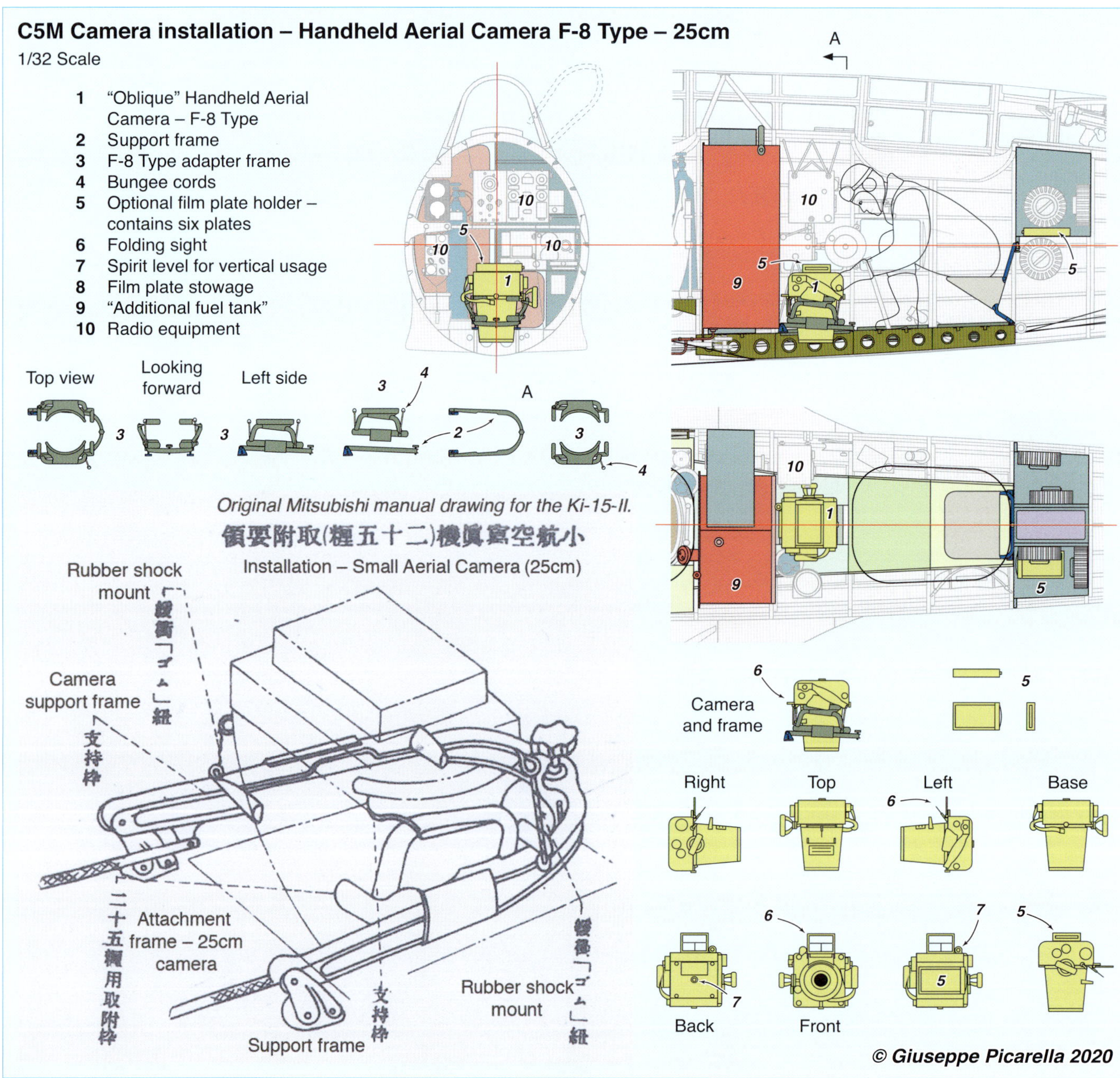

Colour images: Late model F-8 with wooden handles.
Photographed at the NASM Udvar-Hazy Centre.
© Giuseppe Picarella 2020

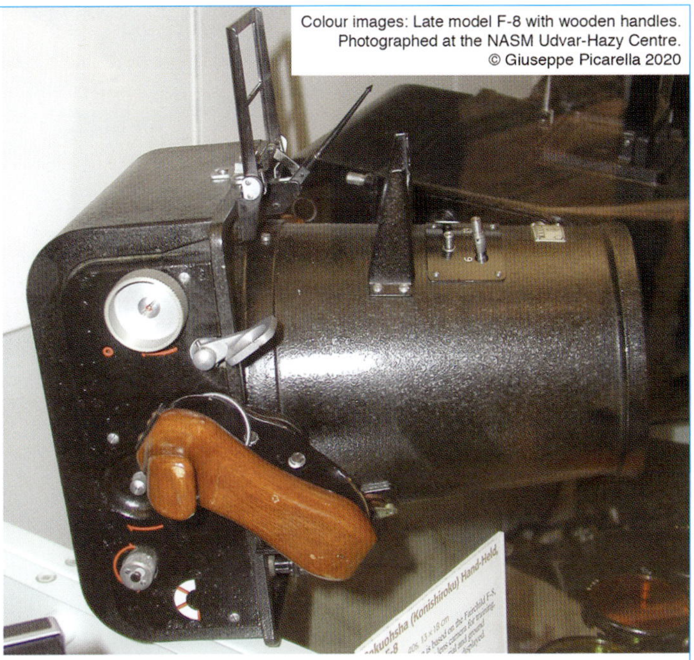

B+W images: F-8 camera with vertical mount fittings.
OPNAV-16V T #232 Report #32
February 1945.

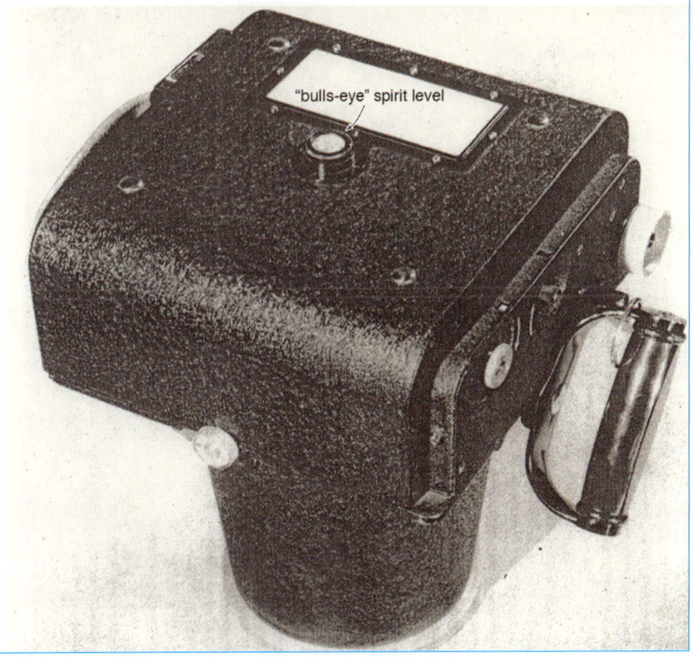

In February 1944, a test report on a captured Japanese F-8 Type camera was produced by TAIC. "**Technical Air Intelligence Center, Report #32, OPNAV.16.V # T 232**". The report concluded that:

"The Japanese F-8 camera was observed to have the following points of advantage.

1. Convenient handles for holding camera.
2. Large "Sports" type viewfinder.
3. Wide range of shutter speeds.
4. Focusing device on lenses."

"While it is not apparent in the test data of this report, the Japanese F-8 camera was considered to have a better focal plane shutter than the Keystone F-8."

The report goes on to recommend that: *"Careful consideration should be given to the possible adoption on U.S. Navy cameras of the following devices:"*

1. More convenient handle and wrist sling.
2. Neck strap to steady and prevent possible loss of camera.
3. Redesign the focal plane shutter."

Support frame – F-8 Type

While the F-8 Type camera used the same vertical support frame as the Army SK-100, its broader lens body and lack of attachment ring fitting rendered this mount incompatible with the Navy camera. To facilitate its installation in the C5M, new C-shaped brackets were attached to the support frame and the camera was secured in position with two bungee cords.

Radio equipment

As would be expected, the Navy had its own radio equipment and designation system, which used the term *"Ku"* from *"kokuki"* or "aircraft" as the designator for airborne equipment.

The C5M1 and C5M2 both received the Navy Type-96 *Ku* Mk.2 "Command" radio. See **C5M2, RO's cockpit and systems**.

Antenna

C5M1 *version 1*

The low quality and limited number of surviving C5M photographs initially seemed to indicate that antennas were not fitted to the C5M1 *version 1*, but the concept of operating a long range reconnaissance aircraft without a radio installed is unrealistic, as it would have severely limited the operational value of the aircraft; what is the point of gathering strategic information if it cannot be transmitted back to base or disseminated to the other aircraft in your formation? The fact remains though, that the aircraft were not fitted with antenna masts and even lacked the standard rear insulator fitting at the top of the fin leading edge. This initially caused some consternation during the preparation of this book, but close examination of surviving photographs reveal a dedicated radio-telegraphy antenna emanated from an insulated fitting mid-way down the starboard side of the fuselage, between FS.5 and FS.6, below to stringer No.5. The lead-in travelled outboard and aft to join an insulator fitting on the main aerial lead running from the starboard wingtip, outboard of WS.23, to a rear insulator fitting located on the mid point of the fin, at FinS.4. Various insulators were included within the aerial circuit and a vibration fitting was installed at the start of the lead-in and fin fitting, to tension the antenna and allow for movement in the airstream.

Obviously this installation is located on the starboard side of the aircraft in order to place it out of the way of the ground and aircrew, who needed to access the port side of the aircraft in order to board the aircraft and open the rear canopy.

As this installation was used for Morse code communications at long range, a trailing antenna installation was also compatible with the Navy Type-96 *Ku* Mk.2 "Command" radio. See **C5M2, Trailing antenna**.

C5M1 *version 2*

An additional antenna installation was fitted to C5M1 *version 2*. This took the form of a 105cm tall mast attached to the TDC of the upper fuselage between FS.6 and FS.7. The thin chord mast was canted forwards approximately 25° and was most likely constructed from a welded steel aerofoil section. The mast exited the centre canopy tunnel through the redundant upper navigation light aperture, and its upper extremity incorporated a streamlined skirt to direct the airstream around the top insulator fitting.

The lead-in is believed to have exited the aircraft via the top of dorsal spine, running forwards to the mast via several insulators, before travelling aft to attach at the standard rear insulator fitting at FinS.7.

Armament

The C5M1 was fitted with a Navy Type-92 7.7mm flexible machine gun (a license-built copy of the Lewis light machine gun) with a rate of fire of 600rpm and a muzzle velocity of 740m/s. This gas-operated weapon was the standard Navy flexible machine gun of the period, which could be fitted with either a "Norman Vane" sight or a ring and bead sight. Illustrations in the C5M2 maintenance manual indicate that five 97-round magazines were carried; one on the weapon and four stowed around the rear storage cabinet. The layout of the magazines would have required the relocation of the rear fuselage canvas divider from FS.9 to FS.10.

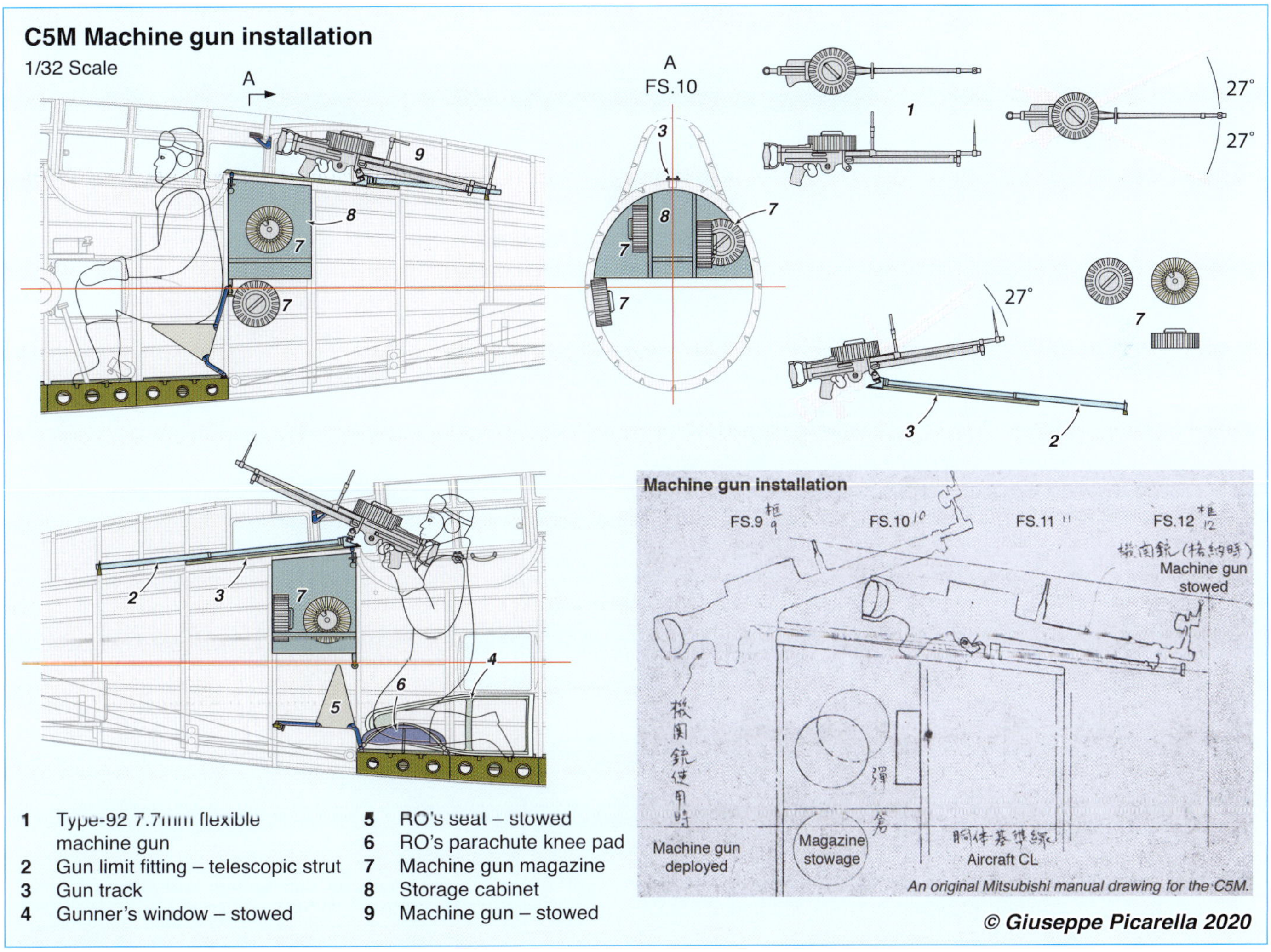

Type-92 machine gun.

Type-92 machine gun.

931

ARMAMENT

7.7 mm. TYPE 92 FLEXIBLE AIRCRAFT MACHINE GUN (LEWIS TYPE) - NAVY

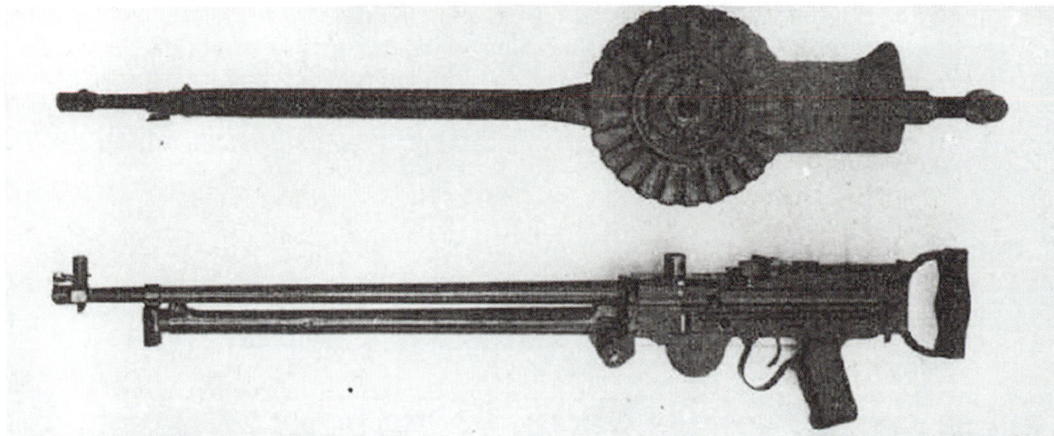

GENERAL

This is almost an exact copy of the British Lewis machine gun, and can fire the British .303 caliber ammunition.

PERFORMANCE

Rate of Fire (est.)	600 rounds per minute
Muzzle Velocity (est.)	2500 feet per second
Effective Range (est.)	600 yards

CHARACTERISTICS

Calibre	.303 inches (7.7 mm)
Overall Length	39 inches
Weight of Gun	18.5 pounds
Type of Feed	Flat Drum Magazine
Magazine Capacity	(a) 47 rds. (b) 97 rds.
Wt. Magazine Empty	3.75lbs.
Wt. Magazine Full	8.8 lbs.
Wt. 100 Linked rds.	-
Charging System	Hand
Firing System	Hand-trigger

A

B

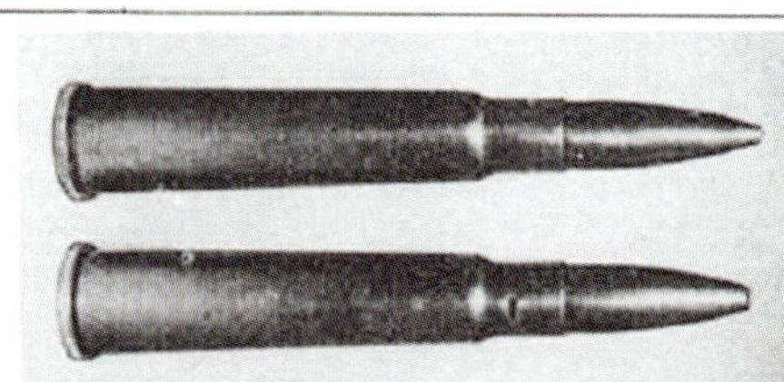

A - Ball
B - Armor Piercing

The color marking is located on the base of the cartridge case.

AMMUNITION

Overall Length	3.06 inches
Case	Rimmed

TYPE	COLOR CODE	PROJECTILE WT. (Grams)
Ball	Black Ring	11.2
AP	White Ring	11.1
Tracer	Scarlet Ring	9.5
Incend.	Green Ring	9.6
HE		
AP/T		
HE/I	Dull Red Ring	9.8
HE/AP		
HE/T		
AP/I		

EXPLOSIVE AND INCENDIARY COMPONENTS

TYPE	CONTENTS
Incend.	Phosphorous
HE	50% PETN - 50% RDX
HE/I	Aluminum & TNT

RESTRICTED DATE March 1945

Mitsubishi Navy Type-98 Reconnaissance Plane Model-11

1. Mitsubishi 875hp Navy *Zuisei 12* (Ha-31) two-row 14-cylinder radial engine – rated at 780hp for take-off
2. Modified cockpit layout and fittings
3. Modular design fuselage main fuel tank – 380 litres
4. Wing leading-edge fuel tank – 43 litres per tank
5. Modular design wing main fuel tank – 100 litres per tank
6. L-shaped "additional fuel tank" – 137 litres

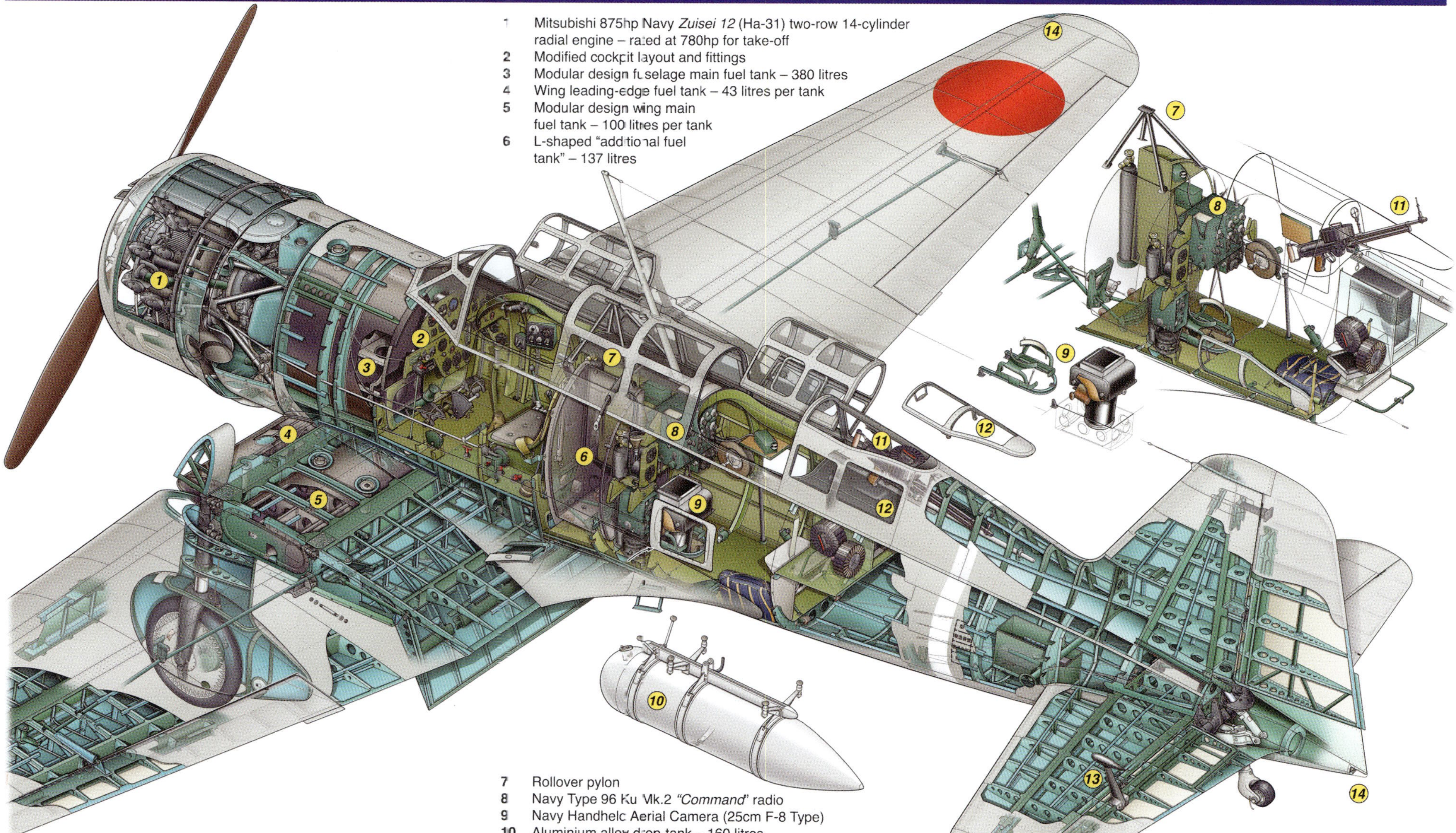

7. Rollover pylon
8. Navy Type 96 Ku Mk.2 *"Command"* radio
9. Navy Handheld Aerial Camera (25cm F-8 Type)
10. Aluminium alloy drop-tank – 160 litres
11. Navy Type-92 7.7mm flexible machine gun five (97-round) magazines
12. Modified gunners' windows
13. Elevator mass balance weights
14. Navigation lights

C5M1 BABS

C5M2

Navy Type-98 Reconnaissance Plane Model-2

Having experienced the high performance capabilities of the C5M1, the Navy attempted to further improve upon the design by developing a fully navalised version of the aircraft. The following technical description is based on the C5M2 maintenance manual (issued in March 1941) and details the known differences between the C5M2 and the Ki-15-II/C5M1 airframes. Unless changes are specifically identified please refer to the C5M1/Ki-15-II technical description.

Nacelle assembly

The installation of the Nakajima *Sakae 12*/NK1C engine required a new cowling and forward fuselage fairing design, which came in the form of an A6M2b *Zeke* style cowling.

Access cowlings

The cowling was a two-part installation with integral nose cowlings and detachable fastener fairings. A chin-mounted carburettor intake was installed at BDC along the full length of the cowling, before turning up between the cowl flaps. At first glance, the cowling looked almost identical to that of the A6M2b, but it was in fact a new design with the upper and rear profile specifically shaped to fit the C5M2 fuselage profile. That being said, it would seem that it utilized many of the components and assemblies from the A6M2b cowling.

Cowl flaps

With the adoption of the A6M2b *Zeke* style cowling and forward fuselage fairings layout, it is also likely that the associated cowl flap assembly was also adapted to fit the C5M2. This differed considerably from that of the Ki-15-II installation, as it used individual actuator arms, attached to the forward firewall assembly. Unlike the A6M2b assembly, the cowl flaps on the C5M2 continued all the way over the TDC of the fuselage and were noticeably shorter in chord. The lower quadrant contained a cut-out to allow for the carburettor intake duct.

Forward firewall

A forward firewall assembly was specifically designed to accept the new engine installation and mount. Once again, this may have been a modified A6M2b assembly.

Mitsubishi C5M2 inboard profile

1/48 Scale

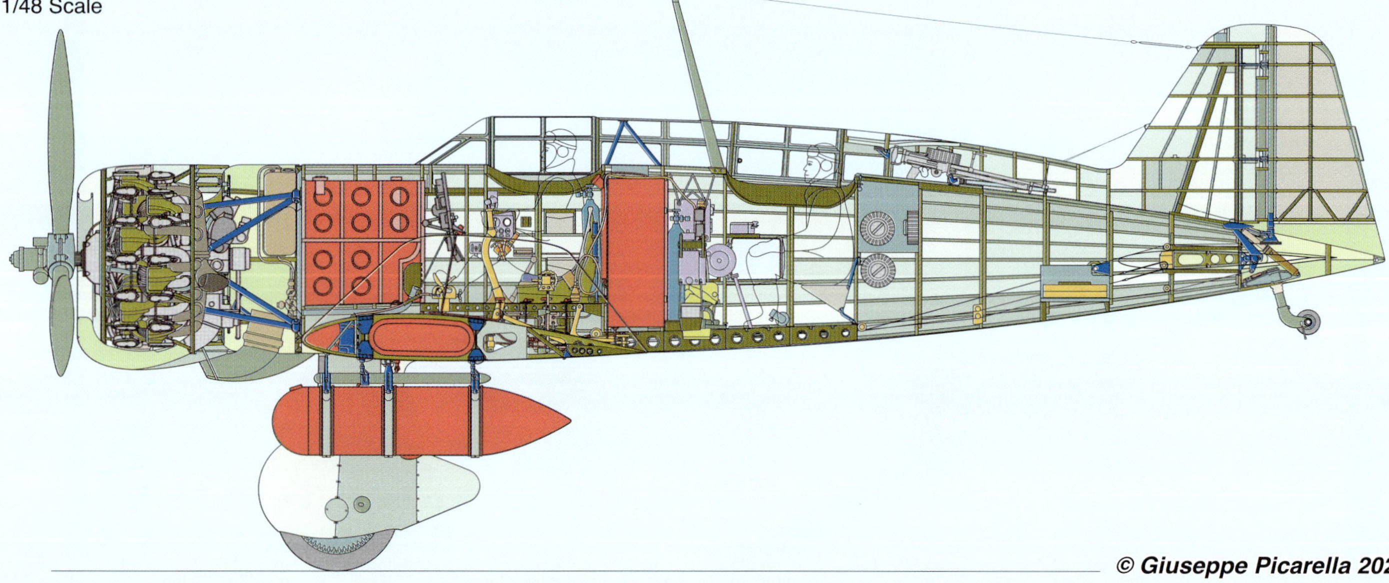

The tightly cowled Sakae engine, with chin-mounted up-draught carburettor intake. Note the large round cut-out in the cowl gills to accommodate the exhaust pipe. (Shoichi Tanaka)

Forward fuselage fairings

An all-new four-part forward fuselage fairing assembly blended the cowling and forward firewall into FS.0. The upper panel would have included an access hatch for the oil filler port. The side panels were assembled with two skins joined at the mid point, while the lower panel would have included a cut-out for the oil cooler intake fairing at BDC. Due to the weight and design of the Nakajima *Sakae 12*, the engine sat further forward of FS.0, which required the forward fuselage fairings to extend further forward than previous installations.

As with the Ki-15, a tightly controlled exit vent (approximately 15mm width) was designed into the rear edges of the fuselage fairings at FS.0, thus ensuring smooth streamlining into the fuselage structure, while allowing adequately pressure cooling of the engine accessory bay, oil cooler and oil tank installation. Unlike the Ki-15, the Navy decided to include 16 Dzus fasteners along the trailing edge of the fairings, which further mimicked the A6M2b installation. These fasteners engaged with dedicated brackets that were located around the circumference of FS.0.

The nacelle assembly was approximately 1,395mm long, from the lip of the cowling to the rear edge of the fuselage fairings (15mm forward of FS.0).

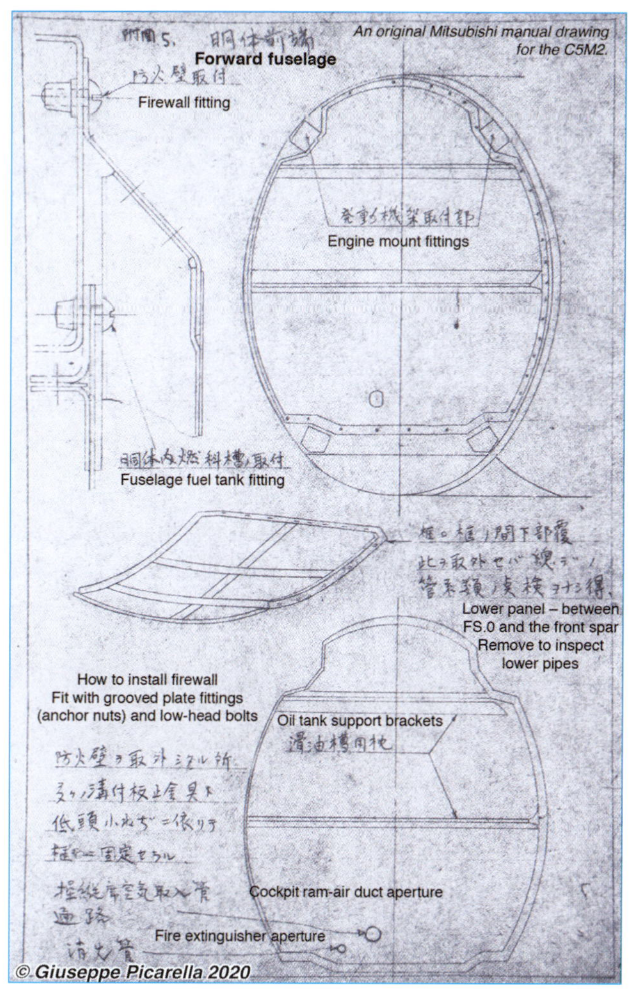

An original Mitsubishi manual drawing for the C5M2.

Canopy

The Navy had some reservations concerning the Ki-15 style sideways hinging bi-fold canopy, most probably stemming from the difficulty of the pilot to exit the aircraft in an emergency. To remedy this situation an all-new sliding canopy was developed for the C5M2.

C5M2 Nacelle assembly

1/32 Scale

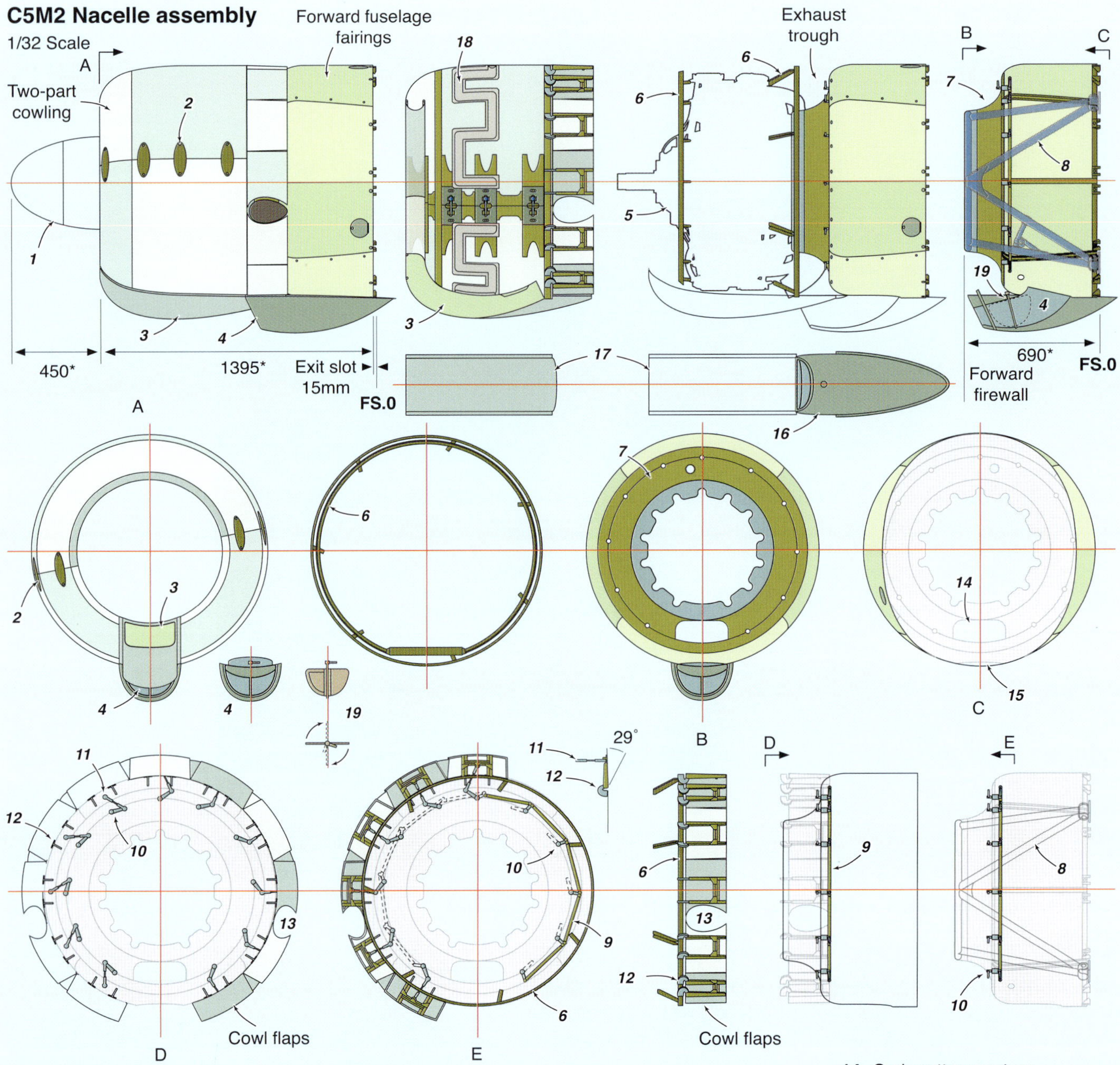

1	Spinner profile based on provisional Mitsubishi drawing	**5**	Nakajima *Sakae 12* engine outline	**9**	Cowl flap torque tube	**14**	Carburettor aperture
2	Cowling latch covers	**6**	Cowling support frames x 2	**10**	Cowl flap bellcrank fitting	**15**	Oil cooler aperture
3	Carburettor intake	**7**	Forward firewall	**11**	Cowl flap armature	**16**	Carburettor intake – looking up
4	Oil cooler intake	**8**	Engine mounting frame	**12**	Cowl flap hinge fitting	**17**	Oil cooler intake – looking up
				13	Cowl flap exhaust aperture	**18**	Asbestos webbing strips
						19	Air-intake shutter – speculative

Below: Photographs of A6M cowling showing similar structure and fittings

* Estimated dimension based on CAD model

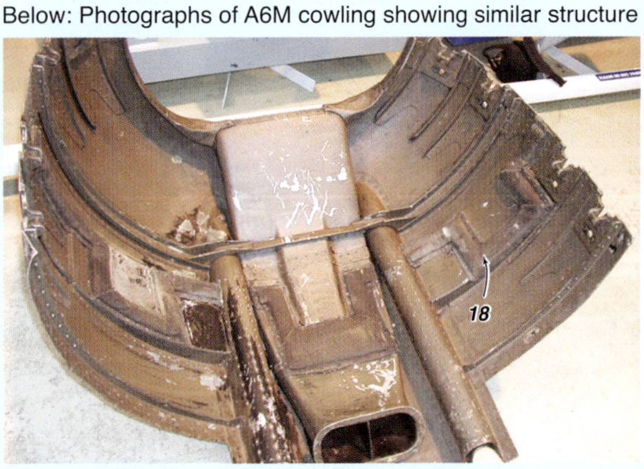

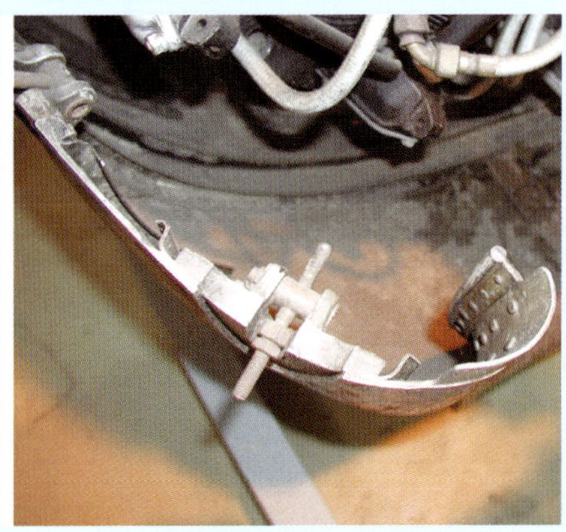

Note: Skin colours used to identify individual panels

The pilot's reward sliding canopy is evident in this photograph. X-14 is a C5M2 version 1 without an antenna mast, while the two aircraft behind are both C5M2 version 2 airframes with masts. (Shoichi Tanaka)

C5M2 Pilot's canopy

1/48 Scale

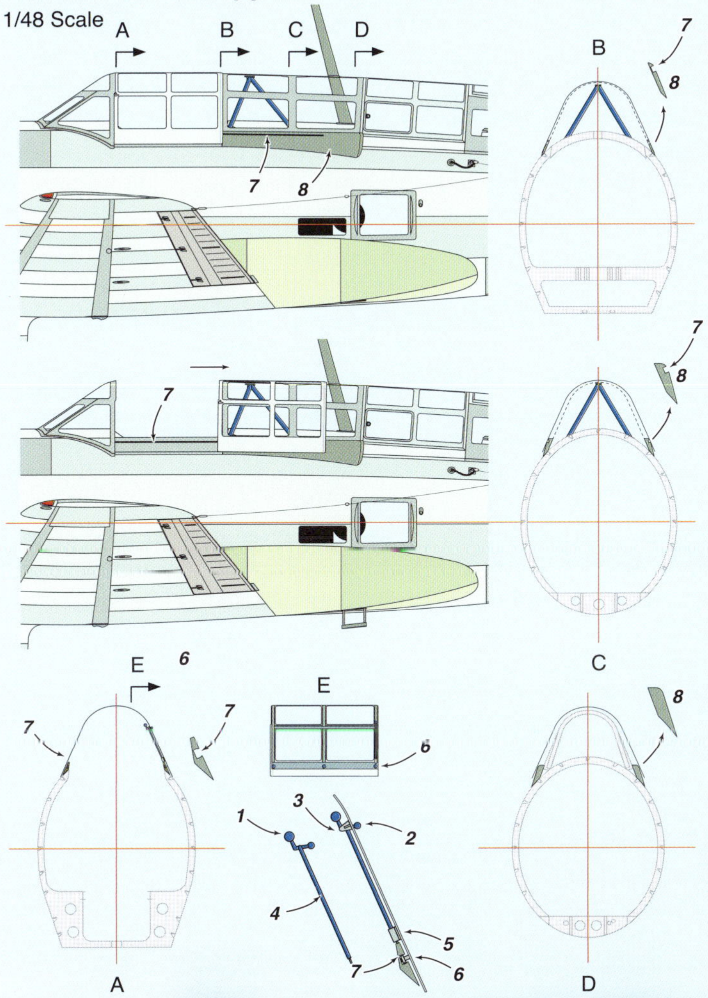

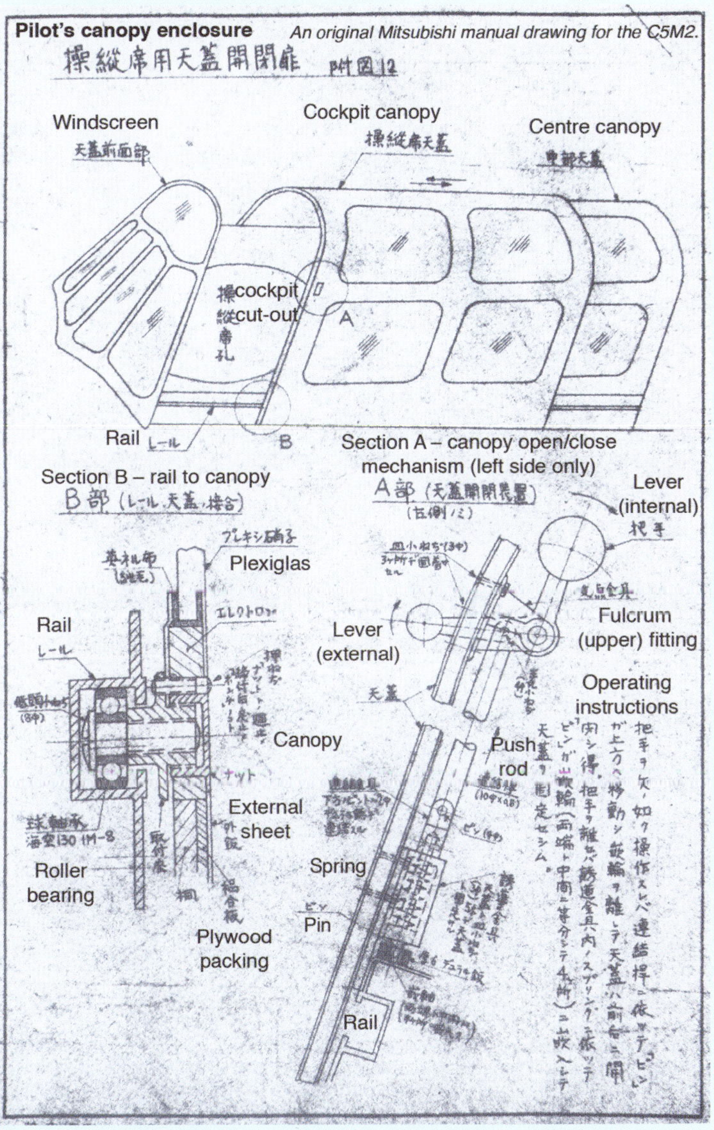

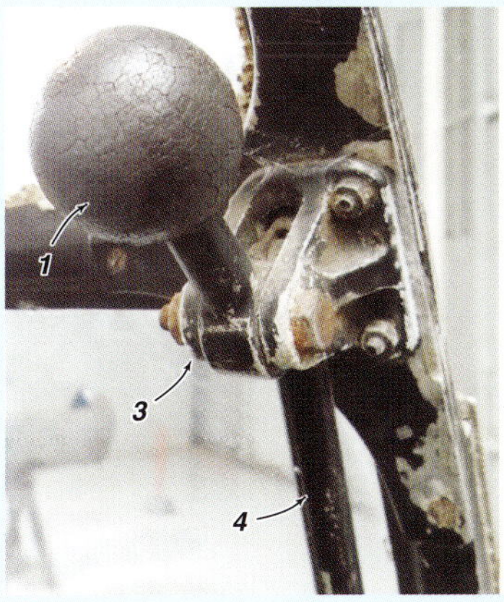

1	Latch internal release handle	**5**	Latch lower bracket
2	Latch external (aerodynamic) release handle	**6**	Canopy roller – 3 per side
3	Latch upper (fulcrum) bracket	**7**	Fuselage mounted rail
4	Latch pushrod	**8**	Runner fairing
		9	Latch position lock

A6M canopy latch fittings: **Far left:** Latch internal release handle. **Top left:** Latch lower bracket. **Bottom left:** Latch external (aerodynamic) release handle – note windscreen/canopy notch.

In order to slide back over the centre canopy tunnel, the new canopy was slightly larger in section, as the original Ki-15 canopy had the constant height and cross-section along the entire centre canopy tunnel. It was also a few centimetres longer, in order for the rear edge to of the canopy frame to bridge the forward edge of the centre canopy tunnel framework.

The increase in height and width of the pilot's canopy also required new windscreen frame, to match the enlarged canopy profile and remove any aerodynamic step between these two sections. The redundant forward runner frame was removed and the lip of the upper hemisphere was notched to accept the new canopy profile, a feature adopted from the *Zeke.*

The new canopy incorporated six roller bearings in its lower frame (three per side), which faced inboard in order to engage into runners installed in the canopy-to-fuselage fairing. The runners were extruded aluminium alloy C-sections, with locator flanges extending from the top and bottom of the C-section. These flanges were set back from the face of the runner in order to allow the installation to be attached behind the canopy-to-fuselage fairing. The side skirts of the canopy were fabricated from several machined components, but also including a plywood insert.

The canopy runner extended aft from the trailing edge of the windscreen, to a position halfway between FS.6 and FS.7, providing approximately 660mm of travel. While the new sliding canopy would improve the pilot's comfort and safety, its design would impact upon the aerodynamics of the centre canopy tunnel. In order for the canopy to slide back and forward, the runners had to remain perfectly parallel, which was problematic for this modification, as the centre canopy tunnel framework narrowed as it progressed aft. The only solution was to install a runner fairing that remained parallel to the canopy, but this resulted in an installation that was approximately 30mm wider (on each side) than the existing centre canopy tunnel at FS.7. In order to "clean up" this installation, a 125mm deep fairing was blended into the fuselage sides, coming to an abrupt end at FS.7 because the fairing could not progress any further aft due to the RO's unaltered canopy installation.

The pilot's new canopy was locked into position by a spring-loaded latch similar to, if not identical to, that found on the *Zeke*. A bellcrank handle assembly was located on the left-hand side of the canopy, at the intersection of the forward and horizontal mid-frame, with a round actuator knob on the inside of the canopy and a smaller (aerodynamic tear-drop shaped) actuation handle on the outside of the canopy. The latch was actuated via a machined attachment fitting and a spring-loaded pushrod, which controlled a locator pin that engaged in holes along the canopy-to fuselage fairing assembly. Four sets of locator holes allowed the canopy to be placed in the closed, slightly open, mid and fully open position. Because the canopy could be set slightly open in flight (for ventilation), the sliding side windows were rendered obsolete. The deletion of these windows and their associated fittings and runners also allowed Mitsubishi to enlarge and redistributed the individual panes, giving the pilot an improved view.

Interestingly, the RO's bi-fold canopy remained unaltered in the redesign, despite being identical in its operation to that of the pilot's original canopy. Although it may seem unusual to have modified one canopy and not the other, it was probably assumed that the pilot would hold the aircraft steady during an emergency, while the RO exited the aircraft.

Rudder

While the rudder horn was visually unchanged, the internal balance-weight attachment system was redesigned and increased in strength. The new C-section attachment bracket was screwed onto the front face of the forward former, with the lead balance weight held in position by three vertical bolts.

The fixed tab was reduced in length and relocated to occupy the space between FinS.3 and FinS.4.

Rudder mass balance *An original Mitsubishi manual drawing for the C5M2.*

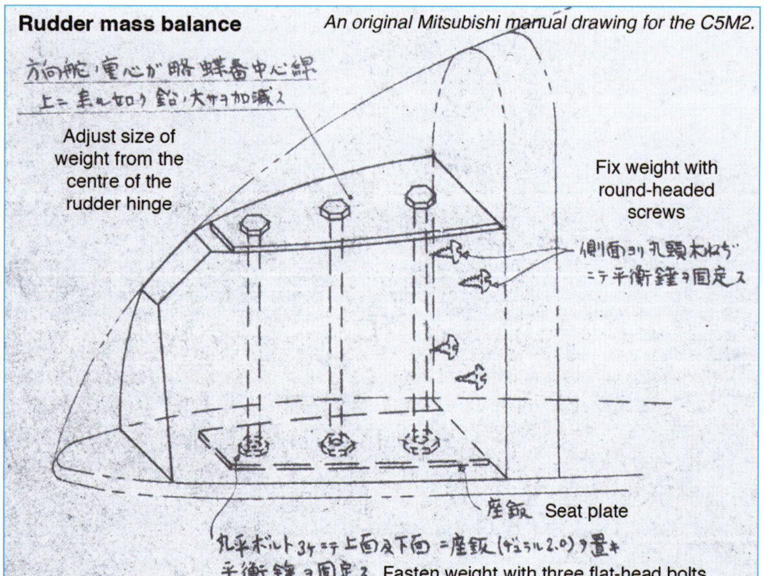

Powerplant.

It is unclear if it was the Mitsubishi Engineering Dept. or the Navy that first suggested utilizing the *Sakae 12* engine installation on the C5M2, but the concept of using this proven long-range engine, whilst also improving equipment commonality in theatre, was inspired. Built by Nakajima under the NAM designation, the "*Sakae*" or "Prosperity" engine installation was the same as that fitted to superlative A6M2b *Zeke*. The engine was also known as the NK1C under the Navy's short designation system.

Nakajima Sakae 12 engine.

A circular cowling support ring was installed on the front of the engine, supported by seven brackets attached to the rocker-covers on the front row of cylinders.

The engine was fitted with a propeller governor, an updraught carburettor at BDC, a vacuum pump, an electric/inertia starter on the aft thrust-line of the accessory casing and a generator at the top of the casing.

The engine could be started by either the electric starter motor or an inertia-starter, via a starter handle inserted in the starboard side lower forward fuselage fairing. The starter handle was stowed behind the pilots seat.

Nakajima *Sakae 12*/NK1C specifications

Rated power	940hp
Compression ratio	7.2
Capacity	27.9 litres
RPM	2,550
Bore/stroke	130/150mm
Length	1,312mm
Height	1,115mm
Width	1,115mm
Weight	530kg

Engine mount

While the engine-mounting frame would have exhibited similarities to that of the installation fitted to the A6M2b, it had been specifically designed for the airframe interface at FS.0, the thrust-line, plus the weight and balance limits of the C5M2 airframe. Integral brackets for the *Sakae 12* oil cooler installation would have been included in the redesign, plus the 13 attachment eyes required for mounting the engine to the attachment ring. Photographs show that the engine mount retained the transverse attachment fittings of the Ki-15, rather than the longitudinal fittings of the A6M mount, as this removed the need to redesign the engine firewall fittings at FS.0. The length of the mount was the longest of all the *Babs* airframes, spanning approximately 690mm from FS.0 to the front face of the mounting ring.

Nakajima 940hp Sakae 12/NK1C engine

1/32 Scale

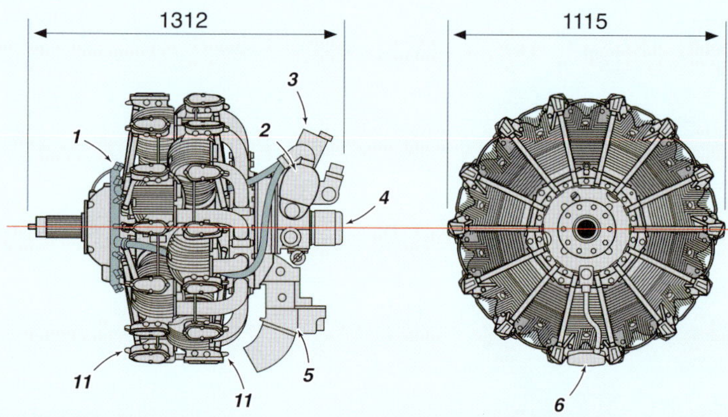

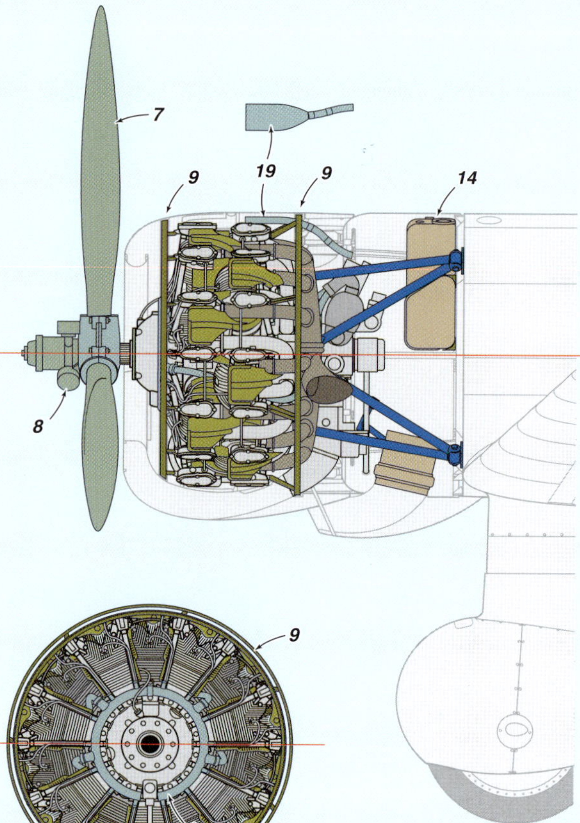

Dressed engine, mount, propeller and lubrication system

1. Ignition harness – front mounted
2. Magneto
3. Generator
4. Inertia starter
5. Carburettor
6. Gearbox oil scavenge line
7. Three-blade constant speed metal propeller
8. Cowling support frames – front and rear
9. Blade counter weights
10. Cylinder cooling baffles
11. Cowling support frame-to-engine attachment points – seven
12. Exhaust collector ring mounted
13. Oil cooler
14. Oil tank – 73 lt
15. Cockpit ram-air intake
16. Engine bay fire extinguisher system aperture
17. Inertia starter handle support bracket
18. Inertia starter handle position
19. Accessory bay ram-air cooling

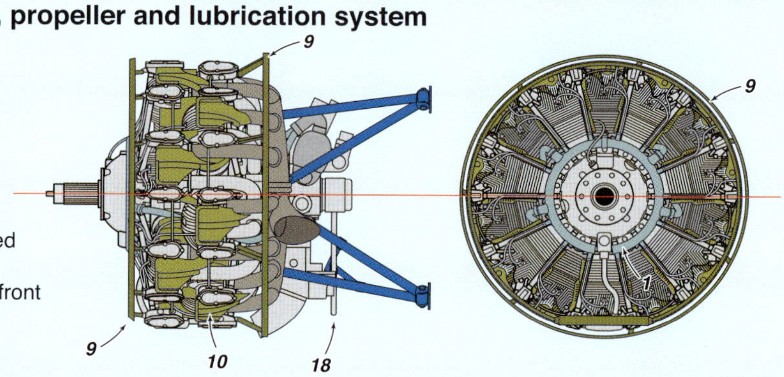

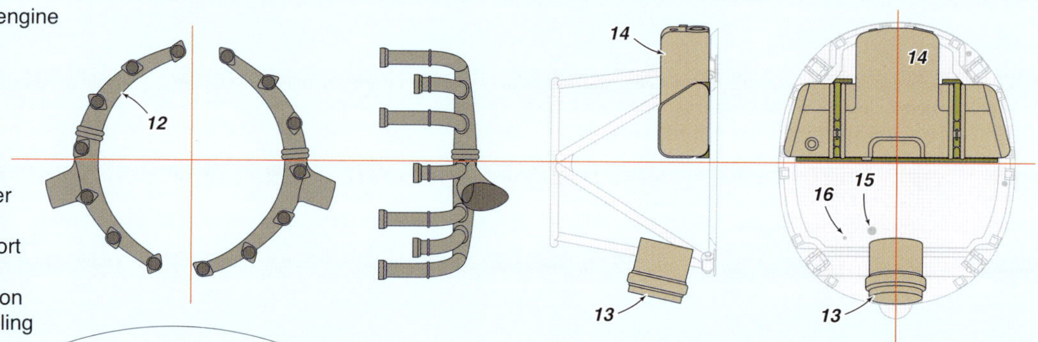

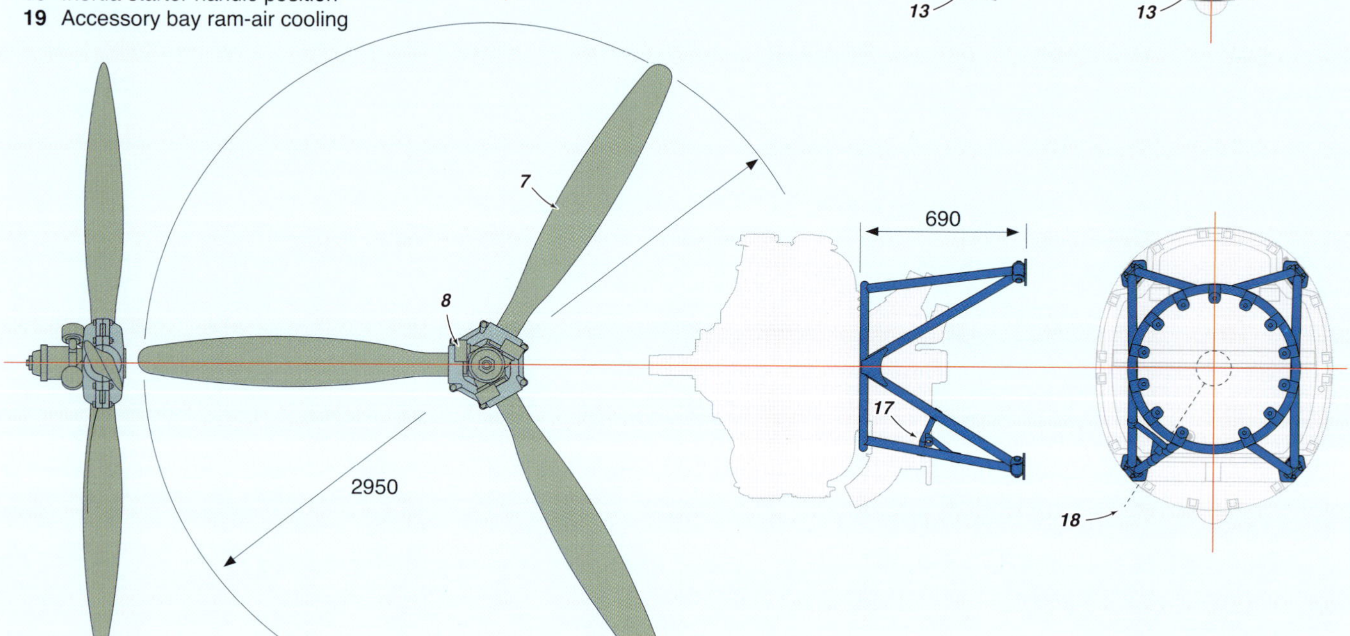

Propeller and spinner

The C5M2 was fitted a propeller that was almost identical to that of the A6M2b (CS40B – Sumitomo Metal Industries, license-built Hamilton Standard type three-blade, constant-speed metal propeller), but the tip of each blade was increased in length by 25mm to give the propeller an overall diameter of 2,950mm. Based on the general arrangement drawing included in the C5M2 maintenance manual, Mitsubishi initially included a spinner as part of the redesign, but the Navy chose not to include one. This is an intriguing choice, given the high-speed nature of the aircraft, as it would have undoubtedly reduced the top speed of the aircraft. It is therefore possible that the deletion of the spinner was an attempt to balance the CG of an aircraft that had already increased in weight by 156kg (344 lb) over that of the Ki-15-II.

Primary systems

Ballast weight

Due to the extensive airframe and engine modifications, all-new weight and balance calculations were required for the C5M2, including an increase in trimming ballast in the rear fuselage. The factory-installed ballast amounted to 33kg in the form of two lead weights (15kg and 18kg) and to support this increase in weight, the ballast box was raised and redesigned to incorporate new attachment structure. Raising the box caused an equipment conflict with the lifting tube assembly (attached to FS.13), which required the box to be cut away in order to fit. The Navy also took the opportunity to eliminating the leather securing straps, replacing them with fixed metallic stringers. The new trimming ballast box was located in the same location (spanning between FS.12 and FS.13) as the Ki-15 and it is assumed from the surviving drawings that the dimension and base panel positioned (270mm below the aircraft CL) were identical. Access to the ballast box was made via the rear cockpit of the aircraft.

Ballast weight box *An original Mitsubishi manual drawing for the C5M2.*

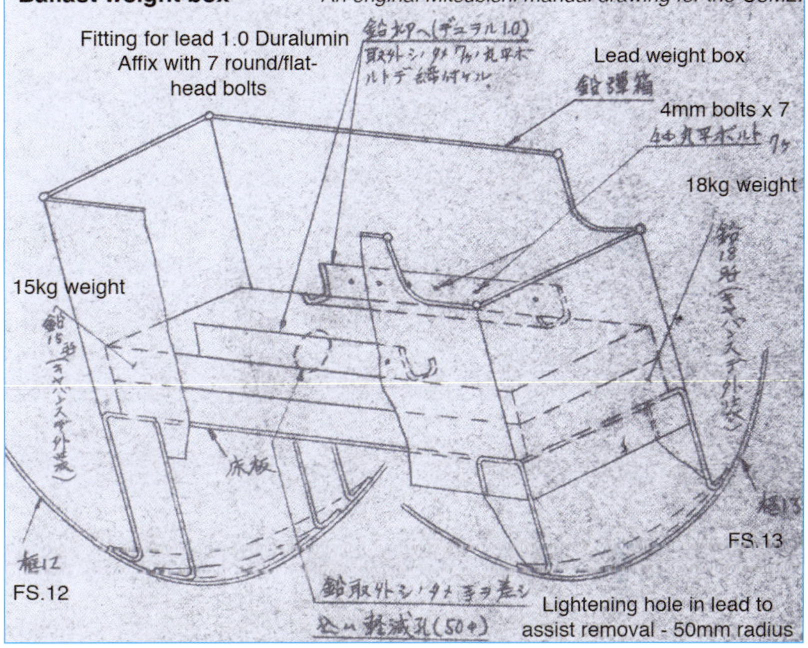

This photograph of the Gasmata C5M2 wreck provides some interesting details of the cockpit. To the right is the steel construction fuselage main fuel tank, with the remains of the rudder pedal bulkhead separating the pedals from the tank. Behind and to the right of the control column is the oil-cooler control handle mounted on FS.3. (Charles Darby)

Fuel system

The internal fuel system layout of the C5M2 was almost identical to that of the Ki-15-II, but due to equipment changes in the RO's cockpit, the requirement to fit the L-shaped "additional fuel tank" became redundant. Just why the Navy decided to retain the smaller 137 litre tank instead of fitting a full width *Kamikaze* style 160 litre tank is unclear, but it is most likely due to CG issues.

Once again Mitsubishi amended its manual to record a slightly different capacity for the C5M2 system as whole. The new fuel figures show a slight increase in the capacity of the fuselage main fuel tank up to 385 litres, while the wing leading edge fuel tanks were both amended to show an increase in fuel capacity up to 48.5 litres. Not including the "additional fuel tank" and drop-tank, this brings the internal fuel capacity of the C5M2 up to 682 litres, which is almost identical to the 685 litre capacity of the Ki-15-I. These new figures would also tend to confirm that the fuel system of the C5M1 (for which we do not have a manual or any engineering data) was identical to that of the Ki-15-I.

Drop-tank

Despite the fact that Mitsubishi schematic drawings of the C5M2 depict a larger drop-tank installation, similar to that of the A5M2 long-range (210 litre) drop-tank, the manual states that the drop-tank volume was still only 160 litres. Photographic evidence confirms that the 160 litre A5M2 style drop-tank was utilized by the C5M2.

Fuel system capacity – C5M2

Tank location	Capacity in litres
Fuselage main tank	385
Wing tanks – starboard	100
Wing tank – port	100
Wing leading edge tank – starboard	48.5
Wing leading edge tank – port	48.5
Additional fuel tank	137
Drop-tank	160
Total	**979**

It is interesting to note that the only C5M2 document to be compiled by the Technical Air Intelligence Unit paints a somewhat confusing picture of the C5M2 fuel system and is worthy of some discussion.

"US intelligence report issued on May 20th 1944. BABS – Additional Information", states that:

"The following details of Type 98 Reconnaissance BABS are available as a result of examining a crashed aircraft.

[Item]3. Fuel tanks were five in number, two located in each wing root and one in the fuselage behind the front cockpit. The latter tank was oval shaped to conform to the fuselage line but had a section cut away on the right side giving access to the rear cockpit."

This report is interesting on many levels, as it calls into question the existence of a main fuselage fuel tank in the C5M2. On the face of it this report is baffling and forces one to ask several questions.

Was a fuselage main fuel tank omitted on some production C5M2 aircraft, or deleted "in the field"? To answer these questions we must ask what the overall benefit would have been by removing the aircraft's main fuel tank?

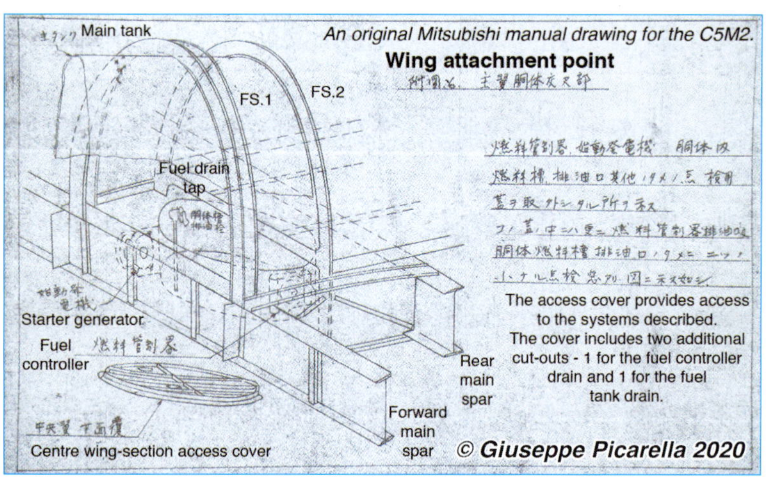

An original Mitsubishi manual drawing for the C5M2.

Could this modification be a weigh or power related issue? In short, both are unlikely as the C5M2 was only 129kg (286lb) heavier than the C5M1 and the *Sakae 12* engine offered an extra 75hp of additional power over the C5M1.

Could there have been a CG issue? This is also unlikely as the fuselage main fuel tank was located at the centre of the aircraft's CG region. In fact, with the main fuselage fuel tank deleted and the "additional fuel tank" filled with fuel, the aircraft's CG would most likely have been out balance. The Ki-15-II pilot's manual actually indicates that by not using the fuel in the "additional fuel tank" the aircraft can be placed out of balance:

"*When the aircraft is fully loaded with fuel in the "additional fuel tank", land only after the fuel in additional tank has been used, or after draining fuel out in "additional tank" during flight.*"

It is perhaps useful to look at how the deletion of the main fuel tank (385 litres) would have affected the fuel load of the C5M2. With the total fuel capacity of the aircraft reduced down to 418 liters (92 gals) internally, or 578 litres (127 gals) with drop-tank, these figures would have been the lowest of any of the *Babs* family, including the prototype C/n1501 (599 litres), which is possibly the biggest reason to discount the idea of a C5M2 operating without a fuselage main fuel tank.

If the idea was to reduce the weight of the aircraft to improve its top speed, for a single short mission, why bother to delete a fuel tank and its systems, when you could just as easily leave the "additional fuel tank" empty, remove the drop-tank or simply limit the total fuel load to 423 litres in the first place?

Could this simply be a maintenance officer's idea of getting his men working? The military takes a dim view of idle hands and the process of assembling a damaged C5M2 into an airfield decoy aircraft is not impossible.

The most obvious solution to this mystery is that fuselage main fuel tank was overlooked by the TAIU field team during its inspection. After all, the *Babs* was an obsolete type and of little importance by 1944. Or, a typographical or interpretation error crept into the documentation during transit or prior to publishing the report?

Oil system

The decision to utilize the proven Sakae 12 engine installation included the oil cooler assembly and a modified intake scoop. It is most likely that the oil cooler air-intake included a butterfly valve (air intake shutter) to control the oil temperature. The installation fitted to the A6M2b utilized a vertical pivot shaft, so it is assumed that the C5M2 included the same arrangement. The 73 litre Ki-15 oil tank was retained on FS.0.

CO_2 fire extinguisher

The C5M2 was the only version of the *Babs* to receive an integral fire extinguisher system. It is unclear if the adoption of this engine bay CO_2 fire suppression system was an attempt at standardization within the Navy, or a perceived requirement following the installation of the *Sakae 12* engine? While the engine typically exhibited high cylinder head temperatures, engine fires were not an issue. That said, it is interesting to note that the A6M2b *Zeke*, which utilized the same engine and cowling installation, also included the same engine bay fire suppression system.

The small CO_2 cylinder would have been installed in the centre fuselage or centre-wing section of the aircraft and was controlled by an actuation handle in the pilot's cockpit. The CO_2 line is identified (in the C5M2 maintenance manual) as passing through the "Extinguisher" aperture in the secondary firewall (FS.0).

Cockpits and secondary systems.

Cockpit access

The installation of the pilot's rearward sliding canopy and runner rendered the flexible upper handhold (located ahead of FS.6) unusable in its original location and it was removed. In its place Mitsubishi incorporated an entry strap made of plaited leather, which allowed the pilot to pull himself up the steep wing root to the cockpit. This type of strap was fitted to other Japanese aircraft, such as the Ki-43 "Oscar".

In order for the strap to be correctly positioned to hang over the canopy-to-fuselage fairing, a dedicated Top hat section attachment frame was added to the left-hand side of the cockpit structure, ahead of FS.5, between stringer No.3 and No.4. The strap contained a brass eye at its anchor point, which connected to a fixed shackle that was fastened to the attachment frame by a 5mm bolt.

Pilot's cockpit and systems

General layout

The equipment layout of the C5M2 cockpit remained similar to that of the C5M1 and Ki-15-II.

C5M2 Cockpit access – pilot

1/32 Scale

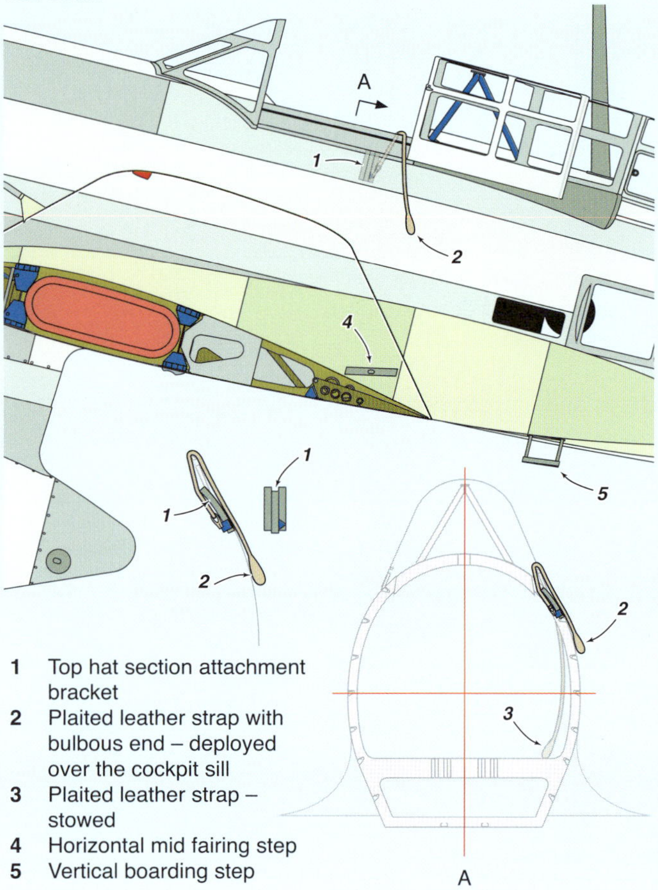

1 Top hat section attachment bracket
2 Plaited leather strap with bulbous end – deployed over the cockpit sill
3 Plaited leather strap – stowed
4 Horizontal mid fairing step
5 Vertical boarding step

Cockpit access strap

An original Mitsubishi manual drawing for the C5M2.

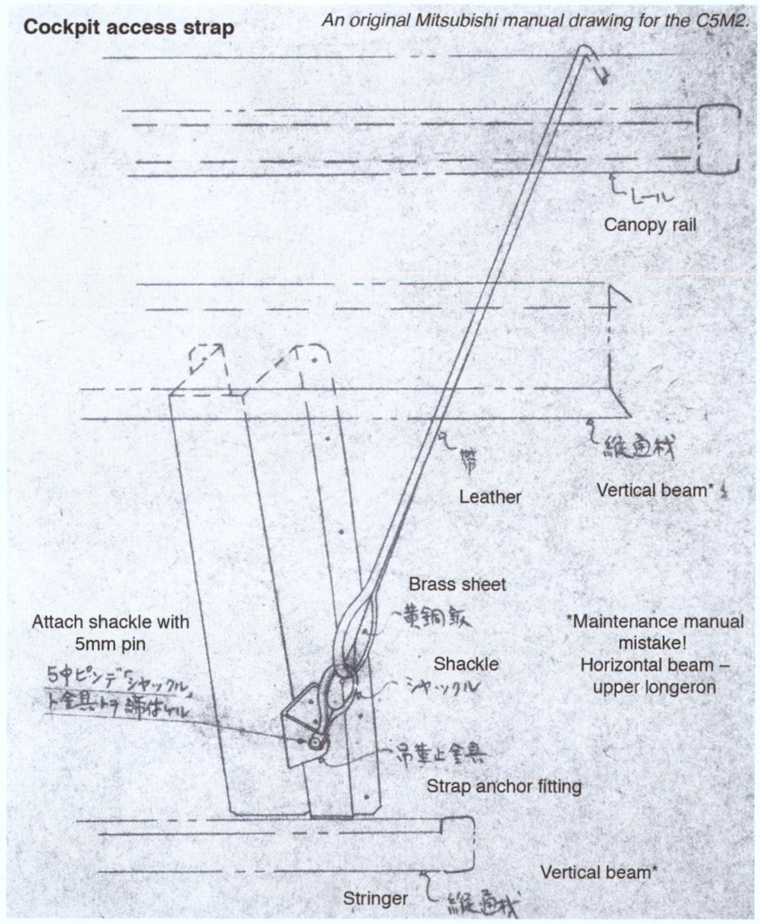

© Giuseppe Picarella 2020

It is possible that the C5M2 (with its Sakae 12 engine installation) utilised an A6M2b Zeke throttle quadrant assembly, minus the rocker switch and gun trigger on the wooden throttle lever.

Pilot and RO's cockpit and systems – C5M2

1/32 Scale

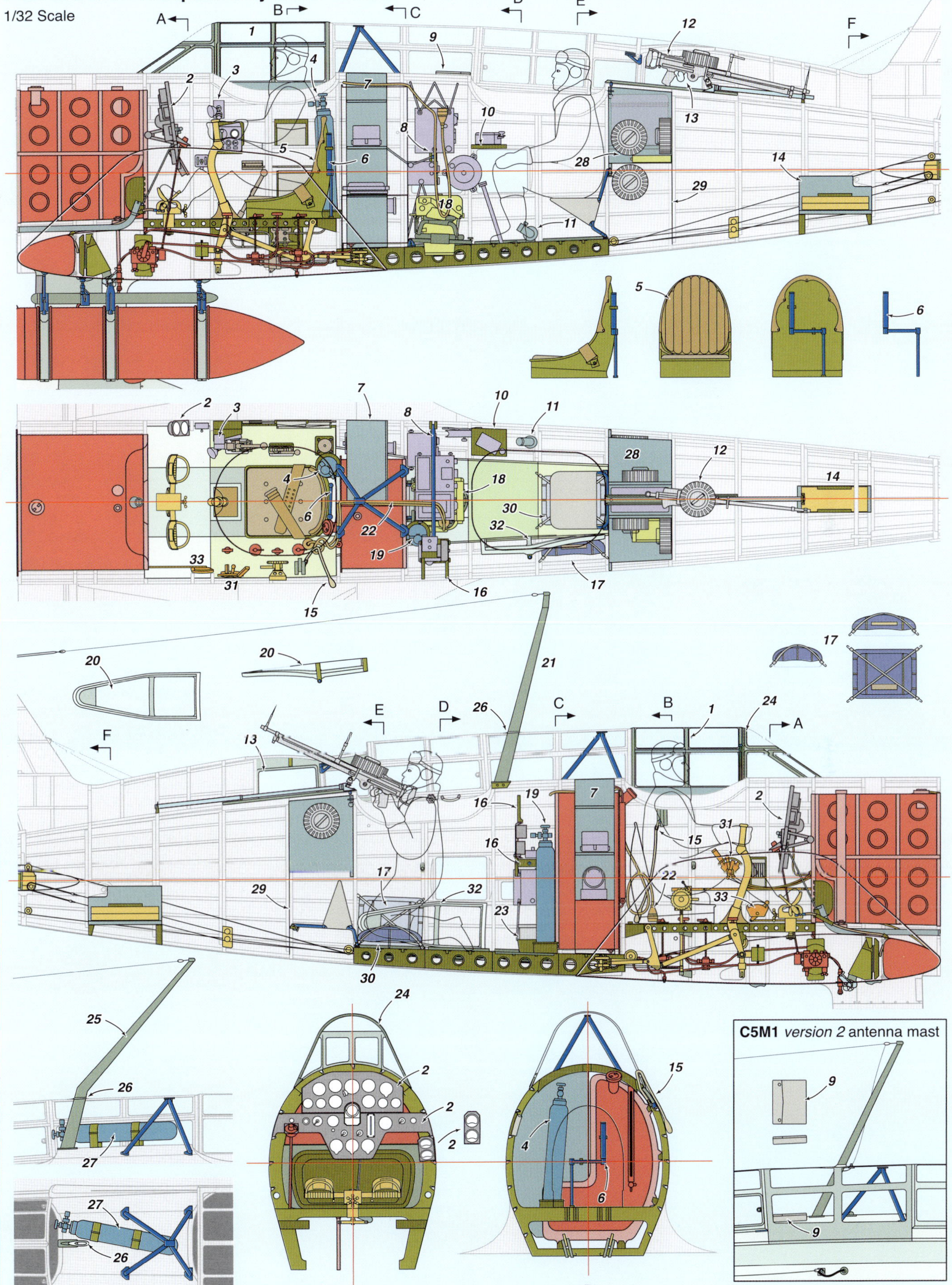

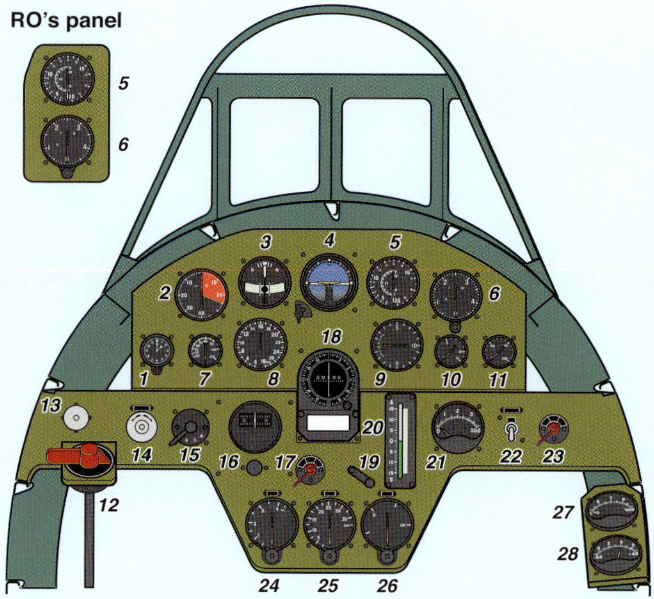

Representative of the production model C5M2

Upper panel

1 Chronometer
2 Manifold pressure Model-2
3 Turn and bank indicator Model-2
4 Artificial horizon Model-1
5 Airspeed indicator Model-3
6 Altimeter Model-2
7 Oil temperature gauge Model-1
8 Tachometer Type-2, Model-3
9 Vertical speed indicator
10 Oil pressure gauge Model-1
11 Fuel pressure gauge Model-2

Lower panel

12 Fuel tank selector
13 Emergency boost control
14 Fuel primer pump
15 Magneto switch
16 Directional gyro
17 Fuel quantity gauge selector – leading edge tanks
18 Navy compass Type-92 Model-2
19 Cockpit ventilation control
20 Inclinometer Model-2
21 Cylinder head temperature gauge Model-1
22 Ignition booster switch
22 Fuel quantity gauge – wing tanks
23 Fuel quantity gauge selector – wing tanks
24 Fuel quantity gauge – leading edge tanks
25 Fuel quantity gauge – fuselage tank
26 Fuel quantity gauge – wing tanks

Auxiliary panel

27 Exhaust gas temperature gauge
28 Inlet manifold temperature gauge

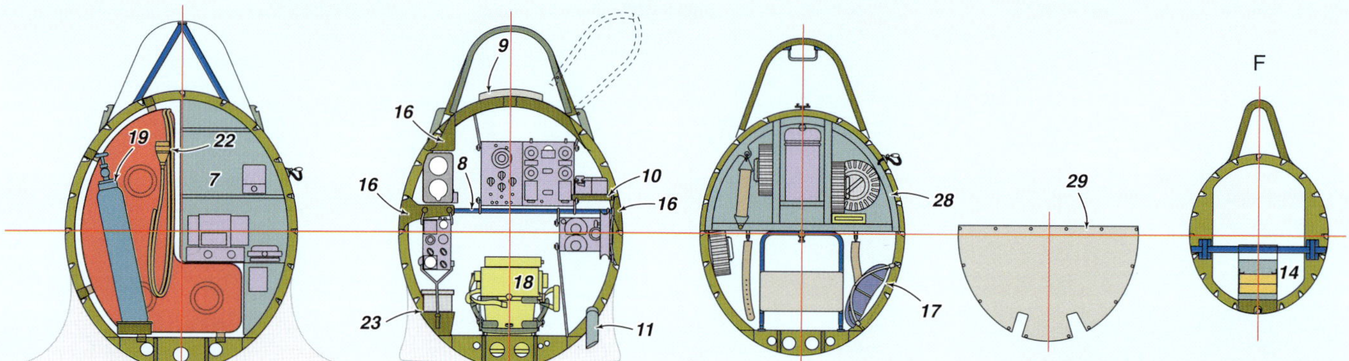

1 Pilot's sliding canopy
2 New instrument panels and auxiliary panel
3 Navalised electrical system
4 Pilot's oxygen cylinder
5 Kapok seat back/flotation aid
6 Engine starter handle – stowed on seat back
7 Redesigned radio cabinet
8 Radio support frame – speculative based on similar installations
9 Document case – *version 1*
10 Desk/Morse key table
11 Relocated trailing antenna down tube
12 Type-92 7.7mm flexible machine gun
13 Additional transparency on dorsal spine – some aircraft
14 Modified ballast box
15 Plaited leather access strap
16 RO's instrument panel/radio support frame structure
17 RO's stowed parachute – stowed on left-hand side
18 F-8 Type Aerial Camera
19 RO's oxygen cylinder
20 Gunner's window additional transparency – some aircraft
21 New antenna mast – C5M2 *version 2*
22 "Gosport" tube
23 RO's Master Compass Model-1 and mounting structure
24 Modified windscreen structure
25 Modified antenna mast fitted to a C5M2 *version 2* – aircraft ***"X-3"*** of the *3rd Kokutai*
26 Antenna streamlined skirt – C5M1 and C5M2 *version 2*
27 Additional oxygen cylinder fitted to aircraft ***"X-3"***
28 Modified storage cabinet
29 Rear fuselage canvas divider (speculative) – relocated to **FS.10**
30 RO's parachute/knee pad – when operating machine gun
31 Modified throttle quadrant
32 Gunner's window – stowed
33 Oil cooler shutter control

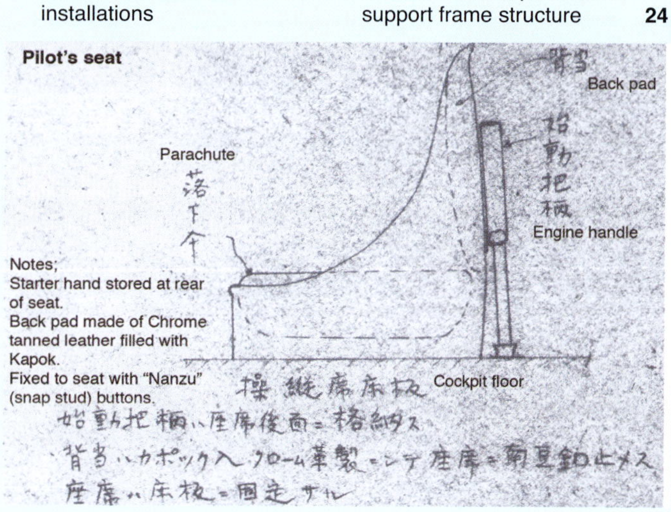

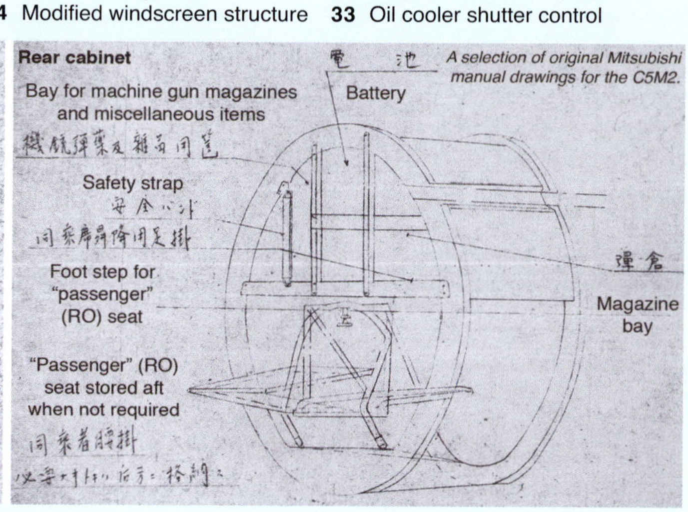

A selection of original Mitsubishi manual drawings for the C5M2.

Note: Skin colours used to identify individual panels

Pitot system

A new type of pitot installation was installed on the C5M2. The support arm was substantially shortened and canted forwards, and the T-shaped pitot head was replaced with a single horizontal pressure head. While the overall effect of this modification lowered the height of the pressure head in relation to the aircraft CL, the tip of the pitot remained approximately the same distance from the wing leading edge.

Instrument panel

The instrument panel took the same three-section layout as previous models of the *Babs*, with primary flight and engine instruments located in the upper panel, fuel and secondary flight instruments fitted in the lower panel and temperature gauges fitted in the auxiliary panel on the right-hand side of the cockpit. The upper panel was inclined away from the pilot and the lower panel more so, with the compass recess bridging the gap between both panels. Interestingly, the schematic image of the instrument panel used in the C5M2 manual is very simplistic indeed and does not fit the fuselage cross-section. The layout depicted herein has been amended to fall within the actual envelope of the forward fuselage structure.

Engine and propeller controls

The installation of the Nakajima *Sakae 12* engine, together with the constant-speed propeller unit, would have required an all-new throttle quadrant assembly for the C5M2, incorporating three controls levers – throttle, mixture and propeller pitch. While this installation would have occupied the same location as the throttle quadrant found on the Ki-15-II, its appearance would most likely have been similar (if not identical) to the throttle quadrant to that found on the A6M2b *Zeke.*

Oxygen system

The oxygen system fitted to the C5M2 was probably similar to that of the C5M1, due to space and weight and balance restrictions.

Interestingly, one C5M2 airframe ("X-3" of the *3rd Kokutai*) was photographed with a single oxygen cylinder located in the centre canopy tunnel, but this may have been a specially modified airframe. See **C5M2, Antenna, C5M2 *version 2.***

Pilot's seat

A new padded seatback was installed in the C5M2. Fabricated from Chrome-tanned leather and filled with Kapok, the seatback could be used as a floatation device in the event of a water landing. The rear face of the pilot's seat was also used as the storage location for the engine starter handle, similar to the installation on the Mitsubishi A6M *Zeke.* Drawings show the "starter-dog" end of handle was placed in a locator cup on the cockpit floor, with the handle held in place by clips.

RO's cockpit and systems

General layout

The layout of the C5M2 cockpit required several modifications to the RO's workstation, due specifically to the size and redistribution of naval equipment.

While the L-shaped "additional fuel tank" remained in the aircraft, the shape of the aperture was too small to accommodate the Type-96 *Ku* Mk.2 "Command" radio, which was 431 x 330 x 266mm (17 x 13 x 10½ inches) in size. This in effect meant that the radio installation had to move forwards by one fuselage frame from FS.5 and FS.6 to FS.6 and FS.7, impacting upon the RO's workstation and overall cockpit area.

Master compass

The Navy Navigator's Compass Model-1 was installed on the left-hand side of the cockpit between FS.6 and FS.7. The compass sat on an aluminium alloy pedestal rising from the cockpit floor up to a height inline with stringer No.8.

Radio cabinet

The adoption of the Type-96 *Ku* Mk.2 "Command" radio rendered the original Ki-15 radio cabinet unfit for purpose; as it had been specifically designed for the smaller Army Type-96 *Hi* Mk.2 "Command" radio. With the relocation of the radio, the cabinet was redesigned to accommodate the ancillary radio equipment.

Instrument panel

The RO's instrument panel was relocated on the left-hand side of the cockpit, between FS.6 and FS.7. An upper support frame was located between stringer No.2 and No.3, and was fitted with a single anti-vibration mount. A mid-point support structure was attached to the fuselage between FS.6 and FS.7, extending into the cabin and centred on stringer No.5, with two anti-vibration mounts to support the lower surface of the instrument panel. The panel contained:

1. Airspeed indicator Model-3
2. Altimeter Model-2
3. Navigator's Compass Model-1 *Kai*

Parachute

It is interesting to note that Mitsubishi drawings show the RO's parachute pack stowed to the side of the seat between FS.8 and FS.9, presumably attached to the fuselage side by bungee cords. The linework technique indicates that the parachute was located on the left-hand side of the seat, as the RO's outline is "dashed" behind the parachute. This new storage location does beg the question as to why the parachute was relocated from under the folding seat, as it was still required as a kneepad when using the machine gun?

Radio equipment

The relocation of the Navy Type-96 *Ku* Mk.2 "Command" radio had a major impact on the ergonomics of the RO's cockpit. The main transmitter/receiver unit was positioned between FS.6 and FS.7, just to the right of the aircraft CL, with the long-wave antenna tuner located directly beneath and to its right. The antenna tuner/wave meter was position to the left-hand side of the radio, suspended between

Upper two images (©Todd A.Pederson) show:
1 Navy Type-96 *Ku* Mk.2 "Command" Radio
2 Equilibrium Capacitor
3 Antenna reel
4 Insulator tube
5 Receiver dynamotor
6 Telegraph (Morse) key
7 Hand microphone
8 Single and dual headphones

Left three images (©Takashi Doi – Yokohama WWII Japanese Military Radio Museum) show size and details of the Wave Meter in relation to the Navy Type-96 *Ku* Mk.2 "Command" Radio

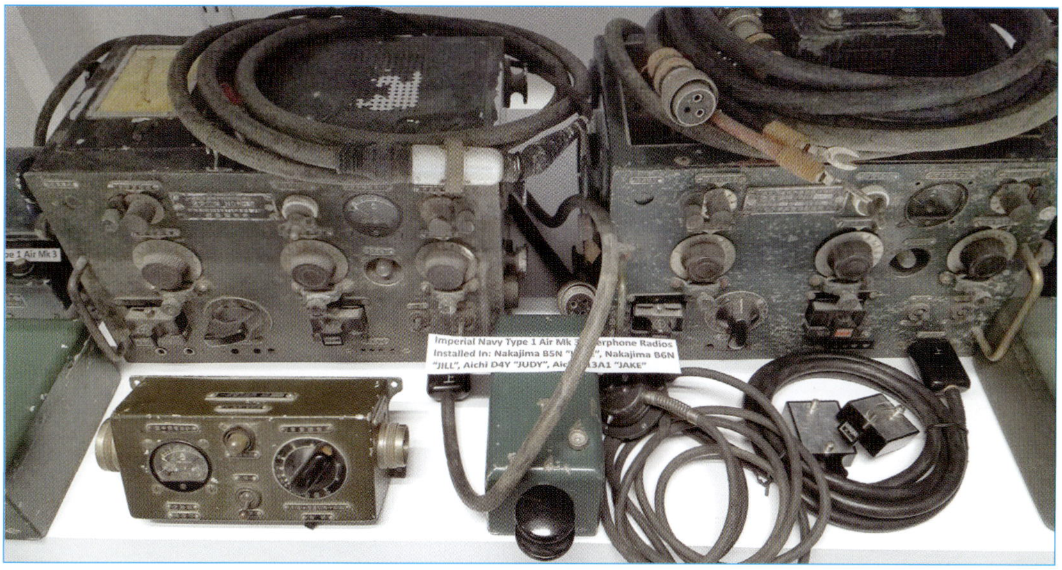

The Navy Type-1 *Ku* Mk.3, *Kai 2* radio. (Todd Pederson)

the compass pedestal and the RO's instrument panel lower support structure. The equilibrium capacitor for the antenna tuner was suspended between the RO's instrument panel and the Navy Type-96 *Ku* Mk.2 "Command" radio.

Delicate items of radio equipment were attached to, or suspended from, the airframe with the aid of anti-vibration bungee cords.

The dynamotor (low to high voltage transformer), vibrator (DC to AC transformer) and voltage controller units were located inside the new radio cabinet installation, and the power junction box was located on its aft face. A trailing antenna reel and guide tube was fitted to the right-hand sidewall of the fuselage, adjacent to stringer No.6, with the antenna exit hole being located aft of FS.8. A telegraph (Morse code) key and folding table was installed on the right-hand side of the cockpit between FS.7 and FS.8, adjacent to stringer No.5.

The Navy Type-96 *Ku* Mk.2 "Command" radio operated within the frequency range of 0.2-0.5/4.5-11.2 Megacycles, with a high/low power output of 27/9Watts (telegraph/voice Watts) and a range of 321km at 3,048m (200miles at 10,000ft). It measured 431 x 330 x 266mm (17 x 13 x 10½ inches) and weighed 21.7kg (48 lb) as a complete unit. One dynamotor and one vibrator unit powered the radio.

It is also possible that the Type-1 *Ku* Mk.3 was installed in later C5M2 aircraft. This radio had a frequency range of 30.0-45.0 Megacycles, a 5Watt power output and a range of 80 km at 3,048m (50 miles at 10,000ft). The size of the radio was 280 x 18 x 168 mm (11 x 7 $1/16^{th}$ x 6 $5/8^{th}$ inches) and the weight of the transmitter/receiver was 11.4 kg (25 lbs). A single vibrator unit powered the radio. A fixed and trailing antenna installation was provided with this radio installation.

Antenna

The C5M2 maintenance manual shows two types of antenna installation as standard, a fixed radio-telephony antenna and a trailing antenna. The Navy Type-96 *Ku* Mk.2 "Command" radio was capable of changing from "telephone" (voice) communications and "telegraph" (Morse code) via a selector on the transmitter unit, thus allowing the RO to switch between the antennas depending on the type of transmission required.

C5M2 *version 1*

The C5M2 *version 1* was similar to C5M1 *version 1*.

C5M2 *version 2*

While the antenna installation fitted to the C5M2 *version 2* was broadly similar to that of the C5M1 *version 2*, the 105cm high mast included several modifications. Canted 13° forward, with a kink at the top, the mast was visibly increased in chord at its base, giving a tapered appearance. This was probably done to reduce vibration issues with the original thin mast. The pilot's new rearward sliding canopy enclosure conflicted with the position of the old mast, which necessitated a 200mm (aft) relocation to allow the canopy to be slid fully open. The base of the new mast was located on the lip of the RO's cockpit at FS.7, with a new aperture at the TDC of the centre canopy tunnel frame. No lead-in was included in this installation as the aerial lead travelled up through the mast, then aft to the standard (FinS.7) rear insulator fitting on the fin.

The long aerial installation (wingtip to wingtip via the fin) was similar to that of the C5M1 *version 2*, but was mirrored on the port side of the aircraft, with its lead-in terminating at FS.8 and FS.9, adjacent to stringer No.4. An insulator fitting was located at the mid point of the fin (FinS.4), together with various insulators within the circuit. It is entirely possible that the port side aerial was part of the RDF installation. See **Radio Direction Finders.**

Navy Type-96 *Ku* Mk.2 "Command" Radio installation

1/32 Scale

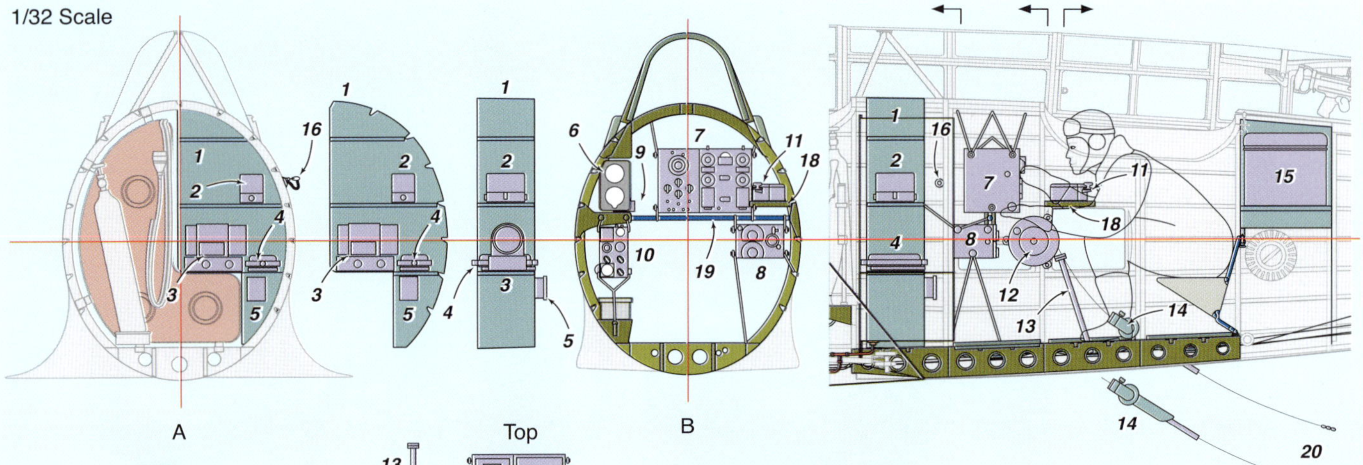

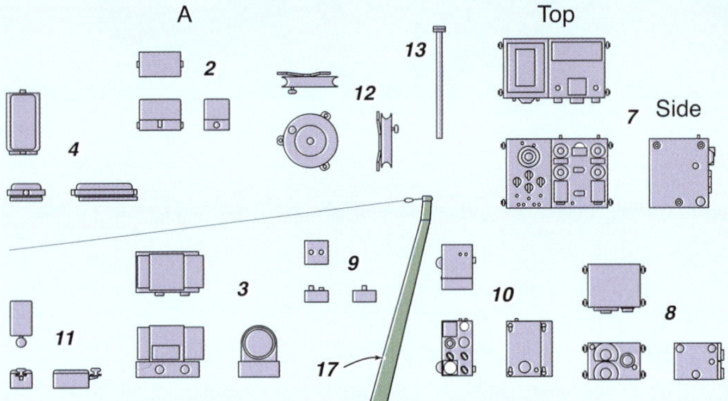

1 Enlarged radio cabinet
2 Dynamotor for receiver
3 Dynamotor for transmitter
4 Transmitter power supply
5 Main power cable junction box
6 RO's instrument panel
7 Type-96 *Ku* Mk.2 "Command" Radio
8 Long-wave antenna tuner
9 Equilibrium capacitor – antenna tuning
10 Wave meter
11 Telegraph (Morse) key
12 Trailing antenna reel
13 Trailing antenna insulator tube – stowed
14 Trailing antenna guide tube
15 Airborne battery
16 Antenna lead-in and insulators
17 Antenna mast – *version 2*
18 Writing/Morse key table
19 Radio support frame – speculative
20 Trailing antenna – deployed

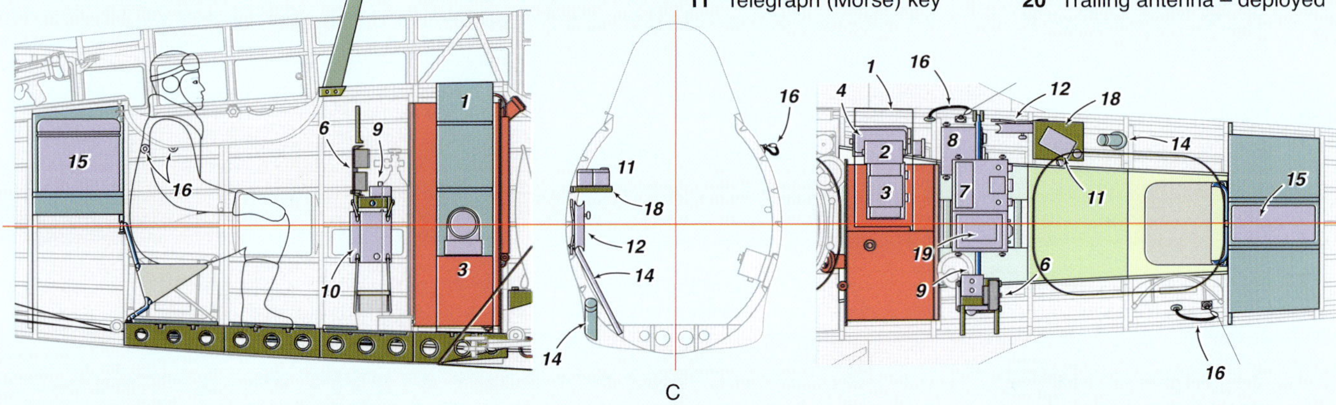

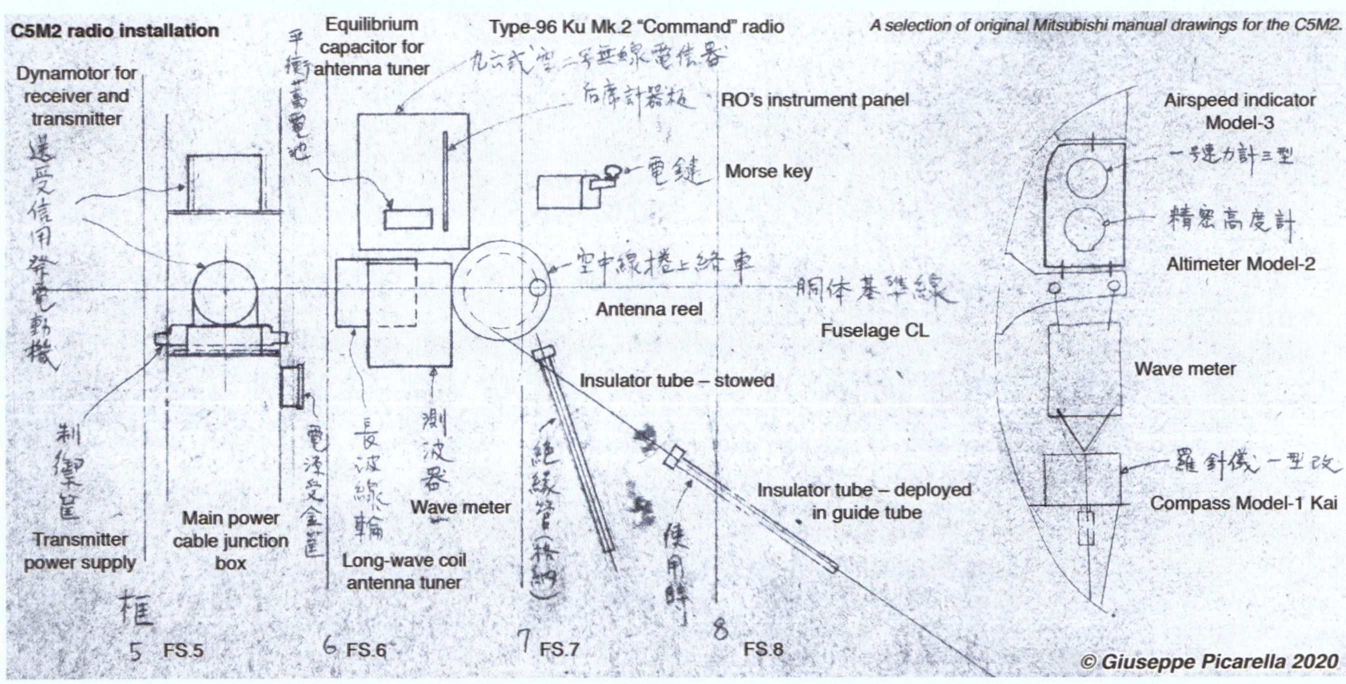

Special missions?

A variation on the **C5M2 *version 2*** antenna mast was installed on aircraft **"X-3"** of the *3rd Kokutai.* While this antenna was located in the new rear location, the mast canted forwards by approximately 39° (after exiting the canopy framework) in an effort to lengthen the aerial lead, possibly denoting that a third type of radio was installed. What is also interesting about aircraft **"X-3"** is the installation of an oxygen cylinder inside the centre canopy tunnel.

Was the oxygen cylinder relocated to provide space for additional radio equipment in the RO's cockpit, or might it indicate that the aircraft was specially modified for long endurance, or high altitude operations over Australia? Whatever the reason, **"X-3"** was subsequently shot down near Bathurst Island, in the Australian Northern Territory on March 22nd 1942. See Chapter 1, **Brothers in Arms.**

Trailing antenna

While the C5M1 *version 1* and C5M2 *version 1* both lacked antenna masts, they were fitted with the aforementioned trailing antenna installations as standard with the Type-96 *Ku* Mk.2 "Command" radio set.

Radio Direction Finders

On the whole, Navy pilots received much more rigorous navigational training than their Army brethren, especially before the start of the Pacific war. The reason for this was quite simple, Navy pilots by definition spent longer periods flying and navigating over the featureless sea, particularly carrier-based aircrews. In order to fly such long missions over water, almost all Japanese Navy aircraft of the period, including single-seat fighters, were fitted with RDF equipment. Ironically these same navigation skills were in great demand following the Navy's entry into the air war over China, where its long-range bomber and reconnaissance crews were tasked with navigating China's vast uncharted expanses.

Therefore the installation of RDF equipment in the C5M aircraft is much more likely than that of the Army's Ki-15. One of the reasons for the continuing confusion surrounding the installation of this type of equipment is perhaps due to the fact that the Ki-15 and C5M were both identified with the same Allied codename *Babs,* within intelligence reports.

Only one piece of wartime intelligence information pertaining to C5M aircraft equipped with RDF equipment could be traced for this book. This came in the form of a (US) Navy Department "*Memorandum*" dated 19th March 1945, which lists the Navy Type-1 *Ku* Mk.3 (RDF) unit as being fitted to the *Babs.* Whether this was fitted to the C5M1 or C5M2 is unknown.

The Navy Type-1 *Ku* Mk.3 RDF operated within the 0.17-1.2 Megacycles range and measured 460 x 230 x 153mm (18 x 9 x 6 inches) in size, and weighed 6.8kg (15 lb) as a complete unit. It would have included a receiver unit, control unit, antenna crank, loop antenna, L/R meter and dedicated dynamotor, but only the control box, crank and L/R meter would need to have been accessible to the RO for the operation usage of the device.

No photographic evidence exists showing a C5M fitted with an RDF loop antenna. Typically such loop antennae were mounted beneath canopy transparencies for better reception, but this was not always the case. The inclusion of aerial leads routed to the wingtip of the C5M could indicate that these were used in place of the standard RDF loop antenna, as aircraft such as the G3M *Nell* carried both loop and wingtip aerial lead equipped RDF equipment.

Armament

Offensive armament

Perhaps the most exotic operational modifications to be utilised by the C5M2 was the installation of an air-to-air bomb, for use against Allied bombers in the Solomon Islands during the summer of 1942. See Chapter 1, **Bothers in Arms.**

Type-99, No.3, Mk.3, *Kai*-1 air-to-air bomb

Originally designed in 1938 for air-to-ground operations (against parked aircraft or ground troops) the Type-99 No.3, Mk.3 aerial-burst or "*San-go*" bomb, was used in the air-to-air role to directly destroy, damage or break-up tight bomber formations, thereby allowing individual aircraft to be singled out and attacked by accompanying fighters. The difference between the initial weapon and the later *Kai*-1 (modified-1) was the inclusion of additional fins installed on the main-body, which increased the speed

Armed C5M2 of the Solomon Islands campaign

1/32 Scale

Small Bomb Dispenser details and (speculative) drop-tank pylon modifications

1/24 Scale

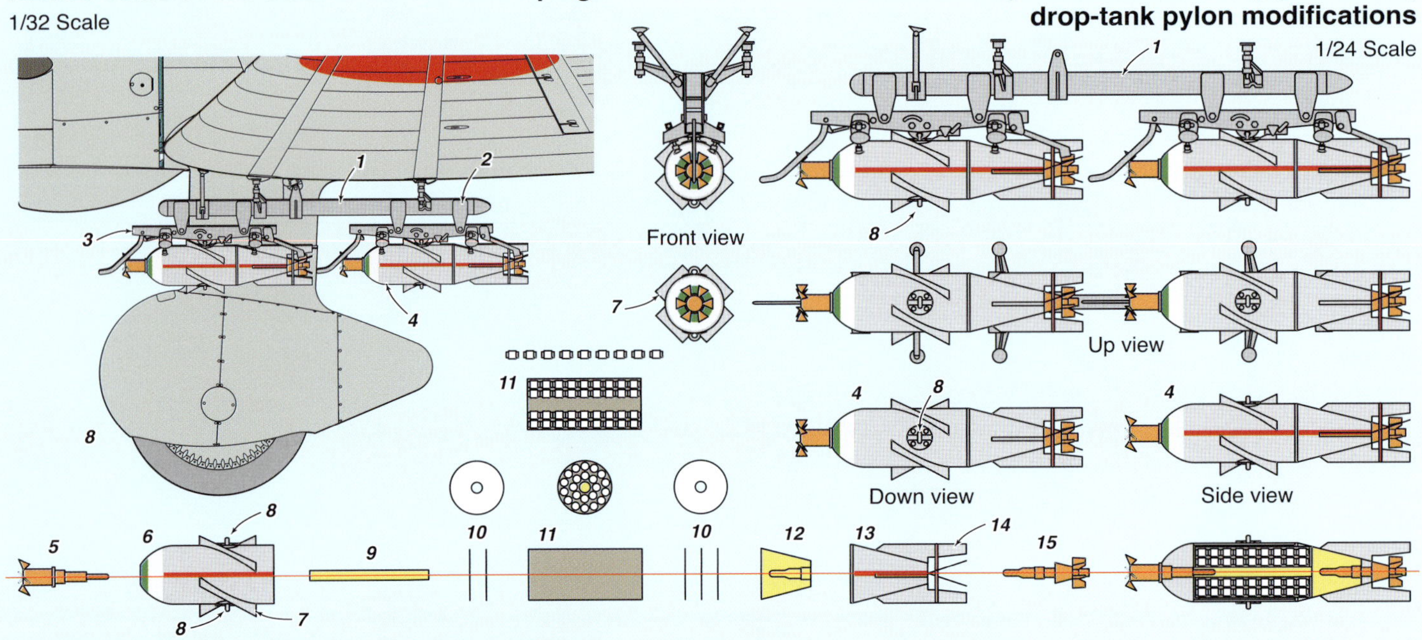

1	Standard C5M drop tank-pylon with modified hoop band arms	**11**	Payload – cardboard tube filled with 198 steel/ phosphorous pellets
2	Modified Bomb Dispenser attachment brackets – four	**12**	Dispersal charge
3	Small Bomb Dispenser for Fighters – two	**13**	Tail-cone
4	Type-99, No.3, Mk.3, Kai-1 air-to-air bomb	**14**	Tail fins – four
5	Nose fuse (impact) – Type-1, Model-2	**15**	Main fuse (Clockwork) Type-99, Mk.3, Model-1
6	Bomb main body	**16**	Bomb sway-brace fittings
7	Main body rotational fins – four	**17**	Nose fuse safety arm – spring-loaded
8	Suspension lugs – two	**18**	Main fuse safety arm – spring-loaded
9	“Burster” tube	**19**	Safety arms – retracted
10	Felt washers – five	**20**	Bomb release fitting

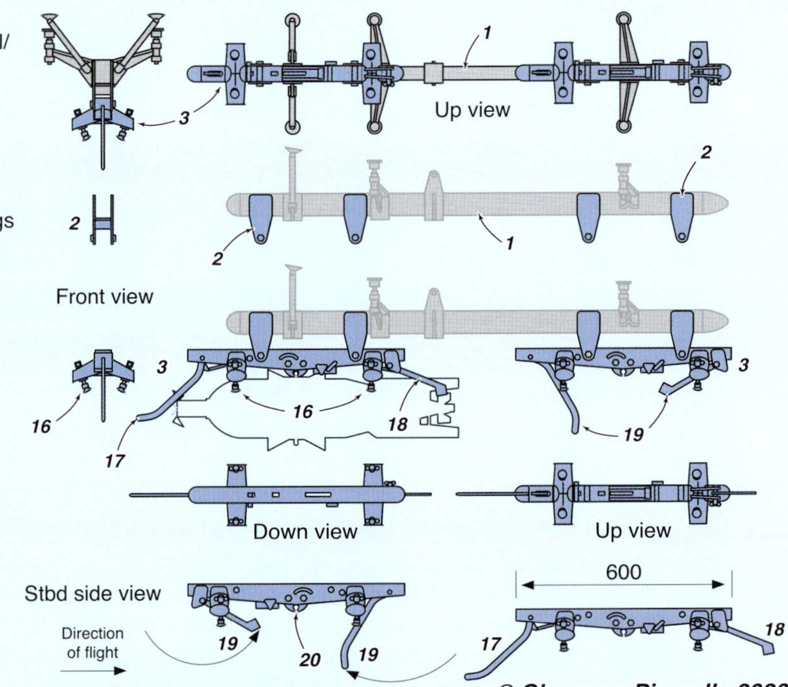

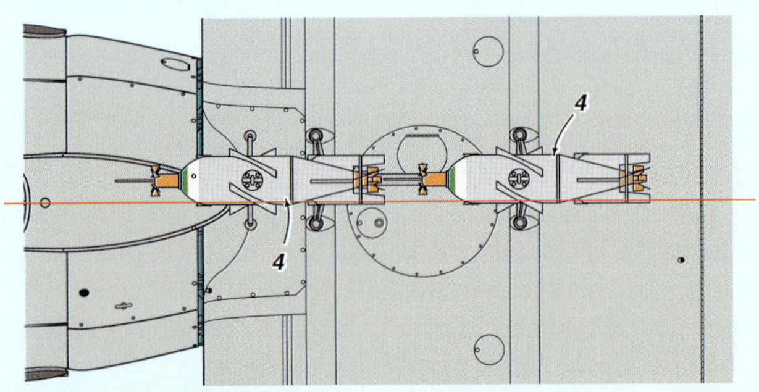

© Giuseppe Picarella 2020

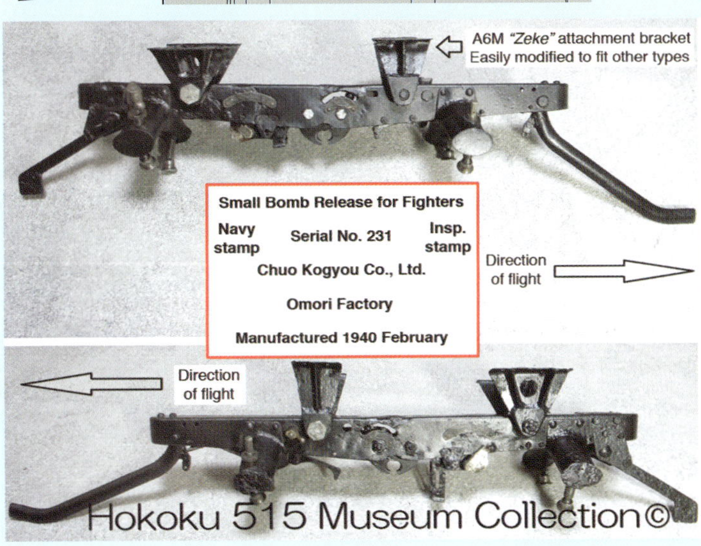

of the bomb's rotational spinning. The weapon consists of a main body, tail-cone, payload, "burster" tube and fuses.

Main body

The main body was constructed from a cast-steel nose-section and rear (threaded) collar, connected by a welded sheet-steel body, which formed a hollow cylinder. The exterior of the cylinder was fitted with two suspension lugs, riveted on opposite sides of the unit, plus four rotational fins. Each of the 35mm x 150mm (1.5 inch x 6 inch) length fins was welded to the body of the weapon at 35° to the longitudinal axis. The cast steel nose section included a threaded cavity to accept a fuse.

Tail-cone

The tail-cone was constructed from a cast-steel tailpiece and forward attachment ring, joined together by a sheet-steel cone. Four rotational fins were riveted to the exterior of the tail-cone and braced by four flat struts. The forward end of the fins were aligned with the longitudinal axis of the weapon, but their trailing edges was angled outwards at an angle of 19° in order to spin the weapon. The tailpiece included a threaded fuse aperture and the remainder of the tail-cone was filled with picric acid (Type-98) explosives to assist in the dispersal of the payload. The tail-cone was screwed on the rear collar of the main body.

Payload

The main body accommodated a cardboard canister containing 198 steel pellets filled with phosphorous, arranged around a central cardboard tube, which fitted over the "burster" tube. The canister was cushioned at both ends with a felt "washer".

Note that some wartime documents list the payload as 144 or 168 pellets.

"Burster" tube

A steel "burster" tube was screwed on to the inner surface of the main body nose-section. Approximately 1.6kg (3.5 lb) of picric acid explosive were included within the "burster" tube and tail-cone cavity.

Fuses

The main fuse of the weapon was a Type-99, Mk.3, Model-1 (D-2 type) clockwork tail fuse, which could be set to detonate the bomb after a predetermined period of time. A Type-2, Model-2 (A3 type) impact type nose fuse was installed as a back up to the tail fuse, to detonate the weapon on contact with the target or the ground. Both fuses would have been "safetied" when the bomb was attached to the weapons pylon.

Operation

Before an attack mission, the clockwork tail fuse of each bomb would be wound and set. The specific time delay required was of course based upon the optimum altitude that the weapon would be deployed over the enemy formation of bombers, the relative or closing speed of the aircraft and the desired height of detonation above the target aircraft. Once dropped from the aircraft, the nose and tail fuse safety wires/arms were withdrawn from the fuse vanes, which were then free to rotate in the airstream and arm themselves. The nose fuse simply withdrew the firing pin to its striking position, in the typical manner. Rotation of the tail fuse vane acted to withdraw an arming spindle from the clockwork timing-mechanism, which started the fuse countdown. As an added safety feature, the clockwork timer was fitted with a centrifugal switch, which only allowed the bomb to arm once it had reached a 1,000rpm spin rate. This was accomplished thanks to the rotational fins on the main body and tail of the weapon. Once the clockwork mechanism had counted down, a spring-loaded firing pin detonating the weapon.

The high rotational spin of the weapon coupled with the "burster" tube explosive charge, acted to disperse phosphorous pellets outwards, while the tail-cone explosive charge pushed the pellets forwards. These combined forces acted to create a cone shaped dispersal pattern for the pellets, which would rain down on the bomber formation. When the phosphorous pellets hit an aircraft, they tended to stick to the aluminium skin and continue burning. Such weapons were obviously most effective when they impacted in the vicinity of a fuel tank, etc.

Colours and markings

Typically, the Type-99 No.3, Mk.3, *Kai*-1 was painted grey with a green band and a silver band applied to the extreme nose of the main body. Some bombs also included silver fin tips, red bracing struts or a thin red stripe down each side of the main body and tail-cone. Both fuses were fabricated from brass.

Deployment

The pilot and RO needed to work together in order to correctly position the C5M2 over the enemy formation and the down-view through the RO's vertical camera window would have been critical for positioning and deployment of the weapon. In fact, it is unclear whether it was the pilot or the RO that actually released the weapon, as the low cockpit canopy of the C5M, coupled with a total lack of downward observation windows, would have made sighting of the weapon almost impossible for the pilot. Regardless of this detail, the fact that two bombs were typically carried, would indicate that two individual release handles were utilized.

Navy Type-99, Number-3, Mk3, Modified 1 Air-to-air bomb

Weight	31.7kg (70 lb)
Length – over-all	62.2cm (24 ½ in)
Length – body	34.3cm (13 ½ in)
Diameter – body	14.6cm (5 ¾ in)
Length – tail	28cm (11 in)
Daimeter – tail	15.6cm (6 1/8in)
Payload	198 phosphorous pellets
Burst charge	1.6kg (3.5 lb) of Type-98 explosives

Weapons pylon

It is unclear what type of weapons pylon was fitted to the C5M2, but given that the aircraft was not designed to deliver weapons, it is likely that the existing drop-tank support pylon was hand modified for attack missions. The most likely weapons delivery system for this field modification was the 600mm long **"Small Bomb dispenser (for Fighters)"** which was designed specifically to allow aircraft like the A6M2b *Zeke* to carry small ordinance. Up to 10 of these simple, pressed-steel pylons could be attached to the underside of the *Zeke* wing, allowing it to carry small practice bombs, or operational weapons such as the 31.7kg (70 lb) Type-99 No.3, Mk.3, *Kai*-1 bomb.

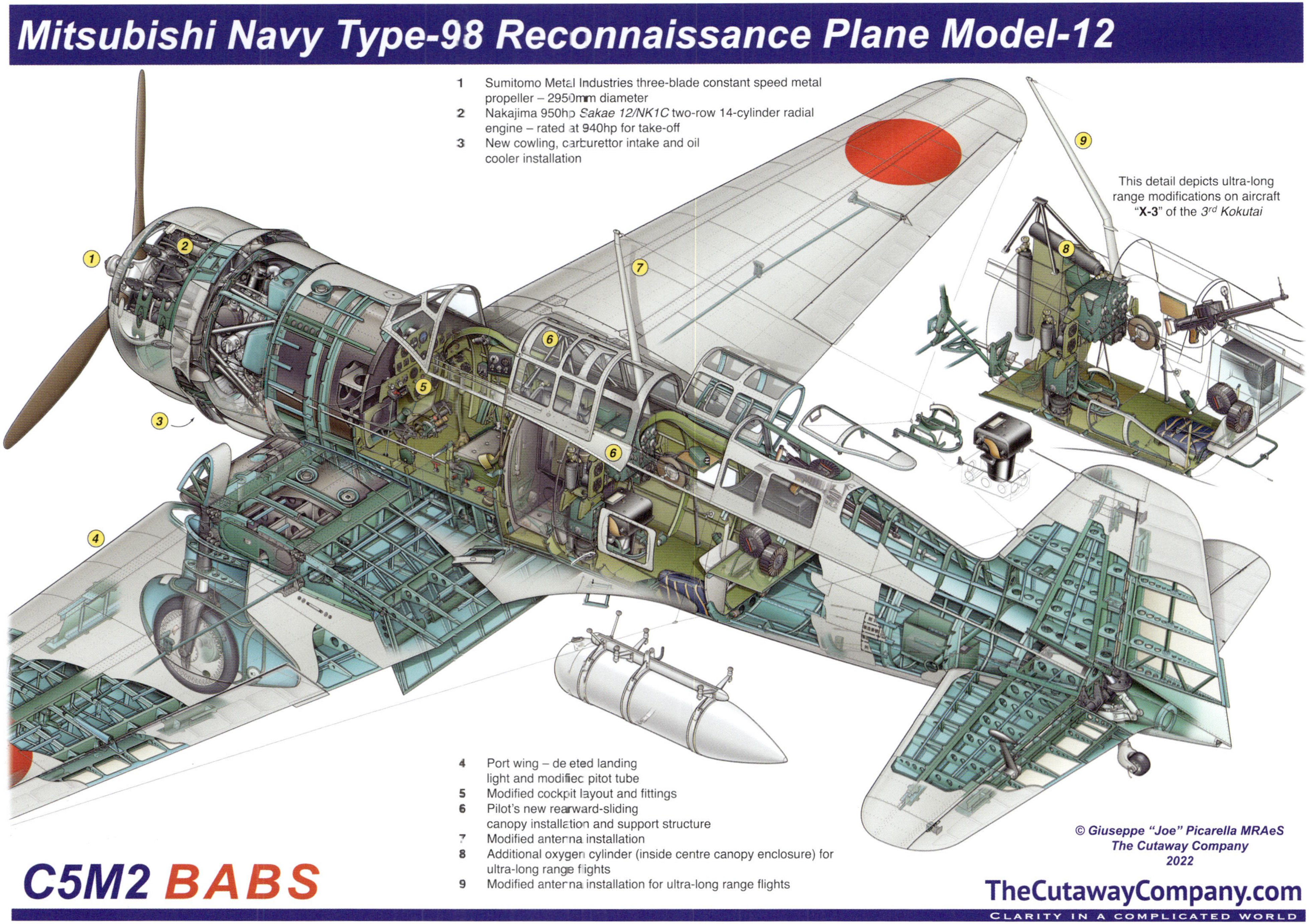
Mitsubishi Navy Type-98 Reconnaissance Plane Model-12
1 Sumitomo Metal Industries three-blade constant speed metal propeller – 2950mm diameter
2 Nakajima 950hp Sakae 12/NK1C two-row 14-cylinder radial engine – rated at 940hp for take-off
3 New cowling, carburettor intake and oil cooler installation
This detail depicts ultra-long range modifications on aircraft "X-3" of the 3rd Kokutai
4 Port wing – deleted landing light and modified pitot tube
5 Modified cockpit layout and fittings
6 Pilot's new rearward-sliding canopy installation and support structure
7 Modified antenna installation
8 Additional oxygen cylinder (inside centre canopy enclosure) for ultra-long range flights
9 Modified antenna installation for ultra-long range flights
C5M2 BABS
© Giuseppe "Joe" Picarella MRAeS
The Cutaway Company
2022
TheCutawayCompany.com
CLARITY IN A COMPLICATED WORLD

Mitsubishi Ki-15-III

While the general layout of the Ki-15-III remained broadly unchanged from that of the Ki-15-II, its design and development would have benefited greatly from all of the small improvements made to the Ki-15-II and C5M2 airframes during their operational careers. With these lessons on hand, and supported by the development of Mitsubishi's new Ki-46 *Dinah* prototype, certain assumptions can be made about the KI-15-III. For general details please refer to the Ki-15-II technical description.

Mitsubishi Ki-15-III Prototype
1/48 Scale

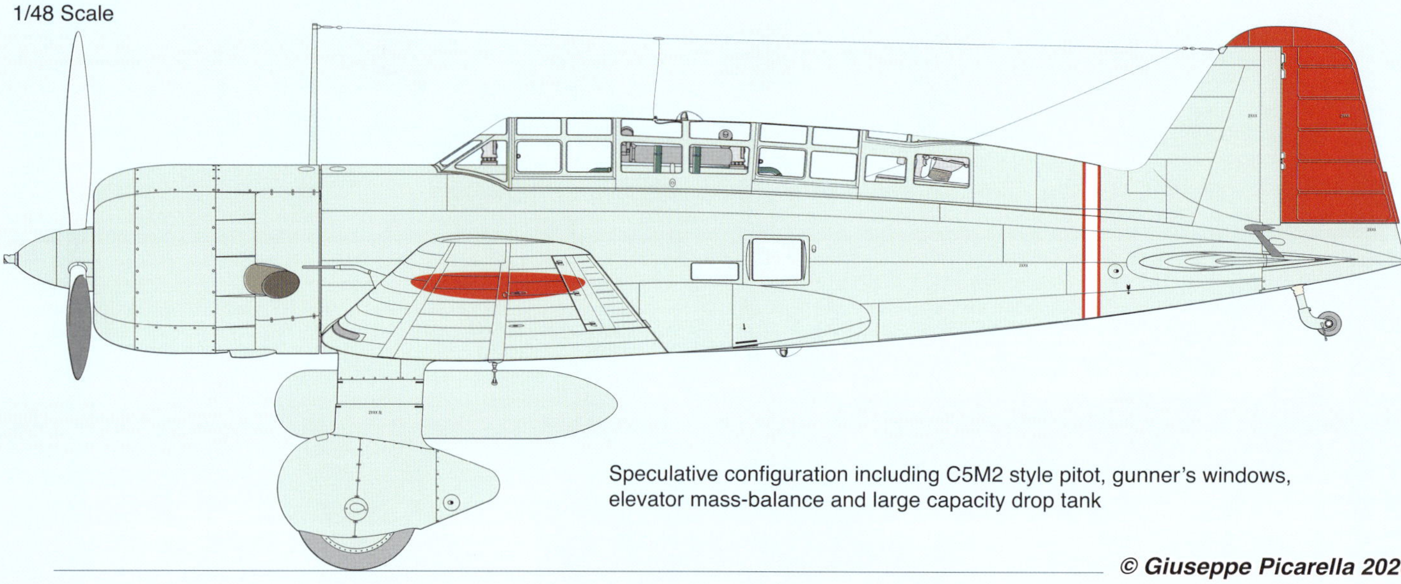

Speculative configuration including C5M2 style pitot, gunner's windows, elevator mass-balance and large capacity drop tank

Nacelle assembly

Cowling

The Ki-15-III would have required an all-new cowling and forward fuselage fairing assembly to accommodate the Mitsubishi Ha-102 engine and it is likely that the advanced aerodynamic research being undertaken for the new Ki-46 would have influenced the design of the engine installation.

At that time there were two potential oil-cooler options available to the designers; the annular radiator, or the ram-air scoop installation. While both systems would ultimately be adopted on the Ha-102

The Mitsubishi Ha-102 engine would be utilised in the Kawasaki Ki-45 KAI-b *Nick*. Note the annual oil cooler.

powered Kawasaki Ki-45 KAIb *Nick* during late 1940, Mitsubishi was not convinced by such an installation and the highly streamlined Ki-46-II design, which also utilized a Ha-102 engine from early 1941, would only incorporate a retractable ram-air scoop which fed a fixed oil cooler in the rear accessory bay, together with a low drag integral carburettor intake on the upper cowling lip.

Powerplant

In 1940 Mitsubishi designed the *Zuisei 21* engine, which was a Ha-26-I fitted with a two-speed supercharger for better performance and redesigned cylinder heads for improved cooling. Unfortunately, the Navy was uninterested in this new engine, but the Army took a different view altogether, giving the engine a new designation – 1,050hp Army Type-1 radial engine, or Ha-102/Ha-31.

The engine was fitted with a quadruple-inlet downdraught carburettor at TDC, a vacuum pump and an electric inertia starter/generator on the aft thrust-line of the accessory casing.

The engine could be started by either the electric starter motor or via a starter handle inserted in the starboard side lower forward fuselage fairing.

Mitsubishi 1,050hp Army Type-1/Ha-102 specifications

Rated power	1,050hp
Compression ratio	7
Capacity	28 litres
RPM	2,700
Bore/stroke	140/130mm
Length	1,473mm
Height	1,118mm
Width	1,118mm
Weight	565kg

Propeller and spinner

The Ki-15-III would have been fitted with a Sumitomo Metal Industries, license-built Hamilton Standard type three-blade constant-speed metal propeller. It is likely that this propeller was the same 2,950mm diameter unit that was fitted to the later Ki-45 and Ki-46-II, as a larger propeller would have been required to absorb the power output of the engine. A Ki-46 style two-part spinner would probably have been fitted to the propeller installation and the "Huck's" type starter would have been reinstated.

Primary systems

Flight control system

Due to the increased performance and weight of the aircraft, it is entirely possible that the elevator mass-balance system of the C5M2 may have been included in the redesign, together with small improvements to the pitot tube, etc.

Fuel system

Given the additional fuel consumption of the Mitsubishi Ha-102 engine, it is likely that an increase in fuel capacity was considered for the upgrade. The options available to the design team included:

- A redesigned "addition fuel tank"
- New fuel tanks in the outboard wing panels
- Increased capacity drop-tank

By adopting a long-range fuel tank system similar to that of *Kamikaze*, the Ki-15-III could have gained approximately 100 litres over the existing capacity of the standard "additional fuel tank". This would have necessitated the removal of the radio cabinet and the relocation of the radio aft, to sit between FS.6 and FS.7, similar to the installation found on the Navy's C5M *Babs*. While the development of new fuel tanks for the outboard wing panels was also possible, the fact that this type of modifications was not adopted in the C5M2, which was produced after the Ki-15-III development phase, would indicate that neither option was pursued.

It is possible therefore that the engineering team considered utilizing a larger drop-tank to regain range, with a capacity of 300 or 400 litres. If this were the case, then the attachment pylon would most

Babs family tree – quick recognition guide

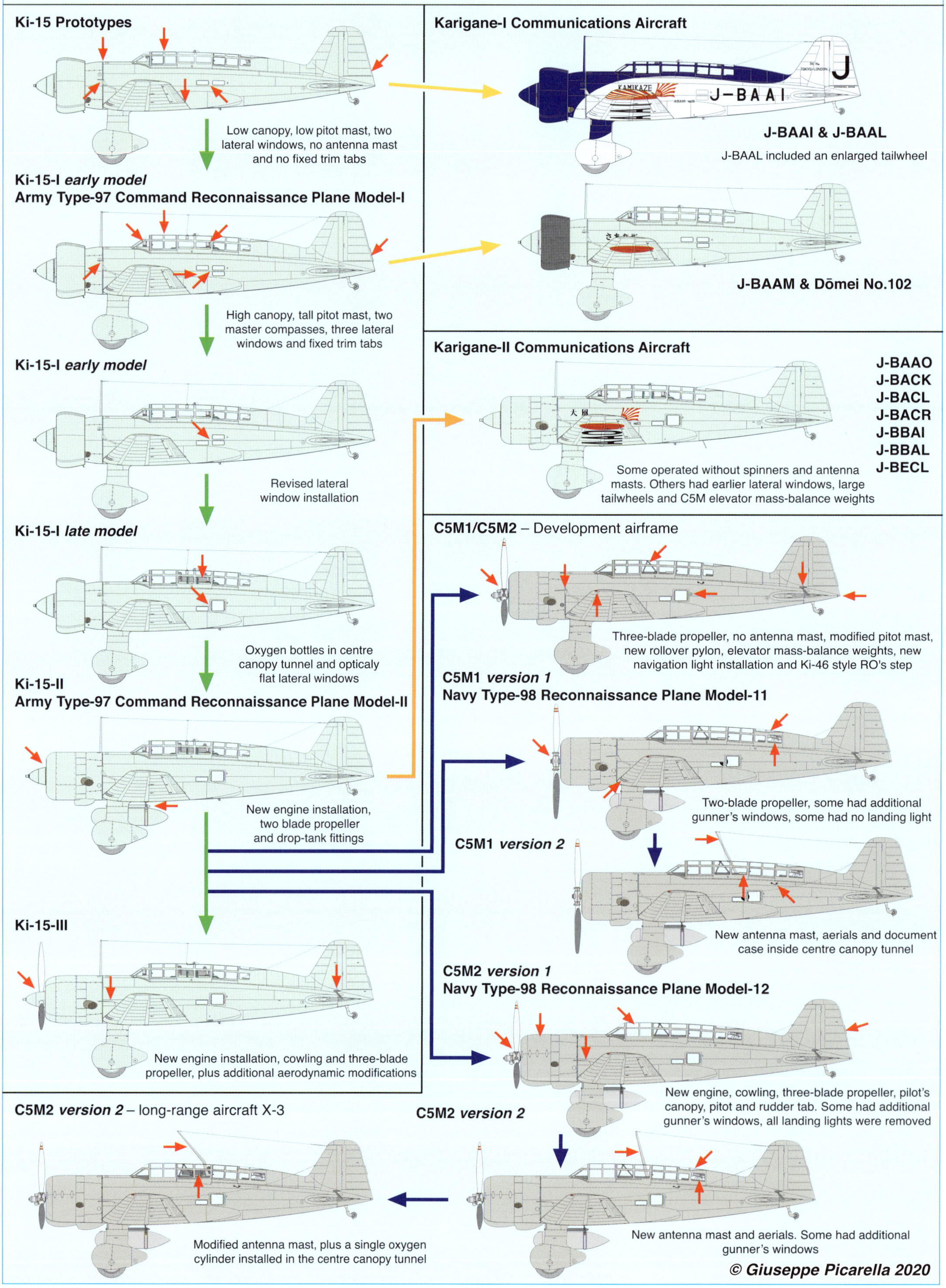

likely have been redesigned to reduce drag and to reposition the tank closer to the lower fuselage, as was the case with contemporary Japanese naval drop-tanks of the period.

Oxygen system

While no evidence of the Ki-15-III oxygen system survives, it is important to understand that the growing trend of higher altitude and longer ranging missions would have required the aircraft to be fitted with as many oxygen cylinders as weight limits would allow. Two oxygen cylinders per crewmember is not an unrealistic assumption, with control of these cylinders being delegated to the RO, as was the case in new Ki-46.

Aerial camera equipment

Had the Ki-15-III entered service instead of the Ki-46, it is possible that it would have carried the Army Mk.1 Automatic Aerial Camera.

This new camera, based on the Navy Fixed Aerial Camera K-8 Type, was undergoing Army evaluations during 1940 and would go on to become standard equipment on the Ki-46, complete with its long 50cm lens. Due to the vertical confines of the Ki-15 rear cockpit, only the Type-2 version of the camera, with its shorter 25cm lens assembly, would have fitted in the aircraft. While this lens installation was optimised for 4,000m to 6,000m (13,000ft to 20,000ft) operations, which fell short of the higher altitudes that were becoming necessary for strategic reconnaissance missions, it still offered a marked improvement over the smaller Army Type-100 Small Aerial Camera (SK-100).

Army Mk.1 Type-2 Automatic Aerial Camera – with 25cm lens

Manufacturer(s)	Konishi-roku/Nippon Kogaku
Shutter speeds	1/50, 1/100, 1/150 sec
Finder	Optical type
Lenses	25cm f4.5
Stock type	Plate/film roll – 24 meter
Image size	24 x 18cm
Dimensions – width/height/depth	–
Weight	–
Operation	Manual or remotely operated
Notes	Heated lens and body – 24 Volts

Radio equipment

The Ki-15-III would probably have been fitted with the Type-99 *Hi* Mk.1 radio and the existing Ki-15-II antenna installation. The highly streamlined Ki-46 retained a fixed antenna installation right up until the last year of the war, when such masts were shortened or removed entirely in order to extract every additional kilometre of airspeed in the skies over the war-torn Japanese mainland.

Armament

When the Army ordered Mitsubishi to develop the Ki-15-III, the inclusion of defensive armament would have been specified as a matter of course. The most likely candidates would have been the trusty Te-4 7.7mm flexible machine gun or the Type-98 7.9mm flexible machine gun. It is also possible that additional rear view windows, similar to those found on the C5M, were also included in the new airframe.

Regardless of this decision, aircrews with operational experience over China had already concluded that evasive flying, coupled with the "clean" high-speed capabilities of the Ki-15, were much more valuable than a handful of rifle calibre bullets.

Chapter 5

Pilot's operating manual

"The cockpits are about four feet apart and the fuel tanks are between them. Both cockpits are roomy and neatly arranged. The rear cockpit has two small windows let into each side at seat level. Dual controls are not fitted. The normal rudder-bar and control column are in the front cockpit."

"The Heavenly Breeze" editorial in The Aeroplane, April 14th 1937.

Type-97 Strategic Reconnaissance Aircraft – Ki-15-II
To be attached to Educational Regulation for Controlling Aircraft

August 1938

Army Air Headquarters

CONTENTS

Controlling the Type-97 Strategic Reconnaissance Aircraft

General

This aircraft is excellent in stability and control.

Adverse reactions following direction changes are small.

Further to the above, any change to the centre of gravity is small between fully loaded with equipment and fuel, or lightly loaded, giving the pilot no significant change in stability and steering.

This aircraft has high inertia. Any change in speed is comparatively slow and coupled to any RPM changes of the engine.

This aircraft yaws to the left due to the propeller rotation, but only small input forces are required on the rudder bar.

This aircraft has poor forward visibility due to engine cowling and fuselage design, and flies faster than any other aircraft currently in use. Special attention is necessary to maintain safe distance to other aircraft while airborne and to other aircraft and obstacles on ground.

Chapter 1

Section 1

Starting

The engine of this aircraft shall be started with either a starting vehicle or the inertia-starter system of the aircraft.

Refer to "The general engine starting procedure" for use of the starting vehicle.

Inertia starting system

1. Confirm master switch is "Off" (item *A* on Mitsubishi Ki-15-II cockpit illustration*)*.
2. Set fuel cock to "wing tank" or "fuselage tank" ***(B)***.

3. Operate fuel pump lever sufficiently until carburettor is filled with fuel *(C)*.
4. Set mixture control lever to closed *(D)*, then slightly open throttle lever *(E)*.
5. Operate injection (primer) pump *(F)* softly but rapidly to inject fuel into impeller casing. Injection strokes are 2 – 3 in summer and 3 – 4 in winter.
6. Shout "Ready to start" to instruct the mechanic to rotate the engine starting handle. Confirm by hand gesture to the mechanic "Ready to ignite", then shout "Ignite"
7. Set magneto switch *(G)* to "On", pull starter T-handle *(H)* with left hand and simultaneously turn master switch *(A)* to "on" with right hand.

Section 2
Engine testing

Let engine run with no power alterations. Watch oil pressure gauge for 20–30 seconds. If pressure does not rise, stop engine immediately. Allow mechanic to inspect the cause of problem.

Warming up shall be done at 800–900 RPM. Select the best RPM where vibration is at its least. Continue in this condition until oil temperature rises appropriately. When oil temperature increases and cylinder head temperature reaches higher than 130°C (oil temperature higher than 40°C), slowly increase RPM and then enter ground tests. During tests careful attention should be paid to cylinder head temperature. Excessive temperature rise shall be avoided on the ground.

Attention shall be paid to tachometer and manifold pressure gauge, check general condition of airframe, indication of gauges and indicators at various RPM settings.

Indications at normal condition under regular rpm are:

1. Oil pressure: 5–6 kg/cm^2.
2. Oil temperature: 40–90°C – shall be lower than 110°C
3. Fuel pressure: 0.1–0.15 kg/cm^2 – when using fuel in wing tank.
4. Fuel pressure when using fuel in fuselage tank is slightly higher than when using fuel in wing tank by 0.04 kg/cm^2.
5. Check airframe vibration, engine sound and exhaust gas are normal.
6. After engine test running is completed, it is necessary to inspect operation of the landing flap. Set flap selector valve lever *(I)* (at right side of pilot seat) to "Down" position. Operate hydraulic pump lever *(J)* manually to deploy flap.
7. Flap angle is indicated on angle indicator *(K)* located on the right side of the cockpit. Maximum down angle is 60°. The hydraulic pump works both ways. If pump is in good working condition, about ten strokes will be enough to set 60° down flap manually. When flaps work, set flap selector valve lever to "Up" position, then operate lever manually to lift flap up.
8. The following list will be helpful for engine testing:
    - During the first test running of the day, or when the engine has been stand idle for a long time, keep engine 800 to 900 RPM.
    - When higher RPM is needed the minimum oil and cylinder temperatures are:
    - Oil temp – 40°C.
    - Cylinder temp – 130°C.
    - Fuel pressure – 5 to 6kg/cm^2 at normal RPM.
    - Oil temp – 40-90°C.
    - Maximum 110 °C.
    - Minimum 40 °C.
    - Fuel pressure 0.1 – 0.15kg/cm^2 at normal rpm.
    - RPM drop at ignition plug selection – less than 50 RPM.
    - RPM during engine testing on the ground:
    - Lower than 400 at slower RPM. At normal RPM, ±0kg/cm^2 approximately 1,200 RPM. At faster RPM, +0.14kg/cm^2, approximately 1,270 RPM.
    - Manifold pressure (normal) ± 0 kg/cm^2.
    - Manifold pressure (maximum) +0.14 kg/cm^2.
9. Other items to be items to be observed during engine testing are as follows:
    - After test running the engine at low RPM settings, operate the throttle lever several times to open/close to clear oiled spark plugs. Then run engine at mid RPM setting for 2 to 3 minutes. Now the aircraft is ready to take off.
    - Maximum manifold pressure is specified at +0.14kg/cm^2, but it is recommended to keep within ±0kg/cm^2.

Stopping

Operate throttle lever to below 800 RPM, then close fuel cock.

When engine sound differs, gradually lower RPM to a natural stop then set ignition switch to "Off" position.

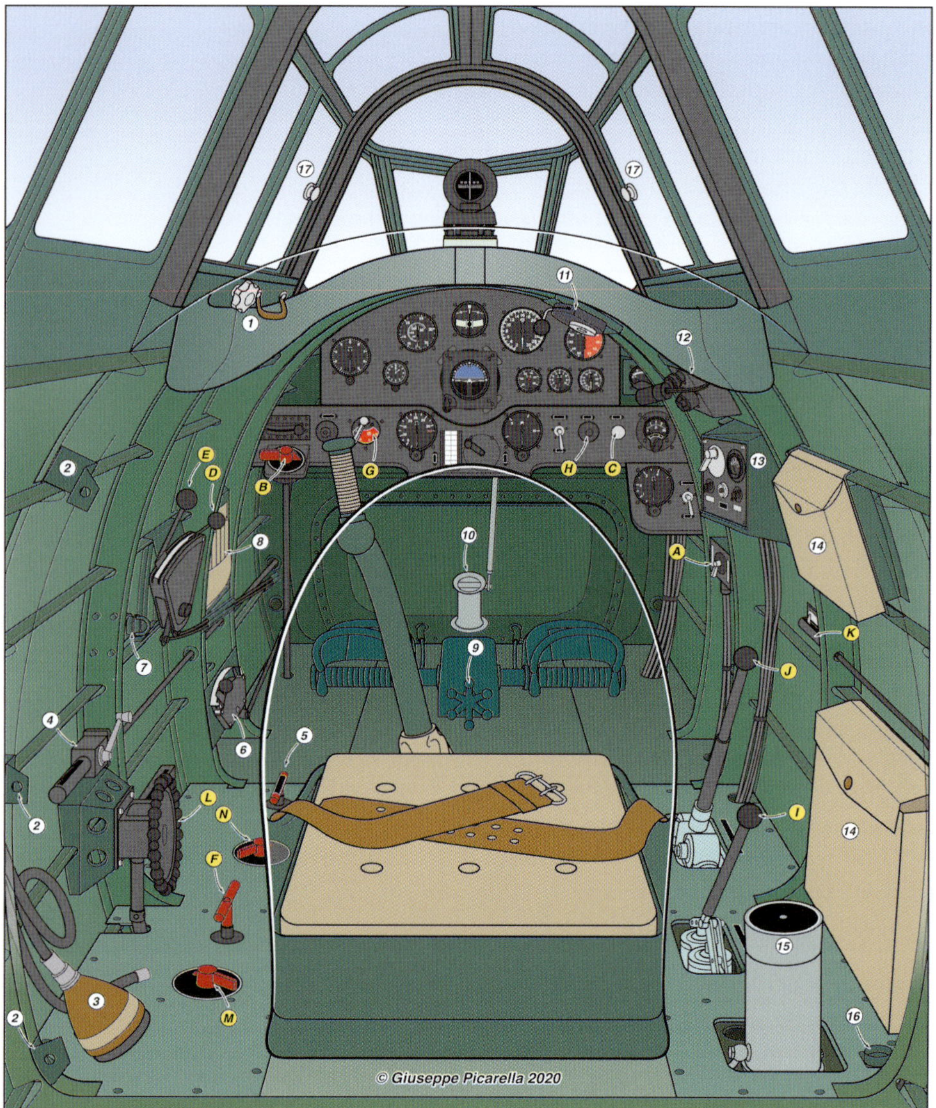

Mitsubishi Ki-15-II cockpit

Cockpit items additional to those highlighted within the Pilot's Operating Manual. For instrument panel details, see Chapter 4, **Technical description**.

1 Canopy lock and leather handle
2 "Additional fuel tank" mounts on FS.5
3 Gosport tube fittings
4 Cowl flap control and position indicator
5 Drop-tank jettison handle
6 Oil cooler shutter control
7 Pilot's boading step internal fittings
8 Pencil holder
9 Rudder pedal adjustment "spider"
10 Fresh air inlet
11 Carburettor dust screen control
12 Cockpit light and control
13 Electrical panel
14 Document case
15 Hydraulic reservoir
16 Radio power source electrical connector
17 Pilot's aft-sliding windows

If you wish to stop the engine by the ignition switch only, fully close throttle lever and after 1-2 minutes of running at minimum RPM set the ignition switch to "off". If the RPM is rather high, the engine may cough and backfire, causing harmful vibration to the airframe and engine. This must be avoided.

When the engine is to be idle for a long period of time, it should be wash-run before storage.

Chapter 2

Ground Taxiing

1. This aircraft has poor forward visibility! Therefore while taxiing on the ground, open the canopy and take care when taxiing around other aircraft and obstacles.
2. On muddy airfields, mud will clog wheel covers and can cause the aircraft to overturn.

In these operating conditions, wheel cover shall be removed for safely purposes, but the pilot should note that the maximum airspeed of this aircraft in level flight will be reduced by approximate 30km/h.

Chapter 3

Taking Off

Special attention shall to be paid to the following items during take-off.

1. This aircraft requires a fairly long take-off run. Always determine the best location for taking off at your airfield, with consideration to available length, surface conditions and prevailing wind direction.
2. When taking off with an excessive load or allowable full load and the runway length is considered short, use flap to reduce length of run. A flap setting of 15 – 20° down is recommended.
3. Set mixture control lever to take-off position during the climb and fly in level flight at full speed.
4. The length of a take-off run under normal loading conditions is approximately 400m and under. For fully loaded conditions allow for approximately 470m.
5. When increasing RPM the manifold pressure should read ±0kg/cm^2. If necessary, +0.14kg/cm2 is allowable, but this setting should be limited to 5 minutes, because excessive use of over boost will reduce the life of the engine.

Chapter 4

Control in the Air

Ascending and Descending

1. The main wheels leave ground at an indicated speed of approximately 150km/h. An indicated speed of approximately 240km/h is appropriate while climbing, but when the "additional fuel tank" is full to capacity, keep indicated airspeed at approximately 220km/h.
2. As the aircraft ascends manifold pressure rises. This is to be balanced periodically with use of the throttle lever.
3. The increase in speed shortly after take-off is rather slow, until the aircraft reaches around 50m AGL. Do not use excessively sharp climb angles.

4. Because forward visibility is poor, pay specific attention to other aircraft flying in your vicinity while climbing.
5. When flap is used for taking off, raise it at around 50m AGL, by placing the flap selector valve lever into the "up" position. It is unnecessary to use hydraulic hand-pump because air resistance retracts the flap as speed increases. Be aware that when the flap is retracted the aircraft will adopt a nose-down attitude. The heavier the aircraft the more pronounced this change in attitude becomes.
6. Properly trim elevators *(L)* for better longitudinal balancing.
7. Descent speed is approximately 270km/h indicated.

Level Flight

1. Level flight at the operational altitude is accomplished at around 0.3kg/cm^2 of manifold pressure, with an indicated airspeed of between 280 and 300 km/h.
2. When flying level at cruising speed, set mixture control lever at "cruising".
3. To maintain longitudinal balance during level flight, properly adjust elevator trim.
4. Do not open the canopies at airspeeds over 200km/h. If this action is necessary, reduce speed to 200km/h by lowering flap to approximately 20°.

Turning

1. It is easy to turn because of good control surface harmonization, but as turning becomes tighter, the reaction of elevator becomes heavier.
2. It is necessary to become accustomed to tight turns, as light vertigo may affect the pilot due to centrifugal forces.
3. Tight turn may cause the engine to run rough. Be aware that such manoeuvres may even cause it stop suddenly.
4. Spiral descents shall be done at 800–900 RPM and around 220km/h indicated air speed.
5. The aircraft can lose approximately 200m in altitude during a tight turn.

Low-speed flight

1. Shall be done with special attention paid to "rate of climb" indication.
2. Recommend altitude of 1,000m at approximately 900 RPM and approximately 200km/h indicated airspeed.

Side-slips

1. Shall be done at slow RPM according to general procedure.
2. Too much banking causes vibration in the airframe. Keep aircraft bank angle lower than 45°.

Chapter 5

Landing

1. Before the aircraft enters the 3rd turn [base leg] over the airfield, lower air speed to 200km/h then lower flap to approximately 20–30°. At end of the 4th turn [finals] lower flap fully upon determining that you are able reach the touchdown point. With flap extended never fly over 200km/h indicated air speed.
2. During descent air speed shall be approximately 170km/h. This will decrease to 150km/h on round-out depending on altitude. When aircraft is heavily loaded, monitor speed and take care not to stall.
3. It is easy to bring aircraft to touchdown, but remember it is dangerous to allow airspeed to drop below 140 km/h, as the aircraft will enter a stall and become uncontrollable.
4. The landing run is approximately 320m as standard. With use of brakes this can be reduced to approximately 230m.
5. When aircraft stops, retract flaps and begin taxiing.
6. Remember that the aircraft has poor visibility in the forward/downward direction. Make a note of potential obstacles both in the air and on ground before landing.
7. In the case of a "touch and go" [go-around] landing, be careful not to lose speed. Raise flap above 50m AGL and be careful of the "nose down" pitch angle associated with the loss of lift.
8. When the aircraft is fully loaded with fuel in the "additional fuel tank", land only after the fuel in "additional fuel tank" has been used, or after draining fuel out of the "additional fuel tank" during flight.

Chapter 6

High-altitude flight

1. When climbing to high altitude, care must be taken to monitor the running condition of engine under decreasing air pressures. Use the mixture control lever to keep manifold pressure indication ±0 kg/cm^2 and gradually open throttle.

2. Start to use mixture control lever when aircraft reaches around 2,000m and gradually open the mixture control while monitoring the engine RPM and sound. At cruising speed it is necessary to constantly adjust the mixture control according to altitude and weather condition. Increased use of the mixture control will also increase RPM. When RPM starts to fall it is at fully leaned out. It is not require to use mixture control for engine running over 0 kg/cm^2 during special tests.
3. When descending, take care that the cylinder-head temperature does not fall below 130° C. If the mixture control lever is closed, then the throttle lever should also be closed. Therefore when opening up the throttle again do not forget the mixture control.

Chapter 7

Controls while in flight

1. Fuel System

Since fuel tank is split into wing tank, fuselage tank and leading-edge tank (plus "additional fuel tank" if the aircraft is so equipped), selection of fuel tanks is up to the pilot's discretion. Be careful to watch fuel level gauges, which can malfunction frequently. Gauges, cocks and piping shall be inspected thoroughly before flight.

2. Warnings for use of "additional fuel tank"

1. The fuel hand-pump lever *(F)* is located on cockpit floor, to the left of pilot seat.
2. The fuel drain cock lever *(M)* is behind the hand pump. The fuel drain cock shall always be placed in "flow" position. Do not touch the fuel drain cock lever except when tank drainage is required.
3. The selector fuel cock lever *(N)* forward of hand pump is set at "forward tank" when fuel in "leading-edge tank " is to be used. When fuel in "additional fuel tank" is to be used, set fuel cock lever to "fuselage fuel tank". When both tanks are not in use, locate these levers in the "stop" position.
4. When draining fuel from the "additional fuel tank", position fuel cock lever *(N)* to "stop" position then position lever of drain cock *(M)* to "drain".
5. Fuel pressure is normally between 0.1 and 0.15 kg/cm^2

3. Oil System

Oil pressure is normally between 5–6 kg/cm^2. When engine is running at normal RPM and oil pressure indicates less than 3 kg/cm^2 then an inspection of the whole system is necessary.

Appropriate oil temperature is between 70–90° C and should never exceed 110°C.

Engine cylinder temperature

The maximum cylinder temperature is 260° C while climbing in summer.

It is normally 180°C in level flight at cruising speed.

Allowable cylinder temperature is 260°C, but care should be taken never to exceed 280°C, even for a short period.

Engine control:

Engine RPM is 2,100 at maximum power. Propeller pitch is adjusted to 2,100 RPM maximum when the carburettor opens fully at 4,300m of altitude.

Be aware that while 2,200 RPM is allowed, it should never be exceed even for a short period, just in case the aircraft dives when the load on the propeller is reduced.

When full-speed flight is attained near to maximum manifold pressure, set fuel control lever at the same position as full climb speed, as per taking off configuration.

Limit continuous high power engine run, at maximum manifold pressure, to 5 minutes.

Chapter 8

Emergency Landing

Follow the same procedure as a normal landing with flap. Be careful to maintain air speed of aircraft. Open canopy in preparation for overturn and fire hazards.

Chapter 6

Dimensions and Performance Figures

"Although the machine seems a robust job. The Heavenly Breeze after which it is called must be a pretty hearty built-in tail-wind because on only 550 hp the machine does not appear to have the performance which it has just achieved."

"The Heavenly Breeze" editorial in The Aeroplane, April 14th 1937.

Dimensions

While many of the basic dimensions for the *Babs* family are well known, certain figures pertaining to different models have simply been assumed and have remained unchallenged since the end of the war. The fact remains that it is impossible for the Ki-15-II, C5M1 and C5M2 to have been identical in length due to the different engine, cowling and spinner installations. The following list of "amended" figures is based on known dimensions and figures taken from the CAD drawings that the author produced for this book. As with the performance figures, these dimensions are offered in good faith.

Interestingly, Mitsubishi specifies the length of the *Kamikaze* as 8.49m (27ft 10 ¼in), with engineering drawings showing this dimension taken from the tip of the spinner dome, because the aircraft was not fitted with a "Hucks" type starter dog. It is therefore likely that the Ki-15-I would be 8.56m (28ft 1in) in length, as its production "Hucks" starter projected out from the front of the spinner by approximately 70mm (2 ¾ in). Ki-15-II drawings on the other hand include the "Hucks" starter within their measurements. Based on the development work that the Aircraft Engineering Dept. was generating for the Ki-46 engine and spinner installation, the estimated length of the Ki-15-III would have been in the region of 8.815m (28ft 11in).

With regards wingspan, the 12m figure issued on general arrangement drawings seems to have been generated with reference to the engineering drawings of the centre wing section and outboard wing sections, which were 2.8m and 4.6m (x2) respectively. While these dimensions are accurate in individual "true" plan form, no consideration was given to the 8° dihedral of the outboard wing panels, which would shorten the assembled wingspan by 90mm, producing a figure closer to 11.91m (39ft 1in).

Given that the dimensions and performance figures for the Ki-15-I would seem to be based on pre-war data, probably issued specifically in support of the *Kamikaze* flight, it is entirely possible that the weight and loading figures for production Ki-15-I were in fact lower than the figures listed above. This is based on the fact that the fuel load of the *Kamikaze* was substantially greater than the capacities of the Ki-15-I **initial, intermediate** and **standard** aircraft.

Babs **dimensions, weights and loading – amended figures shown in bold**

Model/ Measurement	Ki-15-I	*"Kamikaze"*	Ki-15-II	C5M1*	C5M2*	Ki-15-III
Span	**11.91m 39ft 1in**	**11.91m 39ft 1in**	**11.91m 39ft 1in**	**11.91m 39ft 1in**	**11.91m 39ft 1in**	**11.91m 39ft 1in**
Length	**8.56m 28ft 1in**	8.49m 27ft 10 ¼in	**8.74m 28ft 8 3/16in**	**8.46m 27ft 9 1/8in**	**8.645m 28ft 4 3/8in**	**8.815m 28ft 11in**
Horizontal height**	3.34m 10ft 11 ½in	3.34m 10ft 11 ½in	3.34m 10ft 11 ½in	**3.465m 11ft 4 3/8in**	**3.71m 11ft 7 5/8in**	3.34m 10ft 11 ½in

Model/ Measurement	Ki-15-I	*"Kamikaze"*	Ki-15-II	C5M1*	C5M2*	Ki-15-III
Three-point height	3.3m 10ft 10in	3.3m 10ft 10in	3.365m 11ft 7in	3.15m 9ft 10 ¾in	3.1m 9ft 10 ½in	3.3m 10ft 10in
Wing area	20.36sq/m 219.152sq/ft	20.36sq/m 219.152sq/ft	20.36sq/m 219.152sq/ft	20.36sq/m 219.152sq/ft	20.36sq/m 219.152sq/ft	20.36sq/m 219.152sq/ft
Empty weight	1.399kg 3,084 lb	1.399kg 3,084 lb	1.592kg 3,51 lb	1.605kg 3,535 lb	1.715kg 3,781 lb	– –
Loaded weight	2,033kg 4,482 lb	2,033kg 4,482 lb	2,189kg 4,826 lb	2,197 kg 4,833 lb	2,345 kg 5,170 lb	– –
MTOW weight	2,300kg 5,071 lb	2,300kg 5,071 lb	2,481kg 5,470 lb	– –	– –	– –
Wing loading	99.9kg/sq/m 20.5 lb/sq/ft	99.9kg/sq/m 20.5 lb/sq/ft	107.5 kg/ sq/m 22 lb/sq/ft	107.9 kg/sq/m 22.1 lb/sq/ft	115.2 kg/sq/m 23.6 lb/sq/ft	– –
Power loading	3.2kg/hp 7lb/hp	3.2kg/hp 7lb/hp	2.6kg/hp 5.7lb/hp	2.8kg/hp 6.2lb/hp	2.5kg/hp 5.5lb/hp	– –

* C5M1 and C5M2 *version 2*

** Height figures seem to be based on loaded weight, with the oleo compressed.

Performance figures

Calculating the missing performance figures of the different *Babs* aircraft is a difficult process because we do not know how the original figures were produced. For example, with regards ranges figures, how were these generated? Were they actual proven distances established by Mitsubishi, Army or Navy testing, or were they calculated on fuel capacity and optimal fuel-consumption? Were these figures produced to demonstrate a maximum possible range, or were they based on actual combat mission profiles, with a maximum speed segment over the target, in order to show the maximum range of a mission? As we do not know the maximum, average and long-range cruise fuel-consumption rates for the various engines, it is impossible to produce 100% accurate figures, so the following information represents an educated guess. Before we can begin to calculate these figures we have to modify the "*Babs* performance figures" table to include each specific Ki-15-I model, so that we can distinguish between **initial, intermediate** and **standard** fuel systems, plus the highly modified *Kamikaze* aircraft. Next, we can include the known cruise speed figure of 280-300km/h, as listed in the captured Ki-15-II manual. For calculation purposes we will work with an average cruise speed of 290k/h (180mph).

In order to produce range figures we need to work out average fuel-consumption for each engine type. A simple rule of thumb for mid-sized radial engines is to divide the engine's rated horsepower (hp) by 20. In the case of the Ha-8 engine, 1/20th of 550hp equals 27.5. This means that approximately 27.5 Imperial gallons (Imperial gals) or 125 litres per hour (lph) would be consumed. This figure can then be divided by the fuel capacity of the aircraft, which in the case of the Ki-15-I *early model* with the **initial** fuel system (without wing leading edge fuel tanks or additional fuel tank) is 599 lt. This gives an endurance (or time in the air) of 4.8 hours. Cruising at a speed of 199mph for 4.8 hours gives a basic range of 1,537km (955mile). It should be noted that there is a big difference between average fuel-consumption figures and running the engine lean (at its lowest fuel-consumption rates), as we shall see.

The "amended" range figure for the *Kamikaze* comes out at 2,377km (1,477miles), which is 99% of the official stated figures – 2,400km (1,491miles). Given the basic 1/20th hp rule of thumb and fuel capacity (850 lt), it would seem to indicate that the most often quoted Mitsubishi performance figures refer specifically to *Kamikaze*, NOT the military variants of the Ki-15-I. Even so, *Kamikaze* would have needed to lean out its fuel-consumption from 125 lph down to no more than 114 lph for one of the long distance legs of the journey. It should also be remembered that *Kamikaze* also sported a highly lacquered finish, which would have greatly reduced drag when compared to a standard finish Ki-15 airframe.

With the wing leading edge tanks of the **intermediate** fuel system and the "additional fuel tank" of the **standard** fuel system, the modified range of the Ki-15-I *late model* is calculated to be in the region of 1,889km (1,174miles) and 2,102km (1,306miles) respectively. These figures are supported by known Ki-15-I flights over China, which were in excess of 1,700km (1,056miles). It should also be remembered that these distances were straight-line distance, between two known locations (a departure airfield and a target airfield or city), so we have to assume that the aircraft "loitered" over the target in order to perform its job. In addition to this, a fuel reserve would have been required for detours, enemy action, bad weather, plus a small safety margin, etc. If we therefore add 30 minutes flight time at maximum speed (255km) and 30 minutes at cruise speed (145km), the total range figure for a 1,700km (1,056miles)

An original Mitsubishi engineering drawing for the Ki-15-I.

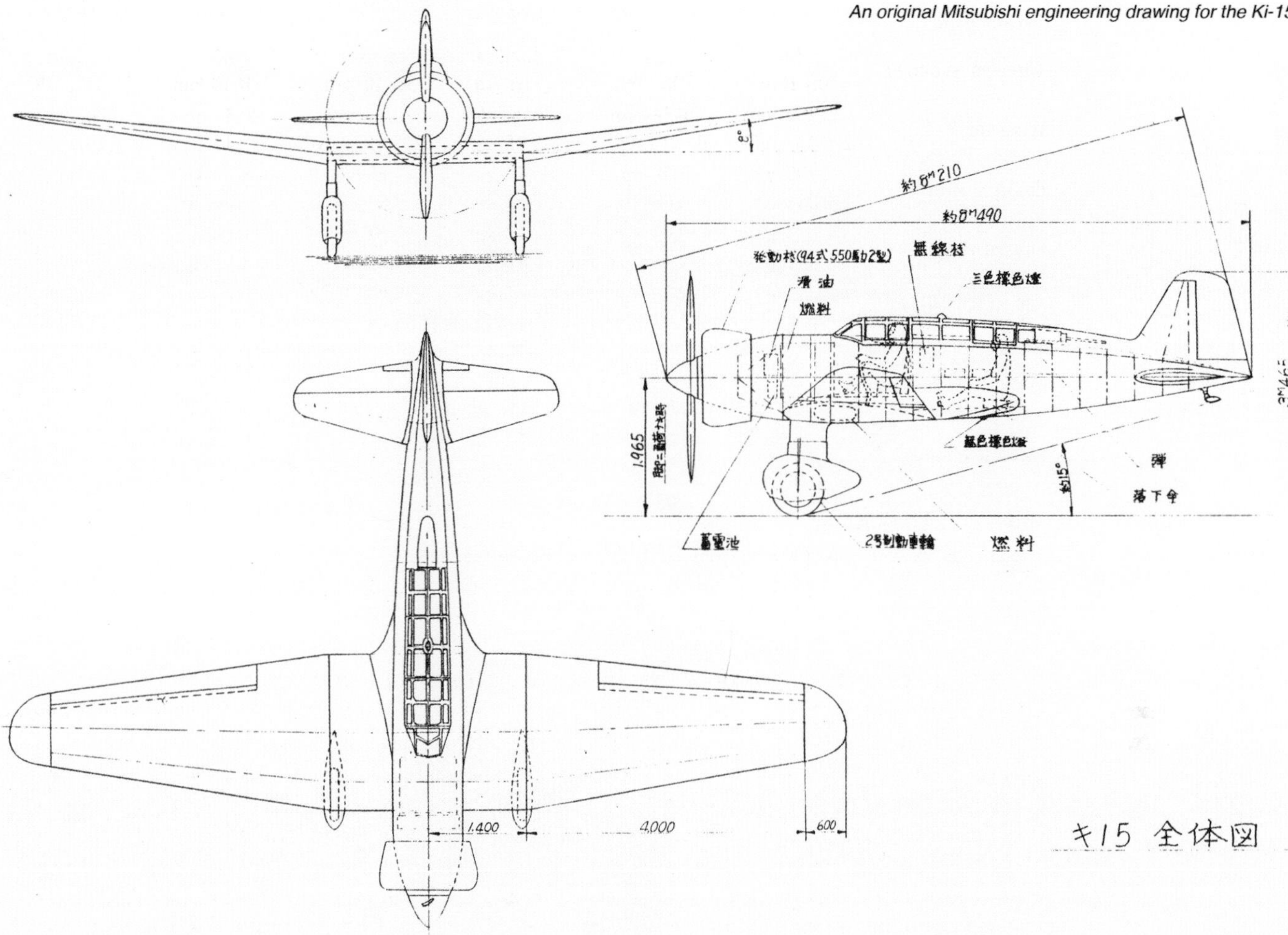

Mitsubishi Ki-15 prototype

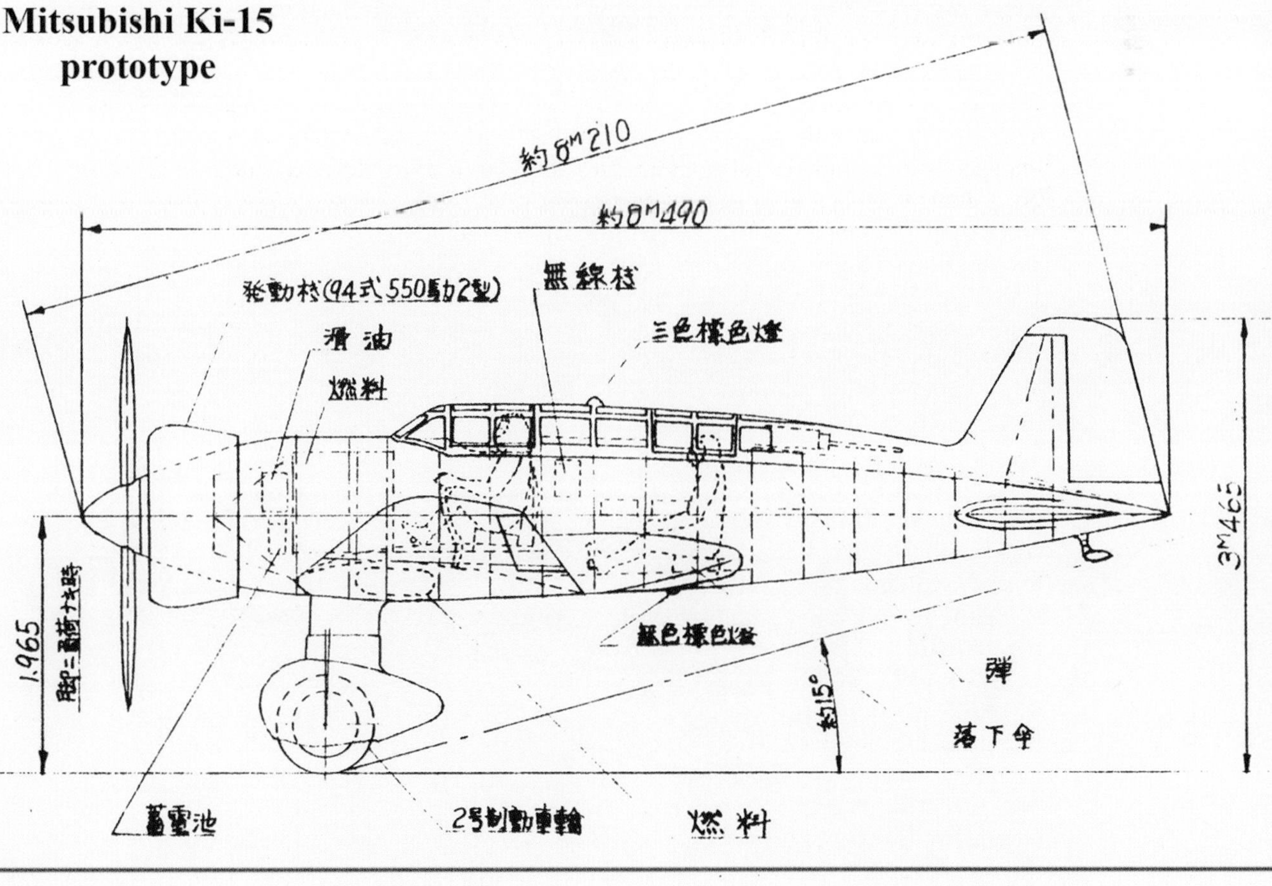

An original Mitsubishi engineering drawing for the Ki-15-II.

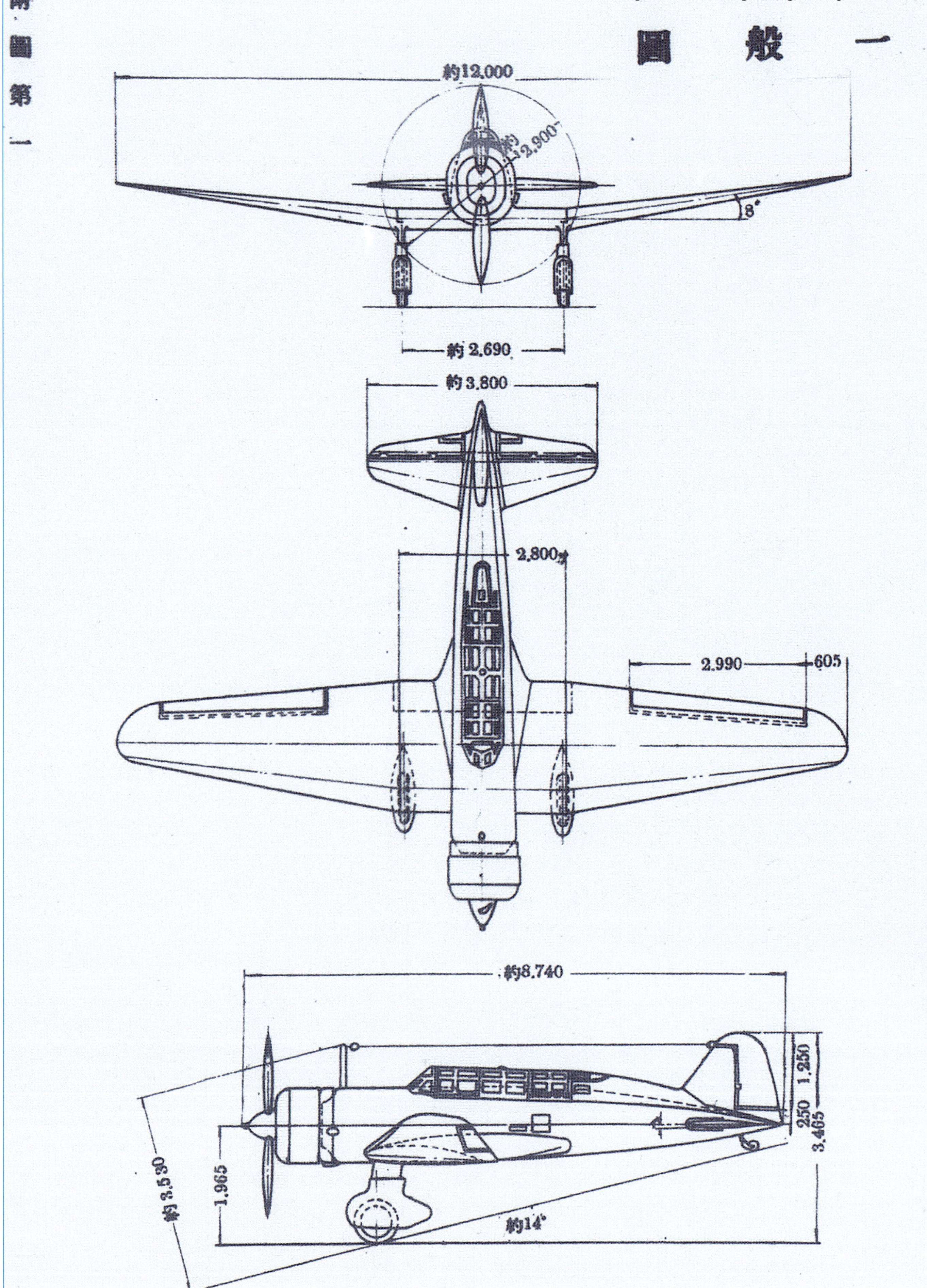

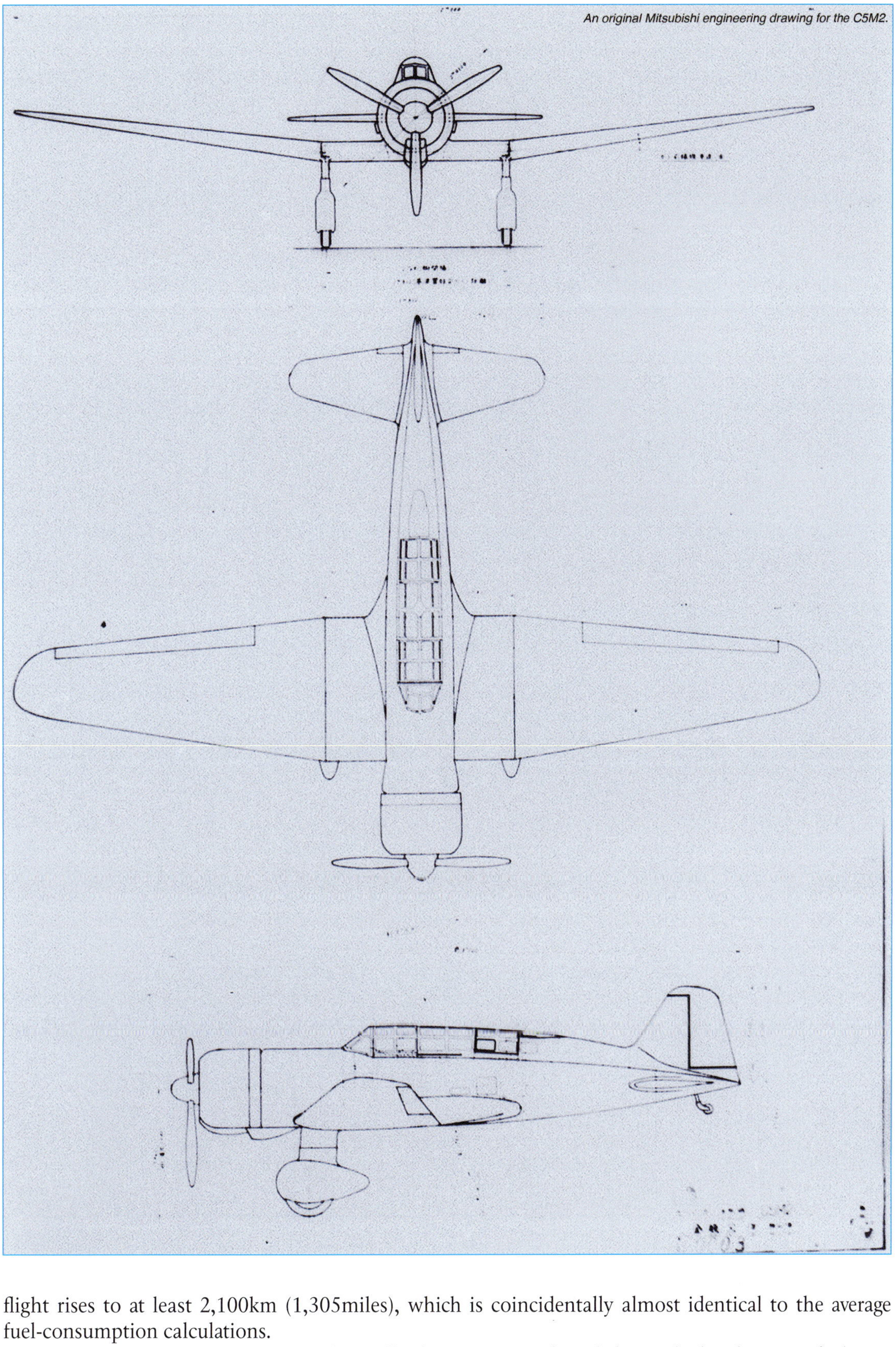

An original Mitsubishi engineering drawing for the C5M2.

flight rises to at least 2,100km (1,305miles), which is coincidentally almost identical to the average fuel-consumption calculations.

The Ki-15-II and the C5M1 were basically the same aircraft and their calculated average fuel-consumption of 204 lph and 195 lph respectively, initially works out to be approximately 63% higher than the Ki-15-I. This increase though does not account for the low quoted range figure of 1,167km (725miles or 630nm), which is barely half the range of the *late model* Ki-15-I! This range figure is also problematic because we know that the C5M1 was operated on missions in excess of 1,850km (1,150miles) over China. What is more, these missions refer to straight-line distance between two locations, so we have to also assume "loiter" time, detours and a fuel reserves were included on top of the basic range figure. If we once again add 30 minutes at maximum speed 468kp/h (291mph) and 30 minutes at cruise speed 284kp/h (176mph), we increase the range by 376km (234miles), which brings the maximum range of the Ki-15-II and C5M1 up to at least 2,226km (1,383miles). If we consider the low quoted figure to be the standard range, the inclusion of a drop-tank would increase the range to 1,400km (870miles), which is lower than that of the prototype Ki-15 with its 599litres fuel capacity! So, is it possible that this figure refers to a "radius of operations", rather than range? If we double the quoted figure of 1,167km (725miles) then a range figure of 2,332km (1,450miles) is produced, which is within 5% of our estimated figure.

Our calculated range figures (2,226km) would indicate that the long-range cruise lean fuel-consumption (for the Ha-26-I/*Zuisei* 12 engine) was at least 121 lph, which is credible. This lean fuel-consumption figure is further supported by the Kawanishi Type-94 Reconnaissance Seaplane, E7K2 or *Alf*, which operated its *Zuisei* 11 engine down to 100 lph or less. If we take an average of these figures (110 lph) then the range of the C5M1 could easily have been in the region of 2,478km (1,540miles), based on its fuel capacity of 963 lt.

Determining the range of the C5M2 is more problematic than any of the other *Babs* airframes due to the extreme lean-cruise capabilities of the *Sakae 12*/NK1C engine. Using the 1/20th average fuel-consumption calculation, a figure of 216 lph (47.5 Imperial gals or 57 US gallons) is produced. Given that the maximum fuel-consumption rate (at maximum rated power) was 345 lph (76 Imperial gals or 91.14 US gallons), then 216 lph represents approximately 62% of that figure, which seem reasonable for similar sized engines of the day. This fuel-consumption rate would have given the C5M2 a range of approximately 1,265km (786miles) or 1,508km (937miles) with drop tank. Once again, the calculated figures are in excess of the official figures 1,112km (691miles), so could this official figure also refer to a "radius of operations"? Alternatively, if we calculate the range of the aircraft (without drop-tank) at full speed and maximum rated power, we get a range of 1,156km (718miles) with an endurance of 2.37hours. It is impossible to say if this forms the basis for the range figure, but it is unlikely as it still exceeds the official figure by a healthy margin.

Where the *Sakae 12*/NK1C engine differed from most other engines in service at that time was in its ability to operate at ultra-lean fuel-consumptions rates, which were documented as low as 62 litres (13.65 Imperial gallons or 16.4 US Gallons) per hour, or just 17.9% of its maximum fuel-consumption rate!

In order to guestimate a set of range figures for the C5M2, we must make a few assumptions. Firstly we need to decide on a cruising speed, which should logically fall somewhere in between that of the C5M1 and the A6M2. We will use 306km/h (190mph or 156kt) for our calculations, but it is important to remember that the C5M2 and A6M2 were often operated in unison during long-range missions, and while the lower cruising speed could have extended the range of the C5M2, the A6M2 had the smaller fuel capacity, so it is likely that the fighters dictated their own higher cruise speed of 333km/h (207mph or 180kt) during such operations.

Secondly we need to decide on the fuel-consumption of the *Sakae 12*/NK1C engine in relation to the C5M2 airframe. Because the engine, propeller and cowling installation, and their relative locations, are practically identical on the C5M2 and A6M2, we will assume that the performance of the engine was identical on both aircraft. Likewise, the general layout of both aircraft was almost identical in dimension and weight, so we have to assume that any difference in performance is based on increased aerodynamic drag, from the increased wetted area of the fuselage, a less efficient aerofoil section and the fixed undercarriage, etc.

A6M2/C5M2 airframe comparison figures

Aircraft/ Performance	Span	Length	Empty weight	Loaded weight	Wing area	Fuel capacity + drop-tank
A6M2	12m 39ft 4 7/16in	9.06m 29ft 8 11/16 in	1,680kg 3,704 lb	2,410kg 5,313 lb	22.44sq/m 241.541sq/ft	535 litres + 865 litres
C5M2	11.91m 39ft 1in	8.645m 28ft 4 3/8in	1.715kg 3,781 lb	2,345 kg 5,170 lb	20.36sq/m 219.152sq/ft	819 litres + 979 litres

Airframe drag is not constant, it is effected by many variables including an object's size, shape, speed, surface area, air pressure and lift, etc., all interlinked and beyond the scope of this description. We do know that the maximum speed of the C5M2 was approximately 10% slower than the A6M2, so for arguments sake lets make the very simplistic assumption that the C5M2 airframe was also 10% less aerodynamically efficient than the A6M2. By increasing the ultra-lean fuel-consumption rate by 10%, this figure rises to 70 lph, which can be divided by the internal fuel capacity of 819 litres, or 979 litres with a drop tank. This gives us an estimated endurance figure of 11.7hours and 14hours respectively, which we can multiply by the cruise speed (306km/h), giving the C5M2 a theoretical range of 3,580km (2,224miles) and 4,284km (2,662miles) respectively. Obviously such figures do not take into account fuel-consumption for maximum power take-off, climb to altitude at full weight, or maximum speed over the target. So lets assume 15 minutes of maximum power for take-off, climb and landing, plus 30 minutes at maximum power over the target area. The combined 45 minutes at maximum rated power would use 260 litres (57 Imperial gallons), leaving the aircraft with 560 litres and 720 litres respectively for ultra-lean cruising. This takes the endurance down to 8hours and 10.3hours, producing a range of 2,448km (1,521miles) and 3,152km (1,958miles) respectively. To this figure we need to add back an additional 100km (61miles) to account for the climb phase, detours, enemy action, bad weather etc., which gives a total of 2,548km (1,583miles) and 3,252km (2,021miles) respectively.

While some may gasp at a potential range of 3,252km, which is 300% above the officially quoted C5M2 figure (1,102km), we know for certain that the C5M2 was used operationally on missions of 8hours and 25minutes endurance, over straight-line distances in excess of 2,606km. This *actual* figure is in excess of our calculated internal fuel range (2,548km), even without the inclusion of "loiter" time over the target, detours and a fuel reserve. See Chapter 1, **Brothers in arms**.

The only data we have for the Ki-15-III is the maximum speed attained during flight-testing and the power output of the Mitsubishi Ha-102 engine. If we assume a cruise speed of approximately 300kp/h (185mph) and an average fuel-consumption of 52.3 Imperial gallons (238 lph), this gives us standard range of 1,011km (628miles), or 1,275km (792miles) with a 208 lt drop-tank. Given the fact that the lean fuel-consumption rate for the *Sakae 12*/NK1C engine was approximately 32% below its calculated average fuel consumption figure, is it safe to assume that the later Ha-102 engine was also capable operating on similar lean settings? If we use a conservative 40% figure to calculate the lean fuel-consumption rate, we arrive at 95.2 litres (21 Imperial gallons) per hour. This would give the Ki-15-III potential range in excess of 2,529km (1,571miles) and 3,180km (1,976miles) respectively.

Babs performance figures – amended figures shown in bold

Model/ Performance	Ki-15-1 *early model* Initial	*"Kamikaze"*	Ki-15-I *late model* Intermediate	Ki-15-I *late model* Standard	Ki-15-II	C5M1	C5M2	Ki-15-III
Max speed	480km/h 298mph	480km/h 298mph	480km/h 298mph	480km/h 298mph	510km/h 317mph	468km/h 291mph 253kt	487km/h 303mph 263kt	530km/h 329mph
Cruise Speed	320km/h 199mph	320km/h 199mph	320km/h 199mph	320km/h 199mph	**290km/h 180mph**	**290km/h 180mph 156kt**	**306km/h 190mph 165kt**	**300km/h 186mph**
Time to altitude	–	–	–	5,000m (16,404ft) 8min 27sec	5,000m (16,404ft) 6min 49sec	3,000m (9,843ft) 4min 51sec	3,000m (9,843ft) 3min 58sec	–
Service Ceiling	–	–	–	11,400m (37,402ft)	–	8,230m (27,001ft)	9,580m (31,430ft)	–
Fuel capacity + drop tank	599litres Not fitted	850 litres Not fitted	736 litres Not fitted	822 litres Not fitted	803 litres 1,011 litres	803 litres 963 litres	819 litres 979 litres	803 litres 1,011 litres
Average fuel-consumption Imperial gallons/litres Ultra-low cruise	**27.5 Igph 125 lph**	**27.5 Igph 125 lph** * **25 Igph 114 lph**	**27.5 Igph 125 lph**	**27.5 Igph 125 lph**	**45 Igph 204 lph** ** **24.2 Igph 110 lph**	**43 Igph 195 lph** ** **24.2 Igph 110 lph**	**47 Igph 213 lph** *** **15.4 Igph 70 lph**	**52.5 Igph 238 lph** **** **21 Igph 95.2 lph**
Average fuel consumption endurance + drop tank	4.8hrs Not fitted	7.43hrs Not fitted	5.88hrs Not fitted	6.57hrs Not fitted	3.93hrs 4.96hrs	4.1hrs 4.94hrs	8hrs 10.3hrs	3.37hrs 4.25hrs
Range + drop tank	**1,537km 955miles**	Quoted range 2,400km 1,491miles	**1,884km 1,171miles**	Quoted range 2,400km 1,491miles **Document range in excess of 2,102km 1,306miles**	**2,548km 1,583miles** **3,252km 2,021miles** **Document range in excess of 2,226km 1,383miles**	Quoted range 1,167km 725miles 630nm **Document range in excess of 2,226km 1,383miles 1,202nm**	Quoted range 1,102km 691miles 600nm **Document range in excess of 2,500km 1,553miles 1,350nm** **3,200km 1,988miles 1,727nm**	**At least 1,011km 628miles + 1,275km 792miles** **** **2,529km 1,571miles + 3,180km 1,976miles**

* Kamikaze calculated fuel-consumption based on 114 lph, but it is likely that the actual figure was below 70 lph.

** Ki-15-II/C5M1 calculated fuel-consumption based on 110 lph, but it is likely that the actual figure was in the region of 80 lph.

*** C5M2 calculated fuel-consumption based on 70 lph.

**** Ki-15-III calculated fuel-consumption based on 95.2 lph, but it is likely that the actual figure was in the region of 80 lph.

Chapter 7

Production figures and construction numbers

"In 1936, the Japanese Army permitted the display, in Europe, of the Kamikaze, a small single-engined reconnaissance plane, prototype of the [Tachikawa Ki-36] Ida...."
The United States Strategic Bombing Survey
Mitsubishi Heavy Industries, Ltd. Corporation Report No.1.

As with all Japanese aircraft production figures, determining exact numbers can be a veritable minefield. In addition to the very obvious fact that many of the documents pertaining to such matters were ordered destroyed by the Japanese military prior to the occupation, the USAAF's own bombing campaigns had been so effective that many important documents were destroyed, burned or damaged before the Japanese could fulfil their own orders.

Clarification of the figures pertaining to the Ki-15, *Karigane* and C5M family of aircraft is further complicated by the fact that three different totals have been put forwards since 1947, in the following publications:

- USSBS Corporation Report No.1, Mitsubishi Heavy Industries, LTD., – June 1947.
- Encyclopedia of Japanese Aircraft 1900–1945, Volume 1, Mitsubishi, Shuppan-Kyodosha., – November 1958.
- Japanese Aircraft of the Pacific War, by René Francillon. Putnam Aeronautical Books., – 1970.

Published production figures

USSBS Corporation Report No.1	Encyclopedia of Japanese Aircraft	Japanese Aircraft of the Pacific War
501	437	439

Note: These figures do not include the universally accepted total of 50 C5M Babs airframes built for the Navy.

Numbers, numbers and more numbers....

In order to better understand the possible variation of 64 aircraft, we need to look more closely at the figures in each of these publications.

USSBS Corporation Report No.1 – June 1947

The main source of data for most of Japan's military manufacturing activities comes from the post-war ***United States Strategic Bombing Survey*** or USSBS, which was established by the then US Secretary of War, Henry L. Stimson, on November 3rd 1944, under the directive of President Roosevelt. The aim of the survey was to conduct an impartial and expert study into the effects of aerial attacks on Germany, which were to be used in connection with increasing air attacks on Japan. The study defined its aim as one of evaluating:

"... the importance and potentialities of air power as a military strategy for planning future development of United States armed forces and for determining future economic policies with respect to national defence."

In effect, the survey was established to determine if large-scale aerial bombing campaigns and the intelligence based activities surrounding this new form of warfare was working effectively and whether they could be improved and perfected. To this end, over 200 in-depth reports were produced for the European campaign, and in order to establish as complete a picture as possible, President Harry S. Truman requested, on August 15th 1945, that a similar survey be initiated looking into the air attacks against Japan. From its headquarters in Tokyo and sub-offices in Hiroshima, Nagasaki, Nagoya and Osaka, 300 civilian and 850 military personal of the USSBS began to send out mobile teams to:

"... *secure reasonably accurate statistics on Japan's economy and war production, plant by plant, and industry by industry.*"

In addition to talking to Japanese production line managers, engineering teams and personnel, the survey also interrogated more than 700 military, governmental and industrial officials in the course of the 3-year survey period. Based on interrogations and surviving documentation, the production statistics for companies such as Mitsubishi were traced back as far as 1930, but in attempting to produce such a mammoth undertaking, various technical and numerical errors found their way into these reports, and in some cases it would seem that estimates and possibly official production orders were interpreted as actual production figures, especially for those programs that originated in the mid 1930s, as demonstrated by the official USSBS "*Ida*" quotation at the head of this chapter.

Typical C/n stencil found on aircraft C/181. The other numbers were applied to photograph in order to identify components in the Soviet report. (NII VVS via Y. Svoyski)

With regards the *Babs*, we know that Army Ki-15s and *Karigane* aircraft were only built at two of Mitsubishi's production facilities – No.1 and No.5 Airframe works.

Mitsubishi No.1 Airframe Works.

Mitsubishi's No.1 Airframe Works operated as the design, research and development facility within the Mitsubishi Aircraft Works at Oe-machi, Nagoya. From its inception in 1921, the Works was responsible for designing, assembling and test flying almost all of Mitsubishi's prototype aircraft, before dispersal plans and air attacks affected the facility.

Airframe production figures by No.1 Airframe Works were understandably small, due to the handcrafted nature and pre-production jig assemblies used for such prototype airframes. Typically output for the No.1 Airframe Works did not exceed more than 1 or 2 airframes per month and delays due to design changes were common. For this reason specific production figures for No.1 Works are not known for the period of 1930-42. It is interesting to note, though, that the figures for No.5 Airframe Works seem to include one Ki-15 prototype, which was produced in 1935 and two in 1936, which most likely represents the three prototypes built by the No.1 Airframe Works.

Mitsubishi No.5 Airframe Works.

Mitsubishi's No.5 Airframe Works also formed part of the Oe-machi facility located on the southern outskirts of Nagoya. Originally established in 1920 for the exclusive purpose of manufacturing airframes for the Army, the facility expanded to include a further six facilities in the local area. These new manufacturing sites supplied assemblies and components to Oe-machi until the earthquake of December 7th 1944. Primarily the No.5 Airframe Works produced Ki-15, Ki-21, Ki-30, Ki-46, Ki-51, Ki-57, Ki-67 and Ki-83 airframes. Production figures for reconnaissance aircraft built at No.5 Airframe Works were included within Appendix F and G of the *USSBS Corporation Report No.1*.

"Appendix F – Aircraft Production (1930-38) Mitsubishi No.5 Works"

Year/ Model	*1930*	*1931*	*1932*	*1933*	*1934*	*1935*	*1936*	*1937*	*1938*	*Totals*
Type-92	*3*	*6*	*74*	*74*	-	-	-	-	-	*157*
Ki-15 "Babs"	-	-	-	-	-	*1*	*2*	*80*	*41*	*124*
Ki-51 "Sonia"	-	-	-	-	-	-	-	-	*3*	*3*
Ki-46 "Dinah"	-	-	-	-	-	-	-	-	*2*	*2*
Totals	*3*	*6*	*74*	*74*	-	*1*	*2*	*80*	*46*	*286*

Note: The Army and the USSBS considered the Ki-51 as a reconnaissance aircraft.

"Appendix G – Aircraft Production, Mitsubishi No.5 Airframe Works (1939-45)"

Year/ Model	*1939*	*1940*	*1941*	*1942*	*1943*	*1944*	*1945*	*Totals*
Ki-51 "Sonia"	*11*	*61*	*2*	*396*	*611*	*177*	-	***1,258***
Ki-15 "Babs"	*137*	*240*	-	-	-	-	-	***377***
Ki-46 "Dinah"	*3*	*20*	*85*	*242*	*479*	*313*	-	***1,142***
Totals	***151***	***321***	***87***	***638***	***1,090***	***490***		***2,777***

These tables produce a combined production total of 501 Ki-15 airframes, which is substantially different from the other two published figures. What is immediately obvious about these figures is the high production total of 80 aircraft in 1937. This is an enormous jump from 2 aircraft in 1936, followed by a similarly strange fall in production in 1938, at a time when the war in China begins to increase in intensity and civilian *Karigane* airframes were recalled into Army service to support the small number of operational Ki-15s. So how do we explain this high production figure? Well, we know from documentation that only four *Karigane* aircraft were built on the No.5 Airframe Works production lines during 1937 and 1938, so these could not account for the increase in production line output. And the first 10 C5M *Babs* airframes built for the Navy were not released from the production line until early 1939, so what could be responsible for the inflated 1937 production figure? The answer is easy to determine if we look more closely at the general document, because within *USSBS Corporation Report No.1* there are numerous accounting irregularities and obvious mistakes. The complete list of production figures shown within Appendix F included 269 Kawasaki Army Type-99 Twin-engined Light Bomber (Ki-48) *Lily* airframes, built between 1936 and 1938. No such airframes were ever manufactured or even assembled by Mitsubishi, and in addition to listing these erroneous Ki-48 production figures; they were also incorrectly collated to produce a combined figure of 369 aircraft in the totals column, not 269! Given these simple errors, it is most likely that the Ki-15 production figure of 80 aircraft listed for 1937 was a typographic or translation mistake. It's not difficult to see how the number 18 could be mistaken for 80, when somebody is dictating notes to a secretary. By transposing the numbers 18 for 80, the figure in *USSBS Corporation Report No.1*, is reduced from 501 aircraft down to 439 – a total that counts the 1st prototype in both the 1935 and 1936 fiscal year! And since the 2nd (C/n1502) and 3rd (C/n1503) airframes were initially built as Army aircraft, before being released to Asahi Shimbun, it seems that these were counted in both sets of figures. Removing these two airframes reduces the Ki-15 production total down to 437 Army airframes.

It should also be pointed out that the two Ki-15-III prototypes do not increase production totals, because they were converted from two existing Ki-15-II airframes.

Army fiscal year orders

All equipment procured by the Army was purchased as part of yearly orders, and for the Ki-15 these production orders covered 1935 through 1940. Each order fell into a specific fiscal year, running from the beginning of April to the end of March the following year. It can be seen that the fiscal year orders, between each April and March period, match the actual production runs, except for the first two aircraft listed in Appendix F of the *USSBS Corporation Report No.1 1*, which accounts for the difference between fiscal year and actual production numbers. In addition to this, if we compare the fiscal orders with the calendar year production figures, we see that 18 aircraft were produced in 1937, not 80, so the theory of a typographic or translation error concerning this figure is vindicated.

Ki-15 production figures – Encyclopedia of Japanese Aircraft 1900–1945

Year	*1936*	*1937*	*1938*	*1939*	*1940*	*1941*	*Total*
Army fiscal year orders	1	29	52	175	180	0	437

Encyclopedia of Japanese Aircraft 1900–1945, Volume 1, Mitsubishi

The ***Encyclopedia of Japanese Aircraft 1900-1945*** was a landmark series of eight volumes, covering the entire history of Japan's aircraft industry. Published between 1958 and 1981, this series detailed the history of every aircraft manufacturer and every known aircraft project in Japan.

The Ki-15 production figures quoted within Volume 1 (Mitsubishi) of the Encyclopaedia match the Army's fiscal year order (437) as listed above, rather than the figure of 439. So why is this?

Given that the 1st prototype (C/n1501) was ordered in July 1935, with a predicted completion date falling in 1936, this aircraft order correctly falls into the 1936 fiscal year. We can see from the completion date of C/n1501 (late April 1936) that construction of the aircraft took nine months to complete, whereas the completion date of the 2nd prototype C/n1502 (March 1937) was 11 months after that of C/n1501. This would indicate that the two prototypes were not constructed in parallel and as such C/n1502 was probably included in the 1937 fiscal year order of 29 aircraft. It should be remembered that while the Ki-15 was an experimental aircraft, its specialized Command Reconnaissance specification was totally unsolicited by the Army and the 1st prototype was probably intended to either prove or disprove the theory, as proposed by Capt. Fujita. As such, if the 1st prototype had been an abject failure, unable to achieve, in the opinion of some, the somewhat unrealistic performance capabilities that had been predicted, then the program may have been terminated outright, and the 2nd prototype would have been cancelled. But the 1st prototype performed beyond all expectations and construction of the 2nd prototype was probably initiated during the autumn of 1936, to complete the Army's original order for two aircraft. At that point in time though, Asahi Shimbun made a request for two aircraft, to participate in their planned Tokyo to London flight, and to the surprise of all involved, the Army agreed to this highly unusual request, as they were probably still unsure about what Command Reconnaissance aircraft could offer them. As Asahi Shimbun's purchase of C/n1502 and C/n1503 was a private venture, falling outside of the Army's 1937 fiscal year order, it is likely that two additional Ki-15 airframes were simply added to the production run, in order for Mitsubishi to fulfil the fiscal order for 29 aircraft, and the two *Karigane* airframes were therefore not included in the fiscal order figures.

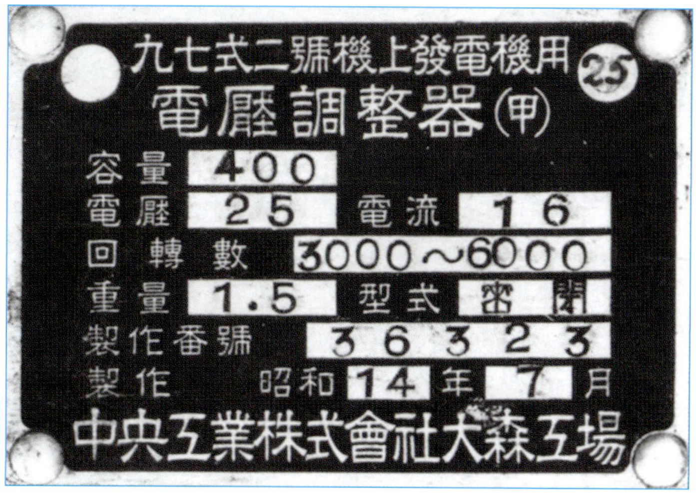

Electrical generator tag with a Japanese calendrical era date of Showa 14 – 7 (1939–July) production date. (NII VVS via Y. Svoyski)

The inclusion of these two civilian aircraft, at the beginning of the Ki-15 production run, would bring the total number of airframes produced at No.5 Airframe Works up to 439. This would seem to be the figure quoted within René Francillon's significant 1970 book.

Possibly more aircraft?

While we can trace all of the Army's Ki 15 fiscal orders through Appendix F and G of *USSBS Corporation Report No.1*, a small note in the same document would seem to indicate that at least eight of the airframes were not included in official production totals. Evidence for an increase in production numbers is found in Appendix G of No.5 Airframe Works report, which includes a footnote that identifies the actual production figure as 188 Ki-15s built: *"For the period April 1940 to March 1941"*.

This figure is at odds with the official figure of 180 Ki-15 airframes for that period, and if we add up the individual monthly production figures for Army Ki-15s, built between April 1940 and March 1941, the total comes to 180 aircraft, which matches the fiscal year order. This official discrepancy probably relates to *Karigane* aircraft, which would imply that the Army allowed certain Ki-15 airframes to be released to civilian operators, after they had completed testing or development programs, etc., with the understanding that Mitsubishi would add additional Ki-15 airframes onto the end of the production run in order to fulfil the Army's fiscal order. After all, the Army was not going to simply give away examples of its newest high-speed military aircraft to wealthy private companies, especially at a time when military budgets were coming under increasing restrictions.

If the first two *Karigane*-I airframes were stricken from the official production figures in 1937 and additional eight airframes was also added to the 1940 production run, it is increasingly likely that all 11 *Karigane* airframes were replaced on the production lines, in order to correct Army fiscal orders. This would increase the Ki-15 production figures for No.5 Airframe Works from 437 to 448 aircraft.

C5M production

Once the Navy had made the decision to order the improved Ki-15 into production as the C5M1, it would be easy to assume that Mitsubishi simply increased the production line tempo at No.5 Airframe Works, in order to deliver 20 additional aircraft in two specific batches? Unfortunately the truth is not so clear-cut because the C5M was a Navy aircraft, which meant that it could not be built on an Army production line. That was not the done thing at that point in time, as rivalry and political manoeuvring between the two services made such a concept almost impossible to undertake.

Mitsubishi *Babs* production figures

Year	Month/Quarter	Army fiscal year orders	Calendar year production	Army Ki-15 monthly production	Ki-15-I/Ki-15-II overlap period	Navy C5M1 monthly production	Ki-15-III production	Navy C5M2 monthly production	Civilian Karigane delivery details	Early Ki-46 production
1935			1							
1936	1Q									
	2Q	1 April 1936 to Mach 1937	2	2						
	3Q									
	4Q									
1937	1Q								3 airframes J-BAAI J-BAAL J-BAAM	
	2Q	29 April 1937 to March 1938	(80) actually 18	18						
	3Q									
	4Q					Ki-15-II First prototype				
1938	1Q								3 airframes J-???? J-BACL J-BECL	
	2Q	52 April 1938 to March 1939	41	41		Ki-15-II First flight		First Karigane-II J-BACL C/n133		
	3Q									
	4Q									
1939	Jan		137	7						
	Feb			7				J-BAAO C/n2012		
	Mar		Ki-15-I C/n181	8						
	Apr	175 April 1939 to March 1940		9		1				
	May			10		3				
	Jun			9		3			2 airframes J-BACK J-BAAO	
	July			11		2				1
	Aug			12		1				
	Sep			16			2 Ki-15-II airframes converted to Ki-15-III configuration and tested			
	Oct			14	Ki-15-I					1
	Nov			16						1
	Dec			18						
1940	Jan		240	19	Production overlap	1				
	Feb			18		1				1
	Mar		Highest known Ki-15-I C/n329	23		1				2
	Apr	180 April 1940 to March 1941		19		1				1
	May			10	Ki-15-II	4				
	Jun			22		2			3 airframes J-BACR J-BBAI J-BBAL	1
	July			22						1
	Aug			17						
	Sep			20						3
	Oct			21						2
	Nov			26						4
	Dec			23						5
1941	Jan							2		6
	Feb							4		7
	Mar							4		4
	Apr							4		3
	May							5		8
	Jun							6		7
	July							2		6
	Aug							3		2
	Sep									9
	Oct									9
	Nov									10
	Dec									14
Totals		437*	439**	438***	–	20*	2****	30*	11*****	108

While it is widely reported that 487 *Babs* airframes were produced between 1935 and 1941 (437 – Ki-15 and 50 – C5M), it is entirely likely that all 11 of the civilian Karigane airframes were not included in Mitsubishi production figures for No.5 Airframe Works, because they were not part of the Army's fiscal orders. The addition of 11 Karigane airframes increases the total *Babs* production figure up to 498 airframes.

* Actual production figures based on fiscal year orders – as used in the *Encyclopedia of Japanese Aircraft 1900-1945.*

** Production figures including C/n1502 and C/n1503, which were originally built for the Army before being sold to Asahi Shimbun – as used in *Japanese Aircraft of the Pacific War.*

*** *USSBS Corporation Report No.1* figures that include the 1st prototype in both the 1935 and 1936 fiscal years.

**** Ki-15-III prototype airframes are not included in the grand total, because they were converted from existing Ki-15-II airframes.

***** It is likely that civilian Karigane airframes were not included within established fiscal year production figures.

The only solution was to set up a dedicated C5M production line at the No.3 Airframe Works, which was formally part of the Naval Aircraft Production section. Ironically, No.3 Airframe Works occupied the same factory complex at Oe-mach, but both sites were operated as individual entities, controlled under the rules of their relative services.

Between April and August 1939 there was a visible reduction in Ki-15 output, which broadly matches the initial batch of 10 C5M1 airframes that were manufactured during that period. This is followed by a slight increase in Ki-15 production once the C5M order was completed which, coincidently, implies that the Ki-15 production line was most likely configured as a single rolling line. What is perhaps most interesting is the fact that the completed C5M airframes are included (for bookkeeping purposes) within the production totals for the Navy's No.3 Airframe Works and not those of the Army's No.5 Airframe Works!

Exactly what percentage of each C5M airframe was assembled on the Ki-15 production line before being completed on the Navy production line is unclear, but given the above clues it would seem that basic Ki-15 airframes were completed at No.5 Airframe Works, before being rolled "next door" to the No.3 Airframe Works to be reworked and navalized! Even though this sounds like a somewhat simple process, the nature of the airframe changes must have been quite time consuming, which is reflected in the slow delivery output of the C5M airframes. The second batch of 10 C5M1s were manufactured between January and June 1940, with a less pronounced fall in Ki-15 production figures, although a 52% drop was observed during the month of May, when the highest output of C5M1s was recorded.

Once the Army's final order of Ki-15-II airframes had been fulfilled at the end of December 1940, Mitsubishi instantly switched production over to the Navy's new C5M2 airframe in January 1941. With only one aircraft type to build, all 30 C5M2s were completed at the No.3 Airframe Works between January and August, with production times being halved when compared to that of the C5M1.

Mitsubishi C5M1/C5M2 production figures – No. 3 Airframe Works

Month/ Year	*Jan*	*Feb*	*Mar*	*Apr*	*May*	*June*	*July*	*Aug*	*Sept*	*Oct*	*Nov*	*Dec*	Totals
1939				1	3	3	2	1					10
1940	1	1	1	1	4	2							10
1941	2	4	4	4	5	6	2	3					30
													50

Babs production figure grand total – 498

Given the above findings and corrections, it is the belief of the author that the total number of Army Ki-15 and civilian *Karigane* airframes produced at the No.5 Airframe Works between 1935 and 1940 stands at 448. By including the Navy's C5M production figure of 50 aircraft, built at the No.3 Airframe Works, the total number of *Babs* aircraft grows to 498.

Construction numbers

For the majority of Japan's WWII military aircraft, individual airframe or construction numbers (C/n) were prefixed with a set of additional numbers in order to conceal actual production figures. From 1932 onwards, all aircraft ordered by the Army were assigned *Kitai* (Ki) or airframe numbers and by the late 1930s, such prototype aircraft carried a construction number that began with the Ki number. For example, the first 12 prototypes of the Kawasaki Army Type-3 Fighter (Ki-61) *Tony* program were identified as C/n6101 through to C/n6112. When the 13th airframe was completed, as the first production representative aircraft, a "100" prefix code was allocated to the aircraft, which officially became airframe C/n113. Thus a "100" prefix code camouflaged true production numbers for the Ki-61-1a series. All subsequent models of the *Tony* that entered mass production received new prefix codes, in order to continue this subterfuge. The Ki-61-Ib received a "500" prefix code, the Ki-61-1c received a "3000" prefix code, the Ki-61-1d received a"4000" prefix code, etc.

Ki-15-I prefix code

Unfortunately, details pertaining to Ki-15 construction numbers were destroyed at the end of the war, but by studying civil registration documents, and *all* of the known Ki-15 photographs, it is possible to identify what prefix codes were used to camouflage the actual production figures.

We know that the first three Ki-15 prototypes were issued with traditional *Kitai* based construction numbers (C/n1501, C/n1502 and C/n1503) and that the first production aircraft was delivered to the Army in May 1937. Given that three aircraft were delivered during May and June, it would seem that either the 4th or 5th airframe represented was the first production machine. The earliest production Ki-

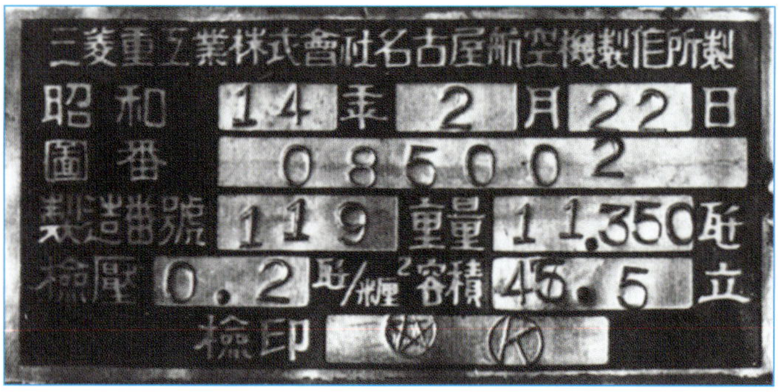

Wing leading edge fuel tank tag with a date of Showa 14 – 2 – 33 (1939 – February – 22nd) production date. (NII VVS via Y. Svoyski)

15 to be officially identified is C/n107, which was registered to Asahi Shimbun as (**J-BAAM**) *Sochikaze* on December 2nd 1937. This tells us that a "100" prefix code was allotted to the Ki-15-I production run.

Interestingly, this registration date does raise the question, why was the 7th production aircraft registration as late as December? Well, we know that the 6th Ki-15 (possibly C/n106) was delivered during June, so the most likely delivery date for the 7th airframe (C/n107) was early August. Given that the 1st prototype Ki-15 (C/n1501) was deployed to China on July 23rd, it is fair to assume that if C/n107 had been available to the Army at the end of July, it too would have been deployed to China in order to bolster operational Ki-15 numbers? In fact, the aircraft was indeed delivered to Asahi Shimbun at the beginning of August, but rather than registering the aircraft with the Civil Aviation Bureau (CAB), it was deployed directly to China in a pseudo military paint scheme, which included the name *Sochikaze* painted along both sides of the fuselage. While in theatre, this aircraft is known to have received battle damage to the leading-edge of the port wing and rudder on November 7th, before being patched up and returned to Japan in December. With so few examples of the Ki-15 available during that period, Asahi Shimbun would also "loan" C/n1502 (**J-BAAI**) *Kamikaze* and C/n1503 (**J-BAAL**) *Asakaze* back to the Army during August, despite the fact that neither aircraft possessed a gunner's windows for defensive armament. C/n1502 was subsequently damaged in a landing accident in November and C/n1503 was returned to Asahi Shimbun in the autumn, presumably when production representative Ki-15s became readily available for operations. At which time C/n107 *Sochikaze* was also returned to Asahi Shimbun and finally placed on the Japanese civil aircraft register on December 2nd 1937, four months after rolling of the production line.

Incidentally, the fact that C/n107 was registered during 1937 adds support to the belief that Appendix F of the *USSBS Corporation Report No.1* was a typographic error, because the total Ki-15 production figures for the period of 1935 through 1937 would have been either 21 or 83 aircraft, depending on which number (18 for 80 aircraft) is accepted as correct. And since Mitsubishi had not yet produced 107 *Babs* aircraft by that point in time, it is impossible for C/n107 to have been the 107th airframe. This proves that C/n107 had to be the 7th production aircraft, which both validates the 1937 production figure of 18 aircraft and the "100" prefix code assumption.

C/n181

Photographic evidence depicting the "100" prefix code is found on several Ki-15s, all the way up to C/n329, the 229th airframe to be built. This includes aircraft C/n181 which was inspected by Soviet forces in mid February 1940. Unfortunately, the Soviets determined that C/n181 was built in December 1939, which is at odds with the "100" prefix code. So, is the Soviet assumption correct?

On the face of it the Soviet report seems very accurate and presents various component data tags, with production dates ranging from February through to September 1939. But the most crucial piece of evidence, the actual airframe data tag, is conspicuous by its absence. In addition to this, the quoted *"December 1939"* production date is also somewhat vague, as the airframe identification tag would have included the year/month/day. Given that the Soviets were not aware of Japanese C/n prefix codes at that time, we can only assume that their perceived production date was based on the most recently dated, or youngest component tag found on the aircraft?

Main landing gear leg tag with a date of Showa 14 – 9 – 16 (1939–September – 16th) production date. (NII VVS via Y. Svoyski)

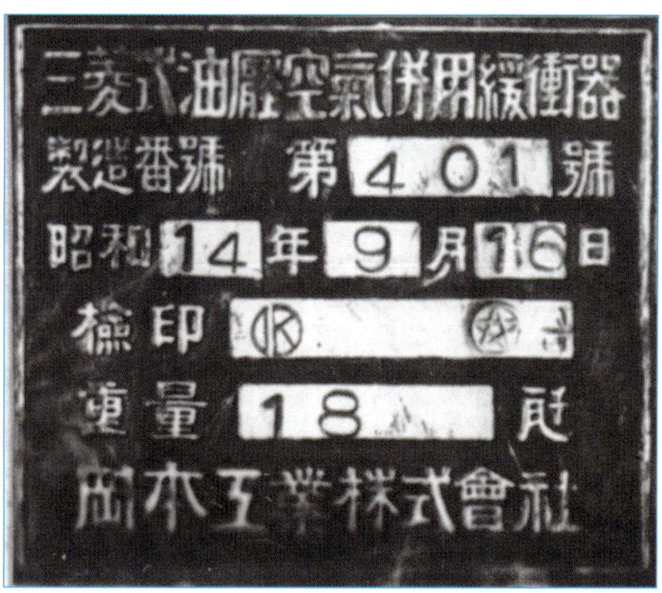

If we include the three or four possible prototype aircraft (C/n1501 – C/n1504) that were produced in 1936 and 1937, together with all of the production Ki-15-I airframes completed through to the end of December 1939, we arrive at a grand total of 198 aircraft built. By comparing the production numbers for each year, it is possible to determine that the 181st production airframe was in fact completed around early December 1939, which initially seems to corroborate the Soviet findings. Unfortunately though this is one of those annoying coincidences that often stalk historians, because if we apply the "100" prefix number code to the 181st production airframe, that aircraft would have been identified as C/n281, and photographs of the captured aircraft definitely shows that it was liberally stencilled with the number "181".

We are therefore left with two options; we can either believe the Soviet report at face value and accept that C/n181 was manufactured in December 1939, and in doing so disprove the "100" prefix code? Or, we can re-examine the Soviet findings in detail?

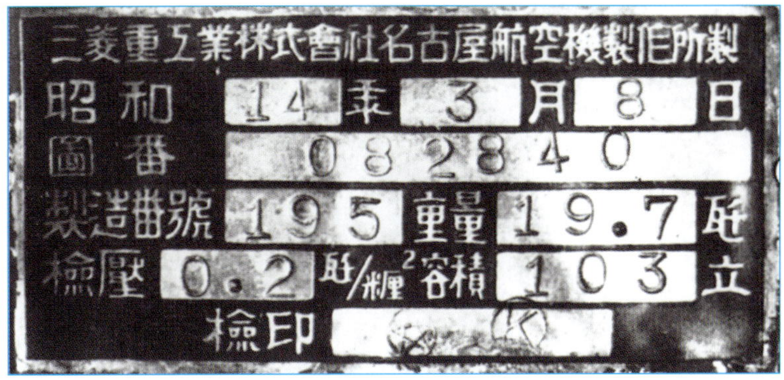

Wing main fuel tank tag with a date of Showa 14 – 3 – 9 (1939 – March – 8th) production date. (NII VVS via Y. Svoyski)

Even if we ignore the possible typographic error of 18 or 80 airframes produced in 1937, Appendix F and G of the *USSBS Corporation Report No.1* lists Ki-15 production for 1938 and 1939 as 41 and 137 airframes respectively, or 178 aircraft in total. If the Soviet production date for C/n181 were accurate, this would mean that only 74 Ki-15s were constructed between aircraft C/n107 in August 1937 and aircraft C/n181 in December 1939, which is obviously not possible because it totally ignores 104 additional airframes that were produced during that period.

If December 1939 is impossible to align with C/n181, can we therefore apply the "100" prefix code to the aircraft and prove that it was in fact the 81st production Ki-15 aircraft? Using the monthly production figures found in Appendix G of the *USSBS Corporation Report No.1*, it is possible to determine that the 81st production Ki-15 was built during the last week of March or first week of April 1939. This is based on the corrected production figure of 18 aircraft during 1937 and the small number of Ki-15-II prototypes and pre-production aircraft that had been built at that time. This date is nine months away from the Soviet production date of December 1939, which may seem like a massive gap, but it does fall well within the quoted components dates listed in the Soviet report – February to December 1939. So why is there a 10 months span of quoted production dates associated with airframe C/n181? The answer to this discrepancy in dates is the result of mass production techniques and the various Ki-15-I modifications and upgrades that were incorporated into the Ki-15, specifically those related to weight and the **initial, intermediate** and **standard** fuel systems. See Chapter 4, **Technical description.**

When the Army issued its initial 1939 production order for 52 Ki-15s (during 1938), the various sub assemblies required to build these aircraft were placed into production within individual departments and divisions at Mitsubishi, or its subcontractors. One department built undercarriage legs, while another assembled the pilot's seats or canopy installations, etc. For example, all of the centre-wing fuel tanks, for the whole fiscal order, may have been fabricated in one production run during February and March 1939. Once each tank was completed it would have been inspected and pressure-tested before its data tag received a completion date, together with an individual item serial number, weight, capacity, inspection date, manufacturers inspection stamp and Army inspection stamp. All of the completed centre-wing tanks for that specific fiscal order would then have been placed in a parts store, where they remained until each tank, or set of tanks, was required for integration into an airframe, which could have been days or even months later.

In the case of C/n181 we are presented with a February 22nd completion date for the wing leading-edge tank and a March 8th date for a centre-wing tank, which fits in well with the last week of March production date for the 81st airframe.

The fact that a MLG tag indicates that the assembly was completed on September 16th 1939 may initially seem problematic, but this could simply indicate that the undercarriage was damaged and replaced in service. In fact, it is more likely that the MLG was replaced with a stronger assembly after the aircraft entered service, due to the increase in maximum take-off weight associated with the adoption of the "additional fuel tank" installation, which added approximately 254 kg (560 lb) of weight to the aircraft. Similarly, the engine electrical generator with its construction date of July and the engine with its construction date of September are both line-replaceable items, which could have been changed at any time after the aircraft entered service in March, therefore they cannot be definitely tied to the aircraft construction date.

It is worth noting that the highest Ki-15-I construction number to be photographically identified is C/n329, which means that at least 229 Ki-15-Is were built under the "100" prefix code system. If we ignore the "100" prefix code for one moment and adopt the Soviet assumption, this would imply that C/n181 was the 181st airframe to be built, and therefore C/n329 would have to be the 329th Ki-15-I airframe. If that were true, it would mean that of all the 448 Ki-15s produced, at least 329 of them were Ki-15-Is, and therefore 119 were Ki-15-IIs. Unfortunately this hypothesis is not supported by the Ki-15-II production data, so the "100" prefix code must hold true for the Ki-15-I.

Ki-15-II prefix codes

Production of the Ki-15-II was officially commenced in September 1939, some 21 months after construction of the first improved Ki-15 prototype, but the exact changeover period from the Ki-15-I and

Ki-15-II is difficult to determine, because Mitsubishi simply provided a monthly production total for *all* Army Ki-15 airframes, regardless of their model. While it would be nice to assume that Ki-15-II production began directly after the completion of the first batch of C5M1 airframes, the evidence points to the fact that Ki-15-IIs were gradually phased into production over a protracted period during the winter of 1939. Although it is not uncommon in the aircraft industry for multiple models of an aircraft to share a production line, such mixed production lines are notorious for causing delays, as one missing component or assembly for a specific model of aircraft could easily reduce the flow of the whole production line.

We know that at least 229 examples of the Ki-15-I were built, because we have photographic evidence of aircraft C/n329. Given an uninterrupted Ki-15-I production run, C/n329 *would* statistically have been completed during mid February 1940, but because Ki-15-II airframes were also under construction on the same production line, that completion date was impossible to achieve. We also know that at least 13 Ki-15-II prototypes and pre-production aircraft were built on the same production line between December 1937 and September 1939, all of which would have pushed C/n329s manufacturing date back into April 1940 at the earliest, almost seven months after production of the Ki-15-II had officially commenced.

While a new prefix code system would be allotted to production Ki-15-II airframes, the initial development aircraft carried "100" prefix codes, because they were converted from partially completed airframes, taken directly from the Ki-15-I production line. This is confirmed with photographic evidence of aircraft C/n133, a Ki-15-II (**J-BACL**) that was documented in September 1938. After one or two development aircraft had been tested, production built Ki-15-IIs were issued with a "2000" prefix code, in order to differentiate between the various models that shared the production line. The earliest "2000" prefix code to be identified is C/n2012 (**J-BAAO**) and the latest is C/n2153, which would indicate that at least 153 production Ki-15-II airframes were built.

Karigane registrations and prefix codes

While the construction and registration dates of the first three *Karigane*-I airframes (**J-BAAI, J-BAAL** and **J-BAAM**) can be determined with some accuracy, the one remaining *Karigane*-I and all seven *Karigane*-II airframes (**J-BAAO, J-BACK, J-BACL, J-BACR, J-BBAI, J-BBAL, J-BECL**) are more difficult to pin down for two reasons. Firstly, in line with the military practice of limiting or concealing information concerning aircraft production and operations, the Japanese CAB ceased all official announcements related to civil aircraft registrations from July 1937 onwards. Secondly, all of the *Karigane* airframes appear to have lived two distinct and separate lives.

The Army and Navy were creatures of habit and pragmatic to the last. Once specialized development, flight-test or early pre-production airframes had fulfilled their intended roles, they were bureaucratically difficult to absorb into service, because they were not completed to production standards, often containing non-standard equipment, alterations and airframe modifications, etc. At which point they were released for sale into the civilian market, a practice that included Ki-15-I prototype C/n1502 (**J-BAAI**), C/n1503 (**J-BAAL**), C/n107 (**J-BAAM**), plus *Karigane*-II C/n133 (**J-BACL**), C/n2012 (**J-BAAO**) and **J-BACK.**

Construction number "2012 Right" applied to the wheel spat of Karigane-II (Ki-15-II) Asakaze. *Note the crimped wheel panels.*

These factors would imply that the fourth *Karigane*-I (**J-????**) was registered after June 1937, but before the first *Karigane*-II (**J-BACL**) in April 1938. And, given the very slow production output during the first half of 1937, it is entirely possible that **J-????** was one of the prototype Ki-15-I airframes, possibly C/n104 through C/n106?

In addition to the registration date "blackout" imposed on CAB documentation, the development of Ki-15-II airframes served to confuse matters further still. The earliest airframe examples of the Ki-15-II/*Karigane*-II were **J-BACL** and **J-BECL**, which were both completed with the three-section (*early model* Ki-15-I) lateral window installations. The exact changeover period for this installation can be narrowed down to mid spring of 1939, because *early model* Ki-15-I – C/n181 was fitted with the same installation during the last week of March 1939, while the optically-flat lateral window installation of C5M1s and *late model* Ki-15-Is began to appear in early and late April respectively. **J-BACL** originally began life as C/n133 (the 33rd Ki-15-I production airframe) during mid April 1938, before being selected as a development airframe for the Ki-15-II. After a short test career **J-BACL** joined the civilian register in September 1938, but was destroyed by fire in October that same year, while **J-BECL** would not appear on the civilian register until post June 1940!

Despite being a later model than the aforementioned *Karigane*-II airframes, **J-BAAO**, with its optically flat lateral windows and centre canopy tunnel oxygen system, carried the earliest (alphabetical) civilian registration. Most likely utilised as a development airframe for the *late model* Ki-15-I and Ki-15-II programs, the aircraft was earmarked for release to Asahi Shimbun, who probably initiated the aircraft's early registration with the CAB in anticipation of its release from testing. But, before the aircraft could be delivered, it was "leased" to the Navy in order to assist with the urgent C5M program. A grainy photograph of **J-BAAO** reveals the construction number stencil on the starboard undercarriage leg to be C/n2012, or possibly C/n2042. The lower construction number falls easily within the Ki-15-II development period without any issues. But, for the sake of the argument, if we assume that the aircraft was in fact C/n2042, modified prior to, or during, the C5M1 production period (March to August 1939), this would imply that 42 production Ki-15-II airframes had already been built before the type was officially ordered into production in September! Given the above discrepancies and airframe details, it is most likely that **J-BAAO** was built during February or March 1939, as C/n2012.

The last Karigane-II to be registered was J-BECL, despite being one of the early Ki-15-II airframes. Note the lateral window installation. (Shoichi Tanaka)

Early photographs of **J-BACK** show the existence of mass balance weights on the elevators, which would indicate that this aircraft was also utilized for C5M development. Almost nothing is known about **J-BBAI** and **J-BBAL**, but given the dual-histories of the other nine *Karigane* airframes, it is likely that they too were employed in some form of development or testing, before being released into civilian market.

Because *Karigane* aircraft were adapted from existing Ki-15 development aircraft, they retained the original Ki-15-I "100" and Ki-15-II "2000" prefix codes.

C5M1 and C5M2 prefix codes

To date, no direct documentation or photographic evidence exists to identify the C/n system that was applied to the Navy's C5M airframes. Without doubt the C5M1 and C5M2 would have received all-new prefix codes (possibly within the "3000" and "4000" ranges respectively), purely to differentiate between the basic airframes on the production line at Mitsubishi's No.5 Airframe Works.

Known Ki-15 and Karigane Construction Numbers (C/n)

Model	Kitai based C/n and Prefix code based C/n	Actual airframe number with Kitai or "100" prefix code removed	Notes
Ki-15-I	1501	1	1st Prototype
	1502	2	2nd Prototype **J-BAAI** *Kamikaze*
	1503	3	3rd Prototype **J-BAAL** *Asakaze*
	107	7	**J-BAAM** *Sochikaze*
	131	31	Kagamigahara training airframe
	132	32	Kagamigahara training airframe
	135	35	*18th Dokuritsu Chutai* aircraft
	181	81	Completed in March 1939. Captured by Soviets in February 1940
	322	222	101st *Dokuritsu Chutai*
	329	229	Possibly *13th Sentai* aircraft
Ki-15-II	133	33	Converted Ki-15-I airframe to Ki-15-II/*Karigane*-II **J-BACL**
	2012	12	**J-BAAO** *Amakaze*
	2073	73	*18th Dokuritsu Chutai* aircraft
	2153	153	*8th Sentai* aircraft

Chapter 8

Models, memorabilia and memorials

"The single engine of the "Divine Wind" used Shell Aviation petrol with Ethyl and AeroShell Lubricating Oil for the westward and eastward flights – both records."

Shell Oil advertisement
Asahi Shimbun commemorative brochure, June 1937.

Models

Given the obscurity of the *Babs* family of aircraft in relation to wartime intelligence and combat reports, one would assume that there would be very few representative model kits available for this subject matter, but this is not the case at all. It would seem that the notoriety of the *Kamikaze* flight has kept the torch of interest alight over the decades.

The first company to produce an injection-molded *Babs* kit was **Marusan** in late 1961, when it launched a 1/50th scale model of *Kamikaze.* This was followed in early 1963 with a Ki-15-I kit, which was in fact the same model with military decals. During late 1963 and 1964 these kits were repackaged with more contemporary box artwork and in 1965 the *Kamikaze* kit was re-issued under a US licensing agreement with **UPC**. Marusan went bankrupt in 1968.

In 1974 **Mania** models launched a 1/72nd scale model of the *Kamikaze,* which seemed to pique the interest of the modeling community and a military version of the kit was soon released, complete with new decals that offered the model as a 2-in-1 kit. This kit was re-issued with new decals in late 1977, just prior to the company being taken over by **Hasegawa**, who continued to offer the Mania kit in re-branded boxes, with new decals, through the late 1990s. To commemorate the 70th anniversary of the 1937 flight, Hasegawa released a special twin kit edition of the model during 2007, which contained two complete kits, with all-new decals for both *Kamikaze* and *Asakaze.*

In 1976 **LS** models launched its own 1/72nd scale model of the *Kamikaze,* followed by versions of the Ki-15-I, Ki-15-II and C5M2. These kits were re-issued several times through the early 1990s, before being re-launched by **ARII** models in 1995.

Smaller kits were issued by **Sankyo** in the form of a 150th scale Navy C5M1, and at least two resin and vacuform kits have been issued by other manufacturers, as limited runs over the years.

In 2018, **FineMolds** issued a high detail 1/48th scale C5M2, complete with two sets of markings. This multi-option kit was designed with interchangeable sections, which allowed FineMolds to re-issue the kit soon after as a Ki-15-I, with three sets of markings. This was followed in quick succession with a model of *Kamikaze,* with two sets of decals depicting the 1937 flight and its post flight markings. The FineMolds range of *Babs* models was completed at the end of the year with the release of the Ki-15-II variant, which also came with two sets of markings.

The number of aftermarket products has also grown over recent years with various etched-brass, resin and clear components being made available for the above kits, together with several decal sheets.

Memorabilia

When Iinuma and Tsukagoshi returned to Japan on May 21st 1937, they were greeted as superstars, the enormity of which had never before been seen in Japan. Wherever the two men or *Kamikaze* appeared, vast crowds would line the streets in order to see them, and it was not long before this notoriety was being exploited for sales, marketing and memorabilia purposes. From cameras and motor oil, through to teacups, sheet music, jewellery and even cider were tenuously connected with the *Kamikaze* brand. Photographs and postcards depicting the Tokyo to London flight were particularly popular in

Marusan/UPC

Mania/Hasegawa

LS

ARII

FineMolds

Japan, allowing people to participate in the national achievement. In every sense, Asahi Shimbun's plan to unite the nation had been successful and would ultimately see their branding expand like never before. This trend continued on into the Pacific war, when postcards depicting military subjects, including images of the Ki-15, were also issued as a form of patriotic support.

Most bizarrely, the final *Babs* "branding" appearance was made in 2009, when an image of a Ki-15-I appeared on a Mozambique postage stamp!

Memories and memorials

In October 1985, a TV documentary-drama was broadcast in Japan, celebrating the 1937 *Kamikaze* flight. Based on Yusuke Fukata's novel "*Bibou nare Showa*", this program was quite fittingly produced by Asahi TV, which used a heavily modified North American T-6 "Texan" to recreate *Kamikaze*.

At the time of writing, not a single piece of Ki-15, *Kamikaze* or C5M is known to exist in a national or private collection. There is, though, a museum dedicated to the life of Masaaki Iinuma, in his childhood home of Minami-Azumi (Azumino), in Nagano Prefecture. Opened in 1989, the ***Iinuma Pilot Memorial Hall*** contains photos and personal items, such as his Aircraft Navigation License, plus maps and memorabilia from the 1937 flight.

Details of the memorial can be found at:
http://azumino-museum.com/iinuma/iinuma.html
http://azumino-bunka.com/facility/iinuma/

A modified North American T-6 was used in the Asahi TV documentary about the 1937 Kamikaze flight. (Shawn DuBois)

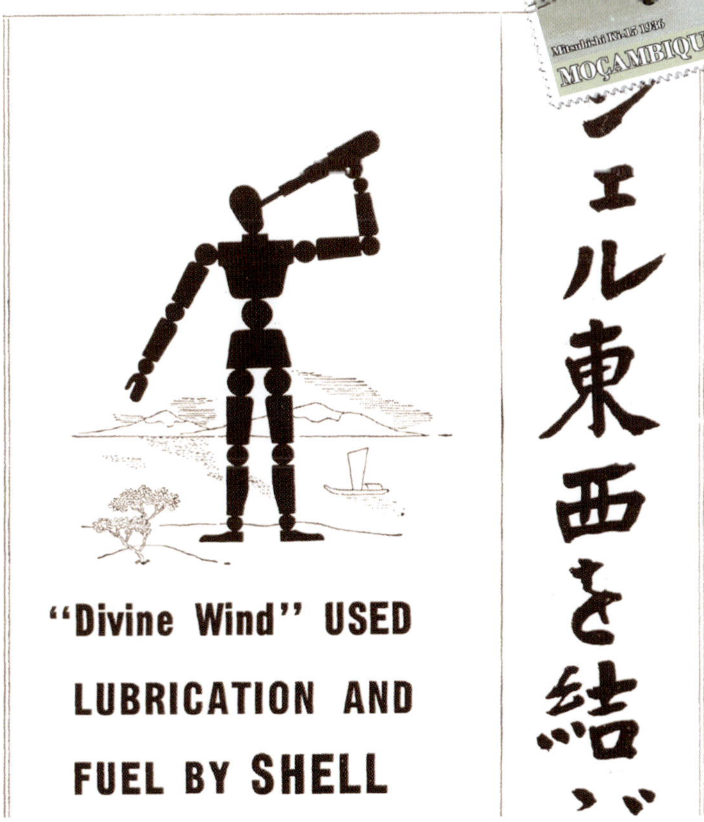

Period postcards, advertisements, branding and stamps depicting the Kamikaze flight and Babs aircraft.

Full-size (**91.5 x 61cm / 36 x 24inch**) high-resolution cutaway posters of the **Mitsubishi Ki-15-I**, ***Kamikaze***, **Ki-15-II**, **C5M1** and **C5M2** are available through ***thecutawaycompany.com*** Each ***Babs*** poster is meticulously detailed and extensively modified, just like the original aircraft, to incorporate type specific equipment, including: propellers, engines, cowls, oil tanks, fuel tanks, wheels, pitots, instrument panels, seats, cockpit fittings, radios, antennas, cameras, canopies and weapons, etc., plus internal and external markings, inboard profiles, technical keys and data figures. And of course ***Percy*** the pig is hidden in each cutaway – enjoy!

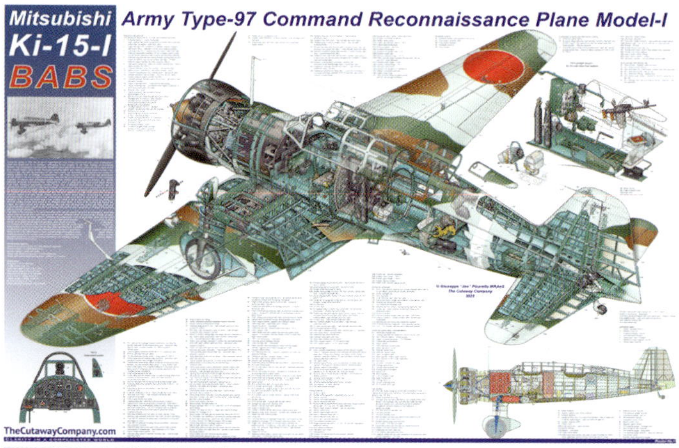

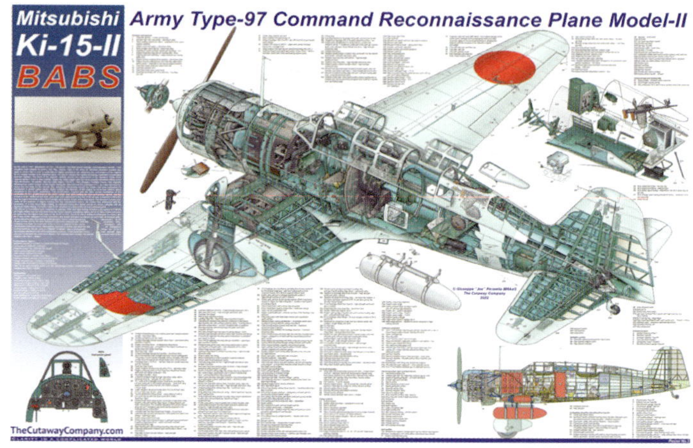

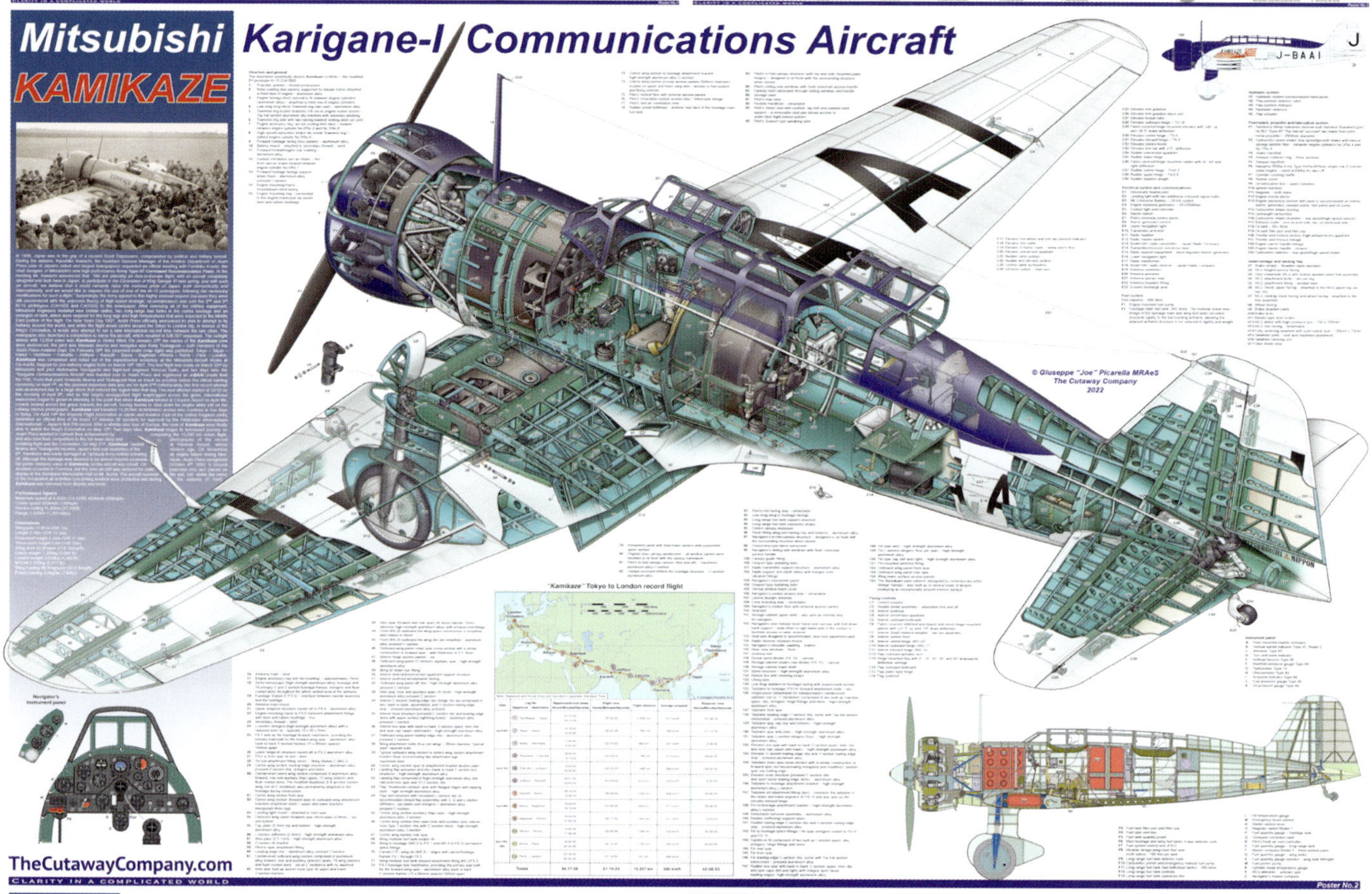

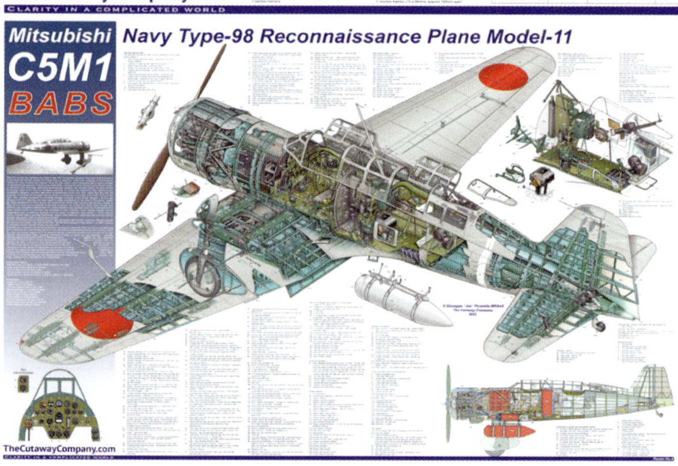

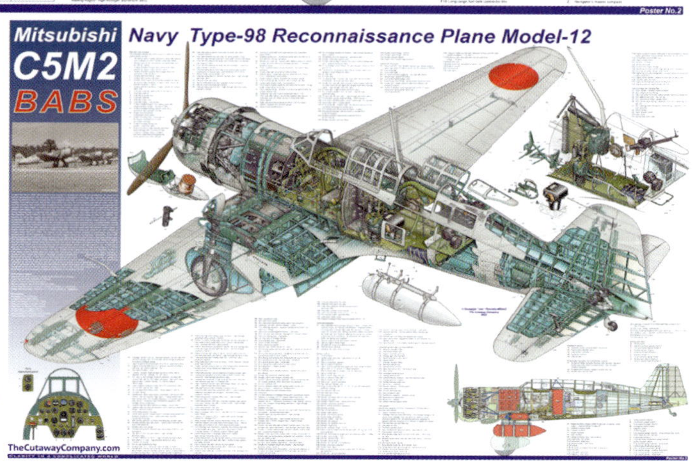

TheCutawayCompany.com

CLARITY IN A COMPLICATED WORLD